The Rise of Eurocentrism

The Rise of
Eurocentrism

ANATOMY OF INTERPRETATION

Vassilis Lambropoulos

PRINCETON UNIVERSITY PRESS

PRINCETON, NEW JERSEY

Copyright © 1993 by Princeton University Press
Published by Princeton University Press, 41 William Street,
Princeton, New Jersey 08540
In the United Kingdom: Princeton University Press, Oxford

Library of Congress Cataloging-in-Publication Data

Lambropoulos, Vassilis, 1953–
The rise of eurocentrism : anatomy of
interpretation / Vassilis Lambropoulos.
p.   cm.
Includes bibliographical references and index.
ISBN 0-691-06949-2
1. Literature—History and criticism—Theory, etc.
2. Canon (Literature)   3. European literature—History
and criticism.   4. Europe—Civilization.   I. Title.
PN441.L36   1992   809'.894—dc20   92-3690

This book has been composed in Bitstream Electra

Princeton University Press books are printed on acid-free paper,
and meet the guidelines for permanence and durability of the
Committee on Production Guidelines for Book Longevity of the
Council on Library Resources

Printed in the United States of America

1 3 5 7 9 10 8 6 4 2

To Gregory

———————————

CONTENTS

ACKNOWLEDGMENTS

I HAVE BENEFITED from the collegial atmosphere of the Department of Judaic and Near Eastern Languages and Literatures of the Ohio State University, where I have been working, first as an assistant and then as an associate professor of Modern Greek. The Chairman, Frederic Cadora, Associate Dean Marvin Zahniser, and Dean Micheal Riley of the College of Humanities assisted my research with grants and many helpful administrative arrangements. Dimitris Mytaras generously gave me permission to use his painting on the cover. Eric Schramm copy-edited the manuscript with great care and sensitivity. Also, I was fortunate once again to work with an editor of Robert Brown's initiative and integrity.

I should like to thank my parents and my in-laws for their unwavering confidence, trust, and support. I am equally grateful to my extended family, Andreas and Maria Mylonas, and Yannis and Katerina Varvarigos. I am grateful to Julian Anderson for her reassuring faith. I thank my research associates Panayiotis Bosnakis, Kostas Demelis, Evangelos Gegas, and Kui Qiu for their diligence and dedication to scholarship. I appreciate the generosity and encouragement of Margaret Alexiou, Victoria Holbrook, Mary Layoun, and Amy Shuman, who gave me the opportunity to present my ideas in seminars, talks, and conferences they organized. Stathis Gourgouris, Eugene Holland, Eleni Vakalo, and Nanos Valaoritis helped with insightful suggestions on particular sections. Gregory Nagy illuminated crucial issues as he responded to the first draft. Nancy Armstrong and Leonard Tennenhouse have consistently provided valuable political lessons. Peter Bien, John Chioles, and Michael Herzfeld read the entire manuscript and guided me with perspicacity and wisdom through many difficult passages. Daphne created and enjoyed all the appropriate emergencies. Without Artemis, I wouldn't have done it and it wouldn't be worth it.

PREFACE: THE RULE OF AUTONOMY

IN A SECULAR CULTURE, there is no time present. Occidental time oscillates precariously between the senses of ruin and anticipation, tradition and restitution. The present of the West has always been hopelessly caught between its Hellenic past and Hebraic future, the reason of the first Messiah (Socrates) and the revelation of the last one. That is why Europe (including its assimilated former colonies, the rest of the West) can only re-form, de-form, trans-form; it can only seek in form, in unmediated presence, the moment that time does not grant in the present moment. Since the great schism of the churches (1054), Europe (i.e., alienated Christianity everywhere) has been pursuing the expression of form, expression in form, the formulation of history. It has been seeking the arrest of time through the illumination of matter: the structure of monotheism in the sculpture of idols. This quest for the suprahistorical form (in which quest the West originated) reached a turning point with the Reformation and its decree against referentiality, against heteronomy, against matters of the world. From now on, matter had to be either spiritual (form) or worldly (material). If the Catholic church had been un-Orthodox, the Protestant denominations were going to be heterodox and heterotrophic, relying only on the organic material of autopoietic form for their spiritual food.

The rule of autonomy is the law of immanence, the reign of secular self-begetting form. Counter-ecclesiastical and anti-dogmatic faith needs to anchor itself in an event other than the (recurring) ritual, and it discovers such an event in form, the spiritual happening of matter. Form (this arrested history, this soteriological event) provides a mimesis of redemption: the redemption of the world through representation, the communion of the word. What forms the form is the verb (as opposed to the unreliable noun of nominalism), the word of the divine Logos; what occurs in the event of form is enunciation; what replaces referentiality is representation. The new ritual, the secular one, is verbal communication, the communion of forms, in which everyone may partake and contribute. The only prerequisite is faith in form—rejection of both scholastic exegesis and nominalist skepticism in favor of belief in literalist meaning. To promote this view, the reformists adopt the text as the preeminent type of form. With its basis in language, the text represents the most eloquent example of secular communion, the communion of tongues that rescues communication from Babel. The text becomes the purest form, the body of all form, and the depth of all immanence. At the same time, a new technology of understanding is created for the penetration of that body and depth, interpretation.

This discipline of communion (which oversees the supreme secular rite) is not imposed from above, from outside, but is bestowed upon, granted to the faithful when its potential (reason) is recognized in the structure of their minds. Its goal is to train people in literalism so that they may receive through reading the body of forms, the spirit of letters. Those people, however, might not be enticed to accept the present of the grace, the gift of an (evangelized) present moment of unmediatedness, if it were not for a promise of freedom, of personal (specifically, spiritual) liberation from subservience to every (other) worldly authority, from worldliness itself, so that humans can now begin doing things with, or even to, this world. Interpretation promised emancipation: acceptance and independence in the civic society. The community of independent interpretation was going to build the kingdom of God on earth (and share it with those qualified). This contract of emancipation through interpretation, of redemption through the letter of the form—this civic covenant proposed by the European middle class marks the inauguration of modernity. By this contract, Christianity abandoned eternal time in exchange for a pledged present.

That present, however, that epiphany, that identity, has never happened. By definition it could not—except in short-lived pagan outbursts of revolution, quickly silenced by accommodating emancipatory arrangements. Nor has liberation transpired, although millions of people have been successfully assimilated in regimes of negotiable rights and responsibilities. What has been happening instead is the Western libration between the Hellenic and the Hebraic poles that have come to represent not only the tension separating a complete past from an unfulfilled future, but also every other contradiction and conflict experienced over the meaning of communion.

This essay, an exercise in nomoscopy, chronicles the development of the Hebraic rule of Hellenic autonomy by studying the techniques of intrinsic governance that have prevailed in modernity. It does not provide a linear history, an interdisciplinary overview, or a consistent narrative. Rather, it is organized as a series of digressions on the issue of the aesthetic, the disinterested contemplation of purposeless beauty, which has dominated definitions of autonomy over the last three centuries of the second millennium. Each chapter begins with a major twentieth-century aesthetic position; but the examination of the interpretive regime diverges from digression to digression. When enough courses and detours have been explored to make the starting point disorientingly conditional and contingent, the chapter stops. As in every passacaglia, however, the bass line (in this case, the Hebraism-Hellenism comparison) keeps reappearing in various guises to reassure readers that the author is indeed still with them. In any case, this kind of composition procedure is justified by playing the game, which is by no means the same as putting the cards on the table.

The book is not "complete" in other respects as well. So far as discussions of the central comparison are concerned, the attentive reader will certainly miss many names, from Blake, Coleridge, and Kierkegaard, to Renan, Nietzsche, and Freud (to mention just a few). For reasons of space, economy, and structure, the study of much relevant material has been postponed for possible future occasions. The same must be said about obvious (and less obvious) bibliographical background which was left out in the hope that the rhythm of what has been devised here compensates for some omissions and that other opportunities may arise for a fuller use of such background. In general, this kind of approach is rather uninterested in two particular criticisms: those demanding exhaustiveness and rational consistency. The strength and insight of so-called contradictions deserve more recognition than they currently enjoy. As the book itself explains, critique (the contumelious controverting of contumacious contradictions) is little more than the confession and expiation of the aesthetic sin of autonomy. Furthermore, in an attempt to move beyond a dialectical understanding of debate, the book, instead of citing its re-sources, re-cites and engages sources directly in a quiet (though sometimes unfaithful) way that makes them parts of, or passages into, its centrifugal digressions.

These and many other strategies of this work are efforts to take different (constructivist) looks at a cluster of related topics, an assemblage of interacting issues. The occasional experimental move, even when unsuccessful, could not have been entirely avoided at a time when all creativity ponders its very possibilities and must therefore experiment. The serenity of certainty during eras of anarchy (that is, dissolution of autonomy) is an unnecessary luxury. The intellectual purview of the book tries to exclude the imperial overviews of theoria (contemplation of universals) in favor of positions of scope (consideration of particulars) like those helpful to a nomoscopy, to the study of regimes of rules. At the same time, while the book presents through its limited scope only some dimensions of a complex development, one hopes that its didactic (as opposed to interpretive or pedagogical) effectiveness has not been compromised.

The Rise of Eurocentrism

Chapter One

THE RITES OF INTERPRETATION

> [T]he criticism of religion
> is the presupposition of all criticism.
> —Karl Marx

THE LAW OF INTERPRETATION

Readers of *Mimesis* will remember the well-prepared and touching comparison in chapter 1, where the two basic types of literary representation in Western culture are dramatically contrasted. The scene of Odysseus' recognition by his old housekeeper Euryclea in the *Odyssey* is examined in great thematic and stylistic detail, and then interpreted against a parallel reading of the sacrifice of Isaac in Genesis. The wide variety of distinct features exhibited in the two texts is organized in two corresponding sets of diametrically opposed character and tone. These sets are then seen as concise pictures of the worldview expressed in the respective works, and are used as the basis for a broad outline of the Homeric and the Biblical systems of thought. At the end of the chapter, the two types are set forth as the starting point for the investigation of European literary representation that the rest of the book conducts through the centuries, from antiquity to modern times.

All this is scrupulously explored and narrated in painstaking philological fashion. Passages are selected carefully and read thoroughly, distinctions are made with an informed eye on stylistic detail, and differences are established with discriminating attention to the particular aspects and the overall pattern of the texts. Both works are considered as epics, but their qualities are found to differ in such a fundamental way that they express (and allow for) opposing modes of understanding and of literary writing. Erich Auerbach (1892–1957) states that he chose to elaborate on this opposition because it operates at the foundations of Western literature, and therefore must be posed at the beginning of his study. But his presentation immediately raises questions. *Mimesis* (1946) does not have an introduction: there is no first, separate section to present its purpose and describe its approach. Instead, the work begins *in medias res*: "Readers of the *Odyssey* will remember the well-prepared and touching scene in book 19, when Odysseus has at last come home" (Auerbach 1953: 3). It begins with a first chapter which, like the rest, bears a neutrally descriptive title, "Odysseus' Scar," and immediately proceeds to conduct a close reading of a classic text. Only after several pages does it become clear that it deals with two texts, rather than one, that it seeks to establish the origins of Western mimetic modes, and that it functions as an introduction to the whole volume. Thus the title is deceptive: while it seems to promise a treatment of a Homeric passage, the chapter is as much about Abraham's sacrifice as it is about Odysseus' scar. It appears, then, that the book is introduced in a surreptitious manner. The suppression of the character of the piece and of its second major topic are closely linked: what at first glance looks like a first chapter and a discussion of the *Odyssey* proves to be an introduction and a comparison of Homer with the Old Testament.

The basic opposition, which the essay establishes but the title does not acknowledge, is posited and developed in a long series of dichotomies, purported to articulate the distinctive features of the Homeric and the Biblical style: external-internal, presence-absence, unity-disconnectedness, totality-fragmentation, illuminated-obscure, clarity-ambiguity, foreground-background, simplicity-complexity, stability-fermentation, serenity-anguish, being-becoming, legend-history. In all these binary oppositions, the first member refers to the Homeric world and the second to the Biblical, while each polarity indicates the antithesis and clash of the two worldviews and mimetic modes. Auerbach argues that the two sets of categories indicate contrasting ways of thinking and dictate contrasting ways of understanding them: each has to be comprehended in its own terms. Consequently, he insists: "Homer can be analyzed . . . but cannot be interpreted" (13), while "the text of the Biblical narrative . . . is so greatly in need of interpretation on the basis of its own content" (15). Auerbach refrains from explicitly defining his terminology; but from the basic sets of categories it may at least be inferred that analysis (which applies to the Homeric) is more of a description of simple incidents, surface meanings, and direct messages, while interpretation (which responds to the Biblical) uncovers hidden meanings, implied messages, and complex significances. This is not the place to discuss the critical validity of such a distinction.[1] It is more important to see how the approach called "interpretation" describes Auerbach's own method of reading literature.

Auerbach is faithful to his position when he reads the scene from Genesis in that he conducts an in-depth, penetrating interpretation which seeks to elucidate all its dimensions. As exemplified in this application, interpretation is the search for an ultimate explanation of both meaning and purpose. It tries to uncover the hidden, obscure, silent, ineffable, multiple meanings of a text, promising and at the same time threatening, retrievable yet always elusive, under the thick layers of language. It also tries to explain the purpose of it all, to describe the overall plan, to specify the final direction toward which everything is moving. In this part of his investigation,

Auerbach is consistent. But he does not show the same consistency in his approach to Homer. For although he argues that the Greek epic allows only for analysis, his discussion exhibits all the unmistakable signs of an interpretive reading: it presents the hidden complexity of the incident with Euryclea, traverses successive layers of significance, exposes invisible assumptions, and finally builds on it a whole theory about Homeric mimesis. Interpretive understanding is again his guiding motive, since he asks persistently why everything in the text happens in this way. Auerbach violates his own epistemological principle and applies an interpretive reading to the *Odyssey*, a Biblical reading to a Homeric text. Although he argues that the two works express opposite worldviews and dictate different readings, he uses for both the approach derived from the second. He does not read Homer against the Bible, as he claims, but rather reads Homer through the Bible: his is a Biblical treatment. Thus his conclusion that Homer cannot be interpreted is an interpretive one, which results from a successful search for deep meanings in his work. Auerbach treats both works in an interpretive fashion, seeking to uncover their artistic essence behind the literary surface.

What appears to be omitted in the title of the essay is the most important element; what is not mentioned is the dominant feature; what is missing is central to what is there—the Biblical mode of mimesis and interpretation. The title promises a study on the recognition of Odysseus' scar, but the essay delivers a model of literary interpretation derived from Abraham's sacrifice; and the number above the title indicates a first chapter but refers to an introduction. These deceptive signs are part of the same tactic: while the essay identifies itself as a chapter on Homer, it is in fact an introduction to the Biblical method of reading; what seems to be an example of representation is nothing less than a model of interpretation. Thus the subtitle of the book, "The Representation of Reality in Western Literature," in order to reflect its approach, should read: "The Interpretation of the Representation of Reality in Western Literature." As the introductory chapter shows, the purpose of the whole project is not to analyze the dominant modes of this representation (i.e., present, describe, show their structure and effects), but rather interpret them (i.e., explain the secret meanings and purposes, unravel the significant pattern of their emergence and development). Auerbach's approach is exclusively Biblical: he comprehends literature according to rules that he finds dictated in the Bible, and consequently sees Western literary tradition as a (secular) Bible.

The purpose of Auerbach's book is to provide a sweeping Biblical view of literary history. His choice of texts alone is ample evidence. All his selections are canonical[2] (and often predictable), made from the revered masterpieces (Cahn 1979) of the dominant European tradition: *Satyricon, Chanson de Roland, Divina Commedia, Decameron, Gargantua et Pantagruel,*

Henry IV, Don Quixote, Manon Lescaut, Luise Millerin, To the Light-house—to mention but a few. These choices make the book "a massive reaffirmation of the Western cultural tradition" (Said 1983: 8). Further-more, selections are made and arranged with the Bible as a model. Accord-ing to Auerbach, the Bible is the greatest canonical book, the Book of books, the absolute Book—the Book containing all the books that are worth reading and preserving. In it (and because of it), there are no other gods, no other books, no other world.[3] "The truth claim of the Bible, Auer-bach says, is so imperious that reality in its sensuous or charming aspect is not dwelt upon; and the spotlight effect, which isolates major persons or happenings, is due to the same anagogical demand that excludes all other places and concerns. Bible stories do not flatter or fascinate like Homer's; they do not give us something artfully rendered; they force readers to be-come interpreters and to find the presence of what is absent in the fraught background, the densely layered (Auerbach uses the marvelous word *ge-schichtet*) narrative" (Hartman 1986: 15). As the central cultural construct of an entire tradition, it constitutes a colossal tautology and self-affirma-tion (and concomitantly a monument of ethnocentrism as well as censor-ship): the book that tells you what to read is both the single one worth reading and the privileged domain of human experience: "it seeks to over-come our reality: we are to fit our own life into its world, feel ourselves to be elements in its structure of universal history" (Auerbach 1953: 15).[4] Auerbach treats the Western literary canon in similar terms: his is a univer-sal history of literature without references, notes, or bibliography; without any room for minor characters, neglected incidents, or marginal works. We are commanded to have no other books before it. As a historical survey, it is organized in autonomous, self-contained units, and deals with a tradition of glorious achievements from its origins through its continuous evolution to the present. The notion of the tradition itself is not discussed, and its authority is recognized unquestionably. The unity, borders, jurisdiction, and goals of that authority are established. The driving implication is that the West has its own Bible, although a secular one, which is its literary canon.

Beyond Auerbach's veneration of the tradition, there is an impressive number and range of similarities that bring *Mimesis* and the Bible even closer—and again I am referring, of course, to *his* Bible, to the conception of the book that emerges from *his* discussion. Here are some characteristics he attributes to the Old Testament:

    — the intent of the stories "involves an absolute claim to historical truth" (14);

    —the narrator "was obliged to write exactly what his belief in the truth of the tradition . . . demanded of him" (14);

—the narrator composed "an effective version of the pious tradition" (14);

—"its claim to truth . . . excludes all other claims" (14);

—"we are to . . . feel ourselves to be elements in its structure of universal history" (15);

—"[it] presents universal history: it begins with the beginning of time . . . and will end with the Last Days . . . Everything else that happens in the world can only be conceived as an element in this sequence" (16);

—"interpretation in a determined direction becomes a general method of comprehending reality" (16);

—"it is pieced together—but the various components all belong to one concept of universal history and its interpretation" (17);

—"the reader is at every moment aware of the universal religio-historical perspective which gives the individual stories their general meaning and purpose" (17);

—"The greater the separateness and horizontal disconnection of the stories and groups of stories in relation to one another . . . the stronger is their vertical connection, which holds them all together" (17);

—an "element of development gives the . . . stories a historical character" (18);

—the style exhibits "development of the concept of the historically becoming, and preoccupation with the problematic" (23).

Although this list includes only characteristics attributed by Auerbach to the Bible, their applicability to his own book is so broad and striking that they may easily be taken as descriptions originally intended for *Mimesis*. They were not; but they do summarize its contents and episodic structure: brief, concise, paradigmatic, didactic, moral stories from the adventures of secular writing in the post-Biblical world, namely, literature.[5] Auerbach did not compose a History of Literature or the history of a particular idea, figure, or theme that would have been yet another all-encompassing, encyclopedic compendium; he wrote the Story of Literature—a selective philological survey which traces the origins and evolution of that chosen art, the art of the Book.

Mimesis is directly and extensively modeled on the Bible, and aspires to work like it: it consists of episodic stories of concentrated tension and high significance; it exhibits a discontinuous and yet evolutionary unity; it is driven by an urgent sense of universal history; it makes absolute claims on historical truth; it has a concrete, stable point of reference which makes everything involved in its sphere meaningful; it is fraught with religious, social, and political background; it employs a multi-layered, multi-dimensional narrative; finally, it seeks canonical authority. *Mimesis* aspires to be recognized as the Old Testament of exegetical philology, the Bible of literary criticism, by presenting and defending history as tradition, reading as interpretation. In its effort to cover Western literature in a definitive way, it employs two principal arguments: there is only one literature worth reading, the very canon which is its subject; and there is only one proper way of reading this canon, Biblical interpretation. By adopting the world-view and reenacting in an intensely dramatic fashion the method of its model, it attempts to achieve the same canonical status in the field of literary studies.[6]

When it outlines in a grand manner the order, the evolution, the laws, the purpose, and the justification of literary tradition, *Mimesis* performs a number of propaedeutic tasks that are important for an exercise of intellectual authority: it gives its readers what they need to know about the world of literature and helps them comprehend it properly; it trains their understanding and cultivates their judgment; and it explains the complex, intricate sense that great literature makes. Out of a large-scale philological explication, based on the orthodoxies of humanism and stylistic exegesis, there emerges a grandiose project: a Biblical interpretation of literature and a monumentalization of its Western canon. While Auerbach gives the modest impression that he is simply attending to the nuances and idiosyncrasies of individual texts, and is not imposing a uniform explanatory method on any of them, his first chapter already testifies to his use of an ahistorical uniformity of standards and universality of principles. His notion of the real is a renunciation of the political: "The argument against 'politics' made throughout *Mimesis* is just this—the realist must surrender himself to his material, suspend all his beliefs, prejudices, and political convictions (which Auerbach *assumes* is possible) in order to achieve a total and direct presentation of reality" (Carroll 1975: 8). (Naturally, this does not mean that his bias is reprehensible, only that his objectivist claims are false.)

Still, the paradox of the chapter's title, which deceives with its unwarranted emphasis on Odysseus, persists: why a discussion of Homer under a misleading heading and in an introduction veiled as a chapter? Given the orientation and methodology of the volume, it appears surprising that Auerbach decided to start with Homer and apply to the *Odyssey* a Biblical treatment, an interpretive reading, instead of simply beginning with the Bible and proceeding from his real model. The problem is not why the second term of the Homeric-Biblical distinction is so heavily privileged, but rather why this very distinction was necessary and what it says about the possible functions of the essay. To answer that any similar project should commence with the Greek epic, an acknowledged classic, would be an inadequate (not to say Eurocentric) response, since it does not solve the problem of the devious title. The basic questions remain: why oppose the Homeric mode of representation to the Biblical one, when what was intended was an adoption, emulation, and propagation of the latter? Why was a discussion of Homer essential to a work modeled on the Bible, a work which aspired to become the Bible of literary criticism? And why did the overwhelming presence of the Bible have to be initially concealed? Auerbach's conception of (what he calls) the Old Testament suggests the answer.

Auerbach believes that the dramatic quality and cultural authority of the Bible is enhanced by an intrinsic dialectic between what is there and what is not, what is present and what is absent, what is said and what is implied, what is mentioned and what is omitted, what happens and what could have happened—the constant, unrelieved tension between presence and absence, voice and silence, promise and fulfillment, being and becoming. His understanding of the Bible depends on polar oppositions which remain unresolvable. The Book of books is constantly valorized as the supreme text because of what it does not state, does not fully narrate, does not reveal, does not name—thus preserving the prophecy about the "fulfilling of the Covenant" (Auerbach 1953: 16) and binding people to its eschatology. This type of valorization through contrast needs a second, almost negative term of comparison, an abject possibility, so that a positive value can be postulated. In the Old Testament, the supreme value is "a single and hidden God" (17), who, after the Fall of Man, "is not comprehensible in his presence, as is Zeus; it is always only 'something' of him that appears, he always extends into depths" (12). He is the hidden or absent God of Abraham whose (condemning) silence enables the Bible to speak (about human guilt). The positive value, then, is constituted as the fundamental otherness, the hidden depth of that ostensibly complete presence, that immediate experience, which defines the negative term of the dichotomy.

The need for defense of a Biblical interpretation like *Mimesis* to include (and even begin with) a discussion of Homer must be explained on the basis of Auerbach's theory about the dialectic inherent in the Old Testament. The Bible is fraught with background, the presence of God's absence: "Since so much in the story is dark and incomplete, and since the reader knows that God is a hidden God, his effort to interpret it constantly finds something new to feed upon" (15). An effective valorization of the Bible would similarly present it as the background haunting Western literature, with its dark presence always in ambiguous retreat, its power constantly felt through its radical difference that allows only something of its depths to appear, inalienable and yet urgent. This presentation requires an absolute contrast to a world of light, immediacy, and fullness, a foreground of false essence and illusionary being. The Homeric epic is called to play this indispensable role, portrayed in every small detail as the negative term of the opposition: in its two-dimensional clarity, it makes readers understand where the Bible is *not*, what it does *not* do, how it does *not* work. Against its foreground, against its unrippling surface, the total difference of the Bible can be recognized as the dramatic, historical, religious, and aesthetic background of all literature.

Analysis too, as a mode of reading, is fraught with the background of interpretation, of that dimension of understanding which feeds on insight rather than vision. The contrast with Homeric analysis highlights the power of interpretation to overcome the charm of appearance and pierce through the spectre of presence. Without analysis, there would be no need for the promise of depth and delivery that interpretation carries. By presenting the Bible as the non-Homeric and non-analytic, Auerbach is in a position not only to praise the originary monument of the canon, but also to show that the kind of reading it invites is the best way to read the whole canon.[7] The purpose of employing the Homeric term is to illustrate graphically the perils of secular representation and understanding. This strategy also explains the character of Auerbach's revisionary reading of the canon. It does not pertain to individual names, works, or events but to the overall approach. The philologist is not interested in changing the entries or their order but rather the way these masterworks are read. He proposes and practices Biblical interpretation as a more powerful approach to the great tradition. In order to do this, he must articulate at his position as the positive term of a binary opposition and construct an idea of the epic as its hostile negative. The tasks of literary interpretation must be established as a moral alternative to the pleasures of Greek physical/material understanding (or analysis).

In addition to critical techniques, the book employs literary devices as well. The systems of thought and style outlined in the description of the Biblical mode bear a very close resemblance to standards of modernist taste (which are not always the same as techniques of modernist writing). Notions like background, interiority, suspense, multi-layeredness, disconnectedness, absence, suggestiveness, fragmentariness, silence, individuality, and others associated with them express qualities of the modernist aesthetic which dominated the first half of the twentieth century. Critics have already noted the successful appropriation of such literary techniques: "With its high respect for randomness and discontinuity, *Mimesis* is another classic of modernism" (Robbins 1986: 49). In his review, René Wellek went even further, suggesting that *Mimesis* "must be judged as something of a work of art." Many years before Roland Barthes or J. Hillis Miller argued for (and pursued) the literariness of criticism, Auerbach had learned from the structural experiments of the post-Flaubertian novel. Thus, in his treatment of the Bible, he is not only tracing the origins of our tradition, but is also suggesting that the Biblical mode has outlasted the Homeric, reigning over the masterful literary representations today, even though the Homeric mode was the first to achieve wide appeal and recognition. The contemporary world is understood and represented in Biblical terms: its

literature itself is, at its best, Biblical. Now that this world has almost overcome the old Greek influence, the Bible is its true, authentic contemporary, since contemporary literature was unmistakably prefigured in it.

In historical viewpoint, *Mimesis* is a work of figural interpretation: it interprets the Western canon as a figure of the Bible and, conversely, claims
that the Bible finds its fulfillment in our literary tradition. Figural or typological understanding constitutes the exegetical approach of the book.
Auerbach's celebrated essay *"Figura"* (1944), written just before *Mimesis*,
may be seen as the missing methodological introduction.

Figuralism or typology[8] originated in early Christian efforts to show that
Jesus Christ was indeed the Messiah and had fulfilled Jewish prophecies, by
retrospectively explaining the Hebrew Bible as the "Old" of the "New Testament"—as the first announcement of a promise that had been kept. A
figura or type is constituted by a historical event or person and can be
identified only when fulfilled by a later event or person in a providentially
structured history, i.e., by its anti-type. The purpose of figurae is "to accommodate the events and persons of a superseded order of time to a new
one" (Kermode 1983: 90). Auerbach explains that the rhetorical *tropos* of
figura acquired its first modern meaning with Tertullian: "*[F]igura* is something real and historical which announces something else that is also real
and historical. The relation between the two events is revealed by an accord
or similarity" (Auerbach 1984: 29). This meaning is connected by definition with the theological *topos* of fulfillment, which is the coming into
being, the historical happening, of what the figure prophetically announced—the revelation of the future originally intimated by it. Thus the
figure is also the prefiguration of things to come, and therefore it is based
on an eschatological view of history. The textual reading which takes figura
as its starting point is called figural interpretation: "[It] establishes a connection between two events or persons, the first of which signifies not only
itself but also the second, while the second encompasses or fulfills the first.
The two poles of the figure are separate in time, but both, being real events
or figures, are within time, within the stream of historical life" (53). Thus
emphasis falls decisively on the typological design of developments and on
fulfillment in history: "Both remain historical events; yet both, looked at in
this way, have something provisional and incomplete about them; they
point to one another and they both point to something in the future, something still to come, which will be the actual, real, and definitive event. . . .
Thus history, with all its concrete force, remains forever a figure, cloaked
and needful of interpretation" (58).

Auerbach's definition of figural interpretation describes both the interpretive project he finds dictated by the Old Testament and his own approach. In opting for a figural narrative of literature, he subscribes to an

eschatological view of history under an unequivocally theological inspiration. The story he tells presents a series of developments that draw their
significance from a higher order, that of a destined completion. As he puts
it, "in the figural system the interpretation is always sought from above;
events are considered not in their unbroken relation to one another, but
torn apart, individually, each in relation to something other that is promised and not yet present" (59). Prefigurative understanding and the language of types allow him to claim the Western tradition for the Biblical
mimesis, and criticism for typological interpretation. Auerbach's view of
the past may also account for the book's organizing typological principle:
"Historical events or literary texts may have their own unique and local
significance—if they have any meaning at all—but in a history's figural
interpretation they are metaphorized as carrying some further significance,
so that some may 'foreshadow' others in a narrative which would grant the
sense of a whole to otherwise self-contained parts" (Bahti 1981: 111).[9] Thus
the appropriation of this Christian exegetical technique for literary criticism, which may be also seen as "another belated repetition of the Christian appropriation and usurpation of the Hebrew Bible" (Bloom 1984: 5),
serves many purposes: it establishes a deeper unity between religious and
secular writing; it argues for a narrative continuity between the ancient and
the modern; it defends the transhistorical modernity of the Bible, making
it the originary event in literature; it intimates the Biblical character of
modernism; lastly, it emphasizes the messianic destination of literature
and the prophetic role of interpretation.[10]

Typology declined around the turn of the nineteenth century with the
emergence of Higher Criticism in Germany. By the time David Friedrich
Strauss published *The Life of Jesus, Critically Examined* (1835), all interest
in it had disappeared. Consequently its revival by Auerbach was quite a
bold move, since his audience could not be expected to have any direct
familiarity with it. Through the concerns of Romance philology, however,
Auerbach was able to provide some informative background, as he did in
Dante: Poet of the Secular World (1929). More importantly, the distance in
time allowed for a return to that method without its original Christian
connotations. Philology and literary history provided a new, scholarly (as
opposed to theological) context. Thus Auerbach employed it while transferring its religious dimension to questions of aesthetic meaning and literary tradition.[11]

For him, philology (as interpretation) is above all an act of faith, and its
theory is the theology of literature, of the secular Scripture. In Auerbach's
hermeneutics, "divinity is not so much removed as secularized. That is to
say, continuity of history is preserved thanks to a new incarnation" (Costa-
Lima 1988: 489). Auerbach understands figural interpretation and practices it in *Mimesis* as an exegesis of prophecy, as divination through explo-

rations of prefigurement, as an explication of promises yet to be fulfilled. Near the end of the essay, he identifies figura with prophecy in explicitly theological language: "In this way the individual earthly event is not regarded as a definite self-sufficient reality, nor as a link in a chain of development in which single events or combinations of events perpetually give rise to new events, but viewed primarily in immediate vertical connection with a divine order which encompasses it, which on some future day will itself be concrete reality; so that the earthly event is a prophecy or *figura* of a part of a wholly divine reality that will be enacted in the future. But this reality is not only future; it is always present in the eye of God and in the other world, which is to say that in transcendence the revealed and true reality is present at all times, or timelessly" (Auerbach 1984: 72). Thus the figure is both a prophecy about an *eschaton* that will occur at the End of Time, and a revelation of that ultimate reality as it is presently encoded in this world, specifically in its re-presentations by Western literature.[12] To return once more to the subtitle of *Mimesis* (which Auerbach never explains): it has become clear that the term "representation" refers to his understanding of all major literature (already prefigured in the Bible) as figura, while "reality" refers to the divine truth that inheres in every present and that will be actualized in/as a unique future, the advent of the Messiah. Rephrased and completed according to its messianic perspective and eschatological yearning, the subtitle should now read: "The Biblical Interpretation of the Prefigurement of the Fulfillment of the Covenant in the Tradition of the Secular Scripture."

In "*Figura*," Auerbach claimed that the figural view of history was active from the early days of Christianity until the eighteenth century. In *Mimesis*, however, the historical origin is replaced with a universalist invariable, the polar distinction between the two modes of Western representation. In the original account, the pagan/archaic/allegorical was what came before the Biblical/Christian/figural. In the new account, the figural is reduced to a variation of the Biblical, one of the two dominant modes—and the same has been done, of course, to all things Christian. The two modes are made to oppose, antagonize each other, and to compete for mastery over human understanding. The Biblical is treated as the most important one, and is used systematically throughout the book as the basic approach to Western literature. On the other hand, the Homeric mode, although almost totally forgotten after the second chapter—receiving brief mention in chapters 5 and 8—returns at the end. Chapters 18 and 19 form the apogee of *Mimesis*, a celebration of the Biblical understanding of history which entered its modern maturity with the nineteenth-century realist novel. But in the last chapter, gloom and doom prevail. This is an age of confusion and hopelessness caused by "the complicated process of dissolution which led to fragmentation of the exterior action, to reflection of consciousness, and to stratification of time" (Auerbach 1953: 552–53), in fiction as well as in real life. The last work examined, Virginia Woolf's *To the Lighthouse* (1927), is compared extensively to the *Odyssey*. Thus the pagan element reappears in obvious response to a question that was tacitly left unanswered in *"Figura"*: what happened after the long domination of the figural view ended? The answer here is implicit, yet ominous: the Homeric, the pagan element, threatens to take over again.

Auerbach is not fighting against Christianity. He is content to indicate the continuity uniting it with Judaism through quiet references to the "Judeo-Christian view of history" (73) or arguments showing that "the first effect of the Judeo-Christian manner of dealing with the events in the world of reality led to anything but rigidity and narrowness. The hidden-ness of God and finally his *parousia* . . . brought about a dynamic move-ment in the basic conception of life . . . which went far beyond the clas-sic-antique norm of the imitation of real life and living growth" (119).[13] Auerbach does not see Christianity as a serious opponent: he skillfully de-velops an idea of the Biblical that includes and appropriates it, reducing it to a variation on the Old Testament. The real enemy is the non-Biblical: the Homeric, the pagan, the Greek.[14] He often alludes to this imminent threat by detecting unsettling parallels between the ancient world and the present order of things, as in the following passage: "Homer . . . likes to bring in the lineage, station, and previous history of his characters. . . . His Greek audiences are schooled in mythology and genealogy; Homer under-takes to give them the family-tree of the character in question as a means of placing him. Just so, in modern times, a newcomer into an exclusive aristocratic or bourgeois society can be placed by information concerning his paternal and maternal relatives. Thus, rather than an impression of historical change, Homer evokes the illusion of an unchanging, a basically stable social order, in comparison with which the succession of individuals and changes in personal fortunes appear unimportant" (28). Auerbach por-trays the Homeric as the enemy of the Judeo-Christian tradition: from the Greek stems everything septic, static, autocratic, absolutist. "'Just so, in modern times,' he writes, in order to demonstrate that Homer's genealogy is not so very different from the Nazis' 'Aryanization' laws, which traced back one's ancestors to three or four removed generations. Homer's my-thology is not so different from the new mythology of the Thousand-Year Reich and its *Volkstaat*" (Green 1982: 42–43). Auerbach's attack on Greek thought becomes anti-Hellenic when he blames the evils of modernity on the Homeric spirit.[15]

Auerbach believes that he is witnessing a critical stage of the historical process, the modern Drama of Europe, and like Ezra Pound (Davie 1975: 17–31) before him in *The Spirit of Romance: An Attempt to Define Some-*

what the Charm of the Pre-Renaissance Literature of Latin Europe (1910), he thinks of "the European possibilities of Romance philology as . . . a task specific to our time" (Auerbach 1965: 6). With great faith in the necessary mission of his discipline, "he sees philological historicism . . . not only as the means by which 'humanity' becomes aware of its own spectacle of 'humanisation,' but also, in traditional idealistic fashion, as the highest point or culmination of that spectacle, the drama of history come to self-consciousness, as it were" (Bové 1986: 164). He is deeply concerned about the present crisis, fearing that "European civilization is approaching the term of its existence." The philologist studying literary history through stylistics proposes, as a way out of this intellectual malaise and historical crisis, interpretive and figural understanding as moral renewal. Interpretation promises spiritual emancipation.

Mimesis represents the epitome of this effort toward a return to Biblical textual faith. The politics behind the Manichean strategy of the book is obvious since Auerbach "conceived of his survey as a unity, as a generalized interpretation of the history of Western civilization and its literature designed and arranged so that two opposing strands or evolutions appear. The one—rigid, restrictive, categorizing, pompous, elitist, hedonistic, decadent, posturing, and ultimately anti-humanity—is meant to be associated with the forces of totalitarianism that were challenging the fate of the world. The other—fluid, open, populist, honest, democratic, moral, serious, and ultimately pro-humanity—is meant to be associated with the best qualities of the democratic Western world" (Green 1982: 62–63). As we have seen, the first strand represents Greek analytical thought, while the second is associated with Biblical figural interpretation. History, tradition, and writing are viewed in terms of this on-going dialectic confrontation, and the only possibility of a synthesis is the eventual assimilation of Christianity into its Biblical roots, resulting in the complete eradication of paganism.

Auerbach's main goal was to study (what he defined as) the Biblical mode of understanding, and promote it as a model for literary and historical knowledge/experience in all its timeliness and urgent relevance. A complementary goal was to show that Christianity is derivative and should faithfully return (as it has been doing for some time) to its religious and historical roots. In both respects, an outstanding feature of his argumentation is the consistent presentation of Greek thought as the negative, alien, and hostile element, which must be neutralized, and finally extinguished. In Auerbach's survey of the canon, the central dialectic evolves between the Homeric and the Biblical, the pagan and the religious, the mythical and the historical, the Hellenic and the Hebraic. The same survey inquires into the possibility of a new (Judeo-Christian) synthesis, whose model has been already prefigured in the representational style of the Old Testament. This synthesis is necessary in order for humanity to survive the modern crisis created by the resurgence of totalitarianism, as the powers of paganism have again increased their influence. Until recently, Western culture seemed to move toward that direction, as indicated, for example, by the historical awareness of realist fiction. But that progress was interrupted by the forces of order, stability, and hierarchy, causing the confusion and hopelessness that modernism reflects. Still, although the possibility of a new synthesis looks at this time very difficult, "the approaching unification and simplification" (Auerbach 1953: 553) remain the only way to a true humanism. The interpretive struggle against the tyranny of antiquity must continue until complete emancipation (of understanding and representing). Thus Auerbach portrays the development of Western literature as the conflict between two incompatible modes of expression, and its larger context of world history as a cosmic battle between the irreconcilable forces of evil and good, or (to put it in the most appropriately banal way) between Athens and Jerusalem (Clark 1984; Eidelberg 1983; Weltin 1987). The pagan evil must be defeated, because it is the source of all anguish, terror, superstition, discrimination, and oppression; the power of God, so magnificently represented in the Biblical prefigural style, will again prevail. In Auerbach's prophecy against the Greek Lucifer of Days, the construction of the Homeric as a paronomastic substitute for the Hellenic served to define and defend not only figural interpretation and historicist realism, but above all the Biblical mode and the Hebraic spirit. *Mimesis*, however, besides being an affirmation, monumentalization, and appropriation of the Western literary canon on behalf of Biblical thought, has a more narrow focal point: it constitutes a revision of that other major modernist *Geistesgeschichte, The Theory of the Novel* (1916) by Georg Lukács (1885–1971).[16]

Lukács' study responded to the Romantic call for "a philosophy of the novel, the rough outlines of which are contained in Plato's political theory" (Schlegel 1971: 198). In the "Dialogue on Poetry" (1799–1800), Friedrich Schlegel had defined the task of this philosophy as "a spiritual viewing of the subject with calm and serene feeling, as it is proper to view in solemn joy the meaningful play of divine images. Such a theory of the novel would have to be itself a novel which would imaginatively reflect every eternal tone of the imagination and would again confound the chaos of the world of the knights. The things of the past would live in it in new forms; Dante's sacred shadow would arise from the lower world, Laura would hover heavenly before us, Shakespeare would converse intimately with Cervantes, and there Sancho would jest with Don Quixote again" (Schlegel 1968: 102–3).

Lukács' book, like *Mimesis*, a work of theory and criticism inspired by Hegelian dialectic (Bernstein 1984), deals with the development of Western literature and is based on a fundamental polarity, discussing from a historico-philosophical perspective the two major forms of epic literature, ancient epic poetry and the modern novel. Lukács differs from Auerbach in so far as he compares the two categories diachronically, not synchronically, and therefore presents them as opposed forms, not antithetical modes. Thus they are compared as paradigmatic expressions of two different ages, not as perennial modalities of thinking and writing. The contrast is absolute but does not allow for direct conflict because it is grounded in historico-cultural circumstances rather than fundamental structures of language and experience.

For Lukács, the epic is the expression of the ancient Greek world, whose primary characteristic was totality of being, completeness of self-being. That world was completely rounded, homogeneous, and meaningful, without any internal gaps or divisions. Dichotomies of experience like interior and exterior, self and other, will and destiny, immanence and transcendence, theory and praxis, and history and philosophy, did not exist, or rather they appeared in an integrated form, articulated in unity. The earthly world and the given moment were the supreme principles in life, and man felt at home everywhere within that all-encompassing, comforting wholeness. Everything was tangible and physical because the world of objects was fully present in its extensive totality. There was no need for theory—no questions, no philosophy: the sensual world of forms was the direct answer, the well-ordered wholeness of immediate reality the only philosophy. The world of the epic is perfectly organic: everything coexists, connects, coheres. All that matters and transpires is the total immediacy of the fully given: there is only foreground, light, form, completeness, unity, as essence and existence become inextricably interwoven into luminous being. That is the meaning of what Lukács calls "integrated civilization," and the epic constitutes its paradigmatic expression.

This understanding of the Greek epic bears many similarities with Auerbach's, as outlined in *Mimesis*: "fully externalized description, uniform illumination, uninterrupted connection, free expression, all events in the foreground, displaying unmistakable meanings, few elements of historical development and psychological perspective" (Auerbach 1953: 19). Although Auerbach borrowed these crucial ideas from Lukács, his rhetoric was quite different. He strengthened the credibility of the argument in two ways: first, he referred to a specific author, Homer, and concentrated on a concrete work, the *Odyssey*; second, he discarded the lyrical, nostalgic incantations of Lukács, using instead the discourse of philology, and the techniques of stylistics in particular. Thus by focusing on one author, one work, one passage, and adopting a respectable scholarly language, he authorized his repetition as an academic study, free from the romantic liberties taken in the philosophical essay.

With regard to the novel (which Goethe had called "a subjective epic" and Hegel the *"bürgerliche epopoeia"*),[17] Lukács believes that it is the contemporary epic—the epic of the age of philosophy, homesickness, and sinfulness, of the fragmented and God-forsaken world. Where there was unity and totality, now there is division and separation. This is the time of the homeless individual, of the unredeemed fall, of decentered metaphysics. "The abandonment of the world by God manifests itself in the incommensurability of soul and work, of interiority and adventure—in the absence of a transcendental 'place' allotted to human endeavor" (Lukács 1971: 97). The transcendental has been displaced by exile, the extrovert hero of the epic by the introspective subject of the novel. Existence is dissonant, uncertain, supposititious; estrangement and nostalgia afflict the tragic soul. The world of objects has been reduced to a fixed category, nature. Nothing bridges the within to the without. Individuality has become an end in itself; autonomy and independence are the desolate spaces humans inhabit. Subject and object, present and past, history and philosophy are irreparably torn apart. Self-reflexivity is the common lot, interiority the sole realm of adventure. Time turns into History as it moves inexorably toward the Last Judgment; totality flees into the heterogeneous. The gods have departed or remain silent; the project of salvation has been left incomplete. This is what Lukács calls the "problematic civilization."

A comparison of this lament of belatedness with Auerbach's description of Biblical representation shows further convergence of opinion: "certain parts brought into high relief, others left obscure, abruptness, suggestive influence of the unexpressed, 'background' quality, multiplicity of meanings and the need for interpretation, universal-historical claims, development of the concept of the historically becoming, and preoccupation with the problematic" (Auerbach 1953: 19). The similarities become more significant in light of Auerbach's aim to establish diachronic equivalences between the Biblical mode and the realist style of fiction. Not only does the novel emerge as a central topic of interest for both critics; an important equation between their oppositions can also be identified: Lukács' Greek epic corresponds to Auerbach's Homeric mode; and Lukács' novel corresponds to Auerbach's Biblical mode (and realist fiction). It is rather superficial to say that the "distinction between the epic and the novel is founded on a distinction between the Hellenic and the Western mind" (de Man 1983: 53). The founding distinction, as articulated by Auerbach, is that between the Hellenic and the Hebraic.

Furthermore, Lukács' conception of the epic, too, is Biblical. Consider his depiction of the Greek world: placed in the context of a binary opposi-

Hymns (174), Job[19] and Oedipus (398), while among the Biblical genres he distinguished Hebrew elegiac, didactic, lyric, idyllic, and dramatic poetry—all of them superior to their Hellenic equivalents. Throughout the book, his stylistic commentary prefigures, so to speak, Auerbach's search for the structure of the ethnic mind. Here is his comparison of the metric capabilities of the two languages: "For the Greek, beyond every other language (and the Latin next to it), is copious, flowing, and harmonious, possessed of a great variety of measures, of which the impression is so definite, the effects so striking, that if one should recite some lame and imperfect portion of a verse, or even enunciate hastily several verses in a breath, the numbers would nevertheless be clearly discernible. . . . But in the Hebrew language the whole economy is different. Its form is simple above every other; the radical words are uniform, and resemble each other almost exactly; nor are the inflexions numerous, or materially different: whence we may readily understand, that its metres are neither complex nor capable of much variety; but rather simple, grave, temperate; less adapted to fluency than dignity and force" (70–71). Like Lowth, who looked at the Hebrew Bible in his search for the fundamentals of poetry and established them by comparing it to Greek writing,[20] Auerbach adopted the same comparativist approach in his own search for the essence of narrative.

Lowth's book is arguably the first work of literary criticism, of that modern reading (called "divine discipline" by Friedrich Schlegel) which isolates texts and analyzes them for their inherent structure and intrinsic qualities. The focus of his attention is uniqueness of style and artistic significance. The fact that such an approach was first applied to the primary religious work of the West is not at all paradoxical. On the contrary, it was the precarious, ambivalent use of the Bible by the believers at that time that dictated the approach. When the voice of the text is no longer heard by its community, "it is *literature* that rises out of the *absence* of Holy Writ, its evasions, withdrawals, and silences" (Needler 1982: 397). Literary criticism emerged as the paradox of secular theology, of a theology that could no longer depend on faith alone for the legitimation of its sources and authority. Literary theory was originally the hermeneutics of that theology, the close reading which was dedicated to extracting from the text itself, from its signifying operations, its meaning and importance. "Saving the Text," to borrow a title (Hartman 1981), was from the beginning its *raison d'être* and rallying cry. That Text has been the Bible.

The very possibility of the project of criticism as a non-theological interpretation was first fully established by Benedict (Baruch) de Spinoza (1632–77), who explored the links between theology, close reading, and politics. Spinoza tried to save the Bible from the devastating Wars of Religion (1560–1660) and the onslaught of empiricist reason in diverse ways: he mediated between Maimonides and Descartes, he dismissed divine inspiration, he wrote a Hebrew grammar. No other effort, though, can be compared with his anonymously published *Tractatus Theologico-politicus* (1670), that "prescient masterpiece of the higher criticism" (Gay 1966: 24), which attracted considerable attention from the start, though until the 1780s in mostly hostile responses. In it, Spinoza attacked superstition and opposed reason to revelation, trying to support Jan de Witt's struggles with Calvinism. While Reformists like Philip Melanchthon (1497–1560) had insisted that philosophy be regarded as *ancilla theologiae*, he distinguished metaphysics as an independent inquiry from theology. This was a bold book that raised issues of understanding (as independent close reading of the Bible), natural rights (such as the right of the individual to interpret), and governance (which should take the Hebrew polity as its model). Spinoza was explicit about his intent and its ideological context: "As I marked the fierce controversies of philosophers raging in Church and State, the source of bitter hatred and dissension, the ready instruments of sedition and other ills innumerable, I determined to examine the Bible afresh in a careful, impartial, and unfettered spirit, making no assumptions concerning it, and attributing to it no doctrines, which I do not find clearly therein set down. With these precautions I constructed a method of Scriptural interpretation" (Spinoza 1951: 8). In response to social upheavals and philosophical disputes that threatened Biblical authority, he devised a new approach that promised to respect the political (but of course not the religious or philosophical) legitimacy of every reading. Spinoza was the first to argue that the right to interpret (the Bible) was a political one, and to demand the philosophical emancipation of that right.[21]

According to his immanentist hermeneutic principle, the Bible must be understood exclusively by itself, its knowledge derived from its own literal meaning. "His *Theologico-Political Treatise* is the first attempt at a philosophical justification and foundation of Biblical criticism" (Cassirer 1951: 184). The book is addressed to Christian philosophers, and its primary goal is to free philosophy from (Christian) theology. "Precisely because Spinoza openly abandoned in the *Treatise* the belief in the cognitive value of the Bible, his maxim to speak 'ad captum vulgi' forced him to assign the highest possible value to the practical or moral demands of the Bible" (Strauss 1952: 197). Reading acquires practical importance: it governs understanding and guides morality. Consequently, any attempt to govern it from outside ignores this useful importance. Spinoza's interpretive "immanentism" (Yovel 1990) was not entirely new. The very concept of interpretation as a personal, independent (and ultimately ascetic) exercise had already been in place for some one hundred fifty years. Erasmus had defended the right of individuals to read the Bible in their common language. As for the idea that knowledge of the Scripture ought to be "looked for in Scripture only" (Spinoza 1951: 100) and that the pursuit of this knowledge was an individual's task and responsibility, it had been propagated by the Reformation since its inception. Spinoza's own original contribution was to politicize the issue by inserting it into discussions of governance.

In Spinoza's work, interpretation, the Reformers' religious duty, became a political right. He claimed that it was political because it was natural (211), civil, and private (207). Instead of being the privilege of the few, "the highest power of Scriptural interpretation belongs to every man" (119)—to the extent, of course, that this is a religious duty and an individual right: this is the democratic Biblical secularism of the *Tractatus*. In a telling passage, the possibility as well as the limits of interpretation as a civil right are defined: "Therefore, as the supreme right of free thinking, even on religion, is in every man's power, and as it is inconceivable that such power could be alienated, it is also in every man's power to wield the supreme right and authority of free judgment in this behalf, and to explain and interpret religion for himself. The only reason for vesting in the hands of the magistrates the supreme authority for the interpretations of law and judgment on public affairs is that they concern questions of public right. Similarly the supreme authority in explaining religion, and in passing judgment thereon, is lodged with the individual because it concerns questions of individual right" (118–19). At issue here is not the legitimacy of personal faith but the right to private understanding. Interpretation can be contested as a right only when it is presented and practiced as private. On the other hand, when the believer becomes a reader of the Bible and when its understanding can be entrusted to him, he can be safely governed.

This distribution of power is not enforced, but guaranteed by a "covenant" (205, 208) between the individual and the sovereign: the sovereign governs, the individual interprets.[22] The "true aim of government is liberty" (259), and liberty is now understood as (that is, limited to) freedom of interpretive judgment. Reason, rights, interpretation, individuality, the Bible, even the government—all are accepted as natural. "In a democracy (the most natural form of government . . .) everyone submits to the control of authority over his actions, but not over his judgment and reason" (263). The emancipation of interpretation is guaranteed by an interpretive understanding of emancipation—an understanding that limits it to areas of knowledge and belief. A few decades before the *Tractatus* appeared the greatest pupil of Erasmus, Hugo Grotius (1583–1645), in his *De jure belli ac pacis* (1635), founded the system of human rights not on divine revelation but on the natural law of reason and social contract of state. He also abolished the medieval distinction between *lex naturae* and *lex divina* by showing that they can both be based on reason. Spinoza extended the contract to include, in addition to choice of government, the exercise of interpretation. They both sought new grounds for strong governmental authority during the period of the Thirty Years' War after the feudal order collapsed and a need arose for an international order in the emerging Europe of nations.

This is the civil covenant to which they contributed: when one submits to authority, one becomes a subject—an individual who has the right to interpret (the Bible) and is entitled to his private opinion (about it). The idea of the self, the independent person, implies that "society is constituted of autonomous, equal, units, namely separate individuals, and that such individuals are more important, ultimately, than any larger constituent group. It is reflected in the concept of individual private property, in the political and legal liberty of the individual, in the idea of the individual's direct communication with God" (Macfarlane 1978: 5). In the theologico-political treatise, interpretation is liberated when it escapes the control of theology and enters the civic world. In order to save the Bible, Spinoza frees interpretation from the law (of theology, faith, court, and tradition) while making it the new Law, the rule of the textual experience of divine meaning—the law of Kant, Kierkegaard, Kafka, and Derrida. This is the order which Auerbach saw in decline and tried to invigorate by returning to the fundamentals of interpretive faith. The problem is that such a return runs against the highest principle of interpretation, the autonomy of understanding. Spinoza's initiative was based on this principle: an autonomous understanding does not need any outside guidance or supervision because it is self-governing; interpretation is the secular law. How wise was it, however, to limit the quest for autonomy, the supreme project of modernity, only to the emancipatory promise of interpretation?

Hebraism and Hellenism

Until the end of the thirteenth century, the Western Church remained the central, all-powerful, unified and unifying institution of its society: religion and church were one, the study of doctrine and the study of the Bible identical. The New Testament was considered the exclusive foundation of the faith, and interest in the Hebrew Bible was limited, as Auerbach has explained, to explorations of prefiguration. By the early fourteenth century, however, preachers and scholars started challenging the exclusive power of the church by questioning its explanatory authority and appealing directly to the Bible itself.[23] "Those scholars and preachers and demagogues (Marsilius of Padua, Wyclif and the Lollards, the Hussites, for example) who challenged the authority of the Church as it was then institutionally constituted, held up the authority of the Bible in its place and argued that the interpretation of Scripture was no matter for the Church to regulate if by the Church was meant the Pope and his cardinals. Instead, the individual must read for himself under the guidance of the Holy Spirit" (Evans 1985: 7). The aim of this new belief was "to challenge the Church both as official interpreter of the Bible and as having authority to decide questions of doctrine" (9). There were also practical considerations dictated by social developments. "On the intellectual level, by the end of the fifteenth century, theology needed a new tool. It had to go back beyond the scholastics and, almost more importantly, beyond Augustine. It had to be evangelical and it had to make the Christian religion correlative to human moral needs" (Levi 1987: 117). As a result, Christians were encouraged to explore personal exegesis, to exercise their own judgment in reading the articles of the faith. Such positions advocated "a devaluation of the collective existence represented by sacraments, saints, and the 'unwritten' tradition of the Church, in favor of a naked confrontation with the scriptures" (Bossy 1985: 97). Similar challenges, based on an increasing attention to the sacred texts, culminated in the Reformation.

With the Protestant Reformation in the sixteenth century, the Church ceased being a unified body of pious believers and became a congregation of attentive readers. Faith, it was determined, not institutional religion, came first; and true faith could only be founded in the Bible. The principal dogma consecrated at the Diet of Worms (1521) was that of *sola scriptura*: "For the reformers the important principle is that the Bible is not only its own witness through the Holy Spirit, but also its own interpreter, proving, judging, illuminating itself" (Evans 1985: 32).[24] The study of the Bible was the road to salvation. Interpretation became a religious duty, and the exercise of personal judgment in private study was actively pursued. A dramatic change, from the ecclesiastic to the interpretive use of the Bible, made possible the Protestant conception of the text: "As the reformers began to dispute hitherto unquestioningly accepted ways of administering grace and truth and power, as the infallible institution of papacy, the rule of cardinals, bishops, and priests, together with the immense power of the confessional was tottering, the most basic levels of religious legitimation were shifted away from the collective bodies and rituals of the Church toward what, in the strength of the personal faith of each believer, was an altogether new emphasis on the reading and interpretation of Scripture as the divine locus of a finished revelation" (Weimann 1986: 452). As the liturgical context disappeared and the institutional support withered, the interpretive imperative provided the only credible religious axiomatic in a world that felt for the first time the experience of popular upheaval as a *social* problem. At the same time, when the colonial West sought to protect and justify its embarrassing riches, the interpretive imperative became probably the first explicatory technique *and* regulatory mechanism to teach the European merchant the wealth of his soul and the rewards of his vocation.

In charting the translation of Western Christianity into the Reformation, three major points of transition may be discerned (Bossy 1985): the shift from a conception of life centered on kin and the social realm to another centered on the individual and his family; the replacement of the ethical code of the Seven Deadly Sins by the Ten Commandments and the rule of their law; and, most importantly for our discussion, the shift from the ritual and symbolism of the Sacraments in a community of kin to the meaning and truth of the Word in a civil society. The Reformation emphasized religious experience, evangelical piety, and moral commitment, while raising questions of the authenticity of faith and ethics. Privacy and interpretation (that is, the depth of interiority) were the enabling conditions of subjectivity, of bourgeois individualism as it emerged in the sixteenth century; and the site of askesis for subjectivity (desert, abyss, or purgatory) was the text of the Bible itself. With this secular soteriology, not only did sin turn into a personal problem, but also reading became a matter of salvation as an integral part of what Max Weber called "worldly asceticism." The new type of reading reconstituted both reader and the object of his devotion. The practice of close (and silent) study brought into relief the character and integrity of the text—its constitution as a series of books and as a unified whole, which its use in church had obscured by making its different parts serve different functions in the service.

Also the split of theology into speculative and exegetical branches during the early twelfth century had taken on dangerous proportions, as by the late fifteenth century the former was following the direction of logic and the latter of grammar, both cultivating a threatening positivism under the strong influence of scientific reasoning. The Reformation brought the two branches together again into the cooperative study of the Bible and gave them a common task: the elucidation of logical and semantic contradictions in the text, and the search for what Huldrych Zwingli called, in his treatise of 1522, the "Clarity and Certainty or Power of the Word of God."[25]

Thus literalism, as this new kind of study became known, was a reaction to nominalism (1350–1500), the dominant trend of late scholasticism, and its rejection of universals. Literalism was offered as the respectable equivalent of naturalism in physics. Its emergence can be traced as far back as the twelfth century, when a "new interest in the literal sense and a new respect for it altered an old balance in favor of the 'spiritual' senses, the allegorical, tropological and anagogical, which had led some of the fathers to regard certain passages as having no literal sense at all" (Evans 1985: 40). At this time, though, literalism was more than just a return to the text—it was the invention of the autonomous, self-justifying and self-explanatory (sacred) text: "'that word' which was in the beginning with God, which was the life and light of men and shone in incomprehensible darkness, was not a personal but a literal word; it was 'it,' not 'him,' instinctively conceived as the word written. It was certainly not the ritual word . . . but the vehicle of truth; and not the social word, but objective, transcendent, addressed to no one and everyone, like the Ten Commandments which were to replace statues and images behind the altars of English churches" (Bossy 1985: 99). The Protestants rejected any interpretive and ecclesiastical tradition that did not agree with the message of the Scripture. With Biblical literalism, the "letter" of the text became more important than the "spirit" of the church.[26] And as the text achieved its independence from the church, the congregation changed into a community of interpreters. The autonomy of the text and that of its readers were mutually authenticating. That was the import of Luther's "priesthood of all believers."[27]

In the late fifteenth century there were two developing directions of educational reform: the Renaissance humanism of Italy and England, and the Evangelical humanism of Germany and the Low Countries. Humanist educational reforms and Protestant religious reforms often assisted each other.[28] Humanists were the first group to support the Reformation, which they saw as an ally in the struggle of their academic movement against scholasticism (Holeczek 1975). The Protestants saw in humanism the interpretive system that would help them win theological debates: "The humanities became for Protestant theologians what Aristotelian philosophy had been to late medieval Catholic theologians, the favored handmaiden of theology" (Ozment 1979: 147). In a sense, the Reformers were scholastics, but of the word, not the argument; hence their literalism of doctrine. "Although the Protestant reformers replaced scholastic dialectic with the rhetorical ideals of humanism when they reformed university curricula . . . , they continued to share the preoccupation of medieval theologians with the definition and defense of church doctrine, albeit on a more homiletical than theoretical level, that is, they were more interested in preaching doctrine than in contemplating it" (136). Still, the two trends together created what the Western university has known until today as Liberal Arts—the set of practices of Protestant interpretation. As Hegel wrote in 1816: "Protestantism is not entrusted to the hierarchical organization of a church, but is, rather, found only in a general intelligence and a general culture. . . . Our universities and our schools are our churches" (quoted in Derrida 1986: 27).[29] The object of worship in these churches has always been the secular scripture.

In the history of Western secular writing, the reader became priest long before the poet (say, William Blake or Vladimir Mayakovsky) became prophet. The language of the service was reduced to a single text, and communal praying was replaced by individual study. The study of that text, though, was the first (universal and, later with Spinoza, civil) right of Man. Conversely, Man's first self-constituting action was that very study. Thus Man (the bourgeois subject), the book (the self-authenticating, self-regulating written document), and interpretation (the search for hidden meaning and intent) came into existence together and supported each other in the Protestant use of the Bible outside the jurisdiction of the Catholic church.[30] "Hence, this new mode of self-authorization, involving as it does some radically different standards of 'knowledge of the truth,' must necessarily situate itself in and bring forth new forms of institutionalization. Within and throughout these, the new forms of authority, for all the emphasis on faith and inwardness, cannot do without—in fact they help to constitute—an increased amount of historical activity. This activity results from the newly sanctioned Protestant text that in the process of its translation, circulation, and reception in the vernacular requires a reading which presupposes and, at the same time, promotes some greater and more highly subjective range of understanding and appropriation. In the crucial years around 1525, the climax of the German peasant revolt, the previous monopoly of the Church in controlling the exegesis of Scripture explodes into everyman's Protestant freedom to write, read, and think about the Bible himself. The new evangelical sources of spiritual authority are dissociated from office, ritual, confessional. They are planted 'in the heart, in faith and love,' that is, in newly active ways of feeling and believing, in some more nearly self-fashioning modes of emotional, intellectual, and political activity, through which alone the Protestant access to the biblical text achieves its supreme power in the lives of the faithful" (Weimann 1986: 460). The Bible in vernacular translation "effectively crushed the unscriptural world of 'good works,' of saint-cults, pilgrimages, purgatory, pardons and minor sacraments" (Dickens 1982: 449).

The new authority was the bourgeois soul and its contact with a personal (printed) copy. If personal Biblical reading was the first act of church disobedience, it was also the first act of civil obedience[31]—the declaration of individuality. In interpretation, a new technology of the self emerged: the interiorization and privatization of meaning. From another viewpoint, it may also be said that in interpretation a new technology of governance emerged: the self as the depth of secular meaning. In both cases, the practices of interpretation, succeeding the rituals of exegesis, promise the emancipation of knowledge from the coercion of outside authority to the extent that it can earn its independence—to the extent that knowledge can achieve its autonomy by judiciously governing (and guarding) itself, by scrupulously observing the rules that it has itself chosen to follow. The law of immanence which rules the secular order—"the perfect law, the law of liberty" (James 1.25)—is the regime of truth that characterizes modernity. As a subject of continuous and fierce contention, this law is claimed at different times by various political paradigms, from rationality to aesthetics and from empiricism to communism. Its presence, however, in the requirement of intrinsic understanding and the promise of liberation is unmistakably manifest.

The emergence of a linguistics of Christian faith was the distant beginning of a debate about the legitimacy of meaning that culminated in Spinoza's politics of interpretation. It raised questions of textual authenticity
and authority that shook the foundations of *corpus Christianum* and
changed its modes of historical understanding. Between the flock and the
Kingdom, the abyss of mediation opened, threatening any attempt at institutional conciliation. Lowth resolved these problems by applying a consistently stylistic approach to the besieged Bible: his answer was criticism as
textual anabaptism. This anabaptism of faith was not in the message, but
in the grace and harmony of the text: its quality, its structural coherence
and perfection would guarantee the required authenticity and authority.

Literalism questioned not just the established, church-authorized significance of the text but its very authenticity. For the first time since the
Middle Ages, the reliability of St. Jerome's *Vulgate* (ca. 404) was disputed
and "the break in the covenant between word and world" (Steiner 1989)
occurred. Signification became an issue not when the infinite interpreta-
bility of the text was discovered, but simply when the Scripture and the
Vulgate were no longer seen as the same, and the latter no longer regarded
as a monument. To document this inadequacy, the Reformists turned
their attention to the original languages of the Bible, Hebrew and Greek,
and the discipline of their study, humanist textualism. Here again humanists and reformers joined forces early. "The art or technique of understanding and interpretation developed along two paths, theological and literary
critical, from one analogous impulse. Theological hermeneutics, as Dilthey
showed, from the reformers' defence of their own understanding of scripture against the attack of the Tridentine theologians and their appeal to
the essential place of tradition; literary critical hermeneutics as a tool of the
humanist claim to revive classical literature. Both involve a revival of something that was not absolutely unknown, but whose meaning had become
alien and unavailable. Classical literature, though constantly present as cultural material, had been completely absorbed within the Christian world.
Similarly, the bible was the church's sacred book and as such was constantly read, but the understanding of it was determined and—as the reformers insisted—obscured by the dogmatic tradition of the church. Both
traditions are dealing with a foreign language and not with the universal
scholar's language of Latin middle ages, so that the study of the tradition
in its original source made it necessary to learn Greek and Hebrew as well
as to purify Latin. Hermeneutics claims to reveal, by specialised techniques, the original meaning of the texts in both traditions, humanistic
literature and the bible. It is significant that the humanistic tradition became united, through Luther and Melanchthon, with the reform" (Gadamer 1979: 153–54). The exegetical authority of the Catholic church was
challenged, its foundations rejected. "Moreover biblical humanism went

on to maintain that an individual interpreter of the Bible armed with the new critical tools in both Hebrew and Greek was entitled to challenge old interpretations of the Scriptures made by popes and other mere office-holders, people ignorant of Greek and Hebrew, who at best had hitherto laid down the law by a blind reliance upon the Latin Vulgate" (Dickens 1982: 497). The fight was over texts and words, origins and sources.

The Reformation was the first modern battle of the books: it raised questions of exegesis, canonicity, interpretive authority, tradition, originality, textuality. (Its arguments about textual legitimacy were rehearsed in the first decade of the sixteenth century, during an earlier battle over the Jewish books which the convert Pfefferkorn, with support from the scholastics, wanted to suppress while some humanists under Reuchlin, Europe's leading Hebraist, struggled successfully to preserve.) During that period, Hebrew and Greek studies emerged as integral components of humanist education. "As a result of the pro-Biblical atmosphere of the Reformation together with the interests of Renaissance humanists, the study of Hebrew became part of the necessary equipment of every enlightened scholar. Continental humanists like Ficino, Pico, and Reuchlin were accomplished hebraists who furthered the study of Hebrew for Gentiles and defended the freedom of pursuing Hebrew studies" (K. Cohen 1975: 13). For example, although Hebrew became part of the university curriculum in the fourteenth century, before 1500 there was no Hebrew grammar available to the interested scholar. Johannes Reuchlin (1455–1522) published *De Rudibus Hebraicis* (1506), a grammar and lexicon in three volumes which compared the *Vulgate* to the original Old Testament and launched Hebrew studies. With the growth of the school of Christian Hebraists, following at the footsteps of Reuchlin, an increasing number of grammars and translations appeared. In the sixteenth century, Henry VIII established Hebrew chairs at Oxford and Cambridge. "In the course of the 17th century, Hebrew language and literature came to be taught in most of the universities of Western and Central Europe, and even the New Testament was interpreted in connection with talmudic teachings" (Ettinger 1961: 204). Its place beside Latin and Greek as a language of faith and culture was established. After Reuchlin showed the need to return to the Hebrew original, Lorenzo Valla (1405–57) and Erasmus (1466–1536) did the same for the New Testament. The Erasmus edition of the New Testament made it universally accessible in the original for the first time, with 1,200 copies printed. The *Novum Instrumentum* (1516) was published in two parts: the first contained the Greek text and Erasmus' Latin translation in parallel columns, and the second contained the *Annotationes in Novum Testamentum*, explaining his deviations from the *Vulgate* by making extensive use of Greek. Luther used this edition as the basis of his German translation of 1522. Erasmus, who in 1505 had designated the translation of the Scripture as "the task of the philologists" rather than the theologians, was now urging theologians to learn the holy tongues of Hebrew and Greek. He compared the Bible favorably to the classics (Baroway 1933: 465–66; Markish 1986: 29), acknowledging the higher authority of Hebrew but attributing more scholarly importance to Greek. The new independent churches observed these trends with some apprehension and suspicion: although the movement to give the Bible to laymen through the vernacular had the advantage of side-stepping the authority of Latin (and of the educational system that supported it), it manifested an uncanny awareness of the differences among languages, periods, and cultures. Nevertheless, scholars of Hebrew and Greek were clearly indispensable, if the interpretive credibility of the Catholic church was to be undermined. The Scripture had to be read in its original languages. Hebrew and Greek, as two areas of linguistic and textual study, developed in parallel for some one hundred fifty years, serving the Reformist construction of the Bible.

The Reformation became a popular movement within the sphere of civic life in the urban centers of the North and the South. Their utopia was religious, not democratic; classical Athens was not their model. "The image of the city of God, aroused by scores of familiar Biblical texts, had been revivified by those triumphs of municipal independence and cohesion which form one of Europe's greatest legacies from the later middle ages. The city of God, the new Jerusalem, now developing into a concrete aspiration for this world, shines forth as the constant factor throughout all the Protestant Reformations: in the Hussites of Prague and Tabor, in Savanarola's godly programme for Florence, in the cities large and small of Luther's Germany, in Zürich under Zwingli and Geneva under Calvin, among the rebellious Dutch Calvinists and the Huguenots with their cities of refuge" (Dickens 1982: 499). It was the Biblical model of the religious community that inspired the newly endowed classes in their search for autonomy and the rule of immanent law. "Among the Reformed Churches the Old Testament loomed larger also because it served to provide a framework for the constitution of a Holy Commonwealth" (Bainton 1963: 17). The law was a serious problem for the Reformers from Erasmus to Calvin and from Martin Bucer to the Antinomians. "The formalism of the Puritan ethic is in turn the natural consequence of its relation to the law" (Weber 1976: 258). In contrast to the apparent cynicism of Niccolò Machiavelli (1469–1527) and the historical republicanism of *Il principe* (published in 1532, written in 1512), the Reformers sought a new order in the rules of interpretive faith. Luther distinguished between the local law (such as the Jewish one contained in parts of the Bible and applying only to Jews) and the universal law (which has the validity of the natural one). "For those who believe in the possibility of a holy commonwealth, there must be some rules for governance. This would apply particularly to Müntzer, Zwingli, and Calvin. And where should those rules more appropriately be found than in the sacred writings which the reformers were endeavoring to rehabilitate?" (Bainton 1963: 35) The importance of the model persisted to the time of Bodin,[32] Hobbes, and Spinoza. "The Old Testament became to political philosophers of the seventeenth century what the 'exemplaria Graeca' were to Horace, and what Horace in his turn became to English Augustans" (Magnus 1928: 491). Thus the first politics of modernity was the textual politics of faith.

The catechetic intent and the concern over governance were accompanied by a complementary interest in civility (Riley 1986). Protestant literacy (Gellner 1988) created for the first time that civic force known as public opinion (Habermas 1989a). A concern about the more general education of the new masses, the Bible readers, is manifest in a special emphasis, not so much on elegance, as on clarity and accuracy of eloquence. In nominal reaction to the obscurity and complexity of Renaissance scholasticism, Reformation rhetoric turned to Greek in search of a model for the persuasive public argument, the argument for the negotiable, common good. In works like Melanchthon's *Oratio* (1549)—probably the first major statement which "sets out a comprehensive case for the precedence Greek ought to take over Latin on all fronts" (Evans 1985: 80)—there is a distinct sense that knowledge is becoming socially accountable, and learning should be differentiated from training. That was the educational dimension of textual humanism: the new scholarship was a political project too. If Hebrew was the language of the new exegesis, Greek was that of the new rhetoric; if Hebrew was the language of interpretation, Greek was that of eloquence; if Hebrew was the language of morality, Greek was that of civility. Greek was the path to the secular. This is how the private morality of faith and the public eloquence of civility were supported and propagated. Thus, in the philological study of the two Testaments by the Reformists, we find the first comparisons of the Hellenic and the Hebraic. The return to the origin through the original (*ad fontes*) drew attention to the two ancient languages and their distinct worlds of meaning and culture. The analysis of the New Testament made possible an awareness of the duality of the classics and a differentiation of Greek from Latin. At the same time, "the notion of Hebrew language and culture as rather different from the Church forces that 'corrupted' it—as, specifically, 'ancient' and 'oriental'— took hold" (Kugel 1981: 208). As the Testaments started competing for priority, so did the contributions of the two old civilizations to Western Christianity.[33] The comparison was part of the Hebrew and Greek study from their very beginning.

Scholars often believe that the Hebraism-Hellenism comparison is a German discussion of the nineteenth century. They acknowledge that "a greatly improved practice in Old Testament exegesis became general, partly through increased knowledge of Hebrew and the influence of Jewish exegesis. In these and other ways it may reasonably be claimed that the Reformation produced a greatly increased Hebraic influence within the Church" (Barr 1966: 42). They have not noticed, though, that the origins of the Hebraic-Hellenic contrast can be traced to Reformation hermeneutics. After the decline of scholasticism and the arrival of print culture, two models of language competed for authority over philosophical grammar: the speech-centered humanist and the text-centered Hebraic models (Elsky 1990). Later, in the work of Erasmus and some Erasmians like William Tyndall (ca. 1494–1536), we discover the beginnings of a comparison on rhetorical grounds that would evolve into stylistic contrasts by the time of Lowth and philosophico-political ones in the work of Hamann and Herder. Traditional views place the beginnings of the discussion at the time of the latter, arguing that "though Romanticism is not anti-Greek for the most part, it is within Romanticism that the cultural concepts which have been applied to the Hebraic and later set against the Greek were fostered" (Barr 1966: 44). The comparison between the Judaic and the Greek heritage, however, started almost as soon as the Reformist persuasion looked at their semantics for a better grasp of its faith and for stronger arguments against Catholic dogma. Understanding the fundamentals of the two languages and the basic operations of the Jewish and the Greek mind was as important to Melanchthon as it was (for obviously different reasons) to Auerbach or Boman.[34]

The comparative approach was an entirely new development. From Tertullian (ca. 160–ca. 230) to Erasmus, occasional comparisons of the Judaic to the Greek were made in the dominant context of the Christianity-paganism opposition and with the additional standard assumption that the Greeks could not even compete in value with the Romans. The real comparison was between the Christian faith and the ancient tradition. The discussion certainly goes back to the Gospels and Paul, where the relation between Jews and Gentiles, given the prospect of their Church membership, became an important question. Even in the work of a purist like Tertullian, who was probably the first to pose explicitly the choice between Athens and Jerusalem and who, in his most militant moments, seemed to reject the classical heritage altogether, the terms of the opposition are essentially Christian and pagan. This was also the case with the other Fathers of the faith: "no effort was made to solve problems through an overt rejection of the Greek mind in favor of the Hebraic. The origin of the modern Hebrew-Greek contrast thus did not lie within the theology of the early Church" (Barr 1966: 41). Early Church Fathers like Justin (ca. 100–ca. 165), Clement of Alexandria (ca. 150–ca. 215), the Syrian Tatian (fl. ca. 172) and Origen (185?–254?), believed that Greek literature and learning had been "borrowed" or "stolen" from the Hebrews.[35] Augustine (354–430), like his mentor Ambrose (333–397), thought the same of Platonic

and Pythagorean philosophy. "Probably the most widespread theory proposed by the fathers to account for the truth in paganism was the suggestion that it had come from the Old Testament. Here they were following a
precedent set by Jewish apologists" (Pelikan 1971: 33). Indeed the dependency theory was common in Hellenistic synagogues. "The roots of this notion are pre-Christian: it was a Jewish bulwark against the inroads of
Hellenization, but one that at the same time helped Jews to accept Greek
learning without conceding it priority or even originality" (Kugel 1981:
143).[36] Jewish intellectuals versed in Hellenistic thought, like Aristobulus
and Philo, were the first to argue that the Scriptures were older than Greek
philosophy, which knew and used them. "Between the antique-pagan and
the patristic poetics, the Hellenized Judaism of the two last pre-Christian
and the first Christian centuries represents an intermediary which came to
exercise a far-reaching historical influence. The Judaeo-Hellenic culture
developed a highly conscious propaganda which did not stop at literary
forgeries (Sibylline oracles, verses attributed to Orpheus). 'One of the
Chief tools of this propaganda was the attempt to show the correspondences between the Jewish law and religion and the teachings of Greek
philosophy' [Otto Stählin]. To this end, the system of allegorical exegesis
developed by the Stoa was taken over. In connection with it appears the
so-called 'authority of antiquity': the sacred writings of the Jews are far
older than those of the Greek poets and sages, who had known them and
learned from them. Thus Josephus, in his treatise against Apion, proved
that the Greek philosophers were dependent upon Moses. All these ideas
were taken over by the early Christian apologists" (Curtius 1953: 446). The
tradition continued well into the new era. "Judaeo-Christian apologetics
and, later, the Alexandrian catechumenical schools taught that the Old
Testament was earlier than the writings of the Greek poets and sages; that
the latter had known the Old Testament and learned from it. This led to
the establishment of parallels between the teachings of the Bible and pagan
myths" (219). This was only one strategy of the large effort to harmonize
Judeo-Christian teaching with Greek thought. Although later Latin theology abandoned the effort when it had no need for it, the comparison was
still occasionally employed, from the sixth to the eleventh centuries, by
poets who used the parallel to defend the idea of the *poeta theologus*.
Isidore of Seville (ca. 570–636), for example, believed that, since Moses was
the first poet, poetry had not begun with the Greeks (Dyck 1977: 33). Comparisons of the Bible with Roman and Greek poetry in the fourteenth century served further explorations of the relationship of theology and poetry,
and also served the justification of imaginative writing on the basis of the
presence of allegory in pagan classics and the Scriptures. That was the time
when allegory was recognized as the fundamental mode of poetry, and typology was widely accepted. In the early sixteenth century, this led to stud-

ies of Biblical style which pursued two main themes: "the attempt to identify in the Bible tropes and figures such as existed in classical rhetoric; and the imputation of classical meters to those songs and books identified as Biblical poetry" (Kugel 1981: 226).

Still, the meaning of the comparison had drastically changed by the time Erasmus started employing the image of the Jew in his religious teachings and using Judaism as a moral category applicable to the contemporary Christianity, even though he was still talking about "the Jews of books, not the Jews of life" (Markish 1986: 6).[37] Curtius has called this transition "the passage from 'Biblical' to 'theological' poetics." A new structure of understanding emerges: "Under the influence of Humanism, theology strives for a new basis and method. From arguments addressed to reason it turns to the arguments of authority and tradition; from scholastic dialectics to study of the original sources; from the 'speculative' to the 'positive' method" (Curtius 1953: 552). French, German, and Spanish Humanisms are all part of "the trend toward philological and historical studies which also include the language of the Old Testament. On the one hand, a turning away from Scholasticism; a conjunction of Hebrew, Greek, and Latin philology on the other—that is the position of Christian Humanism in the first third of the sixteenth century." This trend is the expression "of a universal, harmonizing attitude of mind which seeks to exploit the intellectual stock of pagan Antiquity too for a Christian philosophy of culture" (553). That was the moment when, in the course of a philological search for the origins and sources of European religious tradition, the Jews, together with the Greeks, were invented, were taken for real people, with their own history, and started gradually becoming objects of interest and study.

Although the first Western interest that focused on ancient Israel and Greece stemmed from religious exigencies and had an exegetical character, its philological methodology did not disappear with the triumph of the new churches. On the contrary, it increased in importance as its interpretive use (which we saw in Lowth's analysis) and propaedeutic role (the training in civility mentioned earlier) were needed more and more for the education of the first independent readers, the bourgeoisie. One example is the forging, in the century following the Reformation, of the Dutch national identity, which was heavily dependent on the use of Biblical analogies (Schama 1987). An earlier and more important one is British Israelitism, the belief that the English people were a remnant of the Ten Lost Tribes (Hine 1871) and today's true Israel. England merits special attention, as it was strongly influenced by a political understanding of predestination, the so-called Israelitism. "The English have had a long romance with the Jews, the mingling of their histories not least significant in our own time. But the conjoining in modern history can be dated precisely with the emergence of Elect Nation in the sixteenth century. At first, the analogue was part of an effort to establish a reformed church; sixteenth-century Protestants sought the authority of Scripture, the language of covenant and election, to challenge Rome. But the language did not remain ecclesiastical. The Protestant agenda broadened to a national program. By the 1640s it was right to speak of something like national election" (Zwicker 1988: 38). The Reformed classes appropriated the privileged destiny for themselves as they were advocating the bourgeois covenant of rights.[38] Autonomy was blessed. "The religious aristocracy of the elect, which developed in every form of Calvinistic asceticism" (Weber 1976: 131), was to pursue its destiny in secular realms too. "From about 1570 onwards, the theme of 'election' came to dominate Reformed theology, and allowed an easy identification of the Reformed congregations and the people of Israel. Just as God had once chosen Israel, so he had now chosen the Reformed congregations as his people. From this moment onwards, the doctrine of predestination begins to assume a major social and political function. . . . The form which this theology took in England—Puritanism—is of particular interest. The sense of being the 'elect people of God' was heightened as the new people of God entered the new promised land—America" (McGrath 1988: 92). British Israelitism was a radical form of Puritanism which laid great stress upon "the divine sovereignty in election, as expressed in the *decretum absolutum*" (McGrath 1986: 168).

There was a fervent tradition of religious dissent supporting that belief. It was in England first, long before the Reformation, that the question of the vernacular translation of the Scripture acquired political significance, as was the case with Wyclif and the Lollard Bible of the 1380s (Hudson 1988). In the sixteenth century the miracle-working painted or sculpted image lost its eminence to the written word, an iconoclasm (Aston 1988) best known from Milton's "Eikonoklastes" (1649) (Loewenstein 1990) that again goes back to the Lollard critique of late medieval iconolatry. With the Protestant return to the sources, Hebrew studies flourished and the centrality of the Hebraic model for the nation's self-understanding was widely accepted. "The newly-emergent nationalistic and religious royalties, in particular, gradually transplanted the destiny of the chosen people from its Biblical context to that of the people of England" (Patrides 1972: 79). The sense of a new covenant invigorated the zeal of the destined classes for a secular mission. "Nowhere in the Christian world did the Old Testament receive such a warm reception or penetrate so deeply into the lives of men as in England" (Kugel 1981: 221). Karl Marx, in *The Eighteenth Brumaire of Louis Bonaparte* (1852), indicates the extent of its influence when he observes that, a century before the French Revolution, "Cromwell and the English people had borrowed speech, passions and illusions from the Old Testament for their bourgeois revolution" (Tucker 1978: 596). Indeed "the Old Testament was the book of the Puritan elect. The triumph of the Hebrew spirit was the triumph of parliament and the rule of Oliver Cromwell" (Zwicker 1988: 39). Furthermore, in what may be called "critical" Israel-itism, it was not uncommon to find the opposition to the Hellenic recur-ring in explorations of the Hebraic, for example in treatises that compared the Bible to Homer, such as *Homerus Hebraizon sive, comparatio Homeri cum scriptoribus sacris quoad norman loguendi* (1658) by Zacharus Bogan; *Homeri, poetarum omnium seculorum facile principis, gnomologia, duplici parallelismo illustrata* (1660) by James Duport, and later *Homeros Hebraios sive Historia Hebraeorum ab Homero Hebraicis nominibus ac sententiis con-scripta in Odyssea et Iliade* (1704) by Gerard Croese.[39]

John Milton (1608–74) was the first writer to lay claim on authorial pre-destination—to translate the dogma of the "elect people" into the position of the elect poet, the recipient of the "inspired gift of God, rarely be-stowed," and to use the authority (Guillory 1983) of the prophetic voice as an artistic one. The argument of the superiority of the Hebraic over the Hellenic played an instrumental role in this strategy. The syncretism of the opening of *Paradise Lost* (1667) is aggressive: the author invokes Urania, the "heav'nly Muse" who inspired Moses, from Oreb or Sinai or the Sion hill to help his song "soar / above th' Aeonian mount" (I, 6–15) Helicon. In this comparison between Sion and Helicon, the city of David and the sanc-tuary of the Muses, and the corresponding originary sources of inspiration, a constitutive tension between the Hellenic and the Hebraic enters West-ern poetry. Torquato Tasso had also begun his *Gerusalemme liberata* (1580) by rejecting the ancient Muse and the laurels of Helicon, but in-stead he invoked the Christian Muse from Paradise. Milton adopts rules of the epic tradition but spiritualizes its heroic virtue in order to confer to his Biblical epic a higher authority, that of religious truth and stylistic sublim-ity. He was writing a poem "doctrinal and exemplary to the nation." Show-ing that Sion supersedes Helicon both philosophically and artistically was an important way of justifying the character of his own project.[40] The argu-ment that the Greeks derived their "artful terms" from the Hebrews is part of his self-authorization and the authorization of his poetry as a kind of artistic Israelitism. As he did explicitly in "The Reason of Church Govern-ment Urged against Prelaty" (1642), Milton compares himself to the an-cient Hebrew writers. The art and inspiration of the divine poet transcends the secular tradition and its myths by returning to the principles and mes-sages of prophetic speech.[41]

It was on Rome and not the Elect Nation that the English political elites during Augustanism chose to model their country. "To put the case as simply as possible, in 1650 the central book of English culture was Scrip-ture; by 1700 the texts men chose to talk about themselves were those of Roman history and Roman politics. By 1700 it was Juvenal, not Jeremiah, whom satirists invoked; the Roman senator, not the Mosaic lawgiver, em-

braced as parliamentary ideal; commercial empire, not the end of time, for
which ministries toiled; Roman virtue, not Hebraic righteousness, that defined civic morality" (Zwicker 1988: 37). This signals "the decline of righteousness as a moral code and prophecy as a political agenda" (37). After
1660, there was a need for defusion of religious acrimony, for negotiation
and reconciliation. "The biblical language of correction and humiliation is
an essential facet of Protestant spiritualism, and as a language of personal
discipline, Scripture endured. But as a language of public correction, Scripture was undercut both by the failure of spiritual politics and by changes in
those public institutions that needed correction" (41). With the Roman-
ization of English literary and political culture, the validity of the sacred
model declined.[42] When it was time to build a public life on honor, integrity, and prudence, the Republican mode served to demystify the politics of
prophecy and revelation. After the Civil War, politics used the language
of classical Republicanism—the vocabulary of Roman virtue and civility
(Pocock 1986). "Rome could authorize republic and empire, monarchy and
aristocracy. It could provide the history of valor and the history of luxury;
it could authorize the rule of the strong sovereign and the inviolability of
the senate. . . . It could provide authority for the conduct, the celebration,
and the censure of public life in a nation bent on or being bent toward
bloodless revolution, commercial empire, and the rage of party politics"
(Zwicker 1988: 47). This trend continued, for some for a century and a half,
for others until the end of the nineteenth century.[43]

The lesson of this transition from visions of iconoclastic eschatology to
plans for progressive history is an important reminder: in modernity, in the
urban landscapes and markets of post-Reformation northern capitalism,
scriptural figuralism or messianism is the discourse of the sacred politics of
community; while imperial republicanism or caesarism is the discourse of
the civic politics of the state. Community politics negotiates identity on
the basis of the Hebraic model, while state politics administers order on the
basis of the Roman one.[44] The Roman mode, however, has been far less
efficient and important (and therefore rarely contested) for many reasons,
among them its association with both the Catholic world and the feudal
system. The main agent and vehicle of order has been another mode—not
a mechanism of imposed administration but the technology of freely chosen self-regulation: the autonomy of cultivation. This is the path to emancipation offered by the Hellenic.

While the Middle Ages had no historical understanding of antiquity
(Herren and Brown 1988) and the Renaissance felt only a certain distance
from its old models, the Reformist return to original texts, and especially
the prominence it gave to the Hebrew Bible, brought an acute sense of
division between both the two parts of the Scripture and the two levels of
experience, the present and the past. With the erosion of feudal and

church power, and concomitant advances in astronomy, colonialism, and trade, the harmony of religious and secular spheres collapsed and the possibility of alternative world orders gained in appeal. After the great crisis of theological and political authority from the mid-fourteenth to mid-sixteenth centuries, the success of the Protestant churches and the achievement of Renaissance humanism gave the seventeenth century the sense of a new order (civic life) and a new beginning (modernity). The symbolic (if not figural) value of the Hebraic-Hellenic opposition in defining this break in time and hierarchy was paramount. The Hebraic was proposed as a model for a better understanding of community politics and morality. In Milton, for example, it represented cultural (including moral) excellence, while in Spinoza human reason and rights. The fate of the Hellenic was more complicated and would not be fully determined before a major intellectual conflict, the Battle of the Books in France and England at the end of the century.

The Modern defined itself in opposition to an irrevocable past and an exhausted tradition—in opposition to History.[45] After the Reformation upheavals, "seventeenth-century society found itself at the crossroads of the two types of history. On the one hand, historical discourse tended to reproduce religious discourse; it was a secular variant of the Bible. On the other hand, the contradictions undermining it, added to the effects of 'the European crisis of consciousness,' were paving the way for a new history. In other words, at the end of the age of Louis XIV, thinkers were just about to grasp what Vico was to formulate clearly—the idea that history is made, not by gods, but by men. Our modern notion of historicity is a result of this discovery" (Apostolidès 1982: 63).[46] The sense of a new beginning was complemented by that of an end, and of an alienation from that which ended.

That whole experience had both a linguistic and a chronological meaning. The linguistic one involved "the split between explicative sense and historical reference, and between narrative depiction or form and its meaning or subject matter" (Frei 1974: 42) evident in Spinoza's *Tractatus*. Before the Reformation, the identity of meaning and text, or text and faith, or faith and church was not questioned. "In a precritical era, in which literal explicative sense was identical with actual historical reference, literal and figurative reading, far from contradicting each other, belonged together by family resemblance and by need for mutual supplementation. Later on, when explication and reference became separated, the two kinds of readings would not only separate but clash" (28). With the emphasis of Protestant interpretation on literal reading and the grammar of meaning, medieval exegesis came apart and its two parts took their separate ways: "Realistic, literal reading of the Biblical narratives found its closest successor in the historical-critical reconstruction of specific events and texts of the Bible. . . . Figural reading, concerned as it was with the unity of the

Bible, found its closest successor in an enterprise called Biblical theology, which sought to establish the unity of religious meaning across the gap of historical and cultural differences" (8).

As for the chronological meaning of the Modern, it involved an acute sense of separation (as opposed to the Renaissance distance) from the past, specifically from antiquity. This historical sense was the belief in an ancient and extinct integrated civilization (like that idealized by Lukács) which was usually identified with Hellas. With this nostalgic belief, a long process, which had begun with the removal of the Scripture from the purview of the church for the bourgeois reader's personal edification, was completed some one hundred years later: as the modern state won the battle of the Book against the church in the name of the individual, the past (of both state and individual) was declared History and called Greek, while the present was proclaimed Modern and defined as Judaic.

Until the Reformers' return to the original language of the New Testament expanded to include questions of cultural signification, there was no interest in Greece, no understanding of Greek civilization, no notion of a real, historical Greece. "It cannot be emphasized enough that, just as to Shakespeare the Ancient Greeks were quarrelsome Levantines, not demi-gods, the Italian Renaissance scholars, artists and patrons identified themselves with Greeks but were not centrally concerned with the Greece of Homer or Perikles, or even with the Olympian gods. They were interested in picking up from pagan Antiquity where it had left off" (Bernal 1987: 151). The Hellenic played no part in any comparisons either: "The possibility of pitting Greeks against the Egyptians, Chaldaeans and others, in the defence of Christianity, did not occur until the Renaissance" (193). When comparisons began, they presented the Greek as derivative, and therefore secondary: "Thus no one before 1600 seriously questioned either the belief that Greek civilization and philosophy derived from Egypt, or that the chief ways in which they had been transmitted were through Egyptian colonizations of Greece and later Greek study in Egypt" (121).

The credibility and urgency of the Hellenic were established around the mid-seventeenth century, with the decline of the Reformation textual politics of faith and the emergence of a fully secular bourgeois culture. By the time Spinoza presented the Modern as Biblical (in terms of both reading and governing), the Hebraic and the Hellenic were becoming the poles on the basis of which modernity would, until today, comprehend its nature and reckon its options. In the transition from the uses of ancient fable in ornament and eloquence (Seznec 1953) to the establishment of the science of (Greek) mythology in the 1720s we can observe, on a small scale, the secular triumph of interpretation as historical criticism; and in the shift of interest from the "learning" of Bacon (*The Advancement of Learning*, 1605) to the "understanding" of Spinoza (*Treatise on the Improvement of Understanding*), Locke ("Essay Concerning Human Understanding," 1690) or of Leibniz ("New Essays," 1704), we can see further how knowledge was transformed from a religious to a human category—that is, how interpretation turned from personal to private, and from Biblical to Hebraic. If the sixteenth century created interpretation and its reader, the seventeenth universalized these fundamental concepts of the bourgeoisie and invented autonomous understanding and the human together, arguing that understanding is human while anything human is related to understanding. The autonomy of interpretation was justified anthropologically.

THE EXERCISE OF REASON

With the emergence of human understanding, the religion of reason succeeds the reason of religion. "As the dogmatic content of Protestantism began to yield in importance to the ethical, and as the correctness of a belief began to seem less significant than its sincerity, so doctrinal respectability became a less impressive claim to liberty than moral and social integrity and political loyalty" (Worden 1989: 610). Because of its respect for the (self-disciplined) individual and its understanding of historical and cultural difference, this age of reason was anxious to exhibit its support for (religious) toleration. English tracts were already defending it in the 1620s (Roth 1964: 150–52), Spinoza pleaded for it, John Locke wrote his *Epistola de tolerantia* (written in 1666, published in 1688) and took a clear stand on the Jewish right to equality, Diderot (1713–84) published his *Traité de la tolérance*, Voltaire his *Traité sur la tolérance* (1763), Lessing (who had already written the play *Der Jude* in 1754) dramatized it in *Nathan the Wise* (1779), and other Deists preached it.[47] Writing in the wake of the Revolution, the advocates of toleration opposed the Calvinist doctrine of predestination and advocated liberty of conscience. "It was in the century after Milton, the century from Bayle to Voltaire, that the intellectual victories of toleration were won. . . . The wake of the Glorious Revolution produced the Toleration Act of 1689 and the end of the licensing of press in 1695" (Worden 1989: 610). Toleration was made possible by the interiorization of knowledge, the new focus of government studies: difference in beliefs could be tolerated so long as personal motives and social integrity could be controlled.

The emergence of the Hebraic as the internal other, i.e., the double, of the West can be placed at the time when the status of Jews in society was first debated—at the time of philosophical discussions of toleration, including the right of Jews to equality, and practical discussions of naturalization, of allowing foreigners, like the Jews, to immigrate to Britain. Here

theological, millenarian, missionary, civic, and mercantilistic interests converged. One cause of the debates was the fact that certain people from a
particular ethnic group had started identifying themselves as Jews, had
started "imagining" (Benedict Anderson) themselves as inheritors of the
Biblical nation the Protestants admired so much. It was probably first in
England that the West met "real" Jews, that it heard personal claims about
Jewishness. "The English developed an identity as Elect Nation in virtual
ignorance of the Jews; the fantasy of election came from a book. The metaphor took shape in a world without Jews; perhaps such are the conditions
for metaphors of national identity: Israel, Arcadia, Arthurian Britain, all
were safely remote. And while it remained unlikely for Englishmen to meet
Arthurian Britons, they did in fact begin to meet Jews in the 1650s. No
longer were the Jews simply history, and though the history remained, the
remnant was not so easily romanticized as the history. And the perception
of that history and its application to national life began to change at a time
when the Jews became a subject of contested inquiry. The sudden attention came with the agitation in favor of and unofficial re-entry of the Jews
into England in the early 1650s" (Zwicker 1988: 42). Books of Jewish apologetics published in Italy, France, Germany, or England in the first half of
the seventeenth century covered the entire range of issues, from theology
to law and from economy to philosophy. Finally, in 1714 the deist John
Toland (1670–1722) published anonymously the pamphlet *Reasons for
Naturalising the Jews in Great Britain and Ireland on the Same Foot with all
Nations; Containing also a Defense of the Jews against All Vulgar Prejudices
in All Countries*, where for the first time he "applied a central principle of
European rationalism—the essential oneness of all human nature—to the
case of the Jews" (Katz 1964: 9). His treatise "appears to be an amplified
continuation of the Hebraist-Judicial trend which admired the Jewish Law
as a model for a political constitution, which respected the Jewish past, and
appreciated the social ability of the Jewish people" (Ettinger 1961: 218).

By that time, however, the Elect Nation model had been made redundant by the mechanisms of republican administration of the modern state.
It was also becoming obvious that the rule of the Mosaic code over morality
was incapable of controlling the new reading public. The private ethics of
the merchant and the industrialist had to be justified in a different way—
one that hopefully would also educate the masses of the bourgeois metrop-
olis. The supervision of the bursting public sphere was eventually entrusted
to taste, a technology of conduct rather than belief. This is how the transition from the politics of faith to that of culture began. This is also how the
legitimacy of conduct and the validity of taste were tested—by applying
these (presumably universal) criteria to those who appeared to be the working Protestants' double: those claiming Biblical continuity for themselves,
the Jews.

Contemporary Jews appeared on the scene of history when, among the modern adherents of the Jewish faith, certain merchants and intellectuals started identifying themselves with the people of the Bible, telling Christians that they were the descendants of the Hebrews. This argument greatly appealed to the Protestant admiration for the ancient Israelites, especially their society and morality. At the same time, it made quite apprehensive those Christians who considered themselves the true (and therefore elect) inheritors of that legacy. The response to the Jewish initiative was correspondingly ambiguous: the promise of assimilation as secular redemption—acceptance into the secular society as delivery to a worldly Promised Land. This response enabled the bourgeoisie to achieve two things: prove their tolerance as well as test its limits. They could prove it by promising to accept fellow bourgeois of a different religious persuasion; and they could test it by observing the possible extent and effects of assimilation. The financially emancipated Jewish middle class provided an ideal test case—that of the other who was already inside, the different but not the stranger (say, non-European, Muslim, or black). Now the Protestants discovered in the Jews their double, and started exploring the possibilities of identity. Could the modern Hebrews overcome their otherness and join the civilized classes? Could they conduct themselves in a civil manner? If they could, all the universal claims (about human rights and reason) would be justified, and would be applicable to, if not mandatory for, everybody else, from the lower classes to foreigners. This is how Hegel described the promise of assimilation in 1798: "The subsequent circumstances of the Jewish people up to the mean, abject, wretched circumstances in which they still are today, have all of them been simply consequences and elaborations of their original fate. By this fate—an infinite power which they set over against themselves and could never conquer—they have been maltreated and will be continually maltreated until they appease it by the spirit of beauty and so annul it by reconciliation" (Hegel 1971: 199–200). Secular redemption would come through the reconciliation that only beauty could bestow. The Jewish question, the question of civility, was originally one of tasteful conduct—an experiment in the universality of reason and taste that would unify the public of the capital above any considerations of private interest.

Tolerance, the morality of the conduct of reason, extended the meaning of interpretation into public lifestyle. "Tolerance is not a particular postulate of philosophy, but rather an expression of its principle; tolerance is of the very essence of philosophy. It expresses the affinity of philosophy and religion" (Cassirer 1951: 169). What was to be tolerated was the individual as interpreter, scholar, member of the polity, and Jew; what was not to be tolerated was imitation (specifically, repetition) of the Greeks. When the struggle for authority over the normative approaches to tradition moved from the Scripture to the rhetorical and artistic uses of language, the late seventeenth century proceeded to challenge the eminence of the Ancients, primarily in oratory and poesy, and the Battle of the Books erupted (Rosen 1989).

The onslaught started in France with the first volume of Charles Perrault's *Paralleles des anciens et des modernes en ce qui regarde les Arts et les Sciences* (1688–97, 4 vols.) and Fontenelle's *Digression sur les Anciens et les Modernes* (1688). The whole Battle was waged in critical writing, and through this bellicose exercise the "autonomy of criticism" (Gay 1966: 304) was achieved. Fontenelle (1657–1757), in his *Digression*, exemplifies the confidence of the historical sensibility: essentially we are all equals, he argues—Greeks, Romans, French; once the Romans were Moderns, one day we shall be Ancients. "The position of the Moderns, which finally won out in official circles, elaborated a new relation with the past: the model was to be no longer Rome, but Paris itself. Louis XIV's contemporaries even went so far as to declare themselves classics. Around 1685, they invented the mythology of the 'Age of Louis XIV,' to which we subscribe even today in spite of contemporary historical studies. In doing away with the obligatory references to Antiquity, the intellectuals of the seventeenth century modified their perception of the past: Rome was no longer an essence that France must reincarnate, but a society of the past which could therefore become the target of objective knowledge. Antiquity was transformed from allegory into knowledge" (Apostolidès 1982: 67). With the same confidence, Richard Bentley (1662–1742), another Modern, would systematically apply the historico-philological method to a classical text in his *A Dissertation upon the Epistles of Phalaris* (1699) and launch classical philology by using only internal evidence to prove that an alleged classical document was forgery.[48] In a parallel development, at the end of the seventeenth century Latin was abandoned as a common language of learning, and the use of ancient genres denounced. The Moderns' initial interest in fable turned to the composition of contemporary fables (later to be christened "novels") while the discipline of myth took shape as Fontenelle published *De l'origine des fables* (written 1690–99, published 1724) and Perrault the first full-length translation of fairy tales (1697). Thus when Marcel Detienne asks: "Why is to speak of mythology always, more or less explicitly, to speak Greek or to be influenced by Greece?" (1986: xi; see also 115, 123), the answer is as follows: because during the Battle, fable turned from Latin into Greek (namely, myth), as writing was transformed from classical to Hebraic (namely, literature).

The Battle was proclaimed, defined, and won by the Moderns (who, by the way, assigned to their opponents the position of the Ancients). While their argument took the form of philosophy versus taste in France and that of science versus faith in England, their greatest success on both fronts was the substitution of art and literature for piety and faith. In the Battle of the Books—the first conscious and open conflict in the West of Old and New, tradition and modernity—the ancient past emerged as past history. Literature and the arts appeared as modern, and intrinsic interpretation was deemed the right approach to them while poetics gradually lost its normative character. Social issues were examined in the context of culture, which now became of central importance, and the theory of progress was applied to it; inquiries were made into its operations as questions of education and creativity centered on the imaginative contributions of literature. Historical sensibility was on its way to its aesthetic destination. In the aftermath of the Battle, the Moderns concentrated on new forms of writing that would evolve toward the discourse of literature (Simonsuuri 1979: 24), and the Ancients interested themselves more with the scholarly study of antiquity. Paradoxically "not until men had disavowed servitude to the dogma of Hellenism did the spirit of Hellas reappear" (Burlingame 1920: 194). Once the dogma of classicism was discredited, the "anastomosis of antiquity, especially Greek antiquity, with a later age in another country" (Ellmann 1977: 567) became not only possible, but an empowering proposition for fledging European classes, professions, and nations.

Toleration and its faith in the autonomy of individual reason went through different phases and tones of relativism: Pierre Bayle's *Dictionnaire historique et critique* (1695, 1697; 2 vols.), George Berkeley's *A Treatise Concerning the Principles of Human Knowledge* (1710), Giambattista Vico's *Scienza nuova prima* (1725; *seconda*, 1729–30; *terza*, op. posth. 1744), David Hume's *Philosophical Essays Concerning Human Understanding* (1748), and Voltaire's *Traité sur la tolérance* (1763) represent the major ones (Kilcullen 1988). From Locke's "Discourse on Miracles" (1702) to Hume's "Of Miracles" (contained in the above collection), the last vestiges of the dogma of revelation were destroyed during the English Deism controversy of the 1690s, which coincided with the Battle of the Books (Burns 1981). "The term 'Deism' is used to refer specifically to the 'Enlightenment philosophy of religion'—the belief that there exists a natural religion prior to and taking precedence over all religions of revelation, which declares to man the objective conditions conducive to his happiness, and in whose observance lies his salvation" (McGrath 1986: 199).

The Deistic critique of revelation, which marked the beginning of modern theology, was the development of seventeenth-century rational theology and was based on the twin pillars of scriptural coherence and natural reason. Initially the Deists were against religion as a mystery, and tried to establish Christianity upon a firm pragmatic foundation by demonstrating its complete rationality. They developed the idea of natural and universal religion, the religion of reason (Byrne 1989), and defended the absolute sufficiency of reason as the foundation of all certitude. Since true religion is natural religion and not any particular one (for example, Christianity), they felt that each individual can attain truth by the free exercise of his private judgment, and consequently strongly advocated religious toleration.[49] These positions became more and more liberal. "Although Deism initially regarded scripture as confirmed by reason, the later Deists subjected scripture to such a devastating critique on the basis of their rationalist presuppositions and methods that it became regarded as at best superfluous, and at worst open to the superstitious interpretations of the clergy which had done so much to further their own interests and hinder the republication of the religion of nature" (McGrath 1986: 202). Between Locke's *The Reasonableness of Christianity as Delivered in the Scriptures* (1696) and Anthony Collins' A *Discourse of Free-thinking, Occasion'd by the Rise and Growth of a Sect call'd Free-thinkers* (1713), both Scripture and tradition had been invalidated as sources of authority.

As we have seen, in the socio-political reality created by the Revolution of 1688, not just new forms of government were required but a new regime of governance, one that would cultivate a "sensus communis" (to use Shaftesbury's title of 1709), an ideology of shared sensibilities (rather than beliefs) and consent (Herzog 1989). The code of conduct as a self-controlled public expression of refined taste was created to play that supervising role. For persons of letters as well as journalists "the cultivation and training of Taste was . . . a problem of great social significance, a proper understanding of which would lead to saner relation-patterns among the various members and groups of society" (Aronson 1946: 229). There was a simultaneous emphasis on harmonious personality and stable social structure. "The problem of Taste, indeed, was to them an essentially human problem which most vitally concerned the common man's attitude to social conduct and his integrity of character. Problems related to behaviour were, throughout the eighteenth century, morally determined and Taste was no exception to the rule" (236).

This development signalled the Hellenization of culture that would last for about two centuries. Taste thwarted political activism, conduct blunted antagonism. If the Hebraization of social life worked as atonement for material concerns (and successes), the Hellenization of culture worked as redemption of political necessities. We can discern in the latter "an evolution representative of eighteenth-century thought, from the Augustan emphasis on external form, polished conduct, and urbanity, to philosophical speculation and an increasingly analytical approach to moral problems. This evolution also coincided with a shift in the social structure of England, from aristocratic behaviour-patterns . . . to middle-class ideals of life, their new insistence on the innate moral qualities in man, their humanitarian religion and 'chearfulness'" (228). In the early eighteenth century Joseph Addison and the 3rd Earl of Shaftesbury expressed the new

values of feeling and "moral sentiment," fully aware that "the new politeness advocated by middle-class writers and journalists demanded not only
external polish, but also sincerity, uprightness, and a realization of positive
social values in human relationships" (229). Taste was here the crucial notion: "It not only became a regulating principle of conduct, but also a moral
obligation" (233). Taste also helped differentiate the sophisticated classes
from those abusing wealth or character. "Not only noblemen were accused
of this lack of 'true' Taste, but the common people as well. And that is
quite in the nature of things; for just as the middle classes rediscovered for
themselves the true meaning of Politeness, Good-breeding, and Wit, so
they also took possession of Taste as their sole property" (231). What they
rejected was both "the 'vulgar' taste of the 'multitude' and the 'artificial' or
'false' Taste of the aristocracy" (232).

Taste, on which the (Hellenic) community of shared feelings was based,
created the first culture—the culture of characters. Once that was fully
tolerated, the religious authority of interpretation seemed in serious doubt:
how could faith be guaranteed in the public sphere? After the Deist critique of miracles and mysteries, Spinoza's project to save the Bible through
enlightened, impartial, personal interpretation could not continue without
a concrete goal different from intuitive faith. Following Hume's critique,
Biblical reason was dead. An alternative, more rewarding reading had to be
applied, transcending the disciplined restrictions of empiricism or rationalism on understanding. Thus the search for intrinsic validity turned from
credibility to beauty: the modernity (and therefore continuing relevance)
of the Bible had to be defended on artistic grounds. The Moderns first
claimed the literary by comparing their works to the ancient ones. The
same had to be done with the Bible, if guaranteeing its authenticity was the
major goal: authority should now become a matter of intrinsic quality. Religious conservatism ushered aesthetic liberalism as a defense against Deism.

Critical interest in the Bible as literature has been traced to at least the
second half of the seventeenth century: "Robert Boyle's *Some Considerations touching the Style of the Holy Scriptures* (1663); Jean Leclerc's *Essai
... où l'on tache de montrer en quoi consiste la poésie des Hébreux ...*
(1688); William Nichols' *Conference with a Theist*, Part IV (1699); Robert
Jenkin's *Reasonableness and Certainty of the Christian Religion*, Book II
(1700); several papers in the *Spectator* ... (1712); Henry Felton's *Dissertation on Reading the Classics* (1713); *The Creation. A Pindarick Illustration
of a Poem, Originally written by Moses. With a Preface to Mr. Pope, concerning the Sublimity of the Ancient Hebrew Poetry* (1720); Charles Gildon's
Laws of Poetry (1721); Fénelon's *Dialogues Concerning Eloquence* (1718);
Calmet's *Dictionnaire ... de la Bible* (1722–24); A. Blackwell's *Sacred Classics defended and illustrated* (1725)—these were but a few of the many
works known to English readers in which ... the style of the Scriptures was

analyzed, its Oriental character demonstrated, and its superiority to the
classical style proclaimed in no uncertain terms" (Crane 1922: 33–34).[50] As
the search for the fundamentals of beauty gradually jelled into the inquiry
of aesthetics, the discourses of interpretation, relieved from the burden of
textual concerns which philological scholarship was happily assuming, took
the form of literary criticism. It all happened in a relatively few years, following the storm over Hume's "Of Miracles": Robert Lowth's *De Sacra
poesi Hebraeorum* . . . (1753), Alexander Baumgarten's *Aesthetica* (1750,
1758; 2 vols.), Johann Winckelmann's *Thoughts on the Imitation of the
Painting and Sculpture of the Greeks* (1755), and Edmund Burke's *A Philosophical Enquiry into the Origin of Our Ideas of the Sublime and the Beautiful* (1756). If the qualities of the new writing style, literature, were first
defended in comparisons with ancient works, the principles of the new
interpretive approach, the discipline[51] of literary criticism, were first tested
on the Bible.[52]

Lowth is credited primarily with the discovery of parallelism, the structuring principle of Biblical meter, which he examined in terms of intrinsic
consistency (rather than Renaissance scansion or Augustan diction, as was
the current practice) and presented as the essence of the poetic dialectic
between thought and expression, words and sense, structure and meaning.[53] His was a very attractive picture of the text: "In the post-Lowthian
revival of Hebraism . . . the dialectical pattern of the Bible became central
to Romantic theories of inspiration" (Prickett 1986: 178). Approaching the
Bible as poetry was the epistemological shift that made Lowth's insight
possible: the search for literary qualities always recovers distinctive features. Neo-classical taste had found much to admire in the Bible. "The
loftiest form of praise, the tribute of stylistic superiority to or parity with
classical literature, is affirmed repeatedly" (Baroway 1933: 465).[54] But
Lowth was the first to treat the Bible as literature (and probably to write
the first work of both literary criticism and literary history) by constructing, according to the "Preface" of the English translation, "a system of
criticism" and a "compendium of critical science," complete with all "THE
GREAT PRINCIPLES OF GENERAL CRITICISM."

The system was based on the first systematic philological comparison of
Biblical and Greek writing, and the expressive economy of the two languages. Lowth rejected the rhetorical approach to the Bible and analyzed
its style, rather than tropes and figures, moving from typology to poetics.
He avoided theological and factual questions, and concentrated on formal
analysis and aesthetic merit. He also appropriated prophecy for poetry by
showing, in some of the best discussions of parallelism, the artistic character of the prophetic books and arguing that they were divine poetry. Conversely, poetry was the natural form of prophetic expression. In his book,
Biblical criticism moved from revelation to poetry, from rhetorical analysis

to literary study. "Lowth's work inaugurated a critical revolution. Not merely did the Bible give a new authority for the prophetic status of the poet as the transformer of society and the mediator of divine truth, but it was also stylistically taken as a model both of naturalness and sublimity" (Prickett 1986: 110). By the time William Blake (1757–1827) outlined his idea of "Genius," the Bible as model for poetry and the role of the poet as prophet were fully established.

Lowth, though, was still devising rules of taste and virtue, thinking, like many of his contemporaries (for example, Rollin in the first volume of his studies), in terms of the importance of poetry for religion and exalting it because its true "office and destination" was serving God. A certain religious polemic informed his entire project. It is therefore important to note that "Lowth's concentration on the literal meaning of the text as a document from a particular concrete historical situation can be seen as less an attempt to abolish the old style of typological and mystical readings, than to put such readings on a sounder scholarly basis—to combat Deist attacks on the authenticity of the Bible in general" (124–25). Between his parallelism of syntactical units and Herder's "parallelism of heaven and earth" (in *The Spirit of Hebrew Poetry*), the intervention of Winckelmann contributed to the complete liberation of the aesthetic. For Winckelmann, the aesthetic did not serve or promote religion—it was the new religion; and it was also (like History and myth before it) Greek.[55]

Developments in Germany, "the belated nation" (Helmuth Plessner), where the socio-political circumstances of emancipation were very different, followed another path. "The experiential fervor of the German Reformation had given way to a Protestant orthodoxy in which assent to truth in propositional form was the primary trait. Faith in revelation meant assent to statements which had been given in an infallible form in Scripture. At the beginning of the eighteenth century, however, this orthodoxy was under attack from two directions, Pietism and the Enlightenment" (Talbert 1970: 4). The former emphasized personal commitment, living faith, piety, and the saving power of grace. "At its best, the movement generally known as pietism may be regarded as a reaction on the part of a living faith against the empty formulae of [Lutheran] Orthodoxy" (McGrath 1986: 169). It saw the community of the faithful as a "priesthood of all believers," the visible church of the elect, with a sense of social responsibility. More than just a religious credo, "Pietism meant simply the penetration of methodically controlled and supervised, thus of ascetic, conduct into the non-Calvinistic denominations" (Weber 1976: 132). Under the Calvinist Hohenzollerns, it became the official Prussian faith (Hsia 1989).

While Pietism stressed personal inwardness and experience, placing the individual above dogma and authority, the German Enlightenment too

questioned the validity of revelation for natural theology. Under the influence of the former, the latter became much more conservative than the
English Deism or the French natural religion, seeking to establish the transcendental foundation of religion. German Deism was dominated by the
Leibnizian doctrine of harmony and the Wolffian principle of similarity
between revelation and reason (Cassirer 1951: 175–76). "The German The-
ists started from conscience and tried to prove the Deity by the inward
revelation of the moral law as it speaks in the bosom of men; and they
invoked the authority of Cartesianism as developed by Leibniz, and set
forth and commented upon by Wolff, which appealed to the innate idea of
a Deity as the strongest proof of its existence" (Karl Hillebrand, quoted in
Pelli 1979: 15), thus protecting the character of Lutheranism. They often
defended the Bible from French and English Deist criticisms, since their
purpose was to support and strengthen, not discredit or destroy it. "Indeed,
German Enlightenment did develop a scientific school of biblical criticism
whose intentions were serious and constructive" (Pelli 1979: 16). Attacking
the law of positive religions, they concentrated on morality instead. For the
German Deists (as for Kant later), religion is the recognition of human
duties as divine commands.

In its German Deist appropriation, reason was transformed from a theological into a philosophical category. "There appears to have been a general
and unquestioned assumption that man's higher consciousness is a constant quantity. In other words, reason was assumed to be a constant, un-
varying and universally distributed conglomerate of moral and spiritual
convictions, essentially independent of the historical and cultural situation
of the rational individual" (McGrath 1986: 209). This principle found its
most comprehensive expression in Wolff's philosophy of "sufficient reason." In his *Theologia naturalis methodo scientifica pertractata* (1739),
Christian Wolff (1679–1754) tries to show that the claims of reason and
revealed religion are absolutely compatible and mutually supportive,
adopting Leibniz's teleology of harmony. "In the system of Christian Wolff
there is no sharp differentiation between the content of faith and that of
knowledge, between revelation and reason. The claims of both are to be
carefully balanced and exactly determined" (Cassirer 1951: 175). Despite
this effort, philosophical reason was no longer investing in an unshakable
faith. "Wolff had indeed succeeded in reconciling faith and reason for his
generation and in making traditional Christian insights relevant once
more. At the same time, however, he had shifted the ultimate criterion of
the validity of religious insights from revelation to reason; he had substituted a natural ethic for a revealed ethic; and he had virtually transformed
man's interest in eternal salvation into mere desire for temporal happiness.
Theology had, in fact, become anthropology, and in the process whole
areas covered by traditional Christian theology had been set aside as irrele-

vant and meaningless for modern man. In the course of German theological development it was the so-called Neologists who adopted this radical
alternative, disseminating their theological reductionism from lecture halls
and pulpits alike" (Stoeffler 1973: 238–39). A revisionary trend was challenging the principles of belief, again on a textual basis.

The interpretation of the Bible was an integral part of the project of the
German Enlighteners. Under pressure from English empiricism and later
inspired by Spinoza's Biblical criticism, and caught in the often violent
clash between orthodox Lutheranism and Pietism, they established Biblical
hermeneutics as a discipline, sometimes known by the name attributed to
it by its opponents: Neologism. "They attempted to resolve the conflict
between reason and revelation by historicizing both. The name of the
movement derisively called Neology was to free the study of religion from
its subservience to either dogmatics or coherent analysis. The Neologists
incorporated many of the rationalist critiques without sacrificing Christianity" (Reill 1975: 81–82). They emphasized the collective, historical, and
cultural origin of the Bible as a collection of books; they examined acts of
composition, understanding, and transmission; they dealt with the Scripture as sacred poetry, and highlighted its moral authority (81–87); and they
also traced in it historical origins of human customs and institutions. It was
the rise of Neology that made Pietism harden its position in the second half
of the eighteenth century, and even ally itself with the declining Orthodoxy
to oppose what they both saw as an Enlightenment threat against the integrity and authority of revelation. The rationalists' emphasis on practical
reason, natural ethic, and conduct seemed to destroy the fabric of a theology based on grace and redemption. Pietism reacted strongly to the pursuit
of secular rewards by the new classes. "Its leaders, supported by the remaining Orthodoxists, now stood resolutely against the autonomy of the human
spirit and for biblical revelation as final authority for faith and life; against
a natural ethic and for a revealed ethic; against the reduction of Christian
theology to reasonable principles of human conduct and for the biblical
affirmations about God's redemptive activity; . . . against the shallow eu-
daemonism which had begun to dominate Western man's private and corporate life and for the reality of the eschatological dimension of human
existence, which makes happiness the ultimate, not the immediate, goal of
the salvatory process" (Stoeffler 1973: 242). Some intellectuals tried to reconcile reason with (Shaftesbury's) sentiment, especially friendship (phila-
delphic Pietism). Despite these reactions, however, fears were exaggerated,
since the German Enlightenment was never radical enough to undermine
belief with skepticist arguments. After all "secularism, antithetical to orthodoxy as well as theocracy, is itself a religious category derived from biblical values" (Zelechow 1990: 35). As Marx and Nietzsche would complain
later, for specific historical reasons German secularism never overcame its

religious identity. "That the *Aufklärung* developed in a theological manner to an extent absent from its English counterpart is generally considered to reflect the different political situations in the two countries. In England, the movement of free inquiry had assumed a political nature which was impossible for its German equivalent, so that the movement was obliged to assert itself in the field of literature and the humanities. Thus the common ideas which found political expression in England could only find cultural and religious expression in Germany. The *Aufklärung* is particularly notable for its transference of this political understanding of the nature and function of the secular State to the religious context (i.e., God), so that God was effectively 'modelled' on the newly-emerging understandings of the State" (McGrath 1986: 213). The Germans were the first Protestants to experience the challenges of belated modernity: they modernized without having either the discourse or the institutions that guarantee the rites of interpretation, the civil covenant of the bourgeois regime of truth. Identity and unity, rather than cohesion and stability, were their major concerns. The works of Georg Friedrich Händel (1685–1759) and J. S. Bach (1685–1750), in their contrasts of structure and function, show how different these concerns could be.

The *Aufklärung* was a *bürgerlich* movement of professionally and culturally prominent groups which sought to reform the body politic by working within the system and without destroying the *Ständestaat* tradition. It may be characterized as "an intellectual movement formed by the conjunction of three elements: the legacy of Leibnizian philosophy, the *Ständestaat* tradition, and the Protestant religious revival generated by the appearance of Pietism. Primarily it was bourgeois in spirit, critical of absolutism, opposed to attitudes associated with the court, but not revolutionary in nature. Its intellectual center was the university and its leading proponents were drawn primarily from the professional classes" (Reill 1975: 7–8). Its members abhorred revolution, and wanted simultaneously to liberalize the corporate order and rescue religion from bankruptcy. "The German Enlightenment did not produce an Adam Smith, a Montesquieu, a Rousseau. It read these authors but its most original contribution to social theory lay not so much in economics and politics as in, surprisingly, aesthetics. Where English and French thought concentrated on the study of civil society and the state, German thought concerned itself with the life of consciousness" (Feenberg 1973: 41). It sought the independence and salvation of the individual, whom it placed above society (but not the government), and it envisioned a science of humanity where the disciplines of religion, history, and aesthetics would prevail. "The notion of redemption as intellectual liberation is characteristic of the *Aufklärung*" (McGrath 1986: 225). Redemption from sin does not come through faith but through moral perfection.

Within this bourgeoisie there existed a group which was unique in West European countries: the *Bildungsbürgertum*—the cultural bourgeoisie with a university education who held privileged positions within the state apparatus and the institutions of national culture. The classical education of *Bildung* distinguished the cultural from the industrial bourgeoisie. Since culture was the highest expression of German identity, the *Bildungsbürgertum* was the cultural aristocracy of the nation, and its mission above all patriotic.[56] This bourgeois group dominated the public sphere but was dependent on state office (including education apparatus). The identification of the "unfree professions" (Jarausch 1990) with the German ideology was too close to allow them to create any other social alliances or espouse liberalism like the progressive intelligentsias of France and England.[57] What distinguished their social project was the increasing importance of aesthetic considerations: "Except for the most unabashed proponent of modern superiority, the problem of excellence of ancient art, to say nothing of the meaning of Holy Scripture, called for a study of the relation of art to science, of the understanding each conveys, and of their connection with the milieu in which they were formed. This became a historical problem touching the core of the triad past-present-future. Aesthetics was forced to incorporate historical problems into its scope. If aesthetics is given its most general meaning . . . then the affinity between history and aesthetics becomes apparent. The Aufklärers were aware of this affinity, as well as of the importance of both disciplines for the study of religion, and combined ideas drawn from all three disciplines; all three—history, aesthetics, and religion—showed a deep concern with the questions of the meaning of language, poetry, myth, metaphor, and artistic representation" (Reill 1975: 59–60). They believed in the possibility of progress and education for the nation and the human race through art and knowledge. It was in their discourse that moral considerations changed to artistic appreciations, that the objects of taste rather than its practices assumed greater importance, that the critical rather than the emotional faculties gained priority. The German "taste-bearing stratum" (Levin Schücking) had no use for rhetoric or the public contests of eloquence and character. They historicized reason and revelation, strongly emphasizing the importance of individual autonomy and national uniqueness. "The plea for freedom for the creative human spirit to develop to its full range is one of the outstanding preoccupations of eighteenth-century Germany. If the form it took tended to be generally cultural, this does not make the ideal any the less politically and socially relevant. It does not seem to be out of harmony with the idea of reform from above, but it *is* accompanied by a strong distaste for social disorder and upheaval. The idealist and non-revolutionary path was the one taken, to a greater or lesser extent, by most major German thinkers" (Menhennet 1973: 20). Envisioning a "beneficent revolution" (Wieland) through persuasive reason and non-violent constitutional transformation, they desired a republican form of government. Reformists, those civil servants who were liberal, well-educated, and cultivated, and who aspired to protect the *Ständestaat* by transforming it into a *Bildungsstaat*, competed among themselves over who understood Spinoza best and who liked Jews most.

Although the Deists often presented Biblical religion as a local law whose validity was limited to its ethnic constituency and time, when they drew similarities with their gospel of morality, they still honored this national religion more than others for its prefiguration of the natural religion of reason. German *maskilim*, the Westernizing intelligentsia who were looking for ways of combining their traditional heritage with the secular demands of modernity, recognized a great potential there: "Affiliated in one way or another with Jewish tradition—this applies especially to the Hebrew enlighteners—they considered deism as a new movement aiming at a revival rather than the destruction of religion. In it the *maskilim* saw religion coming to terms with the demands of the new era of the European Enlightenment, an era based on reason and science, and dedicated to tolerance" (Pelli 1979: 18). This development could solve many internal conflicts between tradition and modern life within their own society.[58] Like those proponents of the German Enlightenment who hoped to liberalize the rule of the state through the law of the nation, the maskilim hoped to moderate the law of tradition through the rule of culture. The historical compromise was reached in the work of Moses Mendelssohn (1729–86), who sacrificed revelation in order to preserve the cultural specificity and communal authority of the Law. Confident in its deeper enlightened character, he rationalized orthodox Judaism, assuming that, while law was its determining principle, conduct was the essence of all religion. The philosopher whom Heine called the "Socrates of our time" was the great cultural mediator. "Mendelssohn attempted to build a bridge between the Jewish culture, which seemed to be declining in Germany, and the powerful, influential, and tempting general culture of the time, the latter playing a decisive role in the eclipse of the former. It was a two-way bridge" (20). Jews could feel more comfortable with Gentile culture, and the Enlightenment could understand its Jewish character better. The way to achieve this was to sacrifice ethnic particularity for a universal claim—to argue that the mission of Judaism was to teach the whole world the natural religion of the God of reason. Mendelssohn's translation of the Pentateuch into German, a repetition of Luther's founding gesture, was only one of his many moves in this direction.

Mendelssohn had to deal with strong feelings of unease and impatience within his own community. "Already in 1771 there was published [in London] the first demand to change the Jewish law according to the conditions dictated by time and place" (27).[59] Internal discussions on reform revolved around *halakhah*, the Oral Law which regulated community life: What was the proper relation between Oral and Written Law? (Was it possible to save the Written as an expression of reason and then sacrifice the Oral as something local that has been superseded? Or was it possible to preserve the Oral simply as an ethnic law?) What was the correct connection between tradition and revelation, reason and practice, religion and education, faith and culture? Two centuries later, Derrida would blame the antinomies of these questions on Hellenic thought.

The maskilim, like the Deists, concentrated on moral reform; but unlike the Deists they could not afford to ignore the dimension of experience, since the legal system of Judaism was closely connected with daily life. For them, questions of law, authority, and governance had double urgency, both internal and external. They pursued them passionately in magazines, schools, salons, intellectual societies. Thus they were confronted with the highest stakes in modernity, the subject of all debates in the cultural spaces of the public sphere—the relation between interpretation and emancipation: What is the liberatory promise of the independent and enlightened reason? What are the rules of understanding? What are the confines of individual ethical action? What is the nomos of autonomy? "When the change came, therefore, at the close of the seventeenth century it was a total 'philosophical revolution which changed the whole concept of Nature and its operations,' initiating modern 'rationalism' and rejecting biblical fundamentalism. The final victory that liberated nature from biblical fundamentalism came on the one side from German pietists and English deists (the heirs of the Protestant heretics of the seventeenth century), and on the other from Descartes and his universal 'mechanical' laws of nature" (Tambiah 1990: 90). The capitalist solution to the quest for autonomy was the differentiation of society, the creation of separate spheres of feeling and activity with their own relative independence. It was the sphere of public morality, inheritor to the visions of community, that adopted the Hebraic as its model, while the sphere of culture, the successor of the practices of taste, proclaimed its Hellenic aspirations.

Aesthetic Faith

A discussion entitled "Hebrews and Hellenes," which introduces the first chapter of the first volume of an "interpretation" of the Enlightenment, defines as follows the period's dualist view of history: "As the Enlightenment saw it, the world was, and had always been divided between ascetic, superstitious enemies of the flesh, and men who affirmed life, the body, knowledge, and generosity; between mythmakers and realists, priests and philosophers. Heinrich Heine, wayward son of the Enlightenment, would later call these parties, most suggestively, Hebrews and Hellenes" (Gay 1966: 33). This may not be an inappropriate exaggeration. During the second half of the eighteenth century, and while the last part of the Battle of the Books was belatedly taking place in Germany, the middle class for the first time began to debate explicitly and at length its mission and options in terms of the Hebraic-Hellenic polarity. Heinrich Heine (1797–1856) discovered the polarity in Ludwig Börne (1786–1837); his contemporary Samuel David Luzzatto (1800–65) considered Abrahamism (or Judaism) superior to Atticism; together they gave universal meaning to the old comparison of (Greek) flowers with (Jewish) fruit (Judah Halevi).[60] The emergence of classical scholarship, following the triumph of the Moderns and the invention of History at the turn of the seventeenth century, made possible a systematic and concentrated interest in Greek culture itself. With the opposition of Rationalism and Pietism to ancient thought,[61] however, Greek writing and art had remained subordinate to Latin or ignored (Trevelyan 1941: 1–12), with only the manuals of fables for artists and the handbooks of mythology for versifiers available as sources of information about the period. "Greek literature was generally considered inferior to Latin; in German schools and universities Greek was studied primarily as the language of the New Testament" (Hatfield 1943: 3–5; see also Hatfield 1964: 8). At the same time, after the Battle of the Books distanced antiquity from the present, historical knowledge (primarily of Greece) became an attractive project for the exploration of the origins of Western identity.

In short, the possibility of Greece, of its "discovery" as a real place, was there, but nothing guaranteed that it should happen. The philological skills required for this exploration, already in use in Biblical studies, did not flourish in England. "Although Bishop Lowth's *De sacra poesi Hebraeorum* and his commentary on Isaiah exercised some influence, they did not succeed in establishing a historical or literary-critical tradition of the Biblical writings in the author's native land" (Frei 1974: 151).[62] The reason may be sought in the factual direction that Deism gave to the question of Biblical historical accuracy: the ensuing search for external evidence that would prove the truth of the text had no use for the close analysis of textual meaning. Philological skills found a much more fertile ground in German Neo-humanist scholarship (Gesner, Ernesti, Christ, Caylus).

Reactions to the excesses of late baroque and the artificiality of French rococo were fired by the enthusiasm over the excavations at Herculaneum, Paestum, and Pompeii. In response to calls for a revival of the Greek architectural orders in the first half of the eighteenth century, David Le Roy published *Les ruines des plus beaux monuments de la Grèce* (1758). The rule of ornament was challenged by the order of style. Now balance was deemed more conducive to civility than elegance. In the second half of the century, British fascination with the reality of the historical Greece began, especially after the success of *The Antiquities of Athens, Measured and Deline-ated* (4 vols., 1762–1830), where James Stuart and Nicholas Revett pub-lished the drawings of Greek remains they produced during their expedi-tion to the country (1751–53). The famous expedition was sponsored by The Society of Dilettanti (established in 1732), a group of young aristo-crats who had made the Grand Tour. What attracted the British to Hellen-ism was travel and a taste for cultural exoticism. The Tour could now be extended to include a new, more ancient (if not alternative), unexplored territory.

Indeed, the recovered treasures, from architectural models to the Elgin (Parthenon) Marbles, put on public display in 1807, did not disappoint anyone. But British interest did not extend much beyond experiments in taste. "Meanwhile the Germans were approaching the shrine by a different road. Like the English, they enjoyed speaking of Hellas in religious lan-guage, but in the manner less of pilgrims than of visionaries" (Jenkyns 1980: 13). They turned to the Hellenic ideal with such exultation that they refused to taint it with any experience. Winckelmann, Schiller, Hölderlin, Hegel, and Nietzsche never visited Greece, while Lord Charlemont, Robert Wood, Byron, James Flecker, and John Symonds, like Gérard de Nerval, Alphonse de Lamartine, Théophile Gautier, Gustave Flaubert, and Le Cor-busier from France, and Americans from Herman Melville to James Merrill, did. (In general, it is also interesting how few novels are set in Greece, ancient or modern. Bourgeois interiority has not found the land hospita-ble.) During his visit to Italy, which provided him with his first direct expe-rience of Greek art, Goethe "received a proposal from the Duke of Waldeck which affected him as a threatening temptation: a visit to Greece. Goethe's reaction was by no means a serene one; he even expressed terror when he wrote: 'Once one takes it upon oneself to go out into the world and enters into close interaction with it, one has to be very careful not to be swept away in a trance, or even to go mad. I am not able to speak a single word at the moment' (28th March 1787). Walter Rehm was the first to realise that this holy terror of Greece—a kind of prohibitive fear of contact—was a typically German phenomenon at that period. Whereas the French and the English were more and more eager to get to Athens, scarcely one of the German philhellenes set foot on Greek soil. This is not only true of Goethe, Humboldt and even Hölderlin, but also of the German architects. . . . Rehm comments on this shying away from direct contact with Hellenic reality which had been idealised and mythicised to the point of refusing to visit the place: 'One has the impression that all of them had willingly made this strange renunciation'" (Vogt 1986: 172). It took a businessman's literal reading of Homer in the 1870s, monumentalized in Heinrich Schliemann's recovery of Troy from the hill of Hisarlik, to make the Germans consider the possibility of an encounter with the place.

In Germany, the theological need for ever-richer Biblical comparisons in the early eighteenth century encouraged the literary-historical quest that would eventually develop into the parallel fields of hermeneutics and aesthetics. "Hermeneutical developed together with historical-critical literature" (Frei 1974: 158). The synthesis of the two must be credited to the discipline of philology, the science of the antiquity of texts. "In the German states in 1770–1810, we witness a profound turn away from the *Altphilologie* as a discipline of text criticism and restoration and the emergence of a genuinely hermeneutic, interpretive philology as a comprehensive discipline aiming at the disclosure of a historical, cultural totality" (Leventhal 1986: 248). If literary criticism tutored secular reading in discrimination, philology undertook to authenticate and integrate its objects of study. "In the beginning, there was philology. As the keystone of law and ethics, and also of history and the history of art, stood the study of language and of literature. Never has further-reaching importance been attributed to literary texts, especially to founding literary texts. . . . And never has literary commentary appropriated with such confidence the right to apply its conclusions to other domains, even to assume that textuality was at the center of all knowledge. The philological science, as it was defined by its founders in the late eighteenth and early nineteenth centuries, was an intellectual totality, a world unto itself, the study of language redefined to give philologists access to the essence of nations. In particular, philology was the science of antiquity, the tool German scholars would use to rehabilitate antiquity and reveal the Greeks as the standard for beauty, grandeur, and national genius" (DeJean 1989: 203–4). Philology is the branch of Protestant interpretation which, once emancipated from theology, turned to the study of a new object of knowledge, (pagan) antiquity. In it, the original exercise of reading reached the systematic articulation of a field.

German Hellenism both defined and served bourgeois cultural ideals in a comprehensive way: it portrayed a land of pure Western descent; it countered Pietist asceticism with Puritan stoicism; it provided an antidote to French skepticism and British empiricism; it integrated leisure in Protestant morality; it counterproposed democratic enjoyment to aristocratic taste; it outlined the conditions of healthy individualism; and it ennobled the project of a national culture. It is this last ideal that held the greatest urgency. What has been said about literature can be generalized about all the arts: "The movement of German authors in the eighteenth century to found a German national literature becomes, as the century enters its second half, increasingly a battle they are obliged to wage on two fronts at once: for beyond the need to establish a basis for works distinctively *national* in character, it appears in addition that some way must be found to create *literature* at all" (Morton 1982: 41). The national and the cultural, as they are still understood today, were produced together, verifying and supporting each other. It is in Germany that culture becomes a conscious project, a means of resistance as well as legitimation, of national differentiation as well as superiority. When it came to internal understandings of community life, the Biblical model was still the most meaningful; but when it was time to "imagine" a national culture, intellectuals looked at Greece. "The intense concern with Greece can usefully be understood as a response to a German crisis of identity. The century from 1660 to 1760 saw the rise of France as a 'new Rome' apparently capable of absorbing all Europe" (Bernal 1986: 14). France could proudly exhibit the glories of its court, arts, and reason. In order to surpass the Latinity of these royal codes, German poets, critics, and historians concentrated increasingly on Rome's predecessor. "Thus while Germany could not become a new Rome she could be a new Hellas" (14). If the Reformation had moved above the Catholic establishment back to the originals of religion, the Aufklärung returned above the Latin system to the origins of art. And if the Reformation played Jerusalem opposite to Rome's Athens, Germany now was ready to play Athens opposite to France's Rome.

Both the bourgeois ideals and the national aspirations found their most eloquent defense in the work of Johann Joachim Winckelmann (1717–68), who defined the "humanity of the Greeks" and advocated it as a cultural model. Winckelmann constructed a complete, total picture of Greece: he made of it a coherent, luminous, organic whole—an aesthetic ideal incorporating moral, cultural, and political elements. To this effect, he scrutinized artworks with minute care and historical sensitivity. He understood questions of origin, growth, change, and decline in terms of stylistic evolution: "Winckelmann's most significant and lasting achievement was to produce a thorough, comprehensive and lucid chronological account of all antique art—but chiefly sculpture—including that of the Egyptians and the Etruscans. No one had done this before" (Haskell and Penny 1981: 101). While his predecessors in the first half of the century had re-presented Greece, Winckelmann narrated it, gave it a story of development. He classified artworks by date, rather than iconography, according to (intrinsic) stylistic criteria, and established for the first time successive stages of art. Although he analyzed mainly sculpture, his approach was primarily literary: for example, he discussed mythology as an intricate web of allegories, bringing allegory back from typology into aesthetics and inaugurating a critical interest in it that was still paramount for Walter Benjamin, Paul de Man, or Stephen Greenblatt.[63]

His was a major reinterpretation of antiquity. In Germany, before Winckelmann, differentiating between Roman and Greek was an insignificant concern: they belonged together to humankind's ancient past. Not only did he distinguish between the two, but also defended forcefully the overwhelming superiority of the latter. Until then, the ancient appeal was moral and juridical; the new Greek inspiration became aesthetic. More importantly, he established the Greek difference in all respects, not only from the Roman but also from the contemporary world. "It was Winckelmann who first insisted that Greek sculpture of the finest period was a product of the very highest excellence, brought about under geographical, political and religious circumstances which could never be recreated" (104). A sense of irrevocable separation was again effected: "As reverence for the Greeks increased, so too did awareness of our distance from them" (104). This was already obvious to Friedrich Schlegel, who noted in 1798: "The systematic Winckelmann who read all the ancients as if they were a single author, who saw everything as a whole and concentrated all his powers on the Greeks, provided the first basis for a material knowledge of the ancients through his perception of the absolute difference between ancient and modern" (Schlegel 1971: 181).

Winckelmann treated art as a social phenomenon, and its style as the expression of a specific culture. Like Lowth, he connected art and culture, style and society organically. In his work, the independent aesthetic found its first full articulation and justification. The project of interpretation outlined by Spinoza reached here an apolitical conclusion: criticism was applied to secular, not religious, beauty; and that beauty did not serve religion but constituted (a new) one. This love of pure beauty, however, was not just a cult of "a noble simplicity and tranquil grandeur" but also an exuberant celebration of the leisure deserved for the cultivated few. From Winckelmann's celebration of ecstatic delight in his "Essay on the Capacity of the Perception of Beauty in Art" (1763) to Roland Barthes' self-consuming hedonism in *The Pleasure of the Text* (1973), leisure has been perceived as a typically Greek vice and (effeminate) privilege, scolded and envied by the Protestant work ethic. Winckelmann interconnected ethical and aesthetic judgment, subordinating religious experience to aesthetic revelation. Thus interpretation matured in the worship of autonomous beauty when the independence of the aesthetic was consecrated in/as Greek culture. Where Spinoza saw Hebrew polity as a community, Winckelmann treated the Greek polis as an organism; whereas the former described a community of interpreters, the latter depicted the Greeks as the aesthetic people—the ones to be interpreted.

And interpreted they were, and still are. "The German Enlightenment looks rather to Greece, an interest which follows from the aesthetic concerns of its philosophy. The integral community, which increasingly emerges as a lost utopia in the bourgeois era, is reflected artistically in its happiest form in Homer. The epics of ancient Greece are the epiphany of a civilization perfect of its kind, a civilization of a total man and the harmonious community, not yet touched by the corrosive forces of division of labor and commercialization. In analyzing this epic world, German thought goes far beyond the narrow concept of virtue to lay the basis for a dialectics of consciousness. . . . The theory of epic literature develops as a reflection on the conditions and nature of human community, a reflection which corresponds in the Germany of the time with an increasing anxiety over the consequences of the unleashing of private self-interest by capitalism" (Feenberg 1973: 42–43). The Greece of Winckelmann is the integrated civilization of the lost Eden which inspires Lukács' nostalgia, as well as the idolatrous threat haunting Auerbach's vision of the promised reading. (It was Winckelmann, after all, who in 1755, with his *Thoughts on the Imitation of the Painting and Sculpture of the Greeks*, made mimesis, Auerbach's topic, a central concern for aesthetics.) Eutopia or dystopia, Hellas has remained the Alien (as opposed to the Hebrew Other or the non-European Barbarian) of modern (that is, post-Reformation) thought: the presence of the past, the periphery of the center, the leisure of culture, the male of the female, the physics of metaphysics, the polis of politics.

The imitation of the Hellenic in Hebraic modernity soon became the central educational concern of the period. Even by the time of Heidegger's reading of the Presocratics or Auerbach's interpretation of Homer, the question had not lost its urgency: If the gap of History is understood in terms of the ancient (Hellenic) and the modern (Hebraic), what is the burden of that past on the responsibility of this present? If interpretation is Biblical, what are the limits of the emancipation it promises? Who or what deserves autonomy in an emancipated world? What is the difference between imitation and assimilation (Gombrich 1966)? Winckelmann's contemporaries were already alarmed by the appeal of his artistic hedonism among the bourgeois.[64] The Hebraic opposition to his proposal for a secular democratic faith in humanism was soon articulated. The theologian Friedrich Gottlieb Klopstock (1724–1803) aspired to become the "Christian Homer" by writing, along with Biblical dramas, *Messias* (1748–73), the pietist epic of the life of Christ in Greek hexameters; he outlined his plans for a German intellectual elite in *Die deutsche Gelehrtenrepublik* (1774), a treatise intended to counter what he perceived as the growing Hellenization of the upper middle class.

The young Hegel, in Part Two (1795–96) of "The Positivity of the Christian Religion," still felt the importance of the ultimate question for national rejuvenation raised by Klopstock in his ode "The Hill and the Grove" (1767): "Is Achaea, then, the Teutons' fatherland?" He responded that "what the poet cried to his people in relation to Greek mythology could be said both to him and his nation with just as much right in relation to the Jewish; they could be asked: Is Judaea, then, the Teutons' fatherland?" (Hegel 1971: 149). The dilemma had attracted his attention since his university years, as indicated by the paper "On Some Advantages which the Reading of Ancient Classical Greek and Roman Writers Secures for Us"

(1788): "The first hint of an explicit contrast between the two heritages of Achaea and Judaea in his mind is to be found in his claim that, in virtue of the constancy of human nature, the study of our classical heritage will enable us 'to explain more naturally and make more comprehensible a great deal of the culture, the habits, the customs, and the usages of the people of Israel, who have had, and still have, so much influence upon us'" (Harris 1972: 77). In a society losing its faith to materialism, the Hellenic path seemed an appropriate training in the respect for morality and a better understanding of its socio-cultural basis. As Mendelssohn had already suggested in his *Jerusalem* (1783), the study of the ancients could serve a better understanding of Israel. Until his last college year, "Hegel remained true to the programme of using classical sources to enlighten the study of the Judaic tradition, which he announced at the outset of his university studies" (117). His later philosophy is full of revisions and sublimations of this project.

The use of Hellenism for modernity also occupied Friedrich Hölderlin (1770–1843), who in the late 1780s, together with Hegel and Schelling, attended the Seminary at the University of Tübingen as a student of theology with the intention of becoming a minister. In 1790, to obtain the degree of *magister philosophiae*, he wrote two papers: one influenced by Herder, "Parallels between Solomon's *Proverbs* and Hesiod's *Works and Days*," and another influenced by Winckelmann, "History of the Fine Arts among the Greeks" (Montgomery 1923: 202–7). The Hebraic-Hellenic comparison had become by that time very common. Hölderlin's position on the subject was fully expressed in the late 1790s, when he started distancing himself from Greece by painting it as Oriental (with an "aorgic," as opposed to organic, element) and opposing it to "Hesperia," the Western and modern world. The distinction between Greek and Hesperian art first appears in the famous letter to C. U. Bohlendorff (1801), where the differentiation relieves Hölderlin "entirely of that imitation of antiquity which Winckelmannian classicism had made obligatory for him, and at the same time it allows him to see the reason why the Greeks are nevertheless 'indispensable' for him. Hölderlin overcomes classicism without turning away from the classical" (Szondi 1983: 262). This is what he calls the "salvaging of the Greek for Hesperia."

Hölderlin was not the only one to see the Greeks in an Oriental light. His British and German contemporaries often surmised Oriental influences on Greek culture. Friedrich Schlegel (1772–1829), for example, who aspired to become the "Winckelmann of Greek Literature" and was the first to detect an ecstatic element in drama and to derive comedy from Dionysian rites, changed his interests, after his conversion to Catholicism in 1808, from Greek to Sanskrit (at that time explored by Wilhelm von Humboldt's comparative philology), from aesthetic to moral values, and from ancient sculpture to Nazarene painting. He too emphasized the Oriental ancestry of Greek wisdom and art, which the Greeks forgot or repressed. But Hölderlin went further than anyone else before him in deciding to correct, so to speak, Greek art by emphasizing its presumed Eastern origin. His plan is captured in a telling passage: "Greek art is foreign to us, but I hope to represent it to the public in a more lively manner than is customary, through national convenience and through errors, with which it has always helped itself along: I would emphasize more greatly the oriental element which it denied, and improve upon its artistic error where it occurs" (quoted in Szondi 1983: 270). Thus, after he abandoned in 1799 his drama *The Death of Empedocles*, partly modeled on Sophocles' *Oedipus at Colonus*, Hölderlin translated *Antigone* and *Oedipus Tyrannus*, and published both in 1804 as *Die Trauerspiele des Sophokles*, with "Notes" appended to each play. He hoped to correct the "errors" which he believed the Greek poet had been forced to make by virtue of his time and place in history. The hermeneutic violence of these translations has often been discussed and admired—although never, to my knowledge, compared to their most audacious successors, Ezra Pound's renditions of *Elektra* (1949) and *Women of Trachis* (1954) by Sophocles; it even influenced German modernism from philosophy (Heidegger) to poetry (Celan) and music (Carl Orff). The corrective dimension of the project, however, the attempt to rectify, repair, remedy the Greek original has not been sufficiently noted, although it permeates the poet's accompanying commentary. The important distinction between Greek and Hesperian modes and natures returns in the Notes. The origin of the former lies in "fire from heaven" and "sacred pathos" and "warmth," of the latter in "sobriety" and "precision and effective flexibility." He identified as the unsurpassable virtue of the Greek nature the "Homeric presence of mind and talent for presentation," a virtue he would later present as the first, the "natural" or "naive" tone of poetry. Given the similarities between this depiction and the portrayal of the Homeric in *Mimesis*, the debt of Auerbach (who was familiar with studies of the Bohlendorff letter by Rosenzweig, Heidegger, Adorno, and Benjamin, among others) to Hölderlin's Hellenism is obvious.[65]

Among Winckelmann's contemporaries, Klopstock and Johann Georg Hamann (1730–88) were the eminent writers who, with their uncompromising religious commitment, rejected his theories completely. Opposing reason from the Pietist side and preaching "salvation by the Jews," Hamann offered a new concept of faith which refers to moral conviction, rather than religious belief. Gotthold Ephraim Lessing (1729–81) responded with his own theory of imitation in *Laoköon* (1766), subtitled "On the Limits of Painting and Poetry," a semiotic defense of modernity; and later Mendelssohn proposed a different cultural politics in *Jerusalem: On Religious*

Power and Judaism (1783), where the philosophical identity of Deism and Judaism was developed. Reaction to Winckelmann's politics of aesthetic appreciation, however, was not expressed in religious opposition or philosophical disagreement as much as in the form of a new articulation of the Hebraic, the discovery of Spinoza. The great respect of the *Aufklärung* for Spinoza is understandable in the context of the ideological tendencies of the movement. Interest in his work was revived in Germany during the furor accompanying Lessing's printing of extracts from *Apologie oder Schutzschrift für die vernünftigen Verehrer Gottes*, an unpublished attack on Christianity by the Deist Professor of Hebrew Hermann Samuel Reimarus (1694–1768), which appeared anonymously under the title *Fragments of an Anonymous* in 1774 and 1777–78. The intensity of that elite interest came to the open when the famous *"Wolffenbüttel Fragmente"* controversy (Bell 1984: 71–96) over Lessing's alleged Spinozism erupted between Friedrich Jacobi (1743–1819) and Mendelssohn under the watchful eyes of Goethe, Kant, and Herder (Beiser 1987). To an extent that has yet to be fully comprehended, the debate was about the primacy of Lessing's debt to Winckelmann or to Spinoza. The Hebraic-Hellenic comparison appeared later in Lessing's *The Education of the Human Race* (1780), which established an analogy between revelation and education by dealing with the religious education of the Hebrews (sections 9–53) and suggested a perspectival approach to religious truth by showing how it necessarily manifests itself in history. In his anonymously published treatise, "Lessing countered Reimarus' attack on the revealed character of the Old Testament with a relativistic conception of revealed religion, whereby each revelation is seen as a historically conditioned accommodation to the community to which it is addressed" (Allison 1966: 149). This constitutes a basic hermeneutic principle, since "it means that each historically conditioned revelation contains a relative perfection or partial truth" (149). In its use of the Leibnizian concept of theodicy in the new understanding of the past, "Lessing's view of religion as a divine plan for the education of humanity is nothing but a theodicy of history, a justification of religion not through a being which has existed from the beginning of time but through religious growth and the goal of this growth" (Cassirer 1951: 192). Thus Lessing tried to save revelation by fusing it with Winckelmann's idea of historicism and ideal of *Bildung* into moral autonomy, effectively combining Hebraic faith and reason with Hellenic culture and education. Contemporary critics could not agree on the importance of each element for his thought. Before this could be resolved, though, the focus of interest had shifted to the work of Spinoza itself. As a consequence, the immediate appeal of Winckelmann was largely diminished.

Nowhere else was the Hebraic-Hellenic opposition debated and negotiated as intensely as in the work of Johann Gottfried Herder (1744–1803), the thinker who after Lessing and before Schiller came to redefine the experience and the tasks of modernity in a major way. Despite his respect for the ideals of the Aufklärers, Herder never trusted their faith in reason, their search for universal truth, or their cosmopolitan leanings. Neither did he approve of Hellenism: he was afraid of Goethe's classicism and Schiller's paganism. "Whereas in his Bückeburg period he felt compelled to combat Enlightenment narrowness and self-assuredness, he became subsequently much less polemical, until in his last decade he felt that philosophy and theology had taken a wrong turn with Kantian criticism, and that Goethe's and Schiller's classicism was harmful for the development of German literature and culture in general. And thus he rose again in grim determination to defend his wide theocentric universe against what he considered to be a narrow anthropocentric dogmatism" (Koepke 1982a: 152–53). Above all, he conducted a life-long battle with Winckelmann, praising him for historical insight but asking for more specific cultural detail that would make the imitation of Greece impossible as an ideal. He would even defend Oriental despotism in order to show that Winckelmann's negative evaluation of Egyptian art was unjust, as he did in the essay "*Auch eine Philosophie der Geschichte zur Bildung der Menschheit*" (1774). The same struggle is also obvious in the memorial essay "Monument of Johann Winckelmann" (1778). During much of this single-minded campaign, he sought inspiration and support in the work of Spinoza. His interest in the Dutch philosopher developed continuously after the late 1760s, when he "consciously gives an interpretation of Spinoza's system as a whole. It is the first full interpretation of Spinoza's philosophy undertaken in Germany and is based on a sympathetic understanding of certain fundamental Spinozist concepts, which are also congenial to Herder's own outlook. *God—A Series of Dialogues* (1787) presented to the public a Spinoza hitherto unknown except to independent individuals like Lessing and Goethe" (Bell 1984: 174). It was in *God* that Herder proclaimed Spinoza more divine than St. John.

As his polemical choice of Spinoza over Winckelmann shows, Herder's ardent cultural nationalism was wholly permeated by the Hebraic-Hellenic opposition, and he regularly argued along these options, as, for example, in his essay "On the Effect of Poetry on the Mores of the Peoples in Ancient and Modern Times" (written in 1778 and published in 1781) or in his *Ideas on the Philosophy of History of Mankind*, 1784–91, 4 vols.). Already in *Critical Woods* (1769) he rated the Old Testament writers better than the classical ones. The most extensive comparison of the two, however, was his return to Lowth's grand subject in *The Spirit of Hebrew Poetry: An Introduction for Lovers of the Same and of the Most Ancient History of the Human Spirit* (1782–83, 2 vols.), a history of Hebrew literature. This book is what remains of the aborted project "Archaeology of the Orient." It is divided in two parts, one dialogic and one expository. In the dialogue, Alciphron, a representative of the radical Enlightenment, is convinced by Euthyphron that the Old Testament is of great poetic and historical value. The second part is a literary evaluation of the same book. It contains scores of detailed comparisons of the Hebrew Bible with Greek poets. (Herder even suggested parallelism as the basic structure of Greek meter.) The book owes its importance and widespread influence partly to the fact that here the epistemological value of poetic language is recognized and the identity of poetry and religion admitted (Clark 1955: 297–98). Essentially the importance of Winckelmann's aesthetics is recognized, while art is asked to serve faith.

The influence on Herder of Lowth's book, which Mendelssohn had endorsed in an influential review, is heavy. Lowth too looked for the origin of poetry in religion and popular imagination but classified Hebrew poetry according to technical categories derived from neoclassical usage. Herder, a superb Hebraist himself, found this formalistic. The intent of his approach was to turn "the Bible, and divine revelation with it, into the fullest expression of the one human spirit under the educative guidance of divine providence" (Frei 1974: 185). Herder, who detested Rationalism and Deism, was influenced by Hamann's Pietism.[66] In a market of capital desire, though, he could not afford to present faith as its own reward. "Unlike the Pietists, Herder wrote at a level naturally combining an aesthetic stance with that of a historical relativist; but he shared the Pietists' conviction that the unitary content of the Bible is the history of saving events, self-differentiated into a sequence of temporal stages" (200). He protected the Bible from the philological criticism of the Neologists by trying to ground it historically: his genetic-historical epistemology explains revelation as a historical event. Thus he was able to see the Bible as "the history book of mankind, written by humans, for the purpose of expressing in poetic-historical terms the ways of God through the course of human history" (Koepke 1982a: 145). He defended its unitary meaning, and therefore its theological authority, on historical and aesthetic grounds. "Figuration changes for him from the connectedness of two temporally widely-separated specific occurrences to a slowly accumulating and general sense of anticipation reaching a climactic fulfillment" (Frei 1974: 193). For Herder, as for Lessing, history is education and revelation. "In human fashion must one read the Bible; for it is a book written by men for men: Human is the language, human the external means with which it was written and preserved; human finally is the sense with which it may be grasped, every aid that illuminates it, as well as the aim and use to which it is to be applied" (quoted in Frei 1974: 184). By making history the time where humans are educated in revelation, and therefore by consecrating reading-in-history, he contributed more than anybody else to the idea, which prevailed in late-eighteenth-century Germany, that "a free and self-conscious self-positioning toward the world is an independent and indispensable factor in shaping the depiction of that world with its bearing on the self" (201). This principle may still be one of the best definitions we have of autonomy—"the idea of absolute being grounded in itself, that is to say of *freedom*" (Schiller 1965: 61)—as the project of modernity.

The great problem of autonomy has always been where the ground of its nomos is, what source of authority justifies the *auto*-claim. The post-Lutheran contribution sought a transcendental ground, in an attempt to guarantee, rather than oversee, the function of that nomos. (Hence the importance of law for thinkers from Kant to Schiller, and of order for composers from Haydn to Beethoven.) The locus of the source could have been one among many things—to use the terminology inherited from Herder's solution, social, ethnic, historical, personal, economic, and so on. But the rejection of rhetoric, the fear of skepticism, the lack of important bourgeois institutions, and the emphasis on national construction made the transcendental path, the one dispensing with a factious public and competing parties, the most viable one. During the eighteenth century, the "age of control" (Menhennet 1973: 21), the reason of the polity (like its mass-reading habits) could not be trusted. In his essay "What is Enlightenment?" (1784), Kant, after distinguishing between revolution, which he rejects, and *Reform*, which he seeks, proposes that the requirement for enlightenment is the least harmful freedom of all—the freedom of using in public one's power of reason, of public expression, and more specifically, the freedom of the writer who is addressing a *Publikum*. The writer is aware of his role as a latter-day Reformist. More than self-referential, autonomy should become self-reflexive, and Herder was determined to devise its constitution—the grammar of nomocracy.

Knowledge is determined by language and not reason; language is *pneuma*, "God's breath," the spirit of God communicated to humankind. Herder thought that the Hebrew language, the speech of Adam and the Tower of Babel, was the *Bildersprache* of the human race in its infancy, and that its poetry remains the best ever made. In taking this position, while suggesting that the Greeks failed to achieve maturity, he was comparing not only languages and literatures but also social systems. His political ideas, based (like those of Spinoza, Lessing, Mendelssohn, Eichhorn, and later Coleridge) on the model of the Hebrew polity, had national identity as their true scope. Indeed, Herder, whose fragmentary work may arguably be considered in its entirety as a *Tractatus aesthetico-politicus*, took a resolutely cultural approach to politics.[67] At a time when a collective sense of German identity was just emerging, he insisted that the foundation of national identity be a common, shared culture—replacing in his system the negotiable social contract (Barnard 1989)—where individual and collective identity become one.[68] The state does not operate like a machine but develops like an organism: to the political machinery is opposed the organic State—and to the political/mechanical, the cultural/organic. The organic State is the state of national tradition and culture, of a coherent ethnic community—the *Volkstaat*. In it, power does not emanate from a sovereign but from an impersonal, immaterial, invisible government—nomocracy, the law inherent in *Volk*. This government is an internal part of the social and national existence, and takes the form of aristo-democracy. For Herder, the ethnic community, the *Volk*, the nation, and the state should ultimately become one indivisible unity and independent entity, preserving its social cohesion and self-determination.[69] The aristo-democrats (cf. Berdyaev's "aristocracy of freedom"), who will be overseeing the nomocracy in this (natural rather than political) entity, will be the intellectuals originating from *dem Volk der Bürger*: "Intellectual and cultural activity has its source in the middle class" (quoted in Barnard 1965: 76). They will also be in charge of education, which equals humanization. Thus Herder's ever-so-appealing (to modernist sensibilities) principle of language-creating man, *Volk*, and culture was only part of the larger bourgeois effort to discredit the knowledge and manners of the nobility and gain power by making nationality, rather than heredity or class, the sustaining force of government. Patriotism, *Humanität*, and *Bildung* are closely interconnected in this system.[70] Education humanizes and cultivates, preserving the continuity of *Volk* and culture: for the individual, it is a right and a duty; for the nation, it is the road to its growth, progress, and perfection.

Herder believes that culture and philosophy should serve the rejuvenation of society. "He develops a conception of literature as an exemplary representation of the (in this case, endless) effort of man to create a coherent expression of himself, and thereby to realize himself as a whole being" (Morton 1982: 56). This is also how the nation realizes itself. "In this, Herder anticipates a characteristic feature of German Romanticism, namely its belief in the possibility of effecting political-national renewal in the sphere of cultural activity (preeminently through the medium of poetic art), and thus of bringing about a revitalization of community through cultivation of individuals toward personal self-realization" (63). Responding to fears of lawlessness and revolution, *Humanität* was the political principle that provided Herder, especially during his last period, with an ideal of emancipation. "*Humanität* is that which gives to individuals their humanity, and at the same time that which recalls nations to their human destiny" (Knoll 1982: 10). With it, emancipation takes on the eschatological promise of fulfillment. No longer a question of interpretation, character, taste, or conduct, Humanity is the liberation of emancipation itself from its narrow, interested, hence selfish, ideals. Historicist sensibility and its canonic readings were born at this juncture of the particular and the universal. "As the many-faceted reality of human existence, *Humanität* encompasses all human qualities and capabilities;—as the goal of humankind, however, it is potential rather than actuality. It is the divine calling which summons humans to rise above their state of nature. *Humanität* thus embraces that religiosity which pervades all of Herder's thought and writings" (11). This is his political imperative of self-controlled freedom (Bauman 1988a).

Intellectuals brought different ideas back from their travels to Italy. Winckelmann, the Prefect of Papal Antiquities in the Vatican, reconciled the ethical and the religious in the aesthetic, the Hellenic ideal; Herder, the Superintendent of Schools, Chief Pastor, and Court Preacher in Weimar, reconciled the social and the aesthetic in the national, the Hebraic vision. He showed that the Bible surpasses the Greek classics, attacked Graecomania, and declared Greece dead. Preoccupied, like his predecessor and many of his contemporaries, with the rise to power of the middle class in a secular state, he adopted Winckelmann's view of Greece in his organic theory of history but derived the concept of *Volk* from Judaic tradition. Herder had a remarkable historical sense which helped him question the constancy of human nature, reject the universality of race, and even doubt the superiority of European culture. "Each age, he believed, must be judged by its own standards; each national culture has its unique, incomparable value. Life on this planet is a triumphant progress—'the movement of God through history'—toward the highest possible development of man's total powers, his *Humanität*" (Hatfield 1964: 45). At the same time, his revulsion toward the theology of the English and the politics of the French Enlightenment point to the cultural traditionalism of the "Hebraic humanism" (Kraus 1956: 114–32) he (like Hamann) was advocating. For example, he treated all Biblical poetry as Oriental and proposed it as a model for German literature, calling to arms the "German-Oriental poets." For Herder, the nation was neither a republic (France) nor a kingdom (England) but a nation—a community of people with a shared language, culture, and tradition. The culturally integrated Hebrew community became his normative example. "Herder presented a picture of the Hebrew genius as a cultural phenomenon; he moved away from the older supernaturalistic pattern, and gave Hebrew culture a place on its own merits in the history of civilization" (Barr 1966: 44). He praised the Hebrews as the best example of *Volk* and *Bildung*, and even defended the ethical significance of "Oriental despotism" (as represented, for example, in Moses' legal code). Indeed, the Mosaic Law was his model when he rejected the notion of natural individual rights, defended the idea of an invisible government, and defined the territorial community of his *Volk*-State (Barnard 1959; 1965: 62–67; 1966). In this he was not alone. The reaction against Latinity included a rejection of Roman administrative methods. "In eighteenth-century Germany many still called for the institution of Mosaic law to cleanse the body politic, and an even larger number felt that Mosaic law justified some of the gorier and more extreme forms of eighteenth-century punishments" (Reill 1975: 196). In general, there are three basic categories in his thought: the individual (whose life-long task is *Bildung*), *Volk* (and its culture), and humanity; and they all are portrayed as independent, irreducible, self-regulating units fashioned after the homologous ideas of the organism, the artwork, and the Hebrew nation. Herder is a paradigmatic modern figure in that he turned his attention to those types of discourse that had been recently associated with the aesthetic, and completed the definition of the project of modernity by aestheticizing the public as national culture.

We saw earlier that the sense of a remote, irrevocable past, which first developed in the seventeenth century, and the identification of that past with History and Greece, entered the discourses of religion and knowledge through treatises comparing the Bible to Homer. Indeed, since the fourteenth century, when he was read again in the original language, Homer, although regularly discussed, had been the subject of disappointment (in the fifteenth century because of his inferiority to Virgil), condemnation (for example, by Joseph Scaliger[71] in the second half of the sixteenth century), and finally rejection (by the Moderns). Still, major English literary translations in the second half of the seventeenth century (Chapman, Hobbes, Dryden) and advances in scholarship (like Bentley's discovery of the Aeolic consonant *digamma*) responded to and cultivated the demands of a dilettante taste for the more exotic aspects of the Western tradition. Interest in Greek epic increased in the eighteenth century, when the Northern bardic tradition was discovered, bringing the exotic back home, and the notion of genius (Murray 1989) was associated with the epic. Mid-eighteenth-century England read epic as the most representative product of its culture and started giving priority to Homer over Virgil for his fuller representation of the national soul: in the Homeric epic the ethnic qualities of the bardic, genius, and originality seemed to converge. This perception made Homer a focal point of many debates about national identity, idiom, and creativity. At that time, comparisons of the Biblical to the Homeric were revived. After myth was isolated from history, the epic was seen as historical account of real events. It was also compared (by Lowth, Heyne, and Herder) to the Hebrew Bible in terms of language, style, religion, and society. The interpretive fate of the two canons was intertwined. In addition, the Bible seemed to allow for creative freedom against eighteenth-century neoclassical standards: "Whether for or against the rules or simply oblivious of them, all the critics agreed on the great merit of Hebrew poetic style. . . . One of the marks of this recognition of the greatness of Hebrew literature is the comparison made with the Greek and Roman, invariably to the advantage of the Hebrew" (Freimarck 1952: 513–14). Since literary and philological criticism of the epic developed along the course set by Biblical studies, Homer's interpretation was influenced by that course. Before the end of the century, both the Hebraist Johann David Michaelis (1717–91) and the classicist Christian Gottlob Heyne (1729–1812) were comparing him to Moses. They both taught at the University of Göttingen (established in 1734), where the influence of Winckelmann was felt most. The Göttingen school of philology developed "source criticism" (*Quellenkritik*) under both Heyne, who first distinguished myth from the poetry in which it was contained, and Michaelis, his colleague in Oriental Languages, who did the same for Biblical studies and annotated Lowth in German. In the scholarship of their school, where Homer was rehabilitated, the epic was often seen as the Bible of the Greeks, although nobody argued that the Bible was the Hebrew epic. Greek influence on the Hebrews was quite inconceivable.

Following in the footsteps of Enlightenment Higher Criticism, the study of Homer achieved scholarly sophistication and recognition in the 1780s until it triumphed with F. A. Wolf's *Prolegomena ad Homerum* (1795).[72] Herder, who also published that same year the essays "Homer und Ossian" and "Homer, ein Gunstling der Zeit," had already talked about the collective folk origin of Homer. In this, he was again adopting Spinoza who, in his *Tractatus*, had declared the Bible a product of many hands, subject to canonic composition and interpolation.[73] Herder's aesthetics had also inspired directly, through their regular correspondence, the Biblical hermeneutics of Johann Gottfried Eichhorn (1752–1827), the Professor of Oriental Languages who put the study of the Bible on a solid scholarly basis in his *Introduction to the Old Testament* (1780–83, 3 vols.). Still, philology, historiography, and aesthetics, the three major disciplines that grew out of Biblical interpretation in the 1750s and 1760s, had never before been combined in such a masterful demonstration of analytical skill. Friedrich August Wolf (1759–1824), a student of Heyne, modeled his *Prolegomena* on Eichhorn's Introduction, adapting principles of Biblical scholarship (especially *The Spirit of Hebrew Poetry*) to the study of the epic, and, like him, often proceeded through a comparative treatment of Homer and the Bible (e.g., Wolf 1985: 223–26).[74] "Although there is little evidence that in writing the *Prolegomena ad Homerum* Wolf had intended to imply questions about the historical credentials of the Bible, his methods and the kinds of questions he posed were cut from the same cloth as contemporary German criticism of the Scriptures and the critical discussions of biblical mythology that had originated with Heyne" (Turner 1981: 142). The success was spectacular:[75] the Homeric question (or what Alan John Bayard Wace has called the "Higher Criticism of Homer") became (and persists in being) central to many philological problems (*Critical Exchange* 1984); classical studies gained unprecedented prominence in the German intellectual climate; and the Greek classics started playing an instrumental role in the humanistic disciplines and education.[76]

In 1795, when Herder and Wolf were taking Homer apart, fragmenting (Winckelmann's) Greek world, and Goethe published the *Bildungsroman Wilhelm Meister's Apprenticeship*, the epic of the cultivation of the artistic self, Friedrich Schiller (1759–1805) printed his *Letters on the Aesthetic Education of Man* and the first two parts of *On Naive and Sentimental Poetry* (1795–96). These works mark the completion of the intellectual course traveled by the Reformed classes from trade to industry, from the Bible to Art, and from reading (sixteenth century) to learning (seventeenth) to understanding (eighteenth) to educating (nineteenth). In Schiller's system, education (whose urgent political necessity became acutely apparent after the French Revolution) found its concrete direction: education of pleasure, through beauty, for ethical leisure. The means of this education, as well as its goal, is aesthetic taste.[77] Taste moderates, shapes, and cultivates the individual: "All those material inclinations and brutal appetites, which oppose with so much obstinacy and vehemence the practice of good, the soul is freed from through the aesthetic taste; and in their place, it implants in us nobler and gentler inclinations, which draw nearer to order, to harmony, and to perfection; and although these inclinations are not by themselves virtues, they have at least something in common with virtue; it is their *object*" (Schiller 1902: 130). Taste is socially useful because it gives the soul a direction which disposes it to virtue. Morality may dictate the rules which distinguish good from bad. "But the aesthetic sense governs the will by the feeling and not by laws" (132).[78] In contrast to the imposition of laws by outside systems or necessity, the aesthetic is the autonomous principle of taste and feeling. Morally and physically unconstrained, independent of rational and sensuous determination, the aesthetic is the true free disposition. "In the midst of the awful realm of powers, and of the sacred realm of laws, the aesthetic creative impulse is building unawares a third joyous realm of play and of appearance, in which it releases mankind from all the shackles of circumstance and frees him from everything that may be called constraint, whether physical or moral. If in the *dynamic* state of rights man encounters man as force and restricts his activity, if in the *ethical* state of duties he opposes him with the majesty of law and fetters his will, in the sphere of cultivated society, in the *aesthetic* state, he need appear to him only as shape, confront him only as an object of free play. *To grant freedom by means of freedom* is the fundamental law of this kingdom" (Schiller 1965: 137). Herder's self-reflexive autonomy reaches in Schiller the celestial harmony of a tautology: it is not word and thing but act and law that become one here.

Schiller's Fifth Letter contains a critique of his time which indicts both low and high classes for corruption and immorality: "Man portrays himself in his deeds, and what a form it is that is depicted in the drama of the present day! Here barbarity, there enervation: the two extremes of human degeneracy, and both of them united in a single period of time! Among the lower and more numerous classes we find crude, lawless impulses which have been unleashed by the loosening of the bonds of civil order, and are hastening with ungovernable fury to their brutal satisfaction.... On the other hand, the civilized classes present to us the still more repugnant spectacle of indolence, and a depravity of character which is all the more shocking since culture itself is the source of it" (35). In addition to the dissolution of the civil bonds that used to safeguard meaning and order in society, Schiller laments contemporary fragmentation. In contrast with integrated life in ancient Greece, he sees modern society as "an ingenious piece of machinery, in which out of the botching together of a vast number of lifeless parts a collective mechanical life results. State and Church, law and customs, were now torn asunder; enjoyment was separated from labour, means from ends, effort from reward. Eternally chained to only one single little fragment of the whole, Man himself grew to be only a fragment; with the monotonous noise of the wheel he drives everlastingly in his ears, he never develops the harmony of his being, and instead of imprinting humanity upon his nature he becomes merely the imprint of his occupation, of his science" (40).[79] According to Schiller, there is a double socio-political problem: lawlessness, on the one hand, and fragmentation, on the other; both externally and internally, the center of public life is disintegrating. "Like Herder before him, who had inveighed against a condition in which men had become 'half thinkers, half feelers' and 'no single member partakes of the whole any more,' Schiller portrayed the central predicament of his period as consisting in man's being divided against himself, both as an individual and in his relations to his human and natural surroundings" (Gardiner 1979: 39).

The Jacobin Johann Benjamin Erhard (1766–1827) had just published *On the Right of the People to Revolution* (1795), where he defined the moral right to civil revolution, presenting this revolution as the end of a people's development, and enlightenment as the end of humanity. The *Aesthetic Education*, Schiller's response to Erhard, finds that neither revolution nor religion can provide the answers: history and faith are bankrupt. Schiller's answer is that "we must indeed, if we are to solve that political problem in practice, follow the path of aesthetics, since it is through Beauty that we arrive at Freedom" (Schiller 1965: 27). Neither the French citizen nor the Prussian patriot seem to know where to seek independence. "Training of the sensibility is then the more pressing need of our age" (50), he argues, and proposes "an education for taste and for Beauty. This last has as its aim the cultivation of the whole of our sensuous and intellectual powers in the fullest possible harmony" (99). This is the new civic religion. Herder's national culture is not enough, since the national bonds do not reach deep into the individual's desires and interests; neither is Kant's ethical imperative (although free from the heteronomy of religious commands) adequate for (not just controlling but also) shaping feelings and beliefs. The new civic religion must be a cultural imperative—the aesthetic faith: "Religion is love of Beauty" (Hölderlin 1984: 91). Schiller acknowledges that "it is an obligation for us to seek the salutary bonds which religion and the aesthetic laws present to us, in order that during the crisis when our passion is dominant it shall not injure the physical order. It is not unintentionally that I have placed religion and taste in one and the same class; the reason is that both one and the other have the merit, similar in effect, although dissimilar in principle and in value, to take the place of virtue properly so called, and to assure legality where there is no possibility to hope for morality" (Schiller 1902: 135). The superiority of the aesthetic is that it can train sensibility, mold conduct, and prepare a new social structure. "The aesthetic is the missing mediation between a barbaric civil society given over to pure appetite, and the ideal of a well-ordered political state" (Eagleton 1990: 106).

Schiller proposes what Hegel would later call, writing about Athenian politics, "an aesthetic democracy" (Hegel 1900: 254). His ideal, like all aesthetic ideals before Modernism, is Hellenic. The Greeks, whom Winckelmann saw as artistic, Schiller portrays as aesthetic: out of their games he produces the idea of play[80] that would transform the pains of labor (Kain 1982: 13–33): "[T]his play impulse would aim at the extinction of time *in time* and the reconciliation of becoming with absolute being, of variation with identity" (Schiller 1965: 74). The object of the play impulse (as well as the realm of reconciliation) is Beauty. "Man shall *only play* with Beauty, and he shall play *only with Beauty*. For, to declare it once and for all, Man plays only when he is in the full sense of the word a man, and *he is only wholly Man when he is playing*" (80). Beauty is the freedom to play (with) freedom.

Schiller opposes the aesthetic condition to toiling and compares it to the Greek city experience, while proposing that the aesthetic remaking of modern man would reconcile him with the state by making him one with it. "Whereas in England and the Romance countries the idea of the sensus communis is not even today just a critical slogan, but is a general civic quality, in Germany the followers of Shaftesbury and Hutcheson did not, even in the eighteenth century, take over the political and social element contained in sensus communis. . . . The concept of sensus communis was taken over, but in the removal of all political content it lost its real critical significance. Sensus communis was understood as a purely theoretical faculty, theoretical judgment, on a level with moral consciousness (conscience) and taste" (Gadamer 1979: 26).[81] In Germany, sensus communis became a matter not of civic quality but of personal attitude. *Bildung* undertook to interiorize taste, since beauty was the politics of the soul. In his article on the meaning of Enlightenment (1784), Mendelssohn defined the meaning of the words Enlightenment, *Kultur*, and *Bildung*, which he found interrelated, proposing that *Bildung* consists of *Kultur* and Enlightenment. The first is more practical, and includes morals, manners, taste, sentiments, and habits—in a word, cultivation; while the second is theoretical, and includes knowledge and reason. People as citizens need the former, as individuals the latter. Like the Greeks who had both, a modern nation, too, needs both. Therefore Luther's community of readers would now be trained to develop into a public. The individual would no longer be a reader (of the Bible), an interpreter of religion, or a private character but a (public) attitude, an outward declaration of inwardness. "Though need may drive Man into society, and reason implant social principles in him, Beauty alone can confer on him a *social character*. Taste alone brings harmony into society. . . . All other forms of communication divide society, because they relate exclusively . . . to what distinguishes between one man and another; only the communication of the Beautiful unites society, because it relates to what is common to them all" (Schiller 1965: 138). Mozart (1756–91) had already volunteered to write the sym-phonies for that audience, the scores of the harmonization of the cultivated public.

In exchange for abandoning political engagement, beauty promised pure independence, Schiller's "Heautonomie." In an effort to reconcile freedom and law, Kant had already formulated, in the *Groundwork of the Metaphysics of Morals* (1785), the principle of autonomy, "in which he made transcendental freedom a postulate of practical freedom but claiming, at the same time, that we are free only through our consciousness of standing under a moral law" (Leidner 1989: 181). The project of the *Critique of Pure Reason* (1781) reaches here its completion. "Human freedom was portrayed by Kant as involving a capacity to act independently of the promptings of desire or inclination. It was, moreover, closely tied to morality through the notion of autonomy: Kant implied that it was only in so far as a man chose to make his actions conform to principles which he himself prescribed as binding upon all rational beings that what he did could properly and in the full sense be described as free" (Gardiner 1979: 28). Developing this principle further, Schiller proposes that the aesthetic disposition "is what first gives rise to freedom" (Schiller 1965: 124) on the condition that social interests be abandoned. "Thus at the basis of the aesthetic reconciliation of the Kantian dualism of being and moral obligation there is a more profound, unresolved dualism. It is the prose of alienated reality against which the poetry of aesthetic reconciliation must seek its own self-consciousness" (Gadamer 1979: 74). Against what Hegel in the *Aesthetics* called "the prose of the world," the impossibility of literature promises the absolute book, the impotence of the fragment preaches the incarnation of writing, the broken tablets of art annunciate the divinity of the secular scripture. "Art emerges in the second half of the eighteenth century as a privileged space of cultural activities; it is increasingly viewed as a realm of reconciliation and redemption that is able to suspend the negative side-effects of the functional and social differentiation of society" (Schulte-Sasse 1989: 86). The aesthetic attitude is the fundamental exercise—both ascetic (in that it achieves self-consciousness by denouncing interest, including moral obligation) as well as hedonistic (in that it plays with itself). In it, the paradox which links doing and renunciation, becoming "the ascetic basis of the bourgeois style of life" (Weber), is transcended. The project of autonomy, the modern task of self-grounding, reaches its limit with the aesthetic because the aesthetic is pure differentiation:[82] in a functionally differentiated society, the aesthetic functions not only as the separate sphere of art but above all as the self-thematization of differentiation itself. "It practically defines aesthetic consciousness to say that it performs this differentiation of what is aesthetically intended from everything that is outside the aesthetic sphere. It abstracts from all the conditions of a work's accessibility. This kind of differentiation is itself a specifically aesthetic one. . . . It is the capacity of aesthetic consciousness to be able to make this aesthetic differentiation everywhere and to see everything 'aesthetically'" (Gadamer 1979: 77). The aesthetic politics of differentiation seeks autonomy for autonomy's sake and requires "a disinterested free appreciation of pure appearance" (Schiller 1965: 132) where the synthesis of knowledge and morality, taste and feeling, labor and leisure is achieved as the other-worldly is thoroughly naturalized into the secular.

In the ascetic realm of the disinterested devotion to the material, beyond any work requirements, capitalist greed and social competition are exonerated as they finally turn into the aesthetic ethic, and human rights are fulfilled in that they are justified according to an entirely tautological teleology: "Everything in the aesthetic State, even the subservient tool, is a free citizen having equal rights with the noblest; and the intellect, which forcibly moulds the passive multitude to its designs, must here ask for its assent. Here, then, in the realm of aesthetic appearance, is fulfilled the ideal of equality which the visionary would fain see realized in actuality also; and if it is true that fine breeding matures earliest and most completely near the throne, we are bound to recognize here too the bountiful dispensation which seems often to restrict mankind in the actual, only in order to incite him into the ideal world" (140). The disinterested aesthetic does not just compensate—it also rewards with cultural capital. Now both artist and reader are involved in "an engagement thus voluntarily contracted" (as Wordsworth wrote in the "Preface" to the *Lyrical Ballads* of 1800), and they expect to profit.[83] For the reader, the aesthetic is the accumulation of an attitude, of a capital that can be invested in the market of any differentiated sphere. At the same time, the aesthetic, as auto-formation, is the highest realization of autonomy because "it combines in itself all the conditions of its origin and of its continued existence" (103). That is why beauty is both means and goal, object and condition, form and life. "In a word, it is at once our state and our act" (122). Thus the aesthetic became not only interpretive but social norm, too: aesthetic education as the training for an aesthetic life (and state)—the humanistic training in the contemplative, disinterested disposition. "The aesthetic state, in short, is the utopian bourgeois public sphere of liberty, equality and democracy, within which everyone is a free citizen. . . . Taste, with its autonomy, universality, equality and fellow-feeling, is a whole alternative politics, suspending social hierarchy and reconstituting relations between individuals in the image of disinterested fraternity" (Eagleton 1990: 111). Spinoza's covenant with sovereign authority and Herder's nomocracy of the invisible government found here their technology of the interpretive regiment of emancipation fully articulated in the artistic self and the aesthetic regime.

The essay on the Naive and the Sentimental complements the exposition of Aesthetic Education by sharply defining, on the basis of the opposition in its title, the cultural moment and the ideological identity of modernity against its Greek History. Here there is no effort to reconcile or balance the two poles because the historical difference is considered to be beyond any mediation: the Hebraic takes over the Greek by making it its totally Other—by contrasting Spinoza's community of interpreters with a city of (consenting) players. The ancient world emerges as the exemplary product of Hebraic historicism: wholly separate and in supreme harmony with itself, without contradiction or conflict. When Biblical scholarship and literary criticism saved the authority of the Bible by detecting in its textual constitution a unique combination of the moral and the artistic, Hellas was designated as the locus of the pure aesthetic. The possibility of the classical in modernity was of great concern to German Romanticism. "More particularly, and because the philosophy of history will emerge precisely from a critical problematic of *imitation* (throughout the last years of the [eighteenth] century), it involves doing better or more than Antiquity: at once surpassing and fulfilling the unfinished or incomplete aspects of Antiquity, wherever it failed to effectuate the classical ideal it envisaged. This amounts, in the end, to performing the 'synthesis' of the Ancient and the Modern—or, if you like, to anticipate the Hegelian word (although not the concept), to sublate, *aufheben*, the opposition of the Ancient and the Modern" (Lacoue-Labarthe and Nancy 1988: 11). Alas, the aesthetic, as

Schiller already knew (and Hölderlin and Hegel were soon to realize) was by (its theological) definition (a) ancient and pagan; (b) old and alien; and (c) elsewhere or over. The aesthetic cultivation was an educational program for the refinement of the Hebraic morality of the bourgeoisie—a training in the invisible government of self-discipline.[84] Schiller, expanding the classical-romantic contrast so popular in his time, monumentalized the division of the opposite worlds, outlining the basic aesthetic (and ethical) choices of the West for the next two centuries: "All poets who are truly so will belong, according to the temper of the times in which they flourish, or according to the influence upon their general education or passing states of mind by fortuitous circumstances, either to the *naive* or to the *sentimental* poets" (Schiller 1985: 191). The work of the young Lukács (Congdon 1983) was still part of the same discussion, as the obvious correspondence of his "integrated" and "problematic" civilizations to the naive and sentimental shows, and contributed the last ideal of the auto-formation of the bourgeoisie—the messianic drive for totality (Jay 1984).[85] Lukács later felt, however, that aesthetic training, as dramatized in the *Bildungsroman*, had failed, and reoriented his educational interests toward the *Bildung* of the proletariat in *History and Class Consciousness* (1923).

THE THREAT OF PAGANISM

The ideal of the aesthetic attitude was translated into a pedagogical project by Wilhelm von Humboldt with the aim of bringing national unity, social cohesiveness, and cultural identity to the state, while liberalizing its autocratic structure. Ancient Greece was used as a model culture and a period where the aesthetic prevailed, influencing every aspect of life. "[Humboldt] and his friends saw study of 'Antiquity in general and the Greeks in particular' as a way in which to integrate students and the people as a whole, whose lives they saw as being fragmented by modern society. More immediately, Humboldt and the others saw the study as a way of promoting an 'authentic' reform, through which Germany could avoid revolution of the type that so horrified them in France. From the beginning, then, *Altertumwissenschaft* in Germany—like its equivalent, Classics, in England—was seen by its promoters as a 'third way' between reaction and revolution. In actuality, however, its effect was to shore up the *status quo*. The educational institutions and the Classical *Bildung* that infused them became pillars of 19th-century Prussian and German social order. At the core of *Altertumwissenschaft* was the image of the divine Greek, both artistic and philosophical" (Bernal 1987: 282). The pedagogical project, though, did achieve its nationalist goal. "By the beginning of the nineteenth century Germans were convinced that they were the 'intellectual instructors of mankind' [Baron Bunsen]. This self-assessment was accepted by most 'progressive' Europeans and North Americans. German philosophy and education provided a middle way between bankrupt traditions and French revolution and atheism" (Bernal 1986: 37–38). As Schiller had planned it, the aesthetic did indeed mediate between the reactionary traditions of nobility and revolutionary tendencies of skepticism, providing an alternative path to emancipation: the autonomy of self-cultivation and the privileges of culture. Aesthetic critique made interpretation a question of attitude to the world, rather than position in society.

Educated Germans saw themselves as the modern Greeks, the inheritors of ancient culture. "And yet, when it came to scholarship and historical research it was to Roman history rather than to Greek history that the German genius made the most important contributions" (Yavetz 1976: 279). Although it was the invention of History that made the construction of Greece possible, the study of Greek history was still limited to culture since nobody found its politics attractive. "Is not the unification of Italy and the conquest of the Mediterranean a sounder ideal than what was scornfully depicted by E. Drerup as 'die athenische Advokatenrepublik'?" (283). This scholarship developed after the defeat of Jena by Napoleon in 1806. "An awakening Germany could not find consolation any more in Greek beauty and in morbid Greek politics, but a young, vigorous, patriotic and optimistic Roman 'Bauerngemeinde' could be set up as a model to be admired" (290). The Roman social order served as a model for nineteenth-century Germany (Whitman 1990). In the Romans, Germans found health, strength, order, nobility, right. The historical Greeks were discovered elsewhere.

Interest in Greek history commenced on a significant scale in the late eighteenth century, when the Greeks were perceived as a useful negative model. "The eighteenth century saw the beginnings of a great change in the way history was written; historians, once concerned almost entirely with political and military events, began to investigate such things as commerce, religion and social habits" (Jenkyns 1980: 163–64). Until then, all models were Roman since history served the instruction of the aristocracy. "Although Greek philosophy had influenced some Renaissance writers and Aristotelian categories still informed science and logic, until the late eighteenth century most educated Europeans regarded their culture as Roman and Christian in origin, with merely peripheral roots in Greece. Europe had a Roman past, and European civilization was congruent with Latin Christendom. . . . Roman law and Roman literature, as well as the Latin church fathers, had dominated Europe's cultural experience. . . . In contrast to this visible, tangible, and pervasive Roman influence, the Greeks simply had not directly touched the life of Western Europe" (Turner 1981: 1–2). Until then the study of Greek history was almost unknown everywhere. When Greek political history was first studied, the result was a very negative picture, one of instability and anarchy. "Eighteenth-century and early nine-teenth-century political commentators had consistently pointed to Athens as a key example of civic lawlessness, political disorder, and the absence of personal security" (189). The same is true about English historians of the eighteenth century, such as John Gillies (*The History of Ancient Greece, Its Colonies, and Conquests from the Earliest Accounts till the Division of the Macedonian Empire in the East Including the History of Literature, Philosophy, and the Fine Arts*, 1786) and William Mitford (*The History of Greece*, 1784–1810, 10 vols.) who, writing the first histories which were at the same time political treatises, warned against the perils of democracy. Rome remained the true model. When there was some praise for Greece, it was for Sparta. "In the view of these writers, as in that of more important Continental authors, among them Montesquieu and Rousseau, Sparta appeared as a strong, stable polity immune from the political unrest, party factions, and turbulent leadership that had marked Athenian political life" (189–90). When greater interest arose, it came again from the conservative side. For example, most educated Germans in the nineteenth century (as well as the twentieth, like Gottfried Benn in his essay "Doric World") considered the Dorians the real Greeks, the most Germanic ones.

"But during the last quarter of the century the American Revolution, the radical movement for reform in Parliament, and later the French Revolution awakened a new interest in the Athenian experience on the part of defenders of the political status quo" (192). As a result, during the time of William Mitford, "there emerged a conservative polemical strategy of portraying the ends of the American revolt and of the Yorkshire Association reform movement as democratic in character and then decrying democracy through enumeration of the disasters and crimes of Athens" (192). But by doing that, they made Greek history a legitimate medium for discussing government and politics. "Just as concerns with the Bible determined the nineteenth-century criticism of Homer, the problems of contemporary political debate shaped the writing of Greek history. In nineteenth-century England Greek history would always mean political history that was as profoundly involved with the present as with the past" (194). Positive views of Greece did not emerge until the *History of Greece* (1835–47, 8 vols.) by Connop Thirlwall, Bishop of St. David's, and *A History of Greece* (1845–56, 12 vols.) by the banker turned radical MP George Grote.[86] In his *History of Greece* (1785–1810), written at the suggestion of Edward Gibbon, "Mitford had condemned modern liberal democratic politics by equating it with the lawlessness of ancient Athens. A half-century later Grote reversed the analysis. He vindicated democratic Athens by arguing that it had achieved the kind of stability and constitutional morality that the British liberal state enjoyed in the mid-Victorian age" (216). At the same time, even during the first half of the nineteenth century, no major general history of Greece appeared in Germany, France, or Italy. And when such histories were written in these countries, the phenomenon lasted for only fifty years. "After 1900 the decline of creative work on Greek history became evident. The age in which practical politicians and moralists were interested in Greek was ushered out by Wilamowitz on the one hand and by John Ruskin on the other" (Momigliano 1966: 67). Literary and anthropological studies became more attractive. Greece had no political relevance and an overview of Greek history was not important, even though scholarly work (in papyrology, philology, or archaeology) continued. An eminent historian could complain in 1952 that "the study of Greek political ideas has become increasingly divorced from the study of political events and institutions" (69). The Hellenic, after losing its monopoly over culture, has been identified in the twentieth century with the dreaded political element and perceived as a threat, symbolizing the danger not of lawlessness but of the barbarism feared by Auerbach.

Positive views of Greek political history, even before the appearance of British revisionary studies, were affected by another development. Inspired by the adoration of Greece in the second half of the eighteenth century, a number of diaspora writers and merchants, who had often been Ottoman subjects, began seriously reconsidering their identity and political role. "In a bold geopolitical calculation Greek-speaking Orthodox Christians of the Ottoman Empire decided in the eighteenth century to orient their ethnic community to a new point of reference—the West. Realizing that the power center was no longer the Ottoman Empire, nor even the Russian Empire, they sought access instead to the expanding capitalist states of Europe. The Greek intellectual and mercantile elites, located throughout central and Western Europe, took a gamble on achieving modernization by means of nationalism. . . . They raced to modernize their ethnic community by introducing into Greece the features emblematic of Western European societies. Chief amongst them was a secular culture, a realm of shared experiences which would replace the ethno-religious identities of the Ottoman Empire and act as a new source of bonding. It would offset local loyalties and linguistic variations by harmonizing them in an imaginary realm of national community" (Jusdanis 1991). It seems that the diaspora elites initially considered three options: staying with the declining Ottoman Empire, joining the rising Russian (Orthodox) one, or adopting the capitalist enterprise of parliamentary democracy. The majority soon embraced the last option, and the Hellenic fervor naturally emerged as a potentially major force of legitimation. Thus the diaspora bourgeoisie, in cooperation with its many contacts on the Greek mainland, decided to claim the Hellenic for itself. This is how modern Greeks invented themselves as Hellenes and appeared on the scene of history, causing a tremendous stir in the liberal artistic and intellectual imagination of the time. "By tapping the current of philhellenism they strove to bring modern Greece to European attention. Their enterprise was successful to the extent that modern Greece was and is regarded as a special case in comparison with other countries on the margins of Europe. The declaration of the War of Independence of 1821, for instance, initiated the most fashionably international cause of the century, a pan-European phenomenon rivaling that of the Spanish Civil War in the following century. The passion with which liberal Europeans supported the struggles of the Greeks may be contrasted to the indifference they showed to the revolts of the Serbians, Bulgarians, and Armenians. None of those ethnic groups could elicit the same concern, let alone the logistical aid of the Europeans; unlike the Greeks they could not relate their own nationalist designs to the core of European identity. The discourse of European Hellenism allowed Greeks access to Europe unavailable to other nations. The only other people to make a similar appeal to the West were the Zionists. While Greeks laid claim to the cultural and secular roots of Western civilization, the Zionists exploited the foundational role of the Hebrew Bible in the Judeo-Christian tradition" (Jusdanis 1991).[87] For a brief period, during no more than the first thirty years of the nineteenth century, people around the world who had been inspired by the watersheds of the American and French revolutions saw with exhilaration nothing less than the eternal Hellas rise from the ashes and break the shackles of slavery. Thus it was "the philhellenic movement which, in the 19th century, occupied what might be called the 'radical wing' of the Romantic movement. Philhellenism tended to share the Romantic rejection of urban industrialization, the universalism and rationality of the Enlightenment, and the French Revolution. On the other hand, while the mainstream of Romanticism turned towards the medieval past and Christianity—especially Catholicism—Philhellenes were sometimes religious sceptics or atheists, and political radicals. As young men, for instance, Hegel and Friedrich Schlegel loved the Greeks, but as they grew older and increasingly conservative they turned to Christianity" (Bernal 1987: 289). Almost any politicization of the intellectuals involved (or sometimes was even inspired by) the Greek revolt.

Not that the progressives were completely enthusiastic about the Greeks they began encountering. "The Philhellenes were more concerned with the Classical Greeks than with their heroic, but superstitious, Christian and dirty 'descendants,' whom some tried to explain away as 'Byzantine Slavs' [Jacob Philipp Fallmerayer]" (292). Most of them supported the Greek struggle of independence believing that "the sacred theocracy of the Beautiful must dwell in a free state, and that state must have a place on earth" (Hölderlin 1984: 108), the one originally destined for it. In their eyes, liberated Greece appeared as the incarnated artwork, art made life. All those committed to the Hellenic model "approached their subjects less from an interest in the past for its own sake than from a firm conviction that what they said about Greece would have an impact on contemporary political, religious, philosophical, and moral discourse" (Turner 1981: 7). (That was generally the case with humanistic scholarship before professional specialization.) Many Philhellenes, though, were more willing to include political factors in their evaluation: "The modern Greek is the descendant of those glorious beings whom the imagination almost refuses to figure to itself as belonging to our kind, and he inherits much of their sensibility, their rapidity of conception, their enthusiasm and their courage. If in many instances he is degraded by moral and political slavery to the practice of the basest vices it engenders—and that below the level of ordinary degradation—let us reflect that the corruption of the best produces the worst, and that habits which subsist only in relation to a peculiar state of social institution may be expected to cease as soon as that relation is dissolved" (Shelley 1898: 99–100).

Above all, Greece was the symbol of the general revival of liberty—the total, magnificent happening of emancipation. Shelley wrote in 1821, in the "Preface" to his drama *Hellas*: "This is the age of the war of the oppressed against the oppressors, and every one of those ringleaders of the privileged gangs of murderers and swindlers, called sovereigns, look to each other for aid against the common enemy, and suspend their mutual jealousies in the presence of a mightier fear. Of this holy alliance all the despots of the earth are virtual members" (100–1). It was during those years that the Hellenic and the political converged for concrete historical reasons, and again only for a brief period. Soon after the creation of the Greek state in 1829, Prince Otto, the seventeen-year-old son of King Ludwig of Bavaria, was offered the "hereditary sovereignty" of Greece and was dispatched with the task of re-civilizing the land of Homer. What has been called "the tyranny of the . . . European experience over that of Greek antiquity" (Turner 1981: 8) was firmly extended to the modern country as well. Thus while Jews were challenged to modernize a tradition, overcome ethnic differentiation, contribute to universal culture, and assimilate into the dominant society, modern Greeks were challenged to modernize a nation, define ethnic distinction, create national culture, and separate from the empire. In both cases, the promise of emancipation was irresistible and the interpretive labor spent enormous. (The tremendous cost for the two peoples and the respective results, however, cannot be examined here.)

In the meantime, while Jews and Greeks were preoccupied with their formidable struggles for recognition, another ideological development redefined the character and context of their effort almost before they had the time to understand its implications: the fabrication of race. The Aryans and the Semites, the archetypes of race, were invented in the late eighteenth century. "With the establishment of the Indo-European language family a new concept emerged, that of two master-races, the Aryans and the Semites. These were seen in perpetual dialectic. The Semites had given the world religion and poetry, and the Aryans manliness, democracy, philosophy, science, etc." (Bernal 1985: 68–69).[88] According to the new historical understanding, inspired by comparative linguistics, civilization was a dialogue between the two equals. "Thus as Humboldt and others created their linguistic hierarchies, inflected Semitic was put on the same top rung as Indo-European, which justified the widespread mid-nineteenth-century view of history as a dialogue between Aryans and Semites" (Bernal 1986: 44). The poles of the Hebraic-Hellenic distinction were transformed into two races—two categories rather than two modes, two natures rather than two qualities. The two master races were considered equal for a long time, as "the idea of a common origin for the Aryans and the Semites was still acceptable in the 1840s. It became less acceptable as the century wore on, but persisted until the climax of anti-Semitism in the 1920s and 30s" (Bernal 1987: 255). Furthermore, from the beginning, the Aryans were different from the Semites but modeled themselves on the other race (Olender 1989), competing with them for election by opposing providence to eschatology. At the same time, those who fully identified with the Aryans had the worst contempt for both their contemporary Jews and Greeks alike, whom they considered, for different reasons, degenerate. The author of the *Essai sur l'inégalité des races humaines* (1853–55, 4 vols.) is a representative case: "For Gobineau saw Greek history as a struggle between the Aryan Greek spirit based to the north of Thebes, and the Semitic spirit of the south, both being reinforced by their racial cousins from outside the country. . . . It must be noted, however, that despite his enthusiasm for the character and institutions of the Aryan Hellenes, Gobineau was convinced that Ancient Greece as a whole had been thoroughly 'blackened' and 'Semitized.' He was among those who maintained that the modern Greeks were so mongrelized that they could no longer be considered as descendants of the Ancients" (Bernal 1987: 361–62). When the Hellenic Alien is encountered in Greece, he is treated like any other outsider—as a Barbarian. The German preference for the trip to Italy was based on a deep aversion. As Victor Bérard wrote in 1894: "This European chauvinism becomes a veritable fanaticism when it is not in Gaul, Etruria, Lucania or Thrace but in Greece that we meet the stranger" (quoted in Bernal 1987: 379).

There is nothing especially paradoxical or immoral about the Eurocentric biases of Philhellenism when examined in the socio-political context which produced the truth of "Greece" to support specific narratives and interests. "Although the Hellenic revival of the nineteenth century involved an international community of scholars and writers, many of whom appealed to the wisdom of Greece in terms of a universal human experience or some concept of uniform human nature, the study and interpretation of Greek antiquity nonetheless occurred within the context of national intellectual communities whose characters bore the distinctive imprints of their respective political structures, university organization, and religious confession. In each of these intellectual communities the exploration and criticism of Greek life reflected the particular political, religious, and philosophical preoccupations of the national culture" (Turner 1981: 8–9). (It is the failure to recognize the constitutive operations of the Hebraism-Hellenism dynamic that creates the dominant impression of an unblemished, idolized Hellas—or a neglected, maligned Israel.) Auerbach's essay is a recent example in this long tradition. His Homeric-Biblical distinction repeats the dialectical tension of other modern oppositions, like Schiller's naive-sentimental, Hölderlin's Hellenic-Hesperian, Lukács' epic-novel or even Nietzsche's Apollonian-Dionysian. Indeed, as Nietzsche's model reminds us, the Hebraic-Hellenic polarity has even operated within the ideal of Hellas itself, which is in turn split into a Hebraic and a Hellenic part. This is the reason why so often, from Winckelmann and Hamann to Stefan George (1868–1933) and Rainer Maria Rilke (1875–1926), two types of attitude and two forms of beauty—the serene and the ecstatic—have been discovered in Greece. The invention of the Dionysian, for example, goes back to Christoph Martin Wieland (1733–1813) and his work of the 1760s. "Winckelmann, Hamann, and Herder had already discovered, comprehended, and formulated the concept of the Dionysian long before [Nietzsche]. Novalis and Hölderlin united it with Christian elements in the form of poetic inspiration; Heinrich Heine and Robert Hamerling, a much-read novelist in Nietzsche's time, anticipated his famous antithesis 'Dionysus versus the Crucified One'; and in the research of the German Romantics in the areas of mythology and classical antiquity the antithesis Apollonian-Dionysian had been employed for decades. Friedrich Creuzer and Johann Jakob Bachofen had written voluminous works in which they placed the Greek, Egyptian, and Indian mysteries under the sway of Dionysus, and approximately sixty years before Nietzsche, in the *Philosophy of Mythology* . . . and the *Philosophy of Revelation* . . . , had described the development of the Greek spirit on the basis of the concept of a threefold Dionysus and had formulated the concept of the Dionysian, in contrast to the Apollonian, as an unrestrained, intoxicated power of creation in the artist and the poetic genius" (Baeumer 1976: 166). Especially through their theories of tragedy, these authors seek to establish a new harmony—the reunification of gods with Jesus, antiquity with Christianity, simplicity with passion, poetry with religion. It is probably in Heine's *Gods in Exile* (1854) that the picture is for the first time entirely negative, the god terrifying and destructive: "The synthesis Dionysus-Christ is transposed to the antithesis Dionysus-Christian, which corresponds to Heine's antithetical formulation Hellenic-Nazarene" (174).[89] For Auerbach too, who constructed his antithesis along

Biblical lines, the Hellenic was clearly dangerous. His opposition was between the complex, inner, three-dimensional world of reflexive maturity
and historical experience, and the simple, outer, two-dimensional world of
innocent naiveté and mythical superstition. The danger inherent in the
second pole, he argues, became manifest again in his time, the time of
confusion and modernism, when the totalitarianism of order and hierarchy
came back to claim Western heritage.

Auerbach feels that this is an age comprising events of such quality and
magnitude that they are necessarily the material of history, not of legend,
and therefore they deserve the realistic treatment dictated by the Biblical,
not the mythical mode expressed in the Greek epic. In our time, he implies,
now that human experience has been invaded by raw history, the understanding of reality must change. His model of such understanding is Biblical interpretation, which he both applies to, and discovers in the literary
canon. Auerbach rereads the canon in order to change our understanding
of it, and ultimately, through a different grasp of the basic representational
modes, our sense of reality itself. His main argument is that our sense of
reality is still heavily influenced by the Greek model of genealogical legends, based on analytical observation of static representations of being, and
lacking in psychological depth, historical background, and dramatic complexity. It is as if the success of literature has overshadowed the Bible, the
triumph of interpretation has made faith impossible. "The problem we
face, strangely enough, is not that we cannot define Scripture but that
having gradually redefined fiction in the light of Scripture we now find it
hard to distinguish between them" (Hartman 1986: 12). The same argument could be made about all literature. The method of figural interpretation, which discovers the prefigured fulfillment, can help recover the Biblical perspective by pointing to this alternative through its best (literary)
representations. "The patristic practice of typology, despite its frequently
anti-Jewish point, is absolutely continuous with midrash and pesher; that
is, it is rooted in the figure of Jesus as the sectarian midrashist who appropriates the sacred text, seeing its meaning in its application to himself"
(Bruns 1987: 635). Auerbach's alternative reality to a world he accuses of
worshiping Greek idols is the Jewish experience of the faith in God and of
the prophetic interpretation of his Word.

    In light of this project of the religious reeducation of mankind through
literary reading, the popularity of interpretation (in different critical
schools, from hermeneutics to deconstruction) during the last quarter of
the twentieth century appears as a not-so-recent intellectual phenomenon.[90] Auerbach already argued for the centrality of interpretation, calling
it "a method rooted in Jewish tradition" (Auerbach 1953: 48) and using it
as the proper critical approach, dictated by the Bible itself. According to his

survey, early Christianity employed it to revise and appropriate the Hebrew Bible. Later, the Church Fathers in the West developed it as a specific method to ground the New Testament in Jewish prophecy and connect Christian dogma with Biblical tradition. The Reformation signalled a new return to it, whereby the Bible was recognized as the paramount expression of Jewish history and law. Finally, in the nineteenth century its influence reached deep into literature and its modes of representation, and gave us realist fiction as a historical understanding of the world which itself demands an interpretive approach.

As such a survey shows, in the Hebraic reading the book internalizes and fixes everything. "Or it disappears entirely in favor of a pure and literal recitation forbidding the slightest change, addition, or commentary. . . . Or else interpretation survives but becomes internal to the book itself, which loses its circulatory function for outside elements: for example, the different types of coded interpretation are fixed according to axes internal to the book; interpretation is organized according to correspondences between two books, such as the Old and New Testaments, and may even induce a third book suffused by the same element of interiority. Finally, interpretation may reject all intermediaries or specialists and become direct, since the book is written both in itself and in the heart, once as a point of subjectification and again in the subject (the Reformation conception of the book)" (Deleuze and Guattari 1987: 127). Auerbach suggests that both our understanding and our representation of reality must be based on the Biblical mode if we want to know ourselves historically, rather than mythically, and order our world according to democratic and egalitarian, not hierarchic and totalitarian, principles. The contribution of philology and literary criticism to this project of emancipation is the interpretive method, the search for universals in the historicity of texts, events, and phenomena.[91] His descendants agree: "The subtle tyranny of secularization theories has made us forget till recently the analogy between criticism and theological discourse" (Hartman 1980: 180). Many of them have been working to make this analogy of the two branches of Protestant interpretation explicit and central for contemporary culture.[92]

The interpretive method has also been expected, at least since the avant-garde attacks on the institution of art, to compensate for the loss of the public cultural sphere at the time of World War I by transcending politics. From the emergence of taste with British Neo-classicism through its apotheosis in the Viennese culture of intellectual "circles," it was possible to seek bourgeois harmony in a world of shared feelings, positions, attitudes or public spaces that redeemed the guilt of profit, pacified dissent, celebrated intellectual liberalism, and discredited social unrest. With the disappearance of the general cultivated public (and the emergence of the educated masses), what is the "function" and "context" of criticism? The modernist and post-modernist writer, critic, or academic responds: "The simplest way to put it is that it provides us with shared texts. We can't live unmediated with each other and, for the sake of the intellect as well as the imagination, need passwords. Some are complicated exchanges. I myself—it may be my own defect—cannot conceive of this taking place without the sharing of texts. That's enough of a social context for me, because as soon as you sit around a table and share a text, you are within a social context. You may go beyond that and say 'Is it the Yeshiva kind of sitting around?' or is it some other kind, and then you do get to institutional analysis, but I think the 'abc' of it is that you agree to study texts together, you discover that these texts are interrelated, that one text has been behind many things" (Hartman 1987: 94). For the Western artist and theorist, the only safe thing left to share is the text, the practice of reading texts, the site created by interpretation: "[W]e are all, still and always, aware of the *Crisis*, convinced that 'interventions' are necessary and that the least of texts is immediately 'effective' ['*opératoire*']; we all think, as if it went without saying, that politics passes through the literary (or the theoretical)" (Lacoue-Labarthe and Nancy 1988: 16–17). After the public covenant of interpretation collapsed, only the contract of "sitting around" common texts, only the consensus of commentary[93] and the standpoint of redemption[94] can provide mediation, a sense of order, the possibility of community—a "textual community" (Brian Stock). If that is achieved, if people consent to study (as opposed to, say, demonstrate) together, then above this community of interpreters descends the mystery of (no longer just shared but) interrelated texts, and finally the one revealed text, the canonic book, like the one studied in "the Yeshiva kind of sitting around" or promoted by *Mimesis*. Fulfilling its promise (to Hebraic thinkers like T. S. Eliot, Edmund Husserl, Ferruccio Busoni, or Viktor Shklovsky) to overcome politics, interpretation no longer proclaims or prepares for emancipation but itself becomes the absolute one.

We saw earlier that Auerbach's survey of the literary canon serves two major ideological purposes in the realm of philology: it portrays the canon as the secular Bible of the Christian West, where a Biblical realism is announced and prefigured; and it presents *Mimesis* as the Bible of criticism, which unfolds the drama of the verbal art. In Auerbach's work for the first time "criticism has usurped the place and character of the sacred Book" (Needler 1982: 404) while claiming it is only serving the authority of that Book. A third purpose of the survey is to outline a theological theory of literature that shows the modes of Jewish religion opposing the tropes of Greek idolatry. Auerbach composes the history of Western literature as a theodicy, vindicating the justice of God in respect to Greek evil pleasures. Our true reality is Biblical, he argues, because our world is God's; we should then comprehend and represent it Biblically; our literature too, as well as its understanding, should be Biblical. To read it is to interpret either the word of God or the word of man about the works of God, and both acts of interpretation must respect the reality represented therein (or its prefigurations). Auerbach does not mention the name of God: God himself is not to be named or represented (as it is done in the Greek mode), only his world. This representation, however, must be the appropriate one, respecting human limitations: it must be Biblical, that is, historical, in the sense of recording and reflecting the history of the people of God in his world. Auerbach's theory of literature (and language) is theological, theocentric, and theocratic, stemming from (his understanding of) the Biblical interpretive tradition. In it, Lukács' anxiety over homelessness and belatedness is effectively countered: while Lukács writes about the Fall, Auerbach writes about the Promised Land. Still, for both critics literature is the Book, criticism is interpretation, and aesthetics is theology: they are theologians of the secular Word, attending to its sacred meaning in a faithless age.[95] "The accreted, promissory narrative we call Scripture is composed of tokens that demand the continuous and precarious intervention of successive generations of interpreters, who must keep the words as well as the faith" (Hartman 1986: 17). The covenant of interpretation protects the authority of monotheism in a churchless world.

The impact of Auerbach's treatise has been tremendous[96] in that it brought the historicity of Higher Criticism into the era of formalism by reclaiming successfully the theological heritage of stylistics. Thanks largely to its influence, the devotion of literary criticism to the Bible,[97] since the 1940s, has taken three main directions: first, the analysis of aesthetic features and qualities in the Scripture (Alter 1981, especially 127–30, where mourning scenes from the *Iliad* and the David story are compared; also Alter 1985), often with particular attention to relevant pedagogical needs (Robertson 1977: 16–32 compares both *Exodus* 1–15, as a "comedy," and the Gospel of Mark to *The Bacchae*); second, the study of a specific literary oeuvre, school, trend, or period on the basis of its Biblical inspiration and resources (Damrosch 1985); and third, the exploration of large areas of the Western tradition according to interpretive rules derived from the Bible (Schneidau 1976).[98] In many of these works the Hebraic-Hellenic comparison predictably influences the approach or the selection of texts. Its corresponding presence in the (American, at least) curriculum seems to be equally strong (as in the course "Humanities 1. The Foundations of Western Civilization: Israel and Greece," offered, according to its 1986 brochure, by the Judaic Studies Program at the University of California, San Diego). Given its pervasive nomothetic and educational influence, it is only fair to say about *Mimesis* that "the book stands as a monument to that postwar phenomenon that may be called 'NATO humanism' and that survives in the countless 'Great Books' courses of our curricula: the organization and teaching of a politicocultural view of the West as a continuous and ultimately consistent body of thought and discourse, the hallmarks of which are historical progress, democratic liberalism, a faith in individual man, and a tolerance of multiple gods. In this context, Auerbach's *Mimesis* continues to do service as an immensely useful—indeed, uncontested— pedagogic tool in this popular dissemination of literary high culture" (Bahti 1985: 127). Thus even before a new wave of Puritanism took power and office in the West in the last quarter of the twentieth century, the anti-Hellenism of literary and humanistic studies in general, from Auerbach to Derrida, was preparing the ground for (and has contributed to) its legitimization.

In order to be heard in a world suspicious of preaching after the departure of gods, the theology of secular writing needs to conceal its nature. So it becomes Theory, and conjures up the spectre of a primordial otherness[99] and the spectacle of a gigantomachy between good and evil, illumination and darkness, freedom and slavery. The struggle for mastery over human destiny is articulated and debated in terms of the Hebraism-Hellenism opposition.[100] In this Wagnerian spectacle, theory dramatizes its emancipatory promise, the annunciation of autonomy as the independence (or, in populist rhetoric, resistance) of interpretation, where interpretation means aesthetic attitude as politics—both action and goal, praxis and redemption. Regardless of their specific function, the Hebraic is the Other of the same, the other side of Western identity, the irreconcilable difference which both questions and affirms this identity; while the Hellenic is the alien element, the source of all alienation, the strange *pharmakon* which disrupts the rites of interpretation as the latter is celebrating the communion of reading. Some fatalistically accept the gigantomachy: "There is, then, no way of eluding the burden except by adding to it: by fighting the Quarrel of the Ancients and Moderns all over again in a historical chaos where nothing is definitely obsolete. The practical critic may be blind to what he is doing and the hermeneuticist too aware, but each interpretation of a work of art is gained only by struggling with a *chaos of texts* that is called, euphemistically, tradition or, more neutrally, literary history" (Hartman 1980: 239). Some reject it vehemently: "Our most famous critics— Northrop Frye, Wayne Booth, Geoffrey Hartman, Hugh Kenner, Harold Bloom—are promoters of religion. They do not, as is often claimed, make literature a substitute for religion. Rather, they make religion a substitute for literature. . . . Religion is the most potent repressive force in America today, but teachers of literature do not raise their voices against it—thinking it irrelevant but all the while honouring the Hartmans and Fryes who promote religious values and attitudes" (Culler 1984: 1328). Others boldly contribute to it: Auerbach, for example, constructs, through his reading of one passage from the *Odyssey*, a Greek model of representation (and a picture of the entire Greek civilization) on which he then proceeds to blame all human excess, from ancient hedonism to contemporary fascism. His survey remains throughout fraught with the haunting Hellenic background. The Homeric mode is the sheer negativity against which the Biblical acquires its apocalyptic power to save humanity from the sins of form and pleasure.

The fabrication of the Hellenic serves this purpose: without its alienating function, without its radically extrinsic existence as Alien, the defense of the Hebraic way would not be possible. By catastrophically invoking its ominous promise of beauty and harmony, Auerbach suggests that it is time for civilization to repent and seek atonement: paganism must be abrogated. Scholars have praised Auerbach's decision to start his book with the comparison since they agree that "the contrast between the Bible and Homer signifies two basic, though opposite, types of conceiving the world—and the word. In the contingent world of Hebrew thought, one must not look to nature for ultimate reality, but to the divine creative word which simultaneously reveals and conceals the hidden God, and He is not to be identified with nature, or any of its forms. The text claims an absolute authority in Hebraic thought which it could not possibly possess for the Greeks" (Handelman 1982: 30). Honoring that authority, explanation should again become interpretation, which is representation, which is repetition: we can repent by representing reality (our historical experience of God), by reinterpreting the canon, by repeating the Book: the canon is our history, the Book our reality. *Mimesis*, with its universal teaching (which brings to mind the quietistic piety of Thomas à Kempis), is the Imitation of Yahweh in the realm of literary studies. With it, the moderation of older comparisons has been lost. It used to be possible to see the Hebraic and the Hellenic as equal, even though priority was generally given to the former.[101] After the Hebraization of the cultural sphere with Modernism, after Scholem's messianic history prevailed in Benjamin's thought over Brecht's epic theater, the opposition could only be portrayed as a rivalry.[102] The "split between Greek cognition and Hebraic spirituality" is now perceived as war and gives rise to strong feelings of Hebraic tribalism and triumphantism: "Christian, Moslem, Jew, or their mixed descendants, we are children of Abraham and not of Achilles" (Bloom 1986: 3). The battle of the books has turned into a campaign of anti-Hellenism (sometimes driven by an alarming, post-Nietzschean enthusiasm for Jacob Burckhardt's antipathy to democracy and admiration for aristocracy).

Consider *Black Athena* by Martin Bernal. Its first volume is a solid critique of the ideology informing the field of classics. The author convincingly exposes its Eurocentric bias and the political (national, racial, and colonial) purposes it has served. At the same time, he revives the Hellenistic and early Christian practice of arguing that the Greeks have stolen everything from the Hebrews, or from the Orient in general. To buttress this idea, Bernal resorts to sensationalism: he manipulates his terminology according to audience demands;[103] he plays the role of the pariah;[104] he conjures up enemies;[105] he uses messianic language.[106] Thanks to his rhetoric (as well as the popularity of essentialist affirmations of difference), he has succeeded where others failed:[107] the reception of his book has been overwhelming[108] (notably in Afrocentric high school and college programs). Nevertheless, there are even more disturbing questions. Although Bernal complains that in the past the positions of certain classicists were dismissed because they were Jews, because people thought that those classicists had a "vested interest" in the positions they defended (Bernal 1989: 19–20), he uses the same criterion when he makes sure to identify the Jews among the scholars he discusses. He cannot see that, like those he justifiably criticizes for discrimination, he is connecting ethnicity and scholarship—with the only difference that, since he happens to agree with the rejected positions, Jewishness for him becomes a positive quality.[109]

Bernal grants the Kuhnian principle that "at least in the humanities, there is no scholarship that can stand outside the social and intellectual paradigms held by the community or communities to which the scholar belongs" (Bernal 1985: 66). Thus he is often able to place classicist inventions in their historical context: "Increased [Jewish] self-confidence, though largely reflected in Zionism and religious revival, has had as a byproduct an attempt to restore the Phoenicians" (69). On the other hand, the closer he comes to the time of his writing, the more he forgets the impact of dominant discourses on his own project. Here is another point: "It was not until the mid 1970s that Jewish scholars, notably Cyrus Gordon and Michael Astour, who had begun to demonstrate the close and fundamental connections between the cultures of the Levant and the Aegean, started to be taken seriously. Externally, they were helped by the rise of Israel as a bastion of European culture in the face of the resurgent 'Third World'" (Bernal 1986: 54). Bernal does not seem to suspect that he may be part of the same trend, since "*Black Athena* is essentially concerned with the Egyptian and Semitic roles in the formation of Greece in the Middle and Late Bronze Ages" (Bernal 1987: 22).

It is unfortunate that his effort to highlight the role of the Phoenicians in the formation of Greece relies as much on the Hebraism-Hellenism opposition as the anti-Semitic historiography he criticizes. He has indeed admitted the Hebraic character of the project. When he was asked in an interview about the movement to prove that the Phoenicians and the Canaanites were the parents of the Greeks and by implication of the Europeans, his response was revealing: "There is such a movement, it is true. It started around the 1920s by some Zionists who reacted to Orthodox Judaism and tried to connect with the land of Palestine. . . . Now as far as I am concerned, the person who influenced me most was a Jew but anti-Zionist: Michael Astour. And I think that for him and in some way for me the pro-Phoenician view is a way out to avoid religious Judaism and Zionism. It is the third way" (Kiosse 1987: 63).[110] As a critic had to remind him, though, the third way, the way of culture and scholarship, does not have to lead into Hellenic territory: "The forces of Israeli and Black American self-assertion, championing Semitic and Pharaonic legacies, lie behind his project of historical revision. These two causes are even less readily compatible than the Chinese and Vietnamese combination where his interests started" (Anderson 1987).[111] There is obviously an emancipatory promise in all this—a liberal vision of a fair world: "The political purpose of Black Athena is, of course, to lessen European cultural arrogance" (Bernal 1987: 73). Bernal appeals to his colleagues' sensitivity toward racial issues when he argues that "the scheme set out in Black Athena is better on ethical grounds, that it is more congenial to our general preferences—to the general liberal preferences of academia—than that of the Aryan Model" (Bernal 1989: 25). His own treatment of Greek civilization, though, lacks even a requisite academic respect for cultural specificity.

Bernal almost never takes into account the ancient Greek socio-political context: reading factual statements empirically in Greek texts, he cannot discern the operative discourse.[112] He therefore takes texts at face value and assumes that the authors indeed believed what they said. "The analysis of context that Professor Bernal has provided so ably in his consideration of modern historiography he has neglected to do for his ancient sources. Professor Bernal has removed the production of his literary texts from their social setting" (Green 1989: 59).[113] The reason for this neglect is his virulent anti-Hellenism. During the period of "fabrication" he surveys, from the 1780s to the present, he sees every expression of interest in Greece as a position for or against the Ancient Model that he thinks had prevailed until then. It is as if every Western view of Greece has been determined by one's view of a Near Eastern civilization—Egyptian, Phoenician, Turkish, etc. The possibility that certain Westerners chose to look at Greece because that culture appealed to them more than others (rather than because they were looking for ways of denigrating the others) is never entertained.[114] He might have considered, for example, "simply the sociological gap between the citizen polis as an institutional form—that which made Greek civilisation truly distinctive in a world-historical perspective—and either the Phoenician towns, coastal variants of a millennial line of Mesopotamian city-states, or the Pharaonic empires of Egypt. What was 'classical' about classical Greece, after all, was not its language or its religion— Athena white, black or brown—but its politics, philosophy and art. To set Greek history in its proper Near Eastern context is a necessary antidote to all miraculism; but to resolve it into that context would be a no less implausible reductionism" (Anderson 1987). But Bernal has no patience with anything that may distinguish Greece. In his scenario of conspiracy, the story of Greece was fabricated by racist Romantics and post-Romantics who believed in progress and used it to justify their devaluation and colonization of Semitic cultures. This point is made particularly clear in his dismissive treatment of the revolution against the Ottoman Empire. Bernal describes the Philhellenic fever that responded to the Greek War of Independence in 1821 in this way: "In such an atmosphere of hysteria there was no room for the Egyptians as founders of civilization. Continental feelings became still more intense. Turkish rule in Greece and the Balkans began to be seen as unnatural" (Bernal 1986: 25). Should it have continued, perhaps, to be seen as natural, so that the Egyptian reputation could be preserved? Similarly, when he claims, disregarding its radical tradition he has acknowledged elsewhere, that "Philhellenism has always had Aryan and racist connotations" (Bernal 1987: 387), isn't he condemning support for a liberation movement comparable to those contemporary ones he seems to espouse?[115] It is certainly true that in the eighteenth century Greece "benefited from racism, immediately and in every way; and it was rapidly seen as the 'childhood' of the 'dynamic' 'European race'" (189). But it also happens to be true that Greece benefited from the revolutionary convictions and politics of the time, aligning itself with the cause of liberation that had not been completely subsumed under Schiller's contract of aesthetic education.

It is exactly in exchange for giving up direct political engagement that Western readers have been granted aesthetic (or disinterested interpretive, i.e., self-policed) autonomy.[116] Over the centuries of modernity, the possibilities of public engagement have taken diverse political directions and have been repeatedly controlled, less often by coercion than by concessions of increased social autonomy. The force that had to be contained over and over again is power—the interests of autonomy. It was finally with the Hellenic contract of humanism that the Hebraic politics of community succeeded in completely separating quests for autonomy from questions of power. "By humanism I mean the totality of discourse through which Western man is told: 'Even though you don't exercise power, you can still be a ruler. Better yet, the more you deny yourself the exercise of power, the more you submit to those in power, then the more this increases your sovereignty.' Humanism invented a whole series of subjected sovereignties: the soul (ruling the body, but subject to God), consciousness (sovereign in a context of judgment, but subjected to the necessities of truth), the individual (a titular control of personal rights subjected to the laws of nature and society), basic freedom (sovereign within, but accepting the demands of an outside world and 'aligned with destiny'). In short, humanism is everything in Western civilization that restricts *the desire for power*" (Foucault 1977a: 221). The humanities has educated the masses of readers in acting as an audience, namely, in docility, through the aestheticization of emancipation. Marx's infamous dictum makes arguably better sense if we replace religion with its modern secular equivalent: "⟨The aesthetic⟩ is the general theory of this world, its encyclopaedic compendium, its logic in popular form, its spiritual *point d'honneur*, its enthusiasm, its moral sanction, its solemn complement, its universal basis for consolation and justification. It is the imaginary realization of the human essence, because the human essence possesses no true reality. . . . ⟨The aesthetic⟩ is the sigh of the oppressed creature, the feeling of a heartless world and the soul of soulless circumstances. It is the opium of the people" (Marx 1971: 116).

At the same time, the "culture of critical discourse," of the specialists of interpretation, with its self-grounded claims to authority, has achieved a high level of "context independence" thanks to its "theoreticity" (Gouldner 1979), its capacity to turn those claims into norms of "good speech," into rules of autonomous reflexivity.[117] The problem remains, though, that the aesthetic ideal, interpretation elevated from exercise to attitude, "grants Modernity its autonomy only on the terms on which Modernity accepts Antiquity" (Lacoue-Labarthe and Nancy 1988: 50) as its model and rival, relative and stranger, resident and alien. The result is autopathy. The neurosis of History. The anxiety of emancipation. Hebraization of culture: "Western revisionism. Or that large subject we haven't got a name for, that has to do with both the glory and the horror, not only of Western literature, but of Western culture: which is the deep split between the fact that its religion and its morality are Hebraic-Christian, and its cognition and aesthetics—and therefore its dominant imaginative forms—are Greek" (Bloom 1987: 68). Fortunately this is not the case for everyone in the world, as the polarity would have us believe: the *Iliad* can still be read as a Caribbean epic (Walcott 1990) without the help of distinctions between "biblical narrative based on resentment and mythical narrative based on desire" (Gans 1985: 203) which ultimately rely on figurae and universals. But to those who are happy to be explained, emancipated, assimilated into the civil rites of interpretation, anyone not sharing the aesthetic communion appears uncivilized and threatening.

The issue acquires great urgency during periods of multiculturalist and tribal ideals (Maffesoli 1988), when separatist trends (from pan-Arabism to Central Europeanism, and from "black planet" to "queer nation") adopt the morality and rhetoric of "Otherness" to fashion a distinct identity and to claim recognition. As the semiolytic genealogy of Hebraism and Hellenism shows, the difficulty with this strategy is that, so far as the post-Reformation West is concerned, the model for the Other is always Hebraic: the essential Other is the Jew who has to pass the test of proficiency in Hellenic culture in order to be emancipated into the civil society of interpretive rights. The advantage of the Hebraic strategy is that it places the party concerned in the position of the Jew, of "the outsider as insider" (Gay 1968a), of the one who is already part of the dominant identity, although he remains at the safe distance of "difference" from hegemony. In other words, (self)proclaimed difference can benefit from its intrinsic relation to sameness granted by dialectics, the metaphysics of Protestantism. On the other hand, the Hellenic test can only be passed through failure since it is commonly acknowledged that the Greeks both cannot and should not be imitated. It is exactly because they cannot be repeated that the test must be, so that the promise of emancipation may remain alive and the imperium of modernity may reproduce itself.[118]

A typical example of the self-defeating enterprise of interpretation is the response of the Orient to Orientalism. The discourse of Orientalism, which emerged much later than that of Hellenism,[119] defined its object from the beginning in counter-Hebraic terms. It is no accident that "one of the important impulses toward the study of the Orient in the eighteenth century was the revolution in Biblical studies stimulated by such variously interesting pioneers as Bishop Lowth, Eichhorn, Herder, and Michaelis" (Said 1978: 17). The Orient presupposes the Hebraic because the Orient signifies the non-Western East, the East that is other-than-Hebraic, the Semitic which cannot be recognized as target of anti-Semitism (27). "Orientalism is premised upon exteriority" (20), but it is its concrete exteriority to Hebraism, rather than the Occident in general, that defines it. Consequently, a critic of Orientalism ought not to defend the historical specificity of the Orient by using the morality and rhetoric of Otherness, since the Other is always a Hebraic model, the figura of the emancipated Jew of modernity, of the virtuoso of the culture of atonement, and will therefore lead to formidable Hellenic tests. The "contemporary Manichean theologizing of 'the Other'" (Said 1983: 291) can only lead to universal assimilation. An alternative understanding of independence and pursuit of liberation is necessary, especially in times when the ideals of freedom and revolt attract little enthusiasm. If the covenant of autonomy, as supported by the twin discourses of Hebraism and Hellenism, instead of delivering people from oppression has led to the aesthetic theocracy of interpretation, it may be time to abandon the two disabling discourses and question not the source, auto- or hetero-, but the monotheism of nomos itself.

Chapter Two

THE CULTURE OF ATONEMENT

The Gods depart, in sorrowing token
That happy childhood is outgrown;
The leading-strings at length are broken,
The ungrateful world can soar alone.

All lovely form with them was taken
To grace the home whence erst they came;
So was the world by Art forsaken,
And Beauty left us but her name.
 —Friedrich Schiller

Like everything today is conscious of being looked at,
 looked at by something else but not by God,
and that's the only way anything can have its own form
and its own character, and . . . and shape and smell,
 being looked at by God.
 —William Gaddis

THE DIALECTIC OF CAPITALISM

The direction of the project of autonomy, the ultimate project of modernity, depended on its definition of governance: If praxis (including knowledge) aspired to move away from church and court authority, and to achieve independence, how was it to govern itself? What kind of laws should it devise and follow? Undertaken by the Reformation, the interpretive approach responded with the law of immanent understanding: if to be free was to interpret freely, the rules of governance ought to be sought in the holy orders of reading and the order of holy texts. According to this approach, the precondition of autonomy was the civil liberation of interpretation. "But it is necessary to note, what has often been forgotten, that the Reformation meant not the elimination of the Church's control over everyday life, but rather the substitution of a new form of control for the previous one. It meant the repudiation of a control which was very lax, at that time scarcely perceptible in practice, and hardly more than formal, in favour of a regulation of the whole of conduct which, penetrating to all departments of private and public life, was infinitely burdensome and earnestly enforced" (Weber 1976: 36). Gradually, as this notion of liberation espoused the Hebraic ideal of emancipation and pursued civil rights, the initial askesis of capitalist self-regulation evolved into the exercise of bourgeois self-cultivation under the inspiration of the Hellenic ideal of the aesthetic. This became the basis of the social contract of (high) culture: autonomy of self-cultivation as completely differentiated from other spheres of activity.

This new meaning of freedom demands the absolute grounding of being in itself according to the law of aesthetic immanence. "What is thought in the concept is the law of what is real itself. The concept of freedom has reality when being free as a manner of Being belongs together with the nature and essential ground of Being. If this is correct, the concept of freedom is no longer an arbitrary one. Thus the question of freedom becomes essentially fundamental. If freedom is a fundamental determination of Being in general, the project of the scientific world view as a whole in which freedom is to be comprehended has as its true goal and center ultimately nothing else than precisely freedom itself. The system to be constructed does not also contain the concept of freedom among many others, but freedom is rather the central point of the system. The system itself is 'the system of freedom.' The essential delineation of the fact of freedom founds the system of philosophy on its real ground" (Heidegger 1985: 21). Hence the principle of the aesthetic seeks autonomy for autonomy's sake. When interpretation becomes disinterested (that is, aesthetic), autonomy is happy to protect its purity by policing itself. The aesthetic signals the transition from self-regulated (-controlled) independence to self-supervised (-disciplined) liberty.

Emancipation succeeded, gaining socio-economic self-sufficiency at the cost of abandoning historical effectiveness. Meanwhile, aesthetic autonomy, the absolute one, allowed for interpretive liberty only. It never learned to adapt to, or even survive in, a world of heteronomous interests; it never learned the language of political claims to freedom. Finally, during the twentieth century, when politics began to adopt aesthetic modes of managing and policing, aesthetic autonomy discovered, to its despair, that its own precious liberty too could be desecrated. If the aesthetic character of autonomy can be defiled, is nothing sacred? This is the question raised in another response to that Novalisean elegy on the homelessness of the aesthetic sensibility, Lukács' *Theory of the Novel*. The work under question is contemporary with *Mimesis* and, like it, takes the *Odyssey* as representative of a basic mode of thought. If Auerbach worked with philology, stylistics, and literary history, this book relies on philosophy, cultural theory, and the history of ideas. What distinguishes the *Dialectic of Enlightenment* (1944), however, from other well-known critiques of modernity[1] is neither its apocalyptic tone nor its elitist disposition but rather its devastating analysis of what Max Horkheimer (1895–1973) and Theodor W. Adorno (1903–69) perceive as the entwining of the mythology of reason and the reason of mythology: this unresolvable tension, this fundamental dialectic, inexorably seals the fate of the human race (which, from their perspective, is limited to the West).

Older surveys of decadence, like Oswald Spengler's *The Decline of the West* (vol. I: 1918; vol. II: 1922), traced a rise and a subsequent (though not unavoidable) decline. In contrast, Horkheimer and Adorno present the course of Enlightenment as one of doom and damnation from the start, because of its inherently contradictory character. Their book is a general critique of (Western) civilization, which concentrates on the predicament of contemporary "man" and traces its origin in the ancient past. It outlines the emergence, development, and final collapse of the project of Enlightenment, and is primarily meant as a severe indictment of modern culture, whose rampant barbarism and totalitarianism illustrate the perils inherent in this project.

In broad terms, the Enlightenment is defined as the long-range movement of human liberation from fear and myth through reflection and reason, which achieved mastery over the world but also led to alienation and exploitation. Self-consciousness, the authors argue, procured both proud independence and destructive autocentrism, as attested by its ultimate product, bourgeois subjectivity. In the plight of the modern individual, the self-defeating logic of Enlightenment can be observed at work in all its irrational excess and pathos. Auerbach, like Lukács, concentrated on the dialectic of literary style in the narrative. Horkheimer and Adorno conduct an anatomy of bourgeois culture as the debasement of style itself—as the collapse of the artistic dialectic into mass consumption under capitalism. Art and society are closely connected in their study as they attempt to expose the aesthetics of politics.

The inherent contradictions of rationality are explored in the first chapter of the book, "The Concept of Enlightenment." The authors begin with a broad definition of the autonomy project: "In the most general sense of progressive thought, the Enlightenment has always aimed at liberating men from fear and establishing their sovereignty. The program of the Enlightenment was the disenchantment of the world; the dissolution of myths and the substitution of knowledge for fancy" (Horkheimer and Adorno 1972: 3). As the primary force in humanity's course during the historical period, the Enlightenment opposes knowledge to myth, trying to overcome superstition through inquiry, belief through exploration—to understand the world with informed reason, not impotent imagination; to comprehend, and not just perceive. The main focus is on the contradictory dialectic of the whole movement and the disturbing irreconcilability of its polar terms. What interests (and fascinates and harms) the authors is the inherent impossibility of the project, due to its self-destructive nature. They attempt to show why Enlightenment fails as soon as it succeeds—what interrupts its progress and aborts its completion. Their description of the fatal interplay of liberation and domination, which constitutes the dialectic character of Enlightenment, concentrates on four main problems: subjectivism, objectivism, positivism, and totalitarianism. These beset the program and throw it back to its dark origins, mythical thinking.

By privileging Man (Weigel 1990), Enlightenment has allowed the individual to emerge as Self, as an independent and autonomous social entity. "The social work of every individual in bourgeois society is mediated through the principle of self" (Horkheimer and Adorno 1972: 29). This is the fallacy of self-reliance, whereby individuality turns to individualism, as man puts himself at the center of the universe and estimates everything according to his interests. The inhumanity of the subject is that it views society only as a struggle among selves, and is therefore bound to participate in that struggle.

The self, the autarchic individual, also objectifies the world: he separates himself from it and makes it an object of observation and potential exploitation. "Men pay for the increase of their power with alienation from that over which they exercise their power" (9). This is the solitary task of knowledge: it makes what man comprehends alien to him, and what he commands foreign; it distances and it abstracts things. The original ideal was to achieve rational understanding and real power over nature; but understanding separates and power alienates.

Enlightenment distances, abstracts, and quantifies too: it turns things into observable objects and quantifiable entities. Positivism is the fallacy of immanence, "the myth of things as they actually are" (x). The principle of immanence operates with standards of equivalence which invent relationships of identity. Although the project of the unique individual, Enlightenment is not interested in the particular but in the general: "its ideal is the system from which all and everything follows" (7). It works with rules, numbers, and equations, measuring and calculating things and phenomena.

Finally, in seeking power over nature, reason totalizes the world into a coherent, abstract, manageable system. "Enlightenment is totalitarian" (6) because it strives for complete independence, full understanding, and total control. Its absolutist goals and strategies subject everything to its rules and domination. Totalitarianism is not the aberration of reason but the triumph of legitimized rationality "objectified as law and organization" (37).

Thus the program of the Enlightenment failed because of its inner contradictions. The grandiose enterprise that was launched to liberate humanity from the grip of mythological thinking has collapsed into a new mythology, which is all the worse, since it is still mesmerized by delusions of power. Horkheimer and Adorno seek the cause in the constitutive, morbid, cacophonous dialectic, and discover the problem of secular faith: "In the enlightened world, mythology has entered into the profane" (28). Before, people were paralyzed by the mythology of superstition; now the reign of reason has produced its own mythology, rationality. In a sense, we have come full circle back into unconscious belief; in another sense, we are even more helpless now, having been deceived by our best potential.

This is the discordant dialectic of Enlightenment between reason and domination, knowledge and power, understanding and authority, self-reflectiveness and self-destructiveness. The project is obviously doomed to fail since "for enlightenment the process is always decided from the start" (24). It is the reason of myth that blinds its course. "Mythology itself set off the unending process of enlightenment in which ever and again, with the inevitability of necessity, every specific theoretic view succumbs to the destructive criticism that it is only a belief" (11). The inevitable necessity is activated within the project by its very origins, which predetermine its circular trajectory. "Just as the myths already realize enlightenment, so enlightenment with every step becomes more deeply engulfed in mythology. It receives all its matter from the myths in order to destroy them; and even as a judge, it comes under the mythic curse" (11–12). The adventures of reason are inescapably influenced by the vile character of their starting point, and they are condemned to repeat it again and again. The authors state this deterministic position in the "Introduction" with an aphorism: "myth is always enlightenment; and enlightenment reverts to mythology" (xvi). The rhetoric and the fatalism of the verdict illuminate the title of their book from another angle: the fundamental conflict is not between myth and reason, but rather mythology (the power of domination) and Enlightenment (the force of liberation). Since the forces of myth are not generated by the movement itself, but have been inherited from the previous state of things, they are not exactly intrinsic to Enlightenment, but represent a power from the past that persists unabated. The myth-reason dialectic is only a reactivation and reenactment *inside* Enlightenment of the prior and much more fundamental dialectic between Enlightenment and mythology, which has not disappeared but rather has been (unwillingly and inevitably) interiorized by the new project.

Given the direction of this critique, the choice of the term "mythology" (which the authors never explain) is quite interesting. By using this word (rather than, say, "ideology" or "faith"), Horkheimer and Adorno indicate that their greatest worry is the persistent survival of the pagan element. The real problem is not superstition, deception, or ignorance but myth, the pagan account of things. They are appalled to discover that Enlightenment has not overcome idolatry, that reason has not restored true faith. The God of Mendelssohn and Jacobi has not prevailed over the gods of Schiller and Hölderlin. As Heidegger's "turn" shows, the search for a third alternative to Schelling's mythology and revelation has failed.[2] If the myth-reason dialectic survives within Enlightenment, emancipation from mythology is impossible. As Schönberg's Aron conceded, the language of idols may be the only one accessible to human understanding.

It appears, then, that mythology is the constitutive element in the conflict—not because of its priority but because of its unassailable negativity: although he speaks it, man can never understand it since, as soon as he wants to know, he is engaged in the project of emancipation. Mythology is thus the basic element because the thinking man can conceive it only in negative terms, in terms of what he/it is not, although it is again itself that allows, through its (temporary) suspension, for the movement of thought. According to the anti-positivistic, counter-Hegelian logic of Horkheimer and Adorno, this pole of the opposition is the more important one for the development of reason. They find that Enlightenment invariably makes people aware of mythology, the domineering thought which quantifies, homogenizes, absolutizes, and totalizes. Enlightenment resists belief and its rationalist sublimation, abstraction, by keeping the possibility of liberation open as it tries to be the critical self-consciousness of mythology. Unfortunately, because of its parasitic dependence on mythology, it fails: anticipation of liberation has been repeatedly frustrated since rationalism finally takes over reason, subjectivism confounds the subject, and positivism invades the positive. Its alert self-criticism remains the only human hope: "the Enlightenment *must consider itself*, if men are not to be wholly betrayed" (xv). So far, though, it has succeeded only in drawing attention to its dialectical opposite, mythology; but once this is done, it grows ensnared by prospects of authority and forgets itself completely, thus abandoning critique for the immediate gratification of power.

Enlightenment is therefore the liberating operation of reason, impaired and eventually canceled by the lures of domination: power corrupts autonomy. Horkheimer and Adorno see it as the unavoidable fall into knowledge, with mythology representing the forces of temptation.[3] The story they tell is a populist version of the "mythic curse," the expulsion from Paradise.[4] Since man has chosen to ask and know, he has liberated himself from the world of identity, from the perfect coincidence of name and thing, but he experiences this independence as a different form of domination: this is his gain and his punishment. There is no point in entertaining either hopes for a return to Eden or illusions of a complete emancipation. Levinas would later ask for a complete denunciation of the "answer," the will to know which sent us into exile in the first place, reserving for humans only the right (indeed, the duty) to ask (the question of responsibility to God).

Likewise, Horkheimer and Adorno propose a hygiene of knowledge which diets on non-answers, on responses which work more as markers of a path (like Abraham's to the sacrifice) than solutions to a problem.

Paradoxically, even though the authors utilize secularization as the narrative of the fall into knowledge, when they give an account of the fatal temptation, instead of following their Biblical model, they turn to a story from the Greek epic. This approach is similar to Auerbach's, who utilized a Greek counter-example to make his interpretive model credible. It is worth exploring what necessitated such an approach in this case. The basic dialectic is examined from the side of mythology in the chapter "Excursus I: Odysseus or Myth and Enlightenment" through a discussion of the *Odyssey*, "one of the earliest representative testimonies of Western bourgeois civilization" (xvi). Their model of the fallen hero of knowledge is not Adam but "the figure from the *Inferno* that can most readily be associated with the idea of *curiositas*: the figure of Odysseus in the twenty-sixth canto" (Blumenberg 1983: 338).[5] The king of Ithaca is presented as the first adventurer of reason who defied divine will. "In the *Paradiso*, Dante can ask Adam about the essence of the first sin, and it is explained to him as transgression of the sign (*il trapassar del segno*). Odysseus is the still unredeemed heir of the original sin that had been the transgression of the limits set for man: he transgresses the sign of the inhabitable world that is 'assigned' to man so as to penetrate into uninhabitable regions" (339).[6] Already in their first, general chapter, "The Concept of Enlightenment," Horkheimer and Adorno include in their comments on mythology references to the Greeks, mentioning the names of Homer, Xenophanes, Parmenides, Plato, Aristotle, as well as the Pre-Socratics, the tragedians, and Athenian democracy. They also include a discussion of the Sirens episode in the epic, where they detect elements of the Enlightenment in allegorical form. But in the Excursus they undertake a systematic interpretation of the dialectic in the *Odyssey*, contending that "there is no work which offers more eloquent testimony of the mutual implication of enlightenment and myth than that of Homer, the basic text of European civilization" (Horkheimer and Adorno 1972: 45–46). This is where, they believe, the first and severest confrontation of the two main forces in Western tradition took place, and its final outcome was decided.

The authors try first to debunk "the usual identification of epic and myth" (43). Their cryptic and elliptic dialogue with Lukács begins here and runs throughout the chapter. They agree with him on a major point articulated in *The Theory of the Novel*: "The epic is the historico-philosophic counterpart of the novel, and eventually displays features approximating those characteristic of the novel" (43–44). They differ, however, on

a fundamental level: "Philosophical criticism shows that the usual identification of epic and myth . . . is wholly illusive. *Epos* and *mythos* are two
distinct concepts, and indicate two stages in an historical process" (43).
Lukács saw the epic as the consummate reflection of an unproblematic
archaic age and its mythical thought, where unity, wholeness, and totality
found definitive expression. Horkheimer and Adorno are determined to
undermine this idyllic conception. The epic is not a reflection of mythology but rather the first clear indication of its dissolution. "The Homeric
spirit takes over and 'organizes' the myths, but contradicts them in the
process" (43), exposing their artificiality and conventionality. The poem,
along with its mythical content, has a strong anti-mythological character
which makes it the first announcement of the Enlightenment. Commentators, the authors suggest, have missed two prominent features: that myth
and epic belong to different stages of intellectual (and artistic) development, and that they share a tendency toward "domination and exploitation" (45). The epic is both the promising and the bitter beginning of the
end of the Enlightenment because it is a false, perverse start, polluted with
lust for total power. With this explanation "Adorno reverses Lukács' reduction of novel to epic: he makes Odysseus into a picaresque character"
(Donougho 1981: 29). The *Dialectic* leaves the impression that Lukács, in
his unreserved admiration for and unqualified glorification of complexity
in completeness, was unable to perceive that the epic is actually about what
can no longer be celebrated—a faith that is shrinking, an order that is dis-
solving.[7]

Horkheimer and Adorno outline the false Enlightenment initiated by
the epic hero along lines strongly reminiscent of the four main problems
which they discern in the dialectical constitution of the Enlightenment in
the first chapter. Thus the hero's portrait can be described in terms corresponding to the categories of subjectivism, objectivism, positivism, and
totalitarianism.

Odysseus is the "knowing survivor" (Horkheimer and Adorno 1972: 47),
and the poem of his praise records the (trans)formations of his subjectivity.
"The eventful voyage from Troy to Ithaca is the way taken through the
myths by the self" (46). He wanders, he suffers, he loses himself in order to
create a self and justify it. "The self represents rational universality against
the inevitability of fate" (58). His most typical (if not archetypal) characteristic is cunning, and the greatest (self)affirmation of his intelligence is
the radical transvaluation of sacrifice. "Odysseus acts as sacrifice and priest
at one and the same time. By calculating his own sacrifice, he effectively
negates the power to whom the sacrifice is made. In this way he redeems
the life he had forfeited" (50). Thus he invents himself by deregulating the
ritual. To the extent that it deprives the ritual of its magic and turns the

sacrifice into a role that can be individually appropriated, this is anti-mythic thinking, based on the intelligence of the subject.

"Cunning is only the subjective development of the objective untruth of the sacrifice that redeems it" (51). With its employment, any manipulation becomes possible. "The deception in sacrifice is the prototype of Odyssean cunning" (50). At the same time, it is the first major statement of defiant individualism exploiting conventions to its own benefit, regardless of their public status. The individual pursues his own goals and seeks the freedom to attain them. "The entanglement of myth, domination, and labor" (32), however, begins here, since with one irreverent gesture Odysseus both claims autonomy and alienates himself from the surrounding environment. After denouncing his home and his origins, from now on he is on his own, and he must himself provide the goals and the support. "The history of civilization is the history of the introversion of sacrifice. In other words: the history of renunciation" (55).[8] To put it in terms of the underlying Biblical model, by eating from the tree of knowledge, people voluntarily exiled themselves from their original motherland. With the transformation of sacrifice into subjectivity begins "a denial of nature in man for the sake of domination over non-human nature and over other men. This very denial, the nucleus of all civilizing rationality" (54), objectifies nature and alienates man. Cunning exploits the distinction between word and fact, name and thing, discovering their conventional relationship and showing that it is arbitrary. With the rhetorical dimension of language emphasized, anything can be objectified, separated from the knowing subject—troped and abstracted.

Odysseus is also the "*homo oeconomicus*" (61). He quantifies the world, measures things according to his selfish reason, and pursues his atomistic interests. His utilitarian thought rejects the traditional system of the communal economy. He feels independent and irresponsible enough to participate in different exchanges by any means that help him procure the desired dividends. His calculations and moral indifference make him the first true bourgeois, and a particularly successful one. Finally, his overall attitude of independence and superiority expresses an unmistakably totalitarian disposition. As the first individual to venture beyond the familiar confines of nature and to construct an absolute and insatiable self, an autocratic and implacable subject, Odysseus carves for himself a position of demand, if not power, from which he negotiates with gods, heroes, common people, nature, the past, even death. In the successive triumphs of his rationality, his totalizing calculation and execution of strategies, moves, and operations are completely justified.

Like Auerbach, Horkheimer and Adorno place their work within the urgency of the present historical moment. While they diagnose in the mythic world of the *Odyssey* a system of negative forces besieging the project of Enlightenment from its inception,[9] they point to the Nazi persecution of the Jews as the lowest point ever reached by civilization and the most atrocious expression of the impasse created by the adventures of its rationality. In the last chapter of their book, "Elements of Anti-Semitism: Limits of Enlightenment," they seek to determine the basic causes and dimensions of the drama that brought the project of Enlightenment to its exterminating conclusion. Here they define anti-Semitism as a complex phenomenon which has been motivated by a variety of forces—economic, social, ideological, religious, and psychological.

To begin with, they suggest that "bourgeois anti-Semitism has a specific economic reason: the concealment of domination in production" (Horkheimer and Adorno 1972: 173). The Jews, who for a long time were denied access to the means of production, have a history of involvement with the circulation sector, and have often found themselves blamed for misfortunes they never caused. They were those who "carried capitalist ways of life to various countries and drew upon themselves the hatred of all who had to suffer under capitalism" (175). They did not choose that role: "Commerce was not their vocation but their fate" (175). They paid for the economic success they pioneered by becoming the scapegoats whenever lower classes revolted: they were the first to spread capitalism, and they are again the first to suffer its consequences.

On the social level, anti-Semitism serves to define and control rational (and especially national) idiosyncrasy. Civilization has outlawed spontaneous, free, adaptive mimesis, and has channeled it into certain behavioral patterns, so that personal expression can be effectively controlled. That which does not abide by the current mimetic rules is immediately perceived as different and alien. Surrounded by obedience and uniformity, "the Jews automatically stand out as the disturbing factor in the harmony of the national society" (185). Their attitude provokes the intolerance of idiosyncrasy which demands total conformity because it stems from a reversed and perverted mimesis.

The ideological forces inciting anti-Semitism aim at pacifying the urge of the masses for equality. The ruling clique uses the Jews as a diverting spectacle, deflecting attention from the real problems. The people who suffer discrimination may forget their own grievances by watching others suffer—an experience that provides the reassuring feeling (as well as the intimidating example) that no one is exempted from the hardships of life. The masses are happy to see the Jews sharing the common lot.

Anti-Semitism has its religious origins in Christianity. "The reflective aspect of Christianity, the intellectualization of magic, is the root of evil" (177). The attempt to overcome primitive fear reached here the heights of blasphemy, as the new religion humanized God and deified the sorcerer in one and the same person, Christ. By projecting itself as/in the man-god, rationalization went well beyond the need for self-preservation, and established the realm of the sacred as separate from that of the profane, with the result that one was rendered to Christianity, while the other to the darkest secular powers. "Worldly authority is confirmed or usurped, and the Christian faith acquires the rights on salvation" (178). These rights had to be safeguarded and defended against the predecessor of Christianity, so that the spiritual and the intellectual could be kept apart, with their respective jurisdiction over human activities intact.

Finally, the psychological persuasiveness of anti-Semitism stems from false projection and ensnares the drives of repressed mimesis. The projection is false because it is unreflective and manic, and therefore paranoiac. The paranoiac will insist on rationality and equality only to the extent that the two may justify his pursuits. This pathology is promoted and manipulated by totalitarian systems, which know how to take good care of consciousness by strictly prescribing responsibilities. When such systems point to the Jews as a natural target, paranoia, as reversed mimesis and perverted desire, turns wishfully against them: the half-educated masses direct their hostility at those who appear to threaten their freedom.

The combination of these motivating forces behind anti-Semitism reveals the bankruptcy of a civilization in which mind cannot always protect itself from its own constructs, in which the liberating power can all too easily decay into authoritarianism. Furthermore, the essay continues its descent into man-made hell when the authors propose that "there are no more anti-Semites" (200). The uniformity of the age, with its stereotyped thought, has made even this form of barbarism redundant. Paranoia has taken over contemporary culture, and nobody is exempt from its paralyzing influence. "The Jewish masses themselves are as prone to ticket thinking as the hostile youth organizations" (207). The omnipresence of tyrannical reason has precipitated the extinction of reflexivity. "In late industrial society, there is a regression to illogical judgment" (201). The individual pursues his self-serving interests while committees take responsibility for decisions and tasks affecting society. It is as if today, everybody, including the Jews, has become anti-Semitic. In these lean years, anti-Semitism is no longer directed solely against the Jews, who seem themselves assimilated into the structures of power, but rather against humanity as a whole: "The ticket mentality as such is as anti-Semitic as the anti-Semitic ticket" (207). In their condemnatory Zeitdiagnose, modeled (Habermas 1982) on Nietzsche's On the Genealogy of Morals: A Polemic (1887), Horkheimer and Adorno universalize anti-Semitism as a sickness which, even when not devouring the Jews, exemplifies the ultimate corruption of Enlightenment. At its most flamboyant, arrogant, and despotic, Enlightenment is anti-Semitism, because it turns against itself and strives for domination, eventually destroying the project of emancipation and imposing a slavery of higher order.

Thus the authors see Enlightenment as the movement of emancipation which in their time stands trapped in its false logic and condemned for the barbarity of anti-Semitism, since it failed to achieve authentic liberation and instead created its own enslaving myths. The reasons for this failure should be sought in its mythic origins, from which it was never completely disentangled. The original delusion was the arrogant belief that such a disentanglement was truly feasible, a belief which deceptively opposed its utopia of self-crowned reason to the world of myths: by totally opposing that world, it forced itself to the other extreme, creating its own myth and blind faith. The ambition to dispose of mythology simply by a determined act of comprehensive self-conscious rejection was founded on illusions of autonomous reason. Mythology, however, can be overcome (rather than abandoned) only through acts of revision and transformation. In an age of utter despondency, the last human hope may still lie here. As they wrote in the "Preface to the New Edition" (1969): "Today critical thought (which does not abandon its commitment even in the face of progress) demands support for the residues of freedom, and for tendencies toward true humanism, even if these seem powerless in regard to the main course of history" (ix–x). This is the penitent sagacity that Adorno (1974) later called "melancholy science"—the ascetic practice of dialectical humanism in the face of despair.[10] Against Nietzsche's "gay" or "joyful" science, the authors counterpropose the sad wisdom of a noble perseverance reckoning and surviving the futility of praxis. "Our conception of history does not presume any dispensation from it; nor does it imply a positivistic search for information. It is a critique of philosophy, and therefore refuses to abandon philosophy" (Horkheimer and Adorno 1972: x).

The position outlined by Horkheimer and Adorno is essentially the project of faith in a godless world, of piety in the age of desacralized ritual. They do not propose it explicitly and they do not offer it in a positive manner. To preserve the resistance of their para-logical dialectic against positivist epistemology, they apply the tactics of negative understanding not by directly affirming a value or principle but rather by working their indirect way to truth through a critique of presence, fullness, and givenness. As they put it: "The task of cognition does not consist in mere apprehension, classification, and calculation, but in the determinate negation of each immediacy" (27). Thus they do not pose, describe, substantiate, elucidate their own program; they oppose it to the dominant one of mythology, which wrecked the prospect of Enlightenment, and let it be read in the interstices of their critique. They only allow some of its qualities to shine through undefined, and yet they leave no doubt about its character: the driving force of their program is the same power which is taken to represent self-conscious, non-totalizing reason—the enduring spirit of Judaism. At the same time, by refusing to name it, they seem to conform to the negation[11] they attribute to it: "In Jewish religion, in which the idea of the patriarchate culminates in the destruction of myth, the bond between name and being is still recognized in the ban on pronouncing the name of God. The disenchanted world of Judaism conciliates magic by negating it in the idea of God" (23).

The name of the hope, the program of the true faith, are not mentioned so that they can be protected from the erasure of dialectical critique. Horkheimer pointed out in an interview that he and Adorno "no longer spoke about God but about the 'longing for the Other'" (Horkheimer 1970: 81). Admitting that this was part of Jewish inheritance, he continued: "In the same way, this utter caution [in the use of God's name] has entered our social theory which we called Critical Theory. . . . The pious Jew attempts to avoid whenever possible the word 'God'; he does not write it but uses an apostrophe. So Critical Theory calls cautiously the Absolute 'the Other.' What moves me is the theological idea applied to a rational theory of society" (81).[12] The idea is part of Hegel's view of God: "He is not One as against an Other already existing, but is himself the Other in the form of determinateness, which, however, because He is only One, exists outside of Him as His negative movement" (Hegel 1895, vol. II: 176). Critical Theory brings this idea into the social domain so that theology may offer a dialectical critique of modernity from the standpoint of Judaism. In Horkheimer's mind, "and perhaps in that of certain of his collaborators, the Jews became the metaphoric equivalent of that remnant of society preserving negation and the non-identical. Indeed, Horkheimer came to argue that underlying the Frankfurt School's refusal to describe the utopian alternative to the present society was the traditional Jewish taboo on naming God or picturing paradise" (Jay 1980: 148). As a result of this homology between God and Jew, "at least in Horkheimer's case, the Critical Theorist was understood as 'the Jew' of the administered society. And conversely, anti-Semitism became a model of the totalistic liquidation of non-identity in the one-dimensional world" (149).

If Horkheimer and Adorno are explicit and thorough in their analysis of mythology as the evil part of the dialectic, their reluctance to define the positive pole is consistent with their theological policy.[13] However, their extensive descriptions of mythology, and especially their depiction of anti-Semitism as not just its cancerous excess, but ultimately its very essence, indicate that the thesis of the outlined antithesis, the element undermined and negated by the abuse of reason, is the Jewish spirit, Judaism itself. This impression is supported by a special dimension of the authors' careful argumentation. Throughout the essay on anti-Semitism, and while presenting the absolutist trends conspiring in it, Horkheimer and Adorno also provide sporadic hints about the Jewish people—who they are, what they believe in, how they developed a tradition. In scattered notes toward an anthropological ontology, despite their admission that "race is not a naturally special characteristic" (Horkheimer and Adorno 1972: 169), the authors endow the Jews with a number of distinct racial (although not exactly native) features. This indirect portrait, sketched between the lines interrogating anti-Semitism, should be taken as the starting point for an inquiry into Judaism as the positive dialectical element in Enlightenment.[14] Indeed, it is against some "essence" of Semitism that the failure of reason and its aftermath are measured.

According to this elliptical portrait, the Jews have a "patriarchal religion" (175), the total faith in one God. "The oldest surviving patriarchate, the incarnation of monotheism, they transformed taboos into civilizing maxims when others still clung to magic . . . : they defused magic by its own power—turned against itself as ritual service of God. They did not eliminate adaptation to nature, but converted it into a series of duties in the form of ritual" (186). In their faith, religion and ritual were closely allied to facilitate mimetic adaptation. Like the great Asian faiths, "Judaism was hardly distinguishable from national life and the general drive toward self-preservation" (178). It rationalized the pagan sacrifice on the basis of the organization of the labor process, and in response to fundamental personal and social needs. "Among the primitive peoples, the attempt to overcome immediate fear led to the organized ritual and became the sanctified rhythm of family and national life in Judaism" (178). Thus a moral code was formed, in which reflexivity did not impose its rules on experience but rather rationality emerged out of the social rules. Religion and society molded and produced one another. "The god of Judaism demands his due and calls to reckoning those who do not give it. He entangles his creatures in the net of guilt and merit" (177). In this way, religion prevailed naturally as a social mechanism of order and control.[15]

In their religion, the Jews "proclaimed individualism, abstract justice, and the notion of the person" (175). On these principles they built their lasting national unity, with great respect for both the organic coherence of the community and the individuality of each member. "Reconciliation is the highest notion of Judaism, and expectation is its whole meaning" (199). The outcome of this communal consensus and effort was a tolerant society which nurtured the hope of a better world. Its members were independent, dynamic, innovative. "The Jews were the colonizers for progress" who looked at the future and "always wanted to be first" (175). Their individuality and cultural independence have been attracting hostile attention to their different tradition. "The existence and way of life of the Jews throw into question the generality with which they do not conform. The inflexible adherence to their own order of life has brought the Jews into an uncertain relationship with the dominant order" (169). By insisting on self-determination, they have challenged the conventional wisdom of various regimes of power and at the same time have drawn themselves into a confrontation of incompatible definitions. For a long time, in the face of crawling insecurity, they championed social change and political adaptation without too much compromise. "From the time when, in their capacity as merchants, they helped to spread Roman civilization throughout Gentile Europe, they were the representatives—in harmony with their patriarchal religion—of municipal, bourgeois and, finally, industrial conditions" (175). In recent times, however, they are paying dearly for their services to civilization: "They are now experiencing to their own cost the exclusive, particularist character of capitalism," they are punished for their pioneering contributions and are "degraded to the condition of a species" (175).[16]

With the vicissitudes of Jewish history representing the self-criticism of reason, the apparent complexity of the dialectic is reduced to a good vs. evil polarity: the conflict between Jewish spirit and Greek intelligence. Like Auerbach, Horkheimer and Adorno feel that the Homeric, pagan element is about to take over. Judaism is depicted as the creative and liberating force of Enlightenment which is threatened with extinction by contemporary barbarity but was first and foremost attacked by the mythic rationality represented in the Homeric epic. According to this schematic explanation, the fallacy of the Enlightenment was inaugurated by Odyssean cunning and destroyed by anti-Semitic paranoia: these are the two landmarks that have tainted Western intellectual inheritance. All this amounts to a rather tidy distribution which takes the form of various dichotomies. Anti-Semitism is the absolute evil in both a narrow and a broad sense—both because it discriminates against the Jews, and above all because it annihilates the Jewish spirit of criticism. In the *Dialectic* (as in the entire Western tradition of interpretation and assimilation), "the Jew, with his pre-Christian rites and physiognomy, represents the ultimate incarnation of Otherness at the heart of European modernity" (Wolin 1990: 37). The Jewish spirit is the inspirational, reflective, conscious force in Enlightenment; but when Enlightenment turns against itself and becomes blind, suicidal, and paranoid, it is transformed into the monster of anti-Semitism; and when it destroys its possibility, it abrogates its Jewish identity.

In this picture, the Hellenic is portrayed as vicious and sterile, while the Hebraic is benevolent and creative. This absolute distinction makes the Hellenic not only evil but also anti-Semitic. In the argumentation of Horkheimer and Adorno, the Greek spirit is accused of plotting world domination and conspiring against the Enlightenment. The Satanism affecting the positions of Auerbach and Lukács develops here into a vehement condemnation of those who revolted against the will of God. There is a major difference in strategy, though, between their work and that of the other theorists with regard to historical demarcations: Lukács saw two distinct periods, those of the integrated and the problematical civilizations; Auerbach (and Bakhtin too) distinguished two different modes of understanding and writing which coexist in continuous competition. Horkheimer and Adorno introduce an absolutization, insisting that all thought, in its dominant forms, has been Greek, and presenting its Jewish counterpart as its unrealized, repressed difference. To show the continuous, exterminating impact of mythology, they intersperse their analysis with massive generalizations which, in their all-encompassing claims, one is forced to call mythical: "From Homer to modern times" (Horkheimer and Adorno 1972: 31) or "from the transition to Olympian religion up to the Renaissance, Reformation, and bourgeois atheism" (31). There are also references to "rulers from the cunning Odysseus to the naive managing directors of today" (36) and to passages where "the hero of the adventures shows himself to be a prototype of the bourgeois individual" (43). There is no paucity of aphorisms either: "Unity is the slogan from Parmenides to Russell" (8). "Since Odysseus' successful-unsuccessful encounter with the Sirens all songs have been affected, and Western music as a whole suffers from the contradiction of song in civilization" (60).

The authors go even further when they blame modern totalitarianism and its most hideous offspring, anti-Semitism, directly on Greek reason. It all started, they argue, with its separation of magic from ritual, sign from thing, man from nature: "The irrationalism of totalitarian capitalism . . . has its prototype in the hero who escapes from sacrifice by sacrificing himself" (55).[17] And it all culminated in the Nazi administration of terror: "The phony Fascist mythology is shown to be the genuine myth of antiquity, insofar as the genuine one saw retribution, whereas the false one blindly doles it out to the sacrifices" (13). This last pronouncement completes the picture: the only difference between the Greek and the Fascist mythology is that the first is genuine while the second is phony; but they both belong to the same category, the same cultural system, and the one is the unavoidably disastrous conclusion of the other. The verdict is unambiguous: the Greeks were the proto-Fascists—a position consonant with Popper's critique of Plato's historicism in his contemporary work *The Open Society and its Enemies* (1945). Under different guises, they reiterated this idea elsewhere. For example, they assert: "The bourgeois . . . is already virtually a Nazi" (155). This is obviously as much a comment on Odysseus as it is on the capitalist, the first member of whose class was the Greek king, according to Horkheimer and Adorno. The authors believe that the bourgeois spirit was historically present before its class terms. "Adorno pushes capitalism back to include the epic world of ancient Greece. He locates the roots of bourgeois individualism as far back as the Greeks' ideological assumption that man has subjugated nature" (Donougho 1981: 28). Another statement asserts: "Polyphemous and the other monsters whom Odysseus tricks are already models of the evolving line of stupid devils of the Christian era up to Shylock and Mephistopheles" (Horkheimer and Adorno 1972: 67). Here the implication by indirect equation is this: what Odysseus did to Polyphemus, Christians (including Fascists) tried to inflict upon Shylock, the Jewish representative of the circulation sector.

At first glance, bold conclusions like these look surprising, since Horkheimer and Adorno profess a strong historical sensitivity and aversion to generalization and simplification—from authors who claim early on to maintain "a theory which holds that the core of truth is historical, rather than an unchanging constant to be set against the movement of history" (ix). But they are far from rare. In fact, statements of a reductionist generality and indiscriminate inclusiveness abound in the book: "For centuries society has been preparing for Victor Mature and Mickey Rooney" (156). It might be more accurate to say that decades of aestheticism have been preparing for quietist philosophy of this kind.[18] Drawing on the anti-heroic novel *Naissance de l'Odyssée* (1925) by Jean Giono (1895–1970), Horkheimer and Adorno have no patience or tolerance for the vicissitudes of history: in their hands, it turns into a homogeneous pattern of contrapuntal processes. Their advocacy of dialectic is falsified by their totalizing understanding of historical development. "As far back as we can trace it, the history of thought has been a dialectic of enlightenment," Adorno (1973: 118) would later declare. Wherever they look, all they discern is the cancellation or abortion of Enlightenment by its Greek origins—an endless series of failures, a structural inability for progress. Their survey of thought is basically ahistorical and, according to their own criteria, totalitarian, since they quantify it by reducing it to one dichotomy (namely, Hebraism vs. Hellenism), objectify it by distancing it into an abstraction, and naturalize it by attributing its course to an inescapable necessity. The survey also adopts cunning, a distinct feature of the Jewish stereotype since the nineteenth century, for its portrait of Odysseus *polumetis*.[19] Furthermore, the negative thinking of the book is marred by a fundamental inconsistency: although Judaism is credited with the self-criticism of reason, it is mythology that is presented as the constitutive element of the myth-reason dialectic. Thus, if "dialectics aims at what is different" (Adorno 1973b: 153), Judaism cannot represent otherness. It is the positivity which depends parasitically on what can only be conceived negatively, namely, mythology. One has to conclude that either the understanding of the Greek in Horkheimer and Adorno is Hebraic (as it is in Auerbach) or that philosophy has no other language than Greek (as Levinas always complains).

The explanatory Hebraism-Hellenism opposition is the myth of the *Dialectic*. Lukács depicted Greek civilization as the edenic stage of primordial innocence and bliss, and modern culture as the fall into philosophy (and

theory).[20] In revising his archaeology of original sin, Horkheimer and
Adorno insist that the Greeks are responsible for the fall into knowledge,
and consequently for evil. The history of thought, they argue, is one of
conflict between reason and myth (as initiated by the epic)—or one of the
knowledge of evil. The crucial issue for them is the "fallen nature of modern man" (Horkheimer and Adorno 1972: xiv); and they trace the aftermath of the fall through stark landscapes of darkness, corruption, desola-
tion, sickness, loneliness, and horror—the whole romantic imagery of the
sublime which fills their pages. They see the epic as the first document of
the fall. Here the fall follows man's aspiration to abandon the home of
nature, the Garden of Eden, and embark on unknown adventures on his
way to Troy and in search of an independent self. After many years, he will
conquer the foreign land and return home. But this new Ithaca is no Paradise; now, as a subject, he will introduce numbers, abstraction, labor, capitalism, domination, and exploitation, and become a tyrant. The original sin
of the Greek hero is his venture beyond the world of animistic faith, sacrificial ritual, and mythic thought, and the use of his cunning intelligence to
create a culture of instrumental and self-sufficient reason.[21]

The philosophical project of Horkheimer and Adorno is a theological
history of (Western) thought. While they apologize for its fragmentariness
(xi, xiii), the whole book betrays signs of well-balanced planning: it opens
with an essay on Enlightenment and reason, and it closes with one on mythology and barbarism; in between come three parts on the impact of Enlightenment on knowledge/science, morality, and art; the whole is framed
by an "Introduction" and a sketchy epilogue. Despite modernist appearances of discontinuity, a rational symmetry prevails. The book chronicles in
highly evocative tones the fall of human intellect from the grace of nature
and God, and explores the possibility of overcoming (Nietzsche's) "bad
conscience" (20, 177), the "guilt" (41) of Christian faith, and of achieving
atonement. For Horkheimer and Adorno, the project is "nothing less than
the discovery of why mankind, instead of entering into a truly human condition, is sinking into a new kind of barbarism" (xi). They extend an urgent
invitation to Enlightenment to consider critically its sins and its crimes,
and repent: "The task to be accomplished is not the conservation of the
past, but the redemption of the hopes of the past" (xv).

The authors do not believe, as Auerbach does, in a Judeo-Christian synthesis. Christianity, in its moral bankruptcy, appears sometimes to be the
immediate and visible target of the *Dialectic of Enlightenment*: "Anti-
Semitism is all that the German Christians have retained of the religion of
love" (176). Hatred and aggressiveness, however, are not attributable primarily to the heretic status of the new religion in relation to its predecessor,
but have deeper roots in its impure descent. Christianity is a regression to
myth, sacrifice, and superstition, and ultimately to Greek paganism. As

evidenced by the barbarism of modern times, it has been overpowered by Hellenism, which simply completes the ancient Enlightenment and seals the fall of man.[22] Thus the main target and the arch-enemy of the book is Greek thought and its devilish survivals: as long as these influence our civilization, man is condemned to the freedom, the knowledge, the exile, the labor, and the abyss that he originally chose. Yet, the authors have an alternative to suggest, one last dim possibility: only Judaism, the religion of expectation, may redeem the hopes of the past through reconciliation with the world (of God).[23] Their verdict on their age is entirely negative; but to the (self)destructive dialectic of the Greek Enlightenment, they counterpropose their philosophy of secular reconciliation[24]—a vision that would later be articulated by Adorno as the (melancholy) science of atonement, based on the "theory of the melancholy disposition" (Benjamin 1977: 142–58),[25] and revised indignantly by Derrida as the (festive) science of grammatology.

THE COVENANT OF EMANCIPATION

The questions raised by the *Dialectic* are: In a world infested with paganism and overtaken by barbarism, is there anything sacred left? If "modernity is pagan" (Lyotard and Thébaud 1985: 16), what is the position of the sacred at a time of spiritual regression? What happens to the divine in a secular age infatuated with its illusionary independence? These questions may have a theological function but they should not be examined on the basis of traditional secularization theories since they are not exactly theological themselves. They attempt to (pre)occupy answer positions which may (or may not) be left vacant by the bankruptcy of Protestantism in a manner comparable to the success of the Reformation in taking over medieval church authority. It is to the Reformation, therefore, that the inquiry into the legitimacy of autonomy needs again to refer. "The Middle Ages came to an end when within their spiritual system creation as 'providence' ceased to be credible to man and the burden of self-assertion was therefore laid upon him" (Blumenberg 1983: 138). A new foundation had to be sought for the rightful place of humans on earth, a certainty that did not need to be guaranteed by the doctrine of the office. The possibility of a self-sustained knowledge seemed within the mind's grasp. "The sole criterion of church doctrine for the whole ordering and forming of truth and knowledge breaks down and yields to the growing predominance of seeking founding itself. The criteria get turned around. The truth of faith and faithful knowledge are now measured in terms of the self-certainty of pure thinking with regard to its correctness. . . . But when the ecumenical office loses the sole power as the first and real source of truth, the total realm of beings as it was formed by Christianity does not disappear from view. On the contrary, the order of beings as a whole—God, the creator, the world of creatures, man, belonging to the world and destined for God—these beings as a whole thus experienced now especially *demand a new assimilation* on the foundation and with the means of knowledge founding itself" (Heidegger 1985: 31).

Without the law of providence, autonomy, with its law of immanent understanding, emerges as the legitimate quest in a world that people must learn to order and inhabit on their own. "The element of *cura* [care] in [Augustinian] *curiositas* now becomes the very root of its meaning, which legitimizes the cognitive appetite as the attentiveness that is provoked by the world. The modern age began, not indeed as the epoch of the death of God, but as the epoch of the hidden God, the *deus absconditus*—and a hidden God is *pragmatically* as good as dead" (Blumenberg 1983: 346). In Heidegger's words: "Being itself withdraws into its truth."[26] Left without providence, without pro-vision, people start engaging in the construction of their own vision: *theoria*—a comprehensive, independent, and lofty view of the world.[27] "[T]he progress of thought at the beginning of the modern age rests essentially on the fact that one began to make assertions about the absence of order and to ascribe to that absence (without the intervention of a transcendent factor) a law of self-regulation" (220). With the withdrawal of the transcendent and the disappearance of cosmic order, both of which culminated in the Nominalist critique of Scholasticism (Luft 1988: 743), the historical position of the divine creative power, no longer adequately occupied by theological explanation, was functionally reoccupied by the secular idea of autonomy.[28] Thus "the age transformed epistemology into anthropology and made truth a function of creative activity" (Luft 1987: 10).[29] In counterdistinction to the thesis (supported by Karl Löwith and Carl Schmitt) which, stressing continuity, believes in the transposition of theological concerns into secular principles, the reoccupation thesis emphasizes that "the modern age does not have recourse to what went before it, so much as it opposes and takes a stand against the challenge constituted by what went before it. This distinction . . . makes worldliness the characteristic feature of the modern age without its having to be the result of secularizations" (Blumenberg 1983: 75). Thus the priesthood of all believers becomes a community of interpreters.

Here it is important to draw a distinction between two directions of autonomy, one that seeks a ground and another that offers a reason. According to the reoccupation thesis, "the Romantic attempt to discredit the Enlightenment, and the continuation of this attempt by Nietzsche and Heidegger, confuse a justified criticism of the Enlightenment's attempt at 'self-foundation' with an unjustified criticism of its ideal of self-assertion" (Rorty 1983: 4). This distinction also helps identify the ideological (as opposed to, say, Horkheimer and Adorno's philosophical) dialectic of Enlightenment, as well as its counter-theological origin. "The absolute certainty founded on human thought itself, which Descartes seeks, is not the 'secularization' of the certainty of salvation, which is supposed to be guaranteed in faith, and its *nuda fiducia* [naked trust], but rather its necessary counterposition, which is theologically demanded and (unexpectedly) legitimized by Luther's thesis [on antidivine self-deification]. . . . If one proceeds from the assumption that human autonomy can henceforth articulate its positive character only outside the Middle Ages, then it becomes clear that only two fundamental positions remain open to it, if it wants to throw off its supposedly 'natural' role: hypothetical atheism, which poses the question of man's potential under the condition that the answer should hold 'even if there is no God'; and rational deism, which employs the 'most perfect being' to guarantee this human potential—the 'most perfect being' that is functionalized by Descartes as the principle of the deduction of the dependability of the world and of our knowledge of it. The double face of the Enlightenment, on the one hand its renewal of a theological optimism and on the other its inclination to atheism, loses its contradictory character if one places it in the context of the unity of the onset of human self-assertion and the rejection of its late-medieval systematic role" (Blumenberg 1983: 179). It is in hypothetical atheism that Horkheimer and Adorno see the pagan evil, the idolatry of mythology, and it is in a critical (and obviously post-rational) deism that they invest their hopes for an assertion without the self, for a covenant without nomos—namely, for a secular (and therefore rationally impossible) faith; or (what with Modernism amounts to the same), for a Hebraic culture.[30]

The specific moment of rupture—which Hebraic Modernism and Postmodernism from Lukács to Derrida are attempting to repeat through reversal—is the reoccupation of faith as an answer position by taste after the Battle of the Books. The moment of the positive quality of taste signals the emergence of a reading public in England and France.[31] This independent community of interpreters read in a secular manner: they no longer believed but they discriminated. The civil liberation of interpretation, however, did not mean the loss of its theological heritage, which was now refunctioned differently. This explains why "the vantage point, the defining concept, and the distinctive vocabulary of art-as-such" did not first appear in eighteenth-century art theory—"indeed they were very old and familiar commonplaces; they had functioned, however, not in the traditional philosophy and criticism of the arts, but in alien realms of metaphysics, and especially theology. These ancient commonplaces were imported into, and specialized for, the theory of fine art—they achieved, that is, a radical novelty of application—only when the new social role of the various arts invited and fostered concepts of a requisite sort" (Abrams 1989: 153).

A typical example is the writings collected in the *Characteristicks of Men, Manners, Opinions, Times* (1711, 3 vols.) by the third Earl of Shaftesbury (1671–1713), "the chief bridge by which the theological term 'contemplation,' together with the ethical-religious term 'disinterested,' crossed over into philosophical analysis of the way we apprehend beautiful objects, including works of fine art" (91). Shaftesbury's main concern is the style of life appropriate to a gentleman, especially the requisite training of sensibility. Although the question is a moral one, the writer, who believes that the connoisseur should become a virtuoso of manners, "transforms Neo-Platonic religious ideas into a secularized religion of aesthetics. The universe for him is a continually changing work of art whose Creator is manifest in formal beauty. Thus human knowledge of moral truth (virtue) must be mediated by aesthetics and transformed by the moral artist, a young male who has been educated in a non-institutionalized manner and who has been divinely inspired during states of enthusiastic contemplation. . . . In this manner the moral artist transforms his own life into a work of art and becomes a 'virtuoso'" (Cocalis 1978: 401). For Puritanism, the "religion of virtuosos" (Weber 1958b: 332), virtue was always a matter of virtuosity.[32] Now virtuosity changes into a question of public performance, rather than personal askesis. The mark of the new virtuosity is taste, which becomes "the basis of all that one has—people and things—and all that one is for others, whereby one classifies oneself and is classified by others" (Bourdieu 1984: 56).

Shaftesbury redefines virtue when he introduces the idea of disinterestedness. In his polemic against the Hobbesian account of self-concern in the dialogue "The Moralists: A Philosophical Rhapsody" (1709), he speaks of "the disinterested love of God," an absolute love that stands above all personal interest and is completely unselfish. Hobbes' "exemplary situation" (Nauta 1985: 368), from which he derived the features of the individual, was the capitalist market. The concept of "interest" was particularly important in debates on ethics, and initially signified a positive quality. "For Shaftesbury, as for his contemporaries, it designates the state of well-being or the genuine and long-range good" (Stolnitz 1961–62: 132). He starts rejecting it when he criticizes selfishness: "The opposite of 'interestedness' begins to appear in Shaftesbury's polemic against egoism in ethics and instrumentalism in religion" (132). In this context, disinterestedness means lack of selfishness: the proper moral attitude inclined toward the "contemplation" of virtue. Here in the realm of religion, we have the first appearance of the aesthetic attitude as a distinct mode of experience: a disinterested view (that is, contemplation) of God above self-regard and consequences. This is the new form of faith, faith for its own sake. Shaftesbury's concern is simultaneously with morals and manners, action and character. The regard of God, no longer anticipatory, is "a mode of attention and concern" (133). The person of modernity, the virtuoso of the gaze, the theorist, emerges in Shaftesbury's description of "the virtuous man as a spectator, devoted to 'the very survey and contemplation' of beauty in manners and morals" (133). The ideal of the "spectator" (the title of Addison's periodical in the 1710s) is pure regard, since "disregard for possession or use is only an inference or a specification of the broader proposition that the aesthetic spectator does not relate the object to any purposes that outrun the act of perception itself" (134). Disinterestedness becomes the distinctive feature of the aesthetic experience when the experience is treated in its own right.[33] During early eighteenth-century English iconoclasm, which broke "idolatrous" art and remade it through the new creative procedure of aesthetics (Paulson 1990), Addison took the next step of making aesthetic perception the foundation of aesthetics, and disinterestedness the requirement for good taste—making aesthetic perception a way of looking not only at moral responsibilities but at the entire world; not only a way of believing but also of being. "Thus, the aesthetic disposition is one dimension of a distant, self-assured relation to the world and to others which presupposes objective assurance and distance. It is one manifestation of the system of dispositions produced by the social conditioning associated with a particular class of conditions of existence when they take the paradoxical form of the greatest freedom conceivable, at a given moment, with respect to the constraints of economic necessity" (Bourdieu 1984: 56). It is the emancipation from interest and the renunciation of use that makes the gaze contemplative and freedom aesthetic.

During the century of Samuel Johnson (1709–84), when a reading public appears in England, "it is the reader of poetry who firmly occupies the centre of interest between the death of Dryden [1700] and the publication of the 1800 preface to the Lyrical Ballads. The Man of Taste is king: the consumer, at last, has won his right of choice. In theoretical criticism—and the eighteenth century is overwhelmingly the age of critical theory—the issue is now joined not on conformity to precept . . . but on the reader's response. . . . How is true taste to be defined? And if a democracy of taste, a mere counting of heads, is not sufficient, what does constitute true taste in reading? These are issues which Dryden never once raises; and Pope raises them for professional critics only. Addison, in the Spectator essays [1711–12], raises them for all polite society" (Watson 1962: 68).

What matters in the democracy of taste is not the position of the maker but of the perceiver; not the process of making but the finished product; not the craft of the execution but the perfection of the result; not the construction of the work but its contemplation. In the claims of polite society to cultural superiority we witness "the tendency of a contemplation theory of art to recuperate aspects of its original context in religious devotion" (Abrams 1989: 156). This functional reoccupation endows the new class with the right of an interpretive approach to the whole world as it makes understanding a question of self-fulfilling learning (taking the required time and aptitude for granted[34]). "The new critical language, accordingly, does not envision a product of art from the traditional point of view of its expert constructor or maker, but from the point of view of the connoisseur, who confronts the work as a completed product which he attends to as an isolated thing, for the sake of the satisfactions that doing so yields" (151). The reoccupation of faith by taste coincides with the bourgeoisie's appropriation of taste from the court through consumption: taste is consumption distinguished by discrimination. Within court culture, taste was invested in ritual—in hierarchy and order—and therefore invisible. In the public society of capitalist leisure, it became a cultural investment, one sought by everyone adept in the open market. "In the seventeenth century taste . . . was still an expression of the aristocratic life style, and to the extent that it was applied to artworks, it was the prerogative of court culture, which articulated itself in the patron's judgement. The court's claim to cultural leadership was first shaken when bourgeois critics were able to appeal to the taste of the public. This took place in England . . . and in France. . . . In these countries, the bourgeoisie's demand for equality proclaimed itself, mediated by the judgment of taste" (Berghahn 1988: 40). Just as faith turned everybody into an interpreter during the Reformation, with the Enlightenment taste transformed everyone into a noble person.

The situation in Germany was very different from England and France, where taste could serve the political claims of the bourgeoisie by galvanizing its claims of status and participation. German Enlightenment aspired to shape through criticism a homogeneous public, literary but above all civil. That never happened. "In France, what had begun with the weapons of criticism was carried to its end by the Revolution; in politically splintered Germany, where counterrevolutionary preventive measures sharpened the censorship, republican-minded forces couldn't even carry the day in the literary public sphere" (77–78). The reason is the absence from Germany of conditions that would allow for an articulate public sphere. The public did not yet exist: together with the republic of taste, it had to be formed. The universalism of citizenship "was lacking in Germany where there was not even a suitable concept to designate a 'citizen.' The term *Buerger* had altogether different connotations. It signified a *Stand* (an estate) or rather the tax-paying subject of an authoritarian state whose government would presumably protect the citizens' rights, but did not regard them as the ultimate source of its own authority. The distinction between 'citizen' and 'burgher' . . . did not exist in Germany. Likewise, the nation was not conceived in politico-moral, but in racial terms. One was a German if one belonged to the *Volk*" (Lichtheim 1968: 327). Under these premature circumstances, "in Germany social progress and national development did not mutually support and promote one another as in France, but rather stood in opposition to each other" (Lukács 1978: 9). Furthermore, the intelligentsia was able to offer little more than a philosophical definition of judgment in defense of secular understanding. The question of governance arose only in relation to the legitimacy of interpretation.

Moses Mendelssohn, for example, tried in the 1750s to orient aesthetics toward questions of reception. "For Mendelssohn the unity of the arts is grounded in the powerful effects they exert upon an audience—in the capacity they exhibit to *move* us. He believes that the central task of a general theory of the arts is to explain this fact of experience" (Woodmansee 1984: 27). With the Enlightenment, Winckelmann's neoclassical "principle of imitation" is succeeded by the "principle of pleasure." By the 1780s, however, the tremendous expansion of the book market, although welcome by the intelligentsia, had distressing effects for those who wished to influence the public sphere. In just a few decades, too many people were reading and writing, too many books and periodicals were circulating for the Enlighteners to control the flow of culture. Pleasing this audience seemed more like satisfying its appetite rather than fulfilling its intellectual needs.

The reason why there seemed to be an audience but not a public is because "German absolutism greatly retarded the formation of a middle class—and, hence, the very preconditions of an energetic world of arts and letters. The creation of these conditions was in large measure the work of a few hundred civic-minded literati—philosophers and poets from Leibniz to Lessing—who divided their time between 'their work' and a variety of projects aimed at extending literacy in the broadest sense: the establishment of theaters, the founding of reading societies and periodicals, and so on" (36). In certain respects, such as the secularization of the book market and the development of writing in the vernacular, these efforts were successful. But they did not anticipate that training might turn into entertainment, or education into a *Kulturindustrie*, with the result that "the pragmatic aesthetic worked out by the generation of Mendelssohn, in which the excellence of a work is measured by its capacity to affect an audience, was felt to be incompatible with artistic integrity" (39–40).

The taste of the audience and the interest the book market took in satisfying its demands seemed to defeat the Enlightenment project, or to put it crudely, to justify other people's writing.[35] The reaction of the intellectuals was to revile the publishers who commercialized their trade by exploiting the lower interests of the audience for their own profit. At the same time, intellectuals criticized the audience for simply wanting to be moved and entertained. The intellectuals' supreme strategy, though, was to turn their artistic standards, which had failed, into an aesthetic, into an entire attitude which did not simply have its distinct morality but was in itself a higher morality. Thus, while they seemed to reject the audience, in fact they made themselves more desirable to the part of the audience which aspired to distinction. The professional writers who could not compete in the free market created a new one whose commercial character was made invisible when they denounced interest. They argued that, instead of marketing to public taste, they were "the hierophants of an unapprehended inspiration" (Shelley) who communicated divine messages—prophets and legislators of a new, higher order. They did not promise diversion but redemption.

They achieved this in two complementary ways: first by taking over the Humanities at the University, which they elevated to the highest realm of learning, the foundation of all others; and by constructing a theology of art offering them "both a convenient and a very powerful set of concepts with which to address the predicament in which they found themselves— concepts by which (serious, or 'fine') Art's *de facto* loss of direct instrumentality could be recuperated as a (supreme) virtue" (46). By claiming that art stands above exchange and interest, redeeming all market concerns, they created an alternative market, that of the aesthetic (as opposed to the work) ethic—an autonomy grounded on the contemplation of immanence. "Art, strictly speaking, is liberal or free, its production must not enter into the economic circle of commerce, of offer and demand; it must not be exchanged" (Derrida 1981a: 5).

According to the laws of this differentiated economy, "the ideal of 'pure' perception of a work of art qua work of art is the product of the enunciation and systematization of the principles of specifically aesthetic legitimacy which accompany the constituting of a relatively autonomous artistic field. The aesthetic mode of perception in the 'pure' form which it has now assumed corresponds to a particular state of the mode of artistic production" (Bourdieu 1984: 30). They effected this by reoccupying Pietist faith with the aesthetic attitude, the new bourgeois piety.[36] "The relationship between a religious ethic and art will remain harmonious as far as art is concerned for so long as the creative artist experiences his work as resulting either from a charisma of 'ability' (originally magic) or from spontaneous play. The development of intellectualism and the rationalization of life change this situation. For under these conditions, art becomes a cosmos of more and more consciously grasped independent values which exist in their own right. Art takes over the function of this-worldly salvation, no matter how this may be interpreted. It provides a *salvation* from the routines of everyday life, and especially from the increasing pressures of theoretical and practical rationalism. With this claim to a redemptory function, art begins to compete directly with salvation religion. . . . As a matter of fact, the refusal of modern man to assume responsibility for moral judgments tends to transform judgments of moral intent into judgments of taste ('in poor taste' instead of 'reprehensible')" (Weber 1958b: 341–42). This is the end of the path that led from the grim asceticism of the Reformation to the emotional religiosity of the late seventeenth century to the secularized notions of sentiment in the eighteenth (Campbell 1987). With the aesthetic, the reoccupation of faith by taste, which has now developed into creative imagination, is complete. The contemplative attitude appropriate to God, Shaftesbury's "disinterested love," becomes the purest, most moral disposition. At the same time, pleasure does not disappear but is incorporated into the higher purpose. That is why the aesthetic attitude is transformed from moral askesis into a system of interpretive exercises.

The Romantic generation of the 1790s was the first to recognize the failure of the politics of taste. "The disintegration in the last quarter of the eighteenth century of the Enlightenment project to establish a bourgeois public sphere . . . reached its apex in Romanticism, where the notion of a bourgeois public sphere completely relinquished its regulatory power over the practice of politics and literature. Disturbed and sensitized by the experience of a mass literary market and repelled by the development of a new bourgeois ethos grounded in economics, the Romantics retreated more and more into an aesthetic praxis, which still claimed to be socially critical but held that a meaningful social critique could be made only from the unalienated position of what proved to be an increasingly esoteric aestheticism" (Schulte-Sasse 1988: 99). The aesthetic turn of modernity took place in Germany when the education of Lessing's "humankind" (namely, the bourgeois public) was abandoned in favor of critique, and may be precisely dated from 1787, when Kant abandoned the early title of his third critique, "Critique of Taste." Justification of judgment now took precedence over the "education of taste" (Kant). "The Romantics thought of their analysis of social totality not in terms of institutions and system theory but in categories that were essentially epistemological or concerned with a critique of the nature of knowledge" (140). Interest in effects was succeeded by inquiries into assumptions. The French Revolution and the threat of social unrest made the inward turn of emancipation even more unavoidable in the eyes of the intellectual elite which was despairing of its public influence: "Under the pressure of dominant social relations, the function of criticism also changed after 1789: it lost its bourgeois-enlightening impetus, shook itself free of all practical ties to life, and became aesthetically immanent. Thus began the 'art period'" (Berghahn 1988: 78), the period of aesthetic autonomy.

The so-called Romantic period is the age of critique, that is, of self-reflective, self-corrective, and above all self-disciplined criticism—of a criticism that relinquishes its public function and is interested only in social legitimacy, in claiming the moral higher ground by appearing disinterested.[37] "The concept of critique emerged in the West at the same time as political economy and, as the quintessence of Enlightenment rationality, is perhaps only the subtle, long-term expression of the system's expanded reproduction" (Baudrillard 1975: 50). Critique is the highest form of bourgeois self-assertion. "The bourgeoisie is the first self-critical class in history, the first class to measure itself by the standards of history" (Feenberg 1973: 42) and to discover its universal superiority precisely in its capacity for self-examination. At the same time, critique (for example, Critical Theory) functions as the system's "bad conscience": "For this reason, the culture of capitalism, to the extent that it truly existed, could consist in nothing but the ruthless critique of the capitalist epoch" (Lukács 1970: 26). Critique is, by its constitution "reformist" (Lyotard), a Reformation by other means; it is the right to interpretation systematized in the exercise of rights, theory elevated to emancipation. "Even historically speaking, theoretical emancipation has a specifically practical significance for Germany. For Germany's revolutionary past is theoretical, it is the Reformation. Once it was a monk's brain in which the revolution began, now it is in the philosopher's. Certainly Luther removed the servitude of devotion by replacing it by the servitude of conviction. He destroyed faith in authority by restoring the authority of faith. He turned priests into laymen by turning laymen into priests. He liberated man from exterior religiosity by making man's inner conscience religious. He emancipated the body from chains by enchaining the heart" (Marx 1971: 123). Critique is criticism that no longer aspires to intervene or interact, criticism that is purified of interests[38] (namely, itself aesthetic), and hence superior even to creativity.[39]

In all areas of culture critique becomes the cardinal activity, and hastens to write the epitaph of contemporary art: "We may well hope that art will always rise higher and come to perfection, but the form of art has ceased to be the supreme need of the spirit" (Hegel 1975a, vol. I: 103). According to Hegel's notorious formulation in the *Aesthetics*: "'The science of art is thus in our time much more necessary than in times in which art for itself as art provided complete satisfaction.' Aesthetic theory, therefore, emerges for Hegel at the time when aesthetic praxis is no longer vital to the articulation of truth" (Bowie 1990: 135). Everything seems to exist in order to elevate itself to (self)criticism.[40] Critique converted the regime of autonomy to the regimen of autoscopy.[41] Above all, it was the individual who was instructed to discipline herself (Petschauer 1989) through this exercise, banking on the anticipation not of a society of characters distinguished by taste but of a community of individuals cultivated through *Bildung*—expecting, that is, not a public of common sentiments and beliefs but a nation of shared attitudes and judgments. "The quest for harmony was basic to the concept of *Bildung* in a Germany touched by the industrialization of Europe, frightened by the French Revolution. The aesthetic was the keystone of that

harmony, linking the intellectual and the moral" (Mosse 1985: 6). Hölderlin, for example, hopes that it will create a community free from political
strife. "He envisages an education through beauty which will fit men for
communal harmony" (Reed 1980: 202). While abandoning his three fragmentary versions of *The Death of Empedocles* (1798–99), he talked about
the *"ästhetische Kirche"* (1799) where the highest reconciliation and unity
would reign. "The mainstay of a social renovation for Hölderlin therefore
can only be a new religion, a new church" (Lukács 1978b: 140). Thus the
(aesthetic) question of social harmony as national unity formed the central
bourgeois issue. Consequently, in Germany "a national literature could develop only as a bourgeois revolutionary literature of combat against the
culture of the petty courts which copied Versailles and impeded national
unification" (Lukács 1978a: 115).

The philosophical interest in the project of the Enlightenment which ani-
mates the *Dialectic* had been a major concern for German thought for at
least two centuries, since the time of Lessing and Mendelssohn, when modernity was left without the support of historical prefigurement. The pursuit of this project was closely associated with the seminal ideal of *Bildung*,
of personal organic growth.[42] The development of the *Bildung* ideal found
fertile ground in the discourse on pedagogy created by the congruence of
printing and Lutheranism in north German states (Luke 1989). Writers
like Winckelmann, Herder, Humboldt, and Schiller, for example, explored
the educational potential of art, science, philosophy, and literature for the
cultivation of an individual's unique character. Horkheimer and Adorno,
however, show no interest in this ideal: they seem to believe that in their
time *Bildung* has been denigrated to bourgeois individualism. In their portrait of Odysseus, what is left of *Bildung* is only self-serving, cynical cunning; their *Odyssey* is the epic of egoistic expansion, not personal development. Its model is *The Worker* (1932) by the conservative anarchist Ernst
Jünger, with its portrait of the self-disciplined working man. Humanist
education has collapsed; private interest and corrupt taste have tainted the
nobility of *Bildung* and have undermined the possibility of a public consensus on the liberating power of Enlightenment.

Bildung was from its inception a hegemonic[43] ideal that sought supervision through the practices of self-cultivation and education. It was an
administrative project that set out to codify bourgeois principles of development and power. While the revolutions of the late eighteenth century
were dealing the final blow to the aristocratic order, it proposed the quest
for inner harmony as an alternative solution to social problems. "*Bildung*
was created by philosophers and belletrists who aestheticized religious and
philosophical notions under the aegis of the Hellenic revival. It emerged
with the neo-humanism in the 1790s and became Protestant Germany's

secular social ideal. *Bildung* corresponded to the needs and experiences of those segments of the bourgeoisie and enlightened aristocracy that had superseded the estate structure, providing an alternative social ideal to the otherworldly Christian, on the one side, and the courtly *galant-homme*, on the other. The *gebildeter Mensch* was held to have achieved individual perfection through self-cultivation and refinement that was tantamount to virtue if not salvation itself" (Sorkin 1983: 66). *Bildung* therefore represented a promise that the new culture would respect each and every person, and would help her develop a well-rounded, balanced character. The promise was democratic and the invitation open: anybody could claim individuality and attain her own character. There would be no discrimination against the self.

The goal of this pedagogical enterprise was modelled on the basic principle of the recent philosophy of beauty, the aesthetic and its integrated autonomy. Like that autonomy, the envisioned character was unique, beautiful, coherent, harmonious, and independent. *Bildung* was basically an aesthetic education—the training in private conduct through the askesis in the disciplines and pleasures of the aesthetic disposition. In an era of religious skepticism, it provided the middle class with the equivalent of a secular faith, where the intellectual (true), the moral (good), and the aesthetic (beautiful) were separated and combined as the main spheres of human experience. When the feudal hierarchy and court ritual lost their authority, these spheres found their profane articulation in a set of interpretive and artistic practices applied to the (bourgeois) self and known by the collective name *Bildung*. This driving principle of the faith in (wo)man as disinterested interpreter (of the Bible as novel) and artist (that is, as aesthetic self) served the middle class for numerous purposes: to establish a common bond and tradition among its members; to counter the privileges of the aristocracy with an egalitarian ideal; to take the power of training away from the guilds and the artisans in general; and to inspire a sense of inner balance and higher purpose during the socio-political upheavals of the time by promoting respect for, and contemplation of the self as a deeper reality.[44] The artists of *Bildung*, all volunteers and virtuosos of subjectivity, taught the philosophers of the Enlightenment and their victorious class that the mastery of the world first requires a new form of governance—voluntary control over one's self.

The chapter on the *Odyssey* in the *Dialectic* follows the conventions of the *Bildungsgeschichte* but deplores its standard conclusion, suggesting that the fall into knowledge and division was an unfortunate one since it could never recover integration and unity: the inescapable fate of self-realization is alienation (Rotenstreich 1989; Schacht 1970). The origins of *Bildungsgeschichte* as a literary genre may be traced to the Christian practice of confession and the allegory of the journey of life. The romantic plot of the circuitous journey in quest of an earthly consummation is a "secular version of the fortunate fall" (Abrams 1971: 208) "from self-unity and community into division, and from contentment into the longing for redemption, which consists of a recovered unity if a higher level of self-awareness" (246). It tells the story of an educational journey of self-formation from alienation (division and exile) to reintegration (new self-unity). "Most Romantic versions of the educational journey . . . incorporate a displaced theodicy, in which error and suffering are justified as indispensable to the self-formation and self-realization of the mature individual, in a span of reference coterminous with his life in this world" (244). Life in modernity is no longer a pilgrimage or an exploration of new lands: it becomes a personal adventure (Loriggio 1988; Nerlich 1987). Thus the *Bildungsgeschichte*, as a theodicy of private life, "translates the painful process of Christian conversion and redemption into a painful process of self-formation, crisis, and self-recognition, which culminates in a stage of self-coherence, self-awareness, and assured power that is its own reward" (Abrams 1971: 96). The world is neither discovered nor denounced: it is simply affirmed as the stage of individual drama. The chronicle of the education of the human race is replaced by the narrative of the cultivation of character.

The journey of the fallen/prodigal individual is best represented by the fate of the post-Revolution intellectual/artist. The thinker as bard and prophet is the most concentrated expression and experience of the self—of the autonomous individual who is now encouraged to seek in this world redemption as a progressive self-fashioning, as the artistic fashioning of a self (Kelly 1987; Nehamas 1985). "In this process the redemptive goal of the history of mankind was shifted from the reconciliation and reunion of man with a transcendent God to an overcoming of the opposition between ego and non-ego, or a reconciliation of subject with object, or a reunion of the spirit with its own other, and this culmination was represented as occurring in the fully developed consciousness of men living their lives in this world: the justification of the ordeal of human experience is located in experience itself. Accordingly, the history of mankind, as well as the history of the reflective individual, was conceived not as a probation for an otherworldly heaven but as a process of the self-formation, or self-education, of the mind and moral being of man from the dawn of consciousness to the stage of full maturity. . . . The course of human life (in the economy of statement made possible by German compounds) is no longer a *Heilsgeschichte* but a *Bildungsgeschichte*; or more precisely, it is a *Heilsgeschichte* translated into the secular mode of a *Bildungsgeschichte*" (Abrams 1971: 187–88). For the haunted wanderer[45] of modernity (the Wandering Greek of the *Dialectic* or the Wandering Jew of *Ulysses*), the sacred and the historical (Gnuse 1989) are reconciled in the narrative of aesthetic self(re)cognition.

Quite often, what makes the journey circuitous is its goal: the return to an ancestral home. Redemption becomes repetition: an origin, a beginning, a homeland, an identity are repeated (but this time authentically reconstituted) at the end of a quest: "Idealism in any form must transcend itself in one way or another, in order to be able to return to itself and remain what it is" (Schlegel 1968: 83). According to this narrative (which one is tempted to call libretto), the script of history is not the scripture of human progress but the epic of individual revelation—"a book of epiphanies" (Joyce). In *Bildung*, the (public) process of enlightenment turns into the (private) experience of illumination. At this point, the neo-classical interest in the *Iliad* gives its place to the romantic fascination with the *Odyssey*, as the disciplines of Man turn attention away from social questions of conduct to the aesthetic pursuit of attitude. Odysseus *polutropos* is perceived as the hero of an attitude that shapes the world according to its own disposition. This change in interest is more than a difference of taste between Pope and Wordsworth: it signals the different experience of alienation after 1789. Thus, when Auerbach or Horkheimer and Adorno criticize the cunning of Odysseus, they enter a discussion that goes back to Hegel and Schelling (as well as Hamann's epiphany in London[46]) as they are attempting to debunk the greatest mythical figure of high modernity.

Although ideas about the education of the individual were an integral part of the Enlightenment, with its emphasis on the capabilities of informed reason, they lost their social dimension as their political relevance seemed to dwindle. Despite pedagogical egalitarianism, the unruly crowds in the streets of the metropolitan city made the ideal of the education of the human race look less and less feasible. After the watershed of the French Revolution, the program of *Bildung* emerged as Enlightenment without politics: centered on the autonomous individual and her organic development, it was a private task practiced for its own sake and taking the form of an "aesthetic education" and a "biographia literaria." Repudiating the "present-day prosaic conditions" (Hegel), it ceased to be civic and became poetic.

From Shaftesbury to Schiller, interest in "the formative development of an adolescent nobleman or bourgeois into an artist or virtuoso" (Cocalis 1978: 407) was paramount as the need arose to train the bourgeoisie not in personal self-control (as the faith of Reformation did) but in character conduct—in private ethics and public manners. Rational conduct on the basis of the idea of the calling, a fundamental element of modern culture, was born from the spirit of Calvinist asceticism. "The God of Calvinism demanded of his believers not single good works, but a life of good works combined into a unified system. . . . The moral conduct of the average man was thus deprived of its planless and unsystematic character and subjected to a consistent method for conduct as a whole" (Weber 1976: 117). The idea of calling dictated a thorough rationalization of behavior for the sake of the world beyond. "The alert self-control of the Puritan flowed from the necessity of his subjugating all creaturely impulses to a rational and methodical plan of conduct, so that he might secure his certainty of his own salvation" (Weber 1963: 255). Adopting this lifestyle, "the Puritan literally works out his interiorized religious disposition" (Whimster 1987: 263). Since calling turned into an enormously profitable enterprise in the seventeenth century—in other words, as works paid too well—the socio-economic success of rationalization undermined the systems of askesis and brought about the practices of self-control.

Now it was again time to develop a new technology of the self, one adequate to the emerging realm of interiority. The transformation of taste into a practice of the inner self, into self-cultivation, began with Winckelmann and Wieland, who introduced "*Bildung* into German intellectual life. Both men equated *Bildung* with the Greek ideal of *kalokagathia*, i.e., with being beautifully formed, well-educated, and morally good. But whereas Winckelmann conceived of *Bildung* as an ideal state of being, such as that immortalized in classical art, Wieland interpreted it as a formative process" (Cocalis 1978: 402). While the question of taste concerned the acquisition of a characteristic, the goal of *Bildung* was the formation of a character. In both cases, the importance of cultivation was central. "In contrast to Shaftesbury, however, who was writing from an aristocratic standpoint about the education of young gentlemen, the Germans extended the scope of *Bildung* to include the middle class" (403). Less than a matter of style and status, *Bildung* was also a quest for legitimacy and distinction. Its pursuit became a vehicle for orderly social reform, an investment in the promise of self-discipline to eschew protest and unrest. Social status should be determined by intellectual achievement rather than blood. In his theory of culture, Herder "sets that ideal in explicit opposition to the political status quo, positing it as a peaceful alternative to revolution" (404–5). When Herder calls: "Awake, German nation!" he advocates "purely cultural self-determination" (Berlin 1976: 182) from an anti-political position. Subscribing to this social ideal, the intelligentsia dedicated itself to the mission of criticism, hoping to contribute to the creation and preservation of a public realm that would make exchange and negotiation possible and peaceful.

This move was particularly visible in the area of writing. "The literature of the Enlightenment supplied the bourgeoisie with meaningful entertainment and moral orientation in the world, and it was this bourgeoisie that made up the public; literary criticism . . . mediated between works and the public on whose behalf it spoke; in its permanent discussions and debates it constituted a literary-bourgeois public sphere" (Berghahn 1988: 95). The new community of interpreters was supposed to be constituted by faith in the individual, the (self)creator, and the omnipotence of reason (Bromwich 1989). The institutions of criticism supporting the public function of art promulgated enlightenment of judgment as the civil Reformation. The optimism, however, did not last long. "It had been self-evident during the Enlightenment that literature had a moral-social and critical-emancipative function, one that could permanently influence the life practices of the readers or audience. During Weimar Classicism a momentous change occurred: art separated itself from life, aesthetics detached itself from ethics, and an elite distanced itself from the real public" (Berghahn 1988: 85). The younger generation realized that the efforts of Wolff, Lessing, and Herder to educate an informed, discriminating audience were failing, despite the success of their campaign against courtly imitations of neoclassicism, because they fell short of influencing the lifestyle and the consumption taste of the new public. The rules of the market were defeating the principles of the *Bildung* community (Campbell 1987). "Anxiety at the power of commodity circulation to disperse individual identities moved the Romantics again and again to reflect . . . on the possibility of an unconstrained, unalienated form of identity within modernity. In their assessment of what art and being an artist should mean in an age of commodity exchange, they were led to a valorization of the individual characteristics (*das Charakteristische*) of artists and artworks: the characteristic is that which remains identical with itself" (Schulte-Sasse 1988: 122).

The Romantics did not have in mind the autonomy of the consumer when they advocated the independence of individual taste. Faced with social irrelevance, they retreated from shared community goals into the defiant isolation of the intellectual coterie (like Rahel Varnhagen's salon, Mallarmé's Thursdays, or Balázs' Sundays)—*Bildung* as lifestyle. "Criticism thus became a conversation about art, conducted within a literary elite, a 'literary association' that defined the taste ideals of the epoch in contrast to the needs of the public" (Berghahn 1988: 90). Philosophical reasoning took precedence over political debate, and historical reality was denounced. All forms and exercises of criticism were subsumed under critique, the theory (and consciousness) of discipline.

This momentous change includes two stages: the aestheticization of autonomy by Kant and the aestheticization of the political by Schiller. After the style of taste and the distinction of *Bildung*, it is the (private) ethics of disinterested contemplation that becomes the model disposition—not a position in modernity but for the first time an attitude toward modernity. "The aesthetic legitimation for such a depoliticization of art and for its turning away from reality is delivered by Kant's concept of autonomy, which now gathers effect: what is beautiful is that which pleases generally, in a disinterested manner. Or, in Schiller's words: 'Art is absolved from everything that is positive or that has been introduced by human convention.' This declaration of art's autonomy is Schiller's answer to the historical crisis following the French Revolution. He distances himself from both the 'barbaric constitution of the State,' which allows for no cultural renewal, and from the dominant culture, which is characterized by division of labor, specialization, and alienation—all of which threaten the totality of the human being. Finally, this declaration of autonomy is directed against any state or religious control over art" (88). Emancipation is identified with the liberation of art from interest and of culture from labor,[47] namely, with the ethics of contemplation. This is the political economy of all post-revolutionary theory: with critique, alienation becomes a moral advantage rather than a social disadvantage.

It should not be assumed that all intellectuals were in favor of the aesthetic turn. The reformation in taste fought against two cultural fronts. The first was what Horkheimer and Adorno called the "culture industry," the "mass-deception" of the public (Brantlinger 1983). As Schelling wrote in his *Philosophy of Art* (1807): "Serious theoretical instruction in art is all the more necessary in this age of the literary Peasant War being waged against everything elevated, great, theoretical, yes, even against beauty itself in poetry and art" (quoted in Schulte-Sasse 1988: 149). The comparison with the sixteenth-century revolt indicates the intellectuals' fearful sense of siege. The second front was what in the 1790s seemed as "plebeian tendencies in literature": "Goethe and Schiller presented their idealistic art program in opposition to the 'literary sansculottes'" (Berghahn 1988: 86). Those were the writers who remained committed to the Enlightenment plan for the education of the public while substituting political for philosophical arguments. To the eyes of the literati, they were little more than pamphleteers, making unconscionable compromises to the expectations of the audience. "To the suppressed (and repressed) past of German literary criticism belongs the republican and Jacobin journalism that decisively pushed for a political public sphere and a public opinion. As political journalism, it would be the counterpart to the apolitical and aestheticized literary public sphere of Weimar Classicism. That it could not prevail vis-à-vis the Classic-Romantic criticism has less to do with its intrinsic quality than with the fact that the political conditions, the censorship, and the dominant aesthetics delayed its reception" (449). Opinion lost out to critique, social concerns to *Bildung*, action to contemplation, the political to the aesthetic.

Bildung originally included a civic role as part of its goal: the social presence, if not always involvement, of the enlightened individual was understood as greatly contributing to (indeed, as a prerequisite for) citizenship. A Pietist moral imperative linked the private task with public responsibility. The elevation of the aesthetic disposition to the aristocratic mark of the bourgeoisie, its effective egalitarian substitution for blood or rank, signalled "the triumph of constitutional *Recht* over imperial *Macht*, of secular culture over religious faith" (Schorske 1980: 31). Commitment to *Bildung* meant commitment to reason and art, to bourgeois *Recht* and *Kultur* (Frykman and Lofgren 1987). The liberal creed of the middle class sought a primarily cultural hegemony: constitutionalism, federalism, the bureaucratization of government, or the parliamentary system were much less important than the promotion of art and scholarship. "The democratization of culture, viewed sociologically, meant the aristocratization of the middle classes" (Schorske 1980: 296). The generation of Hegel, Beethoven, Hölderlin, and Wordsworth (all born in 1770) was probably the first to reap fully the benefits of that democratization.

With the functional differentiation of art and the creation of the aesthetic realm, the critic no longer tries to mediate between culture and its public but begins to defend the former against the indiscriminate preferences of the latter (which have made taste a bad quality). "Undoubtedly, the Classical authors use the autonomy postulate to defend the highest level of art against the market-dominated entertainment literature and the crudity of the public taste. But they thereby alienate themselves more and more from the real public. Indeed, over time they exclude the real public from the enjoyment of art" (Berghahn 1988: 89). At the same time, at least for some ten years before and after the turn of the century, they still hoped to create within culture a counterspace with its own public, based on exchanges among those trained in the exercises of *Bildung*—individuals involved in creating their lives and acquiring a biography, like Byron, Jean Paul, Goya, Foscolo, Chateaubriand, Turner, Paine, Kleist, Scott, or de Staël. Not unlike the members of the Frankfurt School, "at least the early Romantics intended (and in so doing they could be regarded as the first avant-garde movement in art) to reconnect art with life: that is, to return art to the realm of experience. . . . [T]he represented modes of communication were supposed to be present, to be acted out, in Romantic groups. . . . For in the eyes of the Romantics, communication through art was the only form of praxis able to free itself from the reified relationships of society" (Schulte-Sasse 1988: 140).

Schiller is again a case in point. After the French Revolution, when he abandoned his belief in direct political change, he concentrated increasingly on *Bildung* as social engineering. "He did not seek to cultivate the features of modern life which contain something public, but attempted rather to create by artistic means an artificial milieu in which the purely private realm is inflated idealistically into the public realm" (Lukács 1978a: 111). During his collaboration with Goethe, which began in the summer of 1794, the possibility of historical change was transposed into the realm of culture—the process of aesthetic cultivation. "Furthermore, by stressing the aesthetic element of *Bildung*, Schiller grants art a self-sufficiency that even Shaftesbury had denied it. For although art had become the principal means of attaining knowledge of truth and virtue, it had always retained a utilitarian function. Schiller, however, expressly posits that aesthetics should be interchangeable with ethics and politics. Instead of mediating virtue, the pursuit of aesthetics becomes a virtue in itself. Likewise, *Bildung* could be regarded as a moral and political act, even in its most individualistic forms, because it implied opposition to a barbaric political system and because it offered its proponents an alternative to revolution for realizing humanitarian goals" (Cocalis 1978: 405).

The liberation of the self, the odyssey of *Bildung*, the autonomy of art, the independence of contemplation, the self-founding of critique—all these are aspects of the aesthetic turn of emancipation, the moment when interpretation placed the laws of meaning within itself and development sought only its own process.[48] "Consequently, *Bildung*, which Herder had associated with specific political demands, becomes a goal in itself that may or may not be shared communally. The apolitical nature of art, which in a time of revolution had qualified art as a political tool, becomes neutralized as soon as the immediate political provocation disappears and art can then be used to sanction wholly individualistic pursuits, as long as they can be called humanitarian" (406). Education becomes wholly internalized, as the first disciplines of humankind, the humanities, prevail in the "conflict of the faculties" (Kant) and acquire institutional authority. From now on, thanks to the academic legitimacy and epistemological supremacy of critique, interpreters will legislate (Bauman 1987).

It is important to remember that "none of the major philosophers since the Scholastics of the 1300s had been an academic. . . . The Idealist revolution represents the academizing of modern philosophy" (Collins 1987: 58). The Idealists were professors who initiated a new university reform. The main thrust of their movement was toward promoting philosophy to the highest position among disciplines. "In 1798, Kant in his last book, *Der Streit der Fakultaeten*, maintained that only the Philosophical Faculty represented rational free inquiry, and hence should be dominant over the other Faculties. It was Kant's program that Wilhelm von Humboldt put into effect when he founded the University of Berlin; and it was Fichte, who had proclaimed that the national greatness of Germany was due to the intellectual and spiritual creativity of its philosophers, who was made its first rector" (61). The victory of Philosophy over the higher Faculties of Theology, Law, and Medicine was best expressed in Fichte's defense of his discipline as critique of all other languages of knowledge. "Kant's 'revolution' was a powerful attempt to raise the new class of cosmopolitan German intellectuals into positions of security and prestige. The outburst of Idealist systems that followed in the 1790s went far beyond Kant in ambitiousness; where he had cut off all speculative Theology as inadmissable efforts to discuss the 'thing-in-itself,' Fichte and his followers replaced Theology with comprehensive Idealist systems. . . . Where Kant pressed to raise philosophy to the level of a science, and to more or less abolish Theology as a rival, Fichte and his followers confidently proposed to take over Theology's territory with a new metaphysical construction, which would also serve as the basis for all other fields of knowledge, including science and history. At their height, they even felt they were creating a new religion, based on rationality" (63). "The Oldest System-Program of German Idealism," with its apostolic ardor, is the earliest gospel of this religion.

In the writings of Wilhelm von Humboldt (1767–1835), starting with the *Limits of State Action* (1791–92), the aspiration of the Enlightenment to reform the state through education was abandoned. Furthermore, all trust in the state as a bureaucratic machine which could be properly regulated was withdrawn, and hope was invested in the sovereignty of the cultivated individual. At best, the state should only protect her independence and preserve the proper conditions for her *Bildung*. Self-education would contribute to social harmony simply by being its own necessary condition and sufficient goal. In this way, politics was turned inside out, or more accurately it was given an inside, a depth, and was encouraged to turn inward towards the experience of the self.

Systematizing *Bildung* into a pedagogical enterprise, Humboldt devises "a coherent program of individual development. He proposes that the state design new institutions that would enable an aesthetic education for any citizen, assuming that whatever is good for the individual must also be good for the state. Museums, art galleries, libraries, archives, and concert halls should be created and opened to the general public. . . . Thus members of the middle class could participate in the same formative development once reserved for the aristocracy and they, as well-bred individuals, could become eligible for posts in a reformed, meritocratic civil service within the existing structure of an absolute monarchy. . . . [B]y involving the middle class in the government, one would insure the stability of the existing political system" (Cocalis 1978: 406–7). This marked the transition from the administrative politics of the Enlightenment to the individual's exercise in managing her own self (Cain 1989; Landes 1988). Aesthetic education and status, though, were increasingly linked, as *Bildung*, the "knighthood of modernity," became more and more not just a sign but also a justification of power. This development can be discerned in two cardinal oppositions of the nineteenth century: high vs. low culture,[49] and culture vs. politics. The first meant that the artistic creations of the masses or the folk were by definition inferior to those of the individual genius, which required for their proper enjoyment all the time (namely, leisure[50]) one could afford. The second opposition legitimized culture as the guardian of morality and stigmatized politics as the origin of social malaise. Commitment to *Bildung*, therefore, meant above all commitment to the politics of High Culture; and the best sign of *Bildung* competence (namely, mastery of the self) was interpretive proficiency (that is, mastery of the canon) as contemplation (of secular scriptures like those studied in *Mimesis*).[51]

Bildung emerged as a precondition for bourgeois politics when the political was banished from the street and became a separate realm of activity—when the practices of governance became the province of government. Furthermore, "in Germany the eighteenth century was a period marked by an increasing social disciplining of the populace in general. (In other countries, most notably Spain, the process had begun much earlier.) Under the pedagogic influence of various social institutions, including the state, the whole of a person's life was regarded as a period of productive labor. . . . Regarding leisure time as the necessary, regenerative side of the labor process was part of the new relationship to time; historically speaking, the emerging necessity of maintaining a productive balance between work and leisure was a precondition for the functional differentiation of the aesthetic realm" (Schulte-Sasse 1988: 170). The plans for the exercises of contemplation converged with other plans for such disciplining, and were used to train people during leisure time. Thus the Romantics proved useful to the capitalist system (which they detested) since the aesthetic became a model for teaching people what kind of autonomy they should seek. Eventually it was the larger regime of aesthetic creativity that would define the idealist version of the state—the Nation as a community of culture (*Volk*).[52]

For the person of *Bildung*, society was either *Volk* or mass. The concept of *Volk* was defined in broad opposition to modernity—to the present, to industrialization, alienation, Enlightenment, reason, social discontent. Thus it was very important for "the unifying element of the Romantic movement in its principal manifestations throughout the key European countries (Germany, England, France, Russia): *opposition to capitalism in the name of pre-capitalist values*" (Sayre and Löwy 1984: 46). As an aesthetic concept, the folk represented an ideal community based on the primordial identity of nature and culture, morality and creativity. "The concept of the folk expressed a political, antimodernist desire for national harmony, because the idea was intended to overcome 'the boundaries of class with the help of a utopian preview of an intact community [*Gemeinschaft*] composed of a synthetic union of citizens, who could *communicate* with one another and understand each other, not just superficially through the medium of the state but in an unmediated fashion through the system of common language [*Umgangsprache*]' [Manfred Frank]. . . . In the discourse of Romanticism 'the people' or 'folk' is primarily a historical category; the concept refers to a time that predated the 'fragmentation' brought on by modernization" (Schulte-Sasse 1988: 172–74). Its radically organic portrait of the nation was the expression of an attempt to recover from the abyss of history a sense of (lost but once possible) order, growth, consensus, roots, collectivity, authenticity, wholeness, and uniqueness: autonomy as autochthony. "National unity was conceived in cultural terms" (Mosse 1970: 10) as culture seemed (first to Herder) the only possible basis for a modern community, and *Bildung* promised membership to it. The analogous aesthetic constructs of *Volk* and *Bildung* mapped the territory and responsibilities of (middle class) culture until the end of Modernism.

Following the humiliation of the Prussian defeat in Jena (1806), treatises like Johann Gottlieb Fichte's *Addresses to the German Nation* (1808) defended the supremacy of the nation. National, rather than personal, education became a priority (Johnston 1989). Above all, popular nationalism found a new attachment to the motherland, rather than culture, and turned into a populist ideology, patriotism. After Napoleon, as far as the middle class was concerned, *Bildung* was nationalized, becoming "an attribute of those who could boast Germanic roots and who alone could appreciate the good, the true, and the beautiful" (Mosse 1985a: 10). This development led to two quite different conceptions. Intellectuals like Humboldt (who headed in 1809–10 the Section for Religion and Education in the Prussian Ministry of the Interior) rejected the idea of patriotic education and chose to abandon considerations of the social relevance of cultivation rather than see *Bildung* serve the state. The lonely path of individuality was the only decent course left to the man of modernity, the thinking person who felt uprooted from his native *Volk*: "Individuality is precisely what is original and eternal in man; personality doesn't matter so much. To pursue the cultivation and development of this individuality as one's highest calling would be a godlike egoism" (Schlegel 1971: 247). As for the rest of his class, now fully entrenched in positions of state control, *Bildung* degenerated into norms of respectability and codes of decorum. The ascetic training in civilization was reduced to "ritual competence" in civility.

An indispensable tenet of the project of autonomy was the self-definition of the modern age as a distinct era, which meant that the age was historically autonomous too. "The modern age was the first and only age that understood itself as an epoch and, in so doing, simultaneously created the other epochs. The problem of legitimacy is latent in the modern age's claim to carry out a radical break with tradition, and in the incongruity between this claim and the reality of history, which can never begin entirely anew" (Blumenberg 1983: 116). Ultimately the question of legitimacy could not be answered foundationally simply because autonomy can only seek its nomos in its own constitution, differentiating its own story from history: there is no self-foundation. "It is impossible to circumvent the necessity of affirming the project of autonomy as the primary position, one which can be elucidated but which cannot 'be founded,' since the very intention of founding it presupposes it" (Castoriadis 1990: 84). The age understands and asserts itself as an epoch. "Its self-understanding is one of the constitutive phenomena of this historical phase in its initial stages. This makes the concept of the epoch itself a significant element of the epoch" (Blumenberg 1983: 468).

Hellas was first identified with the ideal of autonomy when the discourses of emancipation looked for an alternative to the system of Neoclassical taste from which German society should free itself.[53] She seemed to present a model more Greek and more ancient than the French one, as well as completely untainted by Roman-Catholic influence. Rejecting the culture of the petty courts, the Enlightenment embraced the new model of organic integration, pursuing "the illusory perspectives which the flower of bourgeois society, which German classicism set itself: realization of the demands and results of the bourgeois revolution, that is, the revolutionary and voluntary liquidation of feudal survivals, in a non-revolutionary way" (Lukács 1978a: 134). An essential part of this pursuit was the creation of a literary theory capable of shaping and educating the reading public. The principles and values of this theory, of this pedagogical enterprise that constituted the non-revolutionary politics of the intellectuals and professionals, were sought in ancient Greece. Thus what later became known as theory was from the beginning a theoria, a view as well as account, of Hellas. "Since the emergence of the bourgeois class, the development of the theory of modern literature, the theory of its specific characteristics and their justification, has always been very closely related to the development of a theory of antiquity. . . . The great period of bourgeois literary theory, which terminated with the imposing world-historical synthesis of the history of literature and art in Hegel's aesthetics, is based entirely on the conception of antiquity as the canon of art, as the unattainable model for all art and literature" (101). As the independence of the aesthetic realm increased and its population pursued more autonomy, the appeal of Greece incorporated principles of social order as it expanded "into a contrast between the splendidly naïve moral ingenuousness of the Greeks and the empty, exaggerated, and false conventions of bourgeois society" (106).

At the same time, Weimar classicism gradually found its Greek ideal less accessible. "The development of young Hegel shows with the greatest clarity how closely related to each other in Germany at that time were the two complexes: on the one hand, approval of the French Revolution and the cultural programme of renovating antiquity, and on the other, the Thermidorean renunciation of revolutionary methods and the conception of antiquity as conclusively past" (112). Eventually, the numbers of those who were willing to pursue democracy in the public sphere dwindled. The Jacobins

(Feher 1988) were the last to believe in creating a new, political Greece again (Parker 1937). "If Greece—in particular the Greece of the pre-Socratics—nourished a rightist imagination, certainly in Germany, there was also a post-Socratic Greece which nourished a leftist imagination and revolutionary philosophy, those of a democratic citizenry (especially in the France of Rousseau to Jaurès)" (Goux 1989: 19). Before too long, though, when they could not recreate the democracy of the polis, people lost faith in the Greek socio-historical ideal.[54]

For about a century, the Hellenic lost almost all connection with politics. "At the height of his own efforts on behalf of antiquity, Schiller thus bluntly rejects the Jacobin renovation of Hellenism, regarding it as 'Graeco-mania'" (Lukács 1978a: 114). The poet of "The Gods of Greece" (1788) denounces politics while elevating the art of the polis to the highest ideal. "The conception of antiquity as past, as something irrevocably lost, is one of the most important aspects of Schiller's conception of history and thus of his judgment of the present. We know with what decisiveness he placed the irrevocably past character of Greek culture and art at the centre of his philosophy of history, with what animosity he fought against the Jacobin enthusiasm for a revolutionary renovation of antiquity" (132). The Romantic apotheosis of the aesthetic explains why "the tragic transition from the heroic age of the polis republic dreamed by Robespierre and Saint-Just into capitalist prose had to be effected in a purely utopian and ideological manner without a preliminary revolution" (Lukács 1978b: 137). The retreat from the politics of the public sphere to the community of Bildung marks the ascendancy of the Hellenic to the order of transcendental harmony— the law of creativity.

Of course, Bildung had always been exclusively Hellenic: Greece had been its land of remembrance, reverie, and return because it was presumably there that the integration of character and citizenship, of private education and public virtue, of morality and culture reached perfect balance. The classical texts, artworks, and monuments were taken as a lasting and inspiring testimony to that achievement. Bildung was not just a revival of the ancient or the classical but specifically an adoration of the Hellenic: its goal was not (Roman) order, as in baroque absolutism, but organic harmony. It constituted nothing less than the idealist appropriation of antiquity that encouraged Enlightenment to replace the republican rule of aristocracy with its own democratic control through culture.

Bildung both aestheticized pedagogy and gendered class. It made manhood a characteristic of the new gentility, as masculinity (Bordo 1987; Brittan 1989; Pleck 1981) was defined in opposition to family and trade—to the domestic (female) (Armstrong 1987; Ellis 1989; George 1988; Kelley 1984; Poovey 1988a; Shevelow 1989; Suganami 1989) and the entrepreneurial (male) spirit in the urban market. It is necessary to emphasize that "male dominance is intrinsic rather than accidental to classical capitalism, for the institutional structure of this social formation is actualized by means of gendered roles" (Fraser 1989: 128). *Bildung* was sexual division and division of labor elevated to intellectual exercise—the consummate aesthetic and homosocial involvement. Friendship became an integral part of this journey: there was always a real or imaginary friend who accompanied Shelley, Leopardi, Pushkin, Hölderlin, or Whitman (or Edith Wharton) in their quest (Koestenbaum 1989). For men and women alike (Faderman 1981; Todd 1980), *Bildung*, perceived as an exercise in Socratic learning, assumed and instilled a male identity (Theweleit 1987, 1988). It also desired the physical beauty of the male body (Friedrichsmeyer 1983). It was only after *Bildung* declined into training for respectability, and self-control into etiquette (Kasson 1990), that beauty was medicalized as health (Conrad and Schneider 1980; Weeks 1981). Until then, until manliness became a norm opposed to sickness (Mort 1987), masculinity as a state (rather than experience) was a major ideal of cultivation (Sedgwick 1985).

Thus the connection between Jews and homosexuals should be made on the basis not of deviance or otherness but of the aristocracy of culture (morality and taste, respectively) they represent. If culture is the eminent quality of bourgeois aristocracy, then moral knowledge and artistic taste are its main elements, representing its Hebraic and Hellenic dimensions. "Jews and homosexuals are the outstanding creative minorities in contemporary urban culture. Creative, that is, in the truest sense: they are creators of sensibilities. The two pioneering forces of modern sensibility are Jewish moral seriousness and homosexual aestheticism and irony. The reason for the flourishing of the aristocratic posture among homosexuals also seems to parallel the Jewish case. . . . Jewish liberalism is a gesture of self-legitimization. So is Camp taste, which has definitely something propagandistic about it. . . . The Jews pinned their hopes for integrating into modern society on promoting the moral sense. Homosexuals have pinned their integration into society on promoting the aesthetic sense" (Sontag 1966: 290). Jews and homosexuals are but two cultural manifestations of the Hebraic and the Hellenic. The care of *Bildung* is the combination of the two senses—the aesthetic as moral, or sensibility as conduct.

Bildung, which succeeded as an invariably Hellenic ideal, was from the very beginning prominent in discussions of the social, political, and philosophical place of the Jew. Lessing's *Nathan the Wise* (1779), for example, the best-known play of the Enlightenment, has as its hero a Jew who incarnates a judicious combination of enlightened knowledge and cultivated character. The problem of Jewish emancipation became a crucial one for the theoreticians of bourgeois culture and virtue. It came to the fore of public discussions in major countries like Germany, Austria, and France in the late eighteenth century and was closely linked with the civil emancipation of the middle class itself. The Jews, who had been invented during the hermeneutic wars of the Reformation, provided the test case for the democratic/liberal project of the bourgeoisie: an old model and a contemporary margin, a religious origin and an economic presence, a safe distance and an attractive proximity, the Other who was an indispensable part of the Same—all this presented a great challenge to promises of universal harmony: Was an organic integration through cultivation possible? Was it truly open to any individual with the required credentials? Could a cultural democracy abolish social distinctions and political inequality? In the period between the recognition of the Jews as citizens by the French Revolution and by Prussia (1812), the middle class engineered a miracle of liberalization that made it feel legitimate and proud because it was not just its own.[55] By 1807 Jews stopped being called a nation in Germany and were asked to assimilate. The generosity of the new system to the person-as-character was obvious: everybody was welcome to join the producers and/or consumers of culture, even the Jews. Thus the Jew was invited to become the model middle class subject and was endowed with all the bourgeois privileges (that is, human rights). This interpellation was premised and based on a secular contract: "emancipation was what the states were to grant, assimilation what the Jews were to give in return" (Sorkin 1990: 18). Its specific character was the Jews' covenant with aesthetic culture.

While the bourgeoisie was confidently congratulating itself for its liberal willingness to accept the Jews into the world of democratic rights, it was also taking a number of self-protective measures: making culture a requisite for citizenship; establishing the aesthetic as the normative ideal of identity (personal, national, sexual, etc.); creating the educational system (from Gymnasium to the University) that would oversee the regular exercise in *Bildung*; isolating the lower classes into the disorderly, uncultivated, dirty crowd of the "masses" (Hamilton and Wright 1986; Mosse 1975); above all, limiting access to the experiment to the Jews, the Other (of the Same)—the true insider of the new dominant identity. The Jew was chosen as the case most appropriate for the testing of this system: representative of the financial territory claimed by the burghers, bearer of learned reason and traditional morality, seeker of equality and tolerance—this (imagined) person, as an educated individual, could potentially become the best example of what the enlightened middle class promised to do for all people.

Not that the case had no troubling aspects—ideas of the Jew as anti-Christian, Semite, untrustworthy, or different were often associated with the specific ethnic group. At the same time, these very aspects made the case safely challenging: the true potential of *Bildung* would be best exhibited (to the aristocrats who were contemptuously watching the middle class experiment with culture and learning, and to the lower classes which seemed given only to greed and hedonism) in the cultivation and reformation of an Other (and yet not a foreigner or outcast)[56] who had so far no part in it. This could prove that the ideal of *Bildung* was, in a truly egalitarian fashion, available to anybody, as long as there was sincere commitment, willingness to cooperate, and no desire for politics (like unreasonable demands, demonstrations, or strikes). Culture through education and cultivation was an open, inviting, rewarding area. Within it, the Jew was used to prove that the Hellenic was truly democratic (and not, say, aristocratic, like the Roman). Thus the Jew, by becoming a respectable member of *Kulturgemeinschaft*, was emancipated into a world of constitutionalism and liberalism (Hodgson 1983) where the state assumed benevolent command of the national life—into the bourgeois world of sweetness and light, art and science, *Bildung* and reason, where culture provided the promise and the means of integration into mainstream society. The Jewish *Bildungsbürger* became the greatest achievement of the German *Bildungsbürgertum*.

The case of Moses Mendelssohn (also known as the "Jewish Socrates"), the model of *Nathan the Wise*, exemplifies this achievement. He has been hailed as the first modern German Jew in that he "was the first Jew to identify himself with the cultural concerns of Germany and to make the German tongue the medium of his literary creativity" (Altmann 1985: 18). He seemed to excel in all intellectual pursuits that constituted the realm of modern culture. In scholarship, he laid the foundations for what was later to become the *Wissenschaft des Judentums*; in criticism, he worked with Bishop Lowth's principles in his Biblical analysis; in philosophy, he proposed Judaism as the true religion of reason; in Bible studies, he translated the Scripture into German; and in politics, he outlined the plan for a secular Jewish state. He acquired immense prestige: the most distinguished figures of his time, from Lessing and Kant to Jacobi and Goethe, discussed his ideas.[57] The Enlightenment embraced and elevated him to a model and a legend: his case proved that the Jew of reason was somebody with whom one could reason.[58] This Gentile invention defined the agenda for theorists of the Hebraic almost until the age of Ernst Cassirer (1874–1945) and Max Scheler (1874–1928). It was only with the generation of Rosenzweig, Scholem, Buber, and Benjamin (with the decay of *Bildung*, the return to mysticism, the new translation of the Bible, Zionism, and revolutionary Messianism) that Mendelssohn's exemplification of the Hebraic became obsolete. The critique by Horkheimer and Adorno of the ideal of Ithaca is an equally strong rejection of Mendelssohn's Jerusalem—of the state of rights and reason which for them was only another Hellenic myth. There was, however, a single commitment which, precisely because of the success of assimilation (called by Mendelssohn "civil acceptance"), remained for them unalterable: the devotion to culture.

Although Jews were excluded for about another century from the sphere of the mandarins and bureaucrats (which included areas like the state institutions or the University), they were encouraged to excel in culture (arts,

sciences, philosophy, journalism) and all the practices of (its) interpretation (beginning with scholarship). This is how the move "from economic to
intellectual vocations" (Schorske 1980: 149), "the so-called Judaicization
of all educated professions" (Theodor Herzl) by a cultivated class excluded
from state bureaucracy and exercise of political power, took place. The
projected Jewish cultural assimilation through interpretive proficiency was
the large-scale experiment in *Bildung* in the late eighteenth and early nineteenth centuries. The experiment was to use the Greeks in order to educate
the Jews—to educate the Other in order to legitimize the knowledge of the
Same, the regime of aesthetic identity; and the condition was that Jews
become good citizens by showing commitment to culture, respect for political authority, and faith to the total separation of the two. "The cultural
and the political were two different worlds, and Jewish emancipation was a
decisively cultural emancipation" (Mosse 1985: 70). The Jewish covenant
with the aesthetic was the supreme realization on a large scale of Schiller's
idea of social engineering through culture.

The aesthetic covenant made the Jew first and foremost a critic. "Assimilation and criticism are but two moments in the same process of emancipation" (Horkheimer 1974: 108). It was the impossible dream of assimilation
that made criticism a simulation of emancipation. The bourgeois insider
who was the political outsider was in the best position to practice culture
as criticism, to exercise critique. When the religion of virtuosos reached its
self-reflective state, seeking to purify nomos of all external support, it
found in its Others the specialists of secular guilt, of ambivalence over
emancipation. "What is more, critique was also the means of Jewish emancipation from Judaism itself. It not only secured an urbane attitude and
worldly tolerance on the part of Christians; it also offered the philosophical
tool with which the grand self-dynamism of the Jewish spirit sought to
master its religious and social destiny. Jewish philosophy, in all its versions,
has remained critique" (Habermas 1983b: 27). Luring the Jews into the
dilemmatic logic[59] of emancipation and assimilation, tradition and progress, identity and difference, the Hebraic and the Hellenic, modernity
could further experiment with a variety of questions, from survival of community to the authority of the law. At the same time, the guests (or hostages) of modernization have not disappointed their hosts. "Those Diaspora Jews who survive and transcend alien cultures . . . are precisely those
who judge it. Critics, interpreters, summarizers of culture who are Jews can
at least breathe, if only transiently, in Diaspora" (Ozick 1970: 273). It is
again the principle of proficiency that prevails here, the need to earn recognition by achieving distinction, by functioning as the conscience of the
reigning truth, its dialectic of enlightenment, its ever-vigilant critique.

The "Jewish Question" became the crucial issue for high modernity because it combined the problems of modernization, cultivation, and assimi-

lation into a single civil right—that of emancipation. The term "emancipation," first adopted in public debates in 1828, was a Jewish appropriation: so far as the Gentiles were concerned, the rights of the Jew (specifically, the right Jew) remained a question—the quest for cultural democracy. Emancipation was "redemption-through-assimilation" (Bauman 1988: 56), and its strategy was culture—excellence in Hellenic (aesthetic) pursuits, in achievements that transcended national boundaries and peculiarities, and reached into the common (Western) heritage. "Emancipation meant not only the flight from the ghetto past but also from German history regarded as an obstacle to integration. . . . The search for common ground transcending history was one reason why Jews as a group tended to support cultural and artistic innovation to a greater extent than did Gentiles. Jews provided a disproportionate share of support for the *avant garde* and for educational experiments as well. . . . Supporting cultural innovation not only helped overcome a handicap of a separate past but also continued the impetus of *Bildung* as a process of self-cultivation. But then, *Bildung* had always concentrated upon culture and all but ignored politics and society. *Bildung* furthered a cultural vision of the world. This . . . blinded those committed to the primacy of the humanistic culture to political realities" (Mosse 1985a: 14–15).

The "Jewish Question" became the only viable social project of *Bildung* since it also expressed the moral responsibility of culture without raising questions of political participation or struggle. Accepting individuality and universality as the premises of assimilation, Jews willfully "followed the precepts Goethe had proposed for the education of his *Wilhelm Meister,* a novel that was to become the great model of middle-class education" (Arendt 1968: 59).[60] Assimilation was achieved instantly—as soon as the conditions for emancipation were accepted (even though by definition they could never be fully met). " 'Assimilation' designated the status and self-definition of post-emancipation German Jewry" (Sorkin 1990: 18). The proposal seemed irresistibly egalitarian, requiring disciplined work and achievement: "Emancipation, although granted to the Jews on clearly defined terms, generous to the individual but intolerant of the group, offered to the Jews economic opportunities and a civil status which their fathers had not even dreamed of. They were, therefore, not only eager to accept the terms but within a short time carried out most of the mental and physical adjustments their fellow-citizens had stipulated. They soon adopted the views of the Germans about their own tradition together with the values and goals of German society" (Schmidt 1956: 39). This is how "Judaism became Jewishness" (Cuddihy 1974: 14)—how social position became a matter of personal identity, emancipation a matter of attitude, and modernity the anxiety of belatedness. Any remaining political connotations disappeared as the *Bildung* quest was further subjected to a moral codification and turned into a search for respectability: the *embourgeoisement* of the Jew was eventually reduced to the "refinement of the Israelites," as she strove to forget her Yiddish and become *raffiné*.

The outcome of the experiment can be seen in Fin-de-Siècle Vienna, in the Leningrad avant-garde, in Weimar Berlin, in the Paris salons, and in the New York intelligentsia: it succeeded because (certain) Jews were culturally integrated, becoming the best representatives of Enlightenment, assimilation, and respectability. "The Jews who took the Enlightenment on its word and identified emancipation with refinement of manners and, more generally, with self-cultivation, had become cultural fanatics. In every Western nation they were the ones who treated national cultural heritage most seriously—in fact, more seriously than expected (mostly as means of national mobilization and state legitimation). Trying to excel in the complex and often elusive task ahead, they sung the praises of national monuments and masterpieces of national art and literature, only to find that the audience comprised mostly people similar to themselves. They read avidly and voraciously, only to find they could discuss what they had read only with other *aspiring* Germans or Frenchmen like themselves. Far from bringing them closer to assimilation, conspicuous cultural enthusiasm and obsessive display of cultural nobility set them aside from the native middle class and, if anything, supplied further evidence of their ineradicable foreignness. . . . In many German or French cultural centers, symphonic concerts and theater premieres came to play the same social role for the assimilated Jews as the weekly ritual of high church service played for the gentile part of the middle class" (Bauman 1988: 53). By excelling in the Hellenic exercises of *Bildung*, the Jews became the true Greeks, the modern virtuosos of culture. It was their conspicuous distinction, their status as eminent producers and consumers of culture, though, that kept them isolated from the masses (including the Jewish masses), as Horkheimer and Adorno bitterly observed. "The Jews, unlike the masses, reached for *Bildung* in order to integrate themselves into German society. The Jews and the German masses entered German social and political life at roughly the same time, but the Jews were apt to reject the world of myth and symbol, the world of feeling rather than reason. Through the process of their emancipation, they were alienated from the German masses" (Mosse 1985: 8).[61] Where interpretive independence had shaped the meaning of liberation for the classes of the Reformation, the ideal of *Bildung* reoccupied bourgeois emancipation, and the Jewish intellectual, the typical self-sufficient and cultivated bourgeois, became (from Heine to Lukács and from Adorno to Alan Bloom) its custodian.[62]

This very success made his position politically precarious. In the nineteenth century, when culture was considered Hellenic and the guardians of its educational value were considered representatives of Hebraic morality (by people like Arnold or Disraeli), faith in the aesthetic religion and membership in the congregation of culture were still relatively strong. But the failure of liberalism early in the twentieth century brought about the identification of culture with the Hebraic, and of social anarchy with politics and the Hellenic. Under this development, "the program which the liberals had devised against the upper classes occasioned the explosion of the lower. The liberals succeeded in releasing the political energies of the masses, but against themselves rather than against their ancient foes" (Schorske 1980: 117). The revolt of the craftsmen and the proletariat against the inequalities created by laissez faire and free trade had spread between the Napoleonic Wars and the Revolutions of 1848 in France, England, Germany, and Austria. Anti-Semitism also played a part in early attacks against liberalism, statism, and capitalism (Lichtheim 1968).[63] The bankruptcy of the liberal ideal (as well as of the High Culture he defended) left the Jew a victim, since for the peasant and the artisan "liberalism meant capitalism and capitalism meant Jew" (Horkheimer and Adorno 1972: 118). The intertwining of anti-capitalist and anti-Jewish positions has a history going back to the collapse of the *ancien régime*. "Anti-Semitism in its secular form was no isolated phenomenon. It was closely linked up with the opposition to laissez-faire capitalism and its forms of trade and industry. It was later linked with resistance to liberalism and the growing political power of the West, notably Great Britain and America. There is no reason to assume that this was a purely German development. It could be found in other Continental countries and was most prominent and effective among the intelligentsia" (Schmidt 1959: 59). No interpretive proficiency or cultural eminence could provide protection under such conditions of disaffection and unrest.

Emancipation and integration happened on the basis of the universalist ideal of a shared humanity that underscored difference the more it advocated equality and justice. The central requirement was the transcendence of the political (socio-economic interest) through culture (Schopenhauer's disinterested "pure contemplation" of beauty and knowledge). This integration, however, was never satisfactorily achieved exactly because it was never assumed to be political. "The commitment to culture as the guardian of morality excluded overt political action; individual *Bildung* would in the last resort solve all problems of life" (Mosse 1985: 33). Those who internalized the liberal ideal of self-cultivation acquired rights and became independent, but they were never politically free: they became the subjects of culture. First of all, assimilation, like its code, *Bildung*, was an individual affair: only individuals could be cultivated and assimilated. Assimilation meant matching achieved economic status with comparable social acceptance through the mediation of style and attitude. Group assimilation was by definition impossible. Thus "the experience of certain individuals notwithstanding, the entrance of Jewry as a *collective* into the body of German society did not mean real integration into any part, stratum, or section of it. It meant, rather, the creation of a separate subgroup, which conformed to the German middle class in some of its characteristics" (Katz 1985: 85). One of the conditions of voluntary (individual) assimilation was the abandonment of ethnic identity.

In this respect, Jewishness was an important negative qualification that had to be overcome. Since autonomy was a matter of self-disciplined privacy, a question of cultivated character, only qualified individuals could be admitted to the democracy of *Bildung*. "Exit visas were a collective matter, whereas entry tickets had to be obtained individually" (Bauman 1988: 51). Neither human reason nor equality of rights were sufficient for membership in the nation of culture: the new allegiance presupposed a denunciation of collective destiny. "It appears to be only when the gifted Jew escapes from the cultural environment created and fed by the particular genius of his own people, only when he falls into the alien lines of gentile inquiry and becomes a naturalized, though hyphenated, citizen in the gentile republic of learning, that he comes into his own as a creative leader in the world's intellectual enterprise. It is by loss of allegiance, or at the best by force of a divided allegiance to the people of his origin, that he finds himself in the vanguard of modern inquiry" (Veblen 1964: 225–26). Jewishness was never emancipated. On the contrary, the overcoming of a communal tradition—in this case, observance of (the law of) Judaism—was part of the *Bildung* exercises. "Indeed, one may argue that from Heine to Proust and Pasternak many of the decisive moments in the modernist movement represent maneuvers of rejection by Jews of their Jewish past" (Steiner 1976: 75).[64] For Judaism to become universal, one had to be Jewish individually. The result was at least paradoxical: "The abandoning of traditional Jewish occupations, which from the assimilants' viewpoint meant *Entjudung* (de-judaization of 'men as such'), appeared to the baffled native public more like the process of *Verjudung* (judaization of heretofore gentile areas)" (Bauman 1988: 54). At the same time, by becoming the aristocracy of culture, Jews became model "state-people." "The new devotion to the state became almost a substitute for their old religion" (Schmidt 1956: 43), as they pledged unconditional loyalty to secular authority. "The ideology of emancipation regarded the State, or rather the rule of law, as the highest level of social life; it did not demand or exact any internal change beyond that implicit in the legal system itself" (Rotenstreich 1959: 8). The virtuosos of *Bildung* behaved like the religious virtuosos whose "genuinely mystic and charismatic search for salvation has naturally and everywhere been apolitical or anti-political in nature" (Weber 1958b: 337). The virtue of this modern virtuosity was the purity, the disinterestedness of contemplation. The aesthetic gaze could not compromise its integrity by paying attention to (let alone dealing with) any law external to its theoretical constitution.

In a certain sense, the situation was not new. "German Jews retained their old timidity towards the authorities in power. As citizens they were always ready to fulfill the behest of the state, to excel in the observation of state laws and to collaborate with the government, even if that government was anything but friendly towards them. . . . Even the open hostility of the Nazi Era found German Jews reluctant to contemplate political opposition as a group. The laws of the state were regarded as sacrosanct, often to the bitter end" (Schmidt 1956: 42). Political power was rarely challenged: respect for the moral authority of institutions prevailed as "most of the German-Jewish leadership understood only too well the importance of respectability for the cause of Jewish emancipation, and they were ready and eager to accept its dictates of conformity, the more so as respectability provided tangible signs as to how life should be lived in Gentile society" (Mosse 1985a: 7).

It is part of the aesthetic condition to believe that it has escaped institutional control because it surveys matters untainted by purposeful considerations, attending only to the freeplay of imagination and intellect, and contributing to the re-enchantment of the world. "Thus the assimilating Jews did not cheat or otherwise fail to play the game according to the rules. . . . They could not challenge that authority without sapping the foundation of their redemptive hopes. The project of assimilation turned out to be a trap. Without control over the rules, it was impossible to win" (Bauman 1988: 56). It seemed as if, so long as they distinguished themselves in Hellenic pursuits, this capital investment would provide both safety and superiority (Wistrich 1989). "If the Viennese burghers had begun by supporting the temple of art as a surrogate form of assimilation into the aristocracy, they ended by finding in it an escape, a refuge from the unpleasant world of increasingly threatening political reality" (Schorske 1980: 8).

Culture and manners, however, could not protect their practitioners and soloists from the violence of discrimination which they had often supported, and even exercised, albeit only in intellectual and cultural affairs. "*Bildung* and *Sittlichkeit*, which had stood at the beginning of Jewish emancipation in Germany, accompanied German Jews to the end, blinding them, as many other Germans, to the menace of National Socialism" (Mosse 1985a: 15). As late as the 1920s, many defended themselves by displaying their grasp of German identity: "In seeking the origins of Germany, German Jews once more turned to those they deemed the originators of the search, the nationalists who could stand beside the internationalists like Lessing and Goethe. . . . This conception of Germany's past and tradition was proffered as the real one. To German Jews the Nazis were the idealizers, the dreamers, seeking or creating a past that had never existed— a past out of touch with reality" (Bolkosky 1975: 138). The disinfected reality of culture still seemed the only worthy domain where dialectical conflicts could be debated and resolved, or where the uncivilized forces and masses could be educated and tamed.[65] Consequently, critique was identified with resistance. Nazi culture, however, despised by intellectual taste, chose to contest the definition of collective identity by other means.[66]

The Hebraic rule over capitalist codes (such as money and the printed word—which, of course, should not be confused with means, materials, wealth, or power) achieved its full legitimacy in Budapest, Vilna, Frankfurt, Vienna, Salonika, Zurich, and Paris. Ironically, in a total inversion of the Romantic model, of the invitation to *Bildung* extended to the Jewish bourgeoisie, by the time of Benjamin, Jakobson, and Lévi-Strauss Jewishness had become a central metaphor for *Bildung*, and the "Man of Letters" was succeeded by the "Jew of Culture," by Benjamin's "intellectual literary-Jew" and "creative culture-Jew" (Rabinbach 1985: 99). Regarding the Frankfurt School position, for example, "at least in Horkheimer's case, the Critical Theorist was understood as 'the Jew' of the administered society. And conversely, anti-Semitism became a model of the totalistic liquidation of non-identity in the one-dimensional world" (Jay 1980: 149).[67] Already before the end of World War I, culture had abandoned its Hellenic character. The Hellenic had been identified with the (pagan and barbaric) political: while Arnold tried to mobilize it to make culture more attractive (Lambropoulos 1989), Buber attacked it because he saw it as a threat to culture. In a parallel development, while in the era of Mendelssohn and Kant the cultural transcendence of politics was the condition of emancipation, by the time of Bloch and Zweig culture had produced the aesthetic ideal of a transcendental politics. If Heine and Marx gave priority to praxis over theory, at the Frankfurt Institute and in the theories of those "searching for a socialism untainted by the demands of politics or the struggle for power" (Mosse 1985: 57), the order was reversed, and at the end of the twentieth century (in the writings on painting of, say, Hilton Kramer or Jacques Derrida), theory (deconstructionist or neo-conservative) is the only praxis available.[68]

The European intellectual tradition reached its climactic end in the work of the *intellektuelle Linke* of the interwar period, when the ideas of totality (Dembo 1989; Grumley 1989; Jay 1984) and difference became central to its aesthetic politics: totality as the overcoming of the fragmented modernity, and difference as the yearning for a messianic fulfillment of time and language. Cultural leftism searched for a model of social change untainted by politics and activism, and found it in a Kantian (Marburg) or Hegelian (Frankfurt) socialism, which can be both subsumed under what Lukács called in 1931 "Romantic anti-capitalism."[69] The former was more interested in ethics, the latter in aesthetics. The Kantian trend explored the dimming prospects of Enlightenment, the Hegelian the dawning threats to *Bildung*. Both flourished in the Weimar Republic and constituted, as extreme forms of Schiller's social program, a last attempt to revive the educational ideals of humanism. They expressed the hope that political consciousness could be formed and directed either by an ethical or by an aesthetic critique, and they scrupulously avoided politics, concentrating exclusively on theoretical investigations. "As for the working classes, perhaps their sole function in the system of aesthetic positions is to serve as a foil, a negative reference point, in relation to which all aesthetics define themselves, by successive negations" (Bourdieu 1984: 57). The artists of *Bildung* and the masters of art fought the last battle of aesthetic emancipation, thinking that "culture was a liberal and left monopoly" (Mosse 1985: 73), and defending Hebraic culture against Hellenic politics.

By that time, not only had culture become entirely Hebraic but also assimilated Jews had identified with it. "A very high percentage of the Weimar left-wing intellectuals combined all the characteristics repugnant to the Germanic ideologists: Francophile, Jewish, Western, rebellious, progressive, democratic, rationalist, socialist, liberal, and cosmopolitan" (Deak 1968: 23). Most of them saw culture (or form-giving critique) as the only resistance possible. Cultural theory became the left-liberal political practice with no connection to other political practices in the factory, the street, the union, or the party. "Just as the Jewish bourgeoisie was increasingly isolated within the German middle class, Jewish left-wing intellectuals were isolated within the workers' movement. . . . The workers' movement and the socialist parties stood in the midst of the political and social struggle, and it is no coincidence that the heirs of such left-wing intellectuals were idealistic and utopian middle-class university students and professors" (Mosse 1985: 67). Thus it was perhaps quite unavoidable for those intellectuals to underestimate Adolf Hitler, the petty bourgeois painter whose education in culture and power took place among the monuments of the Ringstrasse in Vienna, since they were busy discovering the Young Hegel and the pre-revolutionary Marx or criticizing the Hellenic origins of capitalism and modernity. This is the heritage which the Frankfurt School, combining aesthetic radicalism with political pessimism, was unable (and did not even try) to overcome.[70]

From Mendelssohn to Adorno and from Hamann to Heidegger, all the examinations of modernity which considered the "Jewish question" its central allegory made comparison to a Greek model the standard approach.[71] There is a rare exception, however, which is also the most controversial treatment of the subject: the essay "On the Jewish Question" by Karl Marx (1818–83). A striking feature of his contribution is that it does not involve the Hellenic at all: there is no mention of Greece, myth, polytheism, the

epic, or the polis. There is no need for such comparison: Marx is the first to
write about the Jews not as people but as a historical construct which exemplifies the spirit of capitalism.

The occasion for Marx's essay was provided by *The Jewish Question*, published by Bruno Bauer (1809–82) first in two articles (1842) and the following year, in revised version, as a book. Bauer, Marx's former collaborator
and an expert in New Testament Higher Criticism,was dismissed in 1842
from his chair of Theology at the University of Bonn because of his polemical essay "Theological Shamelessness" (1841). Bauer and Marx, both
members of the generation Bauer called "the Reformation of the nineteenth century," had announced in 1841 (the year of Ludwig Feuerbach's
The Essence of Christianity) plans for a co-edited journal that never materialized, *Atheistic Archives*, and began writing together a book called *Trum-
pet of the Last Judgement on Hegel the Atheist and Antichrist* (1841), which
Bauer completed and published anonymously. At that time, "the emanci-
pationist demand relied on the fact of religious reform. The advocates of
emancipation, especially the Jews, maintained that Judaism had already
undergone the process of internal reform that was a *conditio sine qua non*
of emancipation" (Rotenstreich 1959: 30). In *The Jewish Question*, Bauer
criticized the religion of Judaism as well as Jewish demands for emancipation, arguing that such demands could not be taken seriously because they
were based on a distinct religious identity: if Jews wanted emancipation,
they ought to emancipate themselves from their Jewishness first, since they
could not expect historical recognition while preserving a non-historical
faith. "Bauer was attacking the very principles of the emancipation and its
underlying ideology as it had crystallized in the movement for religious
reform. Bauer argued that Judaism was basically un-historical, i.e., impervi-
ous to change and immutable" (12). While taking the Jews as a metaphor
for humanity in his narrative of true liberation, he also rejected Christianity, which he presented as a continuation and extension of Judaism.
His ultimate target was the foundation of bourgeois society, the Christian
idea of privilege. While Feuerbach, though, had proposed the "resolution
of theology into anthropology,"[72] Bauer brought out the connections of
emancipation with an issue often neglected among Gentiles but always
identified by enlightened Jews with the challenge of modernity: religious
reform.

For Marx even this approach did not go far enough. He responded in his
review of Bauer's book, published in 1844 (the year of the Paris *Economic
and Philosophic Manuscripts*), and in *The Holy Family: Critique of Critical
Critique; Against Bruno Bauer and Consorts* (1845), his first book, which he
co-authored with Friedrich Engels (1820–95). According to Marx, although Bauer analyzed the constitution of the Christian state and exposed
its structural flaws, his discussion of the political emancipation of the Jews

was limited to religion. Marx's complaint is that he "dealt with *religious* and *theological* questions in the *religious* and *theological* way" (Marx and Engels 1956: 149). Because he focused on the antagonism between state and church, he did not offer anything more than a criticism of the Jewish religion. Thus Bauer, whom the academic establishment had expelled from its ranks as the "Robespierre of Theology," is, in his critic's eyes, "St. Bruno"—a theologian who still adheres to a religious view. In *The German Ideology* (1845–46), Marx and Engels would attack all Hegelians from the same standpoint: "The Old Hegelians had *comprehended* everything as soon as it was reduced to an Hegelian logical category. The Young Hegelians *criticized* everything by attributing to it religious conceptions or by pronouncing it a theological matter. The Young Hegelians are in agreement with the Old Hegelians in their belief in the rule of religion, of concepts, of a universal principle in the existing world. Only, the one party attacks this dominion as usurpation, while the other extols it as legitimate. . . . It has not occurred to any one of these philosophers to inquire into the connection of German philosophy with German reality, the relation of their criticism to their own material surroundings" (Tucker 1978: 148–49). In opposition to Bauer's approach, Marx mounts a critique of emancipation itself, which extends to the practices of the political state, and bourgeois society in general.

He sees as the basic presupposition of the political state, the modern state that the middle class built, a sharp differentiation between the public and the private person, which elevates the latter to a pure, independent, capital essence: Man. The political state assumes the inviolable sovereignty of each and every monad, of the individual. This Man is a member of the civil society invested with "human" (namely, civil) rights: liberty, property, equality, and security. Together these rights constitute his freedom of man-as-monad, safeguard the preservation of person, and produce his separation from other men. Thus the citizenship of Man amounts only to the rights of the bourgeois individual which promise security but disappear when the pursuit of freedom comes into conflict with political life. People, therefore, were not freed but rather granted freedom of religion, property, and trade. The Man of the civil society is natural, individual, and private; the Man of the political state is unpolitical. Marx concludes that bourgeois emancipation brought the dissolution of the feudal order but cost the abolition of the political character of society. Human rights are but a new form of control: behind the appearance of civil liberty, they limit freedom. Although they are called rights, in opposition to the aristocratic privilege that reigned before, they are a mechanism of political privilege which suppresses any challenge to the civil system. "*Anarchy* is the law of civil society emancipated from disjointing *privileges*, and the *anarchy* of *civil society* is the basis of the modern *public system*, just as the public system is in turn the guarantee of that anarchy. To the same extent as the two are opposed to each other they also determine each other" (Marx and Engels 1956: 158).

Freedom of religion, for example, is one of the rights supported in the Christian/civil state: individuals feel that they have been emancipated from religion when their disposition toward it becomes a private matter. The political state, however, can afford to take a democratic attitude and non-religious posture because bourgeois emancipation leaves religion intact: the right does not affect the ideology. "Precisely the slavery of civil society is in appearance the greatest freedom because it is in appearance the perfect independence of the individual. . . . Right has here taken the place of privilege" (157). After all, as proved by the secular rites of interpretation, "religion develops in its *practical* universality only where there is no *privileged* religion (cf. the North American States)" (156). In a related observation, Marx notes a consequence: "It is in the North American states—or at least a part of them—that the Jewish question loses its theological importance for the first time and becomes a really *secular* question" (Marx 1971: 90). Freedom of religion, like the other human rights, is granted on the provision that man accepts that he is human and not political. When, therefore, the Jew demands civil rights in the civil state, he acts in a civil manner: he demands his share of modern privileges. He does not realize that he "has already emancipated himself in a Jewish manner" (110), and that in addition he is already part of the dominant system.

Moreover, it is the mutually supportive pairing of Man and Jew that needs to be noticed. "Hence, the *political* emancipation of the Jews and the granting to them of the *'rights of man'* is an act the two sides of which are mutually interdependent. . . . The Jew has all the more right to the recognition of his 'free humanity' as 'free civil society' is thoroughly commercial and Jewish and the Jew is a necessary link in it" (Marx and Engels 1956: 153). Without using the term, Marx proposes that emancipation is only the civil dimension of Hebraization. "The Jews have emancipated themselves in so far as the Christians have become Jews. . . . Indeed, the practical dominance of Judaism over the Christian world has reached its unambiguous, normal expression in North America" (Marx 1971: 111). Emancipation has been successful not because it overcame differences but because, by appearing to tolerate, even eliminate them, it made them transparent. If, therefore, granting rights to the Jews is not an obligation but a precondition of bourgeois society, it can be argued that "the politically perfect, modern state that knows no religious privileges is also the perfect *Christian* state, and that hence the perfect Christian state, not only *can* emancipate the Jews but has emancipated them and by its very nature must emancipate them" (Marx and Engels 1956: 150). In claiming that "the true essence of the Jew has been realized and secularized in civil society" (Marx 1971: 114) and that the whole world today "is Jewish to the core" (Marx and Engels 1956: 148), the author is not referring to a liberation or fulfillment of Jewish tradition: he shows how the image of the middle-class Jew has been produced in civil society as a true essence of his destiny and its history.

If Marx does not introduce to his analysis any Hellenic elements,[73] this is because the historicity (rather than the authenticity, as is usually the case) of Judaism attracts his attention—its political, rather than ethnic, signification. Positing the "Jewish question" as the question of the Hebraic (to use the terminology of this study), he approaches the "actual Jew" (Marx 1971: 110) as a historical construct—a product, a model, and an icon of the middle class and its civil state—and tries to extract his "imaginary nationality" (113). He insists that "real, *worldly* Jewry and hence *religious* Judaism *too*, is being continually produced by the *present civil life* and finds its final development in the *money system*" (Marx and Engels 1956: 147). As he puts it elsewhere: "From its own bowels civil society constantly begets Judaism" (Marx 1971: 110). He looks at the Jew of the civil society, of the human rights, of the free trade, and of the bourgeois culture—the Jew produced by an emancipation that needed his independence for its own legitimacy. Civil society, modern state, human rights, political emancipation, and Judaism are all interconnected and interdependent, and ought to be examined together. For Marx, Jewish rights are not an issue at all. At the time he wrote his review exposing the "Jewish question" as an ideology, he was also engaged in his critique of Hegel's *Philosophy of Right* (1821, 1833), the introduction to which he published, together with the review, in the same issue of *Deutsch-französische Jahrbücher*. As it is known from that complementary piece, his understanding of "rights" was radicalized by a socio-political questioning of modernity. While Bauer asked for the emancipation of Jews from Judaism,[74] Marx proposed the emancipation of society from the Hebraic bourgeois regime, concluding his essay with the aphorism: "In the last analysis the emancipation of the Jews is the emancipation of humanity from Judaism" (110).

Although there were many Jewish and non-Jewish reactions to Bauer's position, apparently there were none to Marx's written in that generation (Rotenstreich 1959: 26).[75] While his contemporary Heinrich Heine was developing the Hebraic-Hellenic opposition into a model of the options of liberal culture (or the possibility of *Bildung* under Manchester capitalism), Marx made a radical turn against Judaism as the most representative expression of bourgeois ideology. Seen in the Marxian context, the *Dialectic of Enlightenment* emerges as a fierce rebuttal of his position. Here the demonization of Lukács' Greece serves to invert Marx's critique of modernity as the Hebraization of the political by the bourgeoisie. Whereas Marx's essay portrayed the Jew as the hero of capitalism, Horkheimer and Adorno attribute this role to Odysseus, this time, in archetypal dimensions; where he asked for emancipation from Judaism, they urge liberation from Hellenism; where he traced capitalism to the construction of Judaism by the civil society, they blame it on the invention of civil society by Hellenism; where he wanted to liberate the political from the state (and later fought for the *Bildung* of the working class), they entertain the possibility of liberating the Enlightenment from mythology (and abandon the potential of *Bildung*). As a consequence, where he demanded the abolition of the modern state, they limit themselves to a critique of reason. What makes their position ahistorical is their disregard for cultural specificity, which allows them to traverse the centuries from epic to jazz without much careful differentiation. In addition, by adopting the Hebraic-Hellenic polarity, they neutralize Marx's interest in politics,[76] and support cultural criticism as resistance to modernity. By so doing, they continue the Marxist aesthetic tradition which "by no means adopts the view of art as ideology, and is concerned with the resistance of art to ideological appropriation" (Bowie 1990: 217–18). It is almost as if anti-Semitism were more a corruption of taste[77] than the perverse excess of a particular social order. By generalizing Judaism, Marx discovered the Hebraic at the heart of capital; by universalizing anti-Semitism, Horkheimer and Adorno eliminate its material reality. Where he thought philosophy should abandon interpretation of the existing world and engage in creating a different one, they find it is too late for such change, and hope that at least a negative interpretation may make the world more bearable. With the decline of *Bildung* into the narcissism of adult melancholy,[78] Marx's political program becomes in their hands an interpretive ethic: the moral purity and superiority of *theoria*.

The loss of the radical Marxian potential in the *Dialectic of Enlightenment* becomes obvious when this book is compared with its contemporary *Réflexions sur la question Juive* (1946), translated as *Anti-Semite and Jew*, by Jean-Paul Sartre (1905–80), which also continues Marx's discussion from the standpoint of dialectic but adopts a very different historical perspective. Sartre defines man as a being in a real (historical, cultural, social, biological, economic) situation which produces and contains the options of his freedom. By applying this principle to the specific subject, he arrives at this methodological starting point: "If I wish to know *who* the Jew is, I must first inquire into the situation surrounding him, since he is a being in a situation." This condition determines identity. "The Jew is the one whom other men consider a Jew" (Sartre 1948: 69). There is no ontological grounding: identity is contingent. "Thus the Jew is in the situation of a Jew because he lives in the midst of a society that takes him for a Jew" (72). This emphasis on historical circumstance and social construction, which is in agreement with Marx's decision to look at the Jew of society, enables Sartre to reject (or rather situate) the issue of authenticity. With all essentialist questions abandoned, he proposes that "it is not the Jewish character that provokes anti-Semitism but, rather, that it is the anti-Semite who creates the Jew. The primary phenomenon, therefore, is anti-Semitism" (143). The Jew is a product of the capitalist society, and anti-Semitism a collective bourgeois crime. The problem, as Marx insisted, is not one of Jewish rights or emancipation. "The Jewish problem is born of anti-Semitism; thus it is anti-Semitism that we must suppress in order to resolve the problem" (147). Sartre is relentless in his criticism of complicity, insisting that "anti-Semitism is not a Jewish problem; it is *our* problem" (152).

With his socio-historical approach, Sartre does not need to trace the origins of anti-Semitism into the epic past or blame the perversity of reason on myth; neither does he need to resort to comparisons with Greece. Steering away from questions of origin, he conducts an anatomy of the situation of the anti-Semites. Most of them "belong to the lower middle class of towns" (25) and have "a fundamental incomprehension of the various forms of modern property" (23). They are culturally and politically the victims of modernity. The Jew plays two main roles: he helps them realize that they have rights (28) and establish "their status as possessors" (25). Sartre calls anti-Semitism "a poor man's snobbery" (26): the disaffected, deprived, frustrated lower classes find somebody to blame for their predicament. But the phenomenon goes deeper than that. In their racism, Sartre discovers a misdirected hostility against the modern political system. "Any anti-Semite is therefore in varying degree, the enemy of constituted authority" (32). This person tries to resist an incomprehensible, rootless, and chaotic modern world. "Anti-democratic, [the anti-Semite] is a natural product of democracies and can only manifest himself within the framework of the Republic" (33). In his thought, the Jew has been identified with bourgeois institutions and authority. This point agrees with Marx's depiction of Judaism as the typical expression of the middle class ideology and achievement.[79]

Sartre's critique indicts not only the anti-Semites but also the rest of society as accomplices. "*Men are accomplices to that which leaves them indifferent*" (Steiner 1964: 21). Even the democrat, who seems eager to protect the victim, in "his defense of the Jew saves the latter as man and annihilates him as a Jew" (Sartre 1948: 56). Bruno Bauer's condition for emancipation is part of his attitude: he prefers to see people as individuals who exist in independence and isolation, and does not accept that a Jewish problem exists because he thinks there is (or there should be) no Jew. While the anti-Semite "wishes to destroy him as a man and leave nothing in him but the Jew," Sartre notes at the conclusion of his critique, the democrat "wishes to destroy him as a Jew and leave nothing in him but the man, the abstract and universal subject of the rights of man and the rights of the citizen" (57). This is the essence of liberal conviction.

The critiques of Marx and Sartre are in many respects complementary: the first exposes Judaism as the bourgeois ideology, and the second describes the actual Jew as the victim of that ideology. They agree on the fundamental premise that the Jews were produced by the culture of the middle class and should be discussed in this context. Because Sartre, like Marx, looks at the historical situation and the socio-economic context, and is able to see the Jew as a cultural (Christian, European, bourgeois) construct, he requires no discussion of the Hellenic. For him, the Jew is the bourgeois myth par excellence. For Horkheimer and Adorno, on the contrary, the Jew is a historical essence—the suspended positivity of secular dialectics. This results in a difference of great significance in their respective positions: whereas for Sartre the Jew is a bourgeois myth, for Horkheimer and Adorno myth is the evil of Hellenism. The former position is consistent with Marx's political critique of Judaism as the logic of capitalism; the latter belongs to the theological tradition of the hermeneutic attack on myth, which was part of the Protestant rejection of miracles and later found its disciplinary articulation in Higher Criticism. Horkheimer and Adorno continued the same theological tradition, believing that "all philosophy is the exegesis of the texts that sought truth" (Friedman 1981: 211). They applied historical readings to texts in order not to situate but to shield them by showing that they constitute the true and only history.

Between Marx's anatomy of the dialectic of bourgeois emancipation and the attack on the false religion of Enlightenment by Horkheimer and Adorno stands *The Protestant Ethic and the Spirit of Capitalism*, a critique of the faith position of modernity by "that bourgeois social philosopher . . . who was neither the *bête noire* nor the *bête blanche* of the German intelligentsia and yet remained its challenging inspiration even where his name remained unspoken" (Fietkau 1986: 169). The *Dialectic* remains faithful to the "re-theologizing of the issues" (173) in the work of Bloch, Lukács, Benjamin, and Carl Schmitt, and systematically ignores Weber's approach because the latter associates reason with the realm that Horkheimer and Adorno were unwilling to criticize—the intrinsic Other of critique: religion. "*The Protestant Ethic* aims at demonstrating the intimate relationship between the rationalization of modern life (with its resultant *Entzauberung*, or desacralization, its transformation into an organized and disciplined market system) and the development of the Lutheran or Calvinistic notion of a *Beruf*, or religiously sanctioned vocation to live ascetically *within* the world itself" (Jameson 1988: 19).

Whereas the authors of the *Dialectic* expose the myth of reason, Max Weber (1864–1920) studies the religion of reason—the enterprise of faith after its withdrawal from the church-controlled economy of other-worldliness. Long before the Frankfurt School denounced instrumentalism, he

had noted the loss of ritual and magic: "The fate of our times is characterized by rationalization and intellectualization and, above all, by the 'disenchantment of the world.' Precisely the ultimate and most sublime values
have retreated from public life either into the transcendental realm of mystic life or into the brotherliness of direct and personal human relations"
(Weber 1958a: 155). In his view, it was the Puritan outlook that determined the development of a rationally controlled life, personal, economic,
or otherwise.[80] The decisive feature of this outlook was "the valuation of
the fulfillment of duty in worldly affairs as the highest form which the
moral activity of the individual could assume. . . . The only way of living
acceptably to God was not to surpass worldly morality in monastic asceticism, but solely through the fulfillment of the obligations imposed upon
the individual by his position in the world. That was his calling" (Weber
1976: 80). The conviction of calling provided an ethical teleology balancing
the sense of homelessness from the church. The individual acquired his
calling and his understanding of rights together: they reinforced each
other, giving the faithful the direction and dignity of personal duty. "The
process of sanctifying life could thus almost take on the character of a
business enterprise" (124). Life turned busy because it had to be not just
lived but run: the fulfillment of duty (that is, the response to the calling)
took the character of labor. "The treatment of labour as a calling became as
characteristic of the modern worker as the corresponding attitude toward
acquisition of the business man" (179). Weber discovers the theological
origins of the capitalist enterprise in this deal between soul and grace, the
marketing of eternity.

Puritans labored willfully under their own calling, profiting at the same
time from the ascetic tasks of life management, the business of salvation.
"The emphasis on the ascetic importance of a fixed calling provided an
ethical justification of the modern specialized division of labour. In a similar way the providential interpretation of profit-making justified the activities of the business man. . . . The whole power of the God of the Old Testament, who rewards His people for their obedience in this life, necessarily
exercised a similar influence on the Puritan who . . . compared his own
state of grace with that of the heroes of the Bible, and in the process interpreted the statements of the Scriptures as the articles of a book of statutes"
(163–64). The business of salvation, reoccupied from the church industry
of indulgence, has been succinctly described by the formula "the rationalization of ends . . . is to the religionalization of means . . . as the rationalization of means . . . is to the 'nonfinalization' of religion" (Jameson 1988: 21),
and elucidated as follows: "This moment of the formula . . . does more than
to suggest that religion is not, as the vulgar Marxist analysis had it, some
mere reflex of infrastructural change. Indeed, it shifts the emphasis from
the relationship between religion and 'ends,' or conscious, superstructural

values, and draws our attention to the effect of religious change on the organization of the means themselves; . . . Thus paradoxically religionalization becomes itself the principal agent in the process of secularization as a whole" (21). The reoccupation of religious positions by new answers or, more specifically, the reoccupation of exegetical positions by interpretation, amounts less to secularization than to deritualization. By pointing out the interior spaces of the sacred, by describing the law of the commandments that succeeded the rites of the sacraments, Weber suggests that "the transition from religion to *Entzauberung,* from the medieval to the modern moment, is effected . . . not by making life less religious but by making it *more* so. Calvin did not desacralize the world; on the contrary, he turned the *entire* world into a monastery" (23). The sacralization of the world and the sanctification of life effected by the Reformation federal theology (Weir 1990), which produced the Puritan *Lebensmethodik* during the process of rationalization, is the object of Weber's work. It is the transformation of this calling from vocation to discipline (Hsia 1989) that would result later in the ideal of *Bildung* (Goldman 1988) as well as the rationalization of work (Campbell 1989).

Without proposing a causal explanation, Weber is reacting to the crude materialism of certain Marxist hypotheses. "Weber's limited thesis was merely that in the formation of this pattern of rationally ordered life . . . the religious component must be considered as an important factor. . . . In tracing the affinity between the bourgeois life pattern and certain components of the religious stylization of life, as shown most consistently by ascetic Protestantism, Weber emphasized the gradual genesis of a psychological habit that enabled men to meet the requirements of early modern capitalism" (Fischoff 1944: 63). He studies the bourgeois revolution, like Marx, using the model (or, in his terms, the "ideal type") of rationalization to highlight a particular dimension of historical change. In response to economist explanations, Weber "rejected the idea that religious ideas were only ideological manifestations of particular social conditions. Ideas for him were, at least in part, autonomous entities with a power to affect social changes" (Burrell 1968: 139–40). Thus he substituted the realm of ideas for the economic one, trying to show the interaction among configurations of meaning and structures of experience. His goal was to show through concrete analysis that ideas and principles, having their own role and power, may contribute to historical formation. Commentators have increasingly seen the compatibility of such a project with the Marxian approach (Antonio and Glassman 1987; Wiley 1987). They have also recognized that his affirmation of the materiality of values is more of "a reaction against historicism, which tended to conceive of man as the more or less unwitting tool of historical development" (Brand 1987: 50).

Of special interest for this discussion is Weber's understanding of the "Jewish question." In a chapter on "Judaism, Christianity, and the Socio-Economic Order" in *The Sociology of Religion*, although he acknowledges that "Judaism played a conspicuous role in the evolution of the modern capitalistic system" (Weber 1963: 248), he observes that "the Jews were relatively or altogether absent from the new and distinctive forms of modern capitalism, the rational organization of labor, especially production in an industrial enterprise of the factory type. . . . Hence, neither that which is new in the modern economic *system* nor that which is distinctive of the modern economic *temper* is specifically Jewish in origin" (250). In his view, there was nothing distinctly Jewish in the Puritan contributions to capitalist development. With this conclusion, he is rejecting the position of the social theorist Werner Sombart (1863–1941), the author of *The Modern Capitalism* (1902, 2 vols.), who in *The Jews and Economic Life* tried to do for Jews what Weber's *Protestant Ethic* did for the Reformation. "It was Werner Sombart, at this time a close collaborator of Weber, . . . who brought Jewry and Judaism into the circle of problems raised by the studies on the Puritan spirit. He emphasized that all those features which Weber had marked as relevant to the rise of capitalism, mainly the disciplined and purposeful direction of life, must be traced back to Judaism. His book *Die Juden und das Wirtschaftsleben* (1911) built a very broad argument around this core, touching on various aspects in order to prove the prominence of the Jewish contribution to the rise of modern capitalism. . . . For Sombart the Jewish migration started by the expulsion from Spain began the new epoch" (Liebeschütz 1964: 50). According to his main argument, "the importance of the Jews was twofold. On the one hand, they influenced the outward form of modern capitalism; on the other, they gave expression to its inward spirit. Under the first heading, the Jews contributed no small share in giving to economic relations the international aspect they bear to-day; in helping the modern state, that framework of capitalism, to become what it is; and lastly, in giving the capitalistic organization its peculiar features, by inventing a good many details of the commercial machinery which moves the business life of to-day, and by co-operating in the perfecting of others. Under the second heading, the importance of the Jews is so enormous because they, above all others, endowed economic life with its modern spirit; they seized upon the essential idea of capitalism and carried it to its fullest development" (Sombart 1951: 21).

Sombart believed that the same ideas shaped the spirit of Judaism and capitalism: rationalism, the contract between God and his people, divine bookkeeping, the conception of profit, and the like. Furthermore, he detected "an almost unique identity of view between Judaism and Puritanism. . . . In both will be found the preponderance of religious interests, the idea of divine rewards and punishments, asceticism *within* the world, the close relationship between religion and business, the arithmetical conception of sin, and, above all, the rationalization of life. . . . Puritanism *is* Judaism" (249). Judaism, Puritanism, Capitalism, Liberalism—all these systems were conflated in Sombart's view of economic understanding, which tended to look for sweeping parallels and disregard specific differences. According to this narrative, the result of the rationalistic transvaluation of economic values was nothing more than a repetition: "The *homo capitalisticus*, who is closely related to the *homo Judaeus*, both belonging to the same species, *homines rationalistici artificiales*" (238). Jews were simply better placed, geographically and philosophically, to pioneer capitalism, because they perfected Protestant ideas much earlier. Judaism has always given Europe life: "Israel passes over Europe like the sun: at its coming new life bursts forth; at its going all falls into decay" (13). Thus modernity is the combined result of two complementary forces: "The capitalistic civilization of our age is the fruit of the union between the Jews, a Southern people pushing into the North, and the Northern tribes, indigenous there. The Jews contributed an extraordinary capacity for commerce, and the Northern peoples, above all the Germans, an equally remarkable ability for technical inventions" (323).

Weber sharply disagreed with Sombart's assessment of the Jewish role. "Weber denied that the features characteristic of modern capitalism were created by the Jews, who never before their assimilation into the life of Western civilization had on their own account organised free labour with the aim of controlling the production of saleable goods according to the possibilities of the market. He agreed that Jewry had played an important part in economic life over many centuries, but had done so by participating in such activities as had existed in all types of advanced civilisation, with money as means of exchange. . . . The considerable skill obtained in all these specialised activities enabled them to become important carriers of modern commerce when it was rising in the seventeenth century. But for Weber their part in this initial period remained definitely different from that of the Protestant middle class who contributed the driving force for the industrial basis of the new enterprise" (Liebeschütz 1964: 51).

With their different but compatible approaches to ideology, Weber and Marx contribute to an analysis of Hebraism on the basis of its Protestant middle-class character that does not conflate it with the history of Jewry. Ahistorical views like those suggested by Sombart or Horkheimer and Adorno confuse the bourgeois uses of the Jew as model with the responses of those who identified themselves as Jews, contesting the Hebraic position, as historical essence, for themselves. Weber's decoding of the Puritan system of life management points to the emergence of conditions favorable to the Hebraization of modernity. Before certain people started claiming

Jewish identity and continuity for themselves, it was the religious stylization of bourgeois self-control (starting with the liberation of Scriptural interpretation into textual immanence) that took Biblical Judaism as a secular model, the covenant as a prototype of capitalist contract. The modern
Jew was emancipated into middle-class culture, the only culture that ever
was. Civil society, human rights, secular understanding, the self, and the
other fundamentals of this culture—questions and ideals that were never
an issue in the rest of the (Christian or other) world—were all invented
under the regime of interpretation, the mode of legitimate self-governance
established when the Reformation successfully projected itself as the originary in Christianity, namely, the Hebraic in faith (and the Hellenic in
knowledge).

Weber's interest in the importance of religion for socio-economic history goes back to the late 1880s. His exploration of Protestantism was part
of a seminal trend away from Dilthey's *Geisteswissenschaft*, which has been
described as *Kulturphilosophie* (Simmel) and *Kulturwissenschaft* (Sombart): the socio-philosophical study of culture produced during and around
the first decade of the twentieth century (by authors born mostly between
1856–66) and including books that appeared between the publications of
Nietzsche and Lukács.[81] The tone characterizing this voluminous production (most of which was presented as research, rather than philosophy or
critique) on the eve of the artistic avant-garde was one of anxiety over a sick
culture, apprehension about its imminent collapse, yearning for an apocalyptic rejuvenation, and a pervasive fear (shared by diverse writers like
Freud, Husserl, Vilfredo Pareto, Jane Harrison, and the early Weber) of
irrational forces that seemed to have eroded its foundations. In that climate, sociology (of culture) emerged as a universal discipline, psychoanalysis as treatment of the bourgeois, the violent end of history as a question of
messianic fulfillment, and the cleansing of signification as a linguistic and
aesthetic concern. Sanitary measures were proposed, therapeutic procedures devised, medicines and diets offered to a world which seemed to
suffer gravely from a social malaise that consumed the public organism
(Weindling 1989). In all these developments, the role of the Jew was an
issue of paramount importance. (Regarding its significance for the creation
of sociology, for example, see Mazlish 1989.) The twin enterprises of the
purification of the public sphere and the restoration of reason (or faith)
were launched at that time, and the administrative society was born. Since
personal temper (which in the past had been assigned to character, taste,
or *Bildung*) could no longer be trusted with Puritan ethic, society as a
whole, and not just individuals, were to be managed. The ideal of Kantian
criticism returned with a vengeance—critique as exorcism. There was a
gnawing suspicion that the Greek spirit of culture had turned suicidal, if
not malevolent, that the Faustian pact with Greek pleasure had to be de-

nounced. The Puritan administration undertook one of its largest projects so far, the treatment of culture for irrationality. The target of all the disciplines of public order became the irrational, most often represented by myth—the old enemy of anti-Hellenic forces like the Moderns, the Enlighteners, or the Left Hegelians.

THE SCIENCE OF MYTH

If there was a product of civilization that the bourgeoisie detested, it was myth. If there was a category of thought they renounced, it was myth. If there was one kind of story they found alien to logic, it was myth. Its continuing appeal seemed utterly puzzling. "Nothing surprised the promoters of the Enlightenment more, and left them standing more incredulously before the failure of what they thought were their ultimate exertions, than the survival of the contemptible old stories—the continuation of work on myth" (Blumenberg 1985: 274). Myth, the presumed structure of the premodern or the savage (ancient, Oriental, African, Asian, Latin American) mind, was the single belief the enlightened class did not tolerate. Discrediting it seemed vital to the superiority of the modern world view. The bourgeois who relied on his analytical reason, his informed knowledge, his unerring self-control, knew with absolute certainty that myth was false and found it a major obstacle to progress (Daniel 1990; Hübner 1983: 229–45). Thus, during the colonization of the Hebrew Bible and of the New Worlds in the sixteenth century, Protestant scholars began creating a number of disciplines to study and stigmatize myth. It took them much time, probably until the late eighteenth century, to admit that the people of Europe had myths too; but then those were called folktales and their study helped in the discovery of national identity.

Myth, of course, has always been posited as fundamentally Hellenic. Heidegger accepted that "myth itself is Greek," and Derrida conceded that there may be no non-Greek mythologies (Derrida 1981: 167). When Horkheimer and Adorno condemn archaic Greece for its creation, they are only repeating (although transposing to the realm of ideology) a blame that is as old as the study of the topic.[82] Ever since exegesis became interpretation at the dawn of the modern era, and the hermeneutic gaze turned from the allegories of the (Roman/Ovidian) fable to the symbols of the (Greek/Homeric) myth—partly in order to explain the heathenism in New Testament miracles by reference to Greek antiquity—myth has been inseparably associated with the Hellenic. Any advocacy of enlightenment presupposes an assault on the gods of Olympus. To return to the question: "Why is to speak of mythology always, more or less explicitly, to speak Greek or to be influenced by Greece?" (Detienne 1986: xi),[83] the answer is, because myth, as a subject of systematic knowledge, has been inextricably associated with

Greece, and at the same time because after the Renaissance and even before the Battle of the Books, the Greek first appeared connected with the mythological. In fact, the Ancients lost the struggle once they granted that they were merely defending false stories. By the time of Fontenelle's *De l'origine des fables* (1724), a science of myth was already in place.

Through its Homeric articulations, myth became the first non-Biblical subject of hermeneutics. The concept itself emerged quite late, only after it separated itself from the constellation of mythology and the concerns of theology. "To begin with, it must be stressed that the word 'myth' was not used in English until the nineteenth century. The word does not occur in eighteenth-century dictionaries or encyclopedias. When a single myth was referred to, it was always as a 'mythological fiction,' a 'poetical fiction,' a 'tradition,' a 'poetical history,' or, most commonly, a 'fable.' Sometimes this last was further refined to 'mythological fiction' in order to prevent confusion with other eighteenth-century uses of 'fable' to mean apologue or modern fable (such as Aesop's or La Fontaine's) and plot or story line. Almost everything relating to what we now think of as myth came, for the eighteenth century, under the heading of the word 'mythology.' This word did not then mean primarily a collection of myths or fables; it meant, first of all, an explanation or interpretation of myths. . . . [T]he most common eighteenth-century meaning of mythology is 'pagan theology,' and . . . religious concerns constitute the usual context in which mythology was discussed. From a Christian point of view, then, mythology is the opposite of true or Christian theology. It is false theology or pagan theology" (Richardson 1978: 10–11). Initially, its study was an examination of the scandalous (or foolish, barbaric, irrational, absurd), where the Hellenic served as an example of corruption and decadence. For some one hundred fifty years, myth (meaning falsehood and idolatry) was explicitly opposed to reason, debunked and rejected.

When theological interest in myth was not denouncing it for corruption, it was detecting Hebrew influences in the origins of ancient thought, and especially religion. "To the orthodox Christian view . . . pagan mythology was thus to be reduced to the context of the Scriptures. The deities and their exploits were more or less disguised or distorted derivations from Biblical revelation and history, and they were meaningful only in so far as they could be traced to Scriptural testimony. In the orthodox conception all religions originated in the one true religion" (Kuhn 1956: 1101). It was this position that Deists from Toland to Bentley attacked, proposing that the work of reason could be discovered even in primitive religions, and furthermore that, before idolatry, there existed a simple, natural, pure faith shared by all people. "For them the myths of the pagans and those of the Old Testament represented an original religion which was at once more reasonable and more catholic than Christianity. Christianity was not *the* one religion; it was one among many which at basis were united in a core of simple, natural, and universal truths" (1115). In this approach, as well as in *Scienza Nuova* (1725, 1730, 1744) by Giambattista Vico (1688–1744), ancient religion gained credibility for the first time. "By showing the similarity between a Greek myth and a biblical story, the deists could turn the orthodox attack on myth back on orthodoxy itself" (Richardson 1978: 12). Thus what mythology really proved was not the superiority of Christianity but the existence of a common origin for all religions, which was taken to be the true, historical revelation. Mythography did not accord Greek myth any special importance. It was the Egyptians and the Orientals (as well as native Druids) who benefited from comparisons in the second half of the eighteenth century, while the antiquity of the Hebrew Bible suffered.

In response to the Deist challenge, Higher Criticism judged the Bible by the ordinary standards of secular history, seeking its defense in a historical, rather than typological, justification. The acceptance of a historical Jesus justified faith in the kerygmatic Christ. "A rationalist and skeptical approach to myth was also evolved by those biblical critics who sought to bolster Christianity not by exalting the whole of the Bible over pagan beliefs and traditions, but by purging it of its mythical elements in order to arrive at a pure and trustworthy historical core that could command belief in a rationalist age. This movement, usually called the higher criticism and most marked in Germany, used an historical-critical approach to the Bible and may be traced back to the same roots as the deists and the rationalist French mythographers. From Bayle, Spinoza, and Richard Simon down through Jean Astruc to Lessing, Reimarus, Eichhorn, and eventually D. F. Strauss, this historical approach to the Bible depended upon the clear opposition of history and myth. The new criticism was textual, critical, and historical and . . . it reversed a long tendency in theological studies toward typology, that technique—also called 'figural realism' or 'phenomenal prophecy'—which, from St. Paul on, interprets the events and figures of the Old Testament as historical prefigurations or prophecies (types) of New Testament events and persons (archetypes). . . . Anything not rationally acceptable or corroborated by external evidence was relegated to the category of myth. . . . The critical historical view of the Bible was intended by the higher criticism as a defense of Christianity, by the deists to defend 'pure' religion, and by atheists to attack both of these; it was used by no one to defend or affirm the value of myth itself" (21–22). Myth was no longer the superstition of belief but the seduction of reason, and thus epistemologically, rather than theologically, discredited.

At the same time, during the eighteenth century, attention to myth in other areas grew much less moral and practical, and much more artistic and spiritual. As criticism defeated theology in the battle for interpretation of the Protestant text, emphasis shifted gradually from the empirical logic of the argument to the expressive strength of the style—something that the person of taste could appreciate and savor. Myth started speaking to people of letters less about sin, more about pleasure; less about idolatry, more about the absolute. Eventually, it liberated itself from theology and entered the aesthetic sphere of contemplation. "Just as the case against myth was made by both Christian and anti-Christian writers, so the eighteenth-century argument in favor of myth had two sides, both having a strong literary element from the start. One affirmation of myth stemmed from an interest in Homer and the other from a literary interest in the Bible" (25).[84] In the 1730s, Thomas Blackwell sought in myth the explanation of Homer's greatness and discovered in it primitive wisdom—social as well as poetic. Two decades later, Lowth protected the Bible from rationalist criticism by suggesting an intrinsic reading, one based on its literary qualities.[85] On the one hand, myth is appropriated through aestheticization by literature and philosophy; on the other, it is appropriated through theologization by Biblical interpretation.

Two kinds of myth emerge: the false one (which is bad history) and the authentic one (which is the narrative of contemplation). Authors from Herder to Coleridge were fascinated by the discovery of its expressive potential: "These writers and critics perceived the affirmative thrust of the higher criticism to be an effort not to destroy the authority of Scripture but to shift it from a reliance upon the historical accuracy of certain events to a reliance upon the mythic truth of the narratives" (35). Syncretic mythography, a popular movement among scholars, churchmen, and connoisseurs which flourished from the 1770s to the 1830s, contributed to this reconsideration. Finally, myth appeared to be endowed with truth of a special order. "What to the Augustans had been preposterous 'fictions' and outworn 'machines' became, through the influence of syncretic mythography, imaginative truth which could express a system of values or ultimate reality as the particular poet might conceive it to be. . . . And it was from this background of mythography that such Romantic poems as Blake's *Jerusalem*, Shelley's *Adonais*, and Keats's *Hyperion*—as well as a host of lesser poems—drew inspiration, material, character, and form" (Kuhn 1956: 1097). Myth was recognized as an alternative mode of comprehension, promising new vistas to the theoretical view of the world.

It was Romantic literature and philosophy that elevated myth to a privileged status, the aesthetic and the absolute. "The historical interest created by the [German] scientific mythologists combines with the poetical interest which is the product of the attitudes of the Romantic poets to make the province of Greek mythology completely respected by the middle of the nineteenth century" (Zwenderling 1964: 456). Idealism, and especially aesthetics, discovered in myth a primary orientation and even an articulation of the spirit of beauty (Winckelmann) or history (Hegel). The Romantic awareness of mythology and its potential (narrative or symbolic) in an age deprived of religious faith was intense as the artists, primarily the poets, discovered in myth a means of addressing modern problems they considered spiritual. "The Romantic concept of myth first of all occurs in reflections on the history of poetry: modern art's confounding chaos and detachment, freed from all confining genres, was attributed to the lack of a collective foundation (which the Romantics considered necessary for poetical freedom) such as that given to Greek art in ancient mythology" (Menninghaus 1988: 295). Furthermore, Romantic scholarship, following the precepts of philology, introduced two cardinal distinctions to the understanding of the Hellenic: the Greek with the two heads, the mythological and the philosophical; and the opposition between mythology and history which obsessed the Left Hegelians (but also Kierkegaard, Nietzsche, and Heidegger). As a result, what was anathema to the Enlightenment (Pépin 1958: 34–41; Starobinski 1989)—the irrationality of myth—became the archetype for Romanticism through its justification by aesthetic coherence and symbolic power.

To be sure, myth was not an alternative to religion but the vision of a higher religion (which the higher criticism of reason had not delivered). For the Romantics, "the separation of myth and belief was not a necessary feature of modernity, but an ill to be remedied if a true culture of community and conviction was to come about. They foresaw a new birth from the pangs of revolution and war which Europe was suffering; revolution was to be, in Friedrich Schlegel's phrase, an 'Inzitament der Religion.' They struggled back towards religion—a new one such as the young Schlegel dreamed of, or the old one to which numerous Romantics converted—as a binding force for the imagination. Sometimes they talked of creating a mythology—from modern physics, Indian philosophy, Shakespeare, Cervantes, Spinoza" (Reed 1980: 194), investing absolute knowledge or beauty with ethical significance and hoping to replace dogmatic theology with sublime revelation. For a while, the potential of myth seemed limitless and its resources inexhaustible: "With fresh Indic and Nordic materials, with the example of Osian to show what could still be done in modern times and in an era of new nationalism, modern writers began to wonder if indeed it might be possible for a poet-prophet to write heroic, perhaps even sacred poetry for the modern age. In Germany, Friedrich Schlegel and in America, Emerson put this aim explicitly as a call for a new mythology" (Richardson 1978: 33). This goal appeared as the first (counter)revolutionary project of the autonomous aesthetic—a revolution of the free spirit: "What, then, does the artist who sees his or her work in terms of the need for a new mythology do in the meanwhile, in a society which seems to be moving further and further away from the integration sought in the new mythology? . . . Widely divergent approaches are possible to this dilemma. The artist may have to give up art altogether, as Hölderlin suggested, in the name of political praxis. In the case of Wagner, art really is supposed to become the mythology of the present" (Bowie 1990: 103). Wagner's *Gesamtkunstwerk* may well be the most comprehensive realization of the project of mythology, as it surveys (a bankrupt) world history and announces a new beginning. Together with Zionism, advanced by Theodor Herzl (1860–1904) in the 1890s,[86] it is also the most grandiose response to the mandate "We need a new mythology" (Hölderlin 1988: 155) of the so-called "Oldest System-Program of German Idealism" (1796?), published by Rosenzweig in 1917 and variously attributed to Hölderlin, Hegel, and Schelling (Hansen 1989).

Klopstock, the "German Milton," had already made "an effort to found a new Protestant mythology to set up against the Greek" (Shaffer 1975: 311). The "System-Program" is a critical one in that it represents the major expression of the crisis associated with the project of mythology, the crisis of autonomy after Kant and the Revolution. It is the program of a transcendental aesthetics, of an aesthetic philosophy that aspires to become art and overcome both critique and politics. Philosophy may achieve that only by transforming itself into art (Lacoue-Labarthe and Nancy 1988: 27–37). The very possibility of autonomy is at stake here. The plan is ambivalent toward Kant: "It wants to re-unify the world that has been split up by Kant's radical critique of traditional metaphysics, at the same time as hanging on to Kant's insistence on our capacity for self-determination" (Bowie 1990: 45). It is equally ambivalent toward the revolution, as it wants to see the revolutionary potential materialized by other means. While the System is still concerned with what Hölderlin was calling in 1795 "public education" and Schelling in 1796 "national education," it announces an ethics of aesthetics and a mythology of reason, promising the re-solution of contra-diction. It preaches complete emancipation from "the entire miserable human construct of state, constitution, government, legislation" (Hölderlin 1988: 154) as well as from the superstition of "a moral world, divinity, immortality" (155), demanding this ideal: "Absolute freedom of all spirits who carry the intellectual world within themselves, and who must search neither God nor immortality *outside of themselves*" (155).

Finally, it proclaims the ultimate reconciliation, asserting that "truth and goodness are united as sisters *only in beauty*" (155). Beauty is not only synthesis but also the total depth, the essence of self-founding autonomy. The new mythology, the mythology of reason, is an aesthetic one in that it seeks its laws only within itself. "If, in Idealism's fundamental myth, only the form of a myth is now meant to be put into effect, with abstract names and in conscious unsurpassability, then this myth has its point in the representation of autogenesis, of the subject's self-production" (Blumenberg 1985: 269). At the same time, this mythology is the religion of autonomy—

the cult of self-rule, the apotheosis of the rule of autonomy: "Monotheism of reason and of the heart, polytheism of the imagination and art, those are what we need!" (Hölderlin 1988: 155). The religion of mythology, the monotheism of polytheism, the reason of beauty, the law of autonomy—all these are variations on the ultimate promise of interpretation (of the effort "to explain something hierarchically lower from something higher," as Karl Mannheim wrote in his review of *The Theory of the Novel*): emancipation as the incarnation of scripture, atonement as the literalization of the spirit— in other words, the Hebraization of Hellenism. "A higher spirit, sent from heavens, will have to found this new religion among us; it will be the last, the greatest achievement of mankind" (156). This is how myth will redeem history.[87]

It is the search for a new mythology[88] that organizes the program and makes the System the central task of Idealist philosophy. "In German Idealism 'system' was explicitly understood as the requirement of *absolute* knowledge. In addition, system itself became the *absolute requirement* and thus the key term for philosophy as such. This change in the idea of system from the seventeenth and eighteenth centuries to that of German Idealism at the beginning of the nineteenth century accordingly presupposes that philosophy understood itself as absolute, infinite cognition" (Heidegger 1985: 35). The subject of philosophy is its own history. This also changes the meaning of reason, turning it into contemplation: it is no longer the order of things but the system of understanding that dictates the rules. "Reason is the faculty of looking out into a view, the faculty of forming a horizon. Thus, reason itself is nothing other than the faculty of system" (37), the imperial exercise of *theoria*: it rules the views it commands. "Reason is the presupposing faculty, what truly reaches out and encompasses. The presupposition which it posits is that unity on the basis of which knowledge of a realm of objects and a world is at all possible. . . . Reason is in itself systematic, at once the faculty and demand of system" (37).

At the same time, however, the will to system, at the very moment it claims to replace religion with its Program, at the moment it promises to redeem history in the aesthetic myth, is forced to repeat the history of this redemption as the truth of history. "Only since the philosophy of German Idealism is there a *history* of philosophy in such a way that history itself is a path of absolute knowing on the way to itself. History is now no longer what is past, what one is finished with and has discarded, but it is the constant form of becoming of Spirit itself. In German Idealism, history is understood metaphysically for the first time. . . . For the thinkers of German Idealism . . . system is the totality of Being in the totality of its truth and the history of the truth" (48). Thought is trapped in a vicious circle because the moment history achieves the status of truth, as it does in this philosophy, is also the moment when truth is burdened with (its) history.

Theoria can only survey the ruins of civilization. In this polarity of myth and history, the ugly Greek again raises her two heads and with her gaze turns the aesthetic body into stone.

The movement from the program to the System, from the mythological to the speculative, from contemplation to identity, is characterized by a contradictory logic. Winckelmann wrote in 1755: "The only way for us to become great, and indeed—if this is possible—inimitable, is by imitating the ancients" (Winckelmann 1985: 33). This attitude, this logic of the imitation of the Greeks,[89] is the double bind of the Hellenic. "Why a logic of the *double bind*? Because the appropriation of the means of identification must both take place, and not take place, through the imitation of the ancients, essentially the Greeks. It must because there is no other model but that of the Greeks (following the collapse of religious transcendence and its corresponding social and political structures: one will recall that it is German thought that proclaimed the death of God and that popular romanticism founded itself on a nostalgia for medieval Christianity). It must not because the Greek model has already served the needs of others" (Lacoue-Labarthe and Nancy 1990: 300). The contradiction of the injunction is quite apparent in another expression of the mandate for a new myth, written a few years after the "System-Program" by Friedrich Schlegel in the "Talk on Mythology" part of his *Dialogue on Poetry* (1799–1800): "The modern poet must create all these things from within himself, and many have done it splendidly; up to now, however, each poet separately and each work from its very beginning, like a new creation out of nothing. I will go right to the point. Our poetry, I maintain, lacks a focal point, such as mythology was for the ancients; and one could summarize all the essentials in which modern poetry is inferior to the ancient in these words: We have no mythology. But, I add, we are close to obtaining one or, rather, it is time that we earnestly work together to create one. For it will come to us by an entirely opposite way from that of previous ages, which was everywhere the first flower of youthful imagination, directly joining and imitating what was most immediate and vital in the sensuous world. The new mythology, in contrast, must be forged from the deepest depths of the spirit; it must be the most artful of all works of art, for it must encompass all the others; a new bed and vessel for the ancient, eternal fountainhead of poetry, and even the infinite poem concealing the seeds of all poems" (Schlegel 1968: 81–82). The poetic ideal can be understood only with reference to the Greeks and yet can be realized only by means that are antagonistic to theirs: there is need for a Greek myth that is completely non-Greek. The treatment proposed for the disease of history (namely, the epigonality of modernity) is allopathy. Because of the way the Hellenic has been articulated, because of the double bind of an autonomy aesthetically defined, "in the modern epoch—even though that epoch reverses, in principle, the

Greek relationship between art and nature—one must indeed repeat that which is most Greek among the Greeks. Begin the Greeks again. —That is to say, no longer be Greek at all" (Lacoue-Labarthe 1978: 71).[90]

If there is no longer anything immediate to imitate or any tradition to continue, if the modern poet is the one who has been creating out of nothing, the promise of mythology is a spiritual one: the totality of the aesthetic praxis. The Moderns, who believe in it, are those who are against the Ancients because they themselves want to be the true Greeks and therefore need the Greeks dead. Indeed, the extinction of Greece is the inadmissible desire at the heart of the post-Reformation world, a desire for which there is no common term (like anti-Hellenism, for example) or tradition of study—no regret or research. If there is a common thread connecting all trends within the project of modernity; if there is a common denominator in all its forms of racism and discrimination; if there is a common element in all fears and persecutions (of otherness, difference, heterology, and skepticism), it is the philosophical colonization of Greece by the Hellenic ideal and her death sentence pronounced by universal proclamations of philhellenism. From the viewpoint of the Hellenic ideal, the Greeks are dead—that is why, unlike other Moderns, no Greek alive, no modern Greek has been compared to Socrates or Pericles, or to any Hebraic figures for that matter. The Hellenic extermination (executed over and over again by masters like Horkheimer and Adorno) is the unspeakable (because originary) violence of all interpretation and emancipation.[91]

As exemplified by a work like the *Dialectic*, Mythology as the (exclusively Christian, regardless of the author's ethnicity) study of myth has not been just another area of specialty but an assemblage of disciplines which together constitute a particular domain of knowledge—the (guilty) moral conscience of epigonal modernity. "To many Christian scholars it was inadmissible that a pagan people ignorant of Revelation could be thought of as living a serenely contented life. The Greeks had not escaped the Fall. The beautiful surface of Greek life and art, the harmonious forms admired by Winckelmann, could only be a covering drawn over intense and unresolved primitive terrors and confusions. It was these scholars who first sought—and found—what has been called the *Nachtseite*, the dark underside of ancient civilization, which they claimed was closely related to the oriental cultures classicism had tried to reject and disavow as barbarian. And it was they who issued the only significant challenge to the neohumanist version of classical antiquity that had established itself as an orthodoxy in the German universities" (Gossman 1986: 46). The disciplines of Mythology have included areas of fields as diverse as philology, comparative mythology, anthropology, folklore, history of religion, psychology, psychoanalysis, literary theory, examinations of ideology, and media studies (Barthes 1972). Any critique of modernity in the nineteenth and twentieth centuries has been based on these disciplines which have constituted the scholarship of cultural criticism, especially after (what the intelligentsia saw as) the failure of the proletariat to rise and demonstrate in, or even take over, the Parisian arcades. These disciplines were also the methodologies of high culture and codifications of discrimination which affirmed the superiority of elite taste. They offered the professional training promised by *Bildung* after it shed its democratic aspirations. They started expressing their abhorrence of popular taste some time before the mid–nineteenth century, when myth was first connected with popular ideology, man's primitive instincts, woman's treacherous sensuality (Kestner 1989), the false consciousness of the masses, and the disruptive power of politics. From the early nineteenth century until the end of World War I, Europe became obsessed with degeneration, individual or collective (Pick 1990). Disciplines and arts from medicine to statistics and social sciences to literature voiced an obsessive fear of the masses (as crowds), the city, criminals, and atheism, while recording and categorizing psychological, sexual, and national pathologies. Malady, perversion, contamination, and decay seemed to threaten order and health. From France to Russia and from Italy to Sweden, intellectuals and administrators, artists and scientists saw the barbarians at the gates. Visions and projects of regeneration developed along with a morbid fascination with the vulgar, the banal, and the transgressive. The alarm was less over revolution than pollution, less over political anarchy than social decline. Above all, it appears that in this "age of declining culture or without culture" (Wittgenstein), civilization has come under attack. A host of philosophers, psychologists, historians, and biologists warned that barbarism could unleash its demonic potential any time. Politicians and educators discerned its Dionysian fury (McGrath 1974) lurking in public squares and state institutions, salons and bedrooms.

Greece provided the central stage and characters for reenactments of this panic. The fear spread that the Grecian urn might turn into a Pandora's box (Frank Wedekind). It was already well-known that the stories of the Greeks were not all harmony and serenity. With the help of Burnouf, Frazer, Harrison, and Dodds, modernism used these narratives to depict disorder, disequilibrium, dissolution. To artists like Léger, Stravinsky, de Chirico, or Richard Strauss, they signified primeval passion; to authors like Hofmannsthal, Joyce, Svevo, Pound, Yeats, D'Annunzio, and Giraudoux, they denoted instability, disorientation, and uncertainty. Similar feelings were shared even by those who found the "mythical method" employed in Joyce's *Ulysses* "a way of controlling, of ordering, of giving a shape and a significance to the immense panorama of futility and anarchy which is contemporary history" (Eliot 1923: 483).

This development of modern art "makes the problem of neo-classicism a touchstone for every interpretation of artistic modernity" (Bürger 1984–85: 118). George, Jung, H. D., Mauss, Kraus, and Gide probed the dark secrets of mythic memory. For Freud, Sartre, Milhaud, or Dali, mythology mediated the problematic relation between philosophy and history. Ambiguous figures like Narcissus (Valéry) or Tiresias (Eliot) emerged as archetypes. From Mallarmé's *Les dieux antiques* (1880) to Wilhelm Wundt's *Mythus und Religion* (1905–9, 3 vols.), Ernst Cassirer's *Language and Myth* (1924), Lévy-Bruhl's *La mythologie primitive* (1935), Georges Dumézil's *Mythes et dieux des Germains* (1939), and Lévi-Strauss's tetralogy *Mythologiques* (1964–71), the exploration of mythic thought became a major scientific, philosophical, and artistic concern for people of all political persuasions. For Modernism, which has been called "myth turned against itself" (Adorno 1984: 34), mythology provided the grand narrative of temptation—one of defiance or seduction, revolt or fall (all represented in the films of Pier-Paolo Pasolini).

Another notable example, this time from theology, is the "demythologizing" of the kerygma (Bartsch 1953) proposed by Rudolf Bultmann (1884–1976). "The 'demythologizing' movement in twentieth-century Protestant theology and exegesis stems precisely from an awareness that the category of myth had subverted that of revealed historicity" (Steiner 1984: 110). For Bultmann, mythology is the use of worldly, human terms to express the other-worldly, the divine. Under the influence of Heidegger, "demythologization cuts to the letter itself. It consists in a new use of hermeneutics, which is no longer *edification* . . . but a boring under the literal meaning, a *de-struction*, that is to say, a de-construction, of the letter itself" (Ricoeur 1974: 389). Demythologization is the first stage of kerygmatic interpretation—not a demystification but an interpretation of myth which follows the intention of the myth (which is to be demythologized). "Demythologization then is only the inverse side of the grasp of the kerygma" (389). It is the proper beginning of the understanding of kerygma as dictated by itself. "Thus, Bultmann's entire undertaking is pursued on the assumption that the kerygma itself wants to be demythologized. . . . It is the kerygmatic core of the original preaching which not only requires but initiates and sets in motion the process of demythologization" (392). The similarities of this principle with the deconstructionist idea that texts set in motion their own deconstruction which the reader only applies—or that the sacred text "assigns the task to the translator, and it is sacred *inasmuch as* it announces itself as . . . to-be-translated" (Derrida 1985: 203)—are obvious.

The disciplines of Mythology studied myth and its Hellenic origins, trying to cleanse modernity ethically, to purify it from an irrationalism that was first perceived as psychological, later intellectual, and finally political. During the period 1880–1920, almost everywhere in the Protestant West there is an endless scholarly fascination with the dark power of irrational forces, from the magical to the physiological. "Scholarship of this type rediscovered the importance of myth as determining the actions of men and society. The study of myths was transferred from anthropology, where it had played a leading role for some time, to the social sciences and the humanities. Myth was no longer confined to the thought of primitive man but was treated as a present concern, an enemy to be defeated and exorcised" (Mosse 1985: 47). By the time it was identified with the political and appeared to threaten the religion of art and cultivation, myth, and with it the Hellenic in general, became the subject of exorcism. If Thomas Mann (1875–1955) was the last representative of self-cultivation, *The Magic Mountain* (1924) is the encyclopedic compendium of these disciplines, and *Doktor Faustus* (1947) the monument of exorcism.[92] Not only did Mythology contribute to the ethnographic construction of the exotic but, from Durkheim to René Girard and from Karl Kerényi to Mircea Eliade, it also responded to the fear that politics "appears to have largely replaced [myth] in modern societies" (Lévi-Strauss 1963: 209). There have been a few valuable reminders of the ideological constitution of ethnography: "To cite, today or tomorrow, that which everyone agrees to call myth is to endorse an out-of-date faithful acceptance of a cultural model that appeared in the eighteenth century when the sum total of accepted ideas concerning pagan divinities between Ovid and Apollodorus are in the realm of *fable* which scholarly erudition then called *mythology*. . . . It thus seems risky to have wished to take it as the subject for a rigidly applied method of scholarly research and to have laid down its rules since the discovery of the West Indies" (Detienne 1986: 131–32). This view, however, cannot be accepted as long as Mythology identifies its subject with the irrational, and proceeds to discover its operations in socio-political turmoil and conflict.[93]

The cathartic and therapeutic treatment of the pathological and the irrational by the disciplines of Mythology is best observed in their maenadic pursuit of Dionysus, the god of mysteries and orgies. "No other Greek god has created more confusion in the modern mind, nor produced a wider spectrum of different and often contradictory interpretations. By the same token, Dionysus has also stimulated more interest than any pagan deity" (Henrichs 1984: 240). In addition to the writings of Rilke, Gide, and Mann, suffice to acknowledge here his presence in the operas *Ariadne auf Naxos* (1916) by Richard Strauss, *Revelation in the Courthouse Park* (1961) by Harry Partch, *The Bassarids* (1966) by Hans Werner Henze, and *Death in Venice* (1973) by Benjamin Britten. Previously the god had appeared in the arts as the exuberant Bacchus. "From the Renaissance until about 1800, the life aspect of Dionysus was the dominant feature. The Romantic reaction rediscovered the death aspect, through direct recourse to Greek literature rather than Latin" (Henrichs 1984: 212).

While Winckelmann was probably the first to contrast the masculine ideal of Apollo with the homoerotic beauty of Dionysus, the dual nature of the latter (which internalized the Apollo-Dionysus opposition) was discovered by the generation of Lessing and Herder. The invention of the Greek with two heads, the split personality, the schizophrenic disposition, the dual nature, may be dated to this internalization of the conflict, this aestheticization of difference, this dialectization of inconsistency. "Eighteenth-century Hellenism was still an Apollo-governed Hellenism; but the Romanticists had dethroned Apollo and set the tragic Dionysos in his place" (Robertson 1924: 22).[94] It was the discipline of dialectics—the self-reflexive exercise of contemplation, the introspective application of aesthetics to the self—that, before the end of the century, constructed, out of the presumably irreconcilable contradictions in tragedy, the model of an inherently torn and divided Greece. "It is known that the Germans discovered, at the dawn of speculative idealism and of romantic philology (in the last decade of the eighteenth century, at Jena, among Schlegel, Hölderlin, Hegel, and Schelling), that Greece, in reality, had been double: there had been a Greece of measure and of clarity, of theory and of art (in the proper sense of these terms), of 'beautiful form,' of virile, heroic rigor, of law, of the City, of the light of day; and a buried Greece, nocturnal, somber (or too blindly bright), the archaic, savage Greece of group rituals, of bloody sacrifices and collective intoxications, of the cult of the dead and of the Earth Mother—in short, a mystical Greece, on which the other, not without difficulty, was raised (through the 'repression' of the mystical one), but which always remained silently present right up to the final collapse, particularly in tragedy and in the mystery religions. One can follow the traces of this doubling of Greece in all of German thought from, for example, Hölderlin's analysis of Sophocles or Hegel's *Phenomenology of Mind* to Heidegger, passing through Johann Bachofen's *Mutterrecht* [1861], Rhode's *Psyche* [1925] and the Apollinian and Dionysian opposition structuring Nietzsche's *Birth of Tragedy* [1872]" (Lacoue-Labarthe and Nancy 1990: 300–301).[95]

The doubling of Greece attributes to the ancient culture the modern syndrome of the double bind—the contradictory injunction of imitation,[96] the Hellenic search for an utterly non-Greek Greek myth and the ensuing anti-Hellenic resentment. The double bind of the relation of the Moderns to the Greeks mandates that "art, so far as it imitates nature, is specifically—and following Winckelmann—Greek art: mimesis is Greek. On the other hand, it is up to the Moderns to accomplish—to see through or bring to term, to complete—what nature cannot carry out. Consequently, it is up to the Moderns to go a step beyond the Greeks—to 'accomplish' them. That is to say, to surpass or surmount them" (Lacoue-Labarthe 1989: 238). That is why modernity, driven by its Hellenic ideal (which overdetermines the project), needs the Greeks tragic (that is, contradictory and self-canceling, and therefore incapable of transcendence) in antiquity and dead in the present. On a more fundamental level, the doubling of Greece reproduces

within the Hellenic the constitutive double bind of modernity, the Jerusalem-Athens opposition, with the result that, beginning with Romanticism,
Greece acquires two natures, one Hebraic and the other Hellenic.[97]

Starting with Hölderlin, the development of the dark side of Greece allowed Romanticism to express less favor for the gods than Weimar classicism. "The old passionate self-abnegation of German mysticism and
pietism returned, and with it the revival of an intensely personal Christianity, a repudiation of the cold deism of the eighteenth century. Indeed, this
religious revival led not a few of the gentler souls of the epoch back into the
fold of the mother Church. . . . The classic age had not felt the need of
tempering its optimistic Christianity with a renunciatory Nazarenism;
deism cherished no antagonism to the joyous serenity of Hellenism. . . .
Something of the hostility of earlier centuries to the Greek ideals returned;
. . . the gods of Greece became once more the gods of heathendom" (Robertson 1924: 20–21). During the first decade of the nineteenth century,
philosophers and scholars like Friedrich Schlegel and Georg Friedrich
Creuzer, the author of *The Symbolism and Mythology of the Ancient Peoples*
(1810–12),[98] traced Dionysus to Indian cults, Asia Minor mysteries, Egyptian mythology, thus orientalizing Greek religion. The Symbolists attacked
the Romantic Hellenism of the classicists and prevailed. Their position was
revised to exclude any Oriental influence, starting with the work that made
the scientific study of myth a key to the Greek mind, Karl Otfried Müller's
Prolegomena to a Scientific Study of Myth (1825); nevertheless the Romantics remained convinced about the need to take a stand in the hostility
between the gods and Christianity. The disciples of Dionysus addressed in
Hegel's poem "Eleusis" (1796) later denounced the mysteries of Ceres and
moved closer to the ideals of Novalis's essay "Europe, or Christendom"
(1800). Where Dionysus used to signify ecstatic inspiration and artistic
creativity, by the time of Heinrich Heine he was associated with sensuality,
intoxication, primal instinct, and darkness (as opposed to the Apollonian
reason, spirit, and light). What Herder saw as "animal-like sensuality"
seemed later more a source of threat than a promise of pagan spontaneity.

After the Symbolists cultivated the fear of the festival and the orgy, mystery was decisively left out of poetry. It is therefore no exaggeration to
claim that "the terrible spiritual conflict in Heine's soul between Nazarenism and Hellenism is . . . the most significant spiritual happening in the
period of declining Romanticism" (Robertson 1924: 24).[99] It was he who
gave to the distinction between Hebraism and Hellenism its modern currency, which he found in the work of Ludwig Börne. In one stroke, Heine
turned against Dionysus, Hellenism, Christianity, and political radicalism.
In his writings, for the first time, the god became the carrier of destruction—a threat to morality, tradition, and balance. The revolution had
turned out to be an orgy. "The case of Heine is particularly interesting with

regard to the past for which he is nostalgic. In his 'aveux de l'auteur' (author's confessions) which conclude *De l'Allemagne*, he reveals that although once a philhellene (like most Jacobin-democrats), he has recently turned back to his Judaic antecedents; and he affirms that the true prefiguration of the French Revolution is neither ancient Greece with its slavery, nor Rome with its legalistic chicanery, but rather Mosaic law and the customs of ancient Judaism" (Sayre and Löwy 1984: 78).[100] In this public atonement, the revolutionary fervor of Jacobinism, with its radical critique of both monarchy and bourgeois oppression, comes to an end—succeeded already by the utopian socialism of Moses Hess and the yearning of *Rome and Jerusalem* (1862).

The pantheistic celebration of mythology was replaced by the dread of barbarism. "In the later nineteenth century the gods of Greece were dead, vanished from the world, without seeming hope of ever coming back" (Robertson 1924: 28). Until Wagner's rereading of tragedy, no creative synthesis of the opposing powers seemed possible. The opposition of Robert Browning (1812–89) to uses of Greek mythology was typical. It was with Nietzsche (and to a lesser degree Walter Pater) in the 1870s that myth was fully upgraded again, becoming the essence of active life, of existence as creative act: "Myth is thus basically the same in both its primitive and its revealed forms; it is the measure of our aesthetic relation to reality, of our ability to take the world as an 'aesthetic phenomenon,' and its development might be called the aesthetic education of man. . . . The state of belonging to a mythical culture and understanding existence in terms of one's myths is thus not really a *state* at all but, rather, a *constantly renewed act* of artistic creation" (Bennett 1979: 423). Thus myth was saved appropriately by Schillerian aesthetics, by the principle of freedom as an aesthetic attitude, becoming the activity of that attitude and the consciousness of that freedom—the narrative (of the legitimacy) of full-fledged human autonomy.

Before long, however, the ritual origins of drama attracted attention when British and German classicists, especially under the spell of Sir James Frazer's *The Golden Bough* (1890, 2 vols.; 1915, 12 vols.) during the first decade of the twentieth century, turned to evolutionary anthropological theories which originated in the 1870s and 1880s (Kluckhohn 1961). The Cambridge School,[101] in particular, studied the way religious ritual influenced the development of ancient drama. For this school of classics, ritual practices predated the formulation of myths. "By using the tools of comparative religion, the theorists were in fact able to construct accounts of the worship of Dionysus and the rites traditionally associated with the origins of drama. . . . High art was shown to evolve out of high ritual" (Payne 1978: 185). The philosophy of religion of the Biblical critic William Robertson Smith (1846–94), author of the *Lectures on the Religion of the Semites*

(1894), which considered myth secondary to ritual, was a major source of inspiration for the Ritualists (as it was for Freud). "What had been true of ancient Hebraism became true for ancient Hellenism" (Turner 1981: 122). Although the impact of the Ritualists was felt mostly in modernist theories of myth, drama, and literature, Dionysiology did not lose its exorcistic character: from books like W. F. Otto's *Dionysos* (1933) and H. Jeanmaire's *Dionysos* (1951) to more recent works by René Girard, Walter Burkert, Marcel Detienne, and Michel Maffesoli (works which often extend the ritualist approach to thought and society in general), Dionysus remains a major figure of ritual, deviation, aggression, sacrifice, and violence.

The position taken by the *Dialectic* against mythical barbarism is heavily indebted to the comprehensive iconomachic campaign at the turn of the century to destroy the idols of profane culture. "Typically, political forces seemed to play no role in checking myth. Instead, culture provided the antidote" (Mosse 1985: 54), together with a massive cross-disciplinary enterprise to comprehend and control the perceived return of an antiquity that had been considered extinct for more than fifty years. "Bloch's warning not to leave irrationalism to right-wingers" (Bürger 1984–85: 125) fell on deaf ears. Creating institutes for its study seemed a better (counter)political strategy. An eminent representative of this strategy of cultural diagnosis was Aby Warburg (1866–1929), who sided with the moralists, trying to exorcise evil with a history of reason. The subject of his scholarship was another return of Greece, the impact of antiquity on fifteenth-century Florence. "Though he saw the Renaissance as an era of conflict between reason and unreason he was entirely on the side of reason. For him the library he collected and wanted to hand on to his successors was to be an instrument of enlightenment, a weapon in the struggle against the powers of darkness which could so easily overwhelm the precarious achievement of rationality" (Gombrich 1986: 13). The edificatory task of the scholar was to help preserve the laws of rationality by dispelling pagan superstition. Within the "Science of Culture" he envisioned, "his principal concern was that of '*das Nachleben der Antike*,' literally 'the after-life of classical antiquity.' . . . [H]e was more concerned with what would now be described as 'revivals,' the reappearance in the Italian Renaissance of artistic forms and psychological states derived from the ancient world. He wanted to know what significance should be attached to these impulses from a pagan past, which he traced in astrological superstitions no less than in the imagery of court pageants" (16). Puzzled by the "continued vitality of the classical heritage" (16), he attempted, as he wrote in 1926, "to understand the meaning of the survival of paganism for the whole of European civilization" (quoted in Gombrich 1986: 307). By looking microscopically at "The Significance of Antiquity for the Stylistic Change in Italian Art in the Early Renaissance" (to use the title of a seminar he gave in the winter of 1925–26 for Hamburg University), he explored how antiquity is imagined.

Warburg's position was clear: "Every age has the renaissance of antiquity it deserves" (238). Accordingly, he intended to contribute to the renaissance he considered appropriate for his time. As part of his defense of the "spirit of Europe," he concentrated on the pathology of collective psychology. "By 'paganism,' as we know, Warburg means a psychological state, the state of the surrender to impulses of frenzy and fear" (308). In studies of representation and social memory, he recognized "in symbolism an aspect of human culture in which the irrational was still very close to the surface. It was the task of a scientific 'psychology of culture' to analyse and explain this form of irrationalism which pervades both religion and art" (75). From his humanistic viewpoint, "the surviving elements of antiquity were always seen as a potential threat to human values, but also as a potential guide towards their expression. Later in his life Warburg was to fall back on the Romantic concept of 'polarity' to formulate the ambivalent role which the classical heritage plays in Western civilization" (87). The notion of polarity, based on Nietzsche's Apollonian-Dionysian dimensions of Greek thought,[102] enabled him to ask how science emerged out of magic, reason out of fear, and to look for the creative potential of dark forces—a positive attitude rejected, together with its faith in enlightenment, by the Frankfurt School. By that time, however, Warburg had no patience for questions of tradition. (For example, he showed no interest in Medieval art—moving in his comparisons directly from the Hellenistic period to the Renaissance.) "While his early research on the Florentine fifteenth century had been based on the concept of development by which one state of mind is replaced by another, he preferred during the last decade of his life to see the rhythm of civilisation represented by the model of polarity and oscillation. . . . [T]his attempt by a scholar completely devoted to historical research to eliminate the time factor as a creative force recalls Franz Rosenzweig's analysis of the Jewish mind which is outside the world and therefore essentially beyond its historical periods" (Liebeschütz 1971: 232). Analyzing history in order to transcend it (for example, studying antiquity in order to undemonize it), examining time in order to redeem it, was a major goal of cultural studies at that time.[103]

Warburg's pursuit of enlightenment may be described with his term "undemonizing." He studied survivals of antiquity in an era he considered similar to his own, the Renaissance, trying to account for their demonic power and thus warn indirectly against their pernicious influence. "It was the move from magic practice and blood-stained sacrifice to the purely spiritual attitude of inward devotion to which he responded with profound enthusiasm" (Gombrich 1986: 278). But unlike Horkheimer and Adorno, who also emphasized the departure from sacrifice, he did not reject ancient thought completely. Subscribing to the standard conception of a double Greece, he saw two opposite forces, one good and one evil, competing for its soul. When he wrote in 1920 that Athens had to be recovered from Alexandria, it was clear which side he chose. "The mind of Aby Warburg, German patriot and German scholar, is evidence that cultivated German Jews saw themselves as part of the Athenian forces—the forces of reason, of enlightenment, of Bildung" (Gay 1975: 40). The Athenian forces of the twentieth century, however, fought with the Hebraic means of high culture. There are few achievements of this struggle comparable to the collection of books that Warburg, the consummate autonomous scholar, built as his own university, exclusively devoted to the study of myth: "If it makes any sense to call Jews the people of the book, the Warburg Library is, almost by definition, the most Jewish of creations" (40), and the grandest physical monument to both the disciplines of Mythology and the conquest of culture by Jewish *Bildung*.

Among the numerous branches of Mythology, such as the history of art promoted by Warburg and his Institute, one area of study whose contribution to the analysis of myth has not been sufficiently recognized is the "Science of Judaism." Its creation is dated in the early scholarly activities of its founder, Leopold Zunz (1794–1886): the publication of his *Notes on Rabbinic Literature* (1818), the establishment of the "Society for the Culture and Science of the Jews" in Berlin (1819), and the publication (for one volume only), under his editorship, of the *Zeitschrift für die Wissenschaft des Judentums* (1822). From the beginning, the practitioners of the Science accepted the current standards of scholarship and promoted the principle of free and objective interpretation. "When it came into being, the Science of Judaism was a powerful and very active force in Berlin, Galicia, Prague, and other centers open to the influence of early nineteenth-century German culture. . . . It arose and took effect under the influence of antiquarian, ideal, and romantic conceptions" (Scholem 1971a: 305). Given the prevailing religious sensitivities, issues of faith were carefully avoided, and consequently Biblical studies systematically neglected.

Two major goals emerged. The first was an internal one: to support the Reform movement with the scientific study of religion. The religious motivation of the Science was strong: it is worth noting that "nearly all the creators and co-workers in the domains of Jewish historiography and Science of Judaism were theologians. The rabbinic share in both the positive and the problematic is enormous; it cannot be overestimated" (305). After the Enlightenment, religiosity had to be based on evidence, not religious laws and communal customs. According to the recommendation of Rabbi Abraham Geiger (1810–74), one of the leaders of the Reform movement as well as a pioneer of the field, a scientific (for example, philological and archaeological) investigation of the sources was needed in order to revitalize the practices of piety. "The Science of Judaism was regarded by Geiger as the only way that led to true Jewish religiosity. . . . Geiger saw in the Science of Judaism the principal tool of renewing Jewish religion" (Wiener 1952: 46). Reform Judaism undertook the task of preserving tradition in an era of rapid modernization through a mediation between faith and *Bildung.*[104] "The integration of Judaism into the frame of modern culture was the absorbing concern of liberal theology in nineteenth-century German Jewry. 'Wissenschaft des Judentums' as a historical science was conceived as the tool for the accomplishment of this end. It was hoped that once one had grasped the development of the Jewish 'idea' as a historical process, its essence would emerge in its unadulterated purity, freed from the encumbrances of tradition, and one had no doubt that the 'refined' (geläutert) type of Judaism thus arrived at would splendidly fit into the world of modern Europe" (Altmann 1956: 193). Hence the urgency of works like the *History of the Israelites* (1820–28, 9 vols.) by Isaac Marcus Jost, the "first Jewish scholar since Josephus to undertake a comprehensive history of the Jews" (Meyer 1975: 330).

The second, external goal was to wrest the analysis of Judaism from theologians and historians of religion, and protect it from Higher Criticism, which was already demolishing the New Testament, by making the historical development of Israel the proper object of study. In the second half of the eighteenth century, certain Talmudists had started calling for a textual criticism based on the authority of reason, rather than tradition. At issue also was the status of the Torah and the relationship between faith and conduct. Similarly, for the first Scientists, freedom of interpretation meant freedom from tradition, especially from Oral Law. They advocated the autonomy of texts and interpretation, proposing the principle that the Science "treats the object of study in and for itself, for its own sake, and not for any special purpose or definite intention" (Wolf 1957: 201). They often encountered resistance to the revisionary approach from more traditional quarters. "It is important to realize, however, that the concept of modern Jewish studies called for a transformation of Jewish learning from a literature of glosses, commentaries, bibliographical lists, and collections of chronographical materials into comprehensive presentations of Judaism as found in its literature, its philosophy, and its history—manifestations of the new vistas of learning, marked by scholarly objectivity, broad scope, meaningful context, proper form and style, and—respectability" (Glatzer 1978: 153).

What the young Scientists were advocating was a major shift of direction in response to the demands of assimilation—one from tales of destiny to histories of progress. The shock of modernity caused a rupture within the Jewish tradition when "the ethnic narcissism of the Jew suffered all at once a grievous trauma by its discovery of nineteenth-century European civilization. In the pre-Emancipation era, Jewry could maintain the illusion of its privileged position by maintaining the plausibility of its expectation of the long-deferred messianic reversal. A credible theodicy was always ready at hand to explain 'the problem of evil'—namely, the present (and hence apparent) inferiority of the Jewish people vis-à-vis the present (and hence apparent) superiority of the surrounding *goyim*" (Cuddihy 1974: 146). The covenant of assimilation, with its promise of secular delivery, challenged the credibility of the normative messianic expectation. The cohesiveness and continuity of the ethnic culture, its particular codes of belief and communication, broke down. "As long as the Jews formed their way of life in accordance with the Jewish tradition, a tradition oriented towards religion, their interpretation of the course of their own history—as far as Jews tried to account for it at all—was dominated by the concept of a historical pattern derived from the biblical prophets: that of a sacred people which, having strayed from the sacred path assigned to it, must languish in exile until it will be saved. . . . In the course of half a century, three historical developments occurred successively in almost all the Jewries of Europe, except those living under Russian rule or influence: enlightenment, political emancipation, and the reform of dogma and liturgy. . . . It is surely no coincidence that German Jews, who had gone through enlightenment, emancipation, and religious reform, who had escaped from the narrowness of a one-sided historical vision, and had been trained during their university studies to arrive at conclusions by scientific method and without preconceived notions—that they, too, were anxious to build a groundwork of scholarly research for a history of their own community" (Herlitz 1964: 69). The Science was going to be the first collective cultural project of emancipation—appropriately enough, a monument to the disciplines of interpretation. Their strategy was to identify monotheism with rationalism. "Wissenschaft was to become a messianic substitute for religion in a secular world" (Biale 1979: 16).

The Scientists encouraged the recognition that "Judaism, as a result of its own inner characteristics, has always remained strange and isolated in relation to the rest of the world" (Wolf 1957: 194). This recognition was a prerequisite for the proposed exodus. The secular challenge was certainly a recent one: "Only when modern history began were the Jews overtaken in the life of culture" (199). The call of modernization was for an active effort to bridge the worlds of synagogue and culture, and reconcile faith with *Bildung*. Both goals, internal and external, are mentioned at the end of the essay "On the Concept of a Science of Judaism" (1822) by Immanuel Wolf, the manifesto of secular scholarship which opened the first issue of Leopold Zunz's short-lived journal. The internal one is dictated by the fact that "the inner world of the Jews . . . has in many ways been disturbed and shaken by the unrelenting progress of the spirit and the associated changes in the life of the peoples. It is manifest everywhere that the fundamental principle of Judaism [earlier defined as the 'religious idea'] is again in a state of inner ferment, striving to assume a shape in harmony with the spirit of the times" (Wolf 1957: 204). The external goal is related to emancipation: "Scientific knowledge must decide on the merits or demerits of the Jews, their fitness or unfitness to be given the same status and respect as other citizens" (204). The three branches of the new science—philology, history, and philosophy—will move away from the isolationist preoccupations of Biblical exegesis to prove that Judaism has been "for most of the history of the world an important and influential factor in the development of the human spirit" (200).

As the Scientists tacitly admitted with their strategic employment of scholarship, so far as Western culture was concerned, there were no Jews before modernity, only Hebrews. The Jew of the West is a (relatively late) by-product (and, as history has brutally shown, an expendable one) of Hebraism. It was Hebraism, some two hundred fifty years after its emergence, that allowed certain people to identify themselves (and/or others) as Jews and claim Judaism as an identity (as Hellenism enabled others to embrace a Hellenic identity). "Hebraism is the tactic of admitting one's inferiority in terms of power in order to claim moral superiority in terms of indigenous spirituality and simplicity. It is a standing temptation for the modernizing intellectual" (Cuddihy 1974: 171). Chosenness is assumed to be the ability to choose freely. The intellectual, the prince of *Bildung*, denounces social power in order to achieve the superior standing of the self-made: cultivated interiority. The same tactic was followed by the Jew of modernity. "'Hebraism' was for the unsynagogued, secular Jewish intellectual what Reform Judaism was for the German Jew still committed to 'formal' membership in a Jewish—albeit a 'reformed' Jewish—community. Both these ideologies elided the 'shameful' Talmudic 'interlude' of *Yiddishkeit*. Both recurred to the Hebrew Bible, traded on its high prestige in the West, and glorified their ancient ancestors as the 'seedbed' of all that was noble in the West. . . . Using invidious comparisons, the 'assaulted intellectuals' of Reform Judaism and Hebraism thus launched their *mission civilisatrice* to Gentile Europe" (171).[105]

The appearance of the Science marked the moment when, after its initial gains, the *Haskalah*, which had emerged in central and eastern Europe in the 1780s, focused more narrowly on theology and ritual, transforming itself into the Reform movement. The maskilim, the Westernizing intelligentsia which sought the emancipation of understanding from the community of the Talmud, saw "the renewal of the religion as essential for the survival of its adherents. Their understanding of assimilation was 'narrow': they thought the continued existence of the Jews and Judaism was beyond the bounds of the emancipation contract. . . . In other words, they wanted a *Deutschtum* that would get them political equality and social acceptance alongside a *Judentum* that would preserve their collective identity" (Sorkin 1990: 21). As part of their conservative program to control discontent and disobedience among the weakening ranks and centrifugal forces of the secularizing community, they started openly taking the rabbinic leadership to task, engineering internal reforms, and at the same time creating a field explicitly devoted to the redefinition of tradition. The stakes were high: How much of tradition could be compromised in the name of civil emancipation? How far could faith go in the direction of reason when the sirens of mythic thought were threatening to lure enlightened minds into superstitious self-confidence? To Immanuel Wolf, two forces seemed to dominate the course of humanity: "In Judaism the divine idea is present as a given, revealed idea. In Hellenism all knowledge has developed from the human spirit itself. Both in their very different ways are the most momentous factors in the cultural history of the human spirit" (Wolf 1957: 196). The Scientists hoped for a Hegelian synthesis of the two forces. In 1836 Zunz confesses: "I cannot agree to the hostile division between revelation and paganism; rather do I see everywhere only emanations of one and the same world spirit [*Weltgeist*]; only in the phenomenal world are there antagonisms, even contradictions, but philosophy resolves them" (quoted in Glatzer 1978: 155–56). Although Horkheimer and Adorno did not share this optimism,[106] approaches to the Hebraism-Hellenism opposition like this one show that the real topic of the *Dialectic* (and even a potential alternative title) is the dilemmas of assimilation.[107]

The initial methodology of the Science was a historicist approach, with emphasis on cultural particularity. "The issue of doctrine, of the binding character of tradition, of truth, could be safely excluded from the investigation. . . . Historicism as applied to the messianic idea helped Zunz to keep the eschatological dynamite from exploding in his structure of Judaism, which he presented as a movement toward humanism, progress, democracy, and Europeanism" (155). The area of culture was naturally an especially important one, and the Protestant interpretive tradition had prepared the ground for the recognition of Hebrew excellence. Jewish writing, for example, was treated by the Science as the epitome of world literature. Treatises like Zunz's *Zur Geschichte und Literatur* (1845) defend positions similar to Lowth's or Auerbach's view of the Western canon: an understanding of Jewish literature is necessary for the understanding of the laws of all literature. Such aesthetic approaches endowed the Hebrew Bible with artistic authority and protected it from Higher Criticism, thus radically revising traditional modes of reading. "To advance this theory [of world importance of Hebrew letters] Zunz had to break with the scale of values of classical Judaism, to which a Biblical commentary or a halakic work was

central and a Jew's treatise on a medical subject peripheral. Zunz superimposed the concept of literature (in the sense of a multifaceted body of
writings) on Hebrew letters, just as he forced the writings of the Jewish
community out of their seclusion into the wider framework of world literature" (157). In general, scholars tried to take over possession of the communal past from the Talmudists and, later, tried to show that Israel's story
was both a true history and an important story for world history. "Thus
Judaism shows itself to be for most of the history of the world an important
and influential factor in the development of the human spirit. . . . An idea,
such as Judaism, which has developed for so many centuries, which has
been alive and productive for such a long period in the history of the world
must for this reason be founded on the essence of humanity itself and thus
be of the greatest significance and importance for the thinking spirit"
(200). As the distinct national character of Judaism was outlined, its significance for the evolution of the West was simultaneously highlighted (and
the role of Christianity underplayed). If Hegel's idea to place Judaism on
the map of world history was to be accepted, its universal importance had
to be justified in terms of the teleological philosophy of the spirit.[108] Thus,
after the Jews were welcomed into bourgeois society, they tried to make not
only Judaism but also Jewishness acceptable by spiritualizing it. Few people
(and not always from the more traditional side) discerned the serious danger of compromising its real life and present character.

Although Hegel's presentation of Judaism as an Oriental system within
world history did not satisfy everyone, interest in the Orient was such that
in 1822 Wolf had no difficulty seeing the Science of Judaism participating
in the Oriental direction of the humanities: "But today the attention of the
scholar, in his attempt to obtain a thorough insight into the history of the
development of the human spirit from the earliest ages of man, is directed,
above all, towards the Orient, this cradle of human culture, this source of
so much that is great and sublime. As this is so, would it not be timely to
subject Judaism, this richest and most widespread fruit of the Orient, to a
thorough examination from a purely scientific point of view?" (Wolf 1957:
203). That was also the time when Greece was often orientalized (for example, by the Symbolist study of myth): "During the late eighteenth and early
nineteenth centuries much speculation had arisen in both Britain and Germany about the possible oriental influence on Greek culture" (Turner
1981: 105). The important advance of the Science was that the Jews were
presented as the historical people par excellence, the ones who were nowhere and everywhere at home, and were therefore truly universal.[109] Long
before homelessness, Heine's predicament, became common fate, as
Adorno observed, it was the new historical identity of the Jews that associated their role with departure and difference—with an exile characterized
by purposefulness without a purpose (as opposed to Odysseus' adventure

of return). If the philosophy of the Enlightenment had universalized He-brew reason, the scholarship of Idealism universalized Jewish history by narrating it as the epic of spiritual development. Following Mendelssohn's idea in *Jerusalem* that Jewish faith was more of a moral legislation than a religion, scholars examined Judaism as the law of the Jewish nation, con-centrating on intellectual and cultural achievements and not on political developments. As the definition of Judaism was broadened to cover all di-mensions of culture, its universal qualities were exalted.[110]

Despite its claims to objectivity, the Science of Judaism never made any secret of its political goals. The professionalization of disciplines had not yet reached the stage where interpretive freedom had to be identified with impartiality. Support for civil equality was explicitly part of its program: "Scientific knowledge of Judaism must decide on the merits or demerits of the Jews, their fitness or unfitness to be given the same status and respect as other citizens. This alone will make known the inner character of Juda-ism and separate the essential from the accidental, the original from the later addition. Science alone is above the partisanship, passions and preju-dices of daily life, for its aim is truth" (Wolf 1957: 204). The cultural poli-tics of the Science also went beyond that. The effort to define Jewish par-ticipation in the historical universal was the scholarly dimension of the larger project to usher Jews into the scene of present history. People who were called and/or considered themselves Jewish and had gone successfully through the cultural training of *Bildung* sought to present themselves as the real (as opposed to abstract—say, literary or philosophical) Jews of the Enlightenment, not only claiming the legendary heritage of Mendelssohn but ultimately seeking to identify themselves with the Hebraic. The recog-nition for Jewish *Bildung*, which they started demanding, meant respect for their superiority in the Protestant Hebraic kingdom. "Ultimately, the only tenable posture for a minority people such as the Jews—even of the State of Israel—to adopt in a world that sees no room for them (and often con-vinces Jews to that effect) is to try afresh in every age to formulate in tran-scendent terms the reason for its continuity" (G. Cohen 1975: xxix).

By appropriating the methods of Higher Criticism for the goals of Higher Historicism, the scholars of Judaism argued that Jews were not just a histor-ical force and model but an active presence too. Hence the urgent call to Jewish scholarship: "But as the formation of a science of Judaism is an essential need for the Jews themselves, it is clear that, although the field of science is open to all men, it is primarily the Jews who are called upon to devote themselves to it. The Jews must once again show their mettle as doughty fellow-workers in the common task of mankind. They must raise themselves and their principle to the level of a science, for this is the atti-tude of the European world. This attitude must banish the relationship of strangeness in which Jews and Judaism have hitherto stood in relation to the outside world. And if one day a bond is to join the whole of humanity, then it is the bond of science, the bond of pure reason, the bond of truth" (204). If the traditional image of Judaism was infested with pagan misconceptions, once that mythic layer was removed, its message to humanity would become legible again. Thus the attack against myth on philosophical and scientific grounds was from the very beginning an integral part of Judaic scholarship.

Surveys of the Science of Judaism which accept the 1860s as the period of its decline are usually influenced by Scholem's attacks on the discipline[111] (following Rosenzweig's suggestion that their generation "smuggle in Jewish knowledge" rather than subscribe to Gentile scholarship) and the emphasis on a new historical reality by Zionist separatism. Such surveys therefore fail to recognize that, after that time, the field did not decline but abandoned its narrowly defined cohesion and moved in the direction of developing its own sub-disciplines. "In the years approaching the First World War, the self-confidence and security of German Jewry was challenged by a new Jewish sensibility that can be described as at once radical, secular and Messianic in both tone and content. What this new Jewish *ethos* refused to accept was above all the optimism of the generation of German Jews nurtured on the concept of *Bildung* as the German Jewish mystique.... For German Jews of that earlier generation the '*Bildungsideal*' of Kant, Goethe and Schiller assured them of an indissoluble bond between Enlightenment, universal ethics, autonomous art and monotheism (stripped of any particularist 'Jewish' characteristics). The mission of the Jews could be interpreted, as Leo Baeck did in his 1905 *Essence of Judaism*, as the exemplary embodiment of the religion of morality for all humanity" (Rabinbach 1985: 78). The radical Modernist sensibility declared the contract of *Bildung* void, divested from Hellenocentric humanism, and concentrated its capital in elite culture. Under the urgency of debates on decline and decadence, which included "the many analyses of the 'sickness of Judaism' written by Jews at the turn of the century" (Mosse 1970: 81),[112] the generation of Rosenzweig responded by transforming the Science into a set of loosely connected sub-disciplines devoted to the Hebraic rejuvenation of civilization. To these belong, among others, the messianic mysticism of Buber (who wrote in 1901 his dissertation on Jacob Böhme), Bloch (who published in 1921 his dissertation *Thomas Münzer als Theologe der Revolution*), Rosenzweig, Shestov, and Scholem; psychoanalysis (which Freud saw becoming "a Jewish national affair"); the school of the Warburg Institute (Aby Warburg, Erwin Panofsky, Ernst Cassirer, Ernst H. Gombrich), which studied the history of classical tradition after Christianity; deconstruction; academic enterprises in "Judaic" or "Jewish Studies" (together with their programs, journals, book series, and conferences); and of course the Frankfurt School (which Gershom Scholem called in 1977 a

"Jewish sect").[113] The effort to establish the autonomy-as-difference of Judaism as a cognitive subject succeeded so much in acquiring scholarly independence and intellectual legitimacy that it was able to produce its own field and epistemology. Moreover, this remains the only Science ever established for the study of a particular ethnic group, for the obvious reason that no other group has required and merited this kind of study.

Even the Jewish intellectual (presumably such as Warburg, Adorno, or Auerbach) is presented by the Science as a "unique entity" (Mendes-Flohr 1982: 143) which demands a special method of analysis. For although educated Jews were not the only members of the *Geistesaristokratie* who found their faith in the egalitarian promise of *Bildung* betrayed by the hierarchy of the Prussian administration (158–61), they were the ones for whom professional failure worked as a sign of distinction. In 1822, a year after the Prussian law concerning Jewish emancipation was introduced, a Royal Order disqualified Jews from academic positions, giving rise to their peculiar occupational patterns. This strengthened their sense of otherness because "in pursuing social integration the German Jew became a cognitive insider—i.e., he obtained an academic education and high German culture—but, nonetheless, he remained a social outsider" (162). Especially since that time, the Jews of Hebraism represent the others of society—not only the historical Jews of modernity but also artists, leftists, perverts, margins, people of color, and the like (but never the non-Western and exotic). At the same time, when culture started losing its national character and acquiring a cosmopolitan one in the second half of the nineteenth century, the Jews of the Science had already assumed a comparable universalist position. The essence and feats of the Jewish intellectual—or "the *genius* of the Jew" (Roback 1929: 40)—have been an area of special (self-reflexive) interest for the Science of Judaism, which applied itself with great zeal to "the documenting of Jewish accomplishments in science and culture" (Deak 1968: 27). This effort was also a response to a common perception: "[M]any Jews . . . accepted the general proposition that there was some 'racial' quality in the Jewish character that emerged most distinctively in the products of high culture: in the exercise of cleverness, of restless intelligence, of a certain unmistakable inwardness. . . . Such self-appraisals are as frequent in the literature of the Wilhelminian as in that of the Weimar epoch" (Gay 1975: 25). This kind of study, which (like the examination of Jewish racial characteristics by Horkheimer and Adorno) searches for "ethnic constants" (George Steiner), is inspired by "the fact, at once flattering and problematic, that the Jewish element has been largely dominant in the revolutions of thought and of sensibility experienced by Western man over these last one hundred and twenty-five years" (Steiner 1976: 64).

The search often uses triumphalist language: "Can it be denied that the leaders of present-day thought and even art are Jews?" (Roback 1929: 43).

In its more populist manifestations, it takes the form of a gallery of Great People (a list of geniuses that would be quite unthinkable for, say, Swedish, Indian, Arab, Zulu, or Mexican cultures). Another standard argument is that the Jew, with his traditional aptitude for study, excels as interpreter, has a "mastery in the field of philology" (62) and is "the critic *par excellence*" (440).[114] Finally, these explorations often rely on the Hebraism-Hellenism contrast for a fuller elucidation of Jewish qualities, noting, for example that "the Greeks were always interested in the *logical*, matter-of-fact view of things. They were keen on definitions, laid the foundation of modern science and evolved a theory of knowledge. The Jews, on the other hand, were racially inclined to trace the *origin of their experience*, to analyze, introspect and discover the manner in which they were affected by them. . . . If there is any concept which characterizes the Jewish bent of mind, it is that of *Purpose*. The Jew, from biblical times on, always asked himself, 'Why?' 'Whither?' This was the purport of the whole prophetic movement. The Greeks asked 'What?' 'How?' In this difference we have the *kernel of the two great world conceptions*" (184–85).[115] Such generalizations sometimes reach a mis-Hellenic pitch.[116] It has been prudently pointed out that, "like notions of Jewish rootlessness and cleverness, the charge—or boast—of presumed Jewish hunger for experiment in the arts and thirst for innovation in literature is largely myth, fostered in part by Jews themselves" (Gay 1975: 26). With the Hebraization of culture, however, it has become difficult to argue that an idea so ardently embraced by so many sides is still a "myth."

The Science of Judaism, like the other disciplines associated with Mythology, saw the pollution of reason by myth as always imminent, and fought to prevent it. The fear of the mythical—the irrational, the orgiastic, the anarchic—haunted modern imagination in the street, the bedroom, the classroom, and the factory. Intellectuals tried to contain and exorcise the threat internalizing (Jung),[117] etymologizing (Cassirer), poeticizing (Yeats), or universalizing (Lévi-Strauss) myth. This narrative of the Dionysian explosion regularly stood for the political claims expressed in popular culture. In works from Ernst Toller's *Masse-Mensch* (1920) and Freud's *Group Psychology and the Analysis of the Ego* (1921) to Elias Canetti's *Masse und Macht* (1960), it was the mass and the crowd (McClelland 1989) that were considered hostile to culture and prone to mythical thinking, heedlessly open to its seductive allure.

The political element is obvious not only in Germanic ideology and Fascist patriotism but also in the "Hellenic polytheism" of Louis Ménard (1822–1901), the author of *Prologue d'une révolution* (1849), who found in Greek concepts of order a more meaningful sense of law than in its biblical enforcements; in the anarcho-syndicalist myth of the "general strike" which Georges Sorel (1847–1922), the author of *Contribution à l'étude pro-*

fane de la Bible (1889), proposed to counter traditional socialist utopia; or in the political myth of cultural criticism of the Right which repudiated rationalism and intellectualism in favor of instinct, "the neopagan turn that pushed Christian themes into the background in favor of a mythologizing recourse to the archaic" (Habermas 1989: 440). Writers like Ludwig Klages (1872–1956), Hermann Alexander Graf Keyserling (1880–1946), and Leopold Ziegler (1881–1958) who rediscovered Johann Jakob Bachofen (1815–87) and the anthropology of romantic conservatism, repudiated reason in the name of instinct, and were absorbed by the aesthetics of Stefan George, who extolled the holiness of the word in "The Poet in Times of Chaos" (1921). The appeal of myth was great for new social groups such as the ones in Austria which, unhappy with the restricted franchise of parliamentary democracy, "raised claims to political participation: the peasantry, the urban artisans, and the Slavic peoples. In the 1880's these groups formed mass parties to challenge the liberal hegemony" (Schorske 1980: 5) and met with great success. The liberal establishment came under serious attack. "The new anti-liberal mass movements—Czech nationalism, Pan-Germanism, Christian Socialism, Social Democracy, and Zionism—rose from below to challenge the trusteeship of the educated middle class, to paralyze its political system, and to undermine its confidence in the rational structure of history" (118).

In general, during the period of the simultaneous Hebraization of culture and demonization of the Hellenic, Greek myth represented the anarchy of the political—the disruption of the civic and the eruption of the popular into the public sphere. The response of the various branches of the Science of Judaism to the mythical impulse of industrial culture was to dehistoricize it: Aby Warburg, who had investigated the interaction between art and patronage in the taste for the antique among fifteenth-century bankers in Florence, looked for the universal laws of creativity (Liebeschütz 1971); Buber related myth to religiosity, then to mysticism, until he found in an area of Jewish *Volk*, the Hasidim, an alternative popular mythology;[118] Freud turned public debates in the main square of Thebes into a Viennese domestic dispute. The nineteenth-century historicism of the discipline was systematically undone in the twentieth, when the Hebraic prevailed in the autonomous domain of culture, as a small part of "the pervasive revolt against industrial society that unfolded among European intellectuals and youth at the turn of the century. A central theme of this revolt was its counterposition of *Kultur* and *Gemeinschaft* with *Zivilisation* and *Gesellschaft*, the former concepts suggesting the sought-after natural, face to face community that would truly meet man's spiritual and creative needs, the latter concepts defining the existing 'society'—mechanized, alienated and destructive of the essential vitality and fullness of human life" (Breines 1970: 9–10).

THE SIN OF ASSIMILATION

The Frankfurt *Institut für Sozialforschung* (established in 1923), more than any other of the branches of the Science, saw myth as the primordial evil of civilization, and made its destruction a primary task. The *Dialectic of Enlightenment*, as anatomy of the mythical predicament of bourgeois society, is an outstanding example of the Mythology research tradition and incorporates many of its dimensions, including the psychoanalytical, the anthropological, the Marxist, and that of literary criticism. Like so many elements of the Frankfurt program, interest in myth was indebted to Neo-Kantianism. Influenced by recent Protestant analyses, Hermann Cohen in the 1880s found the messianic message emancipatory because the prophets made the future possible by liberating history from myth. "He never made a conscious break with his original intention to bring Judaism and Christianity as near together as possible; but with the advent of the new century the emphasis changed. Cohen still recognised the possibility of understanding the doctrine of incarnation as a symbol for the power of the human mind to legislate on good and evil; but the accent is now on a critical discussion of its derivation from myth. The justification of Judaism is now based on the thesis that no other creed had succeeded in liberating man radically from this primitive stage of belief. Christianity is by its very nature based on the existence of one person; the mythological form of thought is also characterized by personification" (Liebeschütz 1968: 24).[119] In *Das Wesen des Judentums* Leo Baeck, Cohen's student and friend, adopts his teacher's position that ethics in Judaism is not just an element, as in every religion, but its very essence. "Myth is therefore categorically excluded from the Jewish realm. Judaism, Baeck asserts, is the only religion which has produced no mythology proper" (Altmann 1956: 199). Rosenzweig, who asserts the primacy of revelation in *The Star of Redemption* (1921), also takes a similar approach when "he compares the mythical world of paganism with the Biblical world of the Word, of dialogue, of openness and love. Paganism presents God, world and man in their mute, closed, unrelated and unrevealed aspects. It is the world of a mythical Olympus, of a plastic cosmos, of the tragic hero, as Oswald Spengler had depicted the Apollonian culture. . . . The world's real drama unfolds only once the isolation of God, world and man is broken and relationship ensues. Revelation breaks the spell, and makes the true history possible" (206). Likewise, the Institute systematically portrayed mythology as the opposite of history. Its members saw the temptations of archaic thought lurking everywhere: in Nazism (Fromm), in Stravinsky (Adorno), in commodities (Benjamin), in identity (Horkheimer), in propaganda (Lowenthal).[120] To them, the archaic was the static, repetitive, stifling, annihilating opponent of reason, and myth, its worldview, was barbarism.[121] If Hegel had found a noble place for myth in his *Bildung* of the Spirit, they, who belonged to the second generation that lost faith in cultivation, attacked its heroes, Odysseus and Prometheus, for their totalitarian behavior.[122] They focused their criticism primarily on the crisis of culture[123] and the decline of taste. Their fastidious contempt for the philistinism of the middle class and their revulsion toward popular art indicate that their understanding of class was based on aesthetic terms: discrimination remained an acquired distinction, and no egalitarian beliefs could do away with the privileges of educated sensibility. The crisis of the aesthetic was nothing less than the sickness of culture.[124] "For them, the search for transcendence was essential for an ideal social and political integration on the basis of a shared humanity. But for these socialists, conscious 'alienation' from the present was a precondition for the 'true consciousness' on which a better future could be built. Only by standing apart could men understand society in its entirety and begin the work for change. Thus outsiderdom itself became a necessary prerequisite for transcendence" (Mosse 1985: 60). The critique of the plebeian corruption, technolatry, and barbarism practiced by the Spenglerian[125] Right was appropriated eventually for the purposes of the Western Marxism—the "Marxism of the superstructure" (J. G. Merquior), of cultural criticism—and combined with an admiration for the moral austerity of radical Modernism.[126] The result was an ethical aestheticism not very different from that of Nietzsche and Heidegger[127] (or even Ernst Jünger's political myth), with one significant difference: the unequivocal denunciation of the Hellenic.

The course of the School was in a way prefigured (as Auerbach would say) in Richard Strauss's turn to three-act bourgeois nostalgia (*Der Rosenkavalier*, 1911), which followed his two one-act "essays" on the Hebraic (*Salome*, 1905) and the Hellenic (*Elektra*, 1909). In the wake of the appearance of *The Will to Power* (1901) and *Being and Time* (1927), few feasible tasks remained to a philosophy witnessing the "darkening of the world": wresting the social sciences from the Weberians, protecting Judaism from critiques directed against Protestantism, and debunking myth were among them. The Frankfurt thinkers also thought that the best way to refute barbarous reality was to dehistoricize it, to neutralize it culturally. Their method was the textualization of philosophy and culture. "Textuality, with Adorno as with some later theorists, thus becomes a rationale for political inertia; *praxis* is a crude, blundering affair, which could never live up to the exquisite many-sidedness of our theoretical insights. It is remarkable how this Arnoldian doctrine is still alive and well today, occasionally in the most 'radical' of circles" (Eagleton 1990: 363). With the Frankfurt School, critique, having long ago abandoned its Enlightenment goal of public education, proudly accepts its own Fall into the abyss of interpretation and the omphaloscopic character of its historiography: "Philosophy, which once

seemed obsolete, lives on because the moment to realize it was missed. . . .
Having broken its pledge to be as one with reality or at the point of realization, philosophy is obliged ruthlessly to criticize itself" (Adorno 1983: 3).
The task of modernity is defined as the exegetical rereading of the canon
after the dissolution of the religious tradition: ascetic contemplation, that
is, commentary: "Philosophy rests on the texts it criticizes. They are
brought to it by the tradition they embody, and it is in dealing with them
that the conduct of philosophy becomes commensurable with tradition.
This justifies the move from philosophy to exegesis, which exalts neither
the interpretation nor the symbol into an absolute but seeks the truth
where thinking secularizes the irretrievable archetype of sacred texts" (55).

The Frankfurt School made interpretation of tradition its only history
and negativity, the proper mode of interpretation, the impossible cleansing
of philosophy from the secular.[128] "The primacy of culture entailed the
primacy of theory" (Mosse 1985: 60), and theory resigned itself to survey-
ing its predicament: sometime between the *Dialectic* and *Minima Moralia*,
it turned into melancholy science (Raulet 1979–80). "The union of freedom as reason and as self-realizing action was split asunder. The Frankfurt
School, following its initial instincts, could only choose reason, even in the
muted, negative form in which it might be found in the administered
nightmare of the twentieth century" (Jay 1973: 279–80). Thus critique, in
concentrating on the murmur of its canonic works in an effort to redeem
its tradition, purged itself from history and reified the locus of bourgeois
identity, the aesthetic.[129]

The attack on myth and the transcendence of politics is the double goal
of the textualization of history, of modernist literalism. "The sacred is at-
tainable only through the texts of history, but it is realized only when it
breaks free of the profane language in which it is rooted. It achieves a partial sacredness on the renewed vision, but its authentic moment is found
only in the historically redeemed Zion that comes after the revolution,
after the Messianic mediation has made the sacred sensually real" (Friedman 1981: 219). Some thought that the redeeming power of art was the
path to the sacred, and proposed the aestheticization of politics;[130] the majority tried to prevent history from returning to mythology and to make it
move forward toward its Messianic fulfillment (Bourgeois 1970). "Judaism,
the most extreme instance of antimodernity in the Western tradition, was
appropriated as the ground from which to resurrect the sacred in order to
undermine the profanity of bourgeois life" (Friedman 1981: 19). Looking
for an answer in a transmission of philosophy that denounces its Hellenic
identity (still accepted in the return to Greece by Lukács and Heidegger),
"the task of philosophy, of Critical Theory, in a profane age is to view the
world through the prisms of the Messianic redemption: to view the world
through the scraps of the divine that have been left in the world in the

Text. Critical Theory, like the Midrash, becomes the profane hermeneutic of the utterly sacred" (101). Thus the critique of myth was not only an attack on the political but a preparation for the messianic.[131] This exegetical approach is clear in Benjamin's contribution to Mythology.

Walter Benjamin (1892–1940) was a theologian of civilization prophesying the redemption of the sin of the sign. He lamented the "Fall" of the "name" from the "name language," the "language mind," to the "human mind" (Benjamin 1978a: 327) and the Fall of understanding into interpretation. He bewailed the corruption of culture by the bourgeoisie. He called his method "redemptive criticism," as he sought, through interpretations of messianic prefiguration, to save the work (and its Word) from wordly consumption, and restore it to its authentic meaning (which equals its name and being). He replaced the older notions of the man of taste and the woman of cultivation with the role he enacted in all his writings, the persona of the collector—the person who wants to possess his *Bildung* and, like Warburg, searches for God in the details of the precious items he owns. "For in one sense Benjamin's life work can be seen as a kind of vast museum, a passionate collection, of all shapes and varieties of allegorical objects" (Jameson 1971: 68).[132] In his theory, Cohen's philosophy of universal Judaism returns to its roots: "And thus the demand upon the philosophy of the future can finally be put in these words: to create on the basis of the Kantian system a concept of knowledge to which a concept of experience corresponds, of which the knowledge is the theory. Such a philosophy in its universal element would either itself be designated as theology or would be subordinated to theology to the extent that it contains historically philosophical elements" (Benjamin 1983–84a: 49). Here the Program-System of philosophy-as-mythology is recuperated for theology.

Like his friends at the Institute, Benjamin studied the myth-Enlightenment dialectic. He viewed Enlightenment as the liberating promise of modernity and myth as the threat of the return of the archaic. In his early work Benjamin "attributes a theological character to logos and truth. That is precisely Cohen's thinking: to liberate thought 'from the entanglement with myth' from the perspective of monotheistic revelatory religion—or, better yet, to make way for it. Above all, Benjamin's early contraposition of divine power and mythical violence is nourished by such a critique of 'myth' *sub specie* religion" (Menninghaus 1988: 300). His critique of mythic consciousness, from which he sought to emancipate philosophy, was based on an opposition between myth and truth. The seductive power of demonic forces appeared to loom large over art and society. "In Benjamin's early writings, the concept of myth occupies the systematic position of a radical, theological gesture of destruction. Myth comes into view for him as a sphere of demonic ambiguity: convicted of fraud and illusion, myth disappears into nothingness in the presence of the authority of the divine name. Although it is still unhistorically and abstractly worded, the concept of myth in the early theological criticism is applied to objects of 'bourgeois society': as a critique of the Enlightenment and the aesthetic autonomy of the beautiful (Goethe's *Elective Affinities*); as a critique of the modern legal state ('Critique of Violence'); and as a critique of a communicative, conventional interpretation of language ('On Language as Such and on the Language of Man'). The characteristics of myth—ambiguity, charm, compulsive repetition, nature's power, mere life—are all mobilized against a bourgeois society conscious of its secularization" (Lindner 1986: 37–38).

But as he moved from ethics to aesthetics, Benjamin substituted history for truth: the approach became historical, its subject modern culture. Like Auerbach, Benjamin discovered truth in the wisdom of the aggadah: "Kafka's work presents a sickness of tradition. Wisdom has sometimes been defined as the epic side of truth. Such a definition stamps wisdom as inherent in tradition; it is truth in its haggadic consistency. It is this consistency of truth that has been lost" (Benjamin 1969a: 143). Once truth was understood as the narrative of history, cultural interpretation and aesthetic materialism served as the critique of the ideology of bourgeois culture.

In an effort to save art not from history but from its barbaric, archaic uses by the middle class, Benjamin attacked the mythical as belief in progress, presence, and permanence. The great enemy was "the dominance of mythical fate. Myth marks a debased human species, hopelessly deprived of the good and just life for which it was determined—banished to a cursed cycle of merely reproducing itself and surviving" (Habermas 1979: 39). In his last major project, the *Passagen-Werk*, he described capitalism as "a natural phenomenon with which a new dream-sleep came over Europe, and in it, a reactivation of mythic powers" (quoted in Buck-Morss 1983: 215). In his view, modernity is asleep under the spell of paganism. "In the *Passagen-Werk*, myth is the indicator for the ambiguous and contradictory co-existence of the return of the archaic and economic technological upheaval, liquidation of experience (*Erfahrung*) and intensification of the social image-space, (anthropological) materialism and (failed) revolution" (Lindner 1986: 39–40). Differentiating the *Passagen-Werk* from Louis Aragon's novel *Le paysan de Paris* (1926) which inspired it, Benjamin adopts Freud's analogy between myth and dream, and talks about the dream waiting for its awakening: "Aragon persistently remains in the realm of dreams, but we want here to find the constellation of waking. While an impressionistic element lingers on in Aragon ('mythology') . . . what matters here is the dissolution of 'mythology' into the space of history. Of course, that can only happen through the awakening of a knowledge of the past that is not yet conscious" (Benjamin 1983–84: 2–3). At the same time, he sought not a philosophy of history, like Adorno, but the revelation of the aesthetic as a secular illumination—a belief related to his onomatopoetic theory of language, which sees a necessary relationship between word and thing. Both as archaic faith and as modern commodity, myth stands in the way of this happening: it taints the immediacy, blurs the vision. Combining a strong interest in the dehellenization of Christian dogma begun by the Lutheran theologian Adolf von Harnack (1851–1930), especially in his *History of Dogma* (1886-89), with a vehement opposition to the uses of myth by the George school (Roberts 1982: 122–33), Benjamin tried to continue Nietzsche's critique of modernity while rejecting the Greek model.

His understanding of myth becomes clearer when he laments its modern political connection: the emancipation of art has not happened because of industrial middle class politics. At this point *Bildung* is relinquished for messianism, and Enlightenment for revelation: as Rosenzweig demanded, (Benjamin's notion of) Jewishness is smuggled in. Since the complementary projects of *Bildung* and Enlightenment have been hopelessly appropriated by the middle class, all that can be done is to expect divine intervention and compose the narrative of the Fall, the pre-history of the modern predicament. As Benjamin wrote to Scholem in 1926, "meaningful *political* goals are non-existent." With the death of the public, he resigned himself to the esoteric function of the intellectual: he continued the Idealist project, practicing critique as the self-criticism of art addressed to an elite group of intellectuals (like the one organized in the Frankfurt Institute). As he wrote in "The Technique of the Critic in Thirteen Theses" around 1925, "the more important court of judgment" is not the public but the colleagues of the critic. Thus the circle of hermeneutics closes with the return of aesthetics to theology and of criticism to illumination.[133] In his late work, Benjamin seems to abandon the messianic and to adopt the apocalyptic, a restitutive apocalyptic in history which he calls by another Greek word, "apokatastasis."[134] The redemptive of his criticism and the catastrophic of his theory of history are combined in a collector's aesthetic view of religion.[135] It is "the retrieval of everything and everyone," the abolition of sin and damnation, the restoration of language and knowledge, the belief that "all souls go to paradise." In his last piece, the "Theses on the Philosophy of History" (1940), we find "the impotent proclamation that salvation is indeed at hand in spite of all the barriers presented to it by actual conditions. . . . In the historico-philosophical theses, Benjamin is about to leap out of historical materialism into the realm of political Messianism where nothing can be done at all. . . . The retranslation of materialism into theology cannot avoid the risk of losing both: the secularized content may dissolve while the theological idea evaporates" (Tiedemann 1983–84: 96). A materialist theology? a politics of salvation? an aesthetic of redemption (Bersani 1990; Wolin 1982)? or what Brecht referred to as Benjamin's "judaisms?" In any case, cultural criticism offers to serve God's plans for humanity once again.

The idea of critique as secular theology in a pagan world which has earned the wrath of God was a constant motif in Benjamin's writing. An early example (which is also a precursor in many respects of the "Elements of Anti-Semitism" in the *Dialectic*) is his "Critique of Violence" (1920–21), which uses the Hebraic-Hellenic opposition (borrowed from the late work of his teacher Cohen). This critique is based on the relation of violence to law and justice, and concerns the justification of its means. Examining current legal philosophy (positive and natural law), he discovers the interest of law in a monopoly of violence that aims at preserving law itself: violence that is not in the hands of the law threatens it by being outside it. That is why modern law divests individuals of all violence. "All violence as a means is either lawmaking or law-preserving" (Benjamin 1978: 287). In any exercise of violence, the law protects and reaffirms itself. From this follows that "all violence as a means, even in the most favorable case, is implicated in the problematic nature of law itself" (287). Violence is "the origin of law" (286). Conversely, law is inextricably implicated in violence. "Among all the forms of violence permitted by both natural law and positive law there is not one that is free of the gravely problematic nature, already indicated, of all legal violence" (293). Violence in lawmaking functions as a means for establishing both law and power as law. "Lawmaking is power making, and, to that extent, an immediate manifestation of violence." It follows that power is "what is guaranteed by all lawmaking violence" (295).

These are strong positions with an anarchist bent and a heavy debt to Sorel's *Réflexions sur la violence* (1907), itself a response to the work on crime by Max Stirner (1806–56). Benjamin, however, reacts against this syndicalist who took a positive attitude to the social function of myth as an expression of mass will and contrasted it with utopia, the daydream of intellectuals. After the critique, Benjamin asks whether there are any "other kinds of violence than those envisaged by legal theory" (293) that could contribute to the solution of human problems. Before proposing his alternative, he collapses both kinds of violence into a new one: mythical violence. This is identical to lawmaking violence and illuminates "fate, which in all cases underlies legal violence" (295). He then proceeds, in response to his question, to propose "divine end making" (295) and oppose it to mythical lawmaking through a comparison of the concept and effects of justice in the Niobe myth and in the Biblical story of Korah (294, 297). What the modern world needs is the pure, immediate violence that would halt the mythical rule—divine violence. "Mythical violence is bloody power over mere life for its own sake, divine violence pure power over all life for the sake of the living. The first demands sacrifice, the second accepts it"

(297). He calls the former "executive" and the latter "sovereign" (300); one is pernicious, the other benevolent. When he asks for the destruction of legal violence, he seeks therefore the abolition not of the state but of mythical forms of law. For Benjamin, the law of the modern state is by nature violent and exercises mythical violence that looks like fate. Contrary to God's will, myth has bastardized pure divine violence with law. "Just as in all spheres God opposes myth, mythical violence is confronted by the divine. And the latter constitutes its antithesis in all respects" (297). There should be no other law but the law of God. Only its violence is justified. The law of the state speaks the language of myth. Only God's violence is totally justified. The violence of Greek thought, legal and mythical, violates God's will with its idolatry.[136]

From this perspective "Benjamin forms the concept of revolutionary violence according to this configuration: It is as if the act of interpretation, which extracts the selective breach in the natural-historical continuum from the past art work and makes this relevant for the present, is invested with the insignia of praxis. This, then, is the 'pure' violence or 'divine' force which strives toward 'the breaking of the cycle maintained by mythical forms of law' [Benjamin 1978: 300]. Benjamin conceptualizes 'pure' violence within the framework of his theory of experience and therefore he must divest it of the attributes of goal-oriented (purposive-rational, *zweckrational*) action; revolutionary violence, like mythical violence, manifests itself—it is 'the highest manifestation of unalloyed violence by the human being' [300]. It follows logically that Benjamin should refer to Sorel's myth of a general strike and to an anarchistic praxis which is distinguished by its banning of the instrumental character of action from the realm of political praxis and its negation of purposive rationality in favor of a 'politics of pure means': 'the violence (of such praxis) may be assessed no more from its effects than from its goals, but only from the law of its means' [292]" (Habermas 1979: 55). Thus praxis becomes autonomous, namely, aesthetic. The violence of aesthetic interpretation is the proper revolutionary praxis. "As teachers in the humane studies, our sacred world must remain the book. . . . An interminable making of interpretations is the duty of the teacher; in this duty he is freer than most other citizens" (Rieff 1972: 6). The connection between emancipation and interpretation is preserved indissoluble.

Like so many of his contemporaries, Benjamin was fascinated by the figure of Odysseus, which represented, always ambiguously, the pagan power of myth over both magic and reason, namely, defiant cunning. Speaking about the group of assistants/messengers who populate Kafka's stories, he observed: "Even the world of myth of which we think in this context is incomparably younger than Kafka's world, which has been promised redemption by the myth. But if we can be sure of one thing, it is this:

Kafka did not succumb to its temptation. A latter-day Ulysses, he let the Sirens go by 'his gaze which was fixed on the distance, the Sirens disappeared as it were before his determination, and at the very moment when he was closest to them he was no longer aware of them.' Among Kafka's ancestors in the ancient world, the Jews and the Chinese, whom we shall encounter later, this Greek one should not be forgotten. Ulysses, after all, stands at the dividing line between myth and fairy tale. Reason and cunning have inserted tricks into myths; their forces cease to be invincible" (Benjamin 1969a: 117). Thus Kafka is portrayed as the true Ulysses, the one who resists temptation. The Odysseus of the *Dialectic*, however, who is depicted as "the first man of the modern State" (Deleuze and Guattari 1987: 355), is the hero who did not resist. Benjamin's comment "becomes fundamental to Adorno's argument in the chapter on Odysseus in *Dialectic of Enlightenment*" (Buck-Morss 1983: 225).[137]

Benjamin also pointed out the importance of cunning for reason. "In his 1935 exposé [on the *Passagen-Werk*], Benjamin wrote: 'Every epoch . . . carries its ending within it, which it unfolds—as Hegel already recognized—with cunning.' For Hegel, through cunning, Reason (consciousness) works its way into history by means of the passions and ambitions of unwitting historical subjects" (224). It is this cunning that Benjamin hoped to enlist against reason itself in order to free it from the grip of myth:[138] "Told with 'cunning,' the *Passagen-Werk* would accomplish a double task: it would dispel the mythic power of present being (*Wesen*) by showing it to be composed of decaying objects with a history (*Gewesen*). And it would dispel the myth of history as progress (or the modern as new) by showing history and modernity in the child's light as the archaic. Told properly, this fairy tale would use enchantment to disenchant the world" (225–26). The course of rationalization, as described by Weber, would be reversed, criticism would redeem modernity and seek the apokatastasis of divine law. "His pedagogy was a double gesture, both the demythification of history and the re-enchantment of the world" (224). "Cunning intelligence" (Vernant and Detienne 1978), the sin of deception and the vice of manipulation, according to Horkheimer and Adorno, is employed in order to reverse the Fall and re-enchant knowledge into Edenic identity. To this end, Benjamin, like a rhapsode, spins "the *Passagen* myth," a modern journey to Hades, with additional similarities to another Aragon epic, *The Adventures of Telemachus* (1922), which in turn rewrote Fénelon's *Les Aventures de Télémaque* (1699): "In ancient Greece one could show places where one descended into the nether world. Our waking existence is likewise a terrain in which places are concealed leading to the underworld, inconspicuous places where dreams flow to the surface. During the day we pass them by, unsuspectingly, losing our way in their dark passages" (quoted in Menninghaus 1988: 309). These places, these thresholds, are the arcades, the Passages. The "Grand Tour" (Burke 1966) of sacred places of antiquity has been reduced to the Parisian prowler's peregrinations in the burial places of bourgeois memory (Macdonald 1988) in search of "fascination" (Baudelaire).

There is another narrative that is being reoccupied here, though, the journey to the epic underworld in the eleventh book of the *Odyssey*. Modernity is drunk asleep like Elpenor, Odysseus' companion who was killed at the palace of the *polypharmakos* goddess Circe. Elpenor was the first soul the king of Ithaca encountered when he went to Hades seeking advice about his future from Tiresias—the seer who, according to the etymology of his name, "interprets *terata*/signs," and also appears as the *theoros* in Apollinaire's play (1918), *The Waste Land* (1922) and Pound's *Cantos*, another "modern Odyssey" (Forrest Read), which begins with Odysseus' search for the underworld. From the character E. P. in *Hugh Selwyn Mauberley* (1920) to the speaker of the *Cantos* (Witemeyer 1969: 161–76), the poet in Pound is Odysseus. Benjamin's work too is a Passage. Like Pound in Canto I (1917), which translates Andreas Divus's Latin version of the Nekuia, Benjamin uses the method of "cultural overlaying." Like Odysseus, he seeks the future, in his case not a *nostos*, a homecoming, but, as he says at the end of the "Theses on the Philosophy of History," "the strait gate through which the Messiah might enter." "This formulation, of the step through a narrow gate, unequivocally satisfies the *Passagen-Werk*'s paradigm of the transfiguring crossing of a threshold, the mythical rite of passage" (Menninghaus 1988: 309). Thus Benjamin plays both Odysseus and Tiresias, hero and prophet.

For the Modernist writer, this rite is itself an ambivalent passage through myth which seeks its destruction but is unwilling to forgo its power: "Benjamin's theory of myth seeks a blasting apart of myth but at the same time does not want to relinquish the whole potential of its forms of experience" (314). In his late work, which develops a counter-mythology of modernity, "the motif of blasting apart myth becomes transfigured into the dialectic of breaking apart *and* rescuing myth" (323). This is a characteristic example of how myth, from the early Benjamin to the late Adorno, was used to make Hellenism represent bourgeois society (in reversion of Marx's critique) and Hebraism stand for either purity (transcendence of the dialectic) or total otherness (negative dialectic). Here is an equivocal attempt to purge culture of paganism which cannot help but both renounce and embrace the cunning to which it owed its potency.

The entire problematic of culture—shared by the Frankfurt group and their contemporaries—which was haunted by mythical echoes of violence and seduction, was first articulated in the sociology of Georg Simmel (1858–1918). In his progress from *Kulturphilosophie* to *Lebensphilosophie*, Simmel saw life as creative becoming, as production of culture, and placed great emphasis on the cultivation of individuality. In his formulation, "culture is the road from a closed unity through an unfolded multiplicity to an unfolded unity" (quoted in Weingartner 1960: 76). Cultivation was expected to heal the distinctions of experience and the divisions of the world. This was the autonomous and pure world of feelings and verses created by George which so fascinated Simmel. For Weber, who was the first to observe that ethical questions were reduced to matters of taste, the lesson derived from George's spirituality of form was that "in the modern era, while having credentials as a form of aesthetic redemptory values, [culture] never really delivers" (Whimster 1987: 277). Hence he opposed artistic (and in general cultural) values. "Weber closes down one avenue, culture, but opens up another, the public realm, however unpromising and unforgiving this realm is" (277). Simmel, however, using Modernism as his model for understanding modernity, hoped that a spiritual aristocracy of creators would help transcend the alienation and objectification studied in the essay "The Tragedy of Culture" (1911). Over the years, as Simmel grew pessimistic about the abilities of personality to develop, and admitted an irreconcilable struggle between experience and process, life and form, it was the generation of people like Bloch (who attended Simmel's seminar) that inherited his stark vision. "For the great question of whether culture is 'possible' . . . turns primarily on whether it is possible to shape *life* itself, if only in ways that, from a historical perspective, may be no more than transitory" (Márkus 1983: 13).

Gyuri von Lukács, the student of Simmel and Weber who made this his central concern, always asked: "[W]hat is the social possibility of culture?" (Lukács 1970: 21) "*Culture* was the 'single' thought of Lukács' life" (Márkus 1983: 3). This thought stood for the unity and harmony of life that would prevail in a post-capitalist world.[139] From the time of *On Spiritual Poverty* (1912), and *Aesthetic Culture* (1913) to *Die Eigenart des Ästhetischen* (1964, 2 vols.), the possibility of culture meant "the question of *whether it is possible to live a life free from alienation*. But behind this question lay his passionate diagnosis of the hostility to culture, the 'crisis of culture,' that characterized modern bourgeois existence, and his own determined rejection of it" (4). The product of culture "possesses real cultural value only *when it is valuable for itself*. The moment cultural productions become commodities, when they are placed in relationships which transform them into commodities, their autonomy—the possibility of culture—ceases" (Lukács 1970: 22).

From his observation that culture in the bourgeois world is impossible, Lukács draws a Schillerian conclusion: authentic culture transcends alienation and makes life authentic. "For authenticity is nothing other than actively using one's abilities to the full, shaping everything that happens to one into a personal destiny that expresses one's innermost nature" (Márkus 1983: 9). It is the aesthetic ideal of *Bildung* that affirms the dignity of life and explains what makes it "more-than-life" (Simmel). "[A]rt is, therefore, the process of investing life with meaning and raising it into consciousness, of transcending the chaos of life. It is a 'judgment on life' and gives 'mastery over things.' The existence of art is proof that the alienation of 'ordinary' life can be overcome" (11). *The Theory of the Novel* discovered the historical possibility of authentic, integrated culture in the Greek polis. "As nearly always in his work, the essential bias is one of subversive, radical conservatism. He solicits the revolutionary future in the name of classic humanistic ideals many of which belong to the leisured civilization and generosities of the bourgeois past" (Steiner 1967: 345). According to his aesthetic view of autonomy, "the question of whether culture is possible, of whether it is possible to shape life, appears . . . to be an *ethical problem*, a question of moral conduct—either active or passive behaviour, but in either case behaviour based on free, individual self-determination or, more generally, a question of the way in which the individual leads his life" (Márkus 1983: 20–21).[140] The generation of Lukács (Gluck 1986) and Heidegger inherited from Cohen's Judaic "turn" the dilemma: ethics or religion? In the 1920s the program of Neo-Kantian philosophy was abandoned and the Marburg School dissolved. At that time Heidegger "said it is the true task of theology, which must be discovered once again, to seek the word that is able to call one to faith and preserve one in faith" (Gadamer 1976: 198). Lukács had already written "Tactic and Ethic" (1919) and Benjamin the essay on violence, both dealing with the nature of ethical norms. Since they felt abandoned by God, they opted for an ethics which they transformed into cultural suprapolitics. Having identified politics with capitalism and barbarism with the taste of the masses, they rejected modernity altogether, save for the program of aesthetic autonomy, which became their ethics. "These young philosophers were moved by eschatological hopes of a new emissary of the transcendent God, and they saw the basis of salvation in a socialist social order created by a brotherhood. For Lukács the splendor of inner-worldly culture, particularly its esthetic side, meant the Anti-Christ, the 'Luciferian' competition with God's effectiveness. But there *was* to be a full development of this realm, for the individual's choice between it and the transcendent must not be facilitated. The final struggle between God and Lucifer is still to come and depends on the decision of mankind. The ultimate goal is salvation *from* the world, not, as for George and his circle, fulfillment *in* it" (Marianna Weber, quoted in Holzman 1985: 91).[141] For Lukács, the total revolution would be a cultural one. Hence the importance of artistic form[142] for the formation of his social theory.

By the end of the Weimar period the ideal of *Bildung* had lost all its pedagogical credibility and philosophical urgency—its market value as cultural capital. The *Dialectic of Enlightenment* accounts for the failure of that investment by blaming it on the capitalist system. "During the 1930s the critical theorists had retained some trust in bourgeois culture's potential for reason which would be released by the pressure of the developing forces of production. . . . [T]he stock of trust was depleted to such an extent at the beginning of the 1940s that Horkheimer and Adorno felt that the Marxist critique of ideology had definitely exhausted itself; they no longer believed that they could fulfill the promises of a critical social theory with the methods of the social sciences. Instead they attempted a radicalization and totalization of their critique of ideology in order to enlighten the En-lightenment about itself. . . . Horkheimer and Adorno therefore consider the basis of the critique of ideology destroyed; and yet they want to hold on to the basic premise of Enlightenment. So they take that which Enlighten-ment did to myth and turn it back onto the process of Enlightenment itself. Critique becomes total: it turns against reason as the foundation of its own analysis" (Habermas 1982: 21–22). They also counter-propose the negative dialectic of (guilt-ridden) autonomous art as the self-immolation of the aesthetic tradition—the Hebraic atonement for the sin of Enlighten-ment, the Fall into Hellenic knowledge. Emancipation is conceptualized as expiation. "A valid theory could only be one which thinks against itself, undoes its every act, achieves a frail evocation of that which its own discur-sivity denies. Emancipatory thought is an enormous irony, an indispensa-ble absurdity in which the concept is at once deployed and disowned, no sooner posited than surmounted, illuminating truth only in the dim glare of light by which it self-destructs" (Eagleton 1990: 347).

Nowhere can this theological project of aesthetic atonement be compre-hended more clearly than in the vindictive theory of contemporary culture outlined in the chapter of the *Dialectic* entitled "The Culture Industry: Enlightenment as Mass Deception." What is offered here as a critique of global culture under capitalism is not only an outline of negative aesthetics but also a theology of Art elaborated on the basis of the binary opposition fall-redemption. According to their contemptuous description, the distin-guishing features of contemporary culture are uniformity, standardization, repetition, conformity, banality, and exhaustion: "the bread which the cul-ture industry offers man is the stone of the stereotype" (Horkheimer and Adorno 1972: 148). An anonymous, omnipresent market produces formu-laic, generic art for the faceless masses, geared toward the sensational ef-fect. All it amounts to is big business: entertainment agencies, company directors, studio hierarchies, and panels of experts calculate and package everything, trying to sell their products and outsell each other. The single purpose is to make people buy and consume, to make a profit. The message of the industry is a very alluring one in its egalitarian promiscuity: there is nothing out of reach. "Everything can be obtained" (161). This is the age of the mechanical mass reproduction of beauty: "only the copy appears"

(143). People are treated like (and finally trapped in a manipulative chamber of mirrors as) potential customers. The culture industry is an unscrupulous business which depends on "classifying, organizing, and labeling consumers" (123), like any other enterprise of that kind and scale. It manufactures their needs and promises amusement goods but never really delivers because it "perpetually cheats its consumers of what it perpetually promises" (139). It promises pleasure and fulfillment, gaining the trust and consent of the aroused audience, without ever supplying full satisfaction. There is one thing people do not realize: "Under monopoly all mass culture is identical" (121). Instead, they duly submit their desires for the customary treatment, each time vainly anticipating better results.

In this era of universal publicity, art, entertainment, and advertising are literally fused, contributing to a "depravation of culture" (143), a hierarchical society, and a justification of domination based on "the false identity of the general and the particular" (121). Hence the pervasive feeling of helplessness and defenselessness of "a culture in the process of self-liquidation" (142). In addition, the "myth of success" (134) has been cultivated through the "idealization of individuality" (140), the praise for subjective independence. By analogy to this society-individual dichotomy, culture has been schizophrenically polarized between the entertainment industry and "its counterpart, avant-garde art" (128), between bourgeois/autonomous/serious Art and its "shadow," its "social bad conscience" (135), light art. Thus division, separation, opposition, and mediocrity prevail.

Horkheimer and Adorno find every single manifestation of modern culture repulsive: radio, television, films, commercials, advertisements, jazz, records, concert relays, reproductions, soap operas, producers, executives, stars—all aspects and members of the realm they call the "pleasure industry." "Finally, in their analysis of mass culture, Horkheimer and Adorno want to demonstrate that *art*, when fused with entertainment, is drained of its innovative power and emptied of all its critical and utopian content. The earlier critique had concentrated on the affirmative aspects of bourgeois culture; it now turns into an impotent rage over the ironic justice of an irreversible judgment which mass culture executes on art which itself had always already been ideological" (Habermas 1982: 17). Pleasure, especially when expressed as sheer enjoyment, they disdain. The most disgraceful and degrading feature of modern art, the authors argue—as others later do about postmodernism (Baudrillard 1981, 1988)—is its exclusive exchange value: it is worth only what it can be exchanged for. Nothing is recognized for its own value, no longer does any artwork seem to possess any inherent merit. Art is not appreciated but exchanged; it has only a social rating and a market price, like any other commodity, but no aesthetic qualities. Like any other industrial product, it is simply marketable, exchangeable, dispensable, replaceable, and therefore utterly debased. "The work of art, by completely assimilating itself to need, deceitfully deprives men of precisely that liberation from the principle of utility which it should inaugurate" (Horkheimer and Adorno 1972: 158). The authors acknowledge that this development was unavoidable under the particular historical circumstances: "Art as a separate sphere was always possible only in a bourgeois society" (157). It won its independence at the cost of being segmented and isolated from the rest of society and culture. Its contemporary status is still determined by capitalist economy, and the complacency (if not complicity) of even the greatest artworks with the exchange system of commodities can hardly be disputed. "It is to its commodity character that art owes its liberation in the first place; it was a liberation for the private enjoyment of the bourgeois reading and theater, exhibition and concert public that came into being in the 17th and 18th centuries. The continuation of this same process, to which art owes its autonomy, also leads to the liquidation of art" (Habermas 1979: 41). With its ability to resist appropriation dramatically diminished, art today is almost happily participating in the fetishization of itself.

This diagnosis is parallel to the authors' critique of contemporary language abuse. Their starting point is the same: "public opinion has reached a state in which thought inevitably becomes a commodity, and language the means of promoting that commodity" (Horkheimer and Adorno 1972: xi–xii). Publicity manipulates language to such a degree that it becomes meaningless, and, in the wheels of propaganda machines like those of fascist regimes, just empty. The reason for this dissolution of signification is that the word has become a sign (164, 165) and, once separated from its vital content, is perceived as conventional. "The absolute separation, which makes the moving accidental and its relation to the object arbitrary, puts an end to the superstitious fusion of word and thing" (164). Whereas before there was unity (even though only superstitious) between language and the world which it was entrusted to represent and preserve, now this unity has been questioned, and language is rationalized, while the world is reduced to information. The name is detached from magic; it becomes a means of manipulation and spreads ideology, that is, new myths. "The demythologization of language, taken as an element of the whole process of enlightenment, is a relapse into magic" (164). Thus the discovery of arbitrariness has led to more arbitrary domination.

It is especially interesting that this critique of modernity shares with the Reformation the same fear and loathing for nominalism, which the authors call "the prototype of bourgeois thinking" (60). Horkheimer and Adorno are, like Benjamin, indebted to the refutation of the arbitrariness of the sign in the essay "The Importance of Names" by Origen (185–254). They find Enlightenment "a nominalist movement" (23) and in the *Dialectic*, their protesting program of a negative interpretive emancipation (and therefore the first outline of Adorno's literalist *Aesthetic Theory*), they chronicle the abuse of signification by the Enlightenment. They show that the original division in language and the dispersion of meaning took place in Greek religion. In the superstitious world of mythology, the sign and the thing, language and the world, were indissoluble, and the "permanence of the signified" (17) was felt everywhere in magical rites and daily life. "In Jewish religion, in which the idea of the patriarchate culminates in the destruction of myth, the bond between name and being is still recognized in the ban on pronouncing the name of God" (23). But with the "Olympian *chronique scandaleuse*" (17), the elements started acquiring some independence and the mythical, under the onslaught of doubt, paled into the fantastic. With the manipulation of the sign by Odysseus, who names absence (Udeis) and so pronounced himself god, the bond of identity dissolves. "Because both the hero and Nobody are possible connotations of the name Udeis, the former is able to break the anathema of the name" (60). What followed was the "clean separation of science and poetry" (17). Science turns the world into a sign which it tries to decipher. "As a system of signs, language is required to resign itself to calculation in order to know nature, and must discard the claim to be like her" (18). Greek Enlightenment effected this change and caused the break: the internal division between signifier and signified culminated in the friction between sign and thing, and led to the estrangement between art and science. The original innocence was lost and now there is no way of return. "The separation of sign and image is irremediable" (18). Dissipation of sense, feeling, and experience is the modern predicament, together with "a utopian yearning for identity which must deny itself under pain of fetishism and idolatry" (Eagleton 1990: 347).

Adorno was later to declare: "All post-Auschwitz culture, including its urgent critique, is garbage" (Adorno 1973b: 367). And yet, this garbage is still indispensable to him because it may prevent another Auschwitz: "Culture keeps barbarism in check; it is the lesser of two evils" (Adorno 1984: 357). This lesser evil is all that is left to defend the integrity of thought. As a result of the negative diagnosis Horkheimer and Adorno offer on modernity, "emancipatory prognoses of necessity took on an unrealistic, utopian hue. Unable to locate progressive emancipatory tendencies in the concrete historical present, the Critical Theorists were constrained to identify *ersatz* repositories of negation—above all, the aesthetic sphere" (Wolin 1990: 35). The dream of emancipation shrinks to this limited territory. For Adorno, "art represents a form of 'salvation' vis-à-vis the 'pressures of theoretical and practical rationalism' that predominate in daily life. Moreover, in Adorno's aesthetics art becomes a vehicle of salvation in an even stronger sense. It takes on a compelling utopian function as a *prefiguration of reconciled life*" (37). This is the theological use of Auerbach's recuperation of typology. "What recommends itself, then, is the idea that art may be the only remaining medium of truth in an age of incomprehensible terror and suffering" (Adorno 1984: 27).

The truth of this art, however, is necessarily a negative one: the expression of suffering under barbarism, combined with messianic anticipation. "Almost always the theodicy of suffering has originated in the hope of salvation" (Weber 1958: 273). In Critical Theory, the salvation promised by art demands the pain of discipline—of the self-discipline of atoning theory: "Suffering, not positivity, is the humane content of art" (Adorno 1984: 369). The *Dialectic* argues that this suffering may only be articulated dialectically by going against norms, rules, and the dictates of tradition through the askesis of style: "Style represents a promise in every work of art. That which is expressed is subsumed through style into the dominant forms of generality, into the language of music, painting, or words, in the hope that it will be reconciled thus with the side of true generality" (Horkheimer and Adorno 1972: 130). Therefore style, like Lukács' culture, is a promise of reconciliation and fulfillment: it confronts and challenges tradition and orthodoxy, promising to create truth by revising the established norms and to fulfill aesthetic needs with genuine artistic satisfaction. It further promises the "reconciliation of the general and particular, of the rule and the specific demands of the subject matter, the achievement of which alone gives essential, meaningful content to style" (130) and its functions. It is an impossible promise but "only in this confrontation with tradition of which style is the record can art express suffering" (130–31)—only in what they call "the necessary failure of the passionate striving for identity" (131). This moralistic view glorifies failure as true success, reification as emancipation, neutralization as critique—in other words, the rule of aesthetic autonomy as the supreme religion of modernity.[143] "There is something perversely self-defeating about this aesthetic, which takes its cue from a notable contradiction of 'autonomous' culture—the fact that art's independence of social life permits it a critical force which that same autonomy tends to cancel out. 'Neutralisation,' as Adorno comments, 'is the social price art pays for its autonomy' [1984: 325]" (Eagleton 1990: 349). Authentic art negates itself because it is aware of its pending failure and yet attempts the impossible: "the style of the great work of art has always achieved self-negation" (Horkheimer and Adorno 1972: 131). Adorno found that this (high modernist) asceticism "has today become the sign of advanced art" (Adorno 1978: 274). Thus style becomes the ethics of autonomous art, confining suffering to the realm of self-righteous contemplation: "Terribilita should remain an aesthetic, not a political, capacity; it rightly belonged to Beethoven and Michelangelo, in their work, not to the condottieri, or Hitler, in theirs" (Bloom 1984: 23). The postmodern style of contemplation is finally reduced to the morality of minimalist commonality, the ethics of lifestyle (Swenson 1990).

The poetic vocabulary employed by Horkheimer and Adorno in these pages is revealing: words like longing, suffering, promise, expectation, reconciliation, fulfillment, and failure are derived from their commentary on Judaism and invoke its theodicy. Their theory of art is modeled on this depiction of the Jewish spirit, their aesthetics patterned on their fundamentals of Biblical monotheism. In both their artistic and philosophical theories the muted referent is the unnamable God. His religion should be understood as the only viable alternative to the false, pernicious project of (Greek) Enlightenment. Not that Adorno was advocating a religious art of "beauty and holiness" (Martin 1990; Brown 1990): "The exalted unity of art and religion is, and always was, highly problematic in itself. Actually it is largely a romantic projection into the past of the desire for organic, nonalienated relations between men, for doing away with the universal division of labor. Probably no such unity ever existed in periods where we might speak of art in the proper sense of freedom of human expression as distinct from the symbols of ritual which are works of art only accidentally" (Adorno 1945: 677). In a differentiated, fragmented world, art and religion have a responsibility to each other to remain separate: art is not the faith but the promise of the faith—not the face but the prefiguration of its *apokalypsis*. "The theological legacy of art consists in the kind of secularized revelation which is the ideal and the limit of every work. To equate art entirely with revelation would amount to an unreflective projection of art's inevitable fetish character on to the theory of art. On the other hand, to eradicate all traces of revelation in art would be to reduce art to a copying machine" (Adorno 1984: 155). The true alternative to the Greek "monoethic" (Lukács) art is a monotheistic art of self-negation which "can keep faith to its true affinity with religion, the relationship with truth, only by an almost ascetic abstinence from any religious claim or any touching upon religious subject matter. Religious art today is nothing but blasphemy" (Adorno 1945: 679).

Despite the Hebraic triumph of the aesthetic, the political, which the Frankfurt School identified with barbarism (specifically, the return of the archaic), did not disappear. Furthermore, because the political, like myth, was often left in the hands of conservatives and reactionaries, it made its presence felt in catastrophic ways. As a consequence, there are those who, in the course of postmodern reconsiderations of the Enlightenment in the West, have denounced assimilation, the whole problematic of the "Jewish question," because they have felt that Hellenic investments in it did not pay off. A separatist kind of criticism, for example, attacks the New Left, "sometimes taken as a 'Jewish' movement" (Ozick 1970: 269) and called "The New Joodeyism" (Rieff 1972: 38), for its emphasis on manners and lifestyle. Instead it proposes "covenant and conduct" (Ozick 1970: 272) as the proper rules for life. The universalist choice of Enlightenment, "to be

Mankind rather than Jewish" (282), was wrong, and its secularization false. "The secular Jew is a figment; when a Jew becomes a secular person he is no longer a Jew. This is especially true for makers of literature" (276). Authors recognized this when they discovered that there are "no Jewish literary giants in the Diaspora" (274). It was the promise of a secular religion, art, that lured people to choose humanity and its disciplines over their own tradition. The novel is a case in point. "The novel at its nineteenth-century pinnacle was a Judaized novel" (272). Things have changed in a secular direction: "Now it is the novel that has been aestheticized, poeticized, and thereby paganized" (271). Its true character has been lost. "At bottom it is not the old novel as 'form' that is being rejected, but the novel as a Jewish force" (272). This attitude, like *Mimesis*, sees the fate of the novel as a Hebraic-Hellenic struggle between faith and idolatry. The choice is between "God or Apollo, Judaism or Art" (Gitenstein 1983: 200). The bitter realization that "the Jewish fiction writer who covets Apollo as god denies Yahweh and His law" (199) dictates a change toward a religious understanding of literature. As Auerbach suggested, the good author is an aggadist (Ozick 1970: 279, 280).

There is, however, a great difference between the modernist and the postmodernist position: the contemporary author resents the canon Auerbach admired because she feels she cannot ever enter its pantheon. The postmodern artist who distrusts art, "though tantalized by the excitement and vitality of secular creativity, recognizes its danger, and fears (even as she lusts after) its magic" (Gitenstein 1983: 199). She earnestly tries to become famous but remains minor. Now she feels betrayed by the emancipatory covenant of culture: "Though I had yearned to be famous in the religion of Art, to become so to speak a saint of Art, I remained obscure" (Ozick 1970: 267) and did not enter the Christian heaven (of universally canonic scriptures). Now she finds that "the religion of Art . . . is the religion of the Gentile nations" (266), a beguiling mythology. In a dramatic change of mind, she rejects the "portrait of the Jew as *Luftmensch*, ennobled by otherness, universalized through wandering, gifted in his homelessness by exceptional sight and judgment, made free by unbelonging" (265). The covenant is denounced, assimilation ridiculed. "Diaspora-flattery is our pustule, culture-envy our infection. Not only do we flatter Gentiles, we crave the flattery of Gentiles" (277). She associates Modernism with sacraments, and in its place advocates a "liturgical" Jewish writing, different from that of "aesthetic paganism." "It was not only an injunction that Moses uttered when he said we would be a people attentive to holiness, it was a description and a destiny" (276). Liturgical writing, described here in ways reminiscent of *Mimesis*, will first appear in fiction. "[T]he liturgical novel will not be didactic or prescriptive; on the contrary, it will be Aggadic, utterly freed to invention, discourse, parable, experiment, enlightenment, profundity, humanity" (280). In a return to the dilemmas of Moses Mendelssohn and his generation, it is suggested that, if "we define ourselves as a religious community" (278), Jews should appropriate, rather than assimilate, and return to their lost, authentic heritage, Yiddish, by treating English the way they treated German. Jews are asked to repent for the sin of emancipation and restore to their art its moral character.

The issue of assimilation was by definition (like all questions of emancipation in modernity after the Battle of the Books) one of Hellenization. Those who were challenged to integrate through modernization were faced with the dilemma of aesthetic paganism: "We can do what the German Jews did, and what Isaac D'Israeli did—we can give ourselves over altogether to Gentile culture and be lost to history, becoming a vestige-nation without a literature; or we can do what we have never before dared to do in a Diaspora language: make it our own, our own necessary instrument, understanding ourselves in it while being understood by everyone who cares to listen or read. If we make out of English a New Yiddish, then we can fashion a Yavneh" (282), a Jerusalem Displaced.[144] Although the aesthetic has been Hebraicized, it seems that it still is what it always has been—inalienably Western.[145] According to the tribalist view, the only place of true consolation and integration remains the traditional community. "[L]ike the Buber-Rosenzweig group in Germany, the alienated American Jewish intellectuals will, I imagine, return to the *integrally alienated*, the highly *individual* Judaism of our literature, and of the remaining Jewish communities which have retained their wholeness" (Halpern 1946: 17). The larger problem is as old as the social disenfranchisement of the early German Romantics: "How to find the community: that, you recognize, is the dilemma of the Jewish intellectual of our day—but not only of the Jewish intellectual! And in this fact that you think you may have discovered a way out. That way is through the community of all the disinherited—the 'alienated,' those who see the world 'as disenchanted'" (15).[146] This time, though, the advice is very different from Schiller's and the proposed solution opposite to Heine's, warning that "you are letting yourself be beguiled by a theory which would endow the condition of 'alienation' with significant psychological compensations exclusively available to you, as a Jew, but denied to him as a Gentile" (15). The answer to the dilemmas of emancipation is a typically postmodern separatism that defiantly goes the way of its difference, pride, and communal tradition.[147]

This decision, inspired by the perceived failure of Enlightenment and assimilation, is accompanied by a deep feeling of disgust and rage of mis-Hellenism. It confesses "a revulsion against the values—very plainly I mean the beliefs—of the surrounding culture itself: a revulsion against Greek and pagan modes, whether in their Christian or post-Christian vessels, whether in their purely literary vessels, or whether in their vessels of *Kulturge-*

schichte. It is a revulsion—I want to state it even more plainly—against what is called, strangely, Western Civilization" (Ozick 1970: 265–66). Christianity, too, becomes a target of contempt: "I am no advocate of some earlier credal organization. In particular, I have not the slightest affection for the dead church civilization of the West. I am a Jew. No Jew in his right mind can long for some variant of that civilization. Its one enduring quality is its transgressive energy against the Jew of culture" (Rieff 1972: 27). There are declarations of religious war that go beyond "the aesthetic warfare between the Hebrew Bible and the New Testament" (Bloom 1984: 13), a perennial problem for Protestant criticism, and that also express hatred: "I am an enemy of the New Testament. My enmity is lifelong and intensifies as I study its text more closely" (4). Beyond the revulsion, the contempt, and the hatred, the open war against Christianity (which has not been met with any protests) is the final assault against the source of all evil, including the gospel of love—pagan orgy and intelligence.[148]

Such attacks on the Hellenic ideal are part of the intellectual-function that has been aptly called the "Jew of culture," and express its constant cultural defensive struggle with and for modernity: "For the sake of law and order, justice and reverence inseparable from their god-terms, we mere teachers, Jews of culture, influential and eternally powerless, have no choice except to think defensively: how to keep ourselves from being overwhelmed by that complex of orgy and routine which constitutes modernization and its totalitarian character type using the language of trust against authority—without which trust cannot exist" (Rieff 1972: 50). For the "Jew of culture," modernity is (under) a constant threat: "The possibility of a permanent barbarism lies before us" (65), he warns again and again. Such apprehension and despair sometimes lead to demands for strict measures that limit civil rights: "In the absence of a supreme interdictory figure, another Moses, a defense by Jews of culture against our democratic orgiasts may be reordered, their preposterous position-taking constrained, from the outside in—by a revival of severe codes of law" (70). There is need for a new order. For example, "consider eliminating the prison system entirely; instead, substitute an order of physical punishment. . . . The supervision of such punishments would again become the right and duty of a would-be ruling class" (72). The task of the intellectual, who today is a "Jew of culture," is to prepare such a class, the interpretive despotism: "You and I, fellow teachers, are the real police, whether we like it or not. No culture can survive without police of our sort—priests, teachers, whoever acts as a responsible draftsman of the ceaselessly redrawn hermeneutic circle, within which is the essential safety, from the danger of living outside it" (43). This exclusive circle cannot be allowed to operate democratically. The advice is simple and direct: "Rehabilitate authority" (72) or "revive the constitution of authority" (73). It is time for culture to rule with all the brute force which has been denied to it (or until now hypocritically denounced by it). Its real enemy is the Dionysian orgiast, the Greek "satyr, who opposes the Jew of culture" (81) and represents contemporary anarchy. Under the rule of culture, he must be disciplined. The democratization of *Bildung* in the industrial era has produced the disruptive politics of mass protest. To save law and virtue, the whole egalitarian project of Enlightenment must be denounced.

The primary target of social criticism and political radicalism, which are presented here as barbarism, is the current intellectual hegemony: "Make no mistake: the figure under siege in our culture is not Johnny Carson, but Lionel Trilling, superior teacher and leading American Jew of culture" (80). Trilling (1905–75) was among the few Modernists interested in *Bildung*, essentially arguing that "literature is concerned with the self." Placing great emphasis on personal style and manners, the disciplines of civility, he made selfhood the highest aesthetic preference. This choice must be seen in the context of his decision to explore how the modern Jew might define himself.[149] For intellectuals of the 1940s, from Adorno to Daniel Bell, from Horkheimer to Mann, and from Auerbach to Sartre that question was one of paramount importance, often taking the form of comparisons between the "estranged Gentile" and the "alienated Jew." The assumption common to most discussions was the familiar plight of the culture and intelligence elite suffering the privilege and purposelessness of autonomy: "The young Jew is left helpless, and aware. He is aware of a distance both from the Jewish culture from which he came and the Gentile culture into which he cannot or will not enter. He is helpless because he cannot find his roots in either. Yet out of this tension of understanding and inhibition has been bred a new kind of Jew, the Jew of alienation, a Jew who consciously accepts this situation and utilizes his alienation to see, as if with a double set of glasses, each blending their perspective into one, the nature of the tragedy of our time" (Bell 1946: 15). Thus for some resistance to assimilation was the ethic of emancipation. They turned the *theoros*'s distant view from above into the prophet's higher moral ground: "The assumption of alienation is a positive value, fostering a critical sense out of a role of detachment; it is, if you will, the assumption of the role of prophet, the one who through an ethical conscience indicts the baseness of the world. . . . Alienation does not mean deracination. It means the acceptance of the Jewish tradition— its compulsion to community—and the use of its ethical precepts as a prism to refract the codes and conduct of the world. As long as moral corruption exists, alienation is the only possible response" (19). Following the precepts of the aesthetic morality and politics first outlined by Schiller and the Tübingen seminary circle, the status of "otherhood" (Benjamin Nelson) is no longer a social predicament but valuable cultural capital accumulated by the true Jews of modernity, the (Protestant) priests of culture. Like any other member of the cultural hegemony, the alienated Jewish intellectual "can live only in permanent tension and as a permanent critic" (19). Jewishness and critique, both aesthetic absolutizations of the Reformation exercise of interpretation, continue to function as the conscience of the Fall of emancipation into idolatry.

Trilling combined the two notions with a nostalgic return not to the German ideal of *Bildung* but to its British equivalent from the age of Empire. "'Culture' early became associated in Trilling's thinking with the social ideal of the gentleman. He took over his conception of the gentleman mainly from nineteenth-century English literature, which became his professional specialty. That ideal of the self is illuminated by Maurice Samuel's polemical book *The Gentleman and the Jew* (1950), which tries to demonstrate the incompatibility of the social types named in its title. Samuel sets up a schema in which the gentleman, actually the English gentleman, is moved by a passion for battle and personal honor. He is pagan, competitive, egotistic. The Jew, on the other hand, is presented by Samuel as peaceable, cooperative, and loving" (Krupnick 1986: 27). Unable to trust the heritage and the support of the Jewish community for its intellectual, Trilling wanted the prestige of the gentleman's image for the Jew. It was in the early 1950s that "he first sharply withdrew from politics. In those years he evolved the conception of an 'opposing self' that existed not so much to oppose specific social arrangements as to oppose 'the culture' in some general sense and to oppose death and lesser evils of the human condition" (167). After *The Liberal Imagination* (1950), which grew out of his notion of the "literary imagination" in the 1940s, he saw the self and culture in conflict, and believed that only art had the power to "liberate the individual from the tyranny of his culture" and allow him to achieve a conscious, distinct, independent identity.[150] Thus the intellectual self became the basis of an "adversary culture," of the aesthetic suprapolitics advocated by Hölderlin, Lukács, and Adorno.

Trilling's faith in art, however, was only the swan song of the assimilationist ideal, which was soon succeeded by separatist calls for ethnic autonomy. During the 1970s, when these calls were systematized into a coherent position, conservative intellectuals like Norman Podhoretz, Jerry Falwell, Irving Kristol, Jeane Kirkpatrick, Alan Bloom, William Bennett, John Silber, Roland Posner, William F. Buckley (to limit ourselves to the United States), and other "Jews of culture" reclaimed public culture for a fundamentalist version of the Hebraic ideology. During the same period, notions and principles of the sacred made a comeback in the humanities, staging the return of scriptural concerns and methods. Both sides, traditional humanism and the professed anti-humanism of scholarship, shared the same faith in higher education: "Because the university must be the temple of the intellect, uniquely unchangeable in that respect, it is a sacred institution, the last in our culture" (Rieff 1972: 7). Conservatives and deconstructionists, moralists and formalists, all reached a remarkable consensus on the place and mission of the education elite: "For us, in our priestly roles, everything there is is there to be interpreted; outside the temple, we are not priests" (13). In this convergence of opinion, the Hebraization of culture finally prevails in higher education and research. "Folding back upon itself, criticism has therefore refused to see its affiliations with the political world it serves, perhaps unwittingly, perhaps not. Once an intellectual, the modern critic has become a cleric in the worst sense of the word" (Said 1983: 292).[151] With the explicit return of the sacred in the disciplines of interpretation, the reoccupation of critique by theology launched in the *Dialectic* appears to have succeeded. "What one discerns today is religion as the result of exhaustion, consolation, disappointment: its forms in both the theory and practice of criticism are varieties of unthinkability, undecidability, and paradox together with a remarkable consistency of appeals to magic, divine ordinance, or sacred texts" (291). This exhaustion and resignation marks the end of the interpretive religious wars.

Both the separatist and the assimilationist positions, both the humanist and the anti-humanist attitudes find in Hebraism the postmodern universal that asserts the moral superiority of contemplation, the cultural ethics of atonement. To the extent that they believe this, they are happy to accept for themselves, *figurae* of the Jew, the situation described by Arnold Zweig in 1933: "The Jews are proletarians. They are proletarians, despite their luxury, their ten-room apartments, their university education, and their intellectual professions" (quoted in Deak 1968: 26). Proletarians of the public sphere and the political arena, intellectuals are content with their priestly function in a society that has benevolently agreed to respect their lack of purpose in exchange for their renunciation of interest.[152] As Paul de Man, a typical Hebraic thinker, had ample opportunity to find out, the situation was one of perfect accommodation: so far as the military, political, economic, and bureaucratic establishment was concerned, theorists were welcome to atone for their autonomy with their opposition so far as this remained a cultural and interpretive one, namely, an aesthetic position. But the proud isolation of autonomy seemed to make them uncomfortable. They worried that they had not managed to formulate in Western language the message of their own singularity. "Until now all we have attempted is an apologetics limited, without great difficulty, to bringing the truths of the Torah into line with the West's noble models. The Torah demands something more" (Levinas 1989b: 286). What a modern Torah like *Mimesis* and the *Dialectic* demand, according to their literalist, and therefore fundamentalist readers, is more than just emancipation or appropriation. "In the singularity of Israel a peak is attained that justifies the very perenniality of Judaism. . . . But this is a singularity that the long history from which we are emerging has left at the level of sentiment or faith. It needs to be made explicit to thought. It cannot here and now furnish rules for education. It still needs to be translated into that Greek language which, thanks to assimilation, we have learnt in the West. We are faced with the great task of articulating in Greek those principles of which Greece had no knowledge. The singularity of the Jews awaits its philosophy" (287).

This dictates the need for the ultimate project of Mythology, which has been called "de-Hellenization": the total elimination of the Greek element from Western thought, an effort pioneered by Adorno and Horkheimer. This is the message of the aphorism: "It is time not for first philosophy but last philosophy" (Adorno 1983: 40). When they proposed Judaism as the project of atonement and return to the kingdom of God, their message to their sinful age was simple: repeat, repent, return. But it might have no urgency or potency without a terrifying enemy, a satanic ghost conjured up as the incarnation of evil. Accordingly, a sinister, frightful model of Greek thought was constructed to play this role and represent thirty wretched centuries of Western civilization, from Odysseus to Hitler.

It is frightfully alarming, however, to realize that, had Horkheimer and Adorno not built this monstrous Hellenic idol and sacrificed contemporary culture to it, had they not invented a mythology of their own, their invocation of the Hebraic God might simply not have been possible at all. It is equally alarming to notice that, in their iconomachic virulence, postmodern plans for de-Hellenization also construct Greek idols on which the absence of justice and freedom are blamed in order to preserve the legitimacy and status of contemplative ethics. In sharp contrast, the socio-political realities in Bucharest, Bombay, Beirut, Buenos Aires, or Birmingham, Alabama, remind us that demonology cannot restore the validity of aesthetic faith. "Theory cannot prolong the moment its critique depended on. A practice indefinitely delayed is no longer the forum for appeals against self-satisfied speculation; it is mostly the pretext used by executive authorities to choke, as vain, whatever critical thoughts the practical change would require" (Adorno 1973b: 3). When the moment of self-referential culture, the rule of autonomy, passes, critique languishes in the mirrors of logology, theory fades into ersatz sacrament: "What is the city over the mountains / Cracks and reforms and bursts in the violet air / Falling towers / Jerusalem Athens . . . / Unreal" (Eliot). Beyond just the privileges of interpretation, the very promise of emancipation is questioned and the quest for independent governance begins again: What can be the auto- of autonomy if not the demos of democracy? The regime in Ithaca, rather than the nostos of Odysseus, is at issue here.

Chapter Three

WRITING THE LAW

Indeed the Holy Scripture is the lock on the portals
of salvation,
But paganism is, sadly, the only key that fits it.
—Ludwig Feuerbach

THE SPIRIT AND THE LETTER

The figures of Abraham and Odysseus as symbols of modernity's supreme right (interpretation) and responsibility (transcendence) became quite common in nineteenth-century discussions of the critical task. They represented two contrasting views of critique (of adventure and trial), one centrifugal and the other centripetal. Thus when Emmanuel Levinas (b. 1905), at the beginning of the period of his Talmudic writings,[1] proposed the Patriarch and the King as alternative models of thought,[2] he was securely relying on their elaborate portraits devised by Kierkegaard and by Horkheimer and Adorno, respectively. *Fear and Trembling* defined the pure interiority of understanding achieved by the transcendence of the social moment, while the *Dialectic of Enlightenment* inspected the ferociously and ruthlessly independent bourgeois consciousness. Levinas combined the two models in an opposition that represented the dilemma of reflection—return or separation: "To the myth of Ulysses returning to Ithaca we can oppose the story of Abraham leaving his fatherland forever for an unknown land and forbidding his servant to lead even his son to the point of departure" (Levinas 1968: 37).

Levinas believes that Odysseus' adventure is circular; his career, which is but a return home, represents the central concern of Greek and most western thought, from Parmenides to Heidegger: the search for self, truth, and Being as the *algos* of *nostos*. Philosophy has long aspired to the totality of homeliness, the ideal of at-homeness (*Heimatlichkeit*) in one's entire existence, and has found its model in the Greek objective (self)representation. "Philosophy is being at home with self, just like the homeliness of the Greek; it is man's being at home in his mind, at home with himself" (Hegel 1955: 152). Being-at-home-with-oneself means to be the ground and origin of oneself, to arise from out of oneself and be in possession of one's life. Independent existence has its own self-justifying value: this is the lesson modern man should learn from antiquity. "When man began to be at home with himself, he turned to the Greeks to find enjoyment in it. Let us leave the Latin and the Roman to the church and to jurisprudence. Higher, freer philosophical science, as also the beauty of our untrammelled art, the taste for, and love of the same, we know to have taken their root in Greek life and to have created therefrom their spirit. If we were to have an aspiration, it would be for such a land and such conditions" (150). Home is where dwelling takes place. According to Heidegger, dwelling is *the basic character of Being in keeping with which mortals exist*" (Heidegger 1971c: 160). His *Introduction to Metaphysics* (1953) suggests, in talking about the Pre-Socratics, that Logos held man rooted and at home when *einai* and *noein* (Parmenides) were still one. Now, however, man finds himself in a "not-at-home" situation, "unhomely" in the world, a stranger (Kristeva 1990). In this search for dwelling, symbolized by the travel back to Ithaca, Levinas detects the incurable nostalgia for the same. "Philosophy's itinerary remains that of Ulysses, whose adventure in the world was only a return to his native island—a complacency in the Same, an unrecognition of the other" (Levinas 1987a: 91).

Abraham, on the other hand, responding to God's command, does not return but leaves his homeland behind for an unknown place. His destination is not self-realization and self-knowledge but separation from one's own, following a command that comes from an "Other." Thought is based on separation, not on Heidegger's "calling into nearness"[3] or on identity. "Separation opens up between terms that are absolute and yet in relation, that absolve themselves from the relation they maintain, that do not abdicate in it in favor of a totality this relation would sketch out" (Levinas 1969: 220). Relation presupposes separation. "Relation is possible only as a function of a separation proceeding from the impossibility of totalization" (Libertson 1982: 311). Hegel, who yearned for autochthonous dwelling, saw Abraham as the personification of the unhappy consciousness: by leaving home and abandoning his culture, he chooses foreignness and becomes a wanderer. In the *Phenomenology of the Spirit* (1807), this move is presented as severance and homelessness. Levinas changes this perspective by making separation, now an ethical category, primary: "Subjective existence derives its features from separation. . . . Separation is the very act of individuation" (Levinas 1969: 299) because it tears existence apart from the personal. "Individuation is an uprooting rather than a rooting within being or within manifestation. But this uprooting is no more an entry into communion than an entry into dispersion" (Libertson 1982: 316). Separation as discontinuity is anterior to subjectivity, and therefore to relation too: it is thought as well as (its) communication. "Every basic term which describes a rapport or relation, in Levinas' philosophy, describes the production of separation by the alteration of being" (317). Alteration, the arrival of alterity, separates and individuates. Ultimately, as the example of Abraham shows, separation is the distance from *Deus absconditus*, the experience of that "moment when God withdraws from the world and veils His face" (Levinas 1979: 218). It is that "distant," "absent," "hidden God" to whom Levinas always refers.[4]

In his examination of the *Akedah*, Levinas foregrounds God's intervention in Abraham's affairs and the demand for obedience. The source of ultimate meaning is the eruption of the "Other" into one's life. The Other opposes the self by the infinity of his transcendence; he commands respect and demands justice (Mouw 1990). The Other is God who commands Abraham out of his being-at-home. Adopting Kierkegaard's ethical imperative from the discussion of Isaac's sacrifice, Levinas argues that serving the Other is more important because it means obeying a command—being called to task, to one's responsibility (which is different from Heidegger's "historical calling," the "call to care"). What is important for the unmediated encounter with the divine is not the leap of faith but the unconditional surrender to the call.

Starting with *Time and the Other* (1947)—if not with his very first book, the dissertation *The Theory of Intuition in Husserl's Phenomenology* (1930), as Derrida (1978: 84) has suggested—Levinas tried to break with what he called the Parmenidean philosophy of Being, "the exercise of the same" which culminated in Heidegger's *Being and Time* (1927), by exploring alterity. Thought which seeks to ground itself in its own dwelling has lost contact with the divine: "Philosophy is atheism, or rather unreligion, negation of a God that reveals himself and puts truths into us. This is the lesson of Socrates's teaching" (Levinas 1987: 49), he suggests, and elsewhere he calls philosophy the "temptation of temptations." Presenting ontology—a term explicitly denounced by Heidegger after 1935—as "a philosophy of immanence and of autonomy, or atheism" (Levinas 1968: 35), he turns his attention to the centrality and irreducibility of the Other. Being is alterity. Against "ontological imperialism," which reduces ethics to knowledge, he "affirms the metaphysical priority of ethics over ontology" (McCollester 1970: 345). Levinas finds the revolt of Kierkegaard against the metaphysics of the Hegelian system valid but not well founded: the real resistance to the totalitarianism of philosophy does not lie in the self but in the face of the Other—in "the epiphany of the absolutely other" (Levinas 1968: 41) and the "absolute of the presence of the Other" (46). Being is sought in the infinity of alterity rather than the totality of identity.

Following Rosenzweig's belief that the reign of "anthropos theoretikos" is over, Levinas concludes: "Already *of itself* ethics is an 'optics'" (Levinas 1969: 29). This position, which is contrasted to "panoramic existence" (Wyschogrod 1974: 294) from Plato to Heidegger, not only revises Sartre's notion of the "look" but offers an alternative to Hellenic theoria. According to Derrida's expansive reading, Levinas's work is a critique of the "imperialism of *theoria*" (Derrida 1978a: 84–85) and the "Greco-Platonic tradition" (91) of light, glance, and presence. Levinas takes as a model for his "metaphysics of the face" (92) Moses' encounter at Sinai. "The face of God which commands while hiding itself is at once more and less a face than all faces" (108). Moving in such a direction, "Levinas already aims for the face-to-face, the encounter with the face. 'Face to face without intermediary' and without 'communion'" (90).[5] It is the face that calls and commands. "The face 'signifies' beyond, neither as an index nor as a symbol, but precisely and irreducibly as a face that *summons me*. It signifies *to-God* (*à-Dieu*), not as a sign, but as the questioning of myself, as if I were being summoned or called, that is to say, awakened or cited as myself. In this summons, the *question* harkens back to its primordial, underived meaning" (Levinas 1983: 112). The alterity of the face is *semeion, arche,* and *ousia*—condition and possibility and fulfillment of subjectivity. This type of encounter seeks to restore and respect the original difference of separation. Levinas prepares for a meeting with the "unforeseeably-other," the "infinitely-other" (91), that dispenses with Christian proximity—with Jesus as intermediary and the rite of communion as mediation. "Face to face with the other within a glance *and* a speech which both maintain distance and interrupt all totalities, this being-together as separation precedes or exceeds society, collectivity, community. Levinas calls it religion" (Derrida 1978a: 95).[6] The new foundation of ethics (Gerber 1967: 185) is the Sinaitic "*re-ligio*" of the private encounter with divine infinity. Levinas seeks in alterity total appearance, full apparition. "The other is not signaled by his face, he is this face" (100). He also seeks "the original unity of glance and speech, eyes and mouth, that speaks" and "precedes, in its signification, the dispersion of senses and organs of sensibility" (100). Thinking of the encounter as an epiphany, he "conceives the face in terms of the 'resemblance' of man and God" (102). The "epiphany of visage," of the other, opens the self to the domain of the divine. The face is the moment of faith. As Levinas concedes: "The Other resembles God." And elsewhere: "Discourse is discourse with God. . . . Metaphysics is the essence of this language with God" (quoted in Derrida 1978a: 108). In Levinas's religion, "God is the other par excellence" (Wyschogrod 1974: 171)—the supreme source of meaning and strength. "Always behind its signs and its works, always within its secret interior, and forever discreet, interrupting all historical totalities through its freedom of speech, the face is not 'of this world.' It is the origin of the world" (Derrida 1978a: 103).

For Martin Heidegger (1889–1976), the most receptive response to the command is listening. "Mortals speak insofar as they listen. They heed the bidding call of the stillness of the dif-ference even when they do not know

that call. Their listening draws from the command of the dif-ference what
it brings out as sounding word. This speaking that listens and accepts is
responding. Nevertheless by receiving what it says from the command of
the dif-ference, mortal speech has already, in its own way, followed the call"
(1971d: 209).[7] The command of the call is to accept. As exemplified in the
commentary on Hölderlin, Heidegger's method involves attentive and re-
spectful listening, and the passive preservation of Being: "To preserve the
work is simply to listen to it, in all passivity, knowing that it is uniquely and
absolutely true. . . . It is not a case of a freedom grasping another freedom
that, like it, attempts to clear a way to the truth: that would be interpreting
and critiquing, and there simply can be no question of interpreting Being;
all that can be done is to receive it and preserve it" (de Man 1983a: 253).
Listen, receive, accept, preserve: these are the commandments of the work
(which is by definition the work of art), and they dictate the disciplinary
practice of reading.

Reacting to Heidegger's quietist hermeneutics, Levinas proclaims that
western philosophy is a philosophy of the response, of the answer, while in
Biblical thought what matters is the question and the search of the question.[8] "There is a question and yet no doubt; there is a question, but no
desire for an answer; there is a question, and nothing can be said, but just
this nothing, to say. This is a query, a probe that surpasses the very possibility of questions" (Blanchot 1986: 9). Abraham does not respond as much as
he is overtaken by the command: he dutifully receives the Other. "It is not
at all a situation where one poses the question; it is the question that seizes
you: what occurs is, you are put into question. All these situations probably
appear differently in the Greek style and in the style which is inscribed very
profoundly in the Biblical tradition. My concern throughout is precisely to
translate this non-Hellenism of the Bible into Hellenic terms and not to
repeat the Biblical formulae in their obvious meaning, isolated from context, which context, at the level of such a text, is the *entire* Bible. Nothing
can be done: philosophy speaks Greek" (Levinas 1982: 137). Suddenly, the
situation of the question changes into the question of translation from one
style to another—translation from the Biblical tradition of question and
separation to the Greek philosophy of response and return, or from alterity
to identity. There is a question and yet it has to be translated. What neces-
sitates this move, Levinas argues, is that philosophy, "the science of the
Greeks" (Husserl), has always spoken Greek. He does not explain why one
should speak philosophy: its priority for (not only western) thought is never
justified, just accepted (like a call) a priori. The possibility of a reverse
translation, from the Greek to the Biblical, is not entertained either. It is as
if, to use Levinas's terms, Biblical tradition, the very thought of the question, had been seized, put into question, by the eruption of the "other,"

Greek philosophy, and had to obey its command. It appears that the question of the question is the Greek character of thought, or at least of the language of existence.

Trying to listen receptively to the same command, Heidegger argued that to ask the question (which, for him, was the question of Being) is not to step outside the limits of philosophy but rather to repeat its originary Greek move. Seeking to restore the question of Being to its inaugural Greek authenticity, he insisted that the very question "what is x?" is the Greek mode of thought—that Greek is the condition and horizon of philosophical inquiry. "If we so stubbornly insist on thinking Greek thought in Greek fashion it is by no means because we intend to sketch a historical portrait of Greek antiquity, as one of the past great ages of man, which would be in many respects more accurate. . . . Rather, our sole aim is to reach what wants to come to language in such a conversation, provided it come of its own accord. And this is that Same which fatefully concerns the Greeks and ourselves, albeit in different ways. It is that which brings the dawn of thinking into the fate of things Western, into the land of evening. Only as a result of this fatefulness [Geschick] do the Greeks become Greeks in the historic [geschichtlich] sense" (Heidegger 1984: 25). It is this reexamination of the Greek dawn of philosophy that Levinas criticizes as return (to philosophy's homeland). Equally concerned about the destiny of western thought, he opposes to its "land of evening" the land that Abraham sought. Still, to the extent that he has to translate the experience of separation into the language of identity, he is condemned to repeat its illusionary return. This is the crucial objection raised by Derrida, who finds that "Levinas's metaphysics presupposes what it seeks to put in question in such a way that it remains haunted by it" (Bernasconi 1987: 127). Like Adorno, who had to diet on the garbage of post-Auschwitz culture, Levinas can address God only in the atheistic language of philosophy. Faith may have been emancipated from the church but not from the spell of Greek idols.

The first philosopher to take an uncompromisingly and unreservedly hostile position against Hellenism from a Hebraic viewpoint was Lev Shestov (1866–1938) in *Athens and Jerusalem* (completed in 1937), where he argued that between the two, no reconciliation or peaceful coexistence is possible. The failures of "the greatest representatives of the human spirit . . . for almost two thousand years" (Shestov 1966: 47) have shown that Jerusalem and Athens, "religion and natural philosophy" (48), are incompatible. At the beginning of his "Foreword," Shestov challenges the traditional conjunctive assumption: "'Athens and Jerusalem,' 'religious philosophy'—these expressions are practically identical; they have almost the same meaning. One is as mysterious as the other, and they irritate modern thought to the same degree by the inner contradiction they contain.

Would it not be more proper to pose the dilemma as: Athens *or* Jerusalem, religion *or* philosophy?" (47) In his earlier work (e.g., 1932: 234–35), Shestov had accepted that the ancient philosophers are eternal and indispensable. Here he insists that an absolute choice must be made between faith and reason, revelation and rationalism, Biblical and speculative thought, religious and secular philosophy.

Shestov's critique is directed against western metaphysics—what he called, before Levinas, Derrida, and Lyotard[9] the "Parmenidean tradition." He criticizes collectively, and most of the time synchronically, all philosophy, and finds it corrupt and seductive from its very (Hellenic) beginning: "Plato and Aristotle, bewitched by Socrates, and, after them, modern philosophy—Descartes, Spinoza, Leibniz, as well as Kant—seek, with all the passion of which men are capable, universal and necessary truths—the only thing, according to them, which is worthy of being called 'knowledge'" (Shestov 1966: 51). Thought since Parmenides remains in the chains of Necessity—of reality, fact, reason, science, truth: "Just as in Hegel, philosophy, in the course of its millennial history, remains one" (271). Christianity is not excluded from this rule of incessant repetition: "Now it appears that the Christian also cannot do without Socrates" (246), which is understandable since "Christian thought in its beginning already admitted two 'Old Testaments'—the Bible and Greek philosophy" (271)—a trend that continued with scholastic thought and modern philosophy.

From Parmenides' revolutionary claim that being is the same as thought, two parallel projects began. The first was metaphysics as a science searching for ultimate truth, which encouraged blind trust on the constraining truths of knowledge. "Metaphysics must be a *parere* (obedience), just like the positive sciences. Parmenides, Plato, Spinoza, Kant, Hegel, 'constrained by the truth itself,' do not choose and do not decide. Someone has chosen, someone has decided, someone has commanded, without them. And this is what is called the truth. . . . All the 'reasons'—theoretical and practical, human and superhuman—have always told us, each in particular and all in general, the same thing throughout the millennial development of philosophical thought: one must obey, one must submit" (151–52). Knowledge has only encouraged submission. "The Greeks, indeed, placed obedience above everything else" (285). The second project was that of an independent discipline of ethics. "In the world ruled by 'Necessity' the fate of man and the only goal of every reasonable being consist in the performance of duty: autonomous ethics crowns the autonomous laws of being" (59). Since the time of the Greeks, Necessity remains sovereign and humankind has made no progress toward true liberation.

If in Shestov's story Parmenides is the first man, Socrates (as in Nietzsche's story) is the great villain.[10] He was the one to formulate the two self-defeating plans of philosophy. "To Socrates belongs the merit of hav-

ing created what was later called 'autonomous ethics.' But it was also
Socrates who laid the foundations of scientific knowledge" (158). He was
the first real sinner, responsible for the fall of thought into knowledge. "In
the eyes of all, publicly, Socrates had to repeat the act which, according to
the ancient myth that no one can attest, Adam had committed" (171).
From Aristotle to Hegel, philosophers have followed his path. "All this constitutes the heritage of Socrates. Since Socrates the truth, for men, has
been confounded with universal and necessary judgements" (167).

In contrast, Shestov is attracted to the figure of the first Patriarch: "Abraham does not ask reason, he refuses to admit the legitimacy of the preten-
sions of knowledge" (319). For Shestov too, the "knight of faith" (Kierkegaard) was the model of the thinker. In two long sections on *Fear and
Trembling, Repetition,* and *The Concept of Dread,* Shestov examines Kierkegaard's view. "Kierkegaard felt Socrates' problem, which is the basic
problem not only of ethics but of all philosophy, no less deeply than Nietzsche. And, like Nietzsche, he strained all his powers to overcome Socrates'
enchantment. It was for this reason alone that he turned to the Bible"
(239). In Abraham he found an imposing alternative and realized that a
choice had to be made. His special problem, however, was that, despite his
preference for the Patriarch, he retained a certain admiration for the philosopher. Kierkegaard could not see Socrates as a fallen man but only as
"man as he was before tasting the fruit of the tree of knowledge" (240).
Despite his severe criticism of Hegel, he could not free himself from the
requirements of the dialectic. He proposed a major reorientation by returning "to faith the position that the Bible had conferred upon it" (332). He
never made the "leap of faith" himself, however, because "he 'understood'
in Abraham only what recalled to him Socrates" (242) and his ethics. He
pointed a way but was unable to follow it; the spell of antiquity and its
knowledge were too strong. "Kierkegaard could never overcome the anxiety
that he felt before Greek wisdom" (248). Shestov offers his own position in
one of the many short sections comprising the last chapter (XIX) of his
book, entitled "Abraham and Socrates." For him, the two men represent
the basic types of thinker, the believer and the scientist, respectively. Their
views and attitudes are opposite and incompatible. "And if philosophy
wishes to attain the promised land . . . , it must adopt the method of Abraham and not that of Socrates and teach men at all events to go forward
without calculating, without seeing anything beforehand, without ever
knowing where they are going" (397). Shestov is unwilling to allow for concessions like those made by Kierkegaard. Mankind, he insists, must accept
"the God of Abraham, the God of Isaac, the God of Jacob, and not the God
of the philosophers" (67). There can be no middle ground.

Shestov's book is a frontal polemic against Greek philosophy: "The
Greeks await salvation from their wisdom founded on knowledge, but they

are going to their ruin, for salvation comes from faith, from nothing but faith" (320–21). His goal is to expose "the indestructible bond between knowledge, as philosophy understands it, and the horrors of human existence" (66). This is a cardinal idea later described by Levinas as the totalitarianism unleashed by Greek thought against what is noblest and purest in man. The hope of transcendence, however, is not lost for Shestov, who sees dialectics only as the latest manifestation of the time-old Greek terror.[11] "We must, before everything else, reject the basic categories of Greek thought, tear out from our being all the postulates of our 'natural knowledge' and our 'natural morality'" (288). He goes back to Tertullian, who is commonly considered the first to articulate this dilemma, and reiterates the question: "*quid ergo Athenis et Hierosolymis?*" (286) An intermediary position is not feasible, he presses, "for what is foolishness for Athens is wisdom for Jerusalem and what is truth for Jerusalem is for Athens a lie" (287). One must select, dedicate himself to, and live with, one or the other.

Shestov, like Kierkegaard, contrasts knowledge, the original sin and lie of speculative philosophy, with faith. "What is important for us is that the faith of Scripture has absolutely nothing in common with faith as the Greeks understood it and as we now understand it" (323). Far from being another feeling of belief, "the faith of the Bible determines and forms being and thus abolishes knowledge with its 'possible' and 'impossible'" (323). His critique is not directed against philosophy but only its Greek ancestry: the opposition he establishes is not between philosophy and faith but rather Greek and Judeo-Christian philosophy. Shestov does not want philosophy abolished or overcome (as did Kierkegaard) but re-directed, re-oriented toward God because what it really aspires to overcome is rationalism, not its own self. Tertullian, Peter Damian, Luther, and Pascal have already shown this path.

As the only alternative to the practices of rationalism, Biblical revelation[12] "is founded on nothing, and is never justified" (274).[13] It is supported only by faith. "Reason wishes to understand" (318). This is the search for the single principle, the ultimate cause. "But 'faith'—again, naturally, the faith of the Bible—concerns itself neither with understanding nor with proofs" (318). With their enslavement to evidence, "the 'first principles' of the Greeks choked the essential truth of the biblical 'revelation.' Not only is not faith a lower form of knowledge, but faith abrogates knowledge" (321). There is a great difference between the eternal truths of reason and the created truth of the Bible (370): "It is in this that the essential opposition between the 'truth' of the Greeks and the 'revelation' of the Bible consists. For the Greeks the fruits of the tree of knowledge were the source of philosophy for all time, and by this very fact they brought men freedom. For the Bible, on the contrary, they were the beginning of enslavement and signified the fall of man" (325). This difference raises inevitably the question of Biblical understanding: Is there a language available for the appropriate approach to God's message? "Is a man educated by the Greeks capable of preserving that freedom which is the condition of the right understanding of what the Bible says?" (278) Obviously not, answers Shestov, since the two categories correspond to totally different modes of comprehension. But if there is an absolute choice between the "metaphysics of knowledge" and "biblical epistemology" (277), then the hermeneutic aporia arises: "How shall we succeed in reading and understanding Scripture not according to the teaching of the great Greek masters but as they who have transmitted to us, by means of the Book of Books, that which they called the word of God wished and demanded of their readers?" (278) The answer has already been given: by absolute faith that does not inquire and does not question. Belief in God is by nature unconditional: "Faith does not examine, it does not look around" (332). Shestov warns: "Human wisdom is foolishness before God, and the wisest of men . . . is the greatest of sinners. Whatsoever is not of faith is sin" (70). Sin is the Hellenic view—rationalism, knowledge, science, culture. The contradiction (with which Auerbach's approach to the Bible is also fraught) is that even the unconditional trust in the word of God, even Abraham's unexamined faith, need to be discussed in terms of (Hellenic) understanding.

The important lesson which Derrida derived from the failures of Shestov and Levinas is this: if the language of response is inescapable even for the thought of the question, then the only viable (non)alternative to the philosophy of return is the rhetoric (and celebration) of repetition—an intrinsic critique of the search for identity exposing its inability to recover the same (origin). In other words, the repetition of the Greeks demanded by modernity should be done in a way that shows the impossibility of a return to Greece. The problem with this practice of endless repetition, this deliberate confusion of the search (and its tongues) is that it can quickly become even more predictable than the destination of the return. The spectacular success of "derrida" (as sign and signature) testifies to that: by the early 1980s it was almost impossible to say anything about "derrida" (at least in English) that was not predictable and banal.[14] At the same time, it became equally inevitable, at least in discussions of art and literature, that something would be said about Jacques Derrida.[15] Banality and predictability were the hallmarks of the reception of his work by everyone (including himself). The wishful impotence of the practice, however, should not entirely subsume the larger project of recasting the Other in the infinity of an immanent otherness.

Jacques Derrida (b. 1930), like Heidegger and Levinas, is interested in the "Greek limits of philosophy" (Clark 1987). In "Violence and Metaphysics: An Essay on the Thought of Emmanuel Levinas" (1964), written on the occasion of Levinas's latest book, *Difficile liberté: Essais sur le Judaïsme*

(1963), Derrida addresses himself to the Greekness of philosophy, the distinctly and exclusively Greek character of (western) thought. "The entirety of philosophy is conceived on the basis of its Greek source. As is well known, this amounts neither to an occidentalism, nor to a historicism. It is simply that the founding concepts of philosophy are primarily Greek, and it would not be possible to philosophize, or to speak philosophically, outside this medium" (Derrida 1978: 81). We still think within the security of Greek knowledge because our very language is Greek. "The knowledge and security of which we are speaking are therefore not in the world: rather, they are the possibility of our language and the nexus of our world" (82). We are all Greeks, Derrida argues, to the extent that we think (and we cannot help thinking) Being and identity, totality and metaphysics.[16]

Derrida views all Western tradition in unperturbed synchronicity as the monstrous trajectory of Greek thought. From Parmenides to Heidegger, almost at a moment of total presence and direct continuity, the whole enterprise appears to him, as it does to Shestov and Levinas, one and the same—that of speaking (in) Greek. The theorist of the different perceives no difference and admits no differentiation among periods, cultures, societies, or languages: in his eyes, all spaces belong to one and the same site, the Site of the Same. They map the era of metaphysics, which imposes notions such as the self, transcendence, presence, plenitude, speech, light, identity, and Being. According to this spectacular tautology, the era of "the Greek domination of the Same and the One" (83) is one and the same. From the ancient to the modern "Greeks named Husserl and Heidegger" (83), the Same has been happening and the One has been occurring again and again.

Derrida's favorite symbol of this oneness—borrowed from the Aryan solar myth of Nazi ideology (Lacoue-Labarthe and Nancy 1990: 309), and therefore, like the *Dialectic of Enlightenment*, associating Greece with that ideology—is the Sun, rising and reigning above the Site of the Same (which is of course the same site, a commonplace). He calls its discourse "photology," its social actuality "heliopolitics," and its thought "heliocentric metaphysics." With Heidegger's "bringing to light" (or even Rosenzweig's "opening up to the light") apparently in mind, he claims that "the entire history of our philosophy is a photology, the name given to a history of, or treatise on, light" (Derrida 1978c: 27)—the light of Being. The Sun is the source of "the light that comes to us from Greece" (Levinas) which makes seeing, presence, clarity and identity possible. The light of the Sun gives us the presence of Being, which Greek reason promises to define and serve; at the same time, it provides for the power of identity, for the sameness of the site. With respect to this tradition, the modern philosophies of phenomenology and ontology are no exception. "Through them, the entire philosophical tradition, in its meaning and at bottom, would make common cause with oppression and the totalitarianism of the same. The ancient clandestine friendship between light and power, the ancient complicity between theoretical objectivity and technico-political possession" (Derrida 1978: 91). Derrida totalizes the history of thought and reduces it to one and the same movement—what Benjamin called *immergleich* (the ever-the-same)—only to warn against totality and identity. What difference does it make, then, if the Sun will again shine on the site of Being? Or is there an alternative in sight for those who have already seen the light?

Derrida supports Levinas's critique of the Greek tradition of philosophy. He praises his questioning of "Western philosophy's very decision, since Plato, to consider itself as a science, as theory" (118) and his "attempt to free the other from the light of Being" (96). He proceeds, however, to deconstruct Levinas's "natural atheism" (103) and show that, to the extent that it privileges speech, the living voice, it has not liberated itself from metaphysics. For although Levinas "places sound above light" (99) and effects "the transcendence of hearing in relation to seeing" (100), he believes that "only living speech is expression" (101). For Levinas, language is preeminently speech. Derrida shows that this assumption keeps him captive to Platonic ideas about writing, and is therefore inconsistent with an effort to define the difference of Judaism. "Moreover," he asks, "how could Hebraism belittle the letter, in praise of which Levinas writes so well?" (102). Derrida perceives in the work of Levinas an "anxious movement within the difference between the Socratic and the Hebraic, the poverty and the wealth of the letter, the pneumatic and the grammatical" (73). He applauds the anxiety but criticizes the hesitation and the final preference for speech, arguing that the anxiety should instead be celebrated and the tension kept alive. "The difference between Derrida and Levinas is the breach between speech and writing, a writing which is itself fissured by spatial and temporal difference" (Wyschogrod 1989: 191). Although they both denounce logocentrism, they disagree over the character of Judaism. For both, that character has to be established with reference to the Greekness of philosophy. They are aware of this inherent limit: "How can the Jew be true to his Jewishness? But what is the essence of Jewishness to which the Jew is to be true? The very question is Greek" (Llewelyn 1988: 282). Levinas feels that only Biblical infinity can transcend the limits of Greek language. For Derrida, on the other hand, (Hebraic) alterity is an intrinsic condition and differential quality of (Greek) identity. He does not believe in the possibility of a prophetic speech: "In effect, such a language would be purified of all *rhetoric*, which is what Levinas explicitly desires" (Derrida 1978a: 147). Instead he shows that rhetoric is the violence within the metaphysics of language.

Despite appearances of resolution, Derrida suggests, everything is not at peace with itself because, far from being just the foundation of metaphysics, "light is the element of violence" (117). There is a war going on in light between violence and metaphysics, a "war within discourse" (117).[17] "The limit between violence and nonviolence is perhaps not between speech and writing but within each of them" (102). Levinas fails to notice this limit and recognize the struggle within metaphysics. "The philosopher (man) *must* speak and write within this war of light, a war in which he always already knows himself to be engaged; a war which is inescapable, except by denying discourse, that is, by risking the worst violence" (117). Where there is light, there is discourse, and where there is discourse, there is violence. "The distinction between discourse and violence always will be an inaccessible horizon. Nonviolence would be the telos, and not the essence of discourse" (116). The logic of philosophy leads from light to discourse to metaphysics to violence. Philosophy is thus trapped between the "inescapable" and the "inaccessible," within the prison-house of its Greek language.

Derrida defines violence in terms that he also attributes to metaphysics—seeing, light, sameness, totality, discourse, time, history. Violence is all we know, or rather all that we do not know about (do not recognize in) metaphysics: it is philosophy's claim to truth and identity, to oneness and sameness. The language and the light are Greek (philosophy); with them comes metaphysics and the violence of its discourse, and the site turns into a battleground, since war "is the very emergence of speech and of appearing" (129)—of speaking a language and of appearing on a site, of a voice and a presence.[18] "One never escapes the *economy of war*" (148). We are thus condemned to the violent economy of language and light, which is the economy of the fall into the site of the same and into the contradictory tautology of identity. But if we accept the Greek premise, the premise of Greek as knowledge or the curse of knowledge, we have to oppose something else to it and oppose it: the Greek is always posited in opposition. Derrida chooses to contrast metaphysics not with something different, as other thinkers of modernity before him did, but with difference itself.

The title of the third and last part of the essay on Levinas, "Difference and Eschatology," enunciates the non-polar dichotomy of Derrida's theory. Levinas opposed eschatology, which "institutes a relation with being beyond the totality or beyond history" (Levinas 1969: 22), to philosophy. In turn, Derrida opposes the radical difference[19] of the undefinable different, of the elusive other, of the ineffable strange, to the eschatology of metaphysics. He is careful to refuse any ontological anchoring to the "infinity of the other" (Derrida 1978b: 114). Although opposed, difference is not the opposite but the negative;[20] it is not the other (as positive) but otherness itself (as not-the-same), the very "alterity of the Other" (123). "*Différance* marks the separation and the relation to the entirely other" (Derrida 1988b: 85), thus superseding Levinas's ethics of alterity. Derrida avoids drawing a line between same and other, demarcating autonomous identities, or affirming qualities of existence; instead, he wishes to respect this reciprocal tension, the alterity of otherness—a letter (letter *a*, as in

228 CHAPTER THREE

différance or altarity; or letter *h*, as in Hamann's "New Apology of the Letter H, by Itself") without voice, a dialectic without synthesis, a conflict without resolution, a difference without eschatology, a faith without salvation. Since "the other cannot be absolutely exterior to the same without ceasing to be other" (126), the tension, the differential character of difference, must be preserved. Same and other are necessarily and mutually implicated: they define each other.[21] Difference is about the otherness of the same, the heteronomy of identity, the multiplicity of the monad, the dark side of light, the extraterritoriality of the site, the war within discourse. Difference is another name for the dilemmas of assimilation.

Derrida's emphasis on difference over identity, distinction over similarity, differentiation over comparison, is far from new: long before his work, philosophy realized that any discourse on identity requires demarcation of differences.[22] In addition, the de-Hellenization of western thought, the project he rightly feels he has inherited from Levinas, remains the same. For this "anti-Hellenic world" (Atkins 1980: 773), the pressing question of a counter-course is still there. What distinguishes his approach from the tradition of the question is that the war of de-Hellenization is conducted not through attack (as was the case with Shestov) or opposition (Levinas) but through contamination and disablement. If a different thought must still speak Greek, it should not denounce but parody it, disassemble it, and eventually appropriate it. If the Greek will, sooner or later, call, question, and seize its different, then a truly anti-Hellenic non-alternative thought ought to try and irrupt it from within (repeating what Heidegger called "irruption of Greek philosophy" in thought), reversing the roles and playing the Greek's infinite (because presumably intrinsic) other. A differential thought is both non-Greek and made possible by *the* non-Greek. Thus to "the Greek element, the Greek thought of Being, the thought of Being whose irruption or call produced Greece" (82), Derrida opposes the "irruption of the totally-other" and calls "this experience of the infinitely other Judaism" (152). "Hebraism, in its difference from onto-theology, provides a stance for a radical re-vision of Hellenic assumptions" (Wolosky 1982: 290). His strategy is to un-Greek philosophy by exposing it to the Judaic difference.[23] "Thus it is not enough to say that Deriddean theory dehellenizes literary criticism, smashing the idols of New Critical scrutiny. In a profound sense, Derrida Judaizes that criticism, recalling the birth of his own proliferative theory in the desert generation of witnesses born to Hebrew women straining over birthstools" (New 1988: 34). Judaization emerges as the properly critical method of de-Hellenization.

What has made the banality of Derridean theory attractive is its playful reliance on the Hebraic-Hellenic dichotomy. Given the philosophical tradition to which the author subscribes, the belief in a vicious Hellenic[24] dominance and a benevolent Hebraic otherness becomes inevitable. He has turned the standard distinction, however, into a dogma, making it the central topic of his investigations, the pivotal concept of his views, the fundamental issue of his writings. Over and over again, he resorts to it, reducing any distinction to a difference and every difference to the infinite and yet imperceptible distance between the two terms, which are confronted and contrasted in an endlessly absorbing array of variations: presence-absence, seeing-hearing, speech-writing, plenitude-lack, voice-silence, and here eschatology-difference. They are all perfect and contagious, appealing to both traditional structuralist dispositions and radical poststructuralist aspirations. But Derrida insists that they are incestuous as well: what we see, understand, and know may be Greek; but the condition for its appearance, its vital supplement, is the elusive Hebraic trace. Hebraism is the experience (in fear and trembling) of the infinitely other, the absolute difference within the heart of philosophical identity. In this regard, the essay on Levinas is exceptionally interesting because here the author, just a few years before introducing the allegorical emblem of *différance*, does not defer (to higher, philosophical or artistic, authorities) but defines the difference as the Hebraic-Hellenic dichotomy, and proclaims that it entails (and can only exist as) war. The essay quotes Matthew Arnold in its motto: "Hebraism and Hellenism—between these two points of influence moves our world" (Derrida 1978a: 79). The title of the essay imitates and reverses that of Arnold's book: Arnold's Hellenic can be either anarchy or culture; Derrida's Hellenic has the potential of both violence and metaphysics. There is an obvious correspondence between anarchy and violence, and culture and metaphysics. The two authors differ in their understanding of the dialectic: while Arnold believed that, since the two ideas are incompatible, people should opt for culture, Derrida criticizes the disjunction and shows that we cannot help living with both, that culture implies anarchy *and* metaphysics—that there is an anarchy of culture *and* a violence of metaphysics. The play of his title with Arnold's polarity, however, indicates that he is equally interested in contesting the cultural sphere.

Derrida's sense of mission is openly apostolic. He addresses the nations: "Are we Jews? Are we Greeks? We live in the difference between the Jew and the Greek, which is perhaps the unity of what is called history" (153). This is the war within discourse. "The history of philosophy is ultimately an argument between Jews and Greeks" (Handelman 1983: 114). The agon is hermeneutic and its battleground textual. " 'The original opening of interpretation essentially signifies that there will always be rabbis and poets. And two interpretations of interpretation,' writes Derrida. There will always perhaps be war between Jews and Greeks, war over Scripture" (177). He envisions a heroic thought which "seeks to liberate itself from the Greek domination of the Same and the One (other names for the light of Being and of the phenomenon) as if from oppression itself—an oppression certainly comparable to none other in the world, an ontological or transcendental oppression, but also the origin or alibi of all oppression in the world" (Derrida 1978b: 83). Like Horkheimer and Adorno, Derrida demonizes the Greeks by blaming all oppression on them. We live under this overwhelming oppression, the tyranny of the light, but at the same time we experience its fundamental tension, the war which is the possibility of discourse. "Between original tragedy and messianic triumph there is *philosophy*, in which violence is returned against violence within knowledge, in which original finitude appears, and in which the other is respected within, and by the same" (131). The tragic and the messianic, the Hellenic and the Hebraic, may determine (and contest for) our world, but within the Hellenic domination Derrida detects the hope for a Hebraic liberation. This hope is not that of freedom, salvation, or even God, at least not in any sense of ontic determination: "But what does this *exclusion* mean if not the exclusion of every particular *determination*? And that God is *nothing* (determined), is not life, because he is *everything*? and therefore is at once All and Nothing, Life and Death. Which means that God is or appears, is *named*, within the difference between All and Nothing, Life and Death. Within difference, and at bottom as Difference itself" (115–16). God is bracketed in/by/as Difference, His coming deferred in all that He differs. "Since Being is nothing (determined), it is necessarily produced in difference (*as* difference)" (150). This is the messianic hope offered by Derrida: he calls on us to depart from the pagan space of the polis, the Greek site, and move, like Abraham, toward the Promised Land of interminable difference, or rather toward what he calls "the Hebraic nostalgia for the Land" (145)—the different and deferred Land which is only known by God's choice and promise: the House of Israel. To the eschatology of presence he opposes the messianism of that promise. If the "speculative dialectic is an eschatology of the identical" (Lacoue-Labarthe 1990: 81), deconstruction is a Messianism of the different. The question of emancipation (this time, from the Greek oppression) comes under a new light.

Thus *différance* is only a figure for the Hebraic-Hellenic opposition, a figure that revises the opposition from a competitive antagonism to an antagonistic interdependence, which is the ground of history. The interdependence is that between the same and its other, the one and the many, language and the unsayable, meaning and its supplement, eschatology and war, metaphysics and violence, or philosophy and its rhetoric. The tension resulting from the indissoluble interdependence is thought. The difference ensues from the relationship of the positive to its internal constitutive other, and this radical difference of the (immanently negative) different Derrida defines as the Hebraic. Levinas identified Hellenism with self, reason, and atheism, while Hebraism with other, experience, and theism (Gerber 1967: 177–78). For Derrida, if the Hellenic is light, speech, and history, the Hebraic is then simply the non-Hellenic—all that makes the Greek possible without allowing for the possibility of itself being posited.

The romantic dimension of Derrida's position raises the old question of originality, of aristocratic (namely, aesthetic) survival in a democratic (that is, bourgeois) tradition: what is left when the imitation of the Greek (namely, the play of high culture) is exhausted? The infinite pursuit of difference, he responds, endless differentiation—play as askesis: "It will not do, however, simply to say that from now on we'll be Hebrews instead of Greeks. We cannot, on religious or any other grounds, airily reject metaphysics: it is sedimented into our language. . . . All we can do is deconstruct instead of destroy, de-constitute or de-sediment the 'metaphysico-theological' concepts and show the roots of their complicities" (Schneidau 1982: 15). But how do we know difference if we cannot posit it? Derrida aptly summarizes the agony when he asks: "will the other of the Greek be the non-Greek? Above all, can it be *named* the non-Greek?" (Derrida 1978b: 82). This question perturbed philosophy and art since their achieved autonomy in modern time—the question about the possibility of the other of the Greek that makes the Greek the founding otherness of western culture. Seeking the non-Greek, yearning for it, has not exorcised the Greek spectre haunting this civilization. "The Greek father who still holds us under his sway must be killed; and this is what a Greek—Plato—could never resolve to do, deferring the act into a hallucinatory murder. A hallucination within a hallucination that is already speech. But will a non-Greek ever succeed in doing what a Greek in this case could not do, except by disguising himself as a Greek, by *speaking* Greek, by feigning to speak Greek in order to get near the king?" (89) The question of philosophy turns into the ultimate bourgeois quest, the quest of (Abraham as) Poet and Jew—the (Jewish) question of freedom and culture in a world ruled by the regime of interpretive rights. But this phrasing also reveals and explains Derrida's strategy, his own compulsive "feigning to speak Greek." He was the first to argue that the Hebraic is not Judaism (the positive different) but its war with the Hellenic (difference itself). The Hebraic can kill the Greek father only by speaking Greek, the language of "alien wisdom,"[25] the language of the Alien. Indeed, the Hebraic *is* the killing of the Hellenic, the un-Greeking of thought. In the aesthetically emancipated postmodern West, the last interpretive project that can protect cultural capital and keep political demands in check is the announcement of a messianic (and therefore already in process) liberation from Hellenism.

Shestov (1932: 158–59) suggested that the fall of philosophy coincides with its beginning, since already its Greek founders pursued unity and totality. Similarly, in Derridean theologesis, the Hebraic stands for Edenic language and the Hellenic for knowledge after the fall. If Hegel wrote his history of philosophy as a *Bildungsroman*, Derrida writes his own as a parable about the fall of man into knowledge (and into the search for answers), where God is the Different—the negative, unreachable otherness—and Greek the Serpent. We are condemned, he suggests, to be blinded by the light of philosophy, deafened by the discourse of return. Since the loss of Paradise (the only true dwelling), since time became history, we can know God only as Difference, and every site as exile. Here an important distinction is made implicitly. In the discourse of the response, God, who is the Different, cannot be known, cannot be spoken about: the Greek language of presence, which guarantees His absence, does not allow for that. What can be dimly perceived, within the violated limits of metaphysics, is our impossible and yet necessary relation with Him, which is one of abysmal difference. The Hebraic (does not simply signify but) is and makes that Difference.

War began with secular language. "Violence appears with *articulation*" (Derrida 1978a: 147–48). As Benjamin taught, arbitrariness disrupted the primordial identity and peace as soon as language lost its Adamic innocence and, instead of calling things, started naming them.[26] Predication, the Greek mode of speech, "is the first violence" (147). The natural immediacy disappeared behind the screen of clarity, of seeing and perceiving a separate world of objects. "Every determination, in effect, presupposes the thought of Being" (140). To speak (Greek) is to articulate, to define, to predicate existence. "There is no speech without the thought and statement *of* Being. But as Being is nothing outside the determined existent, it would not appear as such without the possibility of speech. Being *itself* can only be thought and stated. It is the contemporary of the Logos, which itself can only be as the Logos of Being, *saying* Being" (143). The unavoidable thought of Being (like the use of God's name) is the mortal sin ever since the fall into language. Logos, predication, Being, metaphysics, are the human lot in a site of glaring light and blaring voices: Derrida's history of philosophy amounts to this sweeping generalization. "What is most striking about Derrida's presentation of the history of writing is that in it he subscribes to something suspiciously like a myth of lost linguistic plenitude, displayed in a binary opposition that takes the form of pluri-dimensionality/linearity" (Scholes 1988: 291). His consolation for the human predicament is equally predictable: the Hebraic nostalgia (as opposed to the Odyssean *nostos*) for the Promised Land.

Derrida's Edenic view of language and poetry is not very different from Heidegger's. In either case, the political lesson of quietism is resignation: "A regard for metaphysics still prevails even in the intention to overcome metaphysics. Therefore, our task is to cease all overcoming, and leave metaphysics to itself" (Heidegger 1972: 24). For Heidegger, thought is actively letting what encounters us (Being) be (in its own way). "Like Wittgenstein with whom he has often been compared, Heidegger returns us exactly to where we are, leaving the whole structure of everydayness comfortingly in place, but allows us to do so in the flattering knowledge that we are consequently in on the deepest conceivable mystery" (Eagleton 1990: 312). Following the quietist admonition, Derrida advises those worried by irreconcilable differences that change is impossible; there is no point in it: just let it/them be. Heidegger's advice on art is adopted as a principle of life: "This letting the work be a work we call the preserving of the work" (Heidegger 1971a: 66). We preserve the work by attending to its separation: "*A work conceived radically is a movement of the Same towards the Other which never returns to the Same*" (Levinas: 1987a: 91). Like the promise which it preserves, the work needs to be let be in its distance (that is, to be aesthetically). "As an orientation toward the other, as sense, a work is possible only in patience, which, pushed to the limit, means for the agent to renounce being the contemporary of its outcome, to act without entering into the Promised Land" (92). The aesthetic disposition acquires the force of an ethical imperative: the askesis of atonement is the letting-be of Being, the thinking of thought, the speculative respect for alterity, and the pious attention to difference. "If to understand Being is to be able to let be (that is, to respect Being in essence and existence, and to be responsible for one's respect), then the understanding of Being always concerns alterity, and par excellence the alterity of the Other in all its originality: one can have to let be only that which is not. If Being is always to be let be, and if to think is to let Being be, then Being is indeed the other of thought. And since it is what it is only by the letting-be of thought, and since the latter is thought only by virtue of the presence of the Being which it lets be, then thought and Being, thought and the other, are the same; which, let us recall, does not mean identical, or one, or equal" (Derrida 1978a: 141). If (Hebraic) Being is the Other of (Hellenic) thought, then the thought of Being is nostalgia for its essence and atonement as letting be. Thus contemplation returns to its theological roots—human interest in God.

When Derrida proposed this askesis as a discipline, he called it "grammatology." It is the science of the uneasy acquiescence, protesting complicity, dissenting acceptance. Grammatology is also the science of the open Book, a new discipline of reading: atheological interpretation. "Grammatology is the world of the text which stands by itself because the portals of the infinite have all been closed up" (Raschke 1988: 136). The hiddenness of God from secular reading determines the conditions of disinterested contemplation. "This lost certainty, this absence of divine writing, that is to say, first of all, the absence of the Jewish God (who himself writes, when necessary), does not solely and vaguely define something like 'modernity.' As the absence and haunting of the divine sign, it regulates all modern criticism and aesthetics" (Derrida 1978c: 10). For writers from Mendelssohn to Horkheimer, interpretation in the absence of God was better known as the Hebraic problem of modernity, the project of assimilation: to them, difference was the abyss opened by the decline of the sacred in a world of autonomous readings—the experience of the Jew (or the intellectual) as the Other bourgeois. For Derrida, however, *différance* is a name (and parable) not only for the Hebraic-Hellenic difference but, in addition, for its textual identity. The debt to Hegel is obvious: "Dialectic . . . interprets every image as writing" (Horkheimer and Adorno 1972: 24). Interpretation deciphers the writing of a hand long gone, the trace of an image long banned. "Recent discussions, notably in the visual arts, have witnessed the ascendancy of the concept of *écriture*, inspired perhaps by certain drawings by Klee that seem to shade over into a human scrawl. This is another instance where a notion of modern art throws light on the past: art in general is like a handwriting. Its works are hieroglyphs for which the code has been lost, and this loss is not accidental but constitutive of their essence as art works. Only *qua* handwriting do they have a language, do they speak" (Adorno 1984: 182).

But the attachment to the text acquires systematic importance: "The way of deconstruction is always opened through reading" (Critchley 1989: 93). The Hebraic is now defined in terms of an ineluctable textual indeterminacy. Grammatology pays differential attention to a text: it treats it first as a New Testament, and asks: What differentiates it from its predecessor? How does it authorize the oldness of the Old one? Above all, what is the violence of its Greek language and the dissemination of its enabling trace? And what is the rhetorical supplement that enables it to claim to supplement? Thus grammatology—the post-Biblical study of *Écriture*/Scripture, rather than an intrinsic pharmakon in western ontology—is the deconstruction of the Logos of the Gospel (compare section 6 of *Being and Time*, "The Task of a Destruction of the History of Ontology"): in claiming its *gramma* (letter) and diminishing its *pneuma* (spirit), it constitutes the most important attack on Christology from the left-Kantian direction.[27] Turning against "*pneumatology*, the science of *pneuma*, *spiritus*, or *logos*" (Derrida 1978c: 9), it deconstructs the incarnation of spirit—Christ as the logos of faith.[28] "The Father as presence and as being becomes manifested to man in Christ. And Christ, as logos, allows man access to the 'spoken/ thought sense' of a 'creator God.' This is, as Derrida demonstrates, the very structure of sign-theory" (Wolosky 1982: 286).

If Derrida approaches the Greeks with deconstructive care and contaminates their language with dissimulated tautologies, his attitude to Christianity is one of destructive onslaught against its sacred signs, especially Christ as the *figura* of incarnation: for the deconstructionists, (Biblical) reading must be purged of the spirit. "Almost every tradition influenced by

Christianity has aspired to a spiritualization of the word, its transformation and even disappearance as it passes from 'word as pointer to word as thing itself.' A logocentric or incarnationist thesis of this kind haunts the fringes of most studies of literature, and explains the welcome accorded at present to semiotic counterperspectives" (Hartman 1981a: 35). The central question is whether *ousia* should be defined in terms of identity/filiation or difference/separation. What is at stake is nothing less than the decision of the Council of Nicaea (325) regarding the *homöousion* (Bloch 1972: 181–83): "First, and above all, stand those great moral doctrines of the Gospel to which the highest place has been assigned beyond dispute in the Gospel itself. But, next after these, ecclesiastical history teaches us that the most vital, the most comprehensive, the most fruitful, has been, and is still,—not the supremacy of the Bible or the authority of its several books, not the power of the Pope or of the Church, not the Sacraments, not Original Sin, not Predestination, not Justification, but the doctrine of the Incarnation" (Stanley 1907: 196). Hebraic thought claims that reading has been enslaved by theories of the logos as incarnated spirit and has forgotten the insistence of the letter in the text. "American criticism, on the whole is 'incarnationist' . . . and it often associates this bias with Christian doctrine. Similarly, then, contemporary anti- or nonincarnationist views would move toward the pole of Hebraism, whether or not influenced by canonical texts from that sphere" (Hartman 1985: 174–75). If the covenant of interpretation has been compromised by demands for presence, fullness, and completeness, a need is felt to renew it by emphasizing not the text but writing itself. The result ought to be a renegotiation of the (Hellenic) aesthetic character of the (Hebraic) social contract.

Consideration of Paul's "new covenant" is indispensable for an understanding of deconstruction as a fundamentally theologico-political project (like Spinoza's). This covenant was given "not in a written code but in the Spirit; for the written code kills, but the Spirit gives life" (2 Corinthians 3.6). If, as Paul states, "the Lord is the Spirit" (3.17), then the Spirit is the highest source of authority. "*For Paul, the giving of the Spirit is the establishment of the law*" (Cranfield 1964: 65). But who is addressed, called by the Spirit? Who is commanded, seized by it—only Jews, or Gentiles as well? The Epistle to the Galatians deals with the identity of Christianity regarding its Jewish roots: Are Christians obliged to observe the Mosaic law? Should a Gentile become a Jew before becoming a Christian? In his discussion of God's promise to Abraham and its relation to the law, Paul proclaims: "Now before faith came, we were confined under the law, kept under restraint until faith should be revealed. So that the law was our custodian until Christ came, that we might be justified by faith. But now that faith has come, we are no longer under a custodian; for in Christ Jesus you are all sons of God, through faith. For as many of you as were baptized into

Christ have put on Christ. There is neither Jew nor Greek, there is neither slave nor free, there is neither male nor female; for you are all one in Christ Jesus. And if you are Christ's, then you are Abraham's offspring, heirs according to promise" (Galatians 3.23–29). There are those who see the early church as an enemy of tradition: "One of Christianity's central interpretive axioms was the distinction between 'spirit' and 'letter.' The severity of this differentiation justified the Church's overthrow of the authority of Rabbinic law, the divine text of the Jews, as mere 'letter.' For the Church, the true 'spirit' was the New Testament through Jesus" (Handelman 1982: 15).

In general, during most of the twentieth century, to raise the question of the Spirit is to ask again who is the true heir to Abraham, Christianity or Judaism. Rosenzweig thought this was a racial issue when he talked about the Jews as an eternal "community of blood" whose eternity is (already) present.[29] Adorno and Levinas argued that the West is heir to Odysseus, not to Abraham. The whole question, however, is a rather recent one. Although writers as early as Samuel Hirsch (1815–89) argued that, after Paul, Christianity broke with Judaism, it was only after *Paul and his Interpreters* (1911) by Albert Schweitzer that a distinction between two Judaisms (a Semitic or Palestinian and a Hellenistic or Diaspora) became popular and, in turn, produced two Pauls (the Jewish and the Hellenistic). Since then the relation of Paulinism to Judaism has been a major topic in Protestant theology. "It is quite significant that all these fresh attempts in the interpretation of Paul's theology try to expel his doctrine of justification by faith from its commanding position" (Koester 1965: 192). A de-Hellenized and apocalyptic Paul has emerged as his debt to philosophy and rhetoric diminished in importance.

In order to answer who is commanded by the Spirit, and therefore who becomes party to the new covenant, Paul must define the relation between law and faith. Before the advent of Jesus, the apostle proclaims, people were like children, and therefore confined under the law which was their custodian. "But when the time had fully come, God sent forth his Son, born of woman, born under the law, to redeem those who were under the law, so that we might receive adoption as sons. And because you are sons, God sent the Spirit of his Son into our hearts, crying 'Abba! Father!'" (Galatians 4.4–6). The Spirit of the Son of God redeems from the law, liberating the faithful from an exclusive set of rules and obligations. What is important is not circumcision or uncircumcision, but living and walking by the spirit, because "if you are led by the Spirit you are not under the law" (Galatians 5.18). Paul does not think about the shortcomings of one's obedience to the Law. Although it was the introspective conscience of the West that attributed to him the question about the Law in general, salvation, and a struggle with one's conscience, "it appears that Paul's references to the impossibility of fulfilling the Law is part of a theological and theoretical scriptural argument about the relation between Jews and Gentiles" (Stendahl 1983: 81). The teaching of Paul the Pharisee (Segal 1990), of Saul from Tarsus, was very different from Luther's "Pauline Christianity." The issues for Paul were: "(1) What happens to the Law (the Torah, the actual Law of Moses, not the principle of legalism) when the Messiah has come? (2) What are the ramifications of the Messiah's arrival for the relation between Jews and Gentiles?" (Stendahl 1983: 84) The major problem facing the new religion was the place of the Gentiles in the church and in the messianic community according to the plan of God. "Yet it was not until Augustine that the Pauline thought about the Law and Justification was applied in a consistent and grand style to a more general and timeless human problem" (85).[30] After this Reformist revision, the "letter" came to signify scholastic exegesis, while the "spirit" the interpretive ideal of private (non-dogmatic) reading (outside the Catholic church).

Given its interpretive understanding of the "letter," Protestant thought still sees Christianity as a textual event.[31] According to a typical view, "to prove its own legitimacy, the Church had at once to undermine the authority of the Jewish people while maintaining (in fact, appropriating) the authority of Jewish texts. For this reason the battle for authority between the Church and Judaism took place within the arena of textual politics" (Ragussis 1989: 137). Although this view creates the impression that the church acted more like a contemporary critical movement, it is far from unique. Along the same lines, it has been also suggested that "the theme of the *purloined letter* can characterize our entire problem of Rabbinic versus Patristic hermeneutics. For as we have stressed, it was above all the question of the nature of the letter, the integrity of the text which was at stake. Stealing the 'letter' is stealing the text, stealing Scripture, and transferring meaning elsewhere. It might be said that Paul stole the letter from the Jews and tried to abolish it by transcending it through the spirit" (Handelman 1982: 163). Furthermore, since this viewpoint accepts the Protestant reification of the text as the only explanatory approach possible, it also evaluates interpretations on the basis of organic integration. Some critics find it in the original Book: "Though Christianity attempted to set the 'spirit' against the 'letter' by treating the Bible as a transcended Book of Laws, or stories blind to what they prophesied, for Jews this split between letter and spirit did not occur, or else was repaired by inventive exegetical methods which kept the law-portion and the story-portion as a single, inalienable donation. Here was God's plenty indeed" (Hartman 1985b: 211). Others find organic integration in the tradition which claims to have inherited that origin: "Christianity is a criticism of the Hebrew Scriptures—not only an interpretation, but an evaluation. . . . For nearly two milennia, Christianity has been little other than a critical enterprise. . . . Indeed, it has become commonplace to say that Christian criticism is the only kind we know"

(Marshall 1989: 4). Such views attest, however, to "the inseparable relationship between criticism and theology" (Atkins 1983: 8), and agree in seeing Christianity as a hermeneutic occurrence and believing that "Jews were 'converted' textually, authorially, by the early Church fathers" (Ragussis 1989: 139). Thus the doctrine of incarnation appears to drive Paul's critique of the law and to produce the new canon: "The Rabbinic word became substantialized into flesh. . . . While claiming to spiritualize Judaism, Christianity in effect literalized it with a vengeance" (Handelman 1982: 17). At the same time, in order to strengthen the interpretive resolve of close reading, alternative examples of ascetic resistance have been offered, such as Levinas's adherence to "the Talmud's steadfast refusal to 'spiritualize' since spiritualization can become a stratagem for evading responsibility" (Wyschogrod 1974: 174). This and any other (Modernist or Postmodernist) example of interpretive resistance accepts an aesthetic assumption about the gentility and supremacy of the text. "If we lose our identity it will be because, as I have warned elsewhere, there is no longer a textual difference between ourselves and the gentiles. To ask what a textual difference can be is to confront the truest question of Jewish cultural identity" (Bloom 1985: 116). Hebraic cultural oligopoly is based on the ownership of the means of textual consumption, of the complete textualization of the social. In other words, interpretive capitalism rests on Protestant rules of reading which define the stock as Hellenic and the market as Hebraic. Hence freedom has been traded for rights.

Derrida's enterprise is quite different. His attack on Christology does not present Hebraism naively as the perfect alternative. Offering a better faith would be inconsistent with his anti-dialectical understanding. His own method is Judaization: Derrida is converting Christians into Jews by leading them through the familiar desert of bourgeois promise, culture. This time, though, culture does not signify liberation—a commodity no longer in high demand among the quite secure intelligentsia—but the renewed moral authority of artistic resistance: "All those who deal or inhabit language as poets are Jews—but in a tropic sense. What the trope comes to is locating the Jew not only as a poet but also in every man circumcised by language or led to circumcise a language" (Derrida 1986a: 340). If Paul said that "there is neither Jew nor Greek," Derrida argues that (to the privileged extent that we are poets, of course) we are all Jews: "Anyone or no one may be Jewish. No one is (not) circumcised; it is no one's circumcision. If all the poets are Jews, they are all circumcised or circumcisers" (341). If Paul said that circumcision is not very important,[32] Derrida argues that, on the contrary, it is our "date" with history: *There must be* circumcision, circumcision of the word, and it must take place once, each time one time, the one time only. This time awaits its coming, it awaits a date, and this date can only be poetic, an inscription in the body of language. How are we to transcribe ourselves into a date? Celan asked. When we speak here of a date of circumcision, we are no longer speaking of history. . . . No, the circumcision of the word is not dated *in* history. In this sense, it has no age, but gives rise to, is the occasion of, the Date. It opens the word to the other, it opens history and the poem and philosophy and hermeneutics and religion" (346). Where Paul saw the Spirit as the Redeemer of humanity from the law, Derrida, in his treatise on the occasion of the date (which recalls Rainer Maria Rilke's celebration of Once in the 9th *Duino* Elegy), presents circumcision as the affirmation of the law, the inscription of the law on the body. This inscription is a textual event too: the poetic date of the body of language with the call, the command of circumcision, which makes everyone who obeys it a Jew. The result of these re-readings is that "Derrida, in moving beyond a dialectics of consciousness (Sartre), beyond a dualistic problematic of 'castration' (Freud), has turned his work into a protracted meditation on the institution of circumcision" (Mehlman 1983: 82). If the Rabbinic word became Christian flesh, the incarnated spirit still cannot escape the Mosaic law, as Derrida has shown by his circumcision of the word "difference." Where Augustin de Narbonne, in his *Jésus circoncis* (1694), suggested that Jesus had to undergo circumcision to prove he was a true Jew, the philosopher argues that people need to be circumcised to achieve the poetic status of Jewishness. Thus to the irruption of the Hellenic dawn, he is opposing the occasion of the Hebraic date. In all these disputations, Derrida is obviously engaged in an unremitting settling of accounts with the most important Hebraic thinker of the twentieth century, Heidegger (Zarader 1990).

History and Exile

The theological foundations of Heideggerian theory have long been noticed: "His teaching constitutes a sort of meta-theology, whose language is immersed, inescapably, in that of Pietism, scholasticism and Lutheran doxology" (Steiner 1978: 63). The basic concepts in *Being and Time* preserve their religious character: "All of them originated in the *Christian* tradition, however much death, conscience, guilt, care, anxiety, and corruption are formalized ontologically and neutralized as concepts of *the Dasein*" (Löwith 1966: 68). Early on Heidegger felt that the Christian tradition was at great risk. "If we ask ourselves what Heidegger's real intention was, what led him away from Husserl toward the problem of historicality, it is obvious today that it was not so much the contemporary problematic of historical relativism that preoccupied him as his own Christian heritage. . . . His question became: how can one successfully resist the alien influence of Greek philosophy upon the Christian message?" (Gadamer 1981: 435). What can be done when, as Nietzsche declared, "God is Dead"—when, as

Heidegger rephrased it in 1945, "the world of the Christian God has lost its effective force in history" (quoted in Lacoue-Labarthe 1990: 39)? Some kind of return seems necessary. In this respect, Heidegger (like Benjamin) contributes to the de-Hellenization of Christian dogma launched by Harnack in the 1880s—a systematic and multifaceted effort of Protestant theology that is still under way.[33] "Hegel attempted to syncretize the Hebraic and the Hellenic; in the course of doing so, he hellenized Christianity. Heidegger's Christianity, on the other hand, is heavily dependent on a theological tradition that sought to bring it back to its primitive, that is, Hebraic roots" (Megill 1985: 314). His critique of forgetfulness as fall and his own change of orientation toward Protestantism intensified the Hebraic character of his thought. "Given Heidegger's enduring interest in religion, it is not surprising to learn that his account of the fall of Western man into the role of the self-deifying subject resembles the Old Testament account of the fall of the ancient Israelites into greed and idolatry" (Zimmerman 1981: 227). Heidegger offers a narrative of sin and redemption (though a different one from Rosenzweig's).

From the beginning of his career and well into the early 1920s, Heidegger presented himself as a Christian theologian. For example, the former Jesuit seminarian was considered in 1916 for the chair of Catholic philosophy in the philosophy department of Freiburg University. At that same University, he taught a lecture course in the winter semester of 1920–21, "Introduction to the Phenomenology of Religion," concentrating on Paul and early Christianity. "Part One of the course introduces a phenomenology dedicated to recovering what was forgotten by the entire Western tradition (including Husserl), but which, even if unthematically, was understood by early Christianity: life in its here-and-now facticity, factical life-experience" (Sheehan 1979: 315). Here the memory of the West is directed not to its Greek roots but to the beginning of its church. "Notice the parallels between Heidegger's approach to early Christianity and his approach to the Greeks. In both cases he sees a lived but unthematized level of experience which was covered over by subsequent ages and which must be recovered by a 'violent' de-construction of the tradition. Note as well the parallels in the content of these two experiences. In both cases the experience is a pre-theoretical, pre-rational lived experience of 'self-exceeding,' of being drawn out beyond one's ordinary self-understanding" (315). While the Greek model had not emerged in his thought yet, the idea of a lost dwelling and a homeless wandering betrays another debt: "In claiming that Western humanity had forgotten the originating event and thus ended in technological nihilism, Heidegger was paradoxically closer to the Jews than to the Greeks. For Heidegger, of course, the originating event was not the Divine Law revealed to the Jews, but instead the event of 'being' revealed to the Greeks. Like the Old Testament prophet, Heidegger reminded his people that they wandered in the technological desert because being had concealed itself from them" (Zimmerman 1988: 1117).

In the years 1916–19, Heidegger's religious conviction underwent a shift from Catholicism to Protestantism, and at the same time his disciplinary alliance changed from theology to philosophy.[34] This break with the past marks the turn to the "historical"; and it is the "historical" as the Protestant bourgeois understanding of tradition that enables him, like the other writers of modernity, to invent the Hellenic by discovering the Greeks. Thus Heidegger's doctrine of temporality is derived from an interpretive approach to early Christianity. "It seems that, perhaps unknown to himself, Heidegger has brought us into the orbit of Biblical Hebrew: . . . a language of the kind into which Heidegger attempts to transcribe German" (Rose 1984: 78). The thought which claims, which needs to claim, that it is speaking ("feigning") Greek is Hebraic. "When Heidegger, then, thinks he is thinking Greek (ur-Greek), he is thinking Hebrew" (Hartman 1981: xix). This apparent contradiction is resolved when placed in the general picture: According to interpretation theory, while Hebraism is the discipline of critique, and the Jew is the model critic, the Greeks are always unreflective— always at home, inhabiting (as Heidegger would say) the essence (of language, world, art) but never thinking it; that is why philosophy in modernity is still a Greek language but is never a Greek activity (for example, one associated with contemporary Greeks). The experience of that language may be Greek, but its truth is proudly presented as a modern discovery as well as the preordained future of Greek. That is why Heidegger was able to assume that German harvests and shelters *logos*: "In this relation a Greek word applies to a German word for safekeeping, and the German word offers its services as bestower" (Rand 1990: 443). Thus the modern invariably emerges as more Greek than the Greek itself, since it becomes the measure as well as the destination of its authenticity.

In Part Two of the 1920–21 course, "A Phenomenological Interpretation of Original Christianity in St. Paul's Epistles to the Galatians and Thessalonians," Heidegger begins the practice of his hermeneutics (which is better known from its later applications to poetry). In his reading of I Thessalonians, he concentrates on Pauline eschatology and discovers in the Christian "awaiting" for the Parousia a meaning very different from that of Jewish awaiting: "The authentic Christian relation to the Parousia is fundamentally not the awaiting of a future event" (Sheehan 1979: 321).[35] The relation to the Parousia (of the Logos) is a matter of temporal experience: "The question of temporality in Christian religious experience becomes a matter of how one lives one's facticity" (322). The Parousia requires authentic presence in the present: "The Christian—or Pauline—meaning of eschatology has shifted from the expectation of a future event to a presence before God, . . . a context of enacting one's life in uncertainty before the unseen God. The weight has shifted to the 'how' of existence" (322). The Logos is *para/ousia*—not ousia but the Spirit of *ousia*. What is important, and what Heidegger seeks to encounter, is that Spirit in its full presence, without the mediation of the Law. "Heidegger seems to give us *Yahweh* without *Torah*: the event seems to include advent and redemption, presence and owning, but not the giving of the law on Mount Sinai, and its repeated disowning" (Rose 1984: 80). As an apocalyptic thinker, he is interested in the call as epiphany, in the encounter as private date: after all, Saul's conversion did not involve any documentation. The Hellenic model would eventually allow Heidegger to bring back from Sinai his own tablets—the Presocratic fragments. "Thus Heidegger displays a monumental, though deeply hidden tension between the Hellenic and the Hebraic" (Megill 1985: 315). While the poet, traveling on "the track of the holy" (Heidegger 1971: 97),[36] brings a trace of the vanished gods into the cosmic night, the responsibility of the philosopher is to discover and preserve it, listening for the absent call. This is the piety of thought.

Levinas adopted the exegetical notion of the trace, a translation of the *ikhnos* of Plotinus (*Enneads* 5), in "The Trace of the Other" (1963) and developed it out of the chapter on "The Dwelling" (1969: 152–74) in *Totality and Infinity* (1960), a book which is "a phenomenological defense of subjectivity taken as neither a personalism nor as an egoism but as the blueprint for the affirmation of the divine" (Gerber 1967: 177). Levinas explains: "The beyond from which a face comes signifies as a trace. A face is in the trace of the utterly bygone, utterly past absent" (Levinas 1969: 103), who does not appear. Paul announced the possibility of full knowledge: "For now we see in a mirror dimly, but then face to face. Now I know in part; then I shall understand fully, even as I have been fully understood" (1 Corinthians 13.12). Levinas rejects this promise. The epiphany of the face does not involve any *phainesthai*, and therefore "the signifyingness of a trace consists in signifying without making appear" (Levinas 1969: 104), without a promise of incarnation. Thus "a trace signifies beyond being" (103), *epekeina tes ousias*. In the trace (the letter from beyond), the law of the gender, the law of separation, and the law of the Lord come together. "Through a trace the irreversible past takes on the profile of a 'He.' The *beyond* from which a face comes is in the third person. . . . The supreme presence of a face is inseparable from this supreme and irreversible absence which founds the eminence of visitation. . . . He who left traces in wiping out his traces did not mean to say or do anything by the traces he left. He disturbed the order in an irreparable way. He has passed absolutely. To be qua *leaving a trace* is to pass, to depart, to absolve oneself" (104–5). Derrida, building on this view,[37] uses the trace of the vanished gods to destroy incarnation, the *omöousion* of the Parousia. If Heidegger deduced thinking from thanking (Eucharist), he consumes like a parasite every host (hostia). The deconstruction of logo-/phono-centrism serves only as a foil for a feast of cannibalism on the body of Jesus—its Dionysian textualization. "As against conventional sign-theory, Derrida proposes a theory of the trace. In this theory, not speech, but writing, becomes the preeminent linguistic sign" (Wolosky 1982: 288). Christ is not a sign, as Kierkegaard thought, but a signified—neither spirit nor ousia but the false idol of a trace. "The thematics of the trace . . . abolishes the Pauline distinction between spirit and letter" (298). There is only writing—the letter of the law and the law of gender: the circumcised body. The trace is Derrida's postcard with Socrates writing, the letter that Paul "stole from the Jews," the circumcised tablets that poets recover from the desert.

The question of ousia came into theological prominence early in the thirteenth century. The Fourth Lateran Council (1215), in its effort to define a unified Christian faith, drew on Aristotle's distinction between "substance" and "accident" and "came up with the doctrine of transubstantiation. This stated that while the substances of bread and wine became the substance of Christ, the accidents remained unchanged. . . . In fact, this apparent solution, which seemed to establish the temperate balance between opposites, heralded the beginning of further conflict. The relation between accidents and substances became increasingly a point of controversy, which coincided with a growing split between a focus on public ritual and ceremony and one on private internalized worship. Long before the Reformation, the doctrine of the 'real presence' of Christ in the Eucharist had been attacked by heretical outsiders reacting against the general materialism of the medieval Church in favor of a more spiritually oriented religion" (Kilgour 1990: 81). The Reformation saw Christianity as a religion of history, of the history of God's revelation to humankind in events taking place in time. Among such events, the incarnation was the most important one.[38] During his explorations of the real presence of Christ, "when Luther . . . came to his fulfilled doctrine of justification by faith he associated it most closely with his doctrine of the sacraments. He shows the eucharist to be the objective declaration and assurance of forgiveness of sins and the place where the incarnate Christ is known and received uniquely in his very flesh and blood for our salvation and eternal life" (Hall 1985: 115). As a consequence, the eucharist was disassociated from the church: "For Luther *sacramentum* speaks directly of Christ and not of the mass" (118), and this position allowed for the great debate of the 1520s about the meaning of "real presence," which centered on the verse "this is my body" (Matthew 26.26). "It seemed to Luther that the whole principle of the clarity of scripture (which he regarded as fundamental to his reforming programme at this point) was at stake over the interpretation of this verse" (McGrath 1988: 121). The specific question was whether the *esti* should be taken literally or figuratively. Luther stressed the *verba* and took it literally, hence his "insistence that the body and blood of Christ are in with and under the elements of bread and wine" (Hall 1985: 127). He wrote various treatises on the subject, like *That these Words of Christ 'This is my Body' still Stand Firm against the Fanatics* (1527). "For Luther the exposition of scripture is always more important than theological system-making and he did not deduce the real presence from speculative theory or philosophical definitions but from the words of scripture itself" (132). During the same decade "Zwingli and others had ceased to regard the sacrament as a means of grace, and reduced it to a sign of divine grace" (130), following a figurative understanding of the sacrament and rejecting the real presence of Christ. Since that time, the debate between the literalist and the figurative or symbolist positions has traversed many areas and stages: from the view of the Port-Royal Jansenist grammarians that the sacramental eating of Christ's body is performed through the grammar of the sentence "this is my body" (Marin 1989, originally called *La Parole mangée*) to the Romantic doctrine of the symbol where "the Eucharist is revised into an ideal of aesthetic communion" (Kilgour 1990: 146); and from the conclusion of Act I of *Parsifal* (1882) to the "accident" of the destruction of the sacramental symbols in Leonard Bernstein's *Mass* (1971). Derrida's thematics of the trace, which ranges from a study of esti (Derrida 1982b)[39] to discussions of absence, contributes precisely to this Protestant debate, while attacking its debt to Pauline Christology.

Derrida radicalized the trace,[40] especially in the lecture *"La différance"* (1968)—a deconstruction of the trace in Heidegger's Anaximander essay (Heidegger 1984)—by making it the mark of the (always already) interpreted text, and the sign of the absent original (Tablets). "For Derrida the trace is of a text and not of the Other" (Bernasconi 1988: 24). Heidegger's facticity (I am always already in a world) becomes Derrida's textuality (a book is always already interpreted). "The question of the text repeats, in at least a formal manner, all the movements that characterize Heidegger's elaborations on Being" (Gasché 1983: 170). Since the Parousia is now replaced with the trace of interpretation, "Heidegger's notion of Being and Derrida's notion of text are akin" (160). But it is the letter of the law, rather than the spirit of communion, that becomes primary.[41] "Reading in the classical context is akin to the celebration of the 'mass,' the assimilation of meanings, the consumption of the god, the transfer of presence. It is clear that 'deconstruction,' which prophesies 'the end of the book,' is founded upon the Hebraic passion for iconoclasm, for de-situating holiness and making it a temporal disclosure" (Raschke 1988: 134). The mass of consumption is disrupted and its book desecrated by the meaning of language:[42] "There is only letter, and it is the truth of pure language, the truth as pure language"[43] (Derrida 1985: 204). The letter is the truth and the law of the text. "Derrida has made it clear that the word text can be substituted for the word Being. Text is a translation for Being" (Gasché 1983: 172). At the same time, text is also the *diaspora* (dissemination) of Being.

The only problem is that in this textualist ontology there-is-no-outside-reading: the interpretive activity, although expanded beyond the boundaries of the autonomous text, remains an autonomous discipline of the response (Derrida's piety of reading), and dissemination is only a festive form of preservation. "Geoffrey H. Hartman has called attention to the absence of any account in Derrida of the passage from the (orally grounded) world of 'imitation' to the later (print grounded) world of 'dissemination.' In the absence of such an account, it would appear that the textualist critique of textuality, brilliant and to a degree serviceable as it is, is still itself curiously text-bound. In fact, it is the most text-bound of all ideologies, because it plays with the paradoxes of textuality alone and in historical isolation, as though the text were a closed system" (Ong 1982: 168–69). Derrida is willing to denounce the Book, any and all books, in order to save reading as a spiritual exercise. When all outside justifications for the disciplined attention to the independent text have been discredited, when the institutional authority protecting depth, quality, and beauty has weakened, the last resort for a last-minute defense of interpretation must pose its validation as a self-sufficient praxis. "The problem of the text is both a logical concomitant and an evolutionary sequel to the loss of the significance of scripture. . . . The problem of the text, as Gadamer has indicated, actually comes from the Romantic preoccupation with historical contingency as well as the early nineteenth century endeavor to find a metaphysical standpoint for the investigation of culture. . . . The text shows itself as text once historical self-reflection has permeated the adventure of inscription and interpretation. Derrida's program of deconstruction betokens the final moment in the progressive self-portrayal of the text. It is hermeneutics that has lost its enthrallment with history, which is exactly what happened during the French structuralist interlude, and must fall back upon the solipsism of reading and writing" (Raschke 1988: 129). Through the notion of writing, autonomy is transferred to reading, which becomes closed rather than simply "close": there is no emancipation other than interpretation.

The text as writing is no longer the letter that kills but the law that gives life. The sanctity of the commentary tradition returns to the scene of instruction while interpretation is elevated to the status of faith. "Giving writing a primal status seems to be a way of retranslating, in transcendental terms, both the theological affirmation of its sacred character and the critical affirmation of its creative character. To admit that writing is, because of the very history that it made possible, subject to the test of oblivion and repression, seems to represent, in transcendental terms, the religious prin-

ciple of the hidden meaning (which requires interpretation) and the critical principle of implicit significations, silent determinations, and obscured
contents (which gives rise to commentary). To imagine writing as absence
seems to be a simple repetition, in transcendental terms, of both the religious principle of inalterable and yet never fulfilled tradition, and the aesthetic principle of the work's survival, its perpetuation beyond the author's
death, and its enigmatic *excess* in relation to him" (Foucault 1979a: 144).
With this position, a long course of inquiry has been completed: revising
Kierkegaard's model of the reader as Abraham, Levinas portrayed the theo-
phanic experience of Moses as the possibility of an encounter with the
author, which Derrida challenged by showing the inaccessibility of the original. We are now left with the Book alone and the trace of its past interpretations. The promised return to the land of the endlessly repeatable (and
always already interpreted, and hence canonical) Text is possible only as a
post-Biblical, and therefore aesthetic, exercise. In the course of this search
for ultimate meaning, one parameter has remained constant: the indispensable assumption that the aesthetic attitude (contemplation), Heidegger's
passive preservation, is the prerequisite for any ethical relation.

The relation between ethics and aesthetics also preoccupied another
prophet of Judaization, Hermann Cohen (1842–1918). In "The Style of the
Prophets" (1901), where Greek and Hebrew moral views are compared, he
argued that Plato creates an autonomous science of morality, ethics, and
expresses disdain for poetry and myth. "The prophets, on the other hand,
consider themselves to be above the web of myths their people had
spun. . . . But though they may neglect the past, they use their rich poetic
endowment to depict the future and thus, in their rhetoric, prove to be
genuine and great poets. . . . They are artists, not philosophers" (Cohen
1971: 106).[44] Elsewhere Cohen differentiated between myth and religion
with regard to guilt, arguing that, while the former is concerned with fate
and suggests that "man is not an individual, but rather the offspring of his
ancestors" (Cohen 1972: 169), the latter "is concerned with man's guilt"
and must be considered as "the origin of the I as individual" (168). Here
the distinction between myth and religion was made not on grounds of
ethics but of aesthetics.

At the same time, although Cohen elevated art to the level of the highest
knowledge, he realized that, if philosophy could no longer support religion,
the risk was great: "The fate of religion hinges on this question. Religion is
not science; subsequently, it can also not be ethics. But does this make its
morality a mere artifact? Are the prophets nothing but artists, and is their
style merely an exercise in aesthetics?" (Cohen 1971: 107). If not on an
epistemological basis, how is the superiority of religion going to be defended? Prophetic religion needs to be seen as both art and more-than-art.
Cohen argued that "by their very opposition to mythology the prophets

create a new kind of religion. The new religion of the One God is the work of art created by and expressive of their particular style" (107). Some two centuries earlier, art had to compare itself to religion to gain respectability. When Cohen presented the prophetic expression as artwork, he was appealing to aesthetics in order to save the credibility of religion. He was also appropriating, in a rare move, the aesthetic from mythology and religion. "As it is, the style of the prophets—who, though neither philosophers nor merely artists, are most creative teachers—expresses the special character of religion in contradistinction to mythology, art, or science" (107). The last three areas are the familiar and glorified expression of the Greek spirit. Prophetic art, on the other hand, is not a secular but a religious expression: the prophets are the best artists in that they created religion-as-art. Cohen justified their prophetic work exclusively on aesthetic grounds. If originally religion (through its Protestant interpretive methods) produced art, now the quality of art is called upon to salvage religion.

Cohen's view of art reached its concise formulation in "On the Aesthetic Value of Our Religious Education" (c. 1914), where quite appropriately he called "the Messianic concept of man the basis of modern aesthetics" (155). This position is explained by "Judaism's notion of individual man; for when we speak of the aesthetic value of the Jewish concept of man, we think primarily of the individual, that is, of his nature and the unity of his body and soul" (158). If the religious concept of guilt is the origin of the individual, the autonomous I, then the individual's aesthetic value inheres in guilt and Messianic hope. Art is the supreme expression of the Messianic hope of the subject, who is always the guilty individual. As Cohen sees it, art is the religion of the individual. "Aesthetic and religious values then are correlated. For the aesthetic value of our ancient texts is due to their basic religious significance which, in turn, so affects man's emotions that he feels continually driven to express his own religious feelings in new aesthetic forms" (158). Religion and art reinforce each other, and the proper attitude to art is the religious one (a position rejected later by Adorno). "We cannot truly appreciate the aesthetic value of any work of art without experiencing a sense of reverence for the eternal genius inherent in all creations of abiding aesthetic value. This holds true especially with regard to the Bible, which awakens in us a feeling of reverence for its religious genius and appreciation for its aesthetic sense" (159). Morality and art are closely related and should progress together. "The relationship of aesthetics and ethics is of crucial importance for the aesthetic value of our religious education" (156). One could go further and envision not just correlation and cooperation of the two but even total identification. Cohen quotes from the Bible and concludes: "Such sayings of our Messianism, reflecting an unmistakable and ingrained sense of aesthetics, tend to eliminate the distinction any systematic philosophy must make between ethics and aesthetics" (156).

Although the distinction had been already questioned by French and English Aestheticism, it is rather interesting to see a Neo-Kantian agreeing in principle with, say, Oscar Wilde that aesthetics is the modern ethics, and that the morality of the subject is that of the artist.

The Hebraization of culture in the twentieth century promised the resolution of antinomies plaguing the relation between ethical tasks and aesthetic exercises in the superior synthesis of the praxis of contemplation. Still, a major issue remained unresolved: Can there be a Hebraic culture at all? This question has beset modernity repeatedly. For if bourgeois culture cannot prove its tolerance by hosting an(y) other tradition and establishing a society of equality based on shared sentiments and practices, it has no universality, and therefore no validity. This challenge creates the anxiety of assimilation. Those who have not been entirely convinced that such a society can be created fear that "American Jewish culture is at best as much an oxymoronic phrase as German Jewish culture was" (Bloom 1985: 111) unless some qualification is introduced: "[Jewish] Culture in our context broadly must mean literary culture, if by 'literary' one means biblical and post-biblical *written* tradition" (109). There seem to be some inhibiting limitations within Hebrew religion: "The prohibition against images obliged a channeling into the written word of imaginal energies. Derrida in this is Hebrew rather than Hellene: aniconic yet intensely graphic" (Hartman 1981: 17). This may mean that, in order to establish the Hebraic identity of culture, Jews have to fight the Greeks not just over texts but over the very meaning of culture. "The work of reading is a sullen art reacting against modern iconomania. It may be too panicky a view that there is a contest between word and image which is being won by the latter" (Hartman 1980: 187), since the graphic letter can play an intensely iconoclastic role. For students of the Hebraic, though, Simmel's dilemma persists: is culture a possibility of the tradition or a condition of modernity?

On the subject of aesthetics in Jewish religious thought, "it has been noted that, however creative Jews have been in such fields as religion, law, literature, science, and economics, until recent times—that is, until large numbers of Jews, and with them their artistic traditions, were assimilated into non-Jewish cultures—no Jewish art was produced, nor were there Jewish artists of any great significance. There can thus be no surprise that there has never been any body of Jewish literature on art or aesthetics. How then Jewish aesthetics—that is, a Jewish theory of art?" (Cohen and Mendes-Flohr 1987: 1). The interdiction of the Second Commandment banished the world of images and idols, condemning it as pagan mimesis.[45] It was only after questions of representation overcame realist demands that "in the twentieth century art has finally begun, by divorcing itself from the pagan aesthetic of nature and from the Christian aesthetic of incarnation, to catch up with the aboriginal Jewish aesthetic (for Jews and Gentiles alike) of a phenomenal world in eternal pursuit of the ideal, divine, or at least messianic world. . . . In modernism, art is assimilating Judaism" (5–6). This narrative discovers a disturbing continuity between mimesis and incarnation, and finds in the Jewish aesthetics of modernist art another revolt against idolatry. Its central document is Arnold Schönberg's opera *Moses und Aron* (1930–32), a "sacred fragment" (Adorno) or counter-*Parsifal*, which cancels itself into a theological inquiry (Altizer 1982: 149–50). As "an extended dramatization of Jewish iconoclasm" (Cohen and Mendes-Flohr 1987: 4),[46] it deals with the incommensurability between image (*Bild*) and idea (*Gedanke*)—the inability of representation to present the "divine idea," the "idea of One Timeless," the "Everlasting One." Schönberg shares the conclusion of Karl Kraus in his last poem (1933): "No word redeems." Still, as his prophet stutters his way through the desert of paganism, he never loses his faith in the promised land of the word (Blanchot)— the transcendence of translation.

Derrida has elaborated an anti-incarnationist theory of Hebraic culture, beginning with the assertion that "for the Jew and the Poet" space and language are not defined by the Greek polis. The Biblical "kingdom of priests" is replaced by culture as the kingdom of Jews. "The thinking of Being thus is not a pagan cult of the *Site*, because the Site is never a given proximity but a promised one. And then also because it is not a *pagan cult*" (Derrida 1978a: 145). Both Jew and Poet are destined for the promised land of language. The same point is amplified in another article of the same year, "Edmond Jabès and the Question of the Book" (1964). This is probably Derrida's only paper that is not an exercise in critique (deconstruction or otherwise) but a straightforward aesthetic appreciation—a book review, in fact, where a literary work recently published is interpreted and evaluated. The article has been rightly placed before "Violence and Metaphysics" in *Writing and Difference* because the two introduce and complement each other. Also in this paper, the by-now-familiar literary incarnations of difference—letter, writing, book, Scripture, Jew—make their first appearance. The traditional romantic culture-nature opposition is here translated into Scripture-Nature (Derrida 1978: 71), and a new equivalence emerges which stands Arnold on his head: Culture is Scripture.

The article is characterized by a strong, occasionally strident tone of French Modernism. Derrida reiterates the Mallarméan "unpenetrated certainty that Being is a Grammar; and that the world is in all its parts a cryptogram to be constituted through poetic inscription or deciphering; that the book is original, that everything *belongs to the book* before being and in order to come into the world" (76–77).[47] He also affirms the Flaubertian textual faith:[48] "everything that is exterior in relation to the book, everything that is negative as concerns the book, is produced *within the book*. The exit from the book, the other and the threshold, are all articulated *within the book*" (76). Jabès (1912–90) himself has expressed the same faith in even more extreme terms: "If God is, it is because He is in the book. . . . The world exists because the book does" (quoted in Handelman 1985: 57).[49] Thus Derrida draws freely from the modernist dogma, accepting such principles as the autonomy of the work, the omnipotence of the author-God (Derrida 1978: 70), and the self-reflexivity of literature.[50] In true formalist fashion he discusses the ways in which "the book becomes a subject in itself and for itself" and "infinitely reflects itself" (65), while acknowledging the impossibility of closure (in works like *Moses und Aron*) and honoring the suffering of form: "The fragment is neither a determined style nor a failure, but the form of that which is written" (71). He glorifies its inconclusiveness and its pain: "Everything enters into, transpires in the book. This is why the book is never finite. It always remains suffering and vigilant" (75). Thus the counter-theory of grammatology, which Derrida developed into a science of gay dialectic, is inspired by modernist writing and the aesthetic ideal of the Book (of books). In a world infected by surplus (of meaning, value, and production), the pharmakon of the infinite totality and reflectivity of the autonomous book, autonomous even from its readings, becomes the model of a general economy: the economy of the pure aesthetic.

If Levinas reconstructs the encounter at Sinai, Derrida is more interested in its interpretive aftermath, the fate of the Law in an aesthetic culture: "The inspired interpreter stands on a mountain apart (like Moses receiving the tablets) in profound communication with the poet" (Fisch 1977: 64). He shares with every vatic critic "a concern with 'tablets,' with text-centeredness and text-obsessiveness" (Bloom 1982: 329). The Hebraism of the Book is the blissful suffering of the text—a pathology of reading already captured in Schiller's notion of the sentimental. The sentimental reader suffers the pure autonomy of writing which, in its absolute sacredness, has already dispensed with its readers. When the aesthetic approach prevails, "in the passional regime the book seems to be internalized, and to internalize everything: it becomes the sacred written Book. It takes the place of the face and God, who hides his face and gives Moses the inscribed stone tablets. God manifests himself through trumpets and the Voice, but what is heard in sound is the nonface, just as what is seen in the book are words. *The book has become the body of passion*, just as the face was the body of the signifier. It is now the book, the most deterritorialized of things, that fixes territories and genealogies. The latter are what the book says, and the former the place at which the book is said. . . . In any case, this is the point of departure for the delusional passion of the book as origin and finality of the world. The unique book, the total work, all possible combinations *inside* the book, the tree-book, the cosmos-book: . . . Wagner,

Mallarmé, Joyce, Marx and Freud: still Bibles. If passional delusion is profoundly monomaniacal, monomania for its part found a fundamental element of its assemblage in monotheism and the Book. The strangest cult" (Deleuze and Guattari 1987: 127). The cult of reading, of total textualization, consumes the body of its passion in rituals of inscription, of circumcision, and speaks in tongues of commentary and territory.

Derrida's attention remains fixed on the Palestine of the literary text: "When a Jew or a poet proclaims the Site, he is not declaring war. For this site is not the empirical and national Here of a territory. It is immemorial, and thus also a future. Better: it is tradition as adventure" (Derrida 1978: 66). The real adventure is not Odysseus' return but the departure into the immemorial land of interpretive tradition. The poet is a Jew, and Judaism is writing.[51] "The Jew who elects writing which elects the Jew" (65) is destined for the land of the total text, the absolute work. Because he aspires to survive outside history, "the situation of the Jew becomes exemplary of the situation of the poet, the man of speech and of writing" (65). They both live in the "Desert of the Promise" (66), the text: "Autochthons of the Book. Autonomous too" (67), like the text they read.[52] The basis of autonomy is no longer contemplation but its object. If, according to the Hebraic model, the Book made the Jew, then the text makes (its) readers. This is the Law of Derrida.

Heine's idea about the Jews as "People of the Book"[53] is here elevated from an ethno-cultural to an aesthetic principle (Eisen 1986).[54] The idea has been basically a narrative of national continuity, like the following one: "That is to say, it was an obsession with study, a condition of text-centeredness, that held the great Diaspora Jewries together. This is the common element in Babylon-Persia, Alexandria, Arabia-Spain, Provence, Renaissance Italy, East Europe and Germany-Austria" (Bloom 1982: 321). Now this idea becomes the sign of *Bildung* as election and destiny: "The dwelling assigned, ascribed to Israel is the House of the Book" (Steiner 1985: 5). Thus the People of the Book are not homeless, because the Book is their dwelling. After Heidegger, in his essay on Georg Trakl, "Language in the Poem" (1959), had talked about the "apartness" of the wandering stranger, Levinas pointed out that the true place of gathering (Greek *synagoge*, synagogue) was indicated in "the Bible's permanent saying: the condition (or the uncondition) of being strangers and slaves in the land of Egypt brings man close to his neighbor. In their uncondition of being strangers men seek one another. No one is at home. The memory of this servitude assembles humanity" (Levinas 1987b: 149). Heidegger, however, had given an aesthetic definition of home, arguing, in his commentary on Hölderlin, that "poetry first causes dwelling to be dwelling. Poetry is what really lets us dwell" (Heidegger 1971b: 215). Home is where poetry is read and preserved. "The poetic is the basic capacity for human dwelling" (228). When he talked about the sacred as a dimension of coming to be at home, via building and dwelling, though, Heidegger meant *Heimat*, homeland as the natural home rooted in a rural locality (Applegate 1990). Jabès, whose collected edition of early writings is entitled *I Built my Dwelling* (1959), reversed the order and talked about poetry and departing,[55] calling the text "the fatherland of the Jews" (67). If poetry causes dwelling, then writing is where one dwells—through exodus rather than return (Gurr 1981). Writing is the call to dwelling, the election to reading.

Together homelessness and exile constitute a major motif of any theory of modernity because they reflect the distance of history from Greece, the only home culture seems to have known. "German philosophy as a whole— Leibnitz, Kant, Hegel, Schopenhauer, to name the greatest—is the most fundamental form of *romanticism* and homesickness there has ever been: the longing for the best that ever existed. One is no longer at home anywhere; at last one longs back for that place in which alone one can be at home, because it is the only place in which one would want to be at home: the *Greek* world!" (Nietzsche 1967: 225). From Novalis to Lukács, the agony of displacement cries for return and restitution. This is an expression of alienation not only from the (Greek) Alien but primarily from a public that seeks knowledge and gratification elsewhere. The typical aesthetic gesture is to turn this alienation to the moral advantage of the intelligentsia: "'It is even part of my good fortune not to be a house-owner,' Nietzsche already wrote in the *Gay Science*. Today we should have to add: it is part of morality not to be at home in one's home" (Adorno 1974: 39). It is especially in the bourgeois home, the home one owns, that aesthetic guilt dictates that one not feel at home. More recently, as the Hebraization of culture indulges itself in tautology, it has turned its gaze from the home lost to homelessness to the land promised to exile—from heathenism to Judaism.

Buber repeated a common formula of the Science of Judaism when he said that "the most deep-seated humanity of our soul and its most deep-seated Judaism mean and desire the same thing" (Buber 1967: 55). Derrida, with his references to "exile as writing" (Derrida 1978: 74), takes this into the heart of aesthetics: the modern artist, literature and culture, he proclaims, are Jewish. In views like this Hebraism has been transformed from the avant-garde of humanistic acculturation to the avant-garde of aesthetic culture. The artist emerges as a figura for the Jew.[56] This is a pervasive, although usually veiled, concern: "The 'thematics of the Jew' most often appears in Derrida in sublimated or disguised form. Judaism is a hidden center and motivation for other issues that might at first glance seem to be entirely unrelated to it" (Megill 1985: 304).

At the same time, this sublimated thematics remains an integral and recognizable part of modern identity. We are all going "the way through the Desert. Writing is the moment of the desert as the moment of Separation. . . . God no longer speaks to us; he has interrupted himself: we must take words upon ourselves" (68). Our plight is quintessentially Jewish: it is not that the gods have departed, as Hölderlin thought, but that God will not address us any longer. Thus reading (his Word) and writing (about that reading) become our tasks. "The Jewish consciousness is indeed the unhappy consciousness" (68) or the "hypertrophied" one, according to Levinas; however, it is not only Abraham's, as Hegel believed, but our own too. Jabès has already hurled at his readers: "You are all Jews, even the antisemites, for you have all been designated for martyrdom" (quoted in Derrida 1978: 75). Other intellectuals (from the Nobel Prize winner Elie Wiesel to the commix artist Art Spiegelman) have declared that the world "has *become* the Diaspora Jew." This applies to everybody: "After the Holocaust, we *are* all Jews . . . *all* of us . . . including George Bush, J. Danforth Quayle, Yassir Arafat, and even Yitzhak Shamir. Now our job is to convince them of that" (Spiegelman 1989: 22). Where Horkheimer and Adorno feared that the entire world, including the Jews, had turned anti-Semitic, Judaism has become (or is on its way to becoming) a universal condition: all of us, poets and rabbis, are Jews.[57] Derrida bestows upon this proclamation its proper aesthetico-theological tone, calling the agent of designation writing, every interpreter a rabbi, the poet a Jew—and finally (like Adorno and Horkheimer) anything Greek "anti-Scriptural" (Handelman 1982: 10) and anti-Semitic.[58] The Jew is the poet, the Scripture is the book, exile is writing, the desert is the Library, the Fall is language, reading is commentary, and all philosophy is interpretation: this is his basic (poetic) narrative of the human condition—an aestheticist, decadent existentialism, to be sure, but endowed with the charm of a seductive irreverence toward the decorum of the profession (whatever Derrida may choose that to be, depending on the occasion) and above all a seemingly irresistible declaration of aesthetic anti-nomy.

Derrida's Judaization of textual exegesis sets out and departs from Jabès' modernist aesthetics. Reading Jabès also serves as an interesting mediation between Levinas's phenomenology of faith and his own negative hermeneutics: it helps ground interpretation in the heteroglossia and repeatability of the text itself. Levinas belongs to the phenomenological tradition of Modernism. His face-to-face encounter is a model of reading derived from the principles of the modernist artwork—an isolated, direct, supra-historical communication with the total, overwhelming presence of a perfect, independent, incarnated voice. "Thus his Talmudic interpretations bear witness not only to a deep indebtedness to Husserlian principles but also to Heidegger's hermeneutical phenomenology" (Wyschogrod 1974: 171). Levinas declares unequivocally the theological identity of his poetics of alterity: "The comprehension of the Other is thus a hermeneutics and an exege-

sis" (Levinas 1968: 39). At the same time, he has to resort to the discourse
of philosophy to validate his Talmudic science. "It is fundamental to Levinas' characterization of himself as thinker to disclaim the role of theologian" (Wyschogrod 1974: 159). Hence the use of the Bible to mediate between philosophy and religion. Jabès transposes Levinas's face-to-face to an
encounter with the supreme text but keeps the text's experience private:
"The Jew remains alone with the divine text. He always faces this text"
(Jabès 1987: 10). The true object of devotion is the Torah: "Facing the text
has replaced facing God" (Jabès 1986: 354). The proper response to the
question is obeying the command of reading: "Whether it is the Bible or
secular texts, man is alone with the text. We have no other reality beside
that which the books give us. This also is one of the ways of Judaism" (Jabès
1987: 11).

Derrida, rejecting the appearance of the face altogether, concentrates on
its two major designations: otherness and writing. He suggests that writing
is not presence and fullness but difference—not peaceful form and repose
but formation through violence, because the work is produced by and situated within a tradition which it recalls and reactivates and reenacts, and it
acquires meaning only from/as its difference from it. Thus contemplation
as the locus of the aesthetic is replaced not by its object but by the condition of the object, which is the contemplation of the theoros by it, "the
action of literature on men" (Levinas).

Furthermore, otherness as separation and strangeness is crucial for the
understanding of both Jew and Poet. Derrida considers the conditions that
"made the Jew into the archetypal stranger—on the same grounds as the
writer and any other creator" (Jabès 1987: 8) and the reason why the "history of the writer and that of the Jew are both but the history of the book
they lay claim to" (Jabès 1985: 27). Thus writing turns gradually from the
homelessness of wandering to the endless deferral of the land and into a
nomadic site (a contradiction in terms): the dwelling of the reader/poet in
the house of the Book.[59] The promise which has been kept is not the Logos
of the Gospel but the nomadic (Attali 1990) meaning of the Bible—the
disseminated presence of the supplement of all interpretation. Even here,
though, in the middle of the desert, the shadow of Heidegger, who was
aware of the difference between the Hebraic destination and the Hellenic
destiny, falls heavy on the open pages: "As it reveals itself in beings, Being
withdraws. In this way, by illuminating them, Being sets beings adrift in
errancy. . . . Without errancy there would be no connection from destiny to
destiny: there would be no history. . . . When we are historical we are
neither a great nor a small distance from what is Greek. Rather, we are
in errancy toward it" (Heidegger 1984: 26). The Hebraic separation is
measured by the Hellenic distance, the distance from Greece. That is the
meaning of the trip (*Wanderung*) to Italy, and especially Freud's hesitation

before crossing the Adriatic: for Winckelmann, Goethe, Herder, Shelley, but also Graves and Henze, it is the errancy toward the Greek (the error of interpretation). Joyce knew that, if the nomadism of errancy is Hebraic, its nostalgia is Greek. That is why he, before Levinas, found the idea of a wandering Greek (in Dublin) implausible.[60]

Derrida completes the grandiose modernist project of claiming the practices of literature for the people of the Book. He, like Blanchot (1986: 141) later, quotes Levinas approvingly: "To admit the action of literature on men—this is perhaps the ultimate wisdom of the West, in which the people of the Bible will be recognized" (Derrida 1978a: 102). Derrida's approach to the project is different, though: against Levinas's Spinozist "natural atheism" he counterproposes a "negative atheology" (Derrida 1978c: 297)[61]—a theology without affirmation, apocalypse, or redemption. It is the theology of the Pharisees, of the interpreters of the letter (whose rise has been explained by some as a reaction to the Hellenistic culture supported by the Sadducees). "Jewish praxis, both ritual and ethical, is prior to understanding. The exemplar of this life is the Pharisee" (Wyschogrod 1974: 167), the custodian of the book—Saul rather than Paul. Derrida continues Heidegger's project of the 1930s, "overcoming aesthetics," but avoids its pitfall—to use the expression of the other major thinker of the time involved in the same project, "the aestheticization of politics" (Benjamin). Playing Benjamin against Heidegger, he pursues an aesthetic way of overcoming aesthetics: "A new transcendental aesthetic must let itself be guided not only by mathematical idealities but by the possibility of inscriptions in general, not befalling an already constituted space as a contingent accident but producing the spatiality of space" (Derrida 1976: 290). This is the postmodernist aesthetic of difference, of the total synchronic availability and play of tradition—autonomy as autology. "Deconstruction is essentially a kind of *formalism* because it interprets as symptoms of a metaphysical syndrome (fissures in a text, structures of supplementarity, positing of a transcendental signified) what are actually the internal reflections of the other historical conditions of a text's production" (Wood 1988: 63). There is a broad debate regarding the epistemological, artistic, and political direction of this formalism.

Certain critics (Ulmer 1984) have portrayed Derrida as a postmodern thinker: "What we seem to find in Derrida is a postmodernist polemic against modernism in art and criticism" (Megill 1985: 300). To them, he is the preeminent aesthetician of the postmodern (and one of its illustrious practitioners), since his concerns focus on the Book as a repeatable origin. Modernism was ahistorical, formalist, epiphanic: it believed in the eternal, fulfilled presence of the pure work. Postmodernism, on the other hand, is not ignorant or innocent of history but rather sees it as the total, synchronic, undifferentiated presence and availability of tradition. While the modernist artwork is about itself and seeks redemption from history through form, the postmodernist is about tradition and surrounds itself happily with history; the former strives to establish its own code, the latter thrives on borrowed codes (and time).[62] The postmodernist work reflects the experience of the library, where everything is available and within reach but placed in an order that eliminates any sense of hierarchical history.[63]

Other critics, however, have argued that certain radical aspects of contemporary art "do not undercut deconstruction so much as they make it, from their vantage points, wholly irrelevant. In this respect Derrida stands to postmodern art much as Schoenberg stands to the new consonance: as an example of a certain intellectualism which is no longer the vogue" (Rapaport 1986: 141). His critique of phenomenology has been turned against his own bracketing of the world within quotation marks: "It is difficult to see, on this point, why Derrida's and others' attacks on structuralism for its courting of formalism and historical aridity do not apply to Derrida as well. Derrida's deconstructive project is formalist through and through. Its synchronic desire for '*the greatest totality*,' for dialogue with a unified tradition (logocentrism), defeats its would-be historicist disposition" (Lentricchia 1980: 177). To the extent that he works simultaneously within and against tradition (Melville 1986), practicing and discrediting critique, Derrida remains strategically ambivalent about the adventures of Enlightenment and the pleasures of culture. "Technically, then, deconstruction would be better described as neo-structuralism rather than post-structuralism" (Boly 1988–89: 180). Whether he is erotically teasing his readers or playing Judas to the Logos (Derrida 1986b: 33a), his is the ethic of tempting the temptation which, as Levinas taught, is philosophy. In his discussions of authors, "Derrida constitutes himself . . . as the other's temptation" (Harpham 1987: 266). To the extent that he remains faithful to the possibility of culture, he sides with the unfinished agenda of modernity; but to the extent that he confounds this by questioning the possibility of assimilation, he works within the framework of a skepticist Modernism. "Derrida belongs squarely within the tradition of modernism, where modernism is taken as a movement from presence to self-presence. So modernism in painting is the movement whereby painting comes to have painting, representing and seeing, as its object; literary modernism is the literary questioning of the practice of writing literature. Derrida is a philosophical modernist with a difference; he does not ask the question 'What is thinking?' but rather the literary question 'What is writing?' *in* philosophy" (Bernstein 1987: 104). In general, "Derrida's *programmatic* hesitation toward his historical situation" (Said 1978: 700) expresses his ambivalence about Hellas, the Protestant allonym for civil emancipation: if Greek is the language of philosophy, then it must be spoken at the House of the Book; and yet the

Book cannot be assimilated into the allochthonous (Hellenic) culture but has to be preserved in difference to it. In Protestantism, where understanding is the result of a happy fall, the theory of interpretation becomes a sermon, a sermon on error, because interpretation is by definition in error, an errancy from the text to which it claims to come so close, an errancy in the sea (Odysseus) or the desert (exile). Errancy is true homeliness.

If Heidegger thought that the time of poetry does not have a history, Derrida knows only the time of the library and interpretation:[64] this, he argues, is the eternal time of Jewish history. Beyond the disciplines of reading he has no interest in cultural or social practices: his consideration of institutionality stops where the yearning for the innocence of (and the pain of separation from) the Other (language) begins.[65] "[W]hatever his more recent pronouncements, Derrida himself has hardly been remarkable for his 'institutional' as opposed to discursive analyses, and is thus performatively askew to what he claims in ways of interest to deconstructive criticism" (Eagleton 1986: 79). His position is again programmatically ambivalent and strategically ambiguous: "On the one hand, Derrida has repeatedly insisted on the political character of deconstructionist practice: 'it is not neutral,' he assures us, 'it intervenes.' On the other hand, he has been rather evasive about just which politics, or approach to politics, it involves. . . . Thus, the debate concerning deconstructionist politics stems in no small measure from Derrida's unwillingness or inability to 'decide' it by word or example" (McCarthy 1989–90: 146). Despite the flaunted undecidability of meaning, margin, and measure, "the 'radicality' of deconstruction,' as Derrida conceives it, inexorably carries it in the direction of the ineffable, and that, while this may be harmless enough when dealing with metaphysics, it is seriously disabling where morals and politics are concerned" (147).[66] After all, the mythic figure of the vatic critic who struggles heroically and in vain to overcome uncertainty and doubt (Mileur 1990) and the complementary one of the "antinomian" (Oscar Wilde) artistic critic who sees style as incarnation are too familiar since the reactions of Herder or Wordsworth to the French Revolution. As a contemporary form of professionalized "cultural prophecy" (Bloom 1982: 318)—namely, autoscopic critique—"it seems that deconstruction is, despite its 'radical' impulses and procedures, truly conservative. . . . It is the quintessence of deconstruction that it responds to the decline of academic literary criticism by inscribing within the academy a project of preservation" (Bové 1983: 17). Before a broader assessment of this project can be made, a study is needed relating deconstruction to the Reconstructionism of Mordechai Menahem Kaplan (1881–1983), which considers Judaism as a cultural social totality. What is already clear is that the iconolatric promise of emancipation has been replaced by the iconomachic ideal of resistance. "In this respect, dissidence is less a set of social and political values than a cultural ethics" (Marx-Scouras 1987: 107).

Derrida moves from the synchrony of the structure, which fascinated the structuralist grammarians, to the structure of synchrony, which gives free entry to any library or museum in the world (as always, to those who have the leisure to seek it). And since Postmodernism is fundamentally about playing (games, roles, works, fashions, codes, genders, arms, etc.), he chooses to perform the part of the Pharisee (Saul) , one of "those misunderstood men of literality" (Derrida 1978a: 68), aspiring to become a (performance) artist of tradition[67] (playing, for example, Plato to Nietzsche's Socrates, or Moses to Levinas's Abraham), not a philosopher of history (like all his predecessors in modernity). "To be a Jew is to believe in the intelligence of the Pharisees and their masters. It is through the Talmud's intelligence that we accede to the Bible's faith" (Levinas 1990: 136). Since Derrida, like the Jew and the Poet, is elected by writing, he chooses to live not in history but in (its) tension, the tension of emancipated tradition: between literality and allegory, nominalism and literalism, philosophy and messianism, the polis and the Land, Hellenism and Hebraism. It is what he calls the violence within metaphysics, the war within discourse, but should rather be seen as the postmodernist aesthetic exercise: interpretation cruising cable TV channels, touring the shopping mall, pillaging the tradition, plundering the canon. "In this regard, the fetishizing of multiplicity, difference, aporia, undecidability merely masks behind another image or myth the secret deployment of the ruling culture's real power: that power generated by its own production of surpluses. . . . Play, laughter, and carnival merely parody the freedom, the luxury, of the ruling class. . . . The surplus of the ruling class, however, is the origin and end of production, the perpetual 'holiday' that structures internally the means of labor" (Rowe 1985–86: 49–50). The aesthetic education of man, which used to involve the Grand Tour or attentive museum pilgrimages, now takes the form of learning to bid at auctions. But then autonomy has always invested in art.

The interplay of Hebraism and Hellenism as conceived by Derrida should be examined within this broad post-industrial, consumerist context, infused with the rampant hedonism of figures (as opposed to the modernist asceticism of forms). Significantly, the violence and the antagonism between the two appear rather one-sided: although the tension is assumed to develop between the Greek and the Jewish, only the latter seems to experience it: the Jewish is difference, but the experience of difference is exclusively Jewish too.[68] "There are the Jews and there is something else. But what complicates things is that the 'something else' is also Jewish" (Vidal-Naquet 1980: 97). Above the supremacy of the Hebraic perspective, the Jew is endowed with divine qualities. "Whether he is Being or the master of beings, God himself is, and appears as what he is, within difference, that is to say, as difference and within dissimulation" (Derrida 1978: 74). The same can be said about the Jew who is, "to purloin Heidegger's image, 'the shepherd of being'" (Steiner 1985: 7)—both trace and difference, absence and supplement, the writing of the Scripture and the letter of metaphysics. "The Jew is responsible for all creation" (Wyschogrod 1974: 166). This is his command and task. "God, after all, like [Joyce's] Poldy, is Jewish" (Bloom 1986: 4). The Jew lives in exile and separation, difference and negativity. "This difference, this negativity in God is our freedom" (Derrida 1978: 67), as well as the very possibility of literature. Thus liberation is understood aesthetically: its Romantic means have become its postmodern ends. If "God separated himself from himself in order to let us speak" (67), so does man separate himself from himself at his most Jewish and divine moment, that of creating literature: "Life negates itself in literature only so that it may survive better. So that it may *be* better. It does not negate itself any more than it affirms itself: it differs from itself, defers itself, and writes itself as *différance*" (78). Like Abraham, who deferred his homeland, and like the Jew, who is split between the two dimensions of the letter, literary writing separates itself from itself in order to give God back His words. "I assert that writing is a revolutionary act, a scrupulously Jewish act, for it consists in taking up the pen in that place where God withdrew Himself from His words, it consists indefinitely in pursuing a utopian work in the manner of God who was the Totality of the Text of which nothing subsists" (Jabès, quoted in Handelman 1985: 65). Here Derrida's romantic equivalence connecting God, Judaism, and literature is repeated with a postmodernist vengeance: Scripture, having long ago claimed (bourgeois) morality, now claims culture. If Hebraism was allegorized by Romanticism and sublimated by Modernism, with Postmodernism it has been wholly identified with the aesthetic attitude.

This development, inaugurated by the rehabilitation of figura in *Mimesis*, marks the return of the sacred back to reading after it was expelled by Higher Criticism two centuries ago. For the first time since early Romanticism, the subject is raised explicitly: "Our relation to literature is a sacred, sacralizing moment, at least by virtue of the fact that a literary text is a text in which the distinction between the signifier and the signified, let's say to be brief, or between form and content, is impossible" (Derrida 1985a: 24).[69] Since the "transvaluation of sacred symbols into secular norms" (Fisch 1977: 68) and during the long era of aesthetic education, literature, as the secular scripture, has been the beneficiary of textual faith. Its appreciation provided a new dispensation—the satisfaction of individual independence and the promise of personal salvation. "The aesthetic is thus the wan hope, in an increasingly rationalized, secularized, demythologized environment, that ultimate purpose and meaning may not be entirely lost. It is the mode of religious transcendence of a rationalistic age" (Eagleton 1990: 88). The "sanctification of literature" (Fisch) legitimized interpretation as a secular,

self-governing practice. With the Hebraization of culture, sacrality gradually returns to interpretation, this time as the already-interpreted: "What
comes to pass in a sacred text is the occurrence of a *pas de sens*. And this
event is also the one starting from which it is possible to think of the poetic
or literary text which tries to redeem the lost sacred and there translates
itself as in its model" (Derrida 1985: 204). Literature and Scripture together find their common origin in writing: "And that, which holds for the
literary text or the sacred text, perhaps defines the very essence of the literary and the sacred, at their common root" (186). This return of the sacred
has been made possible, to a large extent, by a particular kind of anti-
Hellenism, the attack on myth.[70] When Walter Benjamin (1969) criticizes
the "aestheticization of politics" or Lacoue-Labarthe (1990) proposes that
National Socialism can be seen as a "national aestheticism" in so far as it
"fictionalized" politics by conceiving the nation-state as a self-organizing,
self-producing work of art, what these writers really object to (and resent)
is mythification, the fact that politics appropriated myth. For them, the
supreme form, indeed conduct, of politics is culture: politics should not be
aestheticized because it taints aesthetics—the supreme politics. That is
why Lyotard (1988) finds Auschwitz a horrible artwork; that is also why
Hartman is haunted by "an ever-present suspicion of political solutions to
aesthetic problems. Hartman is troubled by the politics of art, though more
because he fears the degradation of art by politics than the aestheticizing
of politics in works of art" (Sprinker 1983: 59). The return of the sacred to
the Scripture is intended to make the Biblical connection of literature visible again. As Derrida's narrativization of philosophy shows, literature is
more than holy writing: it is sacred history.

Consequently, the discipline of Grammatology, one of the postmodern
branches of the Science of Judaism, prescribes that the task of reading in a
scriptural culture is an a-theistic commentary: the aesthetic repetition of
the Bible. To borrow the conclusion of Hölderlin's hymn to impossible
nearness, "Patmos":

> what the Father
> Who reigns over all loves most
> Is that the solid letter
> Be given scrupulous care, and the existing
> Be well interpreted
>
> (Hölderlin 1980: 477)

Commentary is the spirit of the law in the House of the Book, as Scholem
taught. "Against both the Jewish existentialists and their rationalist predecessors, Scholem asserts that commentary and not theology is the
correct discipline for understanding Jewish tradition" (Biale 1979: 98).
Like Judaism, theology cannot be assimilated. Commentary, however, the
Hebraic discipline of contemplation qua praxis, may reoccupy the answer

position left vacant by the defunct askeses of *Bildung*. "The necessity of commentary, like poetic necessity, is the very form of exiled speech. In the beginning is hermeneutics" (Derrida 1978: 67). The interminable, subservient, belated task of commentary, "the interpretive imperative" (67), follows from Derrida's conflation of theology and aesthetics, and articulates the new nomos, an interdiction against freedom. "In this activity known as commentary which tries to transmit an old, unyielding discourse seemingly silent to itself, into another, more prolix discourse that is both more archaic and more contemporary—is concealed a strange attitude towards language: to comment is to admit by definition an excess of the signified over the signifier; . . . but to comment also presupposes that . . . by a superabundance proper to the signifier, one may . . . give voice to a content that was not explicitly signified. By opening up the possibility of commentary, this double plethora dooms us to an endless task that nothing can limit. . . . Commentary rests on the postulate that speech (*parole*) is an act of 'translation,' that it has the dangerous privilege images have of showing while concealing, and that it can be substituted for itself indefinitely in the open series of discursive repetitions. . . . This is an exegesis, which listens, through the prohibitions, the symbols, the concrete images, through the whole apparatus of Revelation, to the Word of God, ever secret, ever beyond itself. For years we have been commenting on the language of our culture from the very point where for centuries we had awaited in vain for the decision of the Word" (Foucault 1975: xvi–xvii). In an era when all the world is a library, interpretation is the play of prayer, prayer as play and ploy: "The original opening of interpretation essentially signifies that there will always be rabbis and poets" (Derrida 1978: 67). Derrida's agenda for postmodernist criticism is simple: interpret—pray, play, and plunder. His (narrativization of) philosophy amounts to a virtuoso affirmative critique of modernist/formalist/structuralist aesthetics and a defense of the favorite postmodernist pastime, turning the hierarchy into a junkyard. Others before him (like Roland Barthes) did it with pleasure, but Derrida was the first to do it with faith, proposing that form should be discarded because it is Greek. Answering the life-long concerns of Lukács and Croce, he declares that difference is the "formation of form" (Derrida 1976: 63), the possibility of philosophy, the Hebraic otherness of culture. His invocation of a synchronic, scriptural, tautological, undifferentiated tradition effectively promised the ultimate liberation—delivery (without transcendence) from history. But the unanswered question remains: why history and whose history?

Part of the Levinas-Derrida dialogue about the meaning and mission of Judaism involves a disagreement over history. For Levinas, history is a nightmare of violence. War, the purest experience of pure Being, constitutes the experience of the movement of history. "We do not need obscure fragments of Heraclitus to prove that being reveals itself as war to philo-sophical thought, that war does not only affect it as the most potent fact, but as the very patency, or the truth, of the real" (Levinas 1969: 21). The conduct of war and the affairs of the polis are closely connected. For Le-vinas, as for Buber and Benjamin—and more recently in books expressing fear of Greek politics and thought, like I. F. Stone's *The Trial of Socrates* (1988) or Joseph Heller's *Picture This* (1988)—the Hellenic, after its ostra-cism from the realm of culture, is identified with the mask of paganism and barbarism, the political. "The art of foreseeing war and of winning it by every means [is] politics" (21). War and politics are denounced as lan-guages of ontology and games of power. Levinas repeats a claim already made by Adorno: "Ontology as first philosophy is a philosophy of power" (46). The social moment, which Kierkegaard represented with Agamem-non's public space of decision regarding (the Trojan) war, politics, and power, is here rejected as the tyranny of history. Levinas, too, seeks an alternative in the privacy of the encounter, in the ethical responsibility of the subject toward the personal call. "In political life, taken unrebuked, humanity is understood from its works—a humanity of interchangeable men, of reciprocal relations" (298). But justice is not based on reciprocity. Politics and ethics are contradictory. "Politics must always be criticized starting from the ethical" (Levinas 1985: 80). Levinas reverses Heidegger's reduction of ethics to ontology, making the ethical prior to all judgment: "Morality is not a branch of philosophy, but first philosophy" (Levinas 1969: 304). Its function is annunciatory: "Morality will oppose politics in history and will have gone beyond the functions of prudence or the canons of the beautiful to proclaim itself unconditional and universal when the eschatology of messianic peace will have come to superpose itself upon the ontology of war" (22). The goal is one of "liberating truth of its cultural presuppositions" (Levinas 1987a: 101), from its social construction which threatens to render it local and relative.[71] The threat of a new nominalism appears imminent: "The saraband of innumerable and equivalent cultures, each justifying itself in its own context, creates a world which is, to be sure, de-occidentalized, but also disoriented" (101). For the philosopher, only the centrality of western thought functions as a firm reference point in today's confused world. "I think that Europe is the Bible and Greece. This is not colonialism—the rest can be translated" (Levinas 1988: 174).[72] Be-yond colonialism and Eurocentrism, above society and history, "before cul-ture and aesthetics, meaning is situated in the ethical, presupposed by all culture and all meaning. Morality does not belong to culture: it enables one to judge it" (Levinas 1987a: 100). Politics, however, is far from eliminated: as an ethical system, it becomes state politics, the politics of divine law: "In the measure that the face of the Other relates us with the third party, the metaphysical relation of the I with the Other moves into the form of the

We, aspires to a State, institutions, laws, which are the source of universality. . . . Metaphysics therefore leads us to the accomplishment of the I as
unicity by relation to which the work of the State must be situated, and
which it must take as a model" (Levinas 1969: 300). Thus ontology (as well
as cultural nominalism) are transcended through an eschatology, the ethics
of the supreme commandment—what Levinas has called "monotheistic
politics."[73]

There is a judgment, however, outside the teleology of history, that of
the prophet, which lifts individuals outside secular jurisdiction. The
prophet of Israel is the voice of justice. "The prophetic word says both the
ethical language of the face and the language of justice which belongs to
society. It therefore says more than philosophy can say, for the saying without the said of the ethical call would seem always to be beyond it" (Bernasconi 1988b: 257). The eruption of the ethical dimension into social life
removes the subject from the realm of culture and politics: "The idea of
infinity delivers the subjectivity from the judgment of history to declare it
ready for judgment at every moment" (Levinas 1969: 25) the command
calls. Subjectivity is that invisible side of human action ignored by history.
Prior to the Logos which regulates the cosmos is the prophetic word which
establishes the possibility of language and law. This is the prophetic exteriority. The prophetic is the non-contextual word which judges history from
without. "It is not the last judgment that is decisive" (23), as Christianity
taught; eschatology should be "distinguished from the revealed opinions of
positive religions" (23) which work with a logic of apocalypse and salvation.
"The eschatological, as the 'beyond' of history, draws beings out of the
jurisdiction of history and the future" (23).

For Hermann Cohen, the prophetic tone had not become an exteriority
yet. In "The Social Ideal as Seen by Plato and by the Prophets" (1916), the
comparison of the two "spiritual guides of mankind" (Cohen 1971: 77) is
made within the secular realm. "Plato and the prophets constitute the two
most important wellsprings of modern culture" (66). The modes of cognition they express correspond to the two elements fundamental for every
harmonious society. "A social ideal represents a fusion of two basic components: a scientific mode of cognition and an ethics formalized as religion.
Plato is and remains a symbol of the former, and the prophets are and
remain that of the latter" (66). Plato developed a philosophy of knowledge
based on his theory of ideas, while the prophets concentrated on man and
sought the development of his social conscience: he dealt with science,
they cultivated morality.

Cohen expands on this basic opposition through three major distinctions concerning history, society, and suffering. "*History* is in the Greek
consciousness identical with knowledge simply. Thus, history for the Greek
is and remains directed only toward the past. In opposition, the prophet is

the seer, not the scholar. . . . The prophets are the idealists of history. Their vision begot the concept of history, as the being of the *future*" (Cohen 1972: 261–62). This is the first, theoretical advantage of prophetism: its orientation toward the future. The second advantage is practical. "For prophetism tolerates no discrimination against men, and no differentiation among them" (Cohen 1971: 75). On the contrary, Plato, with his system "which regards intellect and reason as the sole principles of cognition" (74), differentiates among men according to their capacity to philosophize, and has to appeal to the supreme authority of one ruler, his philosopher-king.

The third advantage of the prophets is ethical and is exemplified in their understanding of suffering. In tragedy, as Kierkegaard observed in his discussion of *Antigone*, suffering is punishment for primordial guilt, and therefore results from fate. The prophets, however, introduced the presence of the benevolent God who cares about the human weakness of the sinner. "The God of the prophets is the God of justice" (73) and not of blind tragic fate. "He is the God of world history, and therefore, will at some time make amends to mankind for the suffering of the individual" (73). Thus suffering is justified, and recognized for its value.

Cohen's dedication to the Platonic ideal remains strong and thorough: "Human compassion is no substitute for knowledge. Without philosophy, mankind's suffering cannot be ended; knowledge must become the cornerstone of the world's social structure. Without it, the cause of man's misery will never be found, let alone eliminated; nor will man be redeemed from its suffering" (74). For the elimination of suffering, both science and morality, "philosophy" and "religion" (Cohen 1972: 9), are necessary, and man must learn and live with both. "Broadly speaking, we might say that world history fluctuates between these two basic orientations, the Platonic and the prophetic, with their conflicts as well as their interactions. In our time, we must gain a twofold insight" (Cohen 1971: 76). "Cohen's goal was the same as that of the other Western spokesmen for Judaism who came after Mendelssohn: to establish a harmony between Judaism and culture, between *Torah* and *derekh eretz*" (Strauss 1983a: 235). At the same time, regarding the world that must be prepared, the future that must be built, Cohen's position is unambiguous: "'All the people a nation of priests'— this fundamental prophetic principle must become the motto of the new world" (76). The moral society of the prophets is the world science/philosophy must help create. From the first three chapters of Spinoza's *Tractatus* to Cohen, and from Bloch to Cornel West (1953), theologians of modernity have found in prophetism a most inspiring emancipatory model.

In Levinas's eschatological view, the People of the Book do not expect— they anticipate. Rosenzweig's "eternal people" possess not a land but the longing for a land, and therefore the future. That is why they are eternally unhistorical. "To be a Jew, for Levinas, is to exist 'outside of history,' in the sense of retaining the ability to judge" (McCollester 1970: 351). The Jew, the shepherd of Being who is responsible for the entire creation, judges history instead of being judged by it.[74] For this reason, he has not been tainted by Hellenic politics. "As the Church entered politics she was often conquered by the very paganism she was trying to convert. Judaism, the victim of power, remained undefiled by the paganism of power" (351). Examining contemporary thought, Levinas concludes that his epoch marks the triumph of paganism, of the attachment to the homeland. "In Heidegger atheism is a paganism, the presocratic texts anti-Scriptures" (Levinas 1987: 53). This raises once again the question of western superiority and the importance of the Scripture for it: "Are not we Westerners, from California to the Urals, nourished by the Bible as much as by the Presocratics" (Levinas 1987b: 148), he asks, wondering about the Greek limits of philosophy and the fate of Biblical translations. "The verses of the Bible do not here have as their function to serve as proofs; but they do bear witness to a tradition and an experience. Do they not have a right to be cited at least equal to that of Hölderlin and Trakl? The question has a more general significance: have the Sacred Scriptures read and commented on in the West influenced the Greek scripture of the philosophers, or have they been united to them only teratologically?" (148). At this juncture, Levinas makes a major decision: faced with the threat of innumerable and equivalent cultures, he denounces "the artist's world, the pagan world" (Levinas). Judaism, maintaining itself on the margins of history, refuses to be seduced by art and has no need for aesthetics. "We alone in the world desire a religion without culture" (Levinas). The true monotheist breaks radically with the idolatry of civilization. Not for him the luxury of ambiguity, the ambivalence of assimilation: "There is no Jewish aesthetic, and cannot be, because of the deep and permanent warfare between Yahweh and all idolatry whatsoever, and yet we cannot deny the aesthetic strength of the Hebrew Bible, since its spiritual authority is inseparable from its rhetorical power" (Bloom 1985: 118). Levinas turns decisively against art, culture, history, politics, and global equality, siding with an ethnic identity which for him is ontologically primary because fundamentally ethical.

This is the decisive move against alien wisdom that makes Derrida dissociate himself from eschatology. He charges that Levinas's system amounts to a new religion, requiring man's unqualified submission to the divine will. His face-to-face, as a model of human encounter, "supposes the face-to-face of the man with bent neck and eyes raised toward the God on high" (Derrida 1978a: 107). Levinas needs God as a positive Other to guard against disorder. "This is why God alone keeps Levinas' world from being a world of the pure and worst violence, a world of immorality itself" (107). Because he sees anarchy as a threat, he posits God as an outsider to guarantee and protect the finite totality and order of human experience. Derrida interprets Levinas as an apocalyptic thinker, whose eschatology envisions a triumph against the powers of evil. He finds that Levinas's understanding of Sinai as face-to-face has overly strong Christian overtones. The failure of Levinas's virulent attack on Christianity proves that rejections of the Protestant Logos as the sin of Greek language are always already expressed in Hellenic terms.[75] Derrida criticizes the acceptance of revelation (*apokalypsis*) as unveiling of truth by Heidegger and Levinas. True Jewish faith, he counters, is messianic (that is, grounded in deferral), not apocalyptic (based on epiphany).[76] "Man, one might say, is a God arrived too early, that is, a God who knows himself forever late in relation to the already-there of Being" (107). Between the too-early and the too-late, between the messianic and the always already, develops this tension which Derrida allegorizes as the Hebraic-Hellenic antagonistic interdependence, and calls human history. Its discipline ought to be Grammatology, and its method deconstruction, namely, the un-Greeking of philosophy and the Judaizing of the aesthetic: disassembling the Hellenic and appropriating it (making it speak) for the Hebraic. Derrida realizes that Levinas's wholesale condemnation of history runs the danger of denouncing the major contemporary Hebraic victory, the conquest of culture in the twentieth century. For the Hebraic to be saved from the judgment of history and the equality of cultures, it should not be exempted from comparisons and made the supreme arbiter of ethics; on the contrary, Derrida's strategy is to promote it to an aesthetic model by showing how it can incorporate Greek art— indeed, how it incarnates Hellenic *Bildung*. The familiar rhetorical tactic insists that the "letter" is the authentic "spirit" and that the "law" is the true "faith."

Derrida's disagreement with Levinas over the character of Judaism[77] (which has to be established with reference to the Greekness of philosophy) is only a recent chapter in a long story that can be traced at least as far back as J. G. Hamann's critique of Mendelssohn—the story of the self-definition of modernity with reference to its intrinsic other, the Hebraic. "The question must be asked: is contemporary life the adversary or the double of Jewish consciousness?" (Wyschogrod 1974: 161). Ever since the Moderns defeated the Ancients, this has been the "Jewish question," that of universal successful assimilation into the bourgeois rule of self-government through rigorous contemplation. Levinas's effort to liberate Judaism from the ontic determinations of being and time (i.e., culture and history) has largely relied on a particular exploration of the question—the dialogue between Franz Rosenzweig and Martin Buber. During the 1940s and early 1950s, when Levinas's work consisted primarily in a polemic against Heidegger which turned *destruktion* against *Dasein*, the (usually unacknowledged) presence of Rosenzweig's existential religion in his system was indispensable.[78] "For Levinas and the group of French Jewish thinkers

grouped under the name of the 'Paris school,' Rosenzweig is the chief influence and inspiration. For Levinas, Buber represents a different tendency in
Jewish thought and spiritually is often more an antagonist than a master"
(McCollester 1970: 344). This is true so far as certain issues are concerned,
especially the Law. "Levinas was initially preoccupied with differentiating
or separating his own position from that of Buber" (Bernasconi 1988b:
100). Starting with the dominance of the *éthique* in his work in the late
1950s in reaction to the influence of Simone Weil, however, the former
antagonist becomes more of a master. With *Totality and Infinity* (1961),
Levinas feels that, by returning to Kierkegaard's ethics of subjectivity, he
has adequately responded to Heidegger's historicization of Parmenides,
and begins directly addressing the religious inspiration of his writings.
Thus he "consciously declares himself a participant in twentieth century
Jewish philosophical tradition" (McCollester 1970: 344). Levinas now seeks
to go beyond Rosenzweig's concept of redemption, which he finds dependent on salvation, rather than justice. He also seems more determined to
resist Christian temptation, and makes no attempt to reconcile it with Judaism. To that effect, Buber's adamant refusal to negotiate provides a
model of consistency: there can be no dialogue with Christianity—the face
of the Other is only that of God. Levinas's theology of the encounter recu-
perates the theology of *I and Thou* (1922) by Martin Buber (Levinas 1967
and 1984). Both are efforts to substitute for the public light of the social
life the private response to the revealed, yet hidden, face of divinity—the
God of the Protestant (immanent) reading. For both, the real apocalypse
is interpretive rather than divine—the revelation of the concealed according to the principle of secrecy: "The sources, the roots, of being lie, in fact,
in that which is hidden and not in that which is revealed: *Deus est Deus
absconditus* (God is a hidden God)" (Shestov 1966: 434).

Franz Rosenzweig (1886–1929), who studied in Berlin under Hermann
Cohen and wrote the preface to his posthumous three-volume *Jewish Writings* (1924), felt that his teacher's Judaization (Cohen and Mendes-Flohr
1987: 5) of Kantianism at the turn of the century represented the most
important breakthrough in the Science of Judaism since its establishment—the end of its first, historicist phase. Thus, when he attended in
1929 the university conference on Kant in Davos, which culminated in the
famous debate between Heidegger and Ernst Cassirer, he rightly saw Cassirer, Cohen's legitimate inheritor, as the representative of the ossified
Marburg tradition, and Heidegger as the true heir to Cohen's later break
with idealism. Following his teacher's lead, Rosenzweig worked on a "hygiene of return" to Judaism for the alienated Jew of advanced modernity,
seeking to contribute to her spiritual health (in ways not entirely different
from Freud's). In his view, Odysseus has made it to Ithaca but is dissatis-

fied with his success. The remedy he proposes for the ills of successful assimilation is a "new thinking": the philosophy of dialogue where another type of discourse, *Sprechdenken* (speech-thought, thinking from language), replaces the monologic method of old thinking. Rosenzweig acknowledges that, although Hegel completed the (ancient) project of idealism "from Ionia to Jena," the "new thought" cannot transcend the project since it remains its counter-project: philosophy still speaks Greek (idealism). For this reason, instead of inventing a new language, he proposes an alternative way of speaking. "Thus, dialogue with the other person becomes a model for the relationship between man and God" (Kaufman 1976: 40). Like his other alienated contemporaries (Wittgenstein, Russell, Freud, Saussure, Heidegger, Schönberg), he is offering a verbal treatment, an entirely new grammar, as an alternative to the Greek language of thought. Emphasizing the temporality of discourse, he finds that thinking properly guided by language becomes "grammatical." Long before Derrida's Grammatology, he argues that interpretation, too, must become "grammatical" through a commentary (in *The Star of Redemption*) on the story of Creation developed in opposition to pagan cosmology.

Following the example of the late Cohen, Rosenzweig writes as a philosopher-become-theologian (in contrast to Heidegger's move from Catholic theology to Protestant philosophy). "Philosophy and theology depend on each other and together produce a new type of theological philosopher" (Löwith 1966: 55). The impasse of idealism produces a type of thinker strongly reminiscent of Hamann (to whose philosophy of language Rosenzweig was so indebted): "The philosopher must at the same time be a theologian in order to be capable of understanding eternal truth, both as it is in itself and as truth for us" (59). Trying to smuggle in Judaism, Rosenzweig "takes up theological concepts and reintroduces them into philosophy as ontological categories" (Levinas 1990: 190). Rosenzweig concentrates on revelation, his most important theological concept, as the vehicle of transcendence. Eternity is the present reality for the Jew: Judaism lies outside history and represents its eschatological goal. "He was deeply troubled by the fact that Christianity played a more significant role in history than Judaism. Therefore, he aimed to clearly differentiate Judaism from Christianity. Yet, at the same time, he wished to maintain that both Judaism and Christianity are facets of the truth, that both Judaism and Christianity have a significant role to play in *Heilsgeschichte*, in sacred history. And he felt that he could achieve this aim by maintaining that Christianity is the eternal way whereas Judaism represents eternal life. In other words, whereas the Jew has his being outside of history anticipating redemption, the Christian is forever on the way" (Kaufman 1976: 46). Like Cohen, Rosenzweig returns to *Jerusalem*, rather than the Second *Critique*, for moral guidance; like Cohen too, he seeks a compromise between the two religions. Their meeting ground is the encounter, which is a mutual responsibility: the I-Thou relationship is reciprocal. Here Rosenzweig appropriates Feuerbach's critique of Christianity in the name of human understanding in real life. Feuerbach located the essence of community in the I-Thou relation. According to Rosenzweig, a person becomes an individual when he receives a call from the other which has to be answered. The encounter is historical since *Sprachphilosophie* means lived speech, that is, time- and situation-specific. Its character, though, is eschatological: the dialogical present happens between an "already" and a "not yet." The former refers to the "already-being-always-in-existence" of the world; it also includes a "not yet." Because communication presupposes trust, the future is already present in it: "'Thou' is future" (313). For a consummated encounter, anticipation, readiness, and openness to the surprising character of the future are required by this religious existentialism. This is Rosenzweig's central topic of faith as experience which became Buber's concept of meeting. "The dialogical Thou is futural, a future that really approaches me" (315). One has to make oneself available to this call. Rosenzweig called his theory of truth the "theory of messianic knowledge."

During the second decade of the twentieth century, a loose alliance of thinkers who opposed transcendental philosophy emerged under the name of "dialogicalism." "Independent of each other, and of the other documents from the early period of dialogicalism, are Cohen's later work composed in the winter of 1917–18, Ebner's "pneumatological fragments," written in the winter of 1918–19, [Gabriel] Marcel's indications in *Journal métaphysique*, which, more or less, from July 1918 on turn on the dialogical principle, and finally, in essence, also *I and Thou* itself" (Theunissen 1984: 266). The structure of the movement itself was dialogical: "No less characteristic than the absence of any connection, however, is on the other side, the close alliance that, especially in the circle around Rosenzweig, made possible a συμφιλοσοφεῖν, the like of which has rarely occurred in the history of philosophy" (267). Describing their approach as "new thought," the philosophers of dialogue inherit Kierkegaard's critique of idealism and call their philosophy a linguistic or grammatical one. Thinking of language as conversation, however, they emphasize speech, since they see the meeting as a linguistic reality. Thus, when Derrida mentions the pneumatic-grammatical opposition, he is alluding to Ferdinand Ebner's *Das Wort und die geistigen Realitäten: Pneumatologische Fragmente* (1921) and *Schriften I. Fragmente, Aufsätze, Aphorismen: Zu einer Pneumatologie des Wortes* (1963) or Rosenzweig's "grammatical" exegesis as much as he is debating Paul's distinction between Spirit and Law. Those discussions sought a way out of Kantian ethics, with its emphasis on individual reason and consciousness, by socializing the subject—by positing conversation as primary and constitutive of the subject's identity: "I take the individual to be neither the starting point nor even the end point of the human world. But I take the human person to be the irremovable central location of the battle between the movement of the world away from God and its movement toward God" (Buber, quoted in Theunissen 1984: 285). Already in their work conversation acquires the character of conversion (Buber 1965: 13–14): both because the meeting, as a happening of the spirit, is usually epiphanic,[79] and especially because the individual experiences this meeting as a call. That is why the dialogists stress the command, the order: their Thou is rooted in the imperative; one has no choice but to respond. By attributing to contemplation the intensity of conversion and a categorical character, these theories prepare the conditions for the postmodern denunciation of emancipation. Contemplation, defined in terms of an epiphanic meeting, is already understood as the purest praxis.

Although Buber's earliest thoughts on the encounter probably go back to his Hasidic studies around 1905, he was first faced with the challenge of the Greek limits when he realized that "the thought about the 'dialogical principle' springs not from a metaphysical experience but from an 'experience of faith' and must, for this reason, first be translated into philosophical concepts" (269). The origins of the subject are found in the Scripture: "The biblical leaders are the foreshadowings of the dialogical man, of the man who commits his whole being to God's dialogue with the world, and who stands firm throughout this dialogue" (Buber 1948a: 131–32). Yet Greek translation requires a philosophical presentation of faith. Thus instead of using Abraham's trial as a model, Buber (who completed the first draft of I and Thou in 1919 under the title "Religion as Presence") abandons his early ecstatic mysticism and follows Ludwig Feuerbach's anthropology outlined in the Principles of the Philosophy of the Future (reedited in 1922), especially his emphasis on human community and the I-Thou interrelationship.[80] Buber accepts that the modern Jew is split between the secular world and his own tradition. As a hygiene of reconciliation, he offers the encounter with the Other and the overcoming of mediatedness—the meeting character of the between. The relation with man is a simile of the relation with God. "The Jewish myth is the I-Thou relationship in which the I is either God or 'a kingdom of priests and an holy nation' and the Thou, conversely, either this chosen people or God" (Bloom 1959: 4). Thus the goal of Buber's dialogicalism is a theology of the between. "As 'theology,' the philosophy of dialogue, like all great philosophy of religion since Kant, can only be the philosophy of the kingdom of God" (Theunissen 1984: 384). God is "the existent reality of the between" (383), its ground, possibility, and destination. Man does not possess God: in the encounter, man is addressed by God (who can only be encountered—neither inferred nor met). In I and Thou the action of the Other is experienced as "coming to me and not as going to me" (279). If God is (the) between, the Other is (the) coming to the meeting. "Here the Other is precisely the one who comes to me with his claim, while I have to correspond" (339). This is the *Messiasproblem* (F. von Hammerstein) in Buber's thought. "Consequently, the originality of the between in the concrete experience of meeting manifests itself as the precedence of being spoken to over speaking to" (339). In the meeting, where man encounters God, he is addressed and seized by the Messiah's coming. Dialogue for Buber is not Rosenzweig's "new thought" but new history—"the final, messianic overcoming of history" (Buber 1948a: 133) which rejects historical time.

Among the messianic thinkers, only Ernst Bloch (1885–1977) makes a consistent effort to connect the political with the Bible. In the three-volume *Hope the Principle* (1954–59)—"the odyssey of a mind from the spirit of exodus" (Habermas 1983a: 63)—he compares two attitudes to history: "It is surprising for how long a time the ultimate fear was neither thought nor dreamed about on the Jewish side. The Jews were as immanently oriented a people as the Greeks, but one whose life had an incomparably more vigorous direction toward the future, toward goals" (Bloch 1970: 93). What accounts for this difference is the Greek sense of politics as a practice in this world, history, and society. "The Greek dreams of things to come were almost always rooted firmly in this world. Life itself was to be improved in them, without any alien increment, in rational, albeit motley, fashion. The most remote islands of Greek wish-fulfillment were still located in a contiguous world, and so was their happiness. Happiness, along with its institutions, was immanently inserted into existing life and held up to that life as an example" (125). This holistic description may not be that original but, as it is meant to elucidate Messianism, it acquires special significance, since the political dimension of the ancient totality is not forgotten. "No social utopia was worked out in the Bible" (125), argues Bloch, because an exodus and a kingdom of a transcendental, transhistorical order was promised there. In the polis, the future is a matter of uncertain, unpredictable negotiation, while in the Bible it is the secured outcome of a trusted promise.

Bloch looks at Messianism from a different angle and compares the Hebraic and Hellenic attitudes toward the future in a short section called "Unavoidable and Avoidable Fate; or Cassandra and Isaiah." Here he finds that the Greek fate, *moira*, is inevitable: "doom rolls on even without guilt. It rolls mechanically, not caused but simply occasioned, and hence inexorable" (205). It is usually experienced as an overwhelming end. "*Moira* is the flat, disparate inevitability that brings not only the mind to a standstill but makes the blood freeze" (205). It constitutes the supreme order in the universe and nobody is exempt from its workings, not even the gods. "The very irony of the Greek fate shows how little depends here on the manner

or direction of *human* acts" (206). The blind belief and attitude of helpless
mortals is personified in Cassandra. Things are different in the Bible.
Cohen already praised monotheism for severing the link between (collective) guilt and suffering by making people, as individuals, responsible for
their acts. This possibility is attributed by Bloch (who wrote his doctoral
thesis under Cohen) to the "open space of messianism" (206) and its ethics. Not only is *moira* not ruling the world: "Fate is completely capable of
being changed, rather; Isaiah, above all, teaches that it depends on the
morality of men and on their *decisions*. This is the active antithesis to the
Greek seer, especially to the mere passive despair of Cassandra's vision: in
the Bible fate hangs in the balance, and the weight that finally decides is
man himself" (206). Biblical fate is not static or finite, it never decides in
the absence of man. "It is not categorical but hypothetical" (207), and its
potential actualization depends on human freedom and faith—the "belief
in a God of time" (207) and the space of independence and free will it
produces. The fate of the believer flows from his faith. There is a divine
commandment inserted there. "And yet this moral insert in the mode of
fate opened a *countermove of freedom* noticeably different from Cassandra,
from mere impotent foreknowledge, from what is called prophecy outside
the Bible" (207). Bloch is talking about the moral freedom blessed by faith
for which Shestov yearned. His Messianism, however, has a different aim in
that it seeks to justify the absence of a social utopia from a future-oriented
book like the Bible. According to Bloch, the reason that Biblical religion,
despite its message of individual freedom and responsibility, was never
concerned with a better world—while Greek thought, despite its pervasive
fatalism, explored (and experimented with) the idea—is that the messianic vision saw a God in time who redeems man from history. In Bloch's
picture, it is not so much the question of fate that matters as the difference between hope and utopia, Messianism and politics, transcendence
and contingency.

Bloch calls Marxism "the leap from the Kingdom of Necessity to that of
Freedom" (Bloch 1972: 69). With this religious conception, he returns the
sacrality of the secular scripture to its source: "So far as it is, in the end,
possible to read the Bible with the eyes of the Communist Manifesto" (69).
He takes this interpretive path resolutely by trying to go behind corrup-
tions in the transmission of the original text which distorted, trimmed,
compromised its subversive potential. "Which means finally, that biblical
criticism needs the broadening that will come from continually tracking
down the interestingly different, rebelliously different readings in the available text. For nothing could completely efface or conceal the way things
stood before the great redactions" (71). In order to discover the other,
suppressed text, he proposes a hermeneutics called "detective Bible criticism" (73). The task of this criticism will be "to identify and save the
Bible's choked and buried 'plebeian' element" (75). To achieve that, what

needs to be rejected is a Zeus- or Cronos-like deity, the "doctor of Israel";
and what needs to be saved is religion as a human utopia. "So the banner
should cry not 'Demythologize!'—without distinguishing Prometheus or
Baal from the 'Kerygma'—but *De-theocratize!*' Only that can do justice to
the Bible's still saveable text" (82). The text will be saved through a close,
intrinsic, deconstructive reading of margins and tensions, silences and differences, and not the demythologizing attacks of historicism. "With this
vision as sign-post, and therefore with a quite different sort of criticism—
criticism *through* the Bible—it is possible to see more acutely than ever
that there are in fact two Scriptures: a Scripture for the people and a Scripture against the people" (83). After the bankruptcy of the historicist approach, only a Biblical reading can save the Bible. The alternative understanding is a literalist one, which marks the textualization of resistance.

The question of translation again inhibits most theologians from doing
justice to eschatology: "It is simply that their systems are bound together
with Greek thought, which is being-oriented and anti-historical, instead of
with the historical thought of the Bible, with its Promise and its *Novum*—
with the *Futurum* as an open possibility for the definition of being, right up
to the point of Yahweh himself" (56). Still, even Bloch cannot purify his
own thought when he compares, for example, the idea of god in Aeschylus
and Isaiah (94), or non-conformists in the Bible with Prometheus (36). In
a section entitled "Patient Sufferer or Hebrew Prometheus?" Bloch portrays Job, the true rebel who turns against the status quo and invests hope
only in Exodus, as follows: "That is the Titan who challenges God, and who
needs no demi-god to be his champion (after the model of the Greek tragedy against Zeus), but who places himself fair and square in the fight and
takes his stand as a man against an enemy he believes to be almighty"
(117). Despite the drive toward an inherently Hebrew understanding, the
problem with Bloch's messianic politics is that its political, like the language of philosophy, remains stubbornly Hellenic.

Levinas's effort to combine Rosenzweig's philosophical criticism of ontology with Buber's theology of faith is in reality a compromising mediation
between the two. On the one hand, "Levinas can be interpreted as a descendant of post-Kantian German idealism. For thinkers of this tradition
religion becomes the arena for ethical activity and the proper field for its
expression" (Wyschogrod 1974: 160). On the other hand, he is writing after
Heidegger's declared hostility to neo-Kantianism which appropriated
dialogicalism for historical thinking. While thinkers like Moritz Lazarus
and Hermann Cohen "give expression to liberal and progressive tendencies, Levinas rejects an interpretation of prophetic futurism which makes
the political arena the sphere of its operation" (160). For him, it is not
enough to Hebraicize the Hellenic—Heidegger's major contribution to
philosophy—since even that cannot stop barbarism. This is because western civilization must be purged completely of the Hellenic (in this case, the

political), and if need be, even the cultural, so that its authentic Hebraic character can prevail. Derrida, who is more aware of the relation of the face-to-face with confession, breaks with this existentialist tradition, exposing the structures of personal faith as religious norms, and proposing the aesthetic disposition as the ethical response proper. Neither redemptive nor apocalyptic, the Hebraic finds in his work a new site, writing. And yet, through his predecessors' discussions and disagreements, through so many returns and revisions, from Bloch and Lukács to Gadamer and Lyotard, the issues debated by Rosenzweig and Buber regarding the visitations of divine justice have remained alive. Indeed, it is not an exaggeration to see their dialogue as setting the agenda (and the commensurate anti-Hellenic tone) for much of twentieth-century interpretive thought. "Ever since Martin Buber split off Kierkegaard's view of the existential from Kierkegaard's Christology, and dressed it up as a universal posture, there has been a dominant inclination to conceive of metaphysical content as bound to the so-called relation of I and Thou" (Adorno 1973a: 16). Whether it seeks an "ideal speech situation" (Habermas)[81] in a rational society or Celan's "Conversation in the Mountains" (to use the title of his 1959 essay); whether it examines humankind's "dialogical situation" (Niebuhr 1989) or, as in Gadamer's early writings, proposes a consensus based on conversation (Sullivan 1990);[82] whether it advocates a "dialogical pluralism" (Robert Wood) or "dialogism" (Handler 1990) as a model for social services in the welfare system; whether it relies on Peirce or on Augustine's notion of complete knowledge as a "face-to-face" encounter in Book 12 of the *Confessions* (400); whether it promotes a "conversation of mankind" (Michael Oakeshott) or a "cultural conversation" (Richard Rorty), dialogicalism has produced a strong research tradition in many disciplines and major antidotes to political theories of organization and change.

Still, the real history of the Buber-Rosenzweig dialogue and the ensuing debate is not its evolution over time but the political history that it has made possible: the historical possibility of Israel, the "date" of Israel with history, the reality of an Israeli state. Buber's Zionism, based on "Hebrew Humanism,"[83] envisioned the creation in Palestine of a dialogical state ("an event in mutuality")—a state of *Gemeinschaften*, of communities of dialogue. This spiritual understanding of Jewish nationhood has been expanded further: "The suffering of the just for a justice without triumph is lived as Judaism. Israel, historical and physical, becomes again the religious category" (Levinas 1979: 218). Justice is a shibboleth.[84] "(And I will add as well, in parentheses, that in its terrifying political ambiguity, *Shibboleth* could today name the State of Israel, the state of the State of Israel)" (Derrida 1986a: 338). The Zionist controversy informs all Hebraic discussions, even when their immediate subject happens to be translation, atonement, or Maurice Blanchot. The "question" for post-Kantians from Cohen to

Lyotard is the code of justice that would make Israel accountable only to ethics and not to history.[85] The Israeli state as the Other of the nations, the nation with a right to exist, represents "Israel's universal vocation which the state of Zion ought to serve only, to make possible a discourse addressed to all men in their human dignity, so as then to be able to answer for all men, our neighbors" (Levinas 1987c: 153). But what happens when the Book is circumcised by the Land? Can there be an encounter between law and politics? "The meaning of Israel has lost its unique quality and has been integrated into the historical process itself. Thus, for Levinas, the Hegelian view of cultures is the most formidable threat to the absolute values presented by the Jewish ethic" (Wyschogrod 1974: 161–62). The comparative discussion of cultures goes back to the time of Herder, when the autonomous (aesthetic) idea of the nation first emerged. Israel as "counterlife" (Philip Roth), however, as it was already clear to Herder or to English Israelites, is the *figura* of the nations,[86] the nation which did not go through a revolution—a normative model announcing collective identity as the basis for the universal.

Some critics (like Gershom Scholem) who still remembered the discursive invention of Hebraism, rejected the theory of mission: "It has been said that the very success of Zionism—meaning the dialectical success it manifests in its historical founding of a state—constitutes a betrayal of the mission of Judaism. But this theory of mission, 'to be a light unto the nations,' which over the last hundred and fifty years was accepted by a large part of Jewry, was invented ad hoc by a people who were aware of their historical impotence, that is, their lack of vital resolve to live as a people. It was invented as a kind of spiritual recompense, a lame justification for the existence of Judaism in the Diaspora. The mission theory is one of the most dialectical (in some ways praiseworthy, in some ways shameful) aspects of Jewish experience since the emancipation. Thus, Zionism may indeed be a betrayal of the mission of the Jews invented by German, French, and Italian Jewry a hundred and fifty years ago" (Cohen and Mendes-Flohr 1987: 507). Levinas, on the other hand, believes that in the contemporary world, Israel "is and must remain anachronistic in the sense that it represents a non-coincidence with its time. Judaism maintains the temporality of interiority against the time of history" (Wyschogrod 1974: 162). His eschatology draws directly from the terms of the covenant: "He presupposes the transhistorical unity of Jewish consciousness and the permanence and continuity of Israel" (171). There can be no concessions to historical or cultural exigencies. "This is Israel's apolitical vision of itself. A people whose history has until extremely recent times been lived in diaspora cannot accommodate its morality to politics" (189). The Law of the Land ought to be one, that this is the Land of the Law.

Thus when Levinas talks about return or separation, or Derrida about nostalgia for the land or deferral, they take positions reminiscent of the efforts of the Haskalah philosopher Nachman Krochmal (1785–1840) to elevate Israel above the contingencies of history, and they reenact the option of Palestine haunting the correspondence between Walter Benjamin and Gershom Scholem.[87] For high and late modernity, the call to task is issued from two supreme texts—the Book and (its) Israel. It can even be argued that they are two columns of the same text, and therefore Israel itself is treated like scripture—that, for the interpretive conscience which appropriated Arnold's culture for Hebraism, the state of Israel is the exemplary modernist work: independent, self-sustained, self-regulated, autonomous, exclusive. The homeland of the late twentieth century is the textual desert: "We are capable of living in a state in which certain things that have happened have not. At the same time that they have. This is The State of Israel" (Ronald Sukenick, quoted in McHale 1987: 99). From Buber to Blanchot and from Shestov to Deleuze, the nature of the aesthetic disposition (by definition alienated by the Hellenic Alien), exilic or nomadic (Petrosino and Rolland 1984), is negotiated in terms directly related to the identity of Israel.

The question of its (historical) constitution, however, has not been settled. Some, like Hannah Arendt, looked in vain for inspiration in Heidegger's notion of dwelling. Others have chosen to limit the problem to the ethnic group most directly affected: "Whether or not Jewish history will be able to endure this entry into the concrete realm without perishing in the crisis of the Messianic claim which has virtually been conjured up—that is the question which out of this great and dangerous past the Jew of this age poses to his present and to his future" (Scholem 1971b: 35–36). Derrida's response has been an invitation to preserve the relevance of the question: that constitution cannot be written because the question itself is already a text, if not the Book that has always been interpreted. "The Jew is split, and split first of all between the two dimensions of the letter: allegory and literality. His history would be but an empirical history among others if he established or nationalized himself within difference and literality" (Derrida 1978a: 75). By transforming the aesthetic into a messianism, Derrida has achieved what Nietzsche suggested: he has transformed history, "the antithesis of art" (Nietzsche 1983: 95), into a work of art. And yet the discursive and political genealogy of the issue is such that it never avoids the language it has tried to silence: when the question is raised whether Israel is a site or a land, and whether it would "like to be an Athens, and not a Sparta" (Avineri 1989: 114), not only does the Greek polis reappear but it also dates the date with the exacting urgency of its own ethics: (Hellenic) politics.

Like Freud or Adorno, Levinas, in his search for the authentic in the nonidentical, is exploring the possibility of a "Jewish science" (Levinas 1979: 217). Whatever the rigor of his anti-Parmenideanism, however, his effort fails because of its trenchant moralism: he is too preoccupied with playing Saul against his contemporary Paul, Simone Weil (1909–43), whose writings started appearing in the late 1940s.[88] The lesson of Hermann Cohen has been that, after historicism, a science of Judaism can only exist as a philosophical critique of the Hellenic, that is, as a Hebraicized culture. Since the polarity cannot be transcended, it must be appropriated. In this light, two anti-mythological traditions stand out. "Nietzsche recalls the Greeks. Left-wing Hegelianism (though it is rarely aware of this fact) recalls the Jews, and for this reason it challenges Jews far more intimately and radically" (Fackenheim 1970: 52). This lineage extends roughly from Feuerbach to Habermas. Its dialectical countercurrent, right-wing Kantianism from Kierkegaard to Levinas, has not been less influential. Deconstruction has sprung out of their cross-breeding, a combination of Kantian ethics with leftist politics, with Derrida portraying *and* playing Nietzsche as a left-wing Kantian. To the extent that he constantly interrogates dialectical tradition, Derrida may be seen as a non-Kantian (Rorty 1982: 93), his "textualism as the contemporary counterpart of idealism" (Rorty 1982a: 140), and deconstruction as "post-philosophical romanticism" (143). Nevertheless, his dominant ideological ancestry is that of philosophical Messianism: Cohen, Buber, Shestov, Bloch, Benjamin, Levinas, Fackenheim— the European idealists whose work concentrated on the moral viability of the Hebraic-Hellenic opposition. All these thinkers reacted to the critique of morality through the invocation of the Greeks by Nietzsche, who wrote in 1885: "Today we are again getting close to all those fundamental forms of world interpretation devised by the Greek spirit through Anaximander, Heraclitus, Parmenides, Empedocles, Democritus, and Anaxagoras—we are growing more Greek by the day; at first, as is only fair, in concepts and evaluations, as Hellenizing ghosts, as it were; but one day, let us hope, also in our bodies! Herein lies (and has always lain) my hope for the German character!" (Nietzsche 1967: 225–26). Some philosophers, like Rosenzweig, Bloch, and Heidegger, attempted a return to Schelling. Derrida's way of thwarting the threat of politics is to promote the aesthetic attitude as ethical condition, and interpretation as iconomachic resistance. Consequently, in his work the question turns into the messianic calling of contemplation.

The Future of Tradition

Derrida opens his essay "Violence and Metaphysics" by proposing a community of philosophers who ask endlessly the unavoidable and unanswerable question of the death of philosophy in remembrance of its own possibility and despite the diaspora of its people: "A community of the question about the possibility of the question" (Derrida 1978a: 80). He defends the idea of a "discipline of the question" (80)—a discipline which he later calls Grammatology—because the question has already begun, has a history, and must be maintained. "A founded dwelling, a realized tradition of the question remaining a question" (80). Maintaining the question means interrogating the discipline of the question (a practice which has been called deconstruction). Heidegger defined a comparable responsibility in the first sentence of his essay "The End of Philosophy and the Task of Thinking": "The title names the attempt at a reflection that persists in questioning" (Heidegger 1977: 373). He also complained that the herme-neutical process of questioning had lost its centrality: "The paralysis of all passion for questioning has long been with us. . . . Questioning as a funda-mental element of historical being has receded from us" (Heidegger 1959: 143). "The question is privileged everywhere by Heidegger as *the* mode of thinking" (Derrida 1987b: 171). The problem is that Heidegger saw the question as one of forgetfulness and recovery—as an errant and repentant return to the ontological foundation: "This question of beings as a whole, the theological question, cannot be asked without the question about be-ings as such, about the essence of Being in general. That is the question about the *on he on*, 'ontology.' Philosophy's questioning is always and in itself both onto-logical and theo-logical in the very broad sense. Philosophy is *Ontotheology*. The more originally it is both in one, the more truly it is philosophy" (Heidegger 1985: 51). Derrida knows that Heidegger's "philos-ophy of heteronomy" leads to sites where the Other may be the *Volk*, the Führer, or Being itself (Wolin 1990a). For Derrida, there is no question of return, revelation, or rediscovery because we are always part of thought's internal audit. "Thus, those who look into the possibility of philosophy, philosophy's life and death, are already engaged in, already overtaken by the dialogue of the question about itself and with itself; they always act in remembrance of philosophy" (Derrida 1978a: 80), committing themselves to "this total repetition" (81): "To a considerable degree, we have already said all we *meant to say*" (Derrida 1981: 65). This autistic entanglement is not the result of an approach to, but the very nature of the enterprise, which is tauto-logical. "Philosophy (in general) can only open itself to the question, within it and by it. It can only *let itself be questioned*" (131). Derrida would never name, let alone answer (as Heidegger did), the al-mighty question: his strategy is to invite readers to ask (the question) rather than question (the established, the already in place, practices of asking). There is no intent to write a history of that asking, of the discourse of the question, of its institutional askability. On the contrary, the goal is to safeguard the authority of that discourse by legitimizing the auto- of autonomy.

Like Heidegger, Derrida seems to accept "the possibility of what we might call an 'internal' audit of the history of philosophy, an assessment which confines itself to the field of its texts. Derrida, like Heidegger, will tell us about the relationship between Marx and Democritus before he will

mention capitalism" (Wood 1985: 38). There is no outside-the-philosoph-
ical-text, no outside-the-interpretive-tradition-of-philosophy, no-outside-
nomos; all activity takes place in the Library and the University, the temples of emancipation. "For both Derrida and Heidegger, the metaphysical
tradition is a massive, inescapable fact; but their responses to this shared
perception are revealingly different. Heidegger believes it both possible and
desirable to go behind this tradition by commemorating its withdrawn origins in traces left in 'early words concerning Being.' Derrida holds out no
such hope for circumvention and return; . . . One cannot get *around* a text
so as to locate its extratextual origin because in the very effort to do so one
meets yet another text; any *soi-disant* 'origin' is always already pre-
inscribed in a text. In short, there is only the re-inscription of one text in
another, the re-marking of one by the other—the tracery of intertextuality"
(Casey 1984: 608). Epistemologically speaking, the interpretive question of
Modernity was first (Spinoza) the question of Philosophy, then (Hegel)
Philosophy as the death of philosophy, later (Heidegger) the Fall of philosophy into metaphysics, and finally the sin (and task) of reading (dead Philosophy). These are the stages of the crisis of tradition and assimilation—of
History as the end of history (and its prophetic judgment), of the self-
governed and self-reflective individual. The question of Modernity has
been reduced to the aesthetic question: Athens + Jerusalem. Romanticism
connected the two words with an "is," Modernism with an "or"; Derrida
has suggested the ambiguous silence of a slash "/." The terms themselves,
however, remain unquestioned. Derrida conducts simultaneously a postmodernist critique of absolutist (or pagan) Modernism and of utopian
(Christian) eschatology which may be defined as messianic aesthetics. The
choice (or rather, invention) of an effective genre for this enterprise was
particularly difficult: philosophy, theology, or literature were clearly inappropriate for a para-Hellenic, deliriously parasitical Hebraism that was
going to declare the entire library a playground for rabbis. As in the case of
the ambiguous, ambivalent, ambidextrous slash (dis)connecting Athens
and Jerusalem, Derrida opted for a contradictory combination: interpretation as ersatz exegesis—contemplation of the ridiculous/sublime.

Nowhere else is this choice better exhibited than in his essay "Of an
Apocalyptic Tone Recently Adopted in Philosophy" (1982), aptly published in both the English poststructuralist literary journal *Oxford Literary
Review* and the American theological journal *Semeia*. The essay is a critique, parody, and reaffirmation of the messianic aesthetic. Its immediate
target is Kant's *Von einem neuerdings erhobenen Vornehmen Ton in der
Philosophie* (1796), where "he attacks a tone that announces something
like *the death of philosophy*" (Derrida 1982: 66). In his piece, Kant, always
concerned about the prestige of his discipline, has a specific group of
professionals in mind: "He brings to judgment those who, by the tone they

take and the air they give themselves when saying certain things, place philosophy in danger of death and tell philosophy or philosophers the imminence of their end" (67). He attacks the "mystagogues," those who indulge in "philosophic mystification" (68) and "never fail to take themselves for lords, . . . elite beings, distinguished subjects, superior and apart in society" (69). Derrida takes Kant to task for distinguishing between "the voice of reason and the voice of the oracle" (70): the former speaks unequivocally and prescribes the rules of cognition while the other is visionary, instinctive, seeking the transcendental. Kant opposes the "false mystery of the mystagogues" (73) to the "true mystery" of practical reason. He complains: "The overlordly tone dominates and is dominated by the oracular voice that covers over the voice of reason, rather parasitizes it, causes it to derail or become delirious" (71). But the weakness of this distinction is revealed when he divides Plato in two, a good and a bad one, in order to account for the course philosophy has followed. "Kant wants at once to accuse and excuse Plato for/of this continuous catastrophe that has corrupted philosophy, the strict relation between the name and the thing 'philosophy'. . . . He wants to accuse *and* excuse him for/of the delirium in philosophy, one would say, in the same movement of a double postulation. The *double bind* against filiation: Plato is the father of the delirium, of all exaltation in philosophy . . . , but without it having been his fault. . . . So we must divide Plato; we must distinguish between the Academician and the presumed author of the Letters, the teacher and the sender" (73–74).

It is true that there is "a constant motif in the German tradition from Hölderlin—or even indeed from Schiller—through to Heidegger, the theme of the two Greeces" (Lacoue-Labarthe 1990: 67). The motif of the "two-headed Greek," which has become equally popular in other traditions and disciplines as well, is but a version of the common theme of Greece and its other (Greece), Israel. If the anxious relation with the Ancient is "one of the general foundations of the modern political sphere, being quite simply the invention of the Modern itself, i.e., of what appears in the era of the delegitimation of Christian theocracies" (78), it is also true that the Modern, the new legitimate theocracy of immanence and depth, is always conceived as Hebraic. Thus whenever twentieth-century culture has failed (its Hebraic identity), it is the Hellenic model that is demonized. It therefore comes as no surprise when a discussion of the fate of the Jews in modernity, for example, resorts to standard comparisons, tracing the history of "Extermination" to the Athenian massacre of Melos (35) and the program of the Holocaust to the Funeral Oration of Pericles (97–98), or uses Hölderlin's poetics of Sophoclean drama to approach Auschwitz in terms of tragedy (41–46). Nevertheless, in the Western vocabulary, Philhellenism has no opposite: by repressing the term, modernity will never admit its constitutive anti-Hellenism.

Thus one can easily guess the rest of Derrida's argument against Kant's two Platos. Having exposed the inherent contradiction *and* mutuality in Kant's opposition, he deconstructs his plan, taking apart its foundation: "This cryptopolitics is also a cryptopoetics, a poetic perversion of philosophy" (Derrida 1982: 74). As a post-Nietzschean left-Kantian, Derrida will pursue the same inverted plan: the poetic perversion of philosophy. He will be both teacher and sender, he will practice both science and delirium, he will defend both reason and the oracle. When the history of philosophy is examined in terms of an (impotent) bind against filiation, "the practice of double reading that Heidegger produces as the way of overcoming metaphysics and aesthetics (aesthetics being the metaphysics of presence in art) is precisely deconstruction as practiced by Derrida. Deconstructive readings are double readings that record a text's compliance with the metaphysics of presence and its exceeding that metaphysics" (Bernstein 1987a: 95–96). Critique absolves itself of complicity.

Kant's complaint against the mystagogues of modernity is that they are not true philosophers but rather use poetic language and apocalyptic prediction to obscure their anti-philosophical tendencies. Derrida finds that this is "a fight around poetics (between poetry and philosophy), around the death or the future of philosophy" (Derrida 1982: 77). Kant offers to his opponents as a pact for peace the requirement for a basic distinction between the philosophical and the aesthetic manner of representing, which should not be confused. Still, this contract is one between discourses of the end which share one major element: eschatological predication. Derrida points out that "the West has been dominated by a powerful program that was also an untransgressible contract among discourses of the end. The themes of history's end and of philosophy's death represent only the most comprehensive, massive, and assembled forms of this" (80). Beyond all disagreements, there is one particular point of common reference: "Haven't all the differences taken the form of a going-one-better in eschatological eloquence, each newcomer, more lucid than the other, more vigilant and more prodigal too than the other, coming to add more to it?" (80). Derrida's complaint against trendy languages of apocalypse has been voiced before: "The end of humanism, of metaphysics, the death of man, the death of God (or death to God!)—these are apocalyptic ideas or slogans of intellectual high society. Like all the manifestations of Parisian taste (or Parisian disgusts), these topics impose themselves with the tyranny of the last word, but become available to anyone and cheapened" (Levinas 1987: 141).[89] After such expressions of intellectual indignation, the impression is given that readers may be encouraged to ask about the interests served by the aesthetic and the apocalyptic, both feared and criticized by Kant; that they may be instructed to look into the ideology supporting their alliance; that they may be guided to think in terms of authority, institutionality, knowledge, and historicity.

Derrida offers a list of basic questions for those who wish "to demystify, or if you prefer, to deconstruct the apocalyptic discourse itself and with it everything that speculates on vision, the imminence of the end, theophany, the parousia, the Last Judgment, and so on. Then each time we intractably ask ourselves: where do they want to come to, and to what ends, those who declare the end of this or that, of man or the subject, of consciousness, of history, of the West or of literature, and according to the latent news of progress itself, the idea of which never went so badly one way or the other, to the right or to the left? What effect do these noble, gentile prophets or eloquent visionaries want to produce? With a view to what immediate or postponed benefit? What do they do, what do we do in saying this? For whom do we seduce or subjugate, intimidate or cause to enjoy, to come?" (Derrida 1982: 82–83). Derrida seems willing to pose many similar questions throughout his paper about "all the interests of the apocalyptic tone today" (87) "or the ends to which the apocalyptic seduces" (90). But his response to these questions forgoes addressing the discursive and the institutional, and instead reaffirms the tautological and repetitious structure of thinking by asserting that "every language on the apocalypse is also apocalyptic and cannot be excluded from its object" (91). He presents the apocalyptic as "the structure of every scene of writing in general" and as "a transcendental condition of all discourse, of all experience itself, of every mark or every trace" (87). It seems that we have never left the site of the same. His conclusion shows that "deconstruction suffers not from a relativistic generosity but from an authoritarian exclusion of discursive possibilities. The charge of relativism misses the point. The problem is not that *différance* treats all discourses as if they were equal but that it treats them as if they were the same" (Boly 1988–89: 181–82). Inescapable and unavoidable, the apocalyptic joins the supplement, the trace, the pharmakon, the letter, the hymen, and so many other terms in Derrida's repertory of sublime/ridiculous violence. Not that it makes any difference: "In the final analysis, the dehellenizing of literary criticism is as futile as it is inevitable" (Atkins 1980: 779). The practice is inherently (and gleefully) impotent: "Deconstruction cannot, *on its own terms*, recognize historical differences between texts. *Différance* faithfully records the same violence within any work. . . . As a result, to the eyes of *différance* all texts begin to assume a tropic sameness" (Boly 1988–89: 198). If anything can be anything else, it might as well be apocalyptic too. But how about the demystification readers were promised earlier? "It is interminable, because no one can exhaust the overdeterminations of the apocalyptic stratagems" (Derrida 1982: 89).

After all, apocalyptic writing can be both very conservative and very useful in misleading censorship and dismantling the established order. Thus Derrida's conclusion is conveniently ambiguous: anything is potentially apocalyptic, and the apocalyptic is potentially good or bad.[90]

Deconstruction can put the question to philosophy but cannot, and never intended to, pose the question of philosophy, of its legitimacy. No form of contemplation can contemplate its own conditions, precisely because contemplation understands itself as the perfect condition. "If there is a question that philosophy, itself so questioning, manages to exclude, this is the question of its own socially necessary conditions. Resembling the artist in this respect, the philosopher sets himself up as an uncreated creator, a creator whom there is no getting around and who owes nothing to the institution. The distance from the institution (and, more precisely, from the socially instituted post) which the institution itself allows him, is one of the reasons why he finds it difficult to think of himself in the framework of an institution; and difficult to cease to be its instrument and its plaything, even in his institutionally directed games with the institution" (Bourdieu 1983: 4). With Derrida, philosophy exchanges its (lost) gravity with a dazzling display of style, ultimately protecting its (reputation for) agility at a time it can no longer defend its relevance. In a social system where the University is no longer actively political, deconstruction is "the purest manifestation, so far, of a postmodernist academy's desire to vindicate itself as radical and liberationist, yet also shield itself from the prospect of having any real cultural effect" (Boly 1988–89: 197). A case in point is Geoffrey Hartman, who enlists Derrida "in an essentially academic enterprise. Deconstruction, or at least that version of it practiced in a text like *Glas*, will breathe new life into a discipline whose ultimate social purpose is to ensure that books continue to be read and taught in institutions like Yale and by professors like Hartman" (Argyros and Flieger 1987: 68).

In order to shield itself from politics, culture denounced it as idolatry and claimed that its own critical function was superior. Postmodern formalism follows the same tactic: "A 'deconstructionist politics' which remains true to both deconstruction and to politics has to make a virtue of necessity—or, in philosophical jargon, to ontologise its own embarrassment. Deconstruction becomes itself a politics" (Howard 1989: 172). According to this position, contemplation is the highest form of emancipation. This is the reason why (as proved in all debates in which Derrida has been involved but did not initiate) "there is one sort of difference which deconstruction cannot tolerate: namely, difference as dispute, as good, old-fashioned, political fight" (Fraser 1984: 142). The very mode of the argument tends to forbid disagreement: "Derrida will always choose to differ, but he leaves no empty spaces for any others who would differ with him" (Handelman 1983: 125). Heidegger, in his Rectoral Address (1933), was probably the first to argue that "the philosophical is the rationale or the foundation of the political" (Lacoue-Labarthe 1982: 426). According to this idea, every political foundation is a priori philosophical: philosophy, the aesthetic recovery of Being in history, is the ground of politics. The message is not that, before we do philosophy we should do politics; it is rather that by doing philosophy we are already doing (a more fundamental form of) politics. Critique is in itself praxis. "The Heideggerian determination of philosophy or the philosophical means first of all (and these are terms I use only for convenience): the unconditional valorization or, if you will, overvalorization of the philosophical. . . . For that is undoubtedly, but I admit that the word must be put between quotes, Heidegger's most radical 'political' gesture" (429). It is this gesture that Derrida repeats with an even greater authority: to counter the totalitarian "aestheticization of politics," instead of politicizing art, as Benjamin proposed, he politicizes aesthetics, endorsing while parodying the project of the Enlightenment: assimilation (taking in one's hands the ends of consumption), rather than revolution (taking in one's hands the means of production), is the only liberation.

Banal and predictable as it may be, this conclusion serves the debunking of Christology well: it rejects apocalypse while respecting the apocalyptic (speaking its language). Since Derrida finds that the Apocalypse signifies "the end, theophany, the parousia, the Last Judgment" (Derrida 1982: 82), he attacks "these noble, gentile prophets or eloquent visionaries" (82), like John the Evangelist, who appropriated Judaism and reduced it to the theme of salvation, of the Christian end. His target in this case is the false prophets, the philosophers, who have thematized the apocalyptic, who announce an end and a judgment, ignoring God's original covenant. "It is possible to see deconstruction as being produced in a space where the prophets are not far away" (Derrida 1984: 119). More precisely, "deconstruction opens the space—the difference between signifier and signified—in which faith is possible" (Mackey 1983: 270). He claims that the tone signifies: "We are going to die, you and I, the others too, the goyim, the gentiles, and all the others, all those who do not share this secret with us, but they do not know it" (Derrida 1982: 84). But who are those others, besides the goyim and the gentile prophets, who are not named? And what is the apocalyptic that Derrida tries to salvage from apocalypse, from having its end being talked about? The fiercely anti-Christian tone of the paper suggests the "secret" is Messianism. Derrida questions Christianity's right to adopt it and transform its promise into one of ending, closure, and punishment. This may apply to the goyim prophets but not to the others. Like earlier post-Kantians, he compares prophetism and philosophy to reveal the superiority of the former's vision of the future, of the promise of the question, while repressing the politics of faith: "The proper bearing of thinking is not questioning but rather listening to the promise [*das Hören der Zusage*] of that which is to come into question" (Derrida 1987b: 175).

For the postmodernist Derrida, the apocalyptic tone is neither about ending (as in Christianity) nor about fulfilling (as in Hebraic Modernism): it is about coming. "'Come' is apocalyptic" (94). In *Totality and Infinity*, Levinas had already transformed Ernst Bloch's utopian Marxist "not yet" into "to-come" (*à venir*). "In Levinas as in Blanchot, the indefinite futurity of the *à venir* or 'yet to come' is correlative of the anteriority or 'always already' which haunts punctuality in repetition" (Libertson 1982: 37). Time is not history because history cannot happen while Being is coming: "Through time, in fact, being is not *yet*; which does not confuse it with nothingness [*néant*], but maintains it at a distance from itself. It is not in a single moment [*d'un seul coup*, all at once]. Even its cause, anterior to it, is yet to come" (Levinas, quoted in Libertson 1982: 37). Others can be even more direct and talk about the (male) Messiah, the overlord who commands: "His being there is, then, not the coming. With the Messiah, who is there, the call must always resound: 'Come, Come.' . . . Both future and past (it is said at least once that the Messiah has already come), his coming does not correspond to any presence at all" (Blanchot 1986: 142). In Derrida, Messianism is not about fulfillment (as the ideal of the perfect and autonomous artwork suggests) but its own process. "I shall come: the coming is always to come. . . . *I come* means: I am going to come, I am to-come in the imminence of an 'I am going to come,' 'I am in the process of coming,' 'I am on the point of going to come'" (Derrida 1982: 85). This coming, which represents and reenacts the originary version of the apocalyptic, is pure affirmation, beyond the grasp of cognition or the expectation of sense; it comes from the other and invites us beyond being; it is not supported by language or identity, a voice or a sight; it is not a present or a future but the promise-as-process of (and invitation to) a future.[91] "This *Viens* [come] is a call prior to all other discourse and to all events, to every order and to all desire, an apocalypse which brings nothing to an end, which reveals nothing" (Derrida 1988b: 81). This is the order that addressed Abraham.

"Come," in a constant state of being/coming, stands above history, language and society: Messianism is not an advent. "'Come' no more lets itself be stopped and examined by an onto-theo-eschatology than by a logic of the event, however new they may be and whatever politics they announce" (Derrida 1982: 93). It is the (be)coming of art, art beyond the canon, culture without politics—the pure aesthetic and not the artwork as an entity, a structure, a monad. "Come" is the postmodernist aesthetic of openness, open-endedness, undecidability—the messianic promise of a transcendental beauty that is about itself without ever being, stopping, descending, appearing; the promise and condition of artisticality, which is different (from Greek art), which differs politics and defers history. "Come" announces an announcing and sends, dispatches for Abraham: "Now here, precisely, is announced—as promise or threat—an apocalypse without apocalypse, an apocalypse without vision, without truth, without revelation, *of dispatches* (for the 'come' is plural in itself, in oneself), of addresses without message and without destination, without sender or decidable addressee, without last judgment, without any other eschatology than the tone of the 'Come' itself, its very difference, an apocalypse beyond good and evil" (94). "Come" announces the triumph of Hebraic Messianism against everything that Christianity read into it—apocalypse, vision, truth, revelation, parousia, destination, last judgment, eschatology, good and evil. While Zionism, as a modernist movement, proposed the State of Israel as the absolute artwork,[92] Derrida defends Messianism as the purest expression of art itself: Israel as a state of coming.[93]

Derrida may also play the Messiah on occasion, on a date, defiantly and unapologetically: "Several times I have been asked . . . why (with a view to what, to what ends, and so on) I have or have *taken on* an apocalyptic tone and proposed apocalyptic themes. Thus have they often been qualified, sometimes with suspicion, and above all, I have noticed, in the United States where one is always more sensitive to phenomena of prophetism, messianism, eschatology, and of the apocalypse-here-now" (90). He is especially addressing America, the promised land of Protestant dissent which, as Arnold noted, tends so much to Hebraicize.[94] "We can't understand the reception that deconstruction has had in the United States without background—historical, political, religious, and so forth. I would say religious above all" (Derrida 1985: 2). Amplifying his emphasis on religion, he notes that "the protestant, theological ethic which marks the American academic world acted all the more 'responsibly,' basically taking deconstruction more seriously than was possible in Europe. Or rather in Europe, paradoxically, the dismantling of the religious element was already further along" (12). In a distinct sense, Higher Criticism has yet to happen in America, since for a long time criticism has operated here as higher faith.

Despite Heidegger's horror of its culture of technology, the American response to the call has always been more intense, more attuned to passive listening, more prone to commentary: "From Emerson and Thoreau to Mencken and Brooks, criticism had been the great American lay philosophy, the intellectual conscience and intellectual carryall. . . . Never more than incidentally concerned, save for men like Poe and James, with problems of craftsmanship and style, it had always been more a form of moral propaganda than a study of esthetic problems" (Kazin 1965: 400–401). This religious culture was secularized drastically after 1930, however, when criticism "became a search for fulfillment by the word, a messianic drive toward social action" (401) and a search for cultural solutions to political problems. "Where the first 'modern' critics in America had been crusaders against Puritanism and materialism, latter-day Victorians, as it were, seeking to find a place for literature in America, the more aggressive critical minds in America now became religious crusaders, as of a world to be saved or lost" (401–402). For those who did not join Marxism, religious practice became exclusively a matter of interpretive activity.

The case of the American formalists is particularly pertinent: "To them literature became not merely a great moral and intellectual activity; it became the only activity. They reduced all human discourse to literature, all literature to poetry, all poetry to the kind of poetry they cared to write and study, and like Talmudists reduced all critical discourse to the brilliant technical exegesis of a particular text" (402). New Critics were fully aware of the ancestry of literary scholarship in scriptural exegesis. They remembered that in the nineteenth century, poetry "was rediscovered as a cultural force and was recruited in the cause of religion. In the now well-known formula, poetry was more and more to take the place of both religion and philosophy" (Wimsatt 1954: 275). New Critics felt that, following in the footsteps of the same interpretive tradition, the quasi-religious mode of justification in literary criticism "has in recent years, with the aid of psychological, anthropological, mythological, and ritual idioms, made considerable advances. The defense of religion is nowadays frequently couched in terms which appeal to the power of poetry, and the defense of poetic imagination, in terms which implicate a defense of religion. Despite the discriminatory efforts of some writers . . . the vocabulary and main assumptions of recent criticism have been developing in a way that makes it now difficult to speak well of poetry without participating in a joint defense of poetry and religion, or at least without a considerable involvement in theology" (276–77). Thus they initiated, and remained open to, a dialogue between the complementary disciplines of reading and faith with the aim of strengthening both their common heritage and their shared values: "There is a broad sense in which Christian thinking ought to be sympathetic to recent literary criticism—a sense arising simply from the fact that recent criticism is criticism; that is, an activity aimed at understanding a kind of value, and a kind which, if not identical with moral and religious values, is very close to these and may even be thought of as a likely ally" (267).

This "new 'seriousness' in criticism" (Kazin 1965: 403) was expressed in institutional terms in the professionalization of literary studies and its identification with humanistic instruction: "Defending itself against those who challenged its validity as a form of knowledge, criticism now significantly proclaimed itself a central moral activity, a beacon in an age of confusions" (405). It was in the academic department, the journal, and the

conference that the administration of the technologies of interpretation
were transferred. "And it was in criticism . . . that the radicalization of the
intellectual middle class made itself most deeply felt" (407). That radicalization was the gradual identification (glorified by masters of Hebraic
thinking like Susan Sontag, Philippe Sollers, Robert Wilson, and Leonard
Bernstein) of the aesthetic attitude with political activism.

If we see the formalist critic, with his exclusive devotion to the text, as
"a kind of Sadducee" and his emphasis on the autonomy of the poem as
"an example of the Written Law superseding and displacing the Oral Law"
(Fisch 1977: 66), then we can understand why Derrida plays the part of the
Pharisee. Some people have been surprised by the success of his performance in the United States. "But America is a theological and philosophical conception of itself, a concept with much Puritanism but little ethnic
mythology at the root, which is to say, oddly, with less politics at the root.
For a long time, Jewish assimilation in America was frequently a process of
somehow becoming more Jewish by assimilating to Puritan Hebraism and
its Election theology" (Bloom 1982: 325). It is the importance of assimilation for his entire work that enables him, the self-conscious outsider, to
address *himself*, to announce *himself* to his audience with the keyword of
the paper on the apocalypse: Come, he tells them, and by announcing it, by
inviting you, I am increasing my seductive power (94); come to me, the end
is near, I am your future; come to me because I am the one who is coming,
I am coming in you, I am your text—meet me, read me, give me a hand,
help me come. This may be seen as an act of "aestho-autogamy" (Flann
O'Brien), of "auto-hetero-affection" (John Llewelyn) reminiscent of outra-
geous heavy metal gigs meant to whip to frenzy their adolescent audience;
or as a performance of typical "Derri-Dadaism," which has been compared
to safe sex (Lawrence Kritzman). The pleasures involved in either are, of
course, only promised and endlessly deferred. "In its final phase as metanoia, *différance* sticks it in the ear, but in such a way that the signifier 'it,'
innocent depersonalization of all writing, mystically yet recuperatively dissolves. The final distribution is nonmembranous and itself impenetrable,
anti-hymeneal, in that it dismisses the intricate anatomies that register
vibration as noise and, potentially, as language" (Boly 1988–89: 190–91).[95]
Still, with these few orgasmic sentences, Derrida, the gay rabbi (as opposed
to the High Priest) of culture, performs the greatest role of his career: he
plays Messiah, the "Other," on Levinas's stage of the Sinai, and issues the
command, trying to seize his audience.[96] "If the irony of revisionism can be
compared (as Harold Bloom has compared it) to Milton's Satan copulating
with his own offspring, Sin, to produce the horrible giant, Death, then
Derrida's Nietzschean or Joycean deconstructive project—the irony of
irony as it were—can be likened to a simulated coitus interruptus, after
repeated artificial stimulation of an eccentric kind" (O'Hara 1983: 119).

Simulated, theoretical sex (*pace* critiques of voyeurism) is clearly the safest of its kind.

One plays Messiah when most positions of mastery have been discredited. Together with Jakobson, Russell, and Sartre, Adorno (who was publicly embarrassed when protesting female students bared their breasts in front of him) was probably the last teacher who, by virtue of the glorious canon he owned and offered, could afford to play convincingly the Master in academic (and intellectual in general) initiation sites. The collapse of the western canon has rendered this mastery impossible. "The ideology of the Western world, whether sounded forth within or beyond the universities, depends upon a literary culture, which explains why teachers of literature, more than those of history or philosophy or politics, have become the secular clergy or clerisy of the West" (Bloom 1985: 111). Auerbach and Curtius had every reason to worry about the declining moral authority and social status of that canon, and made a final, grandiose effort to redefine and defend it. In postmodern consumer culture, with no respect for the exercises of *Bildung*, the Great Books have no eminent value. "There is a profound falling-away from what I would call 'text-centeredness' or even 'text-obsessiveness' among the current generation of American undergraduates, Gentile and Jewish alike" (Bloom 1982: 319). The autonomy of the scriptural text is void. This situation has the formalist critics, the virtuosi of interpretation, worried: "In the posthistoricist market of genial productions, moreover, pedagogy itself becomes a topic of advanced study. How do we develop and defend reading, which used to be linked to a select, canonical body of works? Now reading must begin in a relative vacuum, with very few shared texts, or in a plenum, where no book can act for long as the intellectual's bible, as a classic with the freshness of a reborn ancient tongue" (Hartman 1985a: 12). Among the specialists of discrimination there has been justifiable cause for alarm: "It sometimes appears as if we have become a remnant" (12). Some have proposed the creation of elite schools of higher education whose sole purpose would be to prepare expert readers as guardians of western civilization and its endangered aesthetic principles (Steiner, Rieff). Avoiding such an aristocratic option, Derrida chooses to begin in a plenum. His philosophy, like Auerbach's view of the western tradition, insists that there are no other books, no other worlds, no other gods: it is destined for autocracy. However, even though his choices are consistently (if not increasingly) canonical, he canonizes not a set of books (like Auerbach) but a particular act of reading: "I will not say it is a metaphysics, metaphysics itself or its closure which is hiding in this 'textualisation' of discursive practices. I'll go much further than that: I shall say that what can be seen here so visibly is a historically well-determined little pedagogy. A pedagogy which teaches the pupil that there is nothing outside the text, but that in it, in its gaps, its blanks and its silences, there reigns the reserve of the origin; that it is therefore unnecessary to search elsewhere, but that here, not in the words, certainly, but in the words under erasure, in their *grid*, the 'sense of being' is said. A pedagogy which gives conversely to the master's voice the limitless sovereignty which allows it to restate the text indefinitely" (Foucault 1979c: 27).[97] Until Heidegger's "call to conscience" and Levinas's "command," philosophers used to invoke/ quote a supreme order coming from above—a spirit descending upon interpretation. Derrida issues such an order himself.[98]

"Come" is an aesthetic and Messianic notion: it is about coming to interpretation and the coming of the Messiah, which is for Derrida the encounter of secular exegesis with writing. The already written (that is, canonic) text, the Scripture, is the coming of the Messiah, which has always happened. This is why interpretation is (its) repetition. "The Torah is already present; there is no freedom anterior to its imposition" (Wyschogrod 1974: 192). Interpretation is itself emancipation; when one is able to interpret, there is nothing (else) from which to seek emancipation. This notion enables him finally to answer the question of philosophy posed at the beginning of "Violence and Metaphysics," to name the difference (between Athens and Jerusalem): it is the "*double bind* of YHWH affording (with the name of his choice, with his name, we could say, Babel) *translation and no translation*" (Derrida 1982: 64), the fundamental tension making the Septuagint possible and unacceptable. "Such is the question: the alliance of speech and Being in the unique word, in the finally proper name. And such is the question inscribed in the simulated affirmation of *différance*" (Derrida 1982a: 27). For Derrida, Being is not a name of God: "He suggests that God as positive infinity might be 'the other name of Being.' Not one word of Being among others . . . nor one eventual determination of the simplicity of Being. . . . But Being and God, twin non-concepts, proving to be the same name!" (Bernasconi 1987: 131). The question of philosophy, the ultimate "question [is] finally that of the proper name" (Derrida 1989a: 838), the Divine Name of Rosenzweig's *The Star of Redemption*—a name like YHWH or *différance* that cannot be pronounced.[99] "And the proper name of God (given by God) is divided enough in the tongue, already, to signify also, confusedly, 'confusion.' And the war that he declares has first raged within his name: divided, bifid, ambivalent, polysemic: God deconstructing" (Derrida 1985: 170). This is the war within discourse which earlier was deceptively attributed to its Greek metaphysics. "Before the deconstruction of Babel, the great Semitic family was establishing its empire, which it wanted universal, and its tongue, which it also attempts to impose on the universe. The moment of this project immediately precedes the deconstruction of the tower" (167). Deconstruction reenacts God's punishing wrath against the arrogance of the universal (be it what Shestov calls rationality or Levinas calls ontology).

If YHWH is the name of the difference (between the Bible and the Septuagint), then "the question of deconstruction is also through and through *the* question of translation" (Derrida 1988a: 1) and of the legitimacy of the New (Testament) versus (its) always already (Old). The difference of the two languages was important to those who attempted to purify the Bible of Luther's German: "The word of Greek antiquity is detached and formally perfected. It is removed from the block of actual spokenness, sculpted with the artful chisel of thought, rhetoric, and poetry—removed to the realm of form. . . . The purity of the Hebrew Bible's word resides not in form but in originality (*Ursprünglichkeit*). Whenever it was subjected to a consciously artistic adaptation it was polluted. Its full biblical force is present in the biblical word only when it has retained the immediacy of spokenness" (Buber 1968a: 214). The dialogical tradition from Ebner to Levinas is intimately familiar with the encounter commemorated by the Septuagint: "Because the word of Greek antiquity is worked over and hammered into shape—because it is a product—it tends to be monological. The atmosphere of the solitary, sculpting spirit still encompasses it on the platform. . . . In the Bible, when an idea is expressed, the speaker regards the listener with concern. . . . Untransfigured and unsubdued, the biblical word preserves the dialogical character of living reality" (215). These discussions culminate in an attack against (the *parousia* in) John's Greek: "The Greek logos *is*; it possesses eternal being (Heraclitus). . . . In the beginning of the Bible's account of creation there *is* no word; it comes to be, it is spoken. . . . The Greeks teach the word, the Jews report it" (215). Derrida's entire work is about the unreadability of the name—a critique of any translation from Hebrew (Torah) into Greek (*nomos*), which necessarily has produced philosophy and metaphysics, and a simultaneous reminder that the original (text of God's voice/face) is irrevocable. This trait alone makes him a (counter)Protestant thinker, one who attempts to reform the Reformation, to restore it to its original purpose. "There is a very real sense in which reformation can be defined as a summons to a fuller, more concrete translation of Christ's teachings both into daily speech and daily life" (Steiner 1975: 245). If Paul stole the letter from the Jews, Derrida snatches the vowels out of the name of the Christian God.

There is no transcendence, of course. The condition of theoria, of atoning culture, is inaugurated by this bitter realization. The fall into language, into names other than YHWH, is the fall into (Greek) translations (of the same name). Nevertheless, together with the fall comes the promise: "Translation, as holy growth of languages, announces the messianic end" (Derrida 1985: 202) which will deliver texts into the proper name. Twentieth-century philosophers concerned with various renderings of the Bible have been driven by the same hope: "Benjamin envisions a progressive and redemptive communion of all languages through translation, an activity that should help them anticipate the ultimate messianic revelation of the lost original tongue (whose kernel remains hidden in discrete languages in the course of human history)" (Rand 1990: 447). Derrida is no exception: "I believe the histories or enigmas of translation I would like to speak about are without solution or conclusion" (Derrida 1982: 63), he admits at the beginning of the paper on the apocalypse. And yet philosophy must speak about its limits, the limits of Greek (translation). The specific work Derrida has in mind is André Chouraqui's translation of the New Testament, an attempt which consists "in reconstituting a new Hebrew original, under the Greek text at our disposal, and in *acting as if* he were translating that *phantom* original text about which he supposes, linguistically and culturally, that it had already had to let itself be translated (if that can be said in a largely metaphorical sense) in the so-called original Greek version" (95). This parasitical work is about the Hebraic *Ur*-original and its Hellenic translatability; here priority is reclaimed and authenticity reenacted.[100] In a major modernist precedent, when Buber and Rosenzweig re-translated the Hebrew Bible into German (*Die Schrift*, 1925–61, 15 vols.), they tried to purify their native language from Luther's grammar of belief and make it speak Hebrew (again). That gesture had a distinct corrective purpose which can hardly be compared to the postmodern colonialist enterprise of denying the New Testament its own (written) language, because this denial assumes that Greek must be superseded at any cost.

Although Buber and Rosenzweig were originally asked by the publisher to revise Luther's translation, they soon declared the task impossible, and decided "to begin anew from the original Hebrew in the hope of freeing German from its Christian overlay" (Jay 1976: 9). Their new objective was the "Hebraization of German" (Greenstein 1983: 28), an effort to translate Jewish faith and its idea of the voice of God. That is why they returned to the literal mode of rendering first introduced, in his own Bible translation, by Moses Mendelssohn, "who wanted to provide German Jews with a Bible in fluent, idiomatic German, to launch them into the stream of secular culture" (20). Thus, in terms of cultural identity, their project was the reverse of his. A more fruitful comparison should be made with Hölderlin's Sophoclean translations. By returning to principles derived from Herder's philosophy of language, they also hoped to undo the Hellenization of German allegedly achieved in the poet's corrective approach to ancient poetry. (Benjamin, who, according to Gershom Scholem, was not satisfied with the Buber-Rosenzweig work, wrote his own 1923 essay on Hölderlin's Sophocles and Pindar, "The Task of the Translator.") Like Chouraqui, and like the translation of "The Five Scrolls" from Hebrew by Meschonnic (1970), they sought a "language prior to language" (Rosenzweig). Their essays, collected in *Die Schrift und ihre Verdeutschung* (1936), show that they saw translation as a restorative and "messianic act" (Rosenzweig). Their work was intended for Gentiles: the strategy was to Hebraicize German by aestheticizing it. Thus they tried to make the text more poetic, taking the Bible (on the basis of Rosenzweig's *Sprachdenken* as well as his attack on the translation of Greek drama by the philologist Wilamowitz) as the spoken word of God, and therefore as remnant of some *Ursprache*. According to this view, the Scripture is the monument of the ultimate I-Thou encounter. The authors were unable to accept that they were re-translating Luther, that they were repeating the Mendelssohn-Kant encounter. When Gershom Scholem celebrated the completion of the task, he raised again the question of strategy: "For whom is this translation now intended and whom will it influence?" (Scholem 1971: 318). The original endeavor of their *Kultur* politics was to feign not just the culture but language itself. As a Hebraic re-writing of the Re-formation, it would signal the triumph of assimilation—the appropriation (rather than just imitation) of German. To the utter desperation of those who believed in it, the result turned out to be "the tombstone of a relationship that was extinguished in unspeakable horror" (318). Soon after the publication of the first volume, *Das Buch im Anfang* (1925, a translation of the Pentateuch), it appeared that the only person who could read it was Heidegger in his crusade for the Christianization of the Greeks. The comparison with Heidegger's Presocratics (Horwitz 1964: 402–3) is important since "what Hebrew is for Rosenzweig is more or less what Greek is for Heidegger" (Greenstein 1983: 39). Many years later, the poetry of Paul Celan would still try in vain to wrestle the project of translation from the philosopher's Pauline grip.

The plundering of tradition obviously will not stop (why should it? which command would make it?) before the founding Christian document. Derrida declares that "what is at stake could be named as the *appropriation* of the apocalypse: that is also the theme of this exposition" (Derrida 1982: 95). He finds it a highly appropriate choice, because it is a direct response to a "Come." He quotes Chouraqui to the effect that his translation "has the *calling* [my emphasis] to search under the Greek text for its historic context and its Semitic substratum" (95). But that is the command of every "Come," a call for metanoia and conversion: renounce the Greek text as a translation, atone for worshiping its idols,[101] research the Semitic substratum,[102] recover the Bible, and return to its (lost) land. "Come" is Heidegger calling a gathering, a synagogue (which Cohen distinguished from the church) of readers into the House of the Book: it is always an invitation to an aesthetic reading of the Scripture, and of anything as Scripture. It is not Ithaca inviting Odysseus back home; it is God's unconditional demand for discipline and sacrifice. "Come" is the postmodern command issued by Derrida's ubiquitous face—the order to return to the feast of the tablets. People can no longer be trusted with self-government. Both *Bildung* and the canon have lost their disciplinary authority. Pure autonomy does not hold. For the first time, the faltering aesthetic sovereignty needs to be preserved by outside means. Hence readers are commanded to come.

Should the audience obey this order? Do they have a right, a choice not to? Levinas would deprive them of any opportunity. As he complains: "Autonomy or heteronomy? The choice of Western philosophy has most often been on the side of freedom and the same" (Levinas 1987: 48). Therefore the ideal of emancipation must be abandoned. His corrective decrees that the response is already determined by the question. "Responsibility is always prior to the realm of choice which is therefore a secondary phenomenon" (Wyschogrod 1974: 158). If for Heidegger passivity is preservation of the work (that is, authentic reading), for Levinas it acquires the centrality of a supreme imperative: "It marks the place where something is prescribed to me, that is, where I am obligated before any freedom" (Lyotard and Thébaud 1985: 37). Levinas calls freedom into question (De Boer 1985: 212), putting justice before it. Ethics requires submission: "All morality is grounded in a heteronomous will. To know God is already obedience to another" (Wyschogrod 1974: 165). Levinas attempts "to save human freedom, while maintaining that human action depends upon the recognition of heteronomy" (165) by claiming that an involvement with alterity can be the most independent individual decision. This claim relies on Shestov's celebration of blind faith as freedom from the chains of rationality.[103] First of all, subjectivity itself is made possible by the opening to heteronomy, the dissymmetrical relation with the other. "In the differential economy, subjectivity is produced and invested by the passivity of communication" (Libertson 1982: 309). Above anything else, the relation with the other communicates hierarchy. It is the passive response to the "dissymmetry" of communication with the other that individuates into the ethics of vulnerability: "The passivity of the vulnerable one is the condition (or uncondition) by which a being shows itself to be a creature" (Levinas 1987b: 147). The subject is a vulnerable, passive hostage under accusation, a hostage of the other. As Levinas adds in a related footnote: "Subjectivity *signifies* by a passivity more passive than all passivity, more passive than matter, by its vulnerability, its sensibility, by its nudity more nude than nudity, . . . by the accusative of the oneself without a nominative form, by exposedness to the traumatism of gratuitous accusation, by expiation for the other" (147).

Levinas drives his vocabulary of punishment, of "being at the question before any interrogation" (Levinas 1981: 49), into a relentless grammar of torture that argues the guilt of K. From command, passivity, exposedness, and vulnerability to denuding, accusative, submission, subjection, and traumatism, the reader is threatened and victimized into virtue with a solemnity of purpose typical of the Grand Inquisitor. The promise is the same—servility as redemption: "Transcendence is ethics, and subjectivity . . . is, as a responsibility for another, a subjection to the other. The I is a passivity more passive still than any passivity because it is from the first in the accusative—oneself [soi]—and never was in the nominative; it is under the accusation of the other, even though it be faultless. It is a hostage for the other, obeying a command before having heard it, faithful to a commitment that it never made, to a past that has never been present" (Levinas 1987c: 165). If the face is "demand" and "authority," the relation with the other is one of rape, of "one-penetrated-by-the-other" (Levinas 1981: 49).[104] In this relation, the Other (who is always male, the Man) becomes "the Overlord, indeed the Persecutor, he who overwhelms, encumbers, undoes me, he who puts me in his debt no less than he attacks me by making me answer for his crimes, by charging me with measureless responsibility" (Blanchot 1986: 19) and eternal guilt. As Kierkegaard proclaimed, man exists as guilt, he only stands accused. Hegel's Master is transformed into divine Highness.[105] "*Autrui* is governed by nothing. *Autrui* is the Governor. He is Master and Teacher. As is Emmanuel Levinas vis-à-vis his reader" (Llewelyn 1988: 275). According to this view, the "responsible passivity" of Kafka's K. is indeed the model of human virtue. Since passivity is a "task," K. responds and never resists: he doubts, he agonizes, he questions, but never resists; he acts with "disarmed responsibility" (Lacoue-Labarthe)—he remains passive. This is the logic of submission: "The value of human life lies not in happiness but rather in suffering" (Cohen 1972: 263). Levinas's vulnerability and Adorno's melancholy converge in this resigned acceptance of suffering which marks one side of the exhaustion of emancipation. Derrida has taken care of the other.

Levinas presupposes, on the one hand, the faith of Kierkegaard's Abraham for his submissive ethical conduct; and on the other, Auerbach's reading of the Bible's tyrannical and autocratic claim to truth which seeks to subject its audience. With Kierkegaard's library and Auerbach's interpretation no longer in place, Derrida has to look elsewhere for a technology of submission and a rhetoric of command—one that dictates without demanding. The modernist Levinas relied on the primacy of the autonomous text: "To receive the Torah is to carry it out even before it is freely accepted" (Wyschogrod 1974: 192). The postmodernist Derrida poses the political supremacy of contemplation. To do that, he draws again on Levinas, who had defended the importance of the Law on two counts: first, to refute Buber's mystical communion of Hasidism, by "asserting the integrity of legal Judaism against the romantic exponents of Hasidism as the appropriate wellspring of authentic Jewish experience" (167); and second, to discredit Christianity as a soteriological community based on sacrament while valorizing Judaism as an ethical community based on formal law and ritual. "God is made real, not through incarnation, but, rather, through the Law" (Levinas 1979: 219). Better than anything else, this maxim commands Derrida's critical mission. With his distaste for "positive" religions, Levinas found in the observance of ritual law a useful discipline toward virtue, although he mainly followed Rosenzweig's advice to give priority to "commandments" over "law." What Levinas borrowed from Rosenzweig and proposed in 1959 is "the substitution of legislation for the totalizing thought of philosophers and industrial society" (Levinas 1990: 200). The law becomes a superior freedom. "Consequently, Judaism—in which the Revelation is . . . inseparable from the commandment—does not in any way signify the yoke of the Law, but signifies precisely love. . . . It therefore transpires that the eminent role of the *Mitzvah* in Judaism signifies not a moral formalism, but the living presence of divine love that is eternally renewed. And consequently, through the commandment, it signifies the experience of an eternal present. The whole of Jewish Law is commanded *today* even though Mount Sinai belongs to the past" (191). Pursuing this direction further in a last-minute effort to salvage the project of autonomy, Derrida returns to major decisions taken during the Spinozist revival of the 1770s, which influenced the formation of middle-class high culture, and revived the importance of the Law.

In all his numerous disquisitions on the suppression of writing by orality, in all his studies of *écriture* from Plato to Lévi-Strauss, in all his deconstructions of *pneuma* and *parousia*, there is one discussion that Derrida will not analyze, will avoid, will esoterically allude to while suppressing, perhaps because it is exactly the cardinal discussion in which his own readings truly participate: the debates on the relation between Oral and Written Law, the Torah (Pentateuch). This is the Enlightenment question for those Israelites (Jews and others) who were challenged to become part of it by participating in the "civilizing process" (Elias 1978) and joining the bourgeois regime of aesthetic culture—the question of interpretation and assimilation. It is the Haskalah problem for Heyne, Lessing, Mendelssohn, Hamann, and their generation: Is it advisable to accept the universal religion of reason while preserving the authority of the law? Is it possible to govern by faith alone? In a more narrow version, the question concerns the proper place in civil society of halakhah—the system of legal (ritual and civil) rulings in rabbinic literature which constitutes, together with aggadah, the sacred tradition of the Oral Law. This is also known as the problem of revelation and tradition, of the relationship between the divinely revealed written Law and the religious tradition which has transmitted it. According to the dialectic of the Enlightenment, Judaism is the universal model (Cohen's *Vernunftreligion*) which already exists but has not been acknowledged, while Hellenism is the one that has disappeared and needs to be recovered and superseded through imitation. Nobody in modernity preaches the recovery of the Hebraic model: people know it is always there but feel it has been often neglected or misunderstood, and therefore it needs to become reedited and reaffirmed; thus if the Hebraic is the intrinsic other, the Hellenic, though no longer part of this world, is the constitutive alien of modernity, its outside point of reference and comparison against which the originality and achievement of that modernity are measured.

Law was first systematically separated from faith by Mendelssohn, who declared that, although the Law, as the determining principle of Judaism, is revealed, the truth of faith is the same as the truth of reason, and therefore does not depend on revelation. Laws were revealed to Israel by God as Jews were given divine legislation—commandments, regulations, prescriptions. "Mendelssohn put to the moderns a view that Spinoza had borrowed from Maimonides: the most ancient monotheism is not a revealed religion, but a revealed Law. Its truth is universal like reason; its rule and moral institutions, Judaism's particular support, preserve this truth from corruption" (Levinas 1990: 274). Mendelssohn was not concerned with demonstrating the superiority but the singular right of Judaism, which he ascribes to elements specific to its tradition. He moved Judaism from the realm of religion into that of *Kultur* by restricting its essence to Law. The particular practices of Judaism should be respected, since they belong to culture—the practical rather than the speculative sphere. Jewish faith is universal, Jewish practice particular. "Judaism conceived as law is by definition a way of life" (Rotenstreich 1968: 28), another culture, not philosophy. Revelation discloses the Law, not the existence of God. To cultivate and perfect awareness of the latter is the responsibility of Enlightenment. "It is thus evident that Mendelssohn was influenced by the teachings of deism, the English counterpart of the Enlightenment, in resenting the intrusion of metaphysical principles into the constitutive meaning of those axioms asserted by faith, in transferring the seat of religion to the sphere of ethics, and in testing religion not by the truths it proclaims but by its utility and social benefits, by its ethical consequences in the regulation of practical affairs and in the perceptible realm of legislation" (29). Religion becomes a question of performance of positive commandments, not of faith. Mendelssohn favors Judaism as a system of religious obligations over Athanasian Christianity as a doctrine. The new egalitarian dogma of cultural difference, more than anything else, made it possible for the Others of capitalism, the people excluded from civil society, to decide to join modernity and seek emancipation through assimilation by becoming the People of the Book. The Book (of interpretation) emerges when the Law disappears (into culture)—when the rule of law governs reading rather than action or logic.

Moritz Lazarus (1824–1903), in his posthumous *The Ethics of Judaism* (1911), socialized Kant's categorical imperative, making it a regulation of social life: Jewish ethics is a social ethics regulating relations among men as well as public affairs. At the same time, in an effort to reconcile the autonomous nature of objective ethics with the heteronomous structure of Jewish ethics—a problem which Levinas later tried to solve with the idea of passivity—he proposed that, for Judaism, religion and ethics are identical. Taking the philosophy of Lazarus as his starting point, Hermann Cohen argued that, as a commandment, the law raises man to the ethical level because it guides him through discipline and obedience. Kant's objective imperative becomes a religious one but it is still ethical because it is an imperative of pure reason addressed to the person of cultivation. The law is both the commandment and the duty to obey it. The religious imperative is a consequence of the correlation between man and God.

It is in the context of an attack on incarnation, and specifically the sacraments, that Cohen turns his attention to custom and law: "The celebration of the eucharist presupposes as a vital element an assumption about the nature of the trinitarian Deity, while obedience to ceremonial laws never implies anything beyond the limits of human action: God teaches moral behaviour by symbolic reminders" (Liebeschütz 1968: 30). In considering the institutions of Jewry, he shows more understanding for ritual, and abandons the denunciation of law which he inherited from the Enlightenment through Kant's ethics. Furthermore, he establishes the superiority of the Law through a comparison with the laws defied by Antigone: "The Greeks distinguished the 'unwritten laws' from the written ones. . . . Even the positive laws require for their more profound verification conformity with the unwritten laws. . . . These unwritten laws contained the morality of the Greek national spirit before it was formulated and motivated by the philosophers. . . . What the Greeks called the unwritten law, the Jews called written teaching. They wanted to disregard in it the connection with reason, asserted elsewhere, because their vision, their interest, was pointed to the future, which they intended to keep connected with the past. Therefore they fix the past as written teaching, in order to strengthen oral teaching as teaching. The Greek from the very outset addresses his criticism to the present, for which he has to lay a foundation in the past. The Jew, however, does not want to deepen the present through criticism, but rather through establishing its connection with the eternal, with written law" (Cohen 1972: 83). If Mendelssohn moved the law away from religion and into culture, and Lazarus turned it into a social regulation, Cohen, revising Hegel's reading of Sophocles, places it at the heart of individual ethical conduct.

As his three-volume *Jewish Writings* (1924) shows, the founder of the Neo-Kantian "Marburg School" who taught "critical Idealism" at the University for forty years was always interested in Judaism (supporting as early as 1867, for example, Heinrich Heine's Jewish Pantheism against Goethe's Hellenic one). However, his systematic concentration on Jewish problems, which he branded "return"—after he had already been identified with another philosophical turn, the "return to Kant"—started materializing in the early 1880s, after he fell out of academic favor because his thought seemed outdated. For a while he tried to negotiate with Protestant historicism, to which he had always objected, and stressed the importance of prophetic Messianism—but it was too late. Like the author who strove in vain to be accepted as a saint of art, he felt betrayed by the Hellenic covenant of the aesthetic. "Cohen had started his life's work with the belief in the vocation of the German people to win over the world for the realisation of humanitarian idealism. He never abandoned this trust in a better future. But in the practice of his working day he transferred more and more of his hope and his belief to the messianic faith of the Jewish people. . . . It remained, however, his intention to convince his German environment that the living Jewish tradition still offered an essential contribution to the continuity and growth of civilisation" (Liebeschütz 1968: 20). Cohen's Jewish return came after the decline of Hegelian historicism, which had sent the Science of Judaism into documentary research and marginality. Thus during the 1910s, when Buber, Bloch, Benjamin, Rosenzweig, Lukács, Shestov, and other disaffected writers emerged and many calls for a reorientation of the Science toward theology were heard, Cohen's ethico-theology had already paved the way for such a move.

It is ironic that he spent his last years teaching at the Berlin Academy for the Advancement of the Science of Judaism, and that he left his strongest mark on the reevaluation of a Science he used to ignore. Cohen was the writer who established a close connection between religion and reason, elevating the former from its lower status (subsumed under ethics) in his earlier work. His *Ethics of Pure Will* (1904), for example, argued that faith and reason are compatible and mutually enhancing because religion, although a sphere separate from reason, flows from reason and takes part in it. Among religions, Judaism, as the religion of universal ethics, occupies a special position because it is the religion of reason par excellence. "In the same way in which the Greeks must be considered the creators of a scientific philosophy shared by all mankind, the Jewish people created the religion of reason" (Altmann 1956: 198). In Judaism, every man is Jesus, and in general every man, through his own moral exertion, can attain the level of Jesus. Revelation is also compatible with reason, since God's revelation is addressed to man's reason and man's reason is a creation of God's revelation. Thus the latter, as a rational relation, discloses reason. Finally, it was during his Jewish period, too, that Cohen, influenced by dialectical theology, introduced the concept of correlation. Defining the problem of ethics as one of correlation (not union), of correlating the individual with society, he discovered man as a "fellow-man." While Christianity seeks the way to salvation in history, Judaism is not concerned with history because it is already an eternal life. At the same time, the idea that the concept of Judaism cannot be derived from history strengthened Cohen's belief in Judaism's social, even socialist, mission in preparation for the messianic future.

Nietzsche's senior by two years, Cohen was the last intellectual for whom assimilation was possible and desirable. Driven by fervent German patriotism, he was never sympathetic to Zionism or any nationalist understanding of Judaism: for him, the Jew is at home wherever he has reason to feel at home because he has successfully assimilated. He always argued the close affinity of Jewish tradition (as a *Kulturreligion*) with German culture, and of liberal Judaism with Protestantism, which he saw as a progressive force. Cohen's Messianism was oriented toward the higher Jewish task, the mission for which Israel has been chosen. In his essay "Religious Postulates" (1907), Cohen laments the aversion of intellectuals, and especially philosophers, to religion. "This attitude, by now almost predominant in our circles, also constitutes the greatest threat and danger to our existence" (Cohen 1971: 44). In opposition to the spiritual poverty of his time, he offers a hierarchy of three basic principles affirming traditional values: God, state, and culture. For Cohen, both state and culture are religious duties. "Love of our country is a necessary corollary of the idea of the Messianic God" (49), and in their turn, as he states elsewhere, all cultural questions are determined by the state (164). Regarding the latter, he preaches harmonious co-existence. "For this reason a distinction must be made between nation and nationality. The modern state requires a uniform nation but by no means a uniform nationality" (48). Jews, therefore, may preserve their national distinctiveness while belonging organically to the nation-state. "It is the duty of any Jew to help bring about the Messianic age by involving himself in the national life of his country" (49). This is the liberal position on assimilation, the one that trusts the citizens' self-governing consciousness of the law to protect the system of interpretive rites.

Against increasingly attractive Zionist aspirations, the philosopher believes that the Messianic message of prophetism points the way to cosmopolitanism and socialism (71). For him, the preservation of religion-as-nationality is sufficient for the protection of Jewish identity. In his reply to Martin Buber's open letter, "An Argument against Zionism" (1916), he emphasizes the unique privilege and universal mission: "We are proudly aware of the fact that we continue to live as divine dew among the nations; we wish to remain among them and be a creative force for them." And later: "Messianic hope alone guarantees our 'reality,' our authentic existence" (168). Not a sectarian and proudly isolated Judaism but "only a universal, mankind-oriented Judaism can preserve the Jewish religion" (169)—a faith he calls "religion of mankind" and "an entirely universal religion" (168). Until the Jews reach their Messianic future, their true home (170), they must work for both the preservation of their (religious) nationality and their "political integration into the modern national state" (169). Elsewhere he states his belief epigrammatically: "As religion demands man's whole, undivided heart, so does the state" (185). In this last respect, the intrinsic relation of Jews with Germany is especially important. Cohen refers to "that innermost accord existing between the German spirit and our Messianic religiosity. The German spirit is the spirit of classical humanism and true universalism" (169), he explains in a clear allusion to the Hellenic-Hebraic polarity. "Therefore it is only natural that we German Jews should feel at one with ourselves, as Jews and as Germans" (169).

This argument is further developed, in all its messianic intensity, in his two-part essay "The German and the Jewish Ethos" (1915, 1916). The essay opens appropriately with another restatement of the Hebraic-Hellenic motif: "With the advent of the Reformation, modern man began to realize that human insights can lead to two different kinds of certitude: that of the exact sciences and that of faith" (176). The author proceeds to review the project of Jewish philosophy that was launched in the ninth century, advanced by Maimonides in the twelfth, and may be reaching maturity with Idealism, especially Kantian ethics. Cohen sees a clear and promising "connection between cultural idealism and the Bible or Judaism" (177). Rejecting the French Enlightenment, he insists on the affinity and alliance bringing Germanism and Judaism together. "For the German idea of mankind has its origin in the Messianism of Israel's prophets, whose spirit doubtlessly affected German humanism profoundly" (180). Cohen proclaims in exaltation this spiritual bond when he confesses that "we derive a sense of the closest religious communion from the accord existing between Jewish Messianism and German humanism. Our feeling for Germany and its people has therefore religious overtones, so to speak, and is marked by a sense of religious affirmation. In perfect equanimity and harmony of soul, we feel as secure in our German patriotism as in our Jewish religion, whose root and crown are the One God of one mankind" (187–88). In this context and for the sake of the German state, science and faith, humanistic idealism and Biblical religion, will merge and blend; and because of the Messianic roots and the Protestant character of that state, they both have an equally important role to play. "Prophetic idealism is therefore not inferior in degree or extent to the idealism with which philosophy views all being" (184). Its contribution, Cohen implies, will be to facilitate that fusion of culture and ethics that will bring about the era of the universal monotheism. "We know that we as German Jews share in a central cultural force destined to unite all nations in the spirit of a Messianic mankind" (183). Jews are an integral part of the German cultural destiny, which is preparatory of a universal monotheism—this is his vision of the future. "The kindred spirit linking Germanism and Judaism is thus focused on the most distant point of the world's historical horizon" (184). Instead of turning their attention to the creation of their own state, Jews should "make the preservation of our religion a religious and cultural mandate of the German state" (186). Cohen is not advocating a national, ethnic state but a global regimen governed by the principles of Judaism. Like Arnold, he realizes that the modern world, threatened by anarchy and skepticism, can achieve this only by culture, and consequently declares that "it is incumbent upon the cultural forces of the world and their leading spirit, Germany, to promulgate the idea of Israelite monotheism" (186). By mobilizing such Hellenic forces as philosophy, Platonism, ethics, knowledge, science, and art, he hopes to help establish the universal state of Messianic religion.

Because he still adhered to the law of the bourgeois state, the liberal law of individual emancipation, Cohen remained a believer in universal messianism, even though around him the old order had collapsed. He trusted the middle-class consensus and its institutions to govern the conduct of people where the disappearance of a shared discourse of obligations and the challenges to the distribution of rights made it increasingly difficult for capital to defend its moral equanimity. However, the bankruptcy of Enlightenment administration, the decline of the *Bildungsideal*, and the failure of the Spirit to be realized made the abandonment of universalism by the younger generation unavoidable. The appearance of racial anti-Semitism sealed the fate of assimilationist idealism. At the same time, while the project of modernization was considered dead, the dream of modernity lived on. In fact the Hebraic utopian vision acquired a special urgency, learning to speak the tongues of anti-rationalism, mystical intellectualism, and radical secular Messianism. The historicism of the Science of Judaism was rejected as assimilationist and complacent. The great lesson that thinkers learned from Cohen's radicalization of the enterprise was that its principles must be presented as directly derived from within the Judaic tradition, rather than from humanism. "The Messianic stance rejects religiosity, the rational and secular Judaism of the middle classes, and the personal Judaism of 'renewal' represented by Martin Buber. Messianism demands a complete repudiation of the world as it is, placing its hope in a future whose realization can only be brought about by the destruction of the older order. Apocalyptic, catastrophic, utopian and pessimistic, Messianism captured a generation" (Rabinbach 1985: 81) of intellectuals disaffected with idealism, historicism, cultivation, but above all, politics. It is the notion of (high) Culture that becomes most important for the generation of "romantic anti-capitalism" which reacts with revulsion against the taste of the masses—consumer culture. Thus critique, under the influence of writers like Simmel, evolves into cultural criticism, and politics into intellectual, and eventually aesthetic, politics. In his esoteric function, the intellectual pursues redemption through contemplation as she envisions a post-political world. The more art withdraws into its exclusive laws, the more impor-

tant its regime appears as a model of self-regulation. This is no surprise in
the context of art's economic history. "Indeed one might risk the rather
exaggerated formulation that aesthetics is born at the moment of art's effective demise as a political force, flourishes on the corpse of its social
relevance" (Eagleton 1990: 368). The principles of the law and the foundations of government will now be sought in the distinctive features of the
artwork itself—in a professionally sanctioned canon of hermeneutically ap-
proved and sealed masterpieces.

As part of this modernist concentration on the formal structure of identity, the *langue* of difference, an exclusive Hebraism, "a Jewishness without
Judaism" (Rabinbach 1985: 82), makes its appearance in marked contrast
to the Enlightenment emancipation of Judaism without Jewishness. Furthermore, in opposition to Hellenic myth (which is blamed for all mass
deception, from consumer culture to politics) the messianism of a purified
language, of an unmediated, Pentecostal code, promises deliverance from
history. "The interest in Judaism now shifts from the ethical to the ontological; that is, it is apprehended as a reality with qualities and relations of
its own, which develop in accordance with a unifying principle. In other
words, Judaism is beginning to be looked upon as a metaphysical, and not
primarily as an ethical system" (Rotenstreich 1968: 105) at the turn of the
twentieth century. Where Mendelssohn developed claims about the valid
particularity of Judaism and Krochmal argued the special Jewish access to
universal reason, now a self-sufficient ground was sought in works like
Baeck's *The Essence of Judaism* (1905). For writers from Rosenzweig to
Levinas, ethnic identity became ontologically primary: "Judaism is no
longer just a teaching whose theses can be true or false; *Jewish existence*
(and I write existence as one word) *itself is an essential event of being;
Jewish existence is a category of being*" (Levinas 1990: 183). Judaism was no
longer simply shielded from history, as was the case with Cohen's messianism: "Instead of hoping for an evolution towards full emancipation, they
wished to escape from history itself and restore the unique place of the Jews
as an eternal people in touch with higher truths" (Jay 1976: 6). The appeal
was made for return (often contrasted to the Odyssean one) to an essential
and personal Judaism, not a communal tradition of customs and rules. The
Jewish Question was now that of being truly, authentically Jewish: Jewishness was elevated to a cultural idea, the ideal type of the bourgeois of culture, and Judaism became the new counter-politics, oppositional culture.
With Cohen, the grandiose project of Enlightenment came to a belated
close: assimilation through interpretation was complete and successful, but
suddenly its masters discovered that they had to fight its greatest enemy,
the dimension they thought the disciplines of paideia had transcended:
politics. At this crucial moment, assimilation was faced with three options:
nationalist (Zionism), theological (Buber/Rosenzweig), and cultural. Al-

most all the masters of Modernism took the last one. Leon Trotsky (1879–1940), Antonio Gramsci (1891–1937) and Bertolt Brecht (1898–1956) were among the few who could work with alternatives other than aesthetic.

For Rosenzweig, who pursued a different alternative, the encounter at Sinai was initially a revelation—the model of dialogic speech, not the giving of law. Later, however, the student of Cohen recognized the importance of halakhah, and disagreed with Buber's rejection of the authority of the law. The law must be personally experienced as a commandment and observed as practice. Where Buber understood this more in the context of community life and ritual, Rosenzweig believed that individual Jews must feel that they are commanded. His ethics of personal response takes care of a major problem for the hygiene of return: the return of the other's call. Since the authority of self-control (as well as that of the external law, the law of Hegel's state) has declined, what can mandate and guarantee control? The general attitude that had pervaded a very wide spectrum of positions was that the collapse of liberal consensus, bourgeois idealism, and the *Bildung* model signaled a significant weakening of aesthetic discipline. The humanistic regime of autonomy, devised in late eighteenth-century Germany, was undergoing a major crisis. The theoros, the soloist of critique, could no longer be left alone, undisturbed, to contemplate if he did not survey. If not managed, people ought to be supervised. Since heteronomy could not be brought back, autonomy would have to be administered through the invocation (though not imposition, at least not yet) of some outside authority. A new grammar of authority, a new code of sovereignty was necessary. Progressives sought it in radical modernism, the glorification of the (art)work itself. Conservatives, including many Marxists, sought it in moral injunction. Rosenzweig was among the latter. "The task of the Jew today, Rosenzweig argued, is to transform law into commandment" (Löwith 1966: 48). This idea was further developed by Levinas, who raised the command to an ontological category and individuating experience in order to secure its unconditional observance. In his thought, the categorical imperative is allowing oneself to be seized by a call which one obeys passively: law is translated into an absolute existential commandment. At the same time, this project of Hobbesian submission owes a great debt to Buber's transformation of the ethical concept of "correlation" (between man and God, and man and man), advanced in the late writings of Cohen (1972, chapter 8), into the ontological one of "relation." Buber's major concern, however, was the element of reciprocity in man's relation to God. Rosenzweig was philosophically (though not politically) committed to Jewish law, unlike Buber, whose phenomenology of life as a meeting was part of a larger effort to ground ethics socially.

The Zionist Buber was also the greatest opponent of Cohen's views on the identity and political future of Judaism. Where Cohen, in his perennial search for synthesis and transcendence, was always happy to devise common grounds and possibilities for unity, Buber took an uncompromisingly Hebraic position. In discussing the courage of moral heroism, for example, Cohen exclaims: "Here Jewish and Greek ethics touch and attest their kinship, which is based on their common relation to reason. Here one can recognize the common denominator of reason, which makes possible the analogy between Socrates and Plato, on the one hand, and the prophets, on the other. Here are the sources that unite Orient and Occident. . . . Upon this original soil of reason, the differences between polytheism and monotheism seem to disappear, as if they were of secondary importance in the face of the main alternative: sensuality or reason" (Cohen 1972: 437). Around the same time, when Buber, following Hölderlin's Orient (Greece)-Occident distinction, conceives "The Spirit of the Orient and Judaism," he chooses to stress the differences separating it from the Occident. In his conception, the Orient is (and has at last by the end of the eighteenth century begun to be seen as) a coherent totality. "The great complex of Oriental nations can be shown to be one entity, an organism whose members, no matter how functionally different, have a similar structure and a similar vitality; and, as such, the Orient holds a position in its own right vis-à-vis the Occident" (Buber 1967: 56–57). The two must be absolutely differentiated: "I would define the Oriental type of human being, recognizable in the documents of Asia's antiquity as well as in the Chinese or Indian or Jew of today, as a man of pronounced motor faculties, in contrast to the Occidental type, represented by, say, the Greek of the Periclean period, the Italian of the Trecento, or the contemporary German, whose sensory faculties are greater than his motor" (57). Buber rejects the racial distinctions which base their explanations on the natural sciences, and instead grounds his theory of history on psychology, or what he understands as the psychic identity of nations: "The basic psychic act of the motor-type man is centrifugal: an impulse emanates from his soul and becomes motion. The basic psychic act of the sensory-type man is centripetal: an impression is made on his soul and becomes an image. Both are perceiving, both acting, men; but the one perceives in motions, the other acts in images. The first, perceiving, has the experience of action; the second, acting, has the experience of shape. Both think; but the thinking of the first means doing, the thinking of the other, form" (58). While objecting to the racism of the positivists, Buber's is a liberal racism that draws more from philosophy than science. Thus he detects similar differences between the types in the area of comprehension. "The Occidental progresses, step by step, from the world's appearance to its truth . . . ; the Oriental carries this truth in the essence of his being, finding it in the world and giving it to the world" (60). The one proceeds by analysis, the other through identification. "To sensory man, guided by the most objective sense, sight, the world appears objectified. . . . To motor-type man, the world appears as limitless motion, flowing through him" (59). And more abstractly: "The Occidental's comprehension of his sensations originates in the world; the Oriental's comprehension of the world originates in his sensations" (59). Adorno would later elaborate on the objectification of the world effected by the senses of the Occidental man and on the ensuing positivism. Another line of the argument was later developed by Levinas. Buber argues: "In the sensory-type man, the senses are separated from each other and from the undifferentiated base of organic life; they are under the preponderant influence of the most detached, most independent, most objective among them: the sense of light. The triumph of the Greeks in the creative sphere of pure form and shape is the work of his hegemony" (58). This is the power and oppression to which Levinas refers in his critique of "Parmenidean metaphysics." Buber alludes to the alternative metaphysics of the hidden face through Cohen's favorite comparison of Plato to the prophets: "When Plato envisions something, there is nothing but the vision; the Jewish prophet envisions God only in order to hear His word" (59). Monotheism, having God on its side, wins.[106]

The last aspect from which Buber compares the two human types and categories is conduct. The Oriental type is driven by the "pathos of command" (61), which is revealed to be the "pathos of a divine command" (66), the desire to be commanded by a higher power. This command is experienced as a demand for a fulfilling life of duty. Through a comparison of Socrates to Buddha, Buber shows that the two types go their separate ways—the former after the contemplated idea and knowledge, the latter after the lived idea and authenticity. In reality, only the Oriental is concerned about the inner substance and destiny of man, and the transcendence of his fundamental conflict. "Being is in the state of duality: the duality of yea and nay . . . of good and evil . . . and of the real and illusory world. . . . Man is called upon to change being from duality to unity. The world is waiting for man, to be unified by him" (62). Unity for Buber, however, does not mean, as it did for his predecessors, some kind of reconciliation or combination between yea and nay, Hebraism and Hellenism.

Even the Oriental-Occidental distinction does not hold Buber's interest for too long. For after outlining it in the first part of his essay, he proceeds to narrow it down to more basic elements, arguing that the two categories are best represented by the Jewish and the Greek nations respectively. The broad characterizations made earlier fully apply to them. "All I have said about the Oriental is especially true of the Jew. He represents the human type with the most distinctly pronounced motor faculties" (64). Doing and acting, not knowledge, is important for him. "For the Greek, the concept is the end of a psychic process; for the Jew, it is the beginning" (64). By his decision and deed, the Jew unifies the world and brings it to fulfillment: his search for perfection brings him in contact with the divine. "From this point it can be seen that of all the Orientals the Jew is the most obvious antithesis of the Greek. The Greek wants to master the world, the Jew, to perfect it. For the Greek the world exists; for the Jew, it becomes. The Greek confronts it; the Jew is involved with it. The Greek apprehends it under the aspect of measure, the Jew as intent. For the Greek the deed is in the world, for the Jew the world is in the deed" (66). Buber sees as the greatest achievement of Judaism the divine command for decision and action in its absolute value. He believes that "through its new magic, the magic of decision, Judaism won the Occident for the teaching of the Orient. By means of this teaching Judaism became the representative of the Orient at its best" (68). This is more appreciated in the broader context of western spiritual poverty: "None of the great religious teachings originated in the Occident. The Occident received and spiritually reworked what the Orient had to offer" (68), and this pattern has lasted for centuries. What Europe lacks "is the pristine knowledge of the meaning of authentic life" (69) which Oriental theories cultivated. Judaism, in particular, the most influential spiritual system of the Orient, "whose proclamation of the way of authentic life challenged every individual directly," was "the Jewish teaching of decision and return" (69). Buber adopts Kierkegaard's notion of individuality in emphasizing that this egalitarian message turned every person into a sinner, responsible for (and guilty of) his deeds. The man called upon to decide and act is called to repent and return because he has failed and fallen.

An experience of duality and of demand for decision emanating from the divine command leads necessarily to conflict. "The Oriental people's spiritual life . . . tended to develop in the form of a struggle: the struggle of creative minds, of leaders and redeemers, against the aimlessness of the people's drives. This struggle was especially intense and fecund in ancient Judaism" (73). The idea of faith as struggle was later adopted by Shestov's existentialism, and aggressively expounded by Derrida into the cosmic concept of "violence." This idea worried Levinas, however; it also worried Buber, who could praise its energy as "Asiatic strength and Asiatic inwardness" (76) but feared its destructive potential after the Jewish progress toward emancipation in the nineteenth century. "We live in the uncertain state that followed these attempts: the last old structure of the Oriental spirit within Judaism appears to be shaken, with no foundation laid for a new one" (75). The specter of anarchy looms large in his understanding of the modern world; but his idea of anarchy is much more specific and has a geographical basis: "Our age will one day be designated as the era of the Asiatic crisis. The dominant nations of the Orient have surrendered partly to the external power of Europe, partly to its internally-overpowering influences. They have not preserved their most sacred possessions, their great spiritual traditions; at times they even relinquished them voluntarily. . . . The soul of Asia is being murdered, and is itself participating in this mur-

der" (77). Buber may be worried but has not lost his faith, especially in the
true Oriental identity of the Jew: "He has preserved within himself the
limitless motor faculties that are inherent in his nature, and their attendant
phenomena, a dominant sense of time and a capacity for quick conceptual-
ization" (76). As long as these natural qualities survive, all is not lost. He
confesses: "On this manifest or latent Orientalism, this base of the Jew's
soul that has endured underneath all influences, I build my faith in a new
spiritual-religious creation by Judaism" (76). This creation will save humanity from anarchy and dissolution. Buber outlines his project for renewal and reorientation as follows: "We need a searching of our souls, a
turning inward, a return. Europe must dare to promote a new era, in which
the Orient will be preserved and an understanding between East and West
established for their mutual benefit and for the humanitarian work they
must share. In this era, Asia will not be overpowered by Europe but will be
developed from within, by its own inner resources; and Europe will not be
threatened by Asia but will be led by it toward the great vital truths" (77–
78). What the world needs is an Asiatic self-examination of European consciousness; a mutual reconciliation; and a new relationship in which Asia
will develop from within and will guide the path of Europe. In these three
successive stages, the Orient, the spiritual leader, will replace Europe as the
dominant power. This Asiatization of Europe is Buber's version of the Judaization of the Occident. It was Judaism that first taught "decision and
return." Jews, with their Orientalism still intact, may help Europe in its
new role because they are a "mediating people that has acquired all the
wisdom and all the skills of the Occident without losing its original Oriental character, a people called to link Orient and Occident in fruitful reciprocity, just as it is perhaps called to fuse the spirit of the East and the
West in a new teaching" (78).[107]

Cohen's advocacy of a possible fruitful combination of humanism and
Messianism in German soil that would prepare the universal state of monotheism was for Buber an occidental illusion that overestimated Hellenic
philosophy and culture. He accepted the conciliatory idea of reciprocity
and fusion but in his view the superiority of Judaism should not only be the
aim (as in Cohen's earthly Kingdom of religion) but also the means toward
its accomplishment. That is why he was unwilling to make any concessions
to Europe: its Hellenic science and knowledge must be led by the new
teaching of return and redemption emanating from Jerusalem (78). The
unification of the Orient and the Occident was not a matter of kinship
between Greek and Jewish ethics, as Cohen thought, but something for the
self-reflexive spiritual inwardness of Judaism to achieve. For the Zionist
visionary, nothing European/Occidental/Hellenic—be it culture, humanism, philosophy, science, or sweetness and light—will effect the desirable
synthesis, but only the religiosity originating in Palestine, the land of actual

return. According to this Biblical literalism, the divine command for action was directing people to the site of the promise and the date of proximity. This separatist position, with its anti-European emphasis on race and culture, made him a major prophet of the essentialist critiques of Eurocentrism that emerged in the end of the second millennium. With hindsight, its crude good vs. bad polarities may sound a warning to delusions awaiting emancipatory appropriations of the Hebraic model of otherness in so far as the idea of the other, tribal or humanistic, can at best seek and breed assimilation.

The messianic ideology of Modernism is best encapsulated in a comparison of prophetism to secular history and the promises of delivery contained within each. The subject of Buber's essay "Plato and Isaiah" is the encounter of the philosopher and the prophet with history. In Plato's case, the philosopher tried to establish his ideal Republic in Syracuse but failed: "The spirit is in possession of truth; it offers truth to reality; truth becomes reality through the spirit. That is the fundamental basis of Plato's doctrine. But this doctrine was not carried out" (107). As a typical sensory-type, he trusted his understanding and brought its conclusions to the world. "Plato is the most sublime instance of that spirit which proceeds in its intercourse with reality from its own possession of truth" (106). His, however, was not the only failure of spirit in the face of historical necessity. There is also the case of Isaiah, who went to the people during the period of King Uzziah but whose message was scorned and rejected. He failed too; but there is a major difference: "He will not suffer disappointment like Plato, for in his case failure is an integral part of the way he must take" (108). What accounts for their attitudes is that Isaiah does not share Plato's belief in man's self-sufficient spirit and power. "Isaiah does not believe that spiritual man has the vocation to power. He knows himself to be a man of spirit and without power" (108). The two also differ in their self-understanding: "Plato believed that his soul was perfect. Isaiah did not. Isaiah regarded and acknowledged himself as unclean" (108). Plato tried to achieve his goal with a firm grasp of, and confidence in, his mind, his theory, and his right to do so. Isaiah's situation was the opposite: "He had no idea; he had only a message. He had no institution to establish; he had only to proclaim. His proclamation was in the nature of criticism and demands" (109). Thus differences extend beyond personal disposition to include the nature of the mission and its purported audience. The philosopher plans to create a new city while the prophet voices criticism and raises demands "directed toward making the people and their prince recognize the reality of the invisible sovereignty" (109). Isaiah's message is direct and personal, calling everyone and the nation as a whole to return to God. "So, the criticism and demands are directed toward every individual on whom other individuals depend, everyone who has a hand in shaping the destinies of others, and that means they are directed toward everyone of us. When Isaiah speaks of justice, he is not thinking of institutions but of you and me, because without you and me, the most glorious institution becomes a lie" (110). While the philosopher's project was political, the prophet's was "metapolitical" (110). These passages formulate a grammar of command instituting a regime of metapolitical (hence invisible) sovereignty.

Plato aspired to create a new Republic, and therefore thought in terms of a polis, in political terms. When he failed to achieve that, history's victory over his spirit was absolute, and his disappointment justifiable. Isaiah, however, experienced no disappointment because he had no political aspirations or chances. That is why he addressed the two fundamental unities of the state—the individual and the nation. Consequently, his failure was of another order—and it could be called one only in strict (that is, political) historical terms. Thus for Buber the two characters represent opposite types of spirit: the political, the uncertain, the risky, the profane vs. the metapolitical, the certain, the transcendental, the religious; one is addressed to the republic and its citizens, the other to the nation and its subjects; the former risks anarchy, the latter expresses the will of God. In this opposition, the Hellenic is not identified with culture but with politics. What is more, the author associates with the Hebraic metapolitical the two greatest artworks of the modern era, the individual and the nation. Heine had already called Abraham an artist because he fashioned the nation of Israel. Buber develops the analogy further, opposing the artistic/Hebraic to the political/Hellenic. Now the Greek is detested not for its culture, the idolatry of form, but for its politics, the attention to history. Buber invokes the vision of a metapolitical and suprahistorical order of time: "We may yet experience an era of history which refutes 'history'" (111). His ultimate Messianic dream is the transcendence of history through national continuity. The aesthetic politics of Jena is replaced by the prophetic metapolitics of Vienna.

As Buber closes his essay with a reaffirmation of the place, the Zionist "topos" (111), and the "misunderstood, misinterpreted, misused" voice of Isaiah, Messianism comes to rest at the national State proposed by Moses Hess. Prophetism—the transcendence of history, and not the search for a Republic—constitutes its politics, the commanded individuals its subjects, ethnicity its identity, and history its horror. Before becoming Professor of the Philosophy of Jewish Religion and Ethics at the University of Frankfurt (1924–33)—the position which paralysis prevented Rosenzweig from accepting in 1922—Buber had discovered in Hasidism an alternative Judaism, one where the law functions as custom and ritual, and therefore founds an authentic mode of life which expresses the identity of a collective. Buber had no great respect for the "vexatious Talmud" (to which Levinas later returned), considering it antithetical to life. He was interested in possibilities for encounter, not the rule of law, and saw the halakhah as enemy of openness. Preferring "inwardness without the law of God," he severed the relation of law and revelation.[108] Custom, on the other hand, is law spiritualized: it constitutes a vital, ethnic (as opposed to national) community.[109] His early discovery was later fulfilled in the prophetic politics of his Zionist conviction: "*Gemeinschaft* is a messianic category, and socialism acts in the direction of the messianic fulfillment; it is a messianic activity to which everybody is called" (Tillich 1959: 198). If Messianism after Cohen is the present dimension of the future, the dialogists, who sought a non-political praxis for life, found that dimension in the time of the meeting. Bloch took the same call for the messianic praxis in a different, utopian direction. In both cases, however, the metapolitics of prophetism required the transcendence of history and the denunciation of secular politics, namely, the life of the polis.

THE ART OF RULING

Among the three options with which autonomy was faced after the collapse of the Enlightenment project, the theological one—represented by Cohen, Rosenzweig, and the early Buber—was obviously the most conservative, the one most attached to a religion before reason (or after Kierkegaard). The Zionist option, adopted by the later Buber and Scholem, proved far more successful but never broke out, perhaps never tried to break out of its proud isolationism. As far as the West is concerned, it is the third option that has had the greatest impact on culture: the pessimism about full assimilation led to an optimism about assimilating others into Hebraism through interpretation whereby the promise of emancipation does not include the entire civic life but is limited to the cultural sphere. "In short the intellectualist mission of the Jews is the western alternative to Zionism" (Rabinbach 1985: 95). Judaism's mission, no longer moral, becomes intellectual. As Benjamin wrote to the author Ludwig Strauss in 1912: "I see three zionist forms of Jewishness (*Judentum*): Palestine Zionism (a natural necessity); German Zionism in its halfness, and cultural Zionism which sees Jewish values *everywhere* and works for them" (quoted in Rabinbach 1985: 96). His choice, and that of the majority, was to concentrate on "the creative culture-Jew" (99). Where earlier people aspired to live in a state of Israelitism, of pure heart and reason, of equal rights and tasks, now intellectuals desire the status of Jewishness (which, of course, hardly translates into more respect or freedom for actual Jews). They turn with apocalyptic fervor to various aesthetic pursuits, like language, art, mysticism, exoticism, or biologism. They discover that Messianism is violent and destructive but also redemptive and restorative. Before the war, the emphasis was more on the visionary and mystical. "The war gave political shape to the

idea of redeeming European culture and to the implication of language in
its crisis. After 1914 we see in Bloch and Benjamin's writings an attempt to
find a secular and theological philosophy which can embody the Messianic
impulse in relation to a *real* apocalypse, and to translate the promise of
European culture into the promise of political redemption" (104). After
the First World War, intellectuals and artists concentrated on the counter-
politics of revolution or cultural critique.

   This was the time, for example, that Bloch was working on his "System
of Theoretical Messianism" which he never completed. Caught between
the assembly line and the party line, between management and bureaucracy, they found the only compensation for the catastrophe of history in
interpretive atonement and aesthetic redemption. History, even as apocalypse, provided no fulfillment. Thus the virtuosos of vocation devised an
interpretive materialist theology of secular society which explained the
signs of culture as allegories of the promise. In the "new" of modernism
they thought they discerned an alternative covenant. "In the critical theory
of the Frankfurt School, the Jewish Messianic idea was subsumed into radical cultural criticism because implicit in both Benjamin and Bloch was the
premise that only those products of culture that were most valuable retained a utopian image of the future" (123).

   This theology of bourgeois culture perceived the lawlessness of contemporary life as a linguistic, rather than institutional, crisis. For Benjamin, Rosenzweig, Saussure, Cantor, Wittgenstein, Shklovsky, Schönberg,
Braque, Eisenstein, Kraus, Whitehead, Freud, or Husserl, grammar did not
hold and thus needed to be changed. State laws, public codes, or moral
regulations were no longer able to heal the arbitrariness of language and
govern understanding, let alone the masses. "The esoteric language of the
intellectual Jew is directed against the language of political instrumentalism. The expressive quality of language carries the promise of redemption
from power and judgment, 'the absolutely unlimited and creative infinity
of the divine word' [Benjamin]" (107). The intelligentsia rethought its
function in terms of a new language that they invented or discovered, so
that the conditions of subjectivity and communication could be remapped.
They saw no contradiction in this legislative ambition—that is why they
could support both social democracy and "spiritual aristocracy" (as Bloch
wrote in 1918), socialism and elite culture. Buber and Rosenzweig concluded: "The times are passive, the word is active" (quoted in Jay 1976: 16).
Their re-translation of Luther was just a representative example of this
faith in language. "The times proved far less passive than they thought, the
word much less active" (22). Not only did they not recover a primal code or
discover a communitarian speech, but they also lost their last battle against
the political sphere, which they never conquered. Thus while between the
two wars the culture elite saw in the messianic (as opposed to the mythical)

the authentic political, after World War II they abandoned politics and proclaimed the aesthetic the authentic messianic. This, in a simplified version, is the story of the Hebraization of western culture—a story for which the career of Paul de Man (1919–83), rather than Buber's Judaization of Europe, provides the typical narrative.

By the time of Modernism, Humboldt's and Arnold's project of an educating culture had been abandoned. Hebraism appropriated culture from Hellenism by identifying it with the aesthetic, specifically with masterpieces and their professional explication—a separate and autonomous realm with its own specialties, institutions, rituals, and passages. Modernism signaled the unqualified triumph of (Hebraic) High Art over (Hellenic) culture. Since then, the threat for Hebraism has not come from the rest of culture but from non-Art, from the outside of the institution of art, from practices questioning its politics. This mythical threat emanating from below, from low art or street turmoil, has been disparaged as the barbarism of politics in consumer capitalism. From the Battle of the Books to Modernism, all defenders of culture were spokespersons for a shared morality and taste, a public code of feelings and conduct, calling upon (Hellenic) culture to serve and promote the cause of (Hebraic) ethics. While the aesthetic regime was still Hellenic, its power was ambiguous: it could develop into either (Dionysian) anarchy or (Apollonian) art, depending on whether contemplation would be more attracted by leisure or discipline. During the second half of the nineteenth century, the threat of anarchy changed from an internal one (immoral culture) to an external one (anti-aesthetic attitude). After culture was split in two seemingly antagonistic parts, art and politics, the former part grew more and more independent, and drew moral authority from its intrinsic value. Finally, what made modernist Messianism the ultimate aesthetic was, on the one hand, its promise of an ethical autonomy, of an autonomy which is formal because it is entirely intrinsic, and on the other hand, its exorcism and exclusion of the political as public, institutional, agonistic, discursive, strategic, purposeful, and interested. In more general terms, Messianism is the aesthetic ideology of the Hebraicized sphere of (high) culture: the law of the genre of the promise.

At the time that Derrida was starting to settle his accounts with Plato (or, to be precise, with Heidegger's Greeks), Leo Strauss was concluding his. One could imagine a parallel between their relation and that of Cohen and Benjamin: Cohen was the last to express a coherent faith in the vitality of a civic and national culture, and Strauss was clinging to his confidence in the benign rule of the canon, while their successors were revising the laws of signification and education. The common element in all their efforts that has not changed over the years (probably because it is the interpretive limit of the question of modernity) is the hermeneutic aporia: what is the non-Greek, what is the other of the (western) other, of the Hellenic, if not our own identity? The answer is also common to all: our Hebraic difference (from antiquity as well as from all contemporary foreigners and barbarians). Strauss, for example, begins his paper "Jerusalem and Athens," first delivered as a Frank Cohen Public Lecture in Judaic Affairs in 1967, with a stock generalization: "All the hopes that we entertain in the midst of the confusions and dangers of the present are founded positively or negatively, directly or indirectly on the experiences of the past. Of these experiences the broadest and deepest, as far as we Western men are concerned, are indicated by the names of the two cities Jerusalem and Athens. Western man became what he is and is what he is through the coming together of biblical faith and Greek thought. In order to understand ourselves and to illuminate our trackless way into the future, we must understand Jerusalem and Athens" (Strauss 1983: 147). After this faith-reason distinction, he proceeds to consider the possibility of an approach through the "science of culture" (149) and rejects it because he cannot trust its claims of neutrality. Instead, he develops his opposition on the basis of wisdom, a notion he considers higher than culture: "We must then try to understand the difference between biblical wisdom and Greek wisdom. We see at once that each of the two claims to be the true wisdom, thus denying to the other its claim to be wisdom in the strict and highest sense. According to the Bible, the beginning of wisdom is fear of the Lord; according to the Greek philosophers, the beginning of wisdom is wonder. We are thus compelled from the very beginning to make a choice, to take a stand. Where then do we stand? We are confronted with the incompatible claims of Jerusalem and Athens to our allegiance" (149). Having established a ground outside the contingencies of culture which made Levinas so apprehensive, Strauss reiterates Shestov's absolute dilemma and need for an exclusive choice, only to face the same epistemological impasse: "We are open to both and willing to listen to each. We ourselves are not wise but we wish to become wise. We are seekers for wisdom, 'philo-sophoi.' By saying that we wish to hear first and then to act to decide, we have already decided in favor of Athens against Jerusalem" (149–50). Like Derrida (and the tradition of thought since Milton), Strauss asks: How can we not think Greek? How can we do philosophy without choosing the Greek one?

For the believer (like Shestov), everything in the Bible has the face-value of truth. "But from the viewpoint of the Bible the unbeliever is the fool who has said in his heart 'there is no God'; the Bible narrates everything as it is credible to the wise in the biblical sense of wisdom. Let us never forget that there is no biblical word for doubt" (150–51). Still, how can a skeptical age that does not believe in miracles read after Biblical criticism, which "reached its first climax in Spinoza's *Theological-Political Treatise?*" (150).

Which rules should govern secular reading? The available means of understanding are of Greek origin and taint. Strauss intends to show how it is possible to "avoid the compulsion to make an advance decision in favor of Athens against Jerusalem" (151). His Spinozist principle is that immanence should rule: attention to the reasoning of the Bible itself can uncover its own logic. Thus in the first part of his essay, "The Beginning of the Bible and its Greek Counterparts," he gives model readings of the stories about Creation, the Fall, Cain and Abel, the Flood, and Abraham, and then compares them to similar stories in Hesiod, Parmenides, Empedocles, and Aristotle. From such a parallel reading of teachings of Hebraic piety and Hellenic philosophy on the creation, he establishes "the fundamental opposition of the God or gods of the philosophers to the God of Abraham, Isaac and Jacob, the opposition of Reason and Revelation" (166). Like Auerbach, he believes that he has gained access to the logic of the Bible without the influence of Greek principles—and like him again, he has achieved it only through a comparison with Greek examples.

If the first part of the essay deals with beginnings, the second, "On Socrates and the Prophets," discusses endings. Strauss intends to revise Cohen's position, which compared philosophy and prophetism, and sought truth in "the synthesis of the teaching of Plato and that of the prophets" (167). His predecessor discerned many of the sharp differences dividing the two attitudes but was deceived by his idealism into accepting the possibility of a creative fusion. "Cohen has brought out very well the antagonism between Plato and the prophets. Nevertheless we cannot leave matters at his view of that antagonism. Cohen's thought belongs to the world preceding World War I. Accordingly he had a greater faith in the power of modern Western culture to mold the fate of mankind than seems to be warranted now" (168). What separates his age from Cohen's, however, is not the First World War but Modernism and its aestheticization of culture. At the time of Rousseau, Schiller, Heine, Arnold, and Cohen, culture as a broad humanistic area of action and creativity was still considered a valid ideal. After art was appropriated by Hebraism, cultural synthesis became impossible, and irreconcilable antagonism between this and the other spheres broke out. The extreme dilemma still confronts thought: "Since we are less certain than Cohen was that the modern synthesis is superior to its pre-modern ingredients, and since the two ingredients are in fundamental opposition to each other, we are ultimately confronted by a problem rather than a solution" (168). At the same time, it may be possible for the first time to discern the beginnings of this problem in the emergence of modernity. "More particularly, Cohen understood Plato in the light of the opposition between Plato-Aristotle—an opposition that he understood in the light of the opposition between Kant and Hegel. We, however, are more

impressed than Cohen was by the kinship between Plato and Aristotle on
the one hand and the kinship between Kant and Hegel on the other. In
other words, the quarrel between the ancients and the moderns seems to
us to be more fundamental than either the quarrel between Plato and
Aristotle or that between Kant and Hegel" (168). The argument between
Jerusalem and Athens is connected directly to the seventeenth-
century quarrel which defined history, language, and culture in the West.
Cohen's Plato, Strauss implies, was not truly Greek but very Kantian, and
therefore Hebraic. When the Athens-Jerusalem opposition is translated
into the ancients-moderns quarrel, modernity emerges as the project of
Protestant Hebraism—of civil interpretive governance through self-rule.

It is with reference to political praxis that the two paths of wisdom have
been separated and cannot be bridged: Strauss, like Derrida, feels that philosophy has to choose between culture and politics, the wisdom of the date
and the wisdom of the polis. "The fact that both Socrates and the prophets
have a divine mission means or at any rate implies that both Socrates and
the prophets are concerned with justice or righteousness, with the perfectly
just society which as such would be free from all evils. To this extent Socrates' figuring out of the best social order and the prophets' vision of the
Messianic age are in agreement. Yet whereas the prophets predict the coming of the Messianic age, Socrates merely holds that the perfect society is
possible: whether it will ever be actual, depends on an unlikely, although
not impossible, coincidence, the coincidence of philosophy and political
power" (171). Although the missions of philosophy and prophetism are
both divine and future-oriented, the former develops plans for a perfect
society while the latter promises the Messianic age; the one searches for
knowledge, the other accepts revelation; the philosopher promotes inquiry,
the prophet preaches faith. Their ideals of justice, too, are totally different.
"The perfectly just man, the man who is as just as is humanly possible, is
according to Socrates the philosopher and according to the prophets the
faithful servant of the Lord" (172). As Buber and Bloch observed earlier,
what accounts for the difference is the contingent, historical, and political
nature of the social project which pursues the possible interaction of philosophy and politics, knowledge and power, and has nothing in common
with the principles of faith and obedience invested in the expectation of a
Messianic age that will redeem all time and violence.

At the end of his essay Strauss does not formulate a specific conclusion.
He finishes with two stories that he finds parallel, Nathan's direct criticism
of King David and Socrates' indirect criticism of the tyrant Critias. They
represent two types of discourse about the future—one messianic, based
on faith in revelation, the other political, based on reason of thought. The
two trends portrayed here may occasionally and temporarily converge, but
essentially they are incompatible and antagonistic. Strauss does not men-

tion reconciliation at all: there can be no negotiation with the political, no place for the rule of the citizens.

By raising the question of the Law again, Derrida turns the appropriation of culture against its internal prohibition, Christianity, and the promise of emancipation against its intrinsic premise, autonomy. It is his way of addressing Strauss's fears of a skeptical age in which Auerbach's canon cannot guarantee the hegemony of culture, let alone the reign of an interpretive profession. Derrida's initiative has been supported by jeremiads lamenting the very creation of a civic egalitarian society: "The substitution of rules for law in modern times seems an attempt not only to demystify power's link to prohibition, but also to free thought from the One by proposing, to everyday human affairs, the multiplicity of undetermined possibilities created by technologies. But there has always been an ambiguity in what goes by the name of law: in its sacred, sovereign guise, it claims to derive from nature; it annexes to itself the noble prestige of the blood; it is not power but omnipotence. There is nothing but the law: whatever it is exerted against, is simply nothing: not humanity, but only myths, monsters, fascinations. Judaic law is not sacred, but holy. In place of nature—which it does not invest with the magic of sin—it puts relations, choices, mandates: that is to say, a language of obligations. In place of the ethnic, it puts the ethical. . . . There remains judgment. It is left for the highest: God alone judges, which is again to say, the One. . . . Saint Paul wanted to emancipate us from the Law: the Law enters into the drama of the sacred, the sacred tragedy, life born of death and inseparable from it" (Blanchot 1986: 143–44). By trying to secure a dominant place for the law and the judgment of God, deconstruction reverses a tradition of two centuries and makes the philosopher a legislator once again. In its work, Hebraic culture offers not aesthetic education (through the canon) but aesthetic legislation (through commentary).[110] "Derrida's move beyond good and evil 'annuls the ethical' in the name of a 'transcendental aesthetic' in a spirit contrary to Nietzsche's genealogy of morals, contrary, that is, to what Nietzsche knew about law" (Rose 1984: 149). The law must simultaneously be cultivated and obscured. To this effect, the suppression of the debate on Oral and Written Law is particularly helpful. "By using the word 'writing' Derrida reduces the meaning of law to differentiation as such and makes it enigmatic" (140). Origin (like, say, influence in Bloom) becomes a mysterious paradox and a mystical tautology: "Is the law in the book or, rather, the book in the law? Does every book have its own law, or every law its book? In other words, does reading and writing mean bowing to the law of the book or, on the contrary, forging by and by a law to submit the book to? The law is an invention of the book, invention of a book with the authority of law" (Jabès 1986: 355).[111] With Derrida's playful tour of the library and virtuosic use of intertextuality, "his reference to writing does not raise the question of the law—it buries it" (Rose 1984: 170). His performance commands and its promise seduces: "Derrida would have us perish without knowing why, for he leaves the law as unknowable as it was before he raised the question of the *graphein*" (168). His own writing aspires to be scripture and law: this is the ultimate method of Judaization, one that successfully returns (in a way that Heidegger failed to achieve) to Christianity's Sinaitic roots. Membership in culture through textualization and observance of the rituals of interpretation confirms the aesthetic superiority of the law and entitles everyone to Jewishness. If Paul's freedom was freedom from the law, aesthetic freedom is freedom from Christianity. If Christianity was originally a reform movement in Judaism (Segal 1990), now Judaism becomes a reform movement in Christianity.

What Hebraism failed to do morally (with the deployment of universal reason), it has achieved aesthetically (with the rule of the undifferentiated aesthetic disposition). This is seen when Lyotard (1990), for example, argues that to the extent that we all have to be faithful to the Divine Law—which first seized the Jews—so long as we remember that we depend on it, we are all "jews." Rosenzweig wanted to help the alienated Jew find her way back to Judaism; when Derrida extends his "Come," he wants to help the deceived Christian find his way toward Judaism. Those few who manage to reject the offer can hardly help but refrain from a Nietzschean sarcasm: "With Heidegger, all philosophers are reduced to the same: they represent various but, when we come to the heart of the matter, indifferent ways of forgetting Being, of thinking Being as presence, and of mixing up presence and that which is, in each case, present. With post-Heideggerians, this will become the unbreakable circle of Greek-Western onto-logo-theo-phallocentrism. But fortunately, we are not yet completely lost. With the help of the *Zeitgeist*, some noises about the possibility of evading this circle through recourse to the Old Testament (not of course the New, hopelessly contaminated by those damned Greeks), are increasingly perceptible. After we had been almost convinced of the nothingness of any 'transcendental signified,' we are now informed that Jehovah, his laws and the ethic of the Hebrews can and must be restored in the place of a (meta-? or post-?) transcendental signified. Dare we hope that we only need to replace philosophy by revelation in order to be saved? No wonder that, a few exceptions apart, philosophy is practiced less and less, and that most of what bears that name today is just commentary and interpretation, or rather, commentary squared and interpretation squared" (Castoriadis 1989: 6–7). For technocrats of interpretation like Lyotard, the question of the law, of the difference between nomos and Torah, is often more a Kantian question of justice.[112] "Then we are faced with one of two things: either the just comes to us from elsewhere, which means that we are never more than the addressees of prescriptions. This, by the way, is what the Jews think. . . . Or we have our situation: for us moderns, prescriptions are not received. And I think that this modernity, in the precise sense of a society that must decide what is obligatory, begins, in Western thought, with some Greeks" (Lyotard and Thébaud 1985: 17). However, in spite of his claim that "modernity is pagan" (16),[113] Lyotard not only discerns "in the position of the Sophists, or at least some of them, the same humor in relation to commands as in an entire Jewish tradition" (65), but he also finds the Hasidim the most modern example of paganism: "What Judaism, and especially the Hasidim, and some Sophists as well, teach us, is how to be suspicious of prescriptions" (66).[114] Thus he seems to effortlessly combine the polis of Castoriadis with Buber's kibbutz, as organic communities.

Returning to the essential question of writing as debated by philosophers from Mendelssohn to Buber, Derrida proposes that "revelation and tradition [are] fundamentally one category, so that the former is immutably one and the latter immutably many and exegetically derived from it (the Pharisaic position)" (Fishbane 1987: 355). He abolishes the distinction between the divinely revealed written Law and the religious tradition of its transmission by seeing the Talmud as a whole—both aggadah and halakhah, both tradition and revelation. Levinas confirmed that "Jewish thought is inseparable from Rabbinic sources" (Levinas 1969a: 31) by taking an integrative approach to tradition: "The Jewish perception of the world is expressed in the Bible—in the Bible as reflected by Rabbinic literature, of which the Talmud and its commentators constitute the most important part" (30). Responding to Levinas's commandment, "To love the Torah more than God," which reversed the priority of YHWH in Heidegger, Derrida argues that the Torah cannot be separated from the Talmud,[115] or the canon from its commentary, and that interpretation (as remembrance of suffering as well as anticipation of the messianic time) is the supreme act of faith. That is why his message does not undermine authority but gives reasons to celebrate it: "I would say that deconstruction is affirmation rather than questioning, in a sense which is not positive: I would distinguish between the positive, or positions, and affirmations. I think that deconstruction is affirmative rather than questioning; this affirmation goes *through* some radical questioning, but is not questioning in the final analysis" (Derrida 1987a: 20). From Auerbach's aggadah (tales and homilies) to Derrida's halakhah as written Law, a similar affirmative tone prevails. Auerbach as well as Derrida take a midrashic approach, viewing interpretation as scriptural exegesis. They concentrate on smaller units of the text and they decode it, while at the same time affirming the authority of the canon *and* its interpretive tradition. Auerbach is still a contemporary of Isaak Heinemann, who saw midrash as a type of "creative philology" and "creative historiography" (quoted in Stern 1987: 618). Derrida writes after the hermeneutics of

Heidegger: his plan is one not of reconstruction, restoration, or retrieval but of restitution—of what Benjamin called apokatastasis, "the conception of redemption in which all are saved" (Buck-Morss 1983: 233). "Restitutive criticism" (Hartman 1989: 32)—like Bloch's "restorative hermeneutic" (Finkelstein 1989: 61), with its emphasis on incompleteness, undecidedness, illumination, and utopia—gives back to the Oral law its proper authority—this time not a legal or civic (which it could never have) but a cultural one. "The great builders of words and thought . . . are teachers and commentators, they are masters of meaning—but outside the Law" (Steiner 1976: 75). Derrida wants to bring them back to the fold.

Deconstruction, as a discipline of the question, may occasionally seem to question authority, but in the end it invariably sanctions it. This is consistent with the discipline, with any discipline, since it confirms the value of control. It is hard to imagine a more potent endorsement of authority than a questioning that leaves it untouched. This discipline of reading endorses interpretation as control, the self-control that knows where to stop (in the margin, the exile of commentary). The law of deconstruction is the structure of the Law. "We cannot be sure there is a way of destructuring Law. You see, deconstruction cannot be transgression of the Law. Deconstruction *is* the Law. It's an affirmation, and affirmation is on the side of the Law. This is rather difficult. Usually we represent deconstruction as a negative or de-structuring movement, which it is not. It is an affirmative movement, first; and then, *as* an affirmation, it is not an affirmation against the Law or going beyond the Law. . . . That is why writing in a deconstructive mode is another way of writing Law. . . . [Kafka's] 'Before the Law' *is* the Law. We are in front of it as in front of the Law. . . . So deconstruction affirms a new mode of Law. It becomes the Law. But the Law is guaranteed by a more powerful Law, and the process has no end. That is why deconstruction is not a movement of transgression, of liberation; of course, it has some effects of—in a given situation—effects of emancipation, of transgression, of liberation, but, in the end, it is not" (Derrida 1987: 197). Derrida deconstructs emancipation from the law, showing that the structure of emancipation was still that of the law, that the structure of autonomy is heteronomous. Deconstruction is the awareness that interpretation and emancipation, reading and (its) freedom, the Hellenic return (of culture) and the Hebraic promise (of redemption), are mutually implicated and supportive as complementary parts of the Protestant project of modernity; it is also a celebration of the fact that, with the success of the project, its Hebraic element has prevailed, leaving the Hellenic outside as the barbaric threat. Levinas felt that he had to command his audience into submission, offering passivity as a task. Some of his followers added to the picture the trope of innocent suffering, borrowed from romantic authoriality: "Responsibility is innocent guilt. . . . My responsibility is anterior to my birth just as it is exterior to my consent, to my liberty" (Blanchot 1986: 22). This brought the penitents closer to the indulgences of Artaud, Bataille, Fassbinder, and Pasolini than to abstinence: "Suffering suffers from being innocent: thus it seeks to become guilty in order to lessen" (41). The lesson for Derrida has been to tolerate and contain excess by making transgression just another rite of atonement, heresy the most radical expression of faith. "Derrida must somehow perpetuate the Law, at least be the father of Writing lest the parricide become an inadvertent suicide" (Handelman 1983: 125). The postmodern mode of law perpetuation is the anarchy of transgression. The model and code of power continues to be the law; now, however, with the privileges of sovereignty suspended, the juridical representation of power changes from a negative to a positive one (Foucault 1978: 90).

This mode has some strong modernist precedents. "The fact that anarchical and law-giving tendencies or instincts conflicted in Schoenberg's thinking" (Dalhaus 1987: 89)—as they did in that of Benjamin, Bloch, or Joyce—indicates the interdependence of these tendencies. At the same time, the aesthetic rehabilitation of anarchy does not mean that its political expressions deserve equal treatment. The Hebraization of culture produces immanent transcendence and results in complete aestheticization. Thus, on the one hand, it makes the profane sacred again; on the other, it can lead to pantheism: if everything is sacred, is the divine everywhere? Benjamin dealt with the question in the essay "*Dialog über die Religiosität der Gegenwart*" (1912), which presents a debate between a pantheist and "the defender of a religious-social ethic" (Rabinbach 1985: 96). The modernist problem was the proper ethic of the aesthetic. Some writers reiterated the Romantic doctrine that "philosophy is an art" (Shestov). Others went further, identifying the two: "Ethics and aesthetics are one and the same" (Wittgenstein 1963: 147). The postmodernist problem is the aestheticization of ethics. When taste acquires moral authority, philosophy claims that it is "an exercise in morality, and therefore, to the degree that it arrives at no firm conclusions, but rather intensifies and enriches our experience of things, complicating and loosening the referent, it is an 'edifying' or 'aesthetic' discourse" (Vattimo 1988: 148). Derrida uses the law of law transgression to control the danger of pantheism. When the ideal of emancipation dies, interpretation becomes a matter of anarchic taste, a celebration of desecrating consumption. With the invocation of the law, "a nameless Law" (Lyotard 1990: 94), Derrida also attempts to preserve the notion of destiny despite the loss of eschatology. This is what makes him a "teleocrat" of postcapitalist society rather than a technocrat of market economy (Martin and Szelényi 1987: 46). So far as the prophetic authority is concerned, which he embraces in order to legitimate his law-giving plan, a comparable example from musical modernism shows that "the state of emergency which Schoenberg induced with atonality, and the renewed state of legality which he hoped to constitute by means of dodecaphony, were similar in character, in that their substance consisted in an act of decision and not in a systematic web of argument or historical derivation" (Dalhaus 1987: 90). Derrida decided that there is a different state of emergency, one concerning freedom itself.

As commentators (Handelman 1982: 222–23; Hartman 1980: 55) have already noticed, deconstructive cannibalism (on the body of the voice, the Spirit, the parousia, the Logos, the communion, the church) may be explained through a short parable by Kafka: the fact that leopards used to break into the temple and drink from the sacrificial chalices is now anticipated and integrated into the ceremony. What these commentators did not notice (and as commentators they could not) is that the story can be seen as a narrative of institutionalization. When the leopards cannot be killed or chased away, then, with the passivity that Levinas recommends and K. exemplifies, they are accepted as an institutionally transparent (that is, natural) part of the ceremony. Thanks to a new interpretation, danger as well as impotence can be textualized and accommodated. People can be even convinced that those who are consumed will be happy or saved: there is nothing in the covenant of (interpretive) rights to prevent that. Derrida renews that covenant, and to the extent that he can strengthen it, he is perfectly willing to dispense with its texts (which postmodernity has discredited anyway). As long as the politics of the Law (the ceremony, the temple, interpretation) is not questioned, as long as people are seduced into "trying to make the facts of their historical catastrophe agree with the exalted promises of their Sacred Book" (Handelman 1982: 223), there will always be rituals, sacred books, readings, textual faith, and legislators (like Jacques Derrida) proposing a new "political theology" (like Carl Schmitt in 1922) after the "re-treat of the political" (Lacoue-Labarthe and Nancy).[116]

Derrida is in search of "what could be a grace beyond the work" (Derrida 1982: 63) and proposes the aesthetic itself as the answer: a grace[117] beyond apocalypse, redemption and the modernist epiphany—an aesthetic Messianism of the letter. "As regards translation, grace would perhaps be when the writing of the other absolves you, at times, from the infinite *double bind*" (64) of YHWH the lawgiver, of oral and written law, of God's turned face and silent absence—in different terms, the double bind of Hebraism and Hellenism. "Grace is always improbable; it can never be proved. But must we not believe that it comes? That perhaps is belief itself" (64). Grace is the trace that comes, and belief is the messianic (as opposed to apocalyptic) faith. Conversely, messianic hope and faith is belief in a grace beyond the work itself, in a gift of what is not at one's disposal, that keeps coming and thus has arrived.

With Derrida's anti-Christology, the Protestant attack on the sacraments, the "channels of grace," is extended to Logos itself, to the incarnation of the Spirit. "In the sacraments of the New Covenant, grace is not merely *signified* or *prefigured*, as in the ceremonies of the Old Covenant; in the New Covenant, grace is contained and conferred: word, material sign (e.g., bread and wine), and grace all converge in the Presence of the Word. . . . The doctrine of the Real Presence in the Sacrament of the Altar of the New Covenant is thus the fulfillment of the Messianic promise—the deconstructive longing for the *deferred* Presence—of the Old Covenant" (Young 1985: 116). Deconstruction attacks the parousia of Christ by exposing it to Law and its prophecies. Thus it is only fair to suggest that Derrida "might be seen as the last scion of the Protestant Reformation, which generally displaced the sacraments with an intense emphasis on *writing—sola scriptura*. Derrida would seem to have taken this development as far as it can go: he is a Moses who has broken the Tablets and will not re-ascend the mountain, who offers only more wandering—more *erring*—in the wilderness, with the Promised Land endlessly deferred" (116). Heidegger's errancy from home becomes Derrida's "'destinerrance' [a wandering that is its own end]" (Derrida 1984a: 29) in the desert of the promise.[118] But his Messianic dispatches are sublime/ridiculous because of their willful, inexorable dependency on Deist and quietist Protestantism, the dogma that issued the first commandment of assimilation: to accept the task of interpretive culture and contemplative taste.[119] "Criticism, the Protestantism of the earth, replaces dogmatism, the Catholicism of the milieus (code)" (Deleuze and Guattari 1987: 339). Theory exposes the fallacy of "the Law of Freedom—rational and valid *because it is Law*, i.e., without ulterior sanction" (Hegel 1900: 251). Its message is that philosophers have tried for too long (and to no avail) to change the world; it is time again to interpret—this time, not the world but its unchangeability. "In Derrida's work it is never a question of belief or lack thereof, but rather of faith—in an almost ultra-protestant sense. . . . Derrida's writing at times seems to be less inflecting an (older) Old Testament than reforming a (newer) New Testament—in its battle against any *katholikós*, in its tension between the 'already' and the 'not yet,' and in its emphasis on that writing-as-son which has been martyred by the carnal and spiritual circumcision practiced by all 'false doctors' of whatever belief. Derrida doth *protest*—religiously—and asks the same of his followers" (Jardine 1985: 180–81). Naturally, his followers have included many Protestant theologians who see "Incarnation as Inscription" (Taylor 1982: 71). Appropriating Derrida's emphasis on "a certain Judaism as the birth and passion of writing" (Derrida 1978: 64), deconstructive theology has celebrated as the resurrection of the Word the death of (a) God who is only God, and has become a *"radical* Christology" (Carl Raschke), one that considers Jesus "our *différance"* (Atkins 1985: 97). "Thus two very different interpretations of the theological implications of Derrideanism, though both Christians and Jews see Derrida as ultimately supportive of their own religion" (Atkins 1983: 15). This response to deconstruction recalls the positive reaction to Buber of theologies from the Episcopalian "relational theology" to the Orthodox existentialism of Nikolai Berdyaev. The dogma of the Derridean aesthetic does not need Kierkegaard's leap of faith, only the ersatz exegesis which colonizes the humanistic tradition. His is a theologesis not of fear but of festivity or, to use the title of an early book by Shestov, an *Apotheosis of Groundlessness* (1905)— a theology of play that plays with theology. To appropriate a comment made about another contemporary theorist, Derrida is aware "that the age of religion has passed and that for this very reason we are tempted to produce an 'aestheticized' religion, an imaginary or hallucinated community, in an age that is neither religious nor social" (O'Neill 1988: 505).[120] If Benjamin searched for the Messianic in the corruption of the commodity, the waste product, Derrida discovers it in the consumption of the commodity, in the expenditures of cultural life as lifestyle. Modernist formalisms have been succeeded by Postmodernist literalisms like the recycling of the classical tradition by the Early Music movement, which repeats the canon on period instruments for the compact disc industry.[121] In his postmodern "theology of culture" (Paul Tillich), aesthetics, which evolved out of Biblical hermeneutics, comes full circle and succeeds theology: faith becomes the aesthetic attitude par excellence. Criticism no longer serves a purpose but is "a means of provisional grace" (Des Pres 1975: 278). That is why Grammatology is a populist doctrine, and its prophet the first global philosopher.[122]

Still, reading-as-faith and aesthetics-as-theology, especially a century after the decadent charms of Aestheticism, are simply kitsch (even for the elite of cultural capital). Like the health industry and its new abstinence, which arose at the same time as deconstruction, they are based on penance, self-denial, discipline, deferral, endlessly renewed promise, pharmaka, supplements, joyful exercise, celebration of form, and renunciation of the social body. These disciplines are covered in the newspapers as fashionable trends: "Non-ism is only viable as a temporary state, but more and more it is being portrayed as a state of grace" (O'Neill 1990: 14). This grace is induced by an aesthetic self-flagellation, an orgy of encratism: "This secret self-ravishment, this artists' cruelty, this delight in imposing a form upon oneself as a hard, recalcitrant, suffering material and in burning a will, a critique, a contradiction, a contempt, a No into it, this uncanny, dreadfully joyous labor of a soul voluntarily at odds with itself that makes itself suffer out of joy in making suffer—eventually this entire *active* 'bad conscience'—you will have guessed it—as the womb of all ideal and imaginative phenomena, also brought to light an abundance of strange new beauty and affirmation, and perhaps beauty itself" (Nietzsche 1969: 87–88). The Protestant ascetic ethic which invented the aesthetic compensation finds here its perverse fulfillment: theology begins reoccupying the answer positions left vacant by the exhaustion of culture. After higher criticism and high art, the last discipline to console faith is high theory, theoria of its own height.

Recent festivities of self-denial have been accompanied from the beginning by the utterly predictable (but no less enjoyable, for that reason) sound of the disco beat, their contemporary dance (to which all exercising takes place). The true sound of deconstruction is what the music business calls "remixing"—playing with the original song by adding, stripping, breaking up, stretching, reversing, quoting. The phenomenon of issuing multiple versions of the same song, especially dance tracks, appeared in the late 1960s: after the single (45-rpm) version, there might follow the album version, 12-inch (extended) version, instrumental version, dub version, club/disco/house version, a cappella version, and other special ones. The first remixers were usually club disc jockeys who felt free to experiment with many songs playing simultaneously on different turntables, in order to keep the music (and the dancing) flowing and at the same time to show off. Gradually, with the success of the technique, the industry started releasing its own remixes. The (main) song used is always already a hit (and therefore, for music fans, the remix is always already collectable). Remixes are commentaries: once they start appearing, no version is original or definitive. In an ever-expanding market for this format, the 1980s witnessed entire albums consisting exclusively of remixes, like Chaka Khan's *Life is a Dance: The Remix Project* (1989), Paula Abdul's *Shut Up and Dance* (1990), Milli Vanilli's *Remix Album* (1990). Like the members of the latter group (who appeared in concerts and videos but never sang on the albums), Derrida does not offer any truly new tablets but lip-synchs the old aesthetic commandments. Synthesized music and synthetic Hebraism have become such an integral part of our environment that we hostages of the law do not even notice their presence: they condition our controlled pleasures and regulated repentances (Neher 1990) automatically. "[Sylvere Lotringer:] —The Law no longer needs to be written or recognized since it is being made everywhere. . . . The Law disappears by spreading over everything. And as it's absent, it's always right. [Paul Virilio:] —The law is no longer a Law in the political sense: a law which eludes politics is not Law, but mythical law. It's fate" (Virilio and Lotringer 1983: 127). The metapolitics of law constitutes the postmodern mythology of the fearful fate of freedom. And yet, as continuing Hellenophobic alarms show, although the Hellenic allotropy is held hostage by its other, it has not been completely neutralized because it is not subject to the law, and therefore it may be expelled but cannot be arrested.

EPILEGOMENA TO MODERNITY

THE MODERN QUESTION of autonomy emerged when the newly empowered Protestant middle class of western Europe was able to exchange the yoke of feudal tyranny for political hegemony, for its own rules of self-control. Thus autonomy was not at first a question of democracy so much as of credible and effective governance: "How to govern oneself, how to be governed, how to govern others, how to accept him who is to govern us, how to become the best possible governor, etc. I think all these problems, in their multiplicity and intensity, are characteristic of the 16th century, which lies, to put it schematically, at the intersection of two processes: the process which, shattering the structures of feudalism, is about to form the great territorial, administrative and colonial states; and, on the other hand, a totally different movement which, starting with the Reformation and then the Counter-Reformation, puts in question the manner in which one is to be spiritually ruled and led on this earth in order to achieve eternal salvation" (Foucault 1979b: 5–6). While the previous regime was devising laws from above and ruling by force, the new order aspired to create a civic realm free from fear, where decisions would be made by consent and people would rule themselves by self-discipline.

The primary condition for such a realm was a public conduct based on internalized governance. Disciplined conduct distinguishes political government from sovereignty because, instead of imposing laws, the government is disposing exercises, modes of regular behavior. Thus the art of government becomes a matter of disposition, rather than law. Its principle is rationalization, attention to and respect for intrinsic rules, namely, the reason inherent in everything. The supreme nomos of autonomy is immanence, the free structure of interiority, the autocracy of divinely ordained, and yet self-grounded, depth. Its three models—the individual, the state, and the artwork—are governed by intrinsic rational principles. The old divine and cosmological laws, as well as the traditional rhetorical and moral rules, are superseded by self-regulating constitution, the unique reality of secular identity. Independence is self-administered, transcendence grounded. The regime of identity, of sameness and otherness, emerges during this search for the ground of legitimate autochthony.

The first modern system, created to organize the universal calling of vocation, was the administrative State of the fifteenth and sixteenth centuries—the period when the enterprise of salvation colonized the world. It was followed by the disciplinary State of the next two centuries, which was based on the exercises of contemplation. The science of aesthetics was established at that time to formulate a compensatory theoria of rationalization. Aesthetic criteria start controlling the status of statements when arguments need to appeal to an intrinsic finality, rather than a divine plan. Thus governance was modeled on the autotelic aesthetic—the disposition that bears its telos within itself and is a law unto itself. The aesthetic became the internalized rule of autonomy, a "lawfulness without a law." If the quest for self-assertion was a demand for freedom from the coercion of the law, the aesthetic fulfilled it by promising a transparent law, the law of self-founding reason.

The practices of contemplative disposition, better known as manners, taste, and style, are the forms of aesthetic conduct. The appropriate public order, the disposition of a shared public culture, was not a question of who should have access to the temples of discrimination but of what was the required attitude entitling one to such access. Thus the first realm regulated by the principles of autonomous rationality was that of public conduct, of the behavior of the emancipated individual who acts as a responsible reader, one who is capable of personal interpretation. The public conduct of the reader expresses the introjection of the law, the assimilation of the interpretive dogma. Since the aesthetic is autonomous self-realization (and its own reflection), the highest bourgeois ideal was to live autonomously, developing human possibility to the fullest according to the organic laws of its divine nature.

It was in the governmental State of the nineteenth century that culture evolved from a mechanism of social education in civility to an elite code of social distinction cultivated by the canon of art. The cultural prestige, however, which gave moral authority to the liberal hegemony, did not mean anything to the masses which started taking over squares, factories, parliaments, and classes before the end of the century. At that point, art abandoned its compensatory and supportive role and claimed its own independence and moral superiority: it became an autoscopic and ethical activity, giving up completely its public functions but keeping for itself the canon and disciplines of interpretation.

The regulatory State of the late twentieth century salvages from administration, discipline, and government the rule of regulation, the only thing that has survived the exhaustion of autonomous modernity. Postmodern appeals to textual laws and interpretive resistance are desperate efforts to preserve the authority of art and literature when there is nothing to read because of the anarchy at the airport bookstore, in the college curriculum, and on the television dial—or when no one interprets because everybody reads. Although the canon does not hold, contemplation remains the only element of the bourgeois cultural tradition still under operation. It is the aesthetic conduct itself, this time a rigorously differentiated position—a disposition of indiscriminate, cannibalistic textualization which consumes everything (things, people, phenomena, history, society, religion, the earth) by turning it into writing—that is, not by ruling it but by regulating it, by demanding from it its law.

Postmodern interpretation, interpretation at its last historical phase, is this scripturalization of the world. Its ideology is still aesthetic, though this time nihilistic, because it believes that there is nothing of God outside the rule of law. However, its faith is no longer apocalyptic but messianic: interpretation, like tradition, is the promise which has always already arrived. It does not matter whether there is a canon; what is read is irrelevant, as long as everything is read, treated like text, interpreted, Biblicized. Interpretation, the first political right of the middle class, the fundamental exercise of reason, remains the last vestige of modernity, a remnant of privilege and status for intellectuals only, to be sure, and yet their influential way of supporting the disappearing high bourgeois order which has been for some time their single source of support. The only emancipation that interpretation can enunciate now is itself—the claims of an interpretation emancipated from all political connection and contingency, from the covenant of emancipation itself. Understanding is free to interpret, without any external constraints or outside responsibilities—free to the extent that it exchanges liberation with self-reflection, obeys the rules of critique, and identifies independence with aesthetic theoria, thus achieving its own transfiguration into pure faith.

Absorbed by fin-de-siècle euphoria, interpretation has abandoned its public role, denounced its historical accountability, and embraced theological politics. The question is whether it can survive by itself, with the contract of emancipation void; whether its cultural capital has any value in a post-industrial, information economy; whether it can serve the sacred in a world where everything is Hebraic. The important issue is not the end of modernity, its date with history and the ancients. It is the adventure of autonomy that needs reexamination. While originally interpretation signaled the rebellion of exegesis against dogma and ritual, five centuries later, in order to insure the survival of the bourgeois dominion, it allies itself with the law and a new regime of regulations modeled on contemplative, observant consumption. The emphasis has shifted again from auto- to nomos. The remarkable difference is that now, instead of pursuing self-grounding understanding, interpretation promotes legislation and legitimacy: knowledge must be not just lawful or legitimate but licit. Contemplation, the aesthetic ethic, is elevated to a theological doctrine, literalist legalism: salvation by good words. Autonomy succumbs to secular theocracy—scriptural autotheism.

Hebraic theoria, however, cannot usurp the summit of Sinai for too long.

The reasons are many. First, the Hellenic is no longer a credible opponent: holy wars are waged now against non-western gods. Although repeatedly idolatrized and demonized, the Hellenic no longer inspires artists, philosophers, or revolutionaries to envision a cultural synthesis, a formal antidote to alienation. Second, in a post-literate society, debates about letter and spirit or iconomachic crusades are of little consequence to the clashes of late capitalism with local identity and territory. Since modernity has lost its exclusively western character, its very monotheism has been questioned. Third, the dream of assimilation has been discredited to such an extent :hat in many places it is not even revised but purposefully reversed. With the end of colonialism (that is, the international project of forced assimilation), there seems to be no interest in mastering the interpretive practices which trained the white masters of the earth. Finally, at a time of particularism and tribalism, when individuals, sexes, classes, cultures, and other identities have become each other's Other, the cultural status of emancipated otherness is greatly diminished. Too many groups around the world are emphasizing their distinctiveness for difference (through its differentiation from sameness) to signify still the status of special access to the dominant identity.

Thus the authority of theoria is severely eroded when the whole world is watching. That is why theoria is forced to discard its higher views and surveys, and seek authorization to legislate. Surveillance is not effective; it is not enough to generate commentaries on the tablets. When anarchy looms large, it is time to come down from the heights of theoria with new tablets. And so the former managers of consciousness surveillance offer their services as doorkeepers before the Law. Their new job is to re-present the law, telling stories about gates, rules, failed appeals, and grave punishments. This time people who come to seek admission notice the great number of entrances and doorkeepers, and try many of them, while exchanging experiences and insights with fellow sinners. Nevertheless, confession and collaboration will not improve their chances until more and more realize that the whole purpose of present doorkeeping is to distract them, to make them believe not that there is no other Law but that there is no outside-the-Law—the actual, pervasive, and yet invisible law of a land which is run only by laws.

And yet there must be other (non-Hebraic?) laws and other (non-Hellenic?) lands, and other ways of doing things, without even laws or lands. But people will not know it before they begin again (as they have done in the past) to question the law of the land and the land of the law—before they start rejecting autonomic behavior for autotelic action. The project of autonomy did not fail—it simply exhausted itself. It deserves credit for many successes, many sacrifices, many achievements. But it is no longer valid or useful. The same must be said about its supreme models, Hebraism and Hellenism, which guided and rewarded the quest for emancipation through interpretation, liberation through self-rule. There is no longer need to play Hebrews and Hellenes to gain admission to civic society, a society presently languishing under fatigue and global challenges. The weariness of autonomy, though, does not entail defection from freedom. On the contrary, it demands a (radically non-theoretical and anti-aesthetic) refunctioning of freedom, a new dedication to current, concrete, and pressing causes of liberation.

The exhaustion of Hebraism and Hellenism may finally allow Jews and Greeks to live and create like every other people, without the self-enslaving and -exterminating advantages accorded to their ideal types by Protestantism. The collapse of autonomy may also create possibilities for diverse initiatives beyond nomothetic concerns and nomocratic regimes. The mystagogues of the aesthetic and the dramaturges of critique will argue against such possibilities by expertly interpreting them—finding inconsistencies and contradictions and multiple binds where others see vivid seas and open paths. Their arguments provide another illustration of why there is need not for new artistic languages of foundation but for alternative public rhetorics of collective assertion. Organic ideals of community, essentialist declarations of otherness, and ascetic exercises of resistance will not suffice either: they have too strong a theological legacy to be effective in a nomolatrous culture still combating its horror of alienation with the counter-myth of religion. The task of a different assertion of self-determination requires much more if members of society are not to remain political prisoners of their civil rights. The next revolt should turn against the court of rights itself, against the interpenetration of nomos and phusis, anarchy and order. This next project is not a question of end or beginning, catastrophe or genesis, prophecy or annunciation, fate or destiny, return or redemption. It is just a matter of (putting together, putting into action, making operative) a good life, the life we want for ourselves, the society we desire to shape, the history we intend to make. It is just another episode of human rebellion against human oppression, a choice of freedom over exploitation, an experiment with some other configurations of an autotelic constitution of society. Just that. A change of our own making in the name of our own lives. A better (in a manner that interests us, namely, those concerned) way of doing things with those we love. Some other kind of public virtue and political ethic.

NOTES

CHAPTER ONE

1. Comparative philology, looking at the common oral-formulaic ground of Biblical and Homeric poetry, concludes that "on the basis of style, the Hebraic mind or worldview cannot be distinguished from the intelligence behind the *Odyssey* or *Iliad*" (Whallon 1966: 113), and that the distinctive features "Auerbach found in Homeric epic are also to be found in Old Testament poetry" (130). Thus it takes Auerbach to task for unjustifiably comparing two different literary provinces, (Homeric) poetry and (Hebrew) prose, instead of comparing the two oral poetic traditions.

2. Since the special issue of *Critical Inquiry* (September 1983) on "Canons" (von Hallberg 1984), the subject has acquired great importance in many fields. Among the better discussions within literary studies, see Butler 1988; Condren 1985; Deleuze and Guattari 1986; Doyle 1989; Fiedler and Baker 1981; Fowler 1982; Fowles 1987; Gilbert 1985; Hernadi 1978 (Part II); Kermode 1985; Lauter 1985; McLaren 1988; Munich 1985; Robinson 1985; Rosenfelt 1982; von Hallberg 1984 and 1985; and West 1987. Rasula 1987 is a postmodern novel about the authority of the text. For a parallel trend in religious studies, see Barr 1983; Beckwith 1985; Blenkinsopp 1977; Coats and Long 1977; Kermode 1987 ("The Canon"); Metzer 1987; Morgan 1990; and von Campenhausen 1972

3. "The Bible's claim to truth is not only far more urgent than Homer's, it is tyrannical—it excludes all other claims. The world of the Scripture stories is not satisfied with claiming to be a historically true reality—it insists that it is the only real world, is destined for autocracy. . . . The Scripture stories do not, like Homer's, court our favor, they do not flatter us that they may please us and enchant us—they see to subject us, and if we refuse to be subjected we are rebels" (Auerbach 1953: 14–15). The author is reiterating a point made by Hegel in *The Philosophy of Fine Art*: "It is only the limited Jewish national god which is unable to tolerate other gods in its company for the reason that it purports as *the* one god to include everything, although in regard to the definition of its form it fails to pass beyond its exclusiveness wherein the god is merely the God of His own people. Such a god manifests its universality in fact only through his creation of Nature and as Lord of the heavens and the earth. For the rest he remains the god of Abraham, who led his people Israel out of Egypt, gave them laws on Sinai, and divided the land of Canaan among the Jews. And through this narrow identification of him with the Jewish nation he is in a quite peculiar way the god of this folk. . . . Consequently this austere, national god is so jealous, and ordains in his jealousy that men shall see elsewhere merely false idols. The Greeks, on the contrary, discovered their gods among other nations and accepted what was foreign among themselves" (Hegel 1962: 182–83).

4. Similar claims have been made about its importance for literature: "Blake described the Bible as 'the Great Code of Art.' The suggestion is that it codifies and

stabilizes rules for the production of meaning that can then be applied to individual texts read anagogically as books and chapters in a secular scripture built up, as Shelley says in the *Defence* [*of Poetry*] from 'the cooperating thoughts of one great mind' " (Rajan 1986: 585).

5. Regarding its narrative modes and structure, the debt of *Mimesis* to the *aggadah* tradition has not been explored. The aggadah is usually defined as the non-legal material of the Talmud, everything in talmudic and midrashic literature which is not *halakhah*: it is the rabbinic storytelling which amplifies the scriptural narrative, filling in its apparent gaps or inconsistencies. It includes parables, legends, anecdotes, humor, expositions, explanations, and elaborations of biblical stories, moral exhortations, and wise sayings (Barth 1984). Although the aggadah and the halakhah together compose the Oral Law, the "aggadah has often been compared, even opposed, to the halakhah. Historically, the latter has frequently been viewed as serious, the former as frivolous. More recently, the terms of the comparison have been reversed, and halakhah now tends to be depicted as the heavy yoke of the law, as the prescriptive and binding side of Judaism, while aggadah is portrayed as free and imaginative, expressing the spiritual, ever-searching heart of religion" (Stern 1987: 11). Auerbach's approach seems to be part of the latter, post-Enlightenment view which contrasts the open-endedness of storytelling with the rigidity of religious dogma: "The genuine opposite to aggadah is not halakhah but dogmatic theology. Standing at the very origin of classical Judaism, aggadah presents the fundamental obstacle to every effort to fix Jewish thought in a static moment, to convert its didactic assertions into systematic discourse. . . . Most playful and novel in form precisely when it is most commonplace in content, aggadah represents all that is quintessentially untheological about Judaism. As such, it is the point of discontinuity against which every theology of Judaism must take a stand in order to make its own beginning" (12). This view shares the same set of aesthetic principles with Auerbach's way of telling the grand narrative through stories. Walter Benjamin defined truth as "haggadic consistency" (Benjamin 1969a: 143).

6. Auerbach's strategy has obviously worked, since he has been appropriated by academics and turned into a "master," a model of the traditional humanist intellectual: "Auerbach is representative for those American critics and students of literature who believe in the enduring cultural importance, not just of literature, but of critical, humanistic scholarship in an age of need. Auerbach functions as a fantastic source for American critics and theorists; his primary function is not as a philological model but as a sign that in an anti-historical, anti-humanistic age of relativism, mass-cultural leveling, and the increasing irrelevance of writers and critics, it is not only possible for critics to perform opportune and important acts, to construct monumental synthetic texts in the face of massive specialization, to invent new techniques for dealing with changed cultural conditions, and to do all this out of the unique intellectual and existential experience of the individual scholar, but also, in so doing, to relegitimate culturally a certain image of the responsible and responsive authoritative critical voice" (Bové 1986: 80–81). An investigation of the "ideological investment in Auerbach's redemptive qualities" (107) shows that the critic's "own claims and much of his own rhetoric nonetheless draw upon and emerge out of the discourse and values" (139–40) of the German mandarin tradition of anthropological humanism which he seems to oppose. Although Auerbach rejects the subservi-

ence of academics to the *Kulturstaat* and their support for the official (educational and other) policy and nationalist ideology, he never loses his faith in an elite in charge of Western tradition. Indeed, in his vision of an aristocracy of cultivation, the mission of the elite transcends national boundaries to take over (like *Mimesis*) the legacy of *Weltliteratur*. The intellectual is called upon to play a universal role. This strategy of (self)legitimation recalls Auerbach's later condition that "the humanist who hopes to be effective in preserving or renewing humanity *must* experience exile and alienation (as he and Dante both did), in order to be able to transcend the traps of nationalism that threaten humanity's very existence" (175). This position of willful alienation is a source of ever greater authority: "By virtue of this total and loving exile, the philologist becomes a universal intellectual whose very 'marginality' to the forces or powers of modernity, as well as to the orthodox effects of a national or institutional tradition, empowers him to do work basic to the humanist enterprise" (177). Thus the "grand strategy of exile" (180) becomes another source of prestige for the socially displaced humanist. Auerbach's identification with Dante must be seen in the context of this effort of authorial canonization (197).

7. Northrop Frye (1912–91), a minister of the United Church of Canada from 1936, appropriated this argument for Christianity, proposing that, since the Bible has provided a mythological framework for Western literature, it should be the basis for all literary training. See his *The Educated Imagination* (1963), *The Secular Scripture: A Study in the Structure of Romance* (1976), *The Great Code: The Bible and Literature* (1982), and *Words with Power: Being a Second Study of The Bible and Literature* (1990).

8. On religious and literary uses of typology, see Bercovich 1972; Brumm 1970; Budick 1986; Charity 1966; Danielou 1960; Korshin 1977 and 1982; Lampe and Woolcombe 1957; Lewalski 1979; Madsen 1968; Meixner 1971; Miner 1971 and 1977; Preus 1969; Schwartz 1988; von Rad 1963; and White 1971.

9. A study of Auerbach's language which correlates his figural history with his figurative style demonstrates how the tension between prefiguration and fulfillment operates in the presentation of Dante and Flaubert as the two critical moments of self-overcoming for European realism, and how, in its turn, *Mimesis* fulfills the *figura* of Dante in Flaubert (Bahti 1985: 138).

10. In the work of some contemporary theologians, "typology is represented as agreeing with the historical emphasis of Hebrew thought, while allegory is represented as serving the Greek disinterest in history and interest in supra-historical timeless ideas" (Barr 1966: 104–5). The connection between typology and Hebrew thought in *Mimesis* is clear, since figural interpretation is the mode of understanding that Auerbach derives from the Bible and uses in his survey of literary tradition.

11. Auerbach's strategy may be fruitfully compared to the return, through literary issues, of Martin Heidegger to Pietism or of Harold Bloom to the Kabbalah. Some commentators have found Auerbach's understanding of typology too Christian and have criticized it for reductionism: "Typology, in the form described by Auerbach, expresses the need to interpret the Old Testament in such a way as to close down the interpretive treadmill and to declare the fulfillment of all prophetic figures in Christ. Philo's writings and/or midrash, on the other hand, are symptomatic of a desire to describe a delayed messianic coming. They affirm the

continuity of interpretation and even make its endlessness part of the essence of divine meaning" (Budick 1986: 208).

12. As a project of secular typology, *Mimesis* has its origins in the abstracted typologies of the late eighteenth century, when figuralism reached into cosmology or history. In works like David Hartley's *Observations on Man, his Frame, his Duty, and his Expectations* (1791, 3 vols.), scriptural typology "becomes the basis for the existence of abstracted typology or for other, analogical, predictive structures, not only in various kinds of literature and learning but in the works of Nature herself. Hartley's sweep is so broad that he prepares the way for the predictive structures of Blake, Wordsworth, Shelley, and Byron by extending typology beyond the narrow theological sphere" (Korshin 1977: 182). Significantly, Hartley dealt with the role of the Jews in the typology of secular history, which he deemed figural of humankind: "Does it not appear agreeable to the whole analogy both of the word and works of God, that the *Jews* are types both of each individual in particular, on one hand, and of the whole world in general, on the other?" (quoted in Korshin 1977: 183) A similar but pessimistic view attributes modern alienation to "the divorce in our contemporary world between moral and secular conceptions. . . . In this situation, the Jew plays a special role. His life and his wanderings are, in a sense, the image of the world's destiny" (Bell 1946: 12). In typological pronouncements like Hartley's we ought to seek the model of the twentieth-century image of the artist as antitype of the Jew. I am not aware of any studies of the Jew as *figura* in contemporary literature, criticism, or theory.

13. The same care to avoid confrontation with Christianity is evident in an exposition of the cardinal role the Bible has played in Western tradition. The project, derived from *Mimesis*, is to tell the story of the West as a conflict between the Biblical (including the belated Christian) and the Greek. A comparison of two opposing cultural modes, the "kerygmatic" (appropriated from Pietist hermeneutics) and the "cybernetic," shows that "we are a kerygmatic not a cybernetic society" (Schneidau 1976: 295). Another corresponding opposition which dominates the book is that between fiction and myth. A *"demythologizing"* (12) thrust in Biblical thought, coupled with skepticism, which was invented by the Hebrews (24), is opposed to Greek mythology. Readers are warned that "the heritage of the Western forms from the Greek ones should not be exaggerated" (260). The value of ancient culture has been secondary: "On the question of Greek influence, we must always remind ourselves that the preservation of Greek traditions in the West was ancillary to religious thought" (261–62). Because of this misdirected attention, the Hebrew influence has been underestimated. The depth of their contribution may be recognized by examining what is probably its greatest achievement—fiction. "The concept of fiction was resisted by the Greeks, in spite of their flourishing poetry and drama, whereas the Hebrews laid the groundwork for the idea though they had no epic, no drama, and only a restricted, if intense, poetry and prose" (278). Thus fiction, and by extension literature, is a Biblical creation. An investigation of "the Yahwist roots of literature" (276) suggests that this art uses the kerygma as a model and is indeed inherently kerygmatic (303), and therefore, as Auerbach said, in need of interpretation. Despite its debt to mythical thought, the West is not Greek: "The West is an island of literature in a sea of myth" (274). Thus the position of *Mimesis* is advanced to the argument that literature as a whole (and not just one of its

modes) is Biblical in that it constitutes the kerygmatic expression of the Hebraic identity of Western culture.

14. This position is quite old. Solomon Formstecher (1808–89) thought that Christianity was promoting Jewish principles which had been tainted by paganism; that alien influence, however, was gradually being eliminated, especially with the advent of Protestantism.

15. This was a rather popular position in the 1940s, when, taking the Nazis' word for Hellenism, intellectuals started blaming various forms of Greek inspiration (or even bad example) for the horrors of the war. See the first volume of Karl Popper's *The Open Society and its Enemies*, entitled *The Spell of Plato* (1943).

16. I can only allude here to the other major work, one of Romance scholarship this time, to which *Mimesis* proleptically responds, Curtius's *European Literature and the Latin Middle Ages* (1948). The antagonistic relationship between Auerbach and Ernst Robert Curtius (1886–1956) has been noted by various commentators. In response to the advent of fascism, Curtius published *The German Mind in Danger* (1932), a polemical pamphlet which concluded with a plea for a new humanism based on a shared understanding of the common (medieval Latin) roots of European culture. Following that, he devoted himself to the composition of his *magnum opus*. In defining its ideological position, he stressed that his "book is not the product of purely scholarly interests, that it grew out of a concern for the preservation of Western culture. It seeks to serve an understanding of the Western cultural tradition in so far as it is manifested in literature. It attempts to illuminate the unity of that tradition in space and time by the application of new methods. In the intellectual chaos of the present it has become necessary, and happily not impossible, to demonstrate that unity. But the demonstration can only be made from a universal standpoint. Such a standpoint is afforded by Latinity" (1953: viii). Auerbach must have been familiar with at least some of its twenty-five parts which appeared as articles in the years 1932–44, before the volume came out. His own alternative to the solution of Latinity (Santirocco 1987) was Hebraism; and to Curtius's defense of a new canon "bound only by the idea of beauty" (397), he counterproposed a canon imitating a moral social order. The idea that Curtius modeled the book on Joyce's novel, on which he had already written with admiration, is intriguing: "He too presents a work in eighteen chapters, structured in the way that he describes *Ulysses*'s structure. Thus we might see the book as Curtius's attempt, in his own fashion, at *Ulysses*" (Dronke 1980: 1104). Given Auerbach's modeling of *Mimesis* on the Bible, this adds significantly to the complexity of any comparison between the two concluding monuments of Romance philology. The importance of Curtius's method of *Toposforschung* for Auerbach's hermeneutic principle of *Ansatzpunkt* became obvious in the latter's essay "Philologie der Weltliteratur" (1952). The title of Auerbach's last book also shows that, at least for him, their contest over the legacy of Karl Vossler, Aby Warburg, and the other Weimar historicists never ended. For both authors, however, the highest critical ideal was the same: to use Curtius's terms, it was the two requirements for "reverent reception and faithful transmission" (1953: 597) of tradition—"devotion and enthusiasm" (597) or "Faith and Joy" (598).

17. Since Henry Fielding, novelists have often defended their genre as the modern epic (Watt 1957). German comparisons of the two genres began in the 1770s.

The tradition of modern literature has also been read as a history of *nostos* as well as negotiation between the Hebraic and the Hellenic positions on classicism which reaches a magnificent expression in Joyce (Perl 1984, especially the chapter "Novel and Epic: Reading Backwards from *Ulysses*").

18. The sublimity of the Bible has been defended by many British writers both before (Robert South in 1715, Anthony Blackwell in 1725) and after Lowth (Philip Dodridge in 1763, S. J. Pratt in 1777). Since Blackwell's *The Sacred Classics Defended and Illustrated*, most writers agree that the Bible is far more sublime than Greek works. Blake thought that Homer had stolen the sublime from the Bible. Coleridge asked: "Could you ever discover anything sublime in our sense of the term, in the classic Greek literature? Sublimity is Hebrew by birth" (Coleridge 1846: 178–80).

19. In his *Table Talk*, Luther recognized dramatic elements in Job. Later, Milton and some of his contemporaries saw it as a short epic. Macaulay writes that the Oriental style of Aeschylus "often reminds us of the Hebrew writers. The book of Job, indeed, in conduct and diction, bears a considerable resemblance to some of his dramas" (1878: 5).

20. In an extension of Lowth's research, John Jebb applied the same principles to the New Testament, arguing that it was not written "in a purely Greek style" but rather that "the phraseology is Hebrew" (Jebb 1820: 91) and that the "whole arrangement of the periods is regulated according to the Hebrew verses" (93). More recently, commentators have argued that all Gospels were translated from Hebrew, and their present form is "translation Greek" (Tresmontant 1989).

21. The Dutch philosopher is the best-known hero of secularism: "Spinoza is more than a father of modernity, he is the father of Jewish modernity. . . . Spinoza is the modern Jew's second country" (Himmelfarb 1973: 5). The history of his reputation, however, shows that he was discovered much later as the "first secular Jew" (and has been used as a *figura* of Jewish modernity) because of his espousal of (interpretive) secularism—his break with tradition (including both religious and cultural associations), as well as interest in government, socio-historical analysis, and the natural sciences. "What can be said confidently is that Spinoza took the first step in the eventual secularization of Jewish life by examining it empirically as a natural phenomenon subject solely to the forces of secular history. In doing so he opened a breach between the Jewish religion and traditional community, on the one hand, and the broader totality of Jewish life on the other" (Yovel 1990a: 95).

22. The humanistic character of this ideal can be traced to the republican and Reformation intellectual politics of the Swiss Confederation in the first half of the sixteenth century.

23. John Wyclif (1329–84), for example, who taught at Oxford, wanted people to read the Bible for themselves and started translating it from Latin into the vernacular (English), thus giving priority to Scripture over church. In his *De Dominio Divino* (1376), he attacked the official doctrine of transubstantiation and argued that dominion is founded on grace and not in institutional power.

24. This religious position became a common aesthetic principle in formalist poststructuralism: "However, the structure of the Bible as a redacted, self-interpreting text has this important exegetical consequence: the Bible effectively blocks any attempt to understand it by reconstruction of its textual history and a working back

to an original, uninterpreted intention. This self-interpreting text is also self-effac-
ing with respect to its origins" (Bruns 1987: 627).

25. All the major Reformation figures (Erasmus, Luther, Calvin, Melanchthon)
devoted themselves to the task of elucidation and wrote many scriptural commentaries.

26. At the same time, that "letter" became more spiritual than the "spirit," and
its meaning was fiercely debated: for example, while Luther invoked the "spirit" of
the Scripture, the humanist Zwingli appealed to its "letter" by requiring philological competence.

27. In the wilderness of Sinai, God tells Moses: "Now therefore, if you will obey
my voice and keep my covenant, you shall be my own possession among all peoples;
for all the earth is mine, and you shall be to me a kingdom of priests and a holy
nation. These are the words which you shall speak to the children of Israel" (Exodus
19. 5–6). For an analysis of the passage, see Moran 1962.

28. The most representative example was the curriculum (including Latin,
Greek, and Hebrew) reform (1516–19) at the University of Wittenberg, where
Luther was a Lecturer in Biblical Studies, under the great-nephew of Reuchlin,
Melanchthon.

29. Starting with Luther's pan-Germanism, national cohesiveness and tradition
have always been the religion of those churches. Near the end of John Osborne's
play *Luther*, Johann von Staupitz, Vicar General of the Augustinian Order, tells the
Reformer: "The world's changed. For one thing, you've made a thing called Germany; you've unlaced a language and taught it to the Germans, and the rest of the
world will just have to get used to the sound of it. As we once made the body of
Christ from bread, you've made the body of Europe, and whatever our pains turn
out to be, they'll attack the rest of the world too" (Osborne 1961: 100).

30. In a chapter entitled "Theology and Aesthetic Judgement," where he rejects
the possibility of a Christian aesthetic, a theologian explores the meaning of artistic
value for the modern believer. "It is especially the Protestant today who faces a
problem when he seeks to define the basis of artistic judgment" (Wilder 1958: 85).
After outlining the difference between Catholic and Protestant aesthetics on the
basis of the Roman doctrine of transubstantiation and the idea of sacred art, he
concludes: "The great exfoliation of art about the Catholic faith is related to its
sacramental conceptions. The Protestant position, with its different view of church
and sacrament, and its emphasis on the ear rather than the eye, suffers greatly with
respect to the whole realm of *sacred art* itself, but opens the door to the secular
expression of the artist, just as it dignifies the secular vocations of men. In this sense
art is liberated, though Protestantism has often, of course, chained the arts in its
own way" (89). In the distinction between Greek epic and Biblical narrative in
Mimesis, his critique of "classical tools and canons" (66) finds an eminent example
of "the contribution that a theologically oriented criticism can make today" (67).
For another example of such criticism, see his study "Biblical Epos and Modern
Narrative" (Wilder 1969: 41–77).

31. "If your prince or temporal ruler commands you to side with the pope, to
believe thus and so, or to get rid of certain books, you should say, 'It is not fitting
that Lucifer should sit at the side of God. Gracious sir, I owe you obedience in body
and property; command me within the limits of your authority on earth, and I will

obey. But if you command me to believe or to get rid of certain books, I will not obey; for then you are a tyrant and overreach yourself, commanding where you have neither the right nor the authority,' etc. Should he seize your property on account of this and punish such disobedience, then blessed are you; thank God that you are worthy to suffer for the sake of the divine word. Let him rage, fool that he is; he will meet his judge. For I tell you, if you fail to withstand him, if you give in to him and let him take away your faith and your books, you have truly denied God" (Luther 1974: 62).

32. "Bodin tried to show that the nature and extent of [political] authority was involved in the history, the structure and the end of political association. He strove to find some principle of order and unity, that should reconcile liberty and subjection, define political obligation and satisfy conscience and reason" (Allen 1961: 407). Jean Bodin (1530–96), in his last work, the "Dialogue of Seven Wise Men" on religion *Heptaplomeres* (1857, op. posth.), surveys seven creeds and favors Judaism as a spiritualization of the natural law. His work "marked a new turn in the appreciation of Judaism, when he stressed the importance of the Mosaic Law as supreme authority which embodies natural law" (Ettinger 1961: 197). His contemporaries sometimes described him as a Jew in religion.

33. Julius Caesar Scaliger (1484–1558) in his *declamatio* "Against the Slanderers of Poetry" exclaims: "Truly, Plato, since you composed poetry (and what poetry! May the gods drive that vice from the earth), and according to your own laws were exiled from your Republic, but did not live in exile, you showed that other poets as well should not be exiled. We for our part shall gladly pass our lives outside of your Republic (as we have said) with our modest wives and children. We shall live with Moses, with Deborah, with the mother of Samuel, with the minstrel King, with the prophets, with Zachariah, with Simeon, with the ever-virgin Mother of God, whose poetry is more important than your whole *Republic* and all your laws" (Hall 1948: 1129–30).

34. *Hebrew Thought Compared with Greek* does what the title promises for two hundred pages of parallel philological ("*Wörterbuch*") deciphering of the deep structures of the racial experience. The author, who endorses Auerbach's position (Boman 1970: 23), knows well that his topic "is, so to speak, in the air in our day" (13) and strives for a balanced view that should make readers equally grateful to both fountains of wisdom: "From the days of Alexander the Great onward, the history of European civilization manifests only mixtures and syntheses of the two ways of thinking, in which now one and now the other prevails" (12). Thus he explains how we owe dynamic, passionate, temporal, and synthetic thinking to the Hebrews, while the static, moderate, spatial, and analytic to the Hellenes. In a typical passage which illustrates his approach and tone, he has the following to say about their differences in historical understanding: "The one thinks causally and consequently in terms of natural science; the other thinks finally or teleologically. The one puts itself outside the events and looks backwards; the other puts itself into the events and thinks itself 'into' the psychic life of the man involved and how they directed themselves forward in thought and will. The one concerns itself with the past, the other with the present and future. It cannot be said that the one way of observing is more correct than the other; both are possible and necessary, and each in its own field works out best; causal thinking in science, final or teleological think-

ing in ethics and religion. The former is Greek, and the latter is Israelite. The Greeks have given to the world the science of history; the Israelites gave to the world historical religion. In contrast to all their neighbours, both peoples knew what history is" (170). A later commentator, concerned about "the Biblically ministerial function of the Church in its confrontation with the world of the modern university" and "the problem of the disturbing Hebraic void in the university's attempt to preserve and transmit the cultural heritage of the Occident" (Harcourt 1963: 353), proposed that "the Church will have to act in some way as the transferential agent of the Hebraic heritage," "as the Hebraic leaven in the academic dough" (354), taking Boman's two types of thinking as a guide in its critique of the curriculum.

35. "Numenius of Apamea, contemporary of Justin and precursor in important respects of Plotinus and Neoplatonism, affirms the theory of dependence without qualification: 'What is Plato,' he asks, 'but Moses in Attic Greek?'" (Chadwick 1966: 15) Second-century philosophers could only respond by reversing the chronological priority: "The dependence is rather the other way round—Jesus had read Plato and Paul had studied Heraclitus. Christianity ([the Platonist] Celsus urges) is a corruption of the primordial truths enshrined in the ancient polytheistic tradition" (23).

36. Regarding the Hebrews as the first philosophers remained a common notion for a long time. "There are versions of the medieval Aristotle legend that would even have us believe that Aristotle was born a Jew or became a proselyte to Judaism! . . . The idea that hidden away in the library of Hebrew books is to be found the source of all philosophy, science, and learning, and notably that of Aristotle and the Greeks, persisted long after [Roger] Bacon and far beyond the limits of the Middle Ages. It was quite seriously held throughout the fifteenth, sixteenth, and seventeenth centuries and only died out even among the learned in the eighteenth century" (Bevan and Singer 1928: 300–1). Jean Bodin wrote in 1566: "Not inconsistently did the Egyptian priest taunt Solon with the fact that the Greeks seemed to him mere children, because they had nothing old. More appropriate, even, the taunt of the Christian who told the Greeks that Moses the lawgiver was older than the gods of the Greeks, for Greece has almost nothing older than Danaus and Cadmus. Of these the one was founder of the race, the other brought letters to the Greeks. But in those same times the Jews flourished, having the highest reputation for valorous deeds" (Bodin 1945: 340).

37. Theologies which have emphasized the Hebraic-Hellenic contrast with a preference for the former have essentially produced a Christian, and therefore "largely a synthetic Jew," for their own ideological purposes. "The apparent philo-Semitism of the contrast has thus always been ambiguous in its relation to the actual Jews of history, whether ancient or modern" (Barr 1966: 59). The dark story of this attitude is well known and should always remain so. Here is an example from British Israelitism: "Messianic enthusiasm was high throughout seventeenth-century Europe. On the whole, however, English Puritans drew a distinction between the Israelites of the Old Testament and their Jewish descendants: they identified themselves with the first (those who had been the chosen people) but looked with suspicion and disdain on their descendants—the successful merchants who had rejected their Messiah and were, in their eyes, heretics" (K. Cohen 1975: 12). The reasons were partly financial: "To the English Puritans, the Jews of their time were

representatives of that type of capitalism which was involved in war, Government contracts, State monopolies, speculative promotions, and the construction and financial projects of princes, which they themselves condemned. In fact the difference may, in general, with the necessary qualifications, be formulated: that Jewish capitalism was speculative pariah-capitalism, while the Puritan was bourgeois organization of labour" (Weber 1976: 271). The Western ambivalence toward contemporary Jews (and Greeks) is a topic of major importance which unfortunately belongs outside the confines of this study. Suffice to quote here what Wittgenstein wrote in 1931: "In western civilization the Jew is always measured on scales which do not fit him. Many people can see clearly enough that the Greek thinkers were neither philosophers in the western sense nor scientists in the western sense, that the participants in the Olympian Games were not sportsmen and do not fit in to any western occupation. But it is the same with the Jews. And by taking the words of our language as the only possible standards we constantly fail to do them justice. So at one time they are overestimated, at another underestimated" (Wittgenstein 1980: 16e).

38. "In this respect, the century which separates this Reformation from the English Revolution is the one when the priestly pre-eminence of its kings was snatched from them by a people resolved to take its destiny into its own hands. In Europe everywhere, the study of the Scriptures and popular unrest brought about new heresies and sects which the Church of Rome called judaistic; but it was only the English who identified themselves wholeheartedly with the people of Moses. The leaders of Puritanism, like Cromwell and Milton, thought of this affiliation in an allegorical Christian manner. They did not pretend that Jews were flesh and blood ancestors of the English. They merely substituted the English for the Jews so that the former became, in their turn, the people chosen by the Almighty for a special and at the same time a universal mission" (Poliakov 1974: 42).

39. The seventeenth century also saw the publication of about ten rhetorics devoted to the Bible, as well as treatises on the biblical verse like *Davidis Lyra, seu nova hebraea S. Scriptura ars poetica, canonibus suis descripta, et exemplis sacris & Pindari ac Sophoclis parellelis demonstrata cum selectorum Davidis, Salomnis, Ieremiae, Mosis, Iobi poematum* (1637) by the distinguished Hebraist Franciscus Gomarus, Milton's contemporary.

40. *In Paradise Regained* (1671), pagan writing is one mode of knowledge with which Satan tempts the son of God:

> All knowledge is not couched in Moses' Law,
> The Pentateuch or what the Prophets wrote;
> The Gentiles also know, and write, and teach
> To admiration, led by nature's light;
> And with the Gentiles much thou must converse. . . .

(IV, 225–29)

Christ's celebrated rebuke consists in a full-fledged comparison. Here is the part on poetry:

> Or if I would delight my private hours
> With music or with poem, where so soon

As in our native language can I find
That solace? All our law and story strewed
With hymns, our Psalms with artful terms inscribed,
Our Hebrew songs and harps in Babylon,
That pleased so well our victors' ear, declare
That rather Greece from us these arts derived;
Ill imitated, while they loudest sing
The vices of their deities, and their own,
In fable, hymn, or song, so personating
Their gods ridiculous, and themselves past shame.
Remove their swelling epithets, thick laid
As varnish on a harlot's cheek, the rest,
Thin shown with aught of profit or delight,
Will far be found unworthy to compare
With Sion's songs, to all true tastes excelling,
Where God is praised aright, and godlike men,
The Holiest of Holies, and his saints;
Such are from God inspired, not such from thee;
Unless where moral virtue is expressed
By light of nature not in all quite lost.

(IV, 331–52)

41. Research into Milton's Semitic studies began in the era of modernist comparativism. When Harris Fletcher's pioneering *Milton's Rabbinical Readings* appeared in 1930, this philological side of the poet surprised many specialists. Forty years later, after the development of a whole scholarly industry around "the Jewish factor, or to take a word of more universal significance, the factor of Jerusalem" (Fisch 1964: 3), a critic could make this generalization: "His knowledge of Hebrew is felt on every page of his writings and pervades the style of his prose as well as his poetry" (K. Cohen 1975: 3). From Werblowsky's *Lucifer and Prometheus* (1952) to Steadman's chapter on "Sion and Helicon" in *Milton's Biblical and Classical Imagery* (1984), parallel discussions of the Hebraic and the Hellenic have become rather common in Milton studies. Some approaches have even taken Milton's comparisons at face value and have added their own anti-Hellenic turn: "The ancient Greeks vanished from history and nobody prevented the Christian Church from interpreting Greek philosophy and literature in such a way that it could be incorporated into Christianity and subordinated to its religious ethos. The Jews, on the other hand, survived the destruction of their state and temple, preserved their religious writings and beliefs, and remained a living influence in Western culture" (K. Cohen 1975: 10). The book which defends the Hebraic cause more openly than any other promises to deal with "the concept of Jerusalem as applied to English Literature and History in the seventeenth century" (Fisch 1964: 13), but develops into an essay on the Hebraic dimension of Puritanism. While it starts with an examination of the "mythical divorce of Jerusalem from Albion" (11) in Blake's *Jerusalem*, it concludes with a discussion of John Locke in terms of Athens and Jerusalem. Characteristically, after Part One, which is a discussion of the Hebraic rhetorical manner of the period, a chapter on method follows entitled "The Logos," where a

term of contrast is abruptly introduced: "Before we come to the central topics of Hebraism therefore it will be as well to describe by way of contrast those Greek modes of thinking which were nourished either in the Middle Ages or the Renaissance. Here, the leading term and structure will be the *logos* which for the Greeks brings together the spheres of Man, God, and Nature" (67). The rest of the book is explicitly based on this polarity. A principal aim is to dispel the "false identification of Hebraism with Puritanism" (227). The attack on the latter by Enlightenment thinkers, Romantic poets, or cultural critics is totally misdirected. "It is really against St. Paul and not Moses that the campaign is waged, against the Greek, Platonic ethic which divides the 'fallen' world of Matter and Flesh from the 'ideal' world of Spirit. Such divisions are unknown to Hebraism" (277). The author laments the dissociation of sensibility and disintegration of faith that occurred between Milton and Blake. In conclusion, he presents the "inconceivably sharp and challenging" (291) dilemma of Western Man: to "seek wisdom by means of the *logos*, by means of intellectual concepts and schemes" (290) or to "conform to our Covenant-bonds, in which case we are united to the Lord of Life" (292). His argument and plea ends with a poignant question: "Paradoxically, we need Divine help to carry out the tasks which God lays upon us. Can it be that Hebraism can yet mediate that help?" (292) This is obviously scholarship as homily. Its dilemma, however, is not very different from that expressed at the conclusion of *Mimesis*.

42. Following Martin Heidegger's suggestion, in the "Letter on Humanism" (1947), that Humanism is a "specifically Roman phenomenon," it has been proposed that "what [Matthew] Arnold, [Irving] Babbitt, [I. A.] Richards, and the contemporary educational establishment allege to be a 'classical,' i.e., Greek, *paideia*, is, in fact, Roman, that, in other words, modern humanistic education, like that of Renaissance Humanism, has its origins in and is finally affiliated not with the originative thinking of ancient Greece, but with the *Humanitas* of ancient Rome, that representational, imitative, and calculative thinking which authorized, enabled, and legitimated the Roman *imperium*" (Spanos 1985: 72).

43. The same trend may be observed in France: "One should not forget that, generally speaking, the Roman model, at the Enlightenment, played a dual role: in its republican aspect, it was the very embodiment of liberty; in its military aspect, it was the ideal schema of discipline. The Rome of the eighteenth century and of the Revolution was the Rome of the Senate, but it was also that of the legion; it was the Rome of the Forum, but it was also that of the camps. Up to the empire, the Roman reference transmitted, somewhat ambiguously, the juridical ideal of citizenship and the technique of disciplinary methods" (Foucault 1979: 146).

44. In this respect it is interesting, for example, that even after Augustan administration prevailed, "Britain had a philo-Semitic tradition which became particularly strong with the rise of the bourgeoisie in the mid-19th century. Thus many Victorians saw themselves as biblical patriarchs, priding themselves on their diligence, thrift, discretion, respect for forms and—above all—their sense of rigid righteousness" (Bernal 1987: 347). If the Biblical model lost its political urgency, it did not lose its authority in configurations of social life based on ideas of community and local ethics. The ethnic character of the model too, with its racial explanatory power, remained distinct: "Despite the association between the English and the Semites, no one compared the English to the Arabs or the Ethiopians. The 'Sem-

ites' they had in mind were Jews and/or Phoenicians" (350). The story of the Arab struggle to gain acceptance in the discursive domain of Semitism has not been written.

45. "In the early seventeenth century, the process began (and this is highly significant) with a change in the concept of the present. The present was reduced to an instant without inherent duration. It was said to depend on secondary causes and human effort for its preservation. This seems to register the loss of common understanding . . . made apparent by religious wars, economic fluctuations, and a geographic and scientific extension of the idea of the world" (Luhmann 1982: 248–49).

46. "In the modern age history emerged as something it never had been before. It was no longer composed of the deeds and sufferings of men, and it no longer told the story of events affecting the lives of men; it became a man-made process, the only all-comprehending process which owed its existence exclusively to the human race" (Arendt 1968: 58). See also Fussner (1962), Guibbory (1986), Rossi (1984), and Struever (1970).

47. In the first of the seven Wolfenbüttel Fragments, "On the Toleration of the Deists," which Lessing published in 1774, Reimarus demands for the Deists the same tolerance exhibited toward Jews and pagans.

48. On Bentley's invention of "an historical science of antiquity," and its influence on nineteenth-century philology, see Brink (1986), who shows that equal standards of scholarship were not attained again before Wolf.

49. A direct literary parallel to Deism has been proposed: "As a theory, resting upon a coherent, or supposedly coherent, body of principles, neo-classicism was, at bottom, neither traditionalist nor authoritarian; it was an expression of the same rationalism of the Enlightenment which was manifesting itself in deism" (Lovejoy 1932: 291).

50. John Husbands, in the Preface to his anthology A *Miscellany of Poems By several Hands* (1731), proposes that contemporary poetry needs to study the Scripture for the best models of writing: "What innumerable Beauties might our Poetry be furnish'd with from those sacred Repositories? . . . These are the Writings which far surpass all human Compositions. . . . They exceed in Beauty and Propriety any Thing that was ever wrote by Man. The greatest Genius's among the Ancients fall infinitely short of the inspir'd Books" (quoted in Crane 1922: 29).

51. Regarding the secularization of writing and the emergence of its modern categories (like literature), the following comments on the disciplining of bodies apply also to the disciplining of texts by criticism, if we substitute "(autonomous) text" for "body" in the original: "These methods, which made possible the meticulous control of the operations of the ⟨text⟩, which assured the constant subjection of its forces and imposed upon them a relation of docility-utility, might be called 'disciplines.' Many disciplinary methods had long been in existence—in monasteries, armies, workshops. But in the course of the seventeenth and eighteenth centuries the disciplines became general formulas of domination. . . . The historical moment of the discipline was the moment when an art of the ⟨text⟩ was born, which was directed not only at the growth of its skills, nor at the intensification of its subjection, but at the formation of a relation that in the mechanism itself makes it more obedient as it becomes more useful, and conversely. What was then being formed was a policy of coercions that act upon the ⟨text⟩, a calculated manipulation

of its elements, its gestures, its behavior. The ⟨text⟩ was entering a machinery of power that explores it, breaks it down and rearranges it. A 'political anatomy,' which was also a 'mechanics of power,' was being born; . . . Thus discipline produces subjected and practiced ⟨texts⟩, 'docile' ⟨texts⟩. Discipline increases the forces of the ⟨text⟩ (in economic terms of utility) and diminishes these same forces (in political terms of obedience). In short, it dissociates power from the ⟨text⟩" (Foucault 1979: 137–38). If this substitution of "text" for "body" is not entirely inappropriate, then it may indicate that the disciplining of bodies was to a great extent modeled on that of texts.

52. It is fair to say that "the modern attitude to the written word could not and did not arise *until scripture had become literature and literature scripture*" (Lewisohn 1932: x). The two changed status together: scripture "having become literature, it was necessary for literature to become scripture" (xiii). This entailed a different reading experience: "A new type of reader arose—one to whom literature was no longer an elegant diversion or an illustration of the foreknown and fixed, but moral research, a road to salvation, the bread of life" (ix). In addition, when the impact of Deistic philology is taken into account, it becomes clear that "a literary approach to the Bible is one that resists the trend of biblical scholarship toward fragmentation" (Ryken 1974: 36).

53. The study of parallelism goes back to the interest in Biblical repetition of the sixteenth century (Kugel 1981). At that time, the idea that Hebrew poetry was simpler than the classical and closer to contemporary vernaculars emerged. Overcoming Jerome's metrical theories, however, took a very long time, and only in the seventeenth century was it possible to distinguish meter from rhythm, as an analogy between the Bible and the vernaculars was established. But even though Lowth's emphasis on the repetition of structures was not totally new, his assumption about the artistic autonomy of those structures was. He amplified his theory in the "Preliminary Dissertation" introducing his translation of Isaiah in 1778, where he defined *parallelismus membrorum*. His approach to Hebrew poetry affected the course of Biblical scholarship and has remained influential, even outside the field. Of particular relevance to this discussion is the attempt of Roman Jakobson (1896–1982) to elevate parallelism to an ever-present, all-important aspect of poetry, regardless of language, form, culture, or time. During the early years of their work, the Russian Formalists, in an effort to free criticism from the metrical concerns of symbolist poetry and structural linguistics, did much research on rhythm and repetition in both poetry and prose. Osip Brik, for example, wrote on sound repetition (Matejka 1964) and Viktor Shklovsky (1973) on retardation. Working in the same direction, Jakobson first drew attention to parallelism as a stylistic device in 1919, in a study of Russian modernist poetry (Brown 1973: 58–82). Forty years later, from the late 1950s until the end of his career, he studied it as the basic feature of the poetic function of language—as the very essence of literariness (*'literaturnost'*) that the Formalists sought to discover. During this long period, he dealt extensively with the subject in general studies (Jakobson 1960, 1966, 1968, 1980) or in close, often collaborative, readings of poems by Baudelaire, Eminescu, Král, Dante, Brecht, Shakespeare, Codax, Majakovski, Sidney, Blake, Pessoa, Cavafy, Blok, Yeats, and others. The study of parallelism in the context of variance/invariance was an integral part of his project for a nomothetic science of language. In the heyday of structuralist

stylistics, his theory was widely debated. (For representative positions, see *American Journal of Semiotics*, Brooke-Rose 1976, Culler 1975, Fowler 1975, Guillen 1987, S. R. Levin 1962, Lodge 1977, *Poetics Today* 1980, Reinhart 1976, Riffaterre 1966, Ruwet 1973, and Werth 1976). Its influence extended beyond literary studies to linguistics, philology, folklore, and anthropology (Fox 1977). This is another case where methods of analysis first applied to the Bible to justify its intrinsic unity and merit provided a model for the study of universals in literature. The work of Henri Meschonnic, which places the semiotics of the sacred at the center of linguistics, provides a more recent example of this tendency. His view of discourse is based on rhythm (1982), the force organizing subject, language, and history, and is a critique of sign and identity. He presents rhythm as a figure for the Jew, the Jew of the Greco-Christian sign, since it is "hidden by the sign as the Jew has been treated by the political theology of the sign" (Meschonnic 1988: 100).

54. Charles Rollin, for example, in the second volume of his *Traité des Études* (1726–31, 4 vols., complete English translation 1734), devoted a section to the eloquence of the sacred writings.

55. It was effeminate, too (Halperin 1986). The endless fascination of the West with its vision of the Greek as homosexual should also be examined in the context of the masculine-feminine dimension of the Hebrew-Greek polarity. For a representative position, see the definition of the Jew (and his fear of femininity) after Spinoza, under the self-explanatory title "Modern, Honorable, Masculine," which concludes: "For us, manly honor is the truth. It is our truth. It makes sense of what we are, or what we want to be" (Himmelfarb 1973: 12).

56. Fustel de Coulanges, author of the conservative interpretation of political life *Cité antique* (1864), complained in 1872: "In France scholarship is liberal, in Germany it is patriotic" (quoted in Momigliano 1977: 329).

57. "The particular form which the theory of taste took in Britain stemmed from the realignment of state and civil society prepared in the revolutions of the seventeenth century. The new theory of civil society hammered out of the Revolution Principles not only reworked the relation between wealth and virtue, but did so on the basis of the faculty of taste. The outcome was a philosophy of taste which differed considerably from the German philosophy of aesthetics. While British philosophers elaborated a justification of a moral civil society, their German contemporaries concentrated on justifying the welfare absolutism of the 'police-state.' The providentially regulated, sensible discriminations of the British theory of taste were appropriate to its efforts to legitimate the harmonious working of civil society apart from the state and law. The German tradition, on the other hand, saw the common welfare as promoted by the legislative discipline of the state" (Caygill 1989: 100).

58. Such conflicts are already apparent in the attacks of the physician and philosopher Isaac Orobio de Castro (c. 1617–87), Spinoza's contemporary in Amsterdam, against those learning secular sciences and questioning the authority of the Oral Law.

59. Regarding civic emancipation, the publication of *On the Civil Improvement of the Jews* by Christian Wilhelm von Dohm in 1781 [2nd ed. 1783] may be accepted as "the commencement of the social movement for the adoption of the Jews as citizens in European countries. That is also, coincidentally, the date of the promulgation of the Edict of Toleration by the Emperor Joseph II of Austria. From then

on, until the full realization of emancipation in the 1860's and 1870's, the civic and social status of the Jew continued to concern both public opinion and state authorities" (Katz 1964: 3). Mendelssohn praised the book, which advocated the acceptance of Jews as full citizens. "Assessed historically, Dohm's importance lies not so much in the shifting of a point of view from the theological to the humanistic and political but rather in the linking of suggestions pertaining to the Jews' position alone to the changes imminent in society at large. Changes in the status of the Jew in society now presupposed, or at least went hand-in-hand with, changes in the whole society" (12). In 1791 the first group of Sephardic Jews in France was granted civil rights.

60. Heine, who was probably the first to connect emancipation directly with the choice between Hebraism and Hellenism, wrote in 1828: "What is the great assignation of our times? It is the emancipation, not only of the people of Ireland, of the Greeks, the Jews of Frankfurt, the blacks of West India and similar depressed peoples, but of the whole world, especially Europe" (quoted in Katz 1964: 21).

61. The following epigram is called "The Impure Philology":

> Once upon a time, a vestal virgin named Philology
> Protected the purity and clear meaning of the sacred fire of antiquity;
> But soon the flame was snuffed out by a reverent sigh,
> For the pietist robbed her of her maidenhood.
>
> (Feuerbach 1980: 181–82)

62. Lowth's influence was far greater in the realm of literature. Some of this territory has been charted, especially in a chapter entitled "Hebraism and Classicism," whose purpose is to show "how the rediscovery of the Bible as literature rather than as religious text helped to wean the eighteenth-century poet away from his classical model and to mould not merely his poetic techniques but also his literary sensibility" (Roston 1965: 18). As the word "rediscovery" indicates, the author sees the change as a return to the poetic truth of the Hebrew Bible: "Between neo-classicism and romanticism a change had occurred which was closely in line with the biblical tradition. For in place of the wit, the stylization, the balance and the restraint of early eighteenth-century verse, the romantic poet, spurning the poetic diction of the preceding generation, was turning from the form to the spirit, from classicism to Hebraism" (40).

63. Positions on the relation between typology and allegory vary widely. Some consider typology a "spiritual" method of interpretation, and allegory a "literal" one. Others disagree: "For typology, the historical value of the text to be interpreted forms the essential presupposition for the use of it. For allegory, on the contrary, this is indifferent or even offensive, and must be pushed to one side to make room for the 'spiritual' sense which lies behind" (Eichrodt 1963: 227).

64. The transgressions of hedonism have been portrayed invariably as a Hellenic trait: "Transgression opens onto a scintillating and constantly affirmed world, a world without shadow or twilight, without that serpentine 'no' that bites into fruits and lodges their contradictions at their core. It is the solar inversion of satanic denial. It was originally linked to the divine, or rather, from this limit marked by the sacred, it opens the space where the divine functions. The discovery of such a category by a philosophy which questions itself upon the existence of the limit is evi-

dently one of the countless signs that our path is circular and that, with each day, we are becoming more Greek. Yet, this motion should not be understood as the promised return to a homeland or the recovery of an original soil which produced and which will naturally resolve every opposition" (Foucault 1977b: 37).

65. Walter Benjamin makes the Hebraic component of the project explicit and pushes the comparison to an apocalyptic opposition: "Hölderlin's translations from Sophocles were his last work; in them meaning plunges from abyss to abyss until it threatens to become lost in the bottomless depths of language. There is, however, a stop. It is vouchsafed to Holy Writ alone, in which meaning has ceased to be the watershed for the flow of language and the flow of revelation. Where a text is identical with truth or dogma, where it is supposed to be 'the true language' in all its literalness and without the mediation of meaning, this text is unconditionally translatable. In such case translations are called for only because of the plurality of languages. Just as, in the original, language and revelation are one without any tension, so the translation must be one with the original in the form of the interlinear version, in which literalness and freedom are united. For to some degree all great texts contain their potential translation between the lines; this is true to the highest degree of sacred writings. The interlinear version of the Scriptures is the prototype or ideal of all translation" (Benjamin 1969: 81–82). Any discussion of these thoughts (or any German analysis of translation) must begin with "Sendbrief vom Doletschen" (1530), Luther's letter on translation.

66. "Herder invented nothing; the ideas of the Sturm und Drang were represented at Königsberg itself by J. G. Hamann, who . . . really belongs to the mystical trend which, from throughout the century, under various names and either through organized sects such as Pietism or through isolated individuals such as Böhme and Franz von Baader, relieves souls oppressed by the tutelage of reason" (Brunschwig 1974: 92).

67. "The [British and German] traditions of taste and aesthetic culminate in Smith and Herder's attempts to uncover the sources of the conformity of judgment and its objects. Both try to sublate the difficulties raised by the repression of the conformity between production and legislation in their traditions; one in a political economy, the other in a philosophy of history. . . . Both traditions separated the elements of judgment, only to force them back together again. In the theory of taste, the law of the discriminations is given by providence, while production becomes a *je ne sais quoi*. In aesthetic, the law is administred upon its subjects and objects, denying them any autonomy. In both cases the proportionality produced by judgment can only be recognized through the pleasure in beauty. Beauty holds the promise of a freedom which legislates and produces for itself, and becomes not only the necessary supplement of the theories of civil society and the police-state, but also their point of crisis and disruption" (Caygill 1989: 184).

68. In 1787 Herder drew the plan for an "Institute of German National Enlightenment" (*Patriotisches Institut für den Allgemeingeist Deutschlands*).

69. "If the French conception of nationhood has been universalist, rationalist, assimilationist, and state-centered, the German conception has been particularist, organic, differentialist, and Volk-centered. Because national feeling developed before the nation-state, the German idea of the nation was not, originally, a political one, nor was it linked with the abstract idea of citizenship. This pre-political Ger-

man nation, this nation in search of a state, was conceived as a cultural, linguistic, or racial community—as an irreducibly particular *Volksgemeinschaft*. On this understanding, it is ethnocultural, not political unity, that is constitutive of nationhood" (Brubaker 1989: 4).

70. "The German word *Bildung* connotes more than its English equivalents, 'education' and 'formation.' It refers not only to the process of education but also to the goal of education, of cultivating the qualities and faculties that characterize humanity. Ideally, it connotes both mastery of knowledge and development of the self" (Reill 1975: 239).

71. Scaliger was the first to discuss the opposition between *Hebraioi* and *Hellenistai* in Acts of the Apostles 6:1, raising the question of Jewish Hellenism in post-Alexandrian antiquity.

72. "Wolf accumulates and carefully analyzes much more evidence than his predecessors, but the more he argues, the more we realize our necessary ignorance of the classical world. He enlarged the area of the unknown and located Homer far within it, beyond the reach of the neoclassical aesthete and the allegorical interpreter, both of whom assumed some form of assured communication with the poet. . . . Wolf effected this removal of the poet in two ways. He oriented speculation not on the poet or his poem but to the media of its preservation: rhapsodes and alphabets, editors and scholiasts. Second, a negative dialectic replaced, where possible, rational guesswork and established a methodological *docta ignorantia*" (Murrin 1980: 189–90).

73. The absolute unity of the literary canon, which can only inhere in fragmentariness, became a cardinal principle of Romanticism: "The new, eternal gospel that Lessing prophesied will appear as a bible: but not as a single book in the usual sense. Even what we now call the Bible is actually a system of books. And that is, I might add, no mere arbitrary turn of phrase! Or is there some other word to differentiate the idea of an infinite book from an ordinary one, than Bible, the book per se, the absolute book? And surely there is an eternally essential and even practical difference if a book is merely a means to an end, or an independent work, an individual, a personified idea. It cannot be this without divine inspiration, and here the esoteric concept is itself in agreement with the exoteric one; and, moreover, no idea is isolated, but is what it is only in combination with all other ideas. An example will explain this. All the classical poems of the ancients are coherent, inseparable; they form an organic whole, they constitute, properly viewed, only a single poem, the only one in which poetry itself appears in perfection. In a similar way, in a perfect literature all books should be only a single book, and in such an eternally developing book, the gospel of humanity and culture will be revealed" (Schlegel 1971: 249–50).

74. Classicists (e.g., Murray 1907: 101–15; Lord 1960: 156–57) continue to draw parallels between the epics and the oldest Biblical documents (especially Jahvist and Elohist), as Wilamowitz had already demanded in the 1880s.

75. "Wolf's theories were at first greeted with enthusiasm in England; the romantics enjoyed the notion that the Homeric epics were the rude, virile utterances of a barbarous people, like those old English and Scottish ballads which so fascinated them. They saw Homer as they saw Shakespeare, spontaneous, natural, gloriously imperfect and unpredictable" (Jenkyns 1980: 197). Higher Criticism of Homer and the Bible emerged together in the 1820s in England. Later attitudes

grew more reserved. "Both clergymen and lay [Victorian] scholars recognized the skeptical implications for the Bible of Wolfian approaches to Homer. They consciously used that apprehension over the Scriptures to inhibit extensive consideration of Wolf's theory and later of Grote's analysis of the Homeric epics" (Turner 1981: 449). For Victorian critics (as for Auerbach later), the interpretation of the Bible sometimes offered a guide to the reading of Homer. Treating a document first as a text rather than a statement of moral principles was the critical approach "that British scholars had resisted in regard to Homer from fear of its implications for the Bible. . . . Once scholars, such as [Benjamin] Jowett, applied the methods of critical philology and history to the Bible, no substantial religious obstacles remained to prevent application of similar methods to classical documents. . . . Ironically, in England many classicists learned the tools of German critical scholarship from the theologians, as [Alexander] Grant had from Jowett" (Turner 1981: 343).

76. See, for example, the advocacy of William Gladstone, Chancellor of the Exchequer, who, after comparing the epic to the Old Testament and granting that it "stands between Paradise and the vices of later heathenism" (Gladstone 1858: 4), insists that Homer still is indispensable to the education of both boys and men (13).

77. "In many respects, then, early romanticism corresponds to the profound economic, social, political, and moral crisis of the latter years of the eighteenth century. . . . [T]he Germany of the period, suffering from economic crisis and profound social problems accompanied by continual revolts, found itself . . . plunged into a triple crisis: the social and moral crisis of a bourgeoisie, with new-found access to culture . . . but who are no longer able to find positions for those sons traditionally destined for the robe or the rostrum (unless the sons no longer wanted these jobs, notably that of the pastor); the political crisis of the French Revolution, a model that disturbed some and fascinated others, and whose ambiguity becomes ever more apparent with the French occupation; and the Kantian critique, finally, which is unintelligible for some, liberating but destructive for others, and which seems urgently in need of its own critical recasting" (Lacoue-Labarthe and Nancy 1988: 5). For a critique of the political fate of liberalism in its inability to attack bourgeois complacency effectively in the nineteenth century, see Craig 1982.

78. The motto of the book comes from Rousseau: "Si c'est la raison qui fait l'homme, c'est le sentiment qui le conduit."

79. "The whole radical aesthetic tradition from Coleridge to Herbert Marcuse, lamenting the inorganic, mechanistic nature of industrial capitalism, draws sustenance from this prophetic denunciation" (Eagleton 1990: 118).

80. For recent discussions of the idea of play, see Derrida 1981: 156–71; the study of Heidegger and Nietzsche in Hyland 1984; Hearn 1976–77; the special issue of SubStance 1980; Baudrillard 1975: 33–41 ("Ethic of Labor; Aesthetic of Play"); the surveys of the philosophy of play in Hans 1981 and Spariosu 1989; Hutchinson 1983; and Guinness and Hurley 1984, which looks at literature as play.

81. "Why, then, did Schiller dismiss democracies as an amalgam of unconsidered decisions and faction? The truth is that from his start as a political commentator to his final theoretical efforts, Schiller remained loyal to Shaftesbury and the English constitutional model as it had been interpreted by its eighteenth-century German admirers. . . . [It] is not democracy but representative institutions that remain the consistent institutional ideal of Schiller's political theory: a happy me-

dium between large and small assemblies, between popular lawlessness and autocratic despotism" (Chytry 1989: 94).

82. "The process of differentiation among fields of practice produces conditions
favourable to the construction of 'pure' theories (of economics, politics, law, art,
etc.) which reproduce the prior differentiation of the social structures in the initial
abstraction by which they are constituted. The emergence of the work of art as a
commodity, and the appearance of a distinct category of producers of symbolic
goods specifically destined for the market, to some extent prepared the ground for
a pure theory of art, that is, of art as art" (Bourdieu 1985: 16).

83. Regarding the role of the artist, William Blake, in his annotations of 1808 to
the first volume of Sir Joshua Reynolds' *Discourses*, writes: "The Foundation of
Empire is Art & Science. Remove them or Degrade them, & the Empire is No
More. Empire follows Art & Not Vice Versa as Englishmen suppose" (Blake 1972:
445). Reynolds writes in his dedication "To the King": "To give advice to those who
are contending for royal liberality, has been for some years the duty of my station in
the Academy." Blake comments: "Liberality! we want not Liberality. We want a
Fair Price & Proportionate Value & a General Demand for Art" (446).

84. "Disciplinary power has as its correlative an individuality that is not only
analytical and 'cellular,' but also natural and 'organic'" (Foucault 1979: 156).

85. The study "Epic and Novel" (1981) by Mikhail Bakhtin (1895–1975) could
also be fruitfully compared to the studies by Auerbach and Lukács. In regard to the
terms in the title, Bakhtin makes two changes: he generalizes their content, making
them mean not just the respective genres to which they normally refer but fundamental modes of writing; and he, like Auerbach, makes them potentially co-exist
and compete for influence and power. For him, the epic stands for all canonical
literature. It depicts a monochronic, idealized past—a closed, finished, complete,
final, self-contained world. It is addressed to the future memory of a nation, trying
to control its past through selective recollection. As for the novel, it stands for what
is always fluid in the history of genres—for the cyclical project of renewal and
modernity, the constant becoming of literature which anticipates and opens the
future. It is the defamiliarization of the commonplace, the transgression of the
normative, the violation of the rules, the parody of the canon. It enunciates
the perennial novelistic spirit of all literature by expressing the present, the real, the
raw, the lower, the transitory, the free. The modernity of the novel, which counters
orthodoxy, is always relevant because it is irreverent. In this reading, Lukács' conception of the novel as the epic of the sinful age is revised. But while in *Mimesis* the
novel prefigures a final synthesis, that of the assimilation of Christianity back into
its biblical roots, in Bakhtin it is privileged because it disturbs every synthesis and
opposes solidification. For him, the novel has nothing to do with the Fall (Lukács)
or Redemption (Auerbach). It is the spontaneous, explosive violation of systems
and transgression of codes. In this respect, Bakhtin's generalization seems the more
generous and promising: it insists on the importance of the festival after the decline
of the religious ritual. But even for him, the demonological dimension of the argument (namely, the construction of a Hellenic negative) is unavoidable and dominates the essay: even in a world where people can apparently celebrate without gods
and rules, the face and the name of evil, in order to be effectively exorcized, had to
be classical. (There is no need to emphasize the remarkable point of agreement

among the three theorists: their faith and trust in "reality." They all believe in a world out there which is true, natural, present, accessible, and reflected in verbal art. Their common assumption is that representation is a basic way of human understanding, and literature its best medium.)

86. "The opening volumes of George Grote's *History of Greece* (1846) set the Homeric question and its implicit relationship to the Bible before the British reading public and permanently associated the issues with rationalist, radical, and utilitarian thought" (Turner 1981: 142).

87. This last parallel should also be made chronologically: it was roughly at the time when the first "real" Greeks were seeking ways to escape the millet system that the first "real" Jews looked for means of freeing themselves from the bondage of the ghetto.

88. The term "Semitic" (and the corresponding linguistic family) was created (in opposition to the "Japhetic" family, better known as Indo-European) in 1781 by A. L. Schlözer, a student and later colleague of Michaelis at the University of Göttingen. The term "anti-Semitism" first appeared in the pamphlet *The Victory of Judaism over Germanism* (1879) by the German Christian convert Wilhelm Marr.

89. In his reply to Schiller's "The Gods of Greece" (1788), another poem under the same title, Heine again finds the Greeks "repugnant" and their gods old, exiled, and defeated.

90. In addition, the continuing popularity of mimesis among students of narrative and representation should be noted. Auerbach returned to the subject with his 1953 paper. For more recent examinations, see Hume 1985, Costa-Lima 1988, Mahoney 1986, Meltzer 1987, Morrison 1982 (which extends the inquiry into cosmology, epistemology, and ethics), Prendergast 1986, Ricoeur 1981, Schweiker 1990, Sörböm 1966, Spariosu 1984, Steele 1988, Weinsheimer 1985, and Wells 1986.

91. This principle has an interesting precedent in Herder's idea of palingenesis (recurrent partials in culture that explain cultural universals) which he opposed to polygenesis (multiple origins of culture). Palingenetic forms are archetypes, universals of the soul that return. Their function explains the recurrence of cultural expressions. The idea, which was first mentioned in 1768, is elaborated in the essay "*Palingenesie: vom Wiederkommen menschlicher Seelen*" (1797).

92. "What we have done since the masked scepticism of Spinoza, since the critiques of the rationalist Enlightenment and since the positivism of the nineteenth century is to borrow vital currency, vital investments and contracts of trust from the bank or treasure-house of theology. It is from there that we have borrowed our theories of the symbol, our use of the iconic, our idiom of poetic creation and aura. It is loans of terminology and reference from the reserves of theology which provide the master readers in our time (such as Walter Benjamin and Martin Heidegger) with their licence to practise. We have borrowed, traded upon, made small change of the reserves of transcendent authority" (Steiner 1985a: 1275).

93. A differentiation between two major modes of Western culture, rhetoric (whose emblem is the tree) and commentary (whose emblem is the source), presents modernity as a scholastic age dominated by commentary (Charles 1986).

94. "The only philosophy which can be responsibly practised in face of despair is the attempt to contemplate all things as they would present themselves from the standpoint of redemption. Knowledge has no light but that shed on the world by

redemption; all else is reconstruction, mere technique. Perspectives must be fashioned that displace and estrange the world, reveal it to be, with its rifts and crevices, as indigent and distorted as it will appear one day in the messianic light" (Adorno 1974: 247).

95. During his visit to Adrian Leverkühn, and after transforming himself into "a member of the intelligentsia, . . . a theoretician and critic" (Mann 1968: 231), the Devil observes: "The religious is certainly my line: as certainly as it is not the line of bourgeois culture. Since culture fell away from the cult and made a cult of itself, it has become nothing else than a falling away; and all the world after a mere five hundred years is as sick and tired of it as though, *salva venia*, they had ladled it in with cooking-spoons" (237).

96. The methodological convenience of Auerbach's simplistic good-and-evil opposition can be quite irresistible. Notice how a critic, in a chapter entitled "From Odysseus' Scar to the Brown Stocking: A Tradition," unwittingly repeats the Hebraic-Hellenic formula by drawing a biographical parallel between the author and Odysseus: "In exile in Istanbul, Auerbach begins with the homecoming of the archetypal wanderer" (Robbins 1986: 26).

97. There have been comparable developments in other fields too. Regarding anthropology, for example, Claude Lévi-Strauss's "work on American Indian mythologies might be understood as an act of atonement for a world destroyed, parallel to the creation of the Talmud" (Fischer 1986: 200). Hermeneutics has been quite important for this discipline. "In this respect, the model of post-modern ethnography is not the newspaper but that original ethnography—the Bible" (Tyler 1986: 127).

98. Reading the Bible as Literature has developed into an interpretive and pedagogical discipline. In addition to those mentioned in the Bibliography, there has been a great number of books with titles like *What is Structural Exegesis?* (1976); *Biblical Structuralism: Method and Subjectivity in the Study of Ancient Texts* (1977); *Structuralism and Biblical Hermeneutics* (1979); *Ways of Reading the Bible* (1981); *Literary Criticism and Biblical Hermeneutics: A Critique of Formalist Approaches* (1985); *The Bible and the Narrative Tradition* (1986); *Theology and Literature* (1988); *Story, Text, and Scripture: Literary Interests in Biblical Narrative* (1988); *European Literature and Theology in the 20th Century: Ends of Time* (1990). The Centre for the Study of Literature and Theology, established in 1986 as part of Hatfield College, University of Durham, has published since 1987 the semi-annual journal *Literature and Theology* (Oxford University Press). It has also become the home of the National Conference on Literature and Religion, established in 1981. *The Times Literary Supplement* devoted its issue of May 23, 1986 to the topic "God." The 1989 Georgetown University Bicentennial Symposium was devoted to "The Bible and Contemporary Literary Theory." The University of Chicago Press began in 1989 a new series, "Religion and Postmodernism," under the editorship of Marc C. Taylor.

99. In comparisons of "The Hebrew Literature, and Other Literatures" (Taylor 1861), "Other" often means only the Greek.

100. In this spirit, authors often examine the identity of their historical moment using the same terms: "We often speak of 'the Greek miracle'; from this point of view we are fully justified in speaking of 'the Hebrew miracle.' For their phenome-

non was equally great, unique, and unexplained as that of the Greeks. And there is another resemblance between the Hebrew and the Greek miracles. Exactly as, from time to time, the world has seemed to forget the Greeks and their accomplishment, or, at least, to ignore them, and then has been compelled to return and again go to school with them; so, again and again, the world has thought that it could ignore the Hebrews and even make jest of that Jehovah whom they expressed. We are now, more or less, in such a time. Yet there are ample signs that the necessity of explaining our thoughts and ourselves is driving us back to seek an explanation of the whole phenomenon of the Hebrews and of their faith in Jehovah" (Macdonald 1933: 9). This author also compares Greek drama with Hebrew poetry, the "Greek Diké" with the "Hebrew Reason" (35), and suggests that "the Hebrews, so far as concerns even the cold workings of their minds, were Platonists rather than Aristotelians" (12).

101. One study of the legacy of Israel in modern literature is a case in point. First, the author compares Arnold's Greek style with Tennyson's Hebrew: "The Greek simile is foreign to English habits of speech, the Hebrew simile has become naturalized" (Magnus 1928: 485). But this is not just a question of literature and style: "The legacy of Israel in the English language is not merely a matter of words and phrases; it is a matter of the association of ideas. It is mental as well as mechanical, and thus, quite apart from the occurrence of occasional Hebraisms in our daily speech, it is intimate of our life and habits. We think and act *more Hebraico* without conscious imitation, as a son enjoying his patrimony does not to remember whence it came" (487). The conclusion draws on the required comparison but attempts to give a balanced view: "For Hellenism and Hebraism are not contrary, but complementary; for if Plato could be called 'Moses Atticus' by a reader in the second century, A.D., readers in the twentieth century would be skilful to discern that modern literature is inextricably Greek and Hebrew, since it inherits and enhances the glory of Greece and the righteousness of Zion" (505).

102. "The poet of *The Iliad* seems to me to have only one ancient rival, the prime and original author of much of Genesis, Exodus, Numbers, known as the Yahwist or J writer to scholars. Homer and J have absolutely nothing in common except their uncanny sublimity, and they are sublime in very different modes. In a profound sense, they are agonists, though neither ever heard of the other, or listened to the other's texts. They compete for the consciousness of Western nations, and their belated strife may be the largest single factor that makes for a divided sensibility in the literature and life of the West. For what marks the West is its troubled sense that its cognition goes one way, and its spiritual life goes in quite another. We have no ways of thinking that are not Greek, and yet our morality and religion—outer and inner—find their ultimate source in the Hebrew Bible" (Bloom 1986: 2–3). Auerbach's point about the exclusive claim of the Bible returns with a vengeance: "If the Bible is unique (in the West, except for the Koran), it is because we remain enclosed by it, whether we overtly believe in it or not. Shakespeare and Freud, rather than Homer and Plato, remain the Bible's only rivals in enclosing us against our wills, determining our responses to life and art" (Bloom 1988: 25). Of course, it is never explained who is meant by "us" here.

103. Although he blames the crude market considerations of his (British? American?) publisher ("black women still sell!") for his decision to keep the present title, it appears that Bernal has always referred to his book as "Black Athena." However,

after being told that it should have been called "Egyptian Athena," Bernal believes that his title should have been "African Athena" (Bernal 1989: 31), conceivably because people have started calling themselves "African Americans" rather than "blacks." It is probably with an eye to market considerations that, in various publications, Bernal has defined the topic of his project as the "African and Levantine Roots of Greece" (1985), the "Afroasiatic Roots of Europe" (1986), the "Egyptian and Semitic Roots of Ancient Greece" (1986: 55), the "Egyptian and West Semitic Components of Greek Civilisation" (1986: 68), and the "Afroasiatic Roots of Classical Civilization" (1987). Changing "1780–1980" (1986) to "1785–1985" (1987) in the subtitle also makes the book look more up to date.

104. Like Harold Bloom (who meticulously fashions himself on Disraeli's Sidonia), Bernal presents himself as an outsider (non-classicist, British Jew), a "public nuisance," a gadfly, and seeks exotic alliances: "Interestingly, I find it easier to place myself and my promotion of the Revised Ancient Model in the spectrum of black scholarship than within the academic orthodoxy. I see myself in Carruthers' second class, whom he damns as 'Negro intellectuals'" (Bernal 1987: 437).

105. Bernal yearns for opponents: he sees conspiracies and reactionaries everywhere plotting against his work, is disappointed when none are found or when recognition comes quickly. To his utter embarassment, the Classics establishment, which he thought he had attacked, has welcomed him. To my knowledge, there has not been a single (professional or other) negative (let alone hostile) review, despite the numerous disagreements—which he has always welcomed. In addition, the record shows "the enthusiastic and uncritical adoption of *Black Athena* by many nonclassicists precisely because of its ideological congeniality impressively buttressed by the academic credentials and broad learning of its author" (Levine 1989: 12). Suffice to mention Bernal's influence on the albums *To the East, Blackwards* (1990) by New York rappers X-Clan and *Neither Fish Nor Flesh* (1989) by Terence Trent D'Arby. This is how D'Arby defines his reading: "I've got a book written by a man who has been at Oxford for 18 years and who spent eight or nine years researching this book called *Black Athena*. Now what this book is saying is when the Romans came to Greece they were fascinated by Greek traditions and the Greeks were dumbfounded as to why the Romans didn't know that most of this came from Africa or Asia, from black and Judaic traditions. Interestingly enough, a few months ago—and this ran in all the major papers and it wasn't a big headline—a group of scientists and anthropologists had evidence concluding that the first person who actually spoke was an African woman and genetically passed language onto us" (D'Arby 1989: 58). Rappers like X-Clan and Brand Nubian sometimes combine Bernal's message with the teachings of the Black Muslim sect, the Nation of Islam.

106. He finds that "the Broad Aryanists led largely by Jewish scholars, both Zionist and anti-Zionist, are gaining ground and will certainly succeed by the end of the century" (Bernal 1985: 70). Here is his promise: "By 1990 we should be back to the Broad Aryan Model. There will be then a period of competition, after which I believe the Ancient Model—with some revisions—will triumph. It should be dominant by the beginning of the third millennium A.D.—if there is one" (Bernal 1986: 54).

107. Bernal mentions *Stolen Legacy: The Greeks were not the Authors of Greek Philosophy, but the People of North Africa, Commonly called the Egyptians* (1954) by

George G. M. James. The book takes as extreme a position as Joseph Yahuda (reported in the *Jewish Chronicle of London* in 1987), who sees Biblical Hebrew as a "camouflaged Greek" language and its speakers as an "ancient Greek tribe," thus transforming the Jews into "Indo-Europeans." Responding with some indignation, a commentator notes that she comes "from an orthodox Jewish ideology which would certainly resent being 'upgraded' to the status of major contributor to Greek civilization and would be downright dismayed at a rewritten version of history which set Jews aswim with Greeks in a common Mediterranean soup" (Levine 1989: 14).

108. To mention a few examples, it has been reviewed in the *Christian Science Monitor* ("The next far-in book?"), the *Village Voice*, and *Z Magazine*; highlighted in the *Chronicle of Higher Education* and the *Utne Reader*; discussed in the *Science* section and the *Letters to the Editor* page of the *New York Times*; praised by Edward Said and Toni Morrison (in the *Michigan Quarterly Review*); it also provided the topic of the conference "Challenging Tradition: Cultural Interaction in Antiquity and Bernal's *Black Athena*," organized by the Departments of Classics and of African-American Studies at Temple University (1990), and of the Presidential Panel "The Challenge of *Black Athena*: The Classicists' Response" at the 1989 Annual Meeting of the American Philological Association.

109. Counting the Jews all the time, Bernal observes that "by the 1970s many of the dominant figures in the field [of Classics] were Jewish" (Bernal 1987: 403). He notes that Cyrus Gordon and Michael Astour "are self-consciously Jewish" (415) and Semitists "mainly Jewish" (434), and refers to Gordon's "mainly Jewish" (419) students. He also records that the movement for a return to what he calls the Broad Aryan Model, which started in 1945, has been "led mainly by Jewish scholars," and adds: "Since the late 1960s, however, the Extreme Aryan Model has been under heavy attack, largely by Jews and Semitists" (442). I was reminded of that positive use of ethnic origin for potentially dangerous race arguments when, after presenting part of this chapter at a conference, the first question I was asked was: "Are you saying these things because you are Greek?"

110. This alternative was by 1912 already obvious to Walter Benjamin, who thought that "the intellectualist mission of the Jews is the Western alternative to Zionism. This 'modern asceticism,' as Benjamin called it, even determines the 'forms' in which Jewish cultural life appears. What he means is evident—'even the Café.' The Jew, to continue in the idiom of Christian discourse, 'is called,' according to the 'new social consciousness' to be what 'the poor in spirit, the enslaved and the meek were for the first Christians.' 'The best Jews today are linked to a valuable process in European culture'" (Rabinbach 1985: 95). The same letter offers a clear distinction: "'I see three zionist forms of Jewishness (*Judentum*),' Benjamin concludes, 'Palestine Zionism (a natural necessity); German Zionism in its halfness, and cultural Zionism which sees Jewish values *everywhere* and works for them. Here I will stay, and I believe I must stay'" (96).

111. Bernal sees the ancient civilization as a Third World country: "Thus in many ways Vietnam and Japan . . . have served as my models for Greece" (Bernal 1987: xii). He has no difficulty in establishing geographical or chronological analogies with his own area of expertise: "I see relations between Greece and the Near East as analogous to those between Vietnam, Korea, or Japan to China" (Bernal 1989: 23).

112. Addressing the best hopes of a philologist or any other empiricist, Bernal has promised to reveal, in the next three volumes of his work, the true character (read: stolen treasures) of Greek civilization—a claim surprisingly and unanimously overlooked even by proponents of ethnographic specificity with exceptional sensitivity to discursive colonialism.

113. Other commentators have been more specific, noting, for example, that Bernal "overlooks another Greek motive: the desire to excel, to outshine and do down one's immediate Greek rivals and predecessors. . . . The Egyptians served as a stick with which Greeks beat other Greeks" (Griffin 1989: 26).

114. Bernal notes in a footnote: "The view of L. Canfora that there was a right wing *usurpazione* of classics at the turn of the twentieth century takes as its base the Jacobin use of antiquity: *Ideologie del classicismo* (Turin 1980), pp. 39–56. Following conventional wisdom in northern Europe, I do not include this in the tradition of *Altertumswissenschaft*/classics" (Bernal 1986: 62, note 131). This is a strange choice for a scholar who takes great pride in going against the oppression of conventional wisdom.

115. At times Bernal gives the impression that he almost regrets the outcome of the War: "Classics as we know it today was created between 1815 and 1830—an intensely conservative period. The same period also saw the Greek War of Independence, which united all Europeans against the traditional Islamic enemies from Asia and Africa. This War—and the philhellenic movement, which supported the struggle for independence—completed the already powerful image of Greece as the epitome of Europe. The Ancient Greeks were now seen as perfect, and as having transcended the laws of history and language" (Bernal 1987: 440–41).

116. "In capitalist societies the educational system, whether lay or clerical, the structure of moral reflexes handed down from father to son, the exemplary honesty of workers who are given a medal after fifty years of good and loyal service, and the affection which springs from harmonious relations and good behavior—all these aesthetic expressions of respect for the established order serve to create around the exploited person an atmosphere of submission and of inhibition which lightens the task of policing considerably" (Fanon 1968: 38).

117. "In other words, a situation comes about in which interpretations are adjudicated almost entirely by interpreters, or rather by interpreters/workers (i.e., interpreters who interpret within the context, ends, etc., of capitalist economic relations), and thus by individuals to whose concrete advantages or disadvantages those adjudications redound. . . . It follows, then, that the adjudicative concerns of the interpreters who compose the body of workers *and* consumers would tend towards establishing—in a tacit and ideological fashion—criteria of adjudication which open markets, presumably by obsolescence, and reduce capital outlays. It also follows . . . that the establishment of such criteria will be facilitated by the absence of gross criteria of applicative success or failure. To put it crudely, critics will value precisely those varieties of interpretation and criteria of adjudication which, whatever their plausibility, allow them to produce more salable interpretations more simply and less laboriously, and these valuations will not be hindered by the results of technological applications" (Hogan 1985: 181–82).

118. "Worst of all, while it opens up a radical prospect by acknowledging the authenticity of other voices, postmodernist thinking immediately shuts off those

other voices from access to more universal sources of power by ghettoizing them within an opaque otherness, the specificity of this or that language game. It thereby disempowers those voices (of women, ethnic and racial minorities, colonized peoples, the unemployed, youth, etc.) in a world of lop-sided power relations" (Harvey 1989: 117). The fundamentally essentialist logic of Otherness, by treating all minorities like Jews of Hebraism, succeeds in giving them moral superiority and cultural status (that is, Hellenic prestige) but no means necessary for political liberation.

119. "The [romantic] Hellenism associated with Bible studies was a very much wider phenomenon than the interest in Greek classical antiquity. Its concern was with the Hellenistic period, the immediate environment of early Christianity both before and after Christ, with the meeting and synthesis of cultures and ideas out of which emerged a distinctive Christian worldview. 'Orientalism' was one aspect of this broad Hellenism" (Shaffer 1975: 14).

Chapter Two

1. During the 1980s, the decade of epigonality (dominated by trends like post-structuralism, new historicism, neo-geo, meta-fiction, and "after Foucault"), modernity as a project or predicament became a very popular issue. In addition to well-known contributions by Jürgen Habermas and Jean-François Lyotard, see Berman 1982; Cahoone 1987; Connolly 1988; Eisenstadt 1987; Galgan 1982; Giddens 1990; Meschonnic 1988a; Sloterdijk 1987; Vattimo 1989; and Xenos 1989. Many journals (such as *Les Cahiers, Cultural Critique, Modern Age, New German Critique, Theory, Culture and Society* have devoted special issues to the topic. For surveys of older discussions, see Barnouw 1988; Benjamin 1989; Frisby 1986; Kolb 1987; and Love 1986. On modernity as a specifically Jewish problem, see Bauman 1989; Eidelberg 1989; Ellenson 1989; and Meyer 1988. In 1988, Wayne State University Press inaugurated a publication series, "The Culture of Jewish Modernity," edited by Alan Udoff.

2. Schelling lectured on "The Philosophy of Mythology" and "The Philosophy of Revelation" in 1815.

3. On sin and the fall, in addition to Paul's Epistle to the Romans 7 and T. S. Eliot's essay "After Strange Gods" (1933), see Addy 1989; Bataille 1988; Carroll 1985; Highfield 1989; Reilly 1988; Ricoeur 1974: 425–39; and Vergote 1988.

4. "There runs through modern criticism the fantasy of a Second Fall of Man. . . . The Second Fall seems to result from the introduction of scientific utilitarian values and modes of thinking into the world of personal choice between good and evil, with the result that values cease to be personal and become identified with the usefulness or destructiveness of social systems and material things" (Spender 1965: 26).

5. A precedent of the Augustinian *curiositas* may be found in the allegory *De migratione Abrahami* by Philo of Alexandria, where it is the Greek *periergia* (curiosity) that inspires Abraham's travels (and spiritual path) from Chaldea to Egypt (Blumenberg 1983: 284–87). This is obviously not Auerbach's Abraham, who obeys without asking questions.

6. Dante and Virgil encounter Odysseus in the Bolgia of the Evil Counselors who abused the gift of reason. He tells them the story of his last trip, beyond the Pillars

of Hercules (considered the western limit of navigation) and "out of the world of man." On the uses of the Ulysses theme, see Stanford 1976.

7. Lukács responded to the *Dialectic of Enlightenment* with his own critique of modernity, *The Destruction of Reason* (1955).

8. An illustration of this introversion is Adorno's own style—an exercise in renunciation, "a discourse pitched into a constant state of crisis, twisting and looping back on itself, struggling in the structure of every sentence to avoid at once a 'bad' immediacy of the object and the false self-identity of the concept" (Eagleton 1990: 341).

9. There are many features that this view of the Homeric world shares with Lucien Lévy-Bruhl's theory of "modern" (as opposed to "primitive") thought presented in *The Mental Functions in the Inferior Societies* (1910). The main characteristics of that thought are "natural orientation," "objectivity," "induction," "logical attitude," and "separation from and mastery of the world" (Horton 1973: 254). Lévy-Bruhl also saw the growth of individualism as crucial for the radical change from primitive to modern thought. In contrast, the portrait of the Jews in the *Dialectic*, with its emphasis on the importance of organized ritual for reflexively rationalizing the pagan fear and sacrifice, is indebted to Émile Durkheim's view, in *The Elementary Forms of the Religious Life* (1912), that religion is that moment in human evolution at which all forms of higher cultural articulation become possible.

10. Melancholy "from its beginning was identified with the artistic personality, which was seen as essentially ambivalent. Melancholy was seen as both a humor and a disease, and, through the merging of the originally opposed theories of Galen and Aristotle, as both curse and blessing. It was a sign of both a *genius* and of a vicious *daemon*, both in the older sense of good and bad presiding spirits and later in the modern sense of innate qualities" (Kilgour 1990: 153).

11. Writing on "The State of Israel" Horkheimer remarked with bitter ambivalence: "Jewry was not a powerful state but the hope for justice at the end of the world. They were a people and its opposite, a rebuke to all peoples. Now, a state claims to be speaking for Jewry, to be Jewry. The Jewish people in whom the injustice of all peoples has become an accusation, the individuals in whose words and gestures the negative of what is reflected itself, have now become positive themselves" (Horkheimer 1978: 206–7). The same historical development has evoked contrasting feelings: "It is the difficult freedom of Israel, which is not to be treated as an ethnographic curiosity but as one extreme limit of human potential" (Levinas 1989a: 279). This position obviously stems from a very different philosophy: "Zionism is a politics and already a non-politics. An epic and a Passion. Wild energy and extreme vulnerability. Zionism, after the realism of its first political formulations, is finally revealed, in the terms of a Judaism of substance, to be a great ambition of the Spirit" (280).

12. "Neither Adorno nor Horkheimer could say anything positive about God. They believed the critical theorist could not represent the Absolute. Speaking about the Absolute, all that can be said is that the present world is a relative one; by saying what the world is, the critical theorist expresses what God is not. In this Adorno and Horkheimer stand in the great tradition of Western negative theology" (Siebert 1983–84: 113). More important than naming, finding, showing God was to protect him from relativism. "In the tradition of mystical negative theology, Adorno

negated God for God's sake" (114). This is why he engaged not in ideology but "in idology—the destruction of the idolatry" (114) of bourgeois religion.

13. Related to this policy is the iconoclastic *Bilderverbot* mentioned by Horkheimer in 1970: "In my opinion, Marx was influenced by Judaic Messianism while for me the main thing is that God cannot be depicted . . . but is the object of our yearning" (quoted in Marcus and Tar 1986: 346). The same taboo, which found its typical modernist expression in the paintings of Mark Rothko (1903–70), was also accepted by Horkheimer's collaborator: "Aesthetic images are subject to the prohibition of graven images" (Adorno 1984: 153).

14. Horkheimer has noted the close relation of German idealism with Judaism: "Among the particular traits to be found both in idealism and emancipated Jewish thought, I can mention here only one essential one: the impossibility of giving a name to the Divine" (Horkheimer 1974: 112–13). After describing the circular course of Hegel's teaching in Berlin, he comments: "The story sounds like one from the Talmud, and the similarity is more than accidental. In both cases the issue is a truth which cannot be isolated and positively stated, but which is there nonetheless. This element of contradiction is inherent in the Jewish tradition as it is in dialectical philosophy where it becomes explicit as a moment in the process of thought as it strives toward the truth" (113). Horkheimer's studies of Jewish culture began in 1939 with the esssay "The Jews and Europe" (Reichmann 1974).

15. Conservative thinkers who admire this mechanism believe that "there can be no culture without guilt" (Rieff 1972: 68). Consequently, they see an urgent need for "masters of the knowledge of guilt" (33) who can bring back the order of fear through moral control, and they ask: "Who are to be our truth-tellers—better say, our guilt-provokers?" (69).

16. "In a letter Horkheimer wrote to [Leo] Lowenthal on July 5, 1946, he talked of the mistrust the peasant had of the urban manipulator of language, which he called partly justified. 'This distrust,' Horkheimer continued, 'is an element of anti-Semitism itself, and the Jew who manipulates language so easily is not free from guilt in the prehistory of what you explain as the fascist handling of language. Here, too, the Jew is the pioneer of capitalism' (Lowenthal collection, Berkeley, California)" (Jay 1980: 146).

17. Compare this point (which alludes to Abraham and Jesus) to another statement: "The mythic compulsiveness of the word in prehistory is perpetuated in the disaster which the enlightened word draws down upon itself. Udeis, who compulsively acknowledges himself to be Odysseus, already bears the characteristics of the Jew who, fearing death, still presumes on the superiority which originates in the fear of death; revenge on the middleman occurs not only at the end of bourgeois society, but—as the negative utopia to which every form of coercive power always tends—at its beginning" (Horkheimer and Adorno 1972: 69).

18. "Adorno's much quoted remark made shortly before his death in 1969, that 'when I made my theoretical model, I could not have guessed that people would try to realize it with Molotov cocktails'" (Jay 1973: 279), best illustrates the political resignation in the face of barbarism which the Frankfurt School first adopted in the *Dialectic*.

19. Ahasverus was often called in medieval legend the "wicked Jew." A study of the agitator devotes a chapter to "The Enemy as Jew" which lists features of the

stereotype: "The Jews are conceived as living by their wits and avoiding physical work. They achieve their goals by means of intellectual machinations, Stock Exchange manipulations, or revolutionary propaganda, but they never seem to toil in the sweat of their brows" (Lowenthal and Guterman 1949: 85). This "resentment against the Jews as wielders of intellectual power" (84) is often combined with anti-intellectualism: "Domination by intellect is experienced as usurpation because it is not backed by actual physical power and ultimately it depends on the consent of the dominated or on deception. Consistently depicted as over-sophisticated, practicing debauch, enjoying forbidden things, tempting the suckers by futile entertainment and pursuing destructive aims, the modern intellectual, as the agitator sees him, is a secular variation of the devil" (85). It is the same alarmist rhetoric that, inverting here Hegel's notion of "the cunning of reason," warns against the Homeric temptations of knowledge and pleasure. (Incidentally, Lowenthal is credited in the *Dialectic* as the co-author of the first three of the seven sections of its last chapter, "Elements of Anti-Semitism.") On the other hand, writers who believe in "innate intellectuality" (Lowenthal and Guterman) have made appeals to "our Jewish cunning" (Bloom).

20. From a comparable perspective, in the short essay "Helen's Exile" (1948), Albert Camus writes: "We have exiled beauty; the Greeks took up arms for her" (Camus 1955: 134). And later he explains: "The historical spirit and the artist both want to remake the world. But the artist, through an obligation to his nature, knows his limits, which the historical spirit fails to recognize. This is why the latter's aim is tyranny whereas the former's passion is freedom. All those who are struggling for freedom today are ultimately fighting for beauty" (137).

21. The critique of instrumental reason is often attributed to Jewish thought: "But where does the ethical passion against instrumentality derive from? From the Enlightenment? No, it is older than the Enlightenment. From 'humanism'? No, it is older than humanism. The ethical passion against instrumentality—intrinsicness, 'personhood'—derives from the beginning of Jewish civilization. We will find it in the first sentence of Chapter Five of the Book of Genesis: The human being is made in the likeness of the Creator" (Ozick 1984: 8).

22. Max Brod, Kafka's first editor after his death in 1924, takes a similar position from a Zionist perspective. After mentioning the ridicule of Greek deities in the operettas of Jacques Offenbach (1819–80), he notes: "This is a typically Jewish criticism of the prolongation of visible ethics into invisible ones. This became quite clear to me when, in 1915, I gave lectures on ancient literature at a school for Jewish refugees from Eastern Europe in Prague. I must admit that it was only on that occasion that I began to understand the historical fight of Judaism with Hellenism (Maccabees) and the permanent difference between the two worlds of civilization" (Brod 1970: 241). The problem with Greek thought is that it takes the material world as something natural and primary. "Paganism in all its forms is the attempt to construct the supernatural world upon the visible one by way of induction" (241). To this, Brod contrasts "the boldness with which the Jews connected an entirely ungraspable meaning of the world with their God, and from there they derived the world in a deductive way" (241). Greek materialism, however, is far from extinct. "Paganism is not an historical type. We are in the midst of paganism right now, with additional Christian ingredients. The following trends in

modern thinking are mainly emanations of a prevailing paganism: evolution, bio-logical-scientific *Weltanschauung*, monism, the Marxist theory of socialism, historicism" (245). The world is dominated by a pagan-Christian "amalgamation" and "collaboration." Brod traces the history of the unholy pact, which is "the history of the Caucasian mankind" (252), to Renaissance Hellenism and capitalism. Thus his accusation against Christianity is one of complicity only. The original sin was what he, like Lukács and Auerbach, defined as the Homeric "flight to the surface of the world" (243). Other students of paganism have felt that the West has inherited two very different traditions, the dominant Christian-Kantian and the pagan one (Casey 1990): although realistic, pragmatic thought belongs to the latter, the dominant view does not allow people to recognize it because faith prevails over ethics.

23. In a letter published in the editorial column of the *New York Times* (national edition) under the rubric "Letter: On Society" and the title "Light of Hope in Face of Decadence," a rabbi worries about "decay and decline" and concludes that "we are decadent. Youth and body and indulgence. What if this is the Hellenization of America? What comes next? . . . We have a holiday that celebrates a triumph over Hellenism. The Jews are ready to share this victory. The holiday is Hanukkah and its lights have lasted a long time, more than two thousand years. Have hope" (Turetsky 1990: 14). The historical event commemorated in this holiday, the Jewish revolt against Hellenization, has also inspired different feelings: "A great opportunity presented itself to mankind when Judaism and Hellenism met—an opportunity which unfortunately was not seized in its entirety. Had these two worlds interpenetrated each other peacefully, an ideal pattern for man's living might have been created. This would have preserved the intellectual alertness and aesthetic sensitivity of Hellenism in synthesis with the Hebraic religious outlook and ethical values. Such a fusion would have abstracted the virtues of both cultures and enabled them to supplement each other. Mankind still entertains the hope that the time may yet come when Hebraic faith and ethics will be harmoniously fused with Hellenistic science, philosophy, and art, into a pattern of living richer than either alone" (Steinberg 1937: 15).

24. "The reconciliation of civilization with nature, which Christianity tried prematurely to contrive by means of its doctrine of the crucified god, remained as alien to Judaism as to the rigorism of the Enlightenment" (Horkheimer and Adorno 1972: 114). The authors seek a higher form of harmony, since "Adorno is repeatedly forced by systematic considerations to take seriously the idea of reconciliation. This Adorno cannot escape" (Habermas 1983: 108). The overcoming of division and dejection is a major theme in the Romantic lyric where "the ancient struggle for the blessedness of reconciliation with an alienated God becomes the attempt to recover in maturity an earlier stage of integrity with oneself and the outer world" (Abrams 1971: 123) through aesthetic reflection.

25. Adorno's minimalist ethics, which draws on "the genuinely theological conception of the melancholic" (Benjamin 1977: 155), is a vivid illustration of the "need on the part of the 'bourgeois' theorist to participate in the historical guilt of not having been one of the victims" (Blumenberg 1983: 118).

26. Structuralist exegesis has traced the silence of God from the Bible to Auschwitz (Neher 1981).

27. The ineffectiveness of Edmund Husserl's moral commitment to "theory as the initial act of European humanity and as a corrective for its most terrible deviation" (Blumenberg 1983: 236) was uppermost in Adorno's concern with the future of civilization.

28. The same development may be observed in criticism: "The antecedents of heterocosmic theory emerged in critics of literature who, beginning in the late fifteenth century, reversed the traditional comparison of God the creator to a human artisan by making the portentous comparison of the literary artisan to God the creator. . . . In the sixteenth century the partial parallel between the poet's making and God's creating, with the corollary parallel between God's created world and the poem as 'an other nature' or 'a second world,' occurred frequently enough to be almost a standard topos in literary criticism" (Abrams 1989a: 172).

29. From a Hebraic perspective, this account has been criticized for failing to discuss "the radical creativity of the God of Genesis or Job. [Blumenberg] characterizes originary activity solely with references to Hellenistic and Patristic sources such as Philo and Irenaeus" (Luft 1987: 24).

30. It is ironic that some commentators have seen the two followers of the Greek king in the same way that others portray Auerbach in Istanbul as Odysseus: "With the image of Odysseus whose impotence is documented in the fact that, being tied to the mast, he is only able to nod his head, Horkheimer and Adorno demonstrate the impotence of the intellectual, of their work in their own period, their position. Did they hear the song of the Sirens, the call to revolution, when they were on their way in the 1930s? In any case, at the time of writing the *Dialectic of Enlightenment* they had to experience their return politically as well as philosophically as the story of a refusal, as allegory" (van Reijen 1988: 426–27). They returned to West Germany in 1950.

31. Taste and public reinforced each other. "Actually this is what I would call classicism: a situation in which an author can write while putting himself at the same time in the position of a reader, being able to substitute himself for his own reader, and to judge and sort out what he has accomplished from the point of view of the reader that he also is. The writer knows the solicitation that is addressed to him; he shares it in his capacity as reader; he answers it in his capacity as writer. Whereas in what we call modernity, he no longer knows for whom he writes, since there no longer is any taste" (Lyotard and Thébaud 1985: 9).

32. "The virtuoso vogue in the seventeenth century . . . had all along been 'strongly class-conscious,' flaunting a leisure-time avocation free of material and utilitarian ends as a sign of social rank unachievable by what a number of virtuosi . . . had called 'the vulgar' and requiring a cultivated knowledge and taste that serves to distinguish the 'polite' class from social climbers. This defensiveness of the landed upper classes against interlopers from below is itself an index to the instability of the established class structure in England, in an era of new wealth acquired by flourishing commercial and manufacturing enterprises" (Abrams 1989: 144).

33. Thus the aesthetic became a quality first of an attitude and then of an object. "It is worth reminding ourselves that in traditional thought, moral edification, 'truth,' or the dignity of the 'real life' model 'imitated' in the work, legislate for the value of the art-object. That the work is autonomous and unique, and that it therefore defies such extra-aesthetic criteria, is an idea which comes into prominence

only after the concept of 'disinterestedness' has established itself. For it is just in its relation to disinterested perception that the work is autonomous—because it is attended to for its own sake—and unique—because such perception dwells upon and relishes its qualitative individuality" (Stolnitz 1961: 99).

34. "The aesthetic disposition, a generalized capacity to neutralize ordinary urgencies and to bracket off practical ends, a durable inclination and aptitude for practice without a practical function, can only be constituted within an experience of the world freed from urgency and through the practice of activities which are an end in themselves, such as scholastic exercises or the contemplation of works of art. In other words, it presupposes the distance from the world . . . which is the basis of the bourgeois experience of the world" (Bourdieu 1984: 54).

35. The situation deeply worried even writers who, since the advent of modernism, were praised as heralds of artistic integrity. Hölderlin begins his "Remarks on *Oedipus*" (1803) with a direct market consideration: "It will be good, in order to secure for today's poets a bourgeois existence—taking into account the difference of times and institutions—if we elevate poetry today to the *mechane* [skill, craft] of the ancients. When being compared with those of the Greeks, other works of art, too, lack reliability; at least, they have been judged until today according to the impressions which they made rather than according to their lawful calculation and their other mode of operation through which the beautiful is engendered. Modern poetry, however, lacks especially training and craftsmanship" and it is therefore "in need of especially certain and characteristic principles and limits. Thereto, then, belongs that lawful calculation" (Hölderlin 1988: 101). As he sees it, the problem is to devise that calculable law that would give poetry reliability, the intrinsic importance necessary for the survival of the bourgeois poet.

36. Weber cited approvingly the view of Albert Ritschl, in his *History of Pietism* (1880–86), that "the purely emotional form of Pietism is . . . a religious dilettantism for the leisure classes" (Weber 1976: 139). Feuerbach mocks this attitude in the epigram "The Pietists in Rome and Athens":

> In order to display to us the pagan world in all its nakedness
> They sit on the toilets of Rome and Athens
> Demonstrating how once the foul heathen sh—
> And how faith now releases us from all the needs of nature.
> (Feuerbach 1980: 190)

37. "As the ancient peoples have experienced their pre-history in imagination, in mythology, so we Germans have experienced our future history in thought, in philosophy. We are philosophical contemporaries without being historical ones. German philosophy is the ideal prolongation of German history. So if, instead of criticizing the incomplete works of our real history, we criticize the posthumous works of our ideal history, philosophy, then our criticism will be at the centre of the question of which the present age says: that is the question. What in developed peoples is the practical conflict with the modern state institutions, in Germany, where these institutions do not even exist, it is a critical conflict with the philosophical reflection of these institutions" (Marx 1971: 120–21).

38. This ideal is best expressed in the "terrorism of pure theory" advocated by Bruno Bauer in the 1840s. "'The true and pure critic,' [Bauer] wrote, 'never puts his

hand to anything.' His task is to struggle for the consistency of our ideals and to oppose all attempts to compromise their immaculate purity by realising them into action. 'The ideal is already realised in itself. Its reality consists in being an ideal in and
for itself. It is the only reality which can exist in the realm of thought. The ideal is
thought and *as such* first elevates things to their true reality'" (Hook 1962: 95–96).

39. The ideal of critique was rapturously celebrated: "At the same time, I noted
with sincere pleasure the progress of our country—not to speak of our age! The
same age in which we too have the honor to live; the age that, to wrap it all up in a
word, deserves the humble but highly suggestive name of the Critical Age, so that
soon now everything is going to be criticized, except the age itself, and everything
is going to become more and more critical, and artists can already begin to cherish
the just hope that humanity will at last rise up in a mass and learn to read" (Schlegel
1971: 261).

40. "The great schism between understanding and not understanding will grow
more and more widespread, intense, and distinct. Much hidden incomprehension
will still erupt. But understanding too will reveal its omnipotence: understanding
that ennobles disposition into character, elevates talent into genius, purifies one's
feelings and artistic perceptions. Understanding itself will be understood, and people will at last see and admit that everyone can achieve the highest degree and that
up to now humanity has been neither malicious nor stupid but simply clumsy and
new" (Schlegel 1971: 269).

41. The character of Western colonialism is closely linked with the autopathic
"self-consciousness of consciousness" (Collins 1989): "Western culture was the first
to critically reflect upon itself (beginning in the 18th century). But the effect of this
crisis was that it reflected on itself also as a culture *in the universal*, and thus all
other cultures were entered in its museum as vestiges of its own image. It 'estheti-
cized' them, reinterpreted them on its own model, and thus precluded the radical
interrogation these 'different' cultures implied for it" (Baudrillard 1975: 88–89).

42. On the *Bildungsroman* (and the overlapping *Erziehungsroman*, *Entwick-
lungsroman*, and *Künstlerroman*), see Alden 1986; Bakhtin 1986; Beddow 1982;
Bruford 1975; Buckley 1974; Lemon 1985; Moretti 1988; Swales 1978; and also
Herbert Marcuse's dissertation (1978). For feminist studies, see Abel, Hirsch, and
Langland 1983; and Labovitz 1987. For approaches based on questions of identity,
see Ratz 1988; and Sax 1987. Important philosophical background is provided in
Gadamer 1979: 10–19; and Smith 1988.

43. Among the studies on Antonio Gramsci (*Selections from Cultural Writings*,
1985) which pay more attention to his notion of hegemony are Adamson 1980;
Bocock 1986; Femia 1981; Laclau and Mouffe 1985; Lears 1985; and Rustin 1988.

44. J. G. Hamann's early short essay "The Merchant" provides a good picture of
the Enlightenment interest in creating a public sphere and of the bourgeois search
for *Bildung*, distinction, and rank. It is a defense of commerce as not just an occupation but a "calling," and therefore an important social position: "Men knew for-
merly very little of the principles of trade. It was pursued rudely, and was so much
condemned, as to be left almost entirely to the Jews. Now, on the other hand, men
have with much sagacity aimed to make a science of commerce" (Hamann 1856:
122). His concern is the need for "forming the merchant" (123), "the true nobleman of our age" (Merlan 1948: 382), through cultivation: "What happy changes

may not the world promise itself from the commercial spirit, now beginning to prevail, if it should be purified by insight and noble impulses?" (Hamann 1856: 122). He finds in its carrier nobility and virtue, and hopes that, if more respect is shown to his class, through rewards and privileges, the merchant will become a model for all.

45. Although very common in romantic music, the theme of wandering, as the artistic expression of alienation, has found its best medium in that ultimate expression of the unfulfilled self, the German *lied*. See especially song cycles from Franz Schubert's *Die Winterreise*, D. 911 (1827) to Gustav Mahler's *Songs of a Wayfarer* (1883). Opera, too, is full of characters wandering into monologues of self-exile.

46. Hamann's self-discovery, which turned a trip to London (1758) into a literary voyage, is the exemplary (in both artistic and philosophical terms) *Bildung* narrative. Its negative model, which Hamann appropriates for literary autobiography, is the journey to England in 1741 of the young *Dozent* Johann David Michaelis (1717–91), who later became an eminent Higher Critic. "Michaelis, as a result of the visit to England, was able to disabuse himself of the notion of supernatural grace as working in human life; Hamann, on the other hand, as a result of his visit to England some seventeen years later, was convinced of the overpowering work of supernatural grace in human life" (O'Flaherty 1950: 177). Hamann's narrative reminds us that, long before Wagner's *Flying Dutchman* (1843), the journey of cultivation was often undertaken as a business assignment (by, say, a merchant like Hamann), and was only later allegorized into an artistic illumination. The universal destiny of art as an allegory for the international destination of capital has received very limited attention. Other legendary conversions include that of Lukács to Marxism in 1919 and Simone Weil's mystical experience of union with Christ in 1938.

47. Schiller found the capitalist division of labor an obstacle to culture: "'The mental state of most men is, on the one hand, fatiguing and exhausting *work* and, on the other, debilitating *pleasure*.' And Schiller sees . . . two dangers for poetry arising out of this social situation: the view that art exists only to provide pleasure and relaxation, and the view that it should serve only to ennoble mankind morally. Schiller recognizes that both these elements contain a kernel of justification. But at the same time he recognizes that the way in which they become operative in the modern age can only lead to the deterioration of poetry and literary culture" (Lukács 1978a: 134).

48. In the journeys narrated in the Romantic *Bildungsreisen* "the crisis, both of history and of the poet's inner life, is the French Revolution and its aftermath. This crisis is resolved on the higher level of comprehensive and unillusioned awareness which is the correlative, whether in a developed culture or a mature consciousness, to the extended prospect from the mountain height to which the traveler, despite the ever wilder and more terrifying terrain, has won his way" (Abrams 1978a: 134).

49. On the high-low culture distinction, see Gans 1974; Hawkins 1990; Levine 1988; MacCabe 1986; and Miles 1987.

50. On leisure, see Bailey 1987; Coalter 1988; Cunningham 1980; Linder 1970; MacCannell 1975; Rojek 1989; Seabrook 1988; Veblen 1899; and Winnifrith and Barrett 1989. For a critique of Veblen pertinent to this discussion, see Adorno 1941.

51. Thus *Bildung* appears superior to *Kultur*, which becomes one of its provinces: "'But if in our language we say *Bildung*, we mean something both higher and more

inward, namely the attitude of mind which, from the knowledge and the feeling of the total intellectual and moral endeavor, flows harmoniously into sensibility and character' (Wilhelm von Humboldt). *Bildung* here no longer means 'culture,' i.e., the development of capacities or talents. The rise of the word *Bildung* calls rather on the ancient mystical tradition, according to which man carries in his soul the image of God after whom he is fashioned and must cultivate it in himself. The Latin equivalent for *Bildung* is *formatio*, and accordingly in other languages, e.g., in English (Shaftesbury), 'form' and 'formation.' In German also the corresponding derivations of the idea of *forma*, e.g., *Formierung* and *Formation*, have long vied with the word *Bildung*" (Gadamer 1979: 11–12).

52. This may answer a question that has not lost its relevance: "through what turn was German Philosophy able to make of Revolution the promise of a true and good State, and of the State the serene and accomplished form of the Revolution? All our submissions find their principle in this double inducement: make the Revolution quick, it will give you the State you need; hurry up and make a State, it will generously lavish on you the reasonable effects of the Revolution. Obliged to think the Revolution, beginning and end, the German thinkers pinned it to the State, and designed the State-Revolution, with all of its final solutions. Thus did the master-thinkers implement an entire mental apparatus, the very one subtending the systems of domination and patterns of obedience of modern societies" (Michel Foucault, quoted in Mehlman 1983: 18).

53. At the beginning of Joyce's *Ulysses*, tempted by Buck Mulligan's exclamation ("Ah, Dedalus, the Greeks!") and exhortation ("God, Kinch, if you and I could only work together we might do something for the island. Hellenise it"), Stephen thinks to himself: "To ourselves . . . new paganism . . . *omphalos*." The idea had already been suggested by Yeats and Wilde. "Joyce's compatriot, Oscar Wilde, had urged 'a new hellenism,' and in his early critical writing Joyce spoke with only the faintest irony of Ireland's becoming 'the hellas of the north'" (Ellmann 1977: 581).

54. "The contrast between vanished Hellas, which must be renewed in a revolutionary manner, and the miserable condition of contemporary Germany constitutes the constant, though always variously recurring, content of [Hölderlin's] lament. . . . It is the complaint of the best bourgeois intellectuals over the loss of the revolutionary 'illusions' of the heroic period of their own class" (Lukács 1978b: 152). The Jacobin poet celebrated the Greek unity of nature and culture in order to contrast "the vanished democratic public character of life" (149) with modern reality and appeal to action. Nevertheless, although he abandoned the "New Letters on the Aesthetic Education of Man," which he considered writing in 1796 in order to move "from philosophy to poetry and religion" (Hölderlin 1988: 132), and instead composed *Hyperion* (1797–99), the long, passionate letter which closes Part One of the novel shows that aesthetic concerns never lost their primacy.

55. "What is the basis of a partial, purely political revolution? It is that a part of civil society emancipates itself and attains to universal domination, that a particular class undertakes the general emancipation of society from its particular situation. This class frees the whole of society, but only under the presupposition that the whole of society is in the same situation as this class, that it possesses, or can easily acquire for example, money and education. No class in civil society can play this role without arousing a moment of enthusiam in itself and among the masses. It is a moment when the class fraternizes with society in general and dissolves itself into

society; it is identified with society and is felt and recognized as society's general representative. Its claims and rights are truly the claims and rights of society itself of which it is the real social head and heart" (Marx 1971: 125).

56. "It may be more to the purpose to note that this intellectual pre-eminence of the Jews has come into bearing within the gentile community of peoples, not from the outside; that the men who have been its bearers have been men immersed in this gentile culture in which they have played their part of guidance and incitement, not bearers of a compelling message from afar or proselyters of enlightenment conjuring with a ready formula worked out in the ghetto and carried over into the gentile community for its mental regeneration" (Veblen 1964: 223–24).

57. The precious, romantic friendship of Jew and Gentile, modeled on that between Mendelssohn and Lessing, is a common biographical topos. Suffice to mention here Marx and Engels, Hofmannsthal and Strauss, Benjamin and Brecht, or Derrida and de Man.

58. The convergence of views expressed in the responses of Mendelssohn and Kant to the question "What is Enlightenment?" has often been noted: "With the two texts published [in 1784] in the *Berlinische Monatschrift*, the German *Aufklärung* and the Jewish *Haskala* recognize that they belong to the same history; they are seeking to identify the common processes from which they stem. And it is perhaps a way of announcing the acceptance of a common destiny—we know to what drama that was to lead" (Foucault 1984: 33).

59. Ferdinand Lassalle (1825–64), aspiring to Hegelianize Judaism, writes in a letter of 1843: "The dilemma I have defined is therefore a double one, and is, briefly, this: The Talmud must be rejected, the restoration of Mosaism cannot be thought of; what will you set up, then, as positive articles of faith? . . . Moreover, it is not yet possible to come out frankly with the true and full contents of our knowledge and thinking. At the same time, however, care must be taken not to lag too far behind the achievements of German science" (quoted in Silberner 1952–53: 161). His suggestion, though, is not one of rejection: "[I]t might be most advisable to preserve the development of Mosaism, so far as this development can hold its own before the critical forum of reason. It might perhaps be best to retain the interpretation of the Talmud, so far as this interpretation can hold its own before the forum of sound reason. This would at least give infinitely great latitude" (162). This position has been called elsewhere "Hebrew dualism" and has been defined as "the tendency to expand and its opposite, to contract" (Bialik 1961: 19).

60. "It is no accident that the Goethe cult at the start of the nineteenth century was created in the salon of Rachel Varnhagen, for it is certain that no one else strove with such intensity to live in accord with the model of Wilhelm Meister, who understood the 'cultivation of personality' so peculiarly and so deceptively as an assimilation of the bourgeois to the nobleman, as did those Jews who were also called 'exceptional Jews of culture'" (Habermas 1983b: 32). Taking Goethe as a great leader, they "found in Germany's hero Judaism's white knight. . . . In short, he was the model for German Jewish nationalism" (Bolkosky 1975: 141). This choice had no inherent justification. Although he studied Hebrew and Yiddish, Goethe's "whole interest in the Jews was no more than an intellectual curiosity" (Rose 1964: 179). His preference was probably more Hellenic, since he declared "to Böttiger in 1795 that humanity would have taken a healthier turn if Homer had been its Bible instead of the Scriptures" (164).

61. A similar pattern has been noticed in the ascendancy of American Jews: "They wanted the full privileges and opportunities of the middle-class society into which, unlike the major immigrant groups, they moved en masse" (John Higham, quoted in Aaron 1965: 33). Their background was also relevant: "The Jews who were actually welcomed by Puritan nations, especially the Americans, were not pious Orthodox Jews but rather Reformed Jews who had abandoned orthodoxy, Jews such as those of the present time who have been trained in the Educational Alliance, and finally baptized Jews" (Weber 1963: 261). For a microscopic study, see Kanfer 1989.

62. This achievement, associated with the so-called "Jewish mystique" (van den Haag 1969), has been celebrated with unabashed triumphalism. The cultural critic Moritz Goldstein wrote in the essay "German-Jewish Parnassus" (1912): "Suddenly Jews are to be found in all the positions from which they are not deliberately excluded; they have made the tasks of the Germans their own; German cultural life seems to pass increasingly into Jewish hands. This, however, the Christians had neither foreseen nor intended when they granted the Pariahs in their midst a stake in European civilization. They began to resist, again they began to call us foreigners, to consider us dangerous in the temple of their civilization. And now we are confronted with the problem: *We Jews are administering the spiritual property of a nation which denies our right and our ability to do so*" (quoted in Goldstein 1957: 237). Claims in the same spirit remain common: "In literature, in the mass media, in drama and music, in certain branches of the mathematical and physical sciences, the American Jew holds a commanding position. It is the gentile who has to break in" (Steiner 1964: 18).

63. For a despicable example of socialist anti-Semitism, which identifies capitalism with the Jews, see Rizzi 1985–86. The most systematic critique of modernity from a left anticapitalist anti-Semitic viewpoint is *La France juive* (1886, 2 vols.) by Edouard Drumont (1844–1917).

64. There have been different explanations of the phenomenon: "But the more eminent a modern Jew is, the less Jewish he becomes, the less is he usually concerned with Jewry, the less is he attached to Judaism. Our great men do not demonstrate the greatness of our distinctive tradition, but rather reveal—by the success of those who abandoned that tradition—its state of sheer exhaustion" (Polanyi 1943: 38).

65. "As they had turned to Lessing and Schiller to examine their enlightened attitudes, German Jews anxious to display their nationalism and national allegiance turned to identification with Herder, Humboldt, Fichte, and again Goethe. . . . The words that described Goethe and Herder were the same as those that described the Old Testament and Old Testament prophets" (Bolkosky 1975: 139).

66. "By one of the cruel, deep ironies of history, the concept of a chosen people, of a nation exalted above others, was born in Israel. In the vocabulary of Hitler there is a vengeful parody of the Judaic claim. The theological motif of a people elected at Sinai is echoed in the pretense of the master race. Thus there was in the obsessed relation of Nazi to Jew a minute but fearful grain of logic. Torturer and victim had chosen each other as they have chosen themselves" (Steiner 1964: 22).

67. The same position was also adopted by the young Walter Benjamin who, "barely out of school at the age of twenty, rejoiced in his newly discovered Jewish

identity. Jewish intellectuals, he wrote in 1912, provide the principal support and dynamic for true culture, which in this case included not only literature and art but also socialism and the women's emancipation movement. Among Jewish intellectuals, he continued, writers were in the vanguard of change; here the otherwise much maligned *Literatenjuden*—Jews as men of letters—took a central role in creating alternatives to the existing order. Jewishness became a metaphor for the critical mind and for *Bildung*; it is through the study of Goethe, he repeats, that the nature of Jewishness is fully revealed. This definition of Jewishness summarized in an almost uncanny manner the Jewish substance . . . not as an idealization of bourgeois society but as an alternative to the present" (Mosse 1985: 66).

68. The same holds true for painters' views, like a manifesto (Kitaj 1989) where the geopolitical reality of the diaspora is reduced to an artistic mode, "Diasporism," and its misreadings.

69. "Generally speaking, it is clear that the producers of the Romantic anti-capitalist worldview are *certain traditional sectors of the intelligentsia*, whose culture and way of life are hostile to bourgeois industrial civilization: independent writers, ecclesiastics or theologians . . . , poets and artists, academic mandarins, etc." (Sayre and Löwy 1984: 90).

70. In a discussion of protests by student activists, the old Adorno still affirmed the superiority of art: "When the political avant-garde disrupts events of the artistic avant-garde, the result is confusion writ large: neither the belief that disruption is revolutionary nor the related belief that revolution is a thing of artistic beauty holds any water. Artlessness is not above art but below it; and commitment is frequently no more than lack of talent or of adaptation, in any event a weakening of subjective strength" (Adorno 1984: 355–56).

71. References to ancient philosophy, religion, or democracy recur in modern definitions of Judaism. A discussion of the two founding traditions of Western high culture, which compares Hebrew "narrative monotheism" and Greek secular literature, asserts in its introduction: "If Western civilization is looked upon as a product of the interaction of Judaic and Hellenic elements, then 'culture' as we know it is given to us by the Greeks. Because the secular perspective of modern society derives rather from the Greek than from the Judaic side of its heritage, the 'anticultural,' iconoclastic component of this heritage tends to go unnoticed, and indeed to be repressed. The Greek contribution to modernity scarcely needs elucidation. The state, authoritarian or democratic, the generalized international exchange-system, science and its technological by-products, as well as the arts and 'humanities,' all have clearly visible Greek antecedents. The Judaic side seems scarcely visible; one might wonder what this Middle Eastern tribe has contributed to the greatness of Western civilization" (Gans 1985: 1). The principle of the aesthetic is here, as always, indispensable for an answer to this last question: "It is not through perversion of its spirit that Western cultural reflection has maintained its gaze fixed on its Greek more than its Hebrew ancestry. The moral imperative may be our greatest cultural force, and its formulation our greatest achievement, but in its purity it cannot be realized as a positive ethic. In the concrete social context, only esthetic culture permits us to construct an imaginary universe of reciprocal relations. It is through the estheticization of social interaction that modern society offers the only possible path to the realization of the moral imperative" (187–88).

72. Feuerbach began his "Theses for the Reform of Philosophy" (1843) as follows: "The secret of theology is anthropology, but the secret of speculative philosophy is theology." The importance of this kind of approach for German philosophy is crucial. "As far as Germany is concerned, the criticism of religion is essentially complete, and the criticism of religion is the presupposition of all criticism" (Marx 1971: 115). To put this maxim differently, all critique, from the Idealists to the Poststructuralists, presupposes and requires a critical involvement with religion.

73. Marx's choice is remarkable in light of his impressive familiarity with Greek thought (he wrote his doctoral thesis in 1841 on the atomic theories of Democritus and Epicurus) and the parallels he saw between the post-Aristotelian and post-Hegelian age. The romantic and idealist versions of the Hellenic, however, do not seem to have a place in his materialist philosophy. His debt to Hebraic thought, on the other hand, is a more ambiguous question: "Even Marx's notorious 'final solution,' his wish to see the Jew absorbed into the anonymity of mankind, is only a parodistic inversion of the prophetic image of a last gathering and confluence of all men at the hour of redemption" (Steiner 1976: 67).

74. Bruno Bauer returned to the "Jewish question" many years later, in an entry he published in the *Political and Social Encyclopaedia* on "The Jews as Aliens" (1863). This time, he wished to erect a permanent barrier between Jews and Gentiles by emphasizing their racial differences (Rotenstreich 1959). His position commanded little attention, as general discussions were influenced by very different studies, like *Rome and Jerusalem* (1863) by Moses Hess.

75. There is an interesting contemporary parallel in the debate between two French socialists in the pamphlet *Les Juifs, rois de l'époque: histoire de la féodalité financière* (1845) by Alphonse Toussenel and Pierre Leroux's article by the same title (1846).

76. The persisting use of the "Jewish question" (which, we must always insist, is as different from the situation of the actual, historical Jews as, say, Orientalism is different from the condition of the Arabs) to ward off considerations of the political became manifest again in the efforts of the German government to distance itself from the recent past: "The reparations treaty [of 1953] was also a social contract *among* Germans: the abandoned Nazi question was replaced by the new 'consensus' on the Jewish Question about which there could be no statute of limitations (this was implicit) or public debate. . . . If the famous paragraph 131 permitted the reintegration of former Nazis into the civil service, the reparations declaration sanctioned the substitution of the Jewish Question for the Nazi question. . . . The reparations settlement circumscribed the discourse of National Socialism within a version of 'metaphysical guilt' in which the state assumed moral responsibility for its legal predecessor. On the other hand, the antifascist concept of political responsibility broadly defined . . . was exiled to West German literary culture" (Rabinbach 1988: 167). When a new socio-political contract was sought, the "Jewish question," a well-tested basis for civil society, was used as its covenant of atonement and restitution. This time, it took the form of "*Judaizing* the memory of the Holocaust" (181). Thus it became "a central fact of the postwar history of the Federal Republic of Germany: every expansion of German political sovereignty has been accompanied—at least subjectively—by a debate about the 'Jewish Question.' . . . Since 1945, the German Question and the Jewish Question have been inseparable" (192).

77. For the advocates of emancipation, assimilation was indeed a question of disinterested taste. "The problem of Diaspora in its most crucial essence is the problem of aesthetics" (Ozick 1970: 273). This is absolutely true provided it stands as a reminder of the aesthetic conditions of emancipation which turned it into a successful apprenticeship in contemplation. To claim nevertheless that the "German Final Solution was an aesthetic solution: it was a job of editing" (273), is to take an aesthetic (that is, contemplative, disinterested, formalist, apolitical) view of the catastrophe.

78. "The melancholy of the adult state arises from our dual, conflicting experience that, on the one hand, our absolute, youthful confidence in an inner voice has diminished or died, and, on the other hand, that the outside world to which we now devote ourselves in our desire to learn its ways and dominate it will never speak to us in a voice that will clearly tell us our way and determine our goal" (Lukács 1971: 86).

79. There have been a few attempts to accept Sartre's re-definition of the "Jewish question" and give voice to the historical (as opposed to the aesthetic) modernity of Jewishness. The result, however, has been to talk not about the Jew of anti-Semitism but the "Catastrophe Jew" (Améry 1980: 25) and his anger at his fate, rather than the "situations" that produced him: "Anti-Semitism and the Jewish Question, as historical, socially determined conceptual phenomena, were not and are not any concern of mine. They are entirely a matter for the anti-Semites, their disgrace or their sickness. The anti-Semites have something to overcome, not I. I would play into their unclean hands if I began investigating what share religious, economic, or other factors have in the persecution of the Jews" (22–23). Like the look at ethnic identity, the view from the existential predicament cannot produce a program for change and often results in little more than cries of anguish to the God who "suffers gusts of murderous exasperation toward the Jews, toward a people who have made Him a party to history and to the brutish infirmity of man's condition. . . . It may have been the Jew who caught Him by the skirt, demanding contract and dialogue" (Steiner 1964: 17).

80. The accuracy of Weber's evidence has often been challenged. An examination of capitalist development in the Dutch Republic, for example, concludes that "trade and industry are not dependent on either the Protestant or the Catholic religion, but on certain secular forces" (Hyma 1937: 161). Many critics find the liberation from religious influence much more important: "Thus it was the spirit of Erasmus, not of Calvin, which in the end set the tone of economic and cultural life in Dutch society, which became the most capitalist nation of Europe. And it succeeded in this precisely in that it institutionalized the typically bourgeois separation between business and religion" (Pellicani 1988: 72). In addition, most medieval historians have argued that the capitalist spirit already existed in the European city of the Low Middle Ages.

81. They included works like Tomas Masaryk's *The Social Question* (1898), Georg Simmel's *The Philosophy of Money* (1900), Sigmund Freud's *The Interpretation of Dreams* (1900), Edmund Husserl's *Cartesian Meditations* (1900, vol. I), Fritz Mauthner's *Contributions toward a Critique of Language* (1901–2), Benedetto Croce's *Estetica come scienza dell'espressione e linguistica generale* (1902), Sombart's *Das moderne Kapitalismus* (1902), Otto Weininger's *Sex and Character*

(1902), Weber's *The Protestant Ethic and the Spirit of Capitalism* (1904–5), Heinrich Rickert's *The Problem of the Philosophy of History* (1905), Ernst Troeltsch's *Protestantisches Christentum und Kirche in der Neuzeit* (1906), Henri Bergson's *L'évolution créatrice* (1907), William James' *Pragmatism: A New Name for Some Old Ways of Thinking* (1907), Friedrich Meinecke's *Cosmopolitanism and the National State* (1908), Georges Sorel's *Réflexions sur la violence* (1908), Lenin's *Materialism and Empirical Criticism* (1909), and Lucien Lévy-Bruhl's *The Mental Functions of the Inferior Societies* (1910). Ferdinand de Saussure, Émile Durkheim, Jean Jaurès, and Theodor Herzl also belonged to the same generation.

82. In a rare Hebraic appropriation, mythology has also been attributed to great Jewish thought (from Marx, Freud, and Durkheim to Wittgenstein, Lévi-Strauss, and Chomsky), where "the mythological element—in the true sense of the word, meaning an articulate, imaged, self-consistent narrative diagnosis of the origins and shapes of human experience—is paramount" (Steiner 1976:74).

83. Others have asked: "Did the Greeks believe in their myths?" (Veyne 1988). Some formulations of the same question admit to sheer exasperation: "Why the unbroken authority of Greek myths over the imagination of the West? Why should a handful of Greek myths, that of Antigone among them, recur in the art and thought of the twentieth century to an almost obsessive degree? Why is there no end to Oedipus, to Prometheus, to Orestes, to Narcissus, no laying to rest in archaeology?" (Steiner 1984: 300).

84. The long evolution of this idea has led to accommodating positions like the following: "Homer and the Bible, literature and sacred history, sum up better than anything else the complementary contribution of Greek and Jew to Western civilization. . . . The biblical text is designed to inspire fear of God, that is, respect for ethical constraints. The Homeric text contents itself with inspiring a love for the text itself, or more precisely, for its position of hearer subordinated to the reciting Subject" (Gans 1985: 7).

85. "Lowth thus places the Bible beyond rationalist disintegration and urges a view that could immediately be transferred to any other early sacred scripture or mythology. Lowth's influence was considerable: in Germany his approach influenced Herder and led to an affirmation of mythical thought and experience that claimed, in essence, that religious truth expresses itself in early noble ages as poetry and myth, which cannot be reduced or explained away but which must be accepted as valid. Myth thus becomes the essential expression of religious truth. . . . Blackwell urged that Homeric myth be taken seriously as Greek wisdom and religion. Lowth urged that the Bible should be approached as poetry. The effect of these two ideas, together with the general climate of preromantic interest in myth, was a tendency, beginning in the late eighteenth century and manifest in most of the romantic poets, to raise mythic truth to the level of religious truth and to regard both as the natural province of the highest poetry" (Richardson 1978: 27–28).

86. "The Zionist movement would be a kind of *Gesamtkunstwerk* of the new politics. Herzl sensed this when he said, 'Moses' exodus would compare [to mine] like a Shrove Tuesday *Singspiel* of Hans Sachs to a Wagnerian opera'" (Schorske 1980: 163).

87. From a comparably religious view but without any confidence in the Hellenic, Adorno revises this position by endowing the historicity of Hebraic art with

the ability to redeem myth, and argues that "what constitutes the redemptive aspect of art is the act through which spirit discards itself in art. Art remains loyal to shudder not by reverting to it, but by preserving its legacy. The spirit of works of art produces shudder by externalizing itself in objects. Thus, art partakes of the course of real empirical history in accordance with the general dynamic of enlightenment, which is that, owing to the self-reflection of genius, elements of reality enter into the imagination there to become conscious of their unreality. The historical evolution of art *qua* spiritualization is therefore not only a criticism of myth but also a redemption of myth, because as the imagination recollects something it also reaffirms its possibility" (Adorno 1984: 173).

88. Concern about the viability of dogma after Higher Criticism led another theorist through a parallel path during the 1790s to a similar quest: "Coleridge's two major interests, Christian theology under the penetrating probes of Enlightenment criticism, and a new poetry of the supernatural, met in the need for a modern mythology" (Shaffer 1975: 32). It could be argued that this need was first answered, albeit through a different synthesis, during the next decade in the classical landscapes of his contemporary, J. M. W. Turner (1775–1851).

89. In his discussion of the Idealist project of the *system*, Heidegger writes: "Like many other words which have left their imprint on the realm of our human existence, whether directly or in translation, the word comes from the Greek. When we state this, we are not just naming the original language of the word, but the people, the creative force of that people which in its poets, thinkers, statesmen, and artists brought about the greatest formative attack on the whole of Being which ever occurred in Western history" (Heidegger 1985: 25).

90. In *The Rights of Man* (1791–92), Thomas Paine declared: "What Athens was in miniature, America will be in magnitude. The one was the wonder of the ancient world; the other is becoming the admiration and model of the present."

91. Although the genealogy of the Hebraic-Hellenic opposition shows that the former term has been consistently privileged over the latter, there has been no scholarship exploring the phenomenon. Furthermore, research has concentrated exclusively on anti-Semitism and phil-Hellenism. For example, while in a single page of a book one may find a variety of words such as "anti-Judaism," "anti-Semitism," "anti-Mosaism," and "judeophobia" (Markish 1986: 6), no comparable vocabulary exists for negative attitudes toward the Hellenic. If there has been only a handful of books on philo-Semites and no study of Greek-haters, this is precisely because these two attitudes are almost never acknowledged as existing and influencing positions and policies. Hebreophilia and mis-Hellenism are the twin ideologies that the post-Reformation world has most strongly repressed (cultivating the impression that they are rather impossible) and can never admit, since their function is cardinal to Western religious identity, the catholicism of civil rites.

92. The aversion of the cultural elite to politics had turned many intellectuals against egalitarian ideals. In his *Reflections of a Nonpolitical Man* (1918), Mann defended the "nonpolitical ethos" against democracy, which he equated with politics, while recognizing and honoring a German resistance against "Roman civilization" and the "Roman West." Anticipating many of Adorno's positions, he also advocated the integrity of art against politics, the superiority of the musical over the verbal, and the purity of the mystical above the rational. A theory of myth is out-

lined in Mann's *Doktor Faustus* by the conservative scholar Dr. Chaim Breisacher. It takes the form of an "anti-cultural" philosophy of culture which portrays civilization as the decline from cult to culture. The figure of Breisacher is based on the historian of mythology Oskar Goldberg, the author of *The Reality of the Hebrews* (1925) and leader of a theosophic circle in Berlin with which Benjamin was involved. Through a discussion of the Pentateuch, Breisacher proposes that a new age of myth should follow the road of Socratic philosophy. "The coming mythical age will be discovered by reason. Goldberg's philosophy of myth presents a classical case for the dialectic of reason that destroys itself 'reasonably' and calls for the magical ritual of the mythical age to counteract the tyrannical rule of technology in our civilization. . . . It speaks for the deep insight of Thomas Mann that he describes the process of reason's self-annihilation by analyzing Goldberg's philosophy of myth" (Taubes 1954: 391–92).

93. Here are a few more recent representative titles which indicate the unabated interest in myth: *Mythe et pensée chez les grecs* (1966) by Jean-Pierre Vernant; *Mythe et épopée* (1968) by Georges Dumezil; *Myth: Its Meaning and Functions in Ancient and Other Cultures* (1970) by Geoffrey Kirk; *Terror und Spiel: Probleme der Mythenrezeption* (1971), edited by M. Fuhrmann; *Mythe et tragédie en Grèce ancienne* (1972), edited by Vernant and Pierre Vidal-Naquet; *Mythe et société en Grèce ancienne* (1974) by Vernant; *The Nature of Greek Myths* (1975) by Kirk; *Philosophie und Mythos: Ein Kolloquium* (1979), edited by H. Poser; *The Best of the Achaeans: Concepts of the Hero in Archaic Greek Poetry* (1979) by Gregory Nagy; *Der kommende Gott: Vorlesungen über die neue Mythologie* (1982) by Manfred Frank; *Mythos und Moderne: Begriff und Bild einer Rekonstruktion* (1983), edited by Karl Heinz Bohrer; *Les Grecques sans miracle* (1984) by Louis Gernet; *Sacred Narrative: Readings in the Theory of Myth* (1984), edited by Alan Dundes; *Faszination des Mythos: Studien zu antiken und modernen Interpretationen* (1985), edited by Renate Schlesier; and *Die Restauration der Götter* (1986), edited by Richard Faber and Renate Schlesier.

94. Starting with German Romantics like Friedrich Schlegel and Schelling, the Dionysian has also been associated with the feminine. "'Dionysian gyneocracy' (rule by women) and 'Apollonian paternity' are the true opposing themes in [Johann Jakob] Bachofen's *Matriarchal Rights (Das Mutterrecht)* of 1861" (Baeumer 1976: 187). Paglia 1990 sees the universe as the product of the tension between two cosmic forces: the Apollonian (masculine, artistic, and logocentric) and the Dionysian (feminine, natural, and pagan).

95. "That is why Germany, having discovered the oriental (mystical, enthusiastic, nocturnal, savage—*natural*) depths of Greece, regularly identified itself with what one might, from an historico-political point of view, term its 'Doric order' (Hölderlin's 'Junonian,' Nietzsche's 'Apollinian': rigorous, circumscribed, solar—*technical*). And it is obviously here that Rome, which received only that heritage . . . becomes superimposed on the image, which was presented as intact, of Greece. The inaugural gesture of National Socialism is no less Roman, for this reason, nor Sparto-Roman, than the founding gestures of the French Revolution, the Consulate or the Napoleonic Empire" (Lacoue-Labarthe 1990: 74).

96. Marx expresses this aporia in his discussion of the arts in the *Grundrisse* (1857–58): "It is well known that Greek mythology is not only the arsenal of Greek

art but also its foundation. Is the view of nature and of social relations on which the Greek imagination and hence Greek mythology is based possible with self-acting mule spindles and railways and locomotives and electrical telegraphs? . . . But the difficulty lies not in understanding that the Greek arts and epic are bound up with certain forms of social development. The difficulty is that they still afford us artistic pleasure and that in a certain respect they count as a norm and as an unattainable model" (Tucker 1978: 245–46).

97. A rare example of the same doubling within the Hebraic is a suggestion by "Bernard Lazare (1865–1903), who before his conversion to Zionism proposed a metaphysical distinction between 'Jews' (bad) and 'Israelites' (good)" (Lichtheim 1968: 331).

98. In his book, Creuzer "presented the symbolism of the Ancients . . . as the expression of a religious consciousness and a religious world view, rather than as the invention of a free poetic imagination. The implication of Creuzer's work, which revived ideas mooted by Vossius (De theologia gentili, 1641) and Kircher (Oedipus aegyptus, 1652), a century and a half before, was that there had been an original religious consciousness, an original knowledge of the Divine, shared by all men and corresponding to the original adamitic language. This original religion had subsequently been corrupted and fragmented into a thousand 'pagan' cults, just as the original language had broken up, after Babel, into a thousand alien tongues. But to the Christian mythologists it had been restored by Revelation" (Gossman 1986: 46–47).

99. "In keeping with his destruction of the Romantic picture of the world, Heinrich Heine also dissolves the tenuous Romantic unification of Christ with Dionysus. . . . For Heine, the Dionysian has an exclusively negative connotation. Every one of the late Romantic images of a terrifying Bacchus is brought forth by him for the purpose of a biting satire on the classical German image of Greece. . . . The ecstatic passion expressed by Bacchus in Heine's works is more base sensuality than anything else. Its function is not the Romantic rejuvenation and poeticization of the world, rather the demythologization and the zestful destruction of the moral and social order; not the ecstatic exaltation and deification of life, but rather an anguished lust for life; not the unification of religion and poetry, antiquity, and Christendom, rather their separation into mutually hostile camps. The synthesis Dionysus-Christ is transposed to the antithesis Dionysian-Christian, which corresponds to Heine's antithetical formulation Hellenic-Nazarene. . . . Just as the Dionysian topos, because of its ecstatic character, had become the appropriate form for thought and expression for the early Romantics, so it is for Heine, writing at the close of the Romantic period, the favorite topos of the period's rapturous dissolution and destruction" (Baeumer 1976: 173–75).

100. Writers and artists have "sensed an affinity between Yahweh and Dionysus. Like Dionysus, Yahweh can seize, tempt, and destroy; his theophanies can be fearful and even horrifying. It is true that the O.T. is pervasively ethical in a way that The Bacchae is not, and that Yahweh has an orderly and rational Apollonian side, possibly connected with one of his other major names, Elohim" (Stock 1989: 52).

101. The most important works of the School were Prolegomena to the Study of Greek Religion (1903) by Jane Harrison, From Religion to Philosophy (1912) by Francis Cornford, Themis: A Study of the Social Origins of Greek Religion (1912) by

Harrison, *From Religion to Philosophy: A Study in the Origins of Western Specula-tion* (1912) by Cornford, *The Origins of Attic Comedy* (1913) by Cornford, *Ancient Art and Ritual* (1913) by Harrison, *Euripides and His Age* (1914) by Gilbert Murray, and *Epilegomena to the Study of Greek Religion* (1921) by Harrison.

102. In the notes for the last meeting of the seminar Warburg conducted at the University of Hamburg, dedicated to a comparison between Burckhardt and Nietzsche, he wrote: "Thus we suddenly see the influence of antiquity in both its currents, the so-called Apollonian and Dionysian. What part does antiquity play in the development of prophetic personalities? Agostino di Duccio and Nietzsche stand on one side of the divide, the architects and Burckhardt on the other" (quoted in Gombrich 1986: 258). "Structure versus line" was the abstract formula-tion he gave to this opposition.

103. The other major concern for Warburg from early on was religion. "In the autumn of 1888 he jots down a scheme for a history of religion:

(A) Personal gods whose power makes itself felt in an arbitrary and incalcula-ble way—sacrifices for particular ends. (B) One personal god, ruling steadily, angry but can be reconciled—clearly prescribed and regular sacrifices. (C) Christ, God is love. Rejection of St. Paul: the crudely sensuous aspect of sac-rifice: sacrifice and ceremony (the law) eliminated from daily life; what re-mains is prayer and a few ceremonies, baptism, Eucharist. (D) God is within us: daily work the same as divine service. (*Fragmente*, 4 September 1988)

Subsequent notes link this evolutionary scale once more with the problem of anxi-ety. Paganism, with its *ad hoc* sacrifices prompted by fear, lacks any sense of secu-rity. Judaism achieves a sense of security by constant sacrifices. Christianity achieves the same sense of security by its spiritual sacrifices and its consecration of work. The scientific world-view finally achieves a sense of security without sacrifices since it regards both life and work as divine" (Gombrich 1986: 71–72). Culture emerges again as the realm of synthesis and reconciliation.

104. "Another element in the process was the formation of liberal Judaism, that is, of Judaism as a confession. Ever since the earthly fatherland won out over the heavenly fatherland, this confession, like others, has been intended solely as a mat-ter of private life. In contrast to Judaism as a principle that determines the life of both individual and society and in large measure prescribes the course of daily life and the relations of Jews with each other, liberal Judaism prides itself that Jewish communities and their members form part of the national state in which they hap-pen to live" (Horkheimer 1974: 108).

105. From this position, the Gentiles are blamed for the condition of the Jews. "The traditional, observant Jew will explain it as part of sacred salvation his-tory—that is, it is a punishment for Israel's sins. The secularizing, intellectual Jew will turn this theodicy inside out, forging it into an instrument with which to blame the Gentile. The older, intrapunitive theodicy becomes an exteropunitive so-ciodicy: 'You made us what we are today,' the secularist intelligentsia of the Dias-pora will insist, indicting the Gentile West, creating what Salo Baron calls the 'lachrymose' historiography of the Jews. The culture of the West being what it is—Christian—the victim-status carries considerable prestige" (Cuddihy 1974: 147). The sociodicy may find even more universal expressions and become again a

view of destiny: "The Jews are a people whom barbarism must choose for its hatred" (Steiner 1964: 20). The same may hold true for views that blur other historical differences (and will predictably see this book with hostility): "Anti-Semites are not just destructive rock throwers or defacers of synagogues; and philo-Semites are not just celebrators of Jewish achievements. Whether they see the Jew as sub-human or as super-human, they share a sense of fear and loathing of the Jew as such" (Horo-witz 1990: 19).

106. This optimism always finds its strongest adherents among humanists: "Western civilization is compounded of three ingredients: local custom and super-stition, Greek science and art, Hebraic religion. The quantity of the several ingredi-ents varies. In some places, such as France, the Hellenic is as great as the Hebraic; in others, such as contemporary Germany, the local is in ascendance over both the Hellenic and the Hebraic; in America, with its strong Anglo-Saxon heritage and Puritan background, the Hebraic is perhaps the most important" (Boas 1939: v).

107. Since Modernism, Hebraic anti-humanist attacks have become increasingly common and aggressive: "I want to dare to observe that if Jewish feminism does not emerge from Torah, it will disintegrate. For Jews the Enlightenment is an idol that will not serve women as it did not serve Jews; Voltaire was an anti-Semite. For Jews humanism is an idol that will not serve women as it does not serve Jews: in the West it is mainly the self-declared humanists who stand in the gutter with other Jew-haters to support Arafat" (Ozick 1984: 9–10).

108. Lassalle writes in a letter of 1844: "The Jewish religion is the religion of harsh servitude under the abstract spirit, God; hence the fate [of the Jews] is also that of harsh servitude. . . . And yet what a speculative kernel lies for the thinker in this ugliness of formation [of the Jewish spirit]. In the Jewish people, the spirit has achieved such a profound consciousness of itself that it has broken with its outward creatural appearance, [and] with the whole of nature itself. The spirit has compre-hended itself as something higher than all nature and creatureliness, to which latter it had been surrendered in all previous religions. For it, naturalness and finiteness are devoid of essence; absolute essence is [to be sought] in the abstract spirit" (quoted in Silberner 1952–53: 163–64).

109. An interesting dimension of this universalization was the cultivation, mainly in the twentieth century, of a nomothetic language theory often based on norms of Jewish expressive culture. In addition to Roman Jakobson's poetics of parallelism, to the same category arguably belong the studies of Fritz Mauthner (1849–1923), Wittgenstein, Benjamin (in its life-long dialogue with the Kabbalah), and Chomsky (whose first work dealt with Hebrew grammar). This body of scholar-ship, which sought the fundamentals of human expression in deep structures or ordinary communication, is marked by the drama of questionable reference specific to the linguistic tension between Yiddish and Hebrew, on the one hand, and Yid-dish and German, on the other.

110. Since that time, promoting Jewish thought as a non-ethnic philosophy "done in a Jewish way" which gives primary emphasis to ethics (Seeskin 1990) has become quite common. Claude Montefiore (1858–1939) proposed the idea of "a new and purified Judaism" that would be non-ethnic and would take over as a universal religion once traditional Judaism and Christianity withered away (Bowler 1988).

111. Scholem and his generation found true Judaism and bourgeois culture incompatible, and rejected the Science as subservient to the latter. At the same time, his debt to its lessons should not be minimized: "Scholem may be seen as the dialectical fulfillment of the original impulse in the Wissenschaft des Judentums, since nineteenth-century Jewish historiography laid the basis for anarchistic historicism but belied its promise by generally succumbing to a rationalist, dogmatic theology" (Biale 1979: 102–3).

112. The last (and best-known) sickness to appear, "self-hatred" (Gilman 1986)—a term which achieved wide currency in 1930, through Theodor Lessing's *Der jüdische Selbsthaß*—has been called "the pathological side of the German Jews' confident assertion of their German identity" (Gay 1975: 61).

113. "German-Jewish scholarship sought to provide a new spiritual framework for German Jewry by rediscovering a colourful, variegated and coherent Jewish past that would also provide the rationale for variety, orderly change and development within the modern Jewish community. German-Jewish scholarship was a massive effort at reinfusing vitality into what many Jews had understandably come to regard as a fossil that was totally irrelevant to contemporary spiritual life. In the reconquest of the past and in the mastery of the dynamics of history—of law, liturgy, philosophy—the scholars hoped to provide the rationale and motivation for adherence and the guidelines for a spiritual rebirth and future creativity. Zunz never pretended otherwise, nor did Geiger or David Hoffmann or Martin Buber or Franz Rosenzweig or Harry Torczyner. *Literaturgeschichte, Ritusgeschichte, Religionsgeschichte* were all oriented towards parallel goals" (G. Cohen 1975: xxvii). Thanks to this broad view of the longer course of the Science, we can see why its project is not over yet: so long as there is faith in interpretive emancipation, and therefore (deconstructionist, feminist, phenomenological, humanistic, Third-World, or any other) critique engaged in idolomachy, the Science of Judaism will remain a vital and often exemplary force in the (aesthetic) dialectic of modernity—(cultural) resistance and assimilation.

114. "Of one thing we may be quite certain, and that is: the Jews excel as interpreters, whether of literature, the acted drama, music or painting. . . . The reason for the peerlessness of the Jew in the realm of interpretation is to be found undoubtedly in his empathic endowment. With his cosmopolitan spirit and universal reach he can . . . readily gain an insight into the purpose of a masterpiece; and all interpretation is, to a certain extent, creation" (Roback 1929: 59).

115. Since "the Jews have preserved their purity of blood to a greater extent than any other nation" (Roback 1929: 425), physiological and hereditary factors are given serious consideration: "The Jews are, as a people, possessed of a nervous system which allows of a readier canalization and, therefore, rapid distribution of nervous energy, thus facilitating adjustment and re-adjustment with greater ease than in the case of perhaps any other race. The Greeks were not endowed with this plastic nervous system and, consequently, in time were reduced to an insignificant nationality" (Roback 1929: 54).

116. "What has become of the powers that teemed with genius? There is a Greek nation just as there is a Jewish people still existing. While the former has exhausted its supply of greatness, the latter is still producing in ever greater numbers and in a variety of fields. Must we not come to the conclusion that there is a *dynamic* quality

to the genius of the Jew in contradistinction to the static properties of the ancient Greeks, and probably of other nations?" (Roback 1929: 49).

117. Jung's internalization of myth followed in the footsteps of Freud's metaphysical attribution of internalization of authority to human nature: "It is in keeping with the course of human development that external coercion gradually becomes internalized—for a special mental agency, men's super-ego, takes it over and includes it among its commandments" (Freud 1964: 13).

118. The flight from the unruly crowd and the longing for a genuine, true community has usually been studied among individual nations and groups. "Yet the similarity between Buber's rediscovery of the Hasidim and the contemporary German revival of mystics like Meister Eckhart and Jacob Böhme is too striking to be ignored. Germans also wanted to go beyond 'liberal' or 'orthodox' Protestantism to an earlier heritage which seemed more dynamic because it was less rationalistic, less fossilized. . . . Buber's Hasidim performed a similar function by embodying a Judaism which was not rationalized, not fossilized, and surely not quiescent. Moreover, the dynamic nature of the Hasidim arose from a mysticism linked to a revived love for the Volk" (Mosse 1970: 85). Mysticism offered a powerful counter-mythology to those, like Buber (Breslauer 1990), apprehensive about a technocratic and materialistic modernity. "Just as the Germans attempted to root this mystical tradition in their national mystique, so Buber eventually attempted to embody this *Mythos* in the Jewish Volk, exemplified by the Hasidim" (87). Another comparable development was the search in the national mystique for a civil religion, "a common objective for those intellectuals and politicians who proposed the formation of a national consciousness for a modern Italy. In this case, the formulation of a new lay religiousness was considered to be an essential component in cultural modernization" (Gentile 1990: 232). The sacralization of politics, combined with the messianism of a new civilization, attempted to create, through a "new faith," a political life based on the national community. "In essence, the construction of a fascist religion, centred around the sacralization of the state, appears to be an attempt to evoke—in order to legitimize the fascist regime—the sacred nature of the Roman archetype as 'an expression of an ethical-religious concept, in which the essential reasons behind the state's existence and power are projected as symbols of faith' [P. de Francisci]" (Gentile 1990: 247–48). The model for these religious constructions linking "deity and domination" (Nicholls 1989) is the "Cult of the Supreme Being," Robespierre's reaction to atheist-anarchist trends that emerged in the early 1790s. The goal of his civil religion was to reconcile the contradictions of the Republic of Virtue, which reason appeared unable to resolve, through the "*sacralizing of the political authority*" (Fehér 1990: 190), the creation of the first political religion. "For Robespierre, 'the happiness of the people' was the major item on the political agenda. And without having ever heard the name Immanuel Kant, he was on this point, as on so many others, in a surprising harmony with Kant (of course, only within an overarching disagreement), who contended that while freedom unites, the quest for happiness divides" (190–91). The success of all these efforts, however, to found a political community on the religion of a national tradition were short-lived since the gradual Hellenization of the political marked it with an unassailably secular character. The twentieth-century community certainly had its politics but could never be political.

119. Hermann Cohen attempted to distinguish mythology from Judaism through a rationalist transformation of messianism. "In Cohen's utopian universalism, we find equally the suppression of the restorative and apocalyptic aspects of messianism. Cohen's utopianism was based on his distinction between mythology and monotheism. Mythology has no real concept of historical progress and instead harks back to an idyllic Golden Age (*das goldene Zeitalter*). Monotheism, on the other hand, does not seek to return to the happiness of the Golden Age, but instead to increase knowledge of the true God. . . . Unlike mythology, which is romantic and reactionary, monotheism is the aspiration for infinite time. The messianic age will truly be an 'age of culture' since it will be the age of complete knowledge" (Biale 1979: 151). The importance of this position for thinkers from Buber, Benjamin, and Scholem to Heidegger, Rosenzweig, and Lukács cannot be overestimated.

120. Adorno's racism surfaces in his many hostile pieces on jazz as commodity, written from 1936 until the end of his life, where he treats its black identity as a myth: "In fact, Adorno argued [in 1936], 'the skin of the Negro as well as the silver of the saxophone was a coloristic effect.' If the Negro contributed anything to jazz, it was less his rebellious reaction to slavery than his half-resentful, half-compliant submission to it. In a later essay on the same subject [1953], Adorno made the point even clearer: 'However little doubt there can be regarding the African elements in jazz, it is no less certain that everything unruly in it was from the very beginning integrated into a strict scheme, that its rebellious gestures are accompanied by the tendency to blind obeisance, much like the sado-masochistic type described by analytic psychology'" (Jay 1973: 186). The Frankfurt School would consistently try to neutralize unruly expressions of rebelliousness by attributing them to a false and pathological myth of revolt. From the same position stem more recent attacks against African-American tradition: "One of the most preposterous proclamations of all is that of 'black culture.' It is a necessary political put-on, a kind of Zionism without Zion and its cultural history. There is American culture, to which blacks belong, mainly as remissive figures in its mythology; there are various African cultures; but no black culture. Thousands of young minds have been violated by this preposterous idea. . . . 'Black culture' is the worst kind of Americanism, a rancorous hiding, behind empty self-assertion and apartheid, of the typically American fear of inferiority. . . . We teachers are creating a cast of crippled black pets (who are expected to bite the feeding hand, of course)" (Rieff 1972: 42).

121. In a book published in 1948 that "should be regarded as an extended appendix" (Adorno 1973: xvii) to the *Dialectic*, Adorno, the twelve-tone composer and student of Alban Berg, explores how Igor Stravinsky's "regression [to archaism] . . . replaces progress with repetition" (164). As usual, he locates the idolatry of myth in its substitution of repetition for (historical) development. "The Romantic religion of art to which Schoenberg subscribed wholeheartedly—a religion of art which his opposite Stravinsky felt to be inadmissible and dishonest, as regards both religion and aesthetics" (Dahlhaus 1987: 82) is the cardinal difference between the two composers that Adorno does not discuss.

122. *The Flight to Lucifer* (Bloom 1979), a philosophical *Star Wars* (or a Tolkien for theorists) about heresies and false gods, tells the story of the giant Perscors, a combination of Prometheus and Odysseus, who travels from Earth to Lucifer, a planet in a Hellenistic time, in search of meaning and self. Among other literary

uses of Prometheus, see *Frankenstein, or the Modern Prometheus* (1818) by Mary Shelley (1797–1851), the epic *Prometheus and Epimetheus* (1881) by Carl Spitteler (1845–1924), *The Book of Promethea* (1983) by Hélène Cixous, and *Wotan Unbound* (1923), the play by Ernst Toller (1893–1939), whose hero, an anti-Semitic barber addicted to Romantic literature, turns dictator. Recent operatic treatments of the myth include *Prometheus Unbound* (1944) by Havergal Brian (1876–1972), *Prometheus* (1966) by Carl Orff (1895–1982), and *Prometeo* (1984) by Luigi Nono (1924–90). Under the influence of the *Dialectic*, Marcuse, in a chapter called "The Images of Orpheus and Narcissus," finds that "the predominant culture-hero is the trickster and (suffering) rebel against the gods, who creates culture at the price of perpetual pain. He symbolizes productiveness, the unceasing effort to master life; but, in this productivity, blessing and curse, progress and toil are inextricably intertwined. Prometheus is the archetype-hero of the performance principle. . . . If Prometheus is the culture-hero of toil, productivity, and progress through repression, then the symbols of another reality principle must be sought at the opposite pole. Orpheus and Narcissus (like Dionysus to whom they are akin: the antagonist of the god who sanctions the logic of domination, the realm of reason) stand for a very different reality. They have not become the culture-heroes of the Western world: theirs is the image of joy and fulfillment" (Marcuse 1966: 161–62). The experience they represent, the *"aesthetic dimension"* (171), negates the performance principle, helps the reconciliation of opposites, and provides gratification. "Orpheus is the archetype of the poet as *liberator* and *creator*: he establishes a higher order in the world—an order without repression. In his person, art, freedom, and culture are eternally combined. He is the poet of redemption, the god who brings peace and salvation by pacifying man and nature, not through force but through song" (170).

123. A point of contrast, which illuminates the often forgotten ideological context of the *Dialectic*, is the "crisis theology" of Karl Barth (1886–1968) and his school launched during World War I. Their interest in protecting religion from culture led them by 1920 to see the former as "the crisis of culture" (Krüger 1966: 148), and later to resist the authority of philosophy with a Christocentric "theology of the Word." (On the importance of autonomy for Barth, see Macken 1990.)

124. In sharp contrast, Bertolt Brecht (1898–1956), who never won any respect from the Institute, sought through his "epic theater" and the political adaptation of myth (which he did not confine to Greek) "to make dialectics into a source of enjoyment," and alienation a matter of strategic viewpoint (rather than social or existential situation). Adorno also had no use for the "utility music" (*Gebrauchsmusik*) of the 1920s associated with Hans Eisler and Paul Hindemith, preferring instead the apparitions of the negative in twelve-tone asceticism. "Radical avant-gardism and neo-classicism remain equally outside Adorno's concept of the modern" (Bürger 1984–85: 122).

125. "Spengler's most direct influence on the Frankfurt School, then, was through his concept that culture (in this case, Enlightenment) moves decadently toward its own annihilation and comes to rest in its antipode: barbarism. His influence conditioned their vision of the historical possibilities. Spengler, more than Marx, created and nurtured the School's historical vision" (G. Friedman 1981: 85).

126. It is interesting to note "the strange alliance that the Frankfurt School forged between such disparate thinkers as Marx and Nietzsche. In part, the perceived commonality was the shared loathing of bourgeois life, but in greater part the appeal to them came from the desire to appropriate the strength of all who had created the crisis discovered at Auschwitz" (G. Friedman 1981: 20). An extreme example of such appropriation was the psychology of Bruno Bettelheim (1903–90), who was influenced by the model of Dachau and Buchenwald, where he was incarcerated, and believed that the Nazi environment of total control could be used for the rehabilitation of children at the Sonia Shankman Orthogenic School in Chicago, which he directed (1944–73).

127. "In a way, Heidegger's project paralleled that of the Frankfurt School. The problem of history was such that we were presented with the end of metaphysics. The fall of metaphysics meant the emptiness of the critical faculty. Neither party was certain that a critical philosophy could be resurrected. Assuredly, none could be resurrected that did not, in some way, resurrect the relationship between truth and beauty that Plato had forged, this time with beauty gaining sovereignty over truth" (G. Friedman 1981: 75).

128. The tradition that has developed out of this Puritan undertaking considers asceticism "as sub-ideological, common to all cultures. In this large sense, asceticism is the 'cultural' element in culture" (Harpham 1987: xi), it declares with Eurocentric confidence. At the same time, with statements of this kind, the tradition reveals its religious ideology and salvation politics, as when it concludes "that literary theory, especially as it concerns interpretation, is therefore a covertly but constantly ethical activity predicated on the ascetic imperative to resist temptation; and that various theories differ only in the forms of temptation they define and the strategies of resistance they prescribe" (240). Religious definitions and defenses of culture, which often assume a tone of moral edification, arrive swiftly at the predictable comparison: "Our anthropological hypothesis concerning the phenomenon of 'culture' is the following: in submitting ourselves to the esthetic (in particular, the discursive) Subject, we accept the localization of our desire within a self-contained universe of discourse, and *at the same time* experience this sacrificial acceptation of constraint as a sign of our integration into a universal ethical community. This synthesis—tentative, problematic, indeed, essentially paradoxical—is, in effect, that of the 'Greek' and the 'Jewish,' the discursive and the moral, elements of modern Western society" (Gans 1985: 11).

129. Bruno Bauer's quietism of critique comes again to mind: "'The critic,' writes Bauer, 'does not take sides. Nor does he want to take sides with any party. He is lonely—lonely in that he loses himself in the object of criticism—lonely in that he sets himself up against it. Criticism separates itself from everything'" (Hook 1962: 106). Distinction discriminates against action and history. "Criticism is the only power which can enlighten us about the self-deception of the existing order and give us the upper hand. History will take care of the crisis, and its outcome" (quoted in Hook 1962: 110). As Heidegger wrote in 1945: "We are to do nothing but wait." This apraxia is further glorified when "we inactivists, we academic men" (Rieff 1972: 27), in order "to prevent the mental disease of praxis" (13), accept alienation as the strength of the impotent: "It is our duty, as teachers, not to be public men; as public men, we cannot teach" (13).

130. "The aesthetic necessity of art supersedes the terrible necessity of reality, sublimates its pain and pleasure; the blind suffering and cruelty of nature (and of the 'nature' of man) assume meaning and end—'poetic justice.' The horror of the crucifixion is purified by the beautiful face of Jesus dominating the beautiful composition, the horror of politics by the beautiful verse of Racine, the horror of farewell forever by the *Lied von der Erde*" (Marcuse 1969: 44).

131. "Critical Theory, therefore, had a threefold task. First, it had to identify and define the texture of the catastrophe that was the ground for the Messianic crisis. Second, it had to identify the Messianic force. Faced with historical catastrophe, the Frankfurt School had to discover, through the hermeneutics of the texts of the tradition that presaged the catastrophic epoch, the name of the force that could break the epoch apart. Once this name was discovered, then they needed, third, to discover the formulas through which the power of the Messiah could be invoked" (G. Friedman 1981: 241).

132. In certain respects, the self that Benjamin built, with his leisurely attention to the returns and repetitions of tradition, was an early postmodern theoros-turned-voyeur: "Since the whole is untruth, metaphysics and theology can only survive in the most minute and inconsequential particulars (i.e., in what Hegel called lazy existence: one indifferent to or opposed to the universal)" (Siebert 1983–84: 109).

133. The mission of the critic according to Lukács provides a splendid example: "Lukács's essayist is a mystic on the path leading toward the vision of the One. . . . 'It is true that the essay strives for truth: but just as Saul went out to look for his father's she-asses and found a kingdom, so the essayist who is really capable of looking for the truth will find at the end of his road the goal he was looking for: life.' Lukács's essayists are the mystics of everyday life. This might seem a peculiar idea until one remembers that it is precisely everyday life that is the locus of *anomie* for the bourgeois" (Holzman 1985: 81).

134. This is a form of transcendental Zionism. "Apocatastasis, 'the retrieval of everything and everyone,' is the figure that most precisely characterizes Benjamin's materialist messianism. In the Jewish apocalyptic and neoplatonic-gnostic traditions, apocatastasis refers to the restoration of an original paradisal state brought about by the coming of the messiah. With this restoration, things would reassume their proper relations to each other, the displacements that characterize the 'dream condition of the world' would be undone. The goal of Benjamin's 'dialectics of cultural history' is thus the abolition of the prevailing context of expression in favor of the original context of being" (Witte 1986: 57).

135. Here is a complementary view: "In their relation to empirical reality works of art recall the theologumenon that in a state of redemption everything will be just as it is and yet wholly different. There is an unmistakable similarity in all this with the development of the profane. The profane secularizes the sacred realm to the point where the latter is the only secular thing left. The sacred realm is thus objectified, staked out as it were, because its moment of untruth awaits secularization as much as it tries to avert it through incantation" (Adorno 1984: 8).

136. According to another suggestion (Rue 1989), to overcome its present crisis the West needs a new cultural mythology, one based on the "root metaphor" of the covenant: the new modern myth should be drawn from the covenantal tradition.

137. "It is no secret that Benjamin's writings exerted considerable influence on the second phase of Critical Theory. The *Dialectic of Enlightenment* . . . develops the motif of a critique of the mythical condition of bourgeois society in the form of a historical reconstruction of the civilizing process. In this process, the 'self-destruction of enlightenment' comes to pass. Just as in myth enlightenment assumed its first and yet uncertain form, self-conscious enlightenment of modern reason veers back to mythology. . . . Myth returns or actualizes itself as instrumental reason, logic of exchange, and logocentrism" (Lindner 1986: 37–38).

138. There are many examples of cunning appropriation of myth in *Das Passagen-Werk*, like the "parallels between the figure of Odysseus in the *Dialectic of Enlightenment* and that of the 'flaneur' in Benjamin's work. The double meaning of 'the passage' in Horkheimer and Adorno's *Dialectic of Enlightenment* corresponds to the 'twilight' of the passages (arcades) in Paris noted by Benjamin. This is to be understood not only literally but also allegorically" (van Reijen 1988: 421). Another example of the flaneur, this time as anthropologist, is Claude Lévi-Strauss (1908), author of *Mythologiques* (1964–71), the largest compendium of mythology in the twentieth century. "Lévi-Strauss's own stylization of the myth analyst as a hero of a fairy tale corresponds with his application to the myths of the morphology of the fairy tale as developed by V. Propp" (Schlesier 1988: 148–49). In his work, which has been called "a surrealist enterprise" (Rodney Needham), the collector and connoisseur ventures into the underworld of mythic thinking itself in search of signs that can show a safe passage home. In general, the flaneur is a conflation of Odysseus and the Wandering Jew—the interpreter whose only possible nostos is commentary, that is, the return to the (textual) passage.

139. Here is an example of his vision: "The *Aufhebung* of commodity relations enables men and cultural products . . . to recover their autonomous character. . . . With the emergence of the product as an end in itself, it will naturally fit into the totality and the final questions of human life. With the *Aufhebung* of human isolation and of anarchic individualism, human society will form an organic whole; its parts—individual members and products—will support and magnify each other in the service of the common goal—the idea of further human development" (Lukács 1970: 29). Ironically, he believed that in philosophy from Kant to Hegel "capitalism [has] produced the idea of a new society whose task is to bring about the destruction of capitalism" (30).

140. The artist becomes, accordingly, the model of modern moral conduct: "Thus it can be said that for Lukács the most basic image of human freedom is not the hero of the novel, for he can never succeed in his quest for ultimate meaning, but rather the novelist himself, who in telling the story of failure succeeds—whose very creation stands as that momentary reconciliation of matter and spirit toward which his hero strives in vain. The creative activity of the novelist is the 'negative mysticism of godless epochs'" (Jameson 1971: 173).

141. Lukács' friend Béla Balázs writes in his diary of the period: "Gyuri's new philosophy. Messianism. The homogeneous world as the redemptive goal. Art as the Luciferean 'better made.' The vision of the world become homogeneous before the actual process of transformation. The immorality of art. Gyuri's big turn toward ethics" (quoted in Holzman 1985: 91). Furthermore, regarding the divergent and yet comparable paths of Heidegger and Adorno, the question of eschatology also

helps explain why "buried deeply beneath philosophical disputes there hovers another theological difference: the demarcation between Jewish and Christian Messianism, the latter characterized by affirmation of divine redemption and incarnation, the former by indefinite postponement of the messianic event" (Dallmayr 1989: 100).

142. Form, "the highest judge of life" (Lukács) becomes for this generation during the first decade of the century a religious issue or, as Lukács wrote in 1911, "the question of the boundary between religion and art" (Congdon 1983: 81). *Soul and Form* was the title of his collection of essays (1908–10) that appeared in Hungarian (1910), and in a revised form in German (1911). The Frankfurt School too found form "the unfolding of truth. . . . It is also a secularized version of the theological notion that God created the world in his own image" (Adorno 1984: 207).

143. It is from this viewpoint that Greeks like Odysseus are accused of being the source of evil by those who "hope for a renascence of guilt" (Rieff 1972: 71) and subscribe to "the ideology of Hebraism—namely, that whereas 'you may be a superior civilization (whatever that is), we, in our political and economic impotence, are a superior moral heritage.' There is Hellenism, which is pagan, perhaps civilized, and with an eye to beauty, but greater still is Hebraism, with its concern for justice and its superior morality. . . . It is the 'moralistic style' of the modern oppositional intelligentsia" (Cuddihy 1974: 183). The moralistic style finds narcissistic entitlement and dignity in resisting what it knows it will reproduce anyway, like the standard account of Western origins: "It is significant, surely, that when, today, an after-dinner speaker refers to the sources of our civilization, he always names Jerusalem and Athens" (Auden 1948: 2), or she observes in a scholarly study that "the history of the West has not only been that of metaphysics, of its structures and dichotomies. It has also been that of Judeo-Christianity: the strange dialogue between the Greek and the Jew—and their sons. . . . For example, if the Greek father was there to confer authority on his son, . . . the Judaic father turned his back on the son and disappeared from the Temple. . . . [I]f Oedipus was able to accomplish his primordial desire through a confrontation with the Father, Abraham was not led by desire, but closed his eyes in order to *listen* to rather than to see God the Father" (Jardine 1985: 79). In 1990 Taylor University, an Evangelical Christian institution in Indiana, organized a three-day series of lectures under the general title "Jerusalem-Athens."

144. For the first time there is even skepticism about the identification with Spinoza's project: "There is much evidence that the modern world may indeed be moving toward something postmodern; except that the Jews, on the whole, remain conservatively attached to the old modernity of Spinoza. In this conservative attachment Jewish intellectuals differ little from nonintellectuals. At least in this they are all Jews together. All are more comfortable with modernity than with anything less" (Himmelfarb 1973: 14). Already in 1955 Levinas expressed his opposition to lifting the anathema pronounced against Spinoza by the religious authorities of his community (Levinas 1990: 106–10).

145. The virtuosos of critique have been the soloists of assimilation: "Consequently, the problem of assimilation is still with us, and is so to the exact extent that we all—in Israel and among the Diaspora, Zionists and non-Zionists—acknowledge western civilization and lay claim to all that it has contributed and contributes still

to our public and intellectual life, open as it is to the world's vast compass. But our belonging to a religious or national or linguistic Judaism is not something purely and simply to be added to our Western inheritance. One or other of the two factors becomes discredited. We must ask ourselves if there is not a permanent risk of the traditional aspect of our existence sinking, despite what affection and good-will may attach to it, to the level of folklore" (Levinas 1989b: 284).

146. "The intellectually gifted Jew is in a peculiarly fortunate position in respect to this requisite immunity from the inhibitions of intellectual quietism. But he can come in for such immunity only at the cost of losing his secure place in the scheme of conventions into which he has been born, and at the cost, also, of finding no similarly secure place in that scheme of gentile conventions into which he is thrown. . . . He becomes a disturber of the intellectual peace, but only at the cost of becoming an intellectual wayfaring man, a wanderer in the intellectual no-man's-land, seeking another place to rest, farther along the road, somewhere over the horizon" (Veblen 1964: 227). Such intellectual wayfarers have been variously called "Jewish heretics" (Deutscher), "meta-rabbis" (Steiner), "prophets of alienation" (Bell), and "slayers of Moses" (Handelman).

147. This attitude harks back to the program of "positive Jewishness" proposed in the late 1940s during comparisons of the "negative" with the "positive" Jew. Warnings about "some of the parallels that have appeared between Jewish and German nationalism—especially the post-1918 variety of the latter" (Greenberg 1950: 428) were responses to the rise of militant separatism.

148. "The Christian mystery cult evolved into the most terrible rationalizing of transgressiveness ever to curse our culture. Nietzsche knew that Christendom's love was a covert form of making war on culture in any form, an expression of the most terrible hatred, envy, revenge. How sad that Nietzsche remained Christian enough to blame the proud, elitist culture of Israel for this curse, derived from Hellenism. . . . Nothings would be instant everythings by imposing a love that was entirely mendacious. Despite his residual Christian sentimentalism, Nietzsche tried to make war on this love. Judged by the results especially among our educated classes, Nietzsche failed miserably. His prophetic message is lost. But we must continue to make war on this Christening love—on all the envies, for and against, that now disguise the particular conditions of transgressive behavior in our society" (Rieff 1972: 74).

149. In Trilling's early work, it is not the satyr who opposes the Jew of culture but rather the Jew as satyr who opposes bourgeois complacency. "In his second *Menorah Journal* story, 'Chapter for a Fashionable Jewish Novel' [1926], the Prufrockian hero imagines himself, self-parodically, as a kind of Jewish Dionysus, come to shock his friends out of their middle-class respectability: 'He began to feel not like a prophet come howling from the wilderness to warn a people defiling holiness, but like a satyr leaped into a respectable home . . . lustfully Hebraic, rowling gloriously, drunkenly, madly, in Jewishness, disgusting the inhabitants by the abandon and licentiousness of his Semitic existence'" (Krupnick 1986: 26).

150. Many of his contemporaries agreed: "Jewishness, insofar as it has to be asserted in a predominantly Gentile world, should be a personal rather than mass manifestation, and more a matter of individual self-reliance" (Greenberg 1950: 431). The communal understanding of the problem was rejected: "What I want to

be able to do is accept my Jewishness more implicitly, so implicitly that I can use it to realize myself as a human being in my own right, and *as a Jew in my own right*" (432).

151. As J. Hillis Miller told a reporter: "I remember [Paul] de Man looking me in the eye . . . and saying, 'For me, the most important questions are religious questions'" (Campbell 1986: 48). According to a *Christian Science Monitor* editorial, "Stewards of the Language" (April 24, 1985), A. Bartlett Giamatti, President of Yale University, said in a talk that same month at Harvard University: "Ours is still a rhetorically based culture, a culture based on Greek ideas of *paedeia*, those cultural values whose textual study is education and whose pursuit forms the good citizen, a concept the Romans would translate under the rubric *studia humanitates*; it is a culture whose Judeo-Christian roots are manifested in sacramental texts, and acts of interpretation, texts of revealed word. Ours is a culture radically imbued with logocentricity, with the ancient, enduring, and finally numinous awe of writing and what is written." The model for this ideal is often a portrait of the intellectual within the traditional Jewish community: "The intellectual has to an unusual degree formed the religious culture and the moral civilization of the Jews at the lower as well as the higher levels: he gave them not only ideology but *mythos*, not only form but matter, not only an ordering but much of the substance of values. . . . Through the deliberate design of intellectuals, we Jews became for centuries a people of priests. It is characteristic of the traditional Jewish intellectuals, of the rabbis and teachers, that they defined the sphere of their activity as Law—posing in this way a demand for the reception by the people of their special attitudes" (Halpern 1946: 16).

152. Thus concludes "the long, dark and fairly dismal drama that modern critics are always writing about. For it is that drama and this kind of spiritual insight that finally explain the pervading tone of modern critical style. The critics have inflated their language and turned their business into melodrama in order to give importance to an otherwise inconsequential occupation. They have developed a woolly cant so as to communicate with the other participants in the mystery, and an inhumane jargon to get at the objectivity of science, while at the same time asserting their peremptory claim to a grander knowledge. Their tone, though—the portentous imitation-mysticism, the blood-and-thunder language of sin and salvation, the conviction of being among the elect—these they have made up as they follow along the glory trail, circuit riders of literature, revivalists of criticism, missionaries of a bleak and desperate back-country religion, whose tears wet the mourners' benches in a dozen critical reviews" (Douglas 1953–55).

Chapter Three

1. *Difficile liberté: Essais sur le Judaïsme* (1963), *Quatres lectures talmudiques* (1968), *Du sacré au saint: Cinq nouvelles lectures talmudiques* (1977), *L'Au-delà du verset: Lectures et discours talmudiques* (1982). Levinas's return to Talmud repeats the recovery of the sacred texts in the *Ethik des Judentums* by Moritz Lazarus (1824–1903).

2. The comparison of the two figures has also served more localized arguments: "If there is an English equivalent of the American Dream, it is essentially domestic;

its literary roots are Homeric: the wanderer is always really on his way home, and home is fairly unsurprising; despite the annoying suitors, Penelope is the same as ever. The American Dream has a more biblical flavor. Our Abraham and Sarah, impelled by some inner command or outward necessity, journey forth into an unknown country, guided by restlessness and faith" (Taylor 1988).

3. In the essay "God's Nearness" (1914), Cohen contrasts the Greek idea of "likeness between man and God" with the monotheistic idea of the nearness of God: "Drawing close to God constitutes man's moral activity and provides, at the same time, a safeguard against that mysticism which is a violation of pure monotheism. The nearness of God—but by no means a union with God—is man's highest good" (Cohen 1971: 155).

4. The notion is indebted to Luther's practice of speaking about *Deus absconditus, occultus*, and especially in his later works, *nudus* (as opposed to *revelatus*) to represent the negative way to God. This doctrine of the incomprehensibility of God dates as early as his first *Lectures on the Psalms* (1513–16). Luther "speaks of the Hidden God as 'God himself'" (Gerrish 1973: 278). According to his message, "faith's object is always the Word of God. The Hidden God is never the object of faith. But faith nonetheless takes on an urgency, perhaps even a passion, because of the Hidden God, who prevents faith from becoming complacent. Faith, in Luther's sense, was a dare, a risk, or—in one of his favorite words—a 'flight.' Under *Anfechtung* [attack], a man must dare against God to flee to God (*ad deum contra deum*). Faith is not repose, but movement. Hence, faith really does take into itself something of the meaning of God's hiddenness even though it is not directed towards that hiddenness: rather it is movement away from the Hidden God" (291).

5. "Not only is language always accompanied by faciality traits, but the face crystallizes all redundancies, it emits and receives, releases and captures signifying signs. It is a whole body unto itself: it is like the body of the center of significance to which all of the deterritorialized signs affix themselves, and it marks the limit of their deterritorialization. The voice emanates from the face. . . . The face is the Icon proper to the signifying regime, the reterritorialization internal to the system. The signifier reterritorializes on the face. The face is what gives the signifier substance; it is what fuels interpretation, and it is what changes, changes traits, when interpretation reimparts signifier to its substance. . . . The signifier is always facialized" (Deleuze and Guattari 1987: 115).

6. "The order, then, that allows us simultaneously to escape the totalitarianism of philosophy, which ignores the anxiety of 'the individual all the same,' and also the anarchy of individual desires; this life that is beyond the book, this philosophy that becomes life instead of becoming politics, is religion. It does not precede philosophy, it follows it" (Levinas 1990: 186). At the same time, his approach is a literalist one: "I do not preach for the Jewish religion. I always speak of the Bible, not the Jewish religion" (Levinas 1988: 1).

7. The existential hermeneutics of Rudolf Bultmann (1884–1976) suggests that one must allow oneself to be questioned by the text and be receptive to its claims. Derrida's study of political responsibility (1988) is also based on a "grammar of the response."

8. The seven-volume poetic *magnum opus* of Edmond Jabès, which was published during the period of Levinas's Talmudic writings, is called *The Book of Questions* (1963–73) (Motte 1990).

9. "JLT [hébaud]: You are saying then that ontology is a specific kind of language game. There is thus the Parmenides game, if it is true that he was the first to play it. JFL[yotard]: Yes, just as there is, on the opposite side, the Moses game" (Lyotard and Thébaud 1985: 54).

10. Shestov also dismisses the acknowledged pioneer of modernity: "Spinoza was Socrates's second incarnation" (Shestov 1966: 248). The other great traitor of Biblical faith, who subjected it to Hellenic criteria of knowledge, was Philo of Alexandria: "Philo's thought has even made its way into Holy Writ and has given the Fourth Gospel a tinge of its own. 'In the beginning was the Word'—that meant: first Athens was, and only later Jerusalem. And consequently everything which proceeded out of Jerusalem must be weighed in the balances of Athens" (Shestov 1932: xxiii).

11. While condemning the horror inspired by rational philosophy, Shestov does not hesitate to threaten his opponents with the Last Judgment: "And when reason and morality will call before their tribunal the prophets and the apostles and along with them Him in whose name they dare defy the Greek philosophy, do you think that Tertullian will be afraid of the judgment, as Leibniz was?" (Shestov 1966: 288).

12. Solomon Ludwig Steinheim (1789–1866), who opposed philosophy because of its rationalism, sought to make faith based on revelation an independent realm of knowledge with its own cognitive content. He identified the religion of reason with idolatry because it accepts natural laws. Revelation, on the other hand, which is based on the principle of creation by a transcendent force, effects a breach in the closed system of reason which is based on causality and allows for no freedom. Revelation dictates and demands faith, not understanding. True freedom is non-rational and open.

13. According to Levinas, "the request that is made of me by the other, by the simple fact that he speaks to me, is a request that can never be justified. The model here is the relation of God to the Jewish people, with God's initial statement to Moses: 'Let them obey me!'" (Lyotard and Thébaud 1985: 22).

14. The commercial success of his ideas has sometimes exasperated his defenders: "Like nuclear war, deconstruction can be staged, filmed in terms of the clichés of a disaster movie and using the same set and the same lighting as its predecessors: 'Skyscraper,' 'Airport,' 'Airplane,' 'The Day After,' and now 'Deconstruction' (with 'Deconstruction II' and 'Deconstruction III' shortly to follow). Definitely a low-budget operation" (Warminski 1985: 48).

15. Following in the footsteps of Heidegger's impact on theology, psychiatry, criticism, historiography, theory of language, philosophy of science, critique of technology and modernity, Derrida has affected the course disciplines like pedagogy (Atkins and Johnson 1985, Johnson 1982); law (Cardozo Law Review 1990); psychoanalysis (Smith and Kerrigan 1983, Spivak 1985); psychology (Parker and Shotter 1990); analytic philosophy (Dasenbrock 1989); Marxism (Holub 1983, Ryan 1982); theology (Altizer 1982, Raschke 1988, Taylor 1982 and 1985); Bible studies (Greenstein 1989, Hart 1990, McKnight 1985); translation studies (Graham 1985); film theory (Brunette and Wills 1990); architecture (Papadakis, Cooke, and Benjamin 1990); and feminism (Poovey 1988).

16. Levinas's own use of words like liturgy, diaconia, epiphany, and ikhnos in "The Trace of the Other" is a representative example of speaking Greek. Levinas protests that this is not peculiar: "I am Greek, it is Greek thought. The thought of

comparison, of judgment, the attributes of the subject, in short, the entire terminology of Greek logic and Greek politics appear. Consequently, it is not true that
my thought isn't Greek. On the contrary, everything that I say about justice comes
from Greek thought, and Greek politics as well. But, what I say, quite simply, is that
it is, ultimately, based on the relationship to the other, on the ethics without which
I would not have sought justice" (Levinas 1988: 174). Using Greek to speak non-
Greek philosophy is not contradictory but necessary. "I believe that Greek philosophy cannot be eliminated. Even in order to criticize the ultimate character of Greek
philosophy, one needs Greek philosophy. That is not at all a contradiction. The
Greeks have taught us how to speak. Not to speak, not the saying [le dire] but to
rediscover ourselves in the said. Greek philosophy is a special language which can
say everything to everyone because it never presupposes anything in particular.
Greek philosophy is the way that people speak in the modern university the world
over. That is speaking Greek. They all speak Greek, even if they don't know the
difference between alpha and beta. It is a certain way of presenting things. It is a
way of using a language which everyone can enter" (178).

17. Scholars have detected in the Bible the models of rhetorical "structures of
conflict" (McKnight 1985: 94) outlined by Derrida.

18. Derrida's presentation of violence as the anarchic side of metaphysics, which
domesticates it within the dominant Western discourse, is indebted to Benjamin's
praise of divine violence. But Shestov had already gone even further: following
Buber's suggestion, he had presented it as the supreme Biblical command. His book
concludes on this appropriate note: "Philosophy is not *Besinnen* [turning backward]
but struggle. And this struggle has no end and will have no end. The kingdom of
God, as it is written, is attained through violence" (Shestov 1966: 443). Another
phrasing is even more explicit: "For it is written: the kingdom of God is conquered
only by violence" (112). Derrida's positive conception of violence is already articulated unambiguously here.

19. Among recent investigations of *différance*, see Barrett 1987; Eisenstein and
Jardin 1985; Harvey 1986; Heath 1978; Irigaray 1987; Taminiaux 1985; and Vattimo
1980.

20. The question of the negative (Budick and Iser 1989) has been very important
for twentieth-century French philosophy (Descombes 1980: 23–26), especially for
Alexandre Kojève's commentary on Hegel (32–39) and the "*philosophie du non*" of
Gaston Bachelard (1884–1962). Adorno stressed its significance for aesthetics:
"Whether negativity is the barrier or the truth of art is not for art to decide. Art
works are negative *per se* because they are subject to the law of objectification; that
is, they kill what they objectify, tearing it away from its context of immediacy and
real life. They survive because they bring death" (Adorno 1984: 193).

21. Here is a similar distinction: "The same never coincides with the equal, not
even in the empty indifferent oneness of what is merely identical. The equal or
identical always moves toward the absence of difference, so that everything may be
reduced to a common denominator. The same, by contrast, is the belonging together of what differs, through a gathering by way of the difference. We can only say
'the same' if we think difference" (Heidegger 1971b: 218).

22. Major examinations of difference and otherness, before Derrida, include
Hegel's section on "Absolute Difference" in *The Science of Logic*, Heidegger's de-

construction of "The Principle of Identity" (1969) and discusssion of "dif-ference"/ "*diaphora*" (1971d: 202–10), and Deleuze (1956, 1968).

23. Some have seen Derrida's Talmudic typography as one example of this strategy: "The columns of *Glas* are cut by the arbitrary 'justification' of the margins and the edginess of pages that interrupt, like a caesura, the words. *Glas* becomes a stylish reprisal against style—that word whose *y grecque* was hellenized into it during the Renaissance. Derrida rescues style from its confusion with Greek *stulos*, column, and so recovers its link both with stiletto, a pointed weapon, and *stiglus* or *stigma* that emphasize cutting, pointing, branding" (Hartman 1985: 41).

24. The entry "Hellenism" by Arnaldo Momigliano in the *Encyclopedia Judaica* does not recognize the early or classical periods of Greek civilization, and instead defines the word as "the term used by historians to refer to the period from the death of Alexander the Great (323 B.C.E.) to the death of Cleopatra and the incorporation of Egypt in the Roman Empire in 30 B.C.E. . . . The word Hellenism is also used to indicate more generically the cultural tradition of the Greek-speaking part of the Roman Empire between Augustus and Justinian and/or the influence of Greek civilization on Rome, Carthage, India, and other regions which were never part of the empire of Alexander" (vol. 8, 290–91). This use follows the model of J. G. Droysen's *Geschichte des Hellenismus* (2 vols., 1836, 1843), which broadened the meaning originally given to the term by Scaliger: "The originality of Droysen was to take Hellenism to mean, not specifically the way of thinking of Jews under the influence of Greek language and thought, but generally the language and way of thinking of all the populations which had been conquered by Alexander and subjected to Greek influence. In other words, he used the word Hellenism to indicate the intermediary and transitional period between classical Greece and Christianity" (Momigliano 1977a: 310).

25. According to the evidence of the Babylonian Talmud, a ban against "Greek wisdom" (Momigliano 1975) was pronounced about 66 B.C. "The Hasmonean revolt in 169–165 B.C.E. has been recorded in Jewish history as the paradigmatic statement of spiritual opposition to the intrusion of foreign practices on traditional beliefs and worship. It is significant that a localized political struggle whose underlying motives were in part economic and social should be perceived in the popular and scholarly imagination as a purely ideological confrontation between Jewish and Greek values. This perception is already well established in the Book of Second Maccabees—an epitome of the lost volumes of Jason of Cyrene—where we first encounter the term *Judaism* (2:21, 8:1, 14:38) and *Hellenism* (4:13) representing opposing spiritual forces" (Satran 1987: 334). The lessons of the religious observance of Hanukkah are explained in an article called "Hellenism: Ancient and Modern," published in 1926, where parallels are discovered between the ancient story and the present: "Can the old Judaism withstand the new civilization, if it degenerates, as it sometimes threatens to do, into an easy acquiescence in things that are diametrically opposed to the Jewish spirit of purity of thought and holiness of living?" (Herzog 1974: 177). Some participants in the debate about the ostensible contradiction between Torah and Madda (or religious tradition and secular learning) propose a reconciliation based on seeing secular study as a sacred activity, and therefore part of worship (Lamm 1990).

26. Shestov (1932: 207) believed that names, by classifying things, cast them in the light of the universal, thus destroying their particularity.

27. Levinas (1977) later joined this attack with his distinction between the pagan *sacre* and the Jewish search for the *saint*. Meschonnic has followed this by attacking the metaphysics of the sacred (which he opposes to history) as a theory of power and identifying it with Christianity. He has questioned Derrida's use of the word "Hebraism" instead of Judaism, and his association of the former with Hellenism: "Now if one takes everything that is biblical and post-biblical—in brief, Jewish culture—from Greek notions and names the exile with Greek words, would this not already be nothing other than Diaspora, to have lost in advance all properly Hebraic anteriority? And in a certain way this is to betray the Jew" (Meschonnic 1988: 456).

28. In 1875, Hermann Cohen "gave a definition of Christianity's central dogma, the incarnation, which brought it into the orbit of his philosophical understanding of Judaism. The doctrine of God's descent into human existence was understood by Cohen as the symbol for the divine force of the moral law which has joined the human mind and enabled Man to act autonomously. The future vocation of Judaism was based on the fact, that the deepest content of the prophetic preaching about God could still not be expressed in this idea of humanisation" (Liebeschütz 1968: 18).

29. At the turn of the century Jews were attracted to racism by the science of race and the racial hygiene movement. There was a great debate among them "as to whether or not Jews were a race" (Mosse 1978: 124), especially before World War I. The major treatise in the field was *The Racial Problem with Special Attention to the Theoretical Foundation of the Jewish Race* (1910) by the Zionist physician Ignaz Zollschan (1877–1948), which adopted the ideas of Houston Stewart Chamberlain. Fears of misgeneration, ideals of purity of blood, projects in eugenics, and dreams of national mystique were in general very popular among both Jews and Gentiles during that time. After World War II, views of race often adopted the terminology of ethnicity: "Judaism cannot be other than ethnic because it can transcend ethical but not political resentment. Politics can enter the monotheistic narrative only as a moral punishment for the failure of ethics" (Gans 1985: 211).

30. This was limited to the Western church. Orthodoxy never developed in this direction. "Judging at least from a superficial survey of the preaching of the Churches of the East from olden times to the present, it is striking how their homiletical tradition is either one of doxology or meditative mysticism or exhortation—but it does not deal with the plagued conscience in the way in which one came to do so in the Western Churches" (Stanley 1907: 85).

31. A recent example was the linguistic turn in theological hermeneutics, the development of a theory of the Word of God which, in Bultmann's words, sees kerygma as a "language event" (Ebeling 1968).

32. The following two passages express Paul's position: "He is a Jew who is one inwardly, and real circumcision is a matter of the heart, spiritual and not literal. His praise is not from men but from God. Then what advantage has the Jew? Or what is the value of circumcision? Much in every way" (Romans 2.29–3.2). "Now I, Paul, say to you that if you receive circumcision, Christ will be of no advantage to you. . . . You are severed from Christ, you who would be justified by the law; you have fallen away from grace" (Galatians 5.2, 4).

33. Even from the Catholic side it is charged that, "if we consider the history of the second millennium of Christianity we are likely to conclude that the progressive alienation between the Christian faith and the secular, real-life experience of mankind, can be principally accounted for by the artificial maintenance of a cultural form of Christianity, namely, the hellenic, which was gradually (but with accelerating rapidity over the last century and a half), outstripped by a historical development of human consciousness characterized above all by its progressive de-Hellenization" (Dewart 1966: 120)

34. This has been a common strategic move. "Philosophy in Germany lives so thoroughly out of the Protestant spirit that Catholics practically have to become Protestant in order to do philosophy, and Catholic thought has scarcely emerged from the ivory tower of Thomism except in nonphilosophical forms" (Habermas 1983a: 70).

35. In contrast, Rosenzweig sees the Christian church as a way from the Incarnation to *Parousia*, from Christ's coming to his return.

36. Compare the last lines from Hölderlin's fragment "Colombo":

> For often, when
> The heavenly grow
> Too lonely, so that
> Alone they hold together
>
>   or Earth; for all too pure is
> Either
>
>   But then
>
>   the traces of ancient discipline,
>
> (1980: 649)

37. "Thus, I relate this concept of *trace* to what is at the center of the latest work of Emmanuel Levinas and his critique of ontology: relationship to the illeity as to the alterity of a past that never was and can never be lived in the originary or modified form of presence. Reconciled here to a Heideggerian intention—as it is not in Levinas's thought—this notion signifies, sometimes beyond Heideggerian discourse, the undermining of an ontology which, in its innermost course, has determined the meaning of being as presence and the meaning of language as the full continuity of speech. . . . This deconstruction of presence accomplishes itself through the deconstruction of consciousness, and therefore through the irreducible notion of the trace (*Spur*), as it appears in both Nietzschean and Freudian discourse" (Derrida 1976: 70).

38. "The idea of the Incarnation is ultimately the result of a fundamental difference between biblical and pagan theology, which can be reduced to the simple fact that the word 'God' left the tongue of the Jews with as much difficulty as it left the tongue of the Greeks with ease. Whether that was connected with the fact that the God of the Old Testament was the protective power allied with *one* people, withdrawn from and to be concealed from the rest of the world, while the Greek gods

were of the world and enjoyers of the world, were receivable and transportable, need not be decided here" (Blumenberg 1983: 594).

39. On the copula see also Adorno 1973: 100–104. The original context of the discussion is set in the Frankfurt sketch (1798) of Hegel's "Faith and Being" (Harris 1972: 512–15). For an interesting comparison, see the section on "Errors concerning abstract essences" in Chapter 46, "Of Darkness from Vain Philosophy, and Fabulous Traditions," in *Leviathan* (Hobbes 1962: 483–86).

40. Derrida's "traces" are similar to what Ernst Bloch in his virtuoso aggadah, *Spuren* (1930), describes as traces and signs through which Hope announces itself (Jameson 1971: 121–22).

41. Luther had the following to say on the spiritual use of the law: "The law of the letter [said he] is whatever is written in letters, said in words, conceived in thoughts, the tropological, allegorical, anagogical or whatever other mystical sense. This is the law of works, the old law, the law of Moses, the law of flesh, the law of sin, the law of wrath, the law of death, damning all things, making us all culprits, increasing concupiscence, killing by so much the more as it is spiritual because the command 'thou shalt not lust' makes many more guilty than the command 'thou shalt not kill.' All of these are carnal and literal when the letter has sway and the spirit is absent" (quoted in Bainton 1963: 19).

42. "When Man died all his attributes (the ability to create or posit) were transferred to Language. Language was given a voice: language began to speak. 'Die Sprache spricht.' Language was divinized" (Hauge 1989: 174).

43. The truth of "pure language" recalls the letter of Benjamin's "pure law." "Pure Language" was the theme of all world-wide 1990 conventions of the Watchtower Bible and Tract Society ("Jehovah's Witnesses"), which had as their topic Biblical literalism.

44. According to an Athens News Agency report, Shimon Peres, the Israeli Foreign Minister, in a speech at Ben Gurion Airport on November 30, 1987 welcoming Greek Foreign Minister George Papoulias, characterized his colleague's "visit as 'a historic event,' not only because it is the first visit of a Greek Foreign Minister to Israel, but because 'the Israelis and the Greeks are the two oldest nations in the region, and the Greeks distinguished themselves in philosophy while the Jews were known for their prophecies.'"

45. "The Greeks were an eminently visual people. They gloried in the visual arts; ... and they created tragedy and comedy, adding new dimensions to visual art. The Hebrews were not so visual and actually entertained a prohibition against the visual arts. Neither did they have tragedies or comedies. ... The Greeks visualized their gods and represented them in marble and in beautiful vase paintings. They also brought them on the stage. The Hebrews did not visualize their God and expressly forbade attempts to make of him an object—a visual object, a concrete object, any object. Their God was not to be seen. He was to be heard and listened to. He was not an It but an I—or a You" (Kaufmann 1970: 33).

46. The question of Jewish iconoclasm is dramatized by Chaim Potok in two novels (1972, 1990) dealing with a Hasidic painter caught in the dilemma of religious orthodoxy and pagan beauty.

47. "Everything, in the world, exists to end up in a book" (Mallarmé 1977: 49). The dark side of this aphorism is the beginning of his poem "Sea Breeze": "La chair

est triste, hélas! et j'ai lu tous les livres" (90). "To the Nietzschean question: 'Who is speaking?' Mallarmé replies—and constantly reverts to that reply—by saying that what is speaking is, in its solitude, in its fragile vibration, in its nothingness, the word itself—not the meaning of the word, but its enigmatic and precarious being" (Foucault 1973: 305). See also Langan 1986.

48. "Removing the bad faith is the program of . . . modern poetry since Mallarmé and the novel since Flaubert" (Fish 1980: 182), a program which has also been elaborated in the other arts. "The faith is bad because it is a faith in the innocence and transparency of language, which is in turn a faith in the innocence and transparency of the mind and in its ability to process and elucidate a meaning of which it is independent" (182).

49. The formalist pathos of word play and puzzle making in the work of Georges Perec (1936–82) is the best contemporary example of this textual faith.

50. Around 1957, Derrida registered his thesis topic under the title "The Ideality of the Literary Object." Jean Hippolyte agreed to direct it. Derrida planned for his thesis a critique of the "Husserlian project of a transcendental aesthetics" (Derrida 1976: 291). "It was then for me a matter of bending, more or less violently, the techniques of transcendental phenomenology to the needs of elaborating a new theory of literature, of that very peculiar type of ideal object that is the literary object" (Derrida 1983: 37), the masterpiece of language. This was the expression of a life-long commitment since "my most constant interest, coming even before my philosophical interest I should say, if this is possible, has been directed towards literature, towards that writing which is called literary" (37). Subsequently Derrida has worked on the transformation of asking about literature into making literature: "Then, since I've always been interested in literature—my deepest desire being to write literature, to write fictions—I've the feeling that philosophy has been a detour for me to come back to literature. Perhaps I'll never reach this point, but that was my desire even when I was very young. So, the problematics of writing, the philosophical problematics of writing, was a detour to ask the question, 'What is literature?' But even this question—'What is literature?'—was a mediation towards writing literature" (Derrida 1987a: 22).

51. The influence of Levinas on thinkers like Blanchot, Lyotard, Paul Ricoeur, and Luce Irigaray illustrates the fact that "Judaism has become adopted as the 'unofficial religion' of so much contemporary writing in France" (Parker 1986: 80). See also Weinberg 1987. This use of "le Juif imaginaire" (Alain Finkielkraut), especially popular in the post-1968 movement "from Mao to Moses," is complemented by simultaneous efforts to merge Frenchness and Jewishness (Friedlander 1990), making Enlightenment and mitnagdic rationalism (as opposed to hasidic mysticism) compatible. The overall picture is a deeply conservative one of religious preservation and renewal. "Contemporary thought in France, taking on the problematics of modernity, is . . . concerned almost wholly with somehow reintegrating the sacred into the Western symbolic system before it collapses" (Jardine 1985: 101).

52. Martin Buber argues that the Biblical and the historical cannot be disentangled because they are mutually authenticating and admit no other evidence from profane parallels: this is the self-confirming law of this document. "All we can do therefore, is to refer to the Bible . . . under the law of its conception of history, its

living of history, which is unlike everything which we are accustomed to call history" (Buber 1948a: 122).

53. A discussion of the traditional Ashkenazic practice of *Lernen* also includes interesting insights into such notions as the always already of the text, translation, "radical traditioning" (Heilman 1983: 63) and "radical contemporization" (64), prefiguration, repetition (242), restoration (*tikkun*), and many others familiar to poststructuralists from the work of Derrida. From another perspective, a dissenting critic notes that "what has been demonstrated overwhelmingly by normative Jewish scholarship of the twentieth century, is that what is supposed to be the very essence of normative Judaism—which is the notion that it is by study that you make your-self a holy people—is nowhere present in Hebrew tradition before the end of the first or the beginning of the second century of the Common Era. It is perfectly clear that the notion reached the rabbis directly or indirectly from the writings of Plato, because it is a thoroughly Platonic notion. And yet it has become more characteristic of normative Jewish tradition than any other Western tradition still available to us" (Bloom 1987: 53).

54. "It is a puzzle why anti-Semitism should have held such sway among those writers representative of high modernism, since the Jew of the period—urban, cosmopolitan, expatriated, ironic, intellectual, and supremely alienated—was in so many ways the modern aesthetic made flesh" (Berman 1989: 57).

55. In Joyce's *Ulysses*, Odysseus becomes a Wandering Jew whose departing is dwelling in the site of Dublin. Here philosophy's itinerary is cyclical and yet differential. Leopold Bloom and Stephen Dedalus have often been seen as representing Hebraism and Hellenism respectively. "Unlike a modern Greek, Poldy is in surprising continuity with a lineage of which he has little overt knowledge. How different would the book have been if Joyce had centered on a Greek living in Dublin? The aura of exile would not be there" (Bloom 1986a: 2). Bloom is also a better person than Odysseus: "Homer's Ulysses may be as complete as Poldy, but you wouldn't want to be in one boat with him (you would drown, he would survive). Poldy would comfort you in every sorrow, even as he empathizes so movingly with the pangs of women in childbirth" (3). The view of *The Authoress of the Odyssey* (1897) by Samuel Butler (1835–1902), which argued that Homer was a woman, is repeated in *The Book of J* (1990), "translated by David Rosenberg and interpreted by Harold Bloom," where it is proposed that the earliest part of the Bible was written by a princess of the line of King David. In addition to Odysseus and Robinson Crusoe, another archetype for Bloom is Spinoza, who is his "philosopher, and in *Ulysses* as a whole Spinoza plays a greater role than any other philosopher, including Aristotle and St. Thomas who appear, surprisingly, rarely and always, with one exception, in the Stephen Dedalus context" (Raleigh 1977: 585). The suggestion that "Spinoza is to Bloom as Aristotle and Aquinas are to Dedalus" (588) may repay closer examination.

56. The best compendium of cultural Hebraism is Paul Celan's Georg Büchner Prize speech, "The Meridian" (1960), whose vocabulary covers the entire repertory of aesthetic alienation: calling-into-question, strangeness, encounter, otherness, silence, path, date, homecoming, circularity, and much more. The same Hebraism is staked in statements like "all the poets are Jews" (Marina Tsvetayeva) or "every writer is a rabbi" (Cynthia Ozick), and stories like "I, a Jew" (1934) by Borges. It is

also examined regularly in academic panels like "The Jew as Artist/The Artist as Jew" (conference on "Creativity and Continuity: Jewish Culture in America," 1985), "The Jew as Writer, the Writer as Jew" (MLA Convention, 1987), "The Jew as Poet, the Poet as Jew" (MLA Convention, 1988), or "The Jew as Writer/The Writer as Jew (conference on "The Writer in the Jewish Community," 1988). In turn, this popular artistic identification creates the need for essays and books which examine writers', philosophers', and artists' attitudes on Jews, from Milton and Spinoza to Goethe, Dostoyevsky (Goldstein 1981), and Joyce (Nadel 1989), since every writer is expected to have one. This unique expectation is not unjustifiable in light of the centrality of Hebraism in culture and aesthetics, which has been strengthened further by the apparent marginalization of reading in popular culture: "Yet if there *is* something undying in the Jewish concern with text, perhaps we might see a saving elitist remnant that in some odd Messianic sense will make 'Jews' of all—Gentile or Jewish—who study intensively" (Bloom 1982: 322).

57. Some feminists (Hélène Cixous, Chalier 1982) have extended the category to include specifically woman: "'Woman as Jew, Jew as Woman.' Now let us add to these: Torah as feminism, feminism as Torah" (Ozick 1984: 10).

58. "Derrida sees the Greco-Christian Dialectic as unfailingly antisemitic, and in his guerrilla warfare with Truth as the ultimate product of any dialectic, Derrida's own texts come to resemble the Judaic Tabernacle itself" (Jardine 1985: 180). In a public debate at the Hebrew Institute of Riverdale in New York, Rabbi Meir Kahane, the founder of the Jewish Defense League and a member of the Knesset, "condemned the Israeli Government for being 'godless Hellenists' and said they had brought 'a magnificent land to despair and defeat.' 'If we walk in God's path,' he said, Israel will flourish. 'If we go in the ways of Cambridge and Harvard and the Hellenists, then surely we will be destroyed.'" (Goldman 1984). Kahane frequently denounced Western culture as "Hellenism." For the importance of the question of Hellenism on another dimension of contemporary Hebrew culture, see Levin 1985.

59. The legend of the Wandering Jew, which was popularized in modern literature by Eugène Sue's best-selling novel *Le Juif errant* (1844–45, 10 vols.), has found its aesthetic echo in "la vérité nomade" (Blanchot 1969: 183). The epic poem *Ahasverus in Rom* (1866) by Robert Hamerling provides another interesting literary example of nomadism: "In the figure of Ahasuerus, the Wandering Jew, utter denial of life and a longing for death are contrasted with the ruthless greed for life and pursuit of sensual pleasure symbolized by the person of 'Nero-Dionysus,' the prototype of the Caesar-craze in the popular tradition of the nineteenth century" (Baeumer 1976: 175). In the sciences, Sombart, drawing partially on Adolf Wahrmund's *Law of the Nomads and Contemporary Jewish Domination* (1887), discussed the "inherent 'Nomadism' or 'Saharaism'" (Sombart 1951: 328) of the Jews, who are a desert people, and distinguished between "the nomadic and the agricultural life, between Saharaism and 'Sylvanism'" (342). He suggested that two factors "make up the Jewish spirit . . . —desert and wandering, Saharaism and Nomadism" (344). He also found that "the modern city is nothing else but a great desert" (334), and called Nomadism "the progenitor of Capitalism" (343). Postmodern writers too have found the notion useful. Economists see the privileged members of the dominant regions of the world turning, in the coming "hyper-industrial" period of service economy, into nomads, as they used to be when the "Order of the Sacred" prevailed

(Attali 1990). Philosophers who oppose nomadology to history (Deleuze and Guattari 1987: 23) make another distinction: "The abstract machine exists enveloped in each stratum, whose Ecumenon or unity of composition it defines, and developed on the plane of consistency, whose destratification it performs (the Planomenon)" (73).

60. The classicist Victor Bérard, author of *La Turquie et l'Héllenisme contemporain* (1893), argued in *The Phoenicians and the Odyssey* (1902–3, 2 vols.) that, while Homer was Greek, he invented nothing and worked only with foreign material because Ulysses was a Phoenician rover. Joyce based his understanding of the *Odyssey* in Bérard's view that the epic was of Semitic origin: "The *Ulysseid* . . . appears to be a Phoenician *periplous* (log-book) transposed into Greek verse and a poetic legend according to certain very simple and typically hellenic principles: anthropomorphic personification of objects, humanization of natural forces, *hellenization* of the raw material. . . . In the Odyssey imagination and fantasy play but a small part. Arrangement and logic were the poet's part in the work. . . . The Hellene is, first and foremost, a skilled arranger. The poet invents nothing. He utilizes the facts given in the 'log.' . . . The poem is obviously the work of a Hellene, while the 'log' is clearly the record of a Semitic traveller. The poet . . . was a Greek; the seafarer . . . was Phoenician" (quoted in Gilbert 1963: 80–81). By making his Odysseus a Jew, Joyce semiticizes again the hero of the epic. During their discussion in the "Ithaca" section, Dedalus (who in the beginning of the book had been tempted by thoughts of Hellenization) explores with Bloom similarities between the Hebrew and Irish traditions.

61. As usual, Derrida has tried equivocally to distance himself from the theological underpinnings of his ideas: "So much so that the detours, locutions, and syntax in which I will often have to take recourse will resemble those of negative theology, occasionally even to the point of being indistinguishable from negative theology. . . . And yet those aspects of *différance* which are thereby delineated are not theological, not even in the order of the most negative of negative theologies, which are always concerned with disengaging a superessentiality beyond the finite categories of essence and existence, that is, of presence, and always hastening to recall that God is refused the predicate of existence, only in order to acknowledge his superior, inconceivable, and ineffable mode of being" (Derrida 1982: 6).

62. A representative example is the work of Stanislaw Lem (1921). *A Perfect Vacuum* consists of sixteen reviews of imaginary books, including one called "Odysseus of Ithaca" (where the full name of the hero is Homer Maria Odysseus) and one "A Perfect Vacuum" by Stanislaw Lem. Three more reviews of imaginary books appear in *One Human Minute*. Books are also invented in the essay "Metafantasia: The Possibilities in Science Fiction" (1985). For a parody of this parody, see Tuleja 1989. For a similar effort in the realm of literary theory, which includes parodies of book-reviewing styles, see Sharratt 1985. Finally, Lem's *Imaginary Magnitude* is a series of introductions to books that may one day be written, where the first introduction introduces the book itself. This particular game goes back to Kierkegaard's book *Prefaces* (1989), which consists of eight prefaces and was published on the same day as *The Concept of Anxiety*, under the pseudonym Nikolaus Notabene.

63. Jorge Luis Borges (1899–1986) has written on the book as Scripture and the universe as library in "On the Cult of Books" (1951); see also his "The Total Library" (1939), and "The Library of Babel" (1945).

64. "The space of language today is not defined by Rhetoric, but by the Library: by the ranging to infinity of fragmentary languages, substituting for the double chain of Rhetoric the simple, continuous, and monotonous line of language left to its own devices, a language fated to be infinite because it can no longer support itself upon the speech of infinity. But within itself, it finds the possibility of its own division, of its own repetition, the power to create a vertical system of mirrors, self images, analogies. A language which repeats no other speech, no other Promise, but postpones death indefinitely by ceaselessly opening a space where it is always the analogue of itself" (Foucault 1977: 67).

65. For instance, right after expressing doubts about the degree to which his research would conform to classical norms of a thesis, he adds: "If, from this moment on, I was indeed convinced of the necessity for a profound transformation, amounting even to a complete upheaval of university institutions, this was not, of course, in order to substitute for what existed some type of non-thesis, non-legitimacy or incompetence. In this area I believe in transitions and in negotiation—even if it may at times be brutal and speeded up—I believe in the necessity for a certain tradition, in particular for political reasons that are nothing less than traditionalist, and I believe, moreover, in the indestructibility of the ordered procedures of legitimation, of the production of titles and diplomas and of the authorization of competence" (Derrida 1983: 42). Derrida's radical conformism has received little attention.

66. An eminent example is the short-lived "Center for Philosophical Research on the Political" (December 1980–November 1984), organized in Paris by Jean-Luc Nancy and Philippe Lacoue-Labarthe, whose orientation from the beginning reflected a *"decision to replace the project of politicizing deconstruction with the project of deconstructing the political"* (Fraser 1984: 137).

67. It is hard to read Nietzsche's description of the ironic intellectual without thinking of Derrida's public performance: "The madly thoughtless shattering and dismantling of all foundations, their dissolution into a continual evolving that flows ceaselessly away, the tireless unspinning and historicizing of all there has ever been by modern man, the great cross-spider at the node of the cosmic web—all this may concern and dismay moralists, artists, the pious, even statesmen; *we* shall for once let it cheer us by looking at it in the glittering magic mirror of a *philosophical parodist* in whose head the age has come to an ironical awareness of itself, and has done so with a clarity which (to speak Goethean) 'amounts to infamy'" (Nietzsche 1983: 108).

68. The rhetoric of the following interdiction is typical: "Auschwitz is something else, always something else. It is a universe outside the universe, a creation that exists parallel to creation. Auschwitz lies on the other side of life and on the other side of death. There, one lives differently, one walks differently, one dreams differently. Auschwitz represents the negation and failure of human progress; it negates the human design and casts doubts on its validity. Then, it defeated culture; later, it defeated art, because just as no one could imagine Auschwitz before Auschwitz, no one can now retell Auschwitz after Auschwitz. The truth of Auschwitz remains hidden in its ashes" (Wiesel 1989).

69. Derrida has referred to the "Puritan integrity" of certain deconstructionists. Among the convictions that Hartman, J. Hillis Miller, and Bloom shared during the 1960s was the following: "For all three, the imaginative consciousness underlying

the words of literature was connected with the sacred—with those impulses and experiences that, before the second Fall, had given rise to religion and theology" (Martin 1983: xxi). This explains their intense dedication to interpretation: "The sacred has so inscribed itself in language that while it must be interpreted, it cannot be removed. One might speculate that what we call the sacred is simply that which must be interpreted or reinterpreted, 'A Presence which is not to be put by'" (Hartman 1980: 248). Bloom in his first book (1959) examined the "mythopoeic aspects" of Shelley's poetry from the viewpoint of Buber's I-Thou relation. "In books like *The Disappearance of God* (1963) and *Poets of Reality* (1965), Miller had not merely delineated the place for these masterworks in what he as a post-structuralist would come to call the logocentric tradition, but with an uncanny sense of the interpenetrability of sacred and secular canon, he identified the mystery of the Incarnate logos as his means of sanctioning their placement" (Pease 1983: 68). His Christomathic interest has always been prominent: "Throughout his earlier work, Miller draws relationships between the role of Christ as mediator and the mediatorial functions of the artwork" (89). The "Puritan, iconoclastic, Jahvist tendency" (Hauge 1989: 168) in Paul de Man's American writings has also been increasingly noticed.

70. To mention an eminent case, Rosenzweig elaborated a dialogic Biblical theology in contrast to Greek pagan consciousness. In a letter to Buber in 1922, Rosenzweig says that for both his *The Star of Revelation* and Buber's *I and Thou* (which Buber was planning as a lecture series on "The Primary Forms of Religious Life"), the crucial problem was the relationship between paganism and religion. Regarding Buber's plan, he writes: "You want nevertheless, if I understand you correctly, to use two pedal points throughout your lectures: magic, which is the 'paganism of all nations,' and prayer, which is 'Judaism in all religion,' one as the decrescendo and the other as crescendo" (quoted in Horwitz 1978: 253).

71. "Hence, this new definition of truth: truth is what passes history by and which history does not notice" (Shestov 1966: 432).

72. Popular versions of this view exhibit no less confidence. They still compare "these two races, master-builders of the gigantic temple of civilization" (Herzog 1974: 211), though on a more simplistic level: "It is universally admitted that the most valuable elements in the cultural wealth of modern humanity are ultimately traceable to the legacies it has received from Israel and Hellas" (211). "Civilization exhibits two forces—religion and science—contending for mastery over the human mind. Science is ultimately traceable to the contribution made by the Hellenic race. Israel, on the other hand, has brought into the world the light of religion in its highest and purest form" (222).

73. "[T]he State, in accordance with its pure essence, is possible only if penetrated by the divine word; the prince is educated in this knowledge; this knowledge is taken up by each person on his own account; tradition is renewal. What is important above all is the idea that not only is the essence of the State not in contradiction with the absolute order, but that it has been called up by that order" (Levinas 1989: 271). Levinas opposes this to "the pagan State, jealous of its sovereignty, the State in pursuit of hegemony, the conquering, imperialist, totalitarian, oppressive State, attached to a realist egoism. As such it separates humanity from its deliverance. Unable to exist without adoring itself, it is pure idolatry" (274). This view is consonant with his distinction between the messianic community and Caesar's state.

74. Independence from the judgment of history, the most ancient claim of Judaism, is "its claim to a separate existence in the political history of the world. It is the claim to judge history—that is to say, to remain free with regard to events, whatever the internal logic binding them. It is the claim to be an eternal people. . . . The thing that attacks this claim to be an eternal people is the exaltation of the judgment of history, as the ultimate jurisdiction of every being, and the affirmation that history is the measure of all things" (Levinas 1990: 199). More than Christianity, atheism, science, or philosophy, it is the challenge of history to the superiority of Judaic judgment that is the greatest threat.

75. A particularly interesting area of Derrida's disagreement with Levinas is the meaning of terms they both appropriate from Heidegger, like dwelling and departing, apartness and nearness, homelessness and rootlessness, sameness and dif-ference, trace, call, and response. Derrida appears the greater supporter. "One might say, then, that Derrida *underwrites* Heidegger, in the various and contradictory senses of that word" (Riddel 1979: 245). In this regard he "floats the possibility, perhaps even necessity of reading Heidegger not from some exterior position but from another place in his interior" (Wood 1987:111).

76. Cohen contrasts eschatology and messianism, as does Derrida, in parallel with tragic to religious moral heroism. He finds that "Platonic courage has only an ending, similar to that of tragedy, in which the hero must go to ruin in order to be victorious in the consciousness of the spectator. In Judaism, on the other hand, the hero does not live only for the sake of his own heroism, but, insofar as he is a man, he is in correlation with God. He is therefore able to live and to defend his life only as God's confederate, as God's servant, and hence as God's hero" (Cohen 1972: 438). To the extent that both Greek and Jewish moral courage reject the sensuality of this life in the name of heroic reason, they are similar and equivalent; but the superiority of the latter inheres in its covenant with God and consequent self-transcendence. Rosenzweig (in *The Star*) and Benjamin (in the 1921 essay "Fate and Character") took the comparison in interesting directions. Buber (1968), on the other hand, distinguishes between the prophetic and the apocalyptic.

77. In *Otherwise than Being*, in response to Derrida's critique of the exteriority of the Other, the notion of exteriority crucial for *Totality and Infinity* "is abandoned as a way of explaining how the Other relates to the self and is replaced by the metaphor of 'proximity' or the idea of, 'the Other *within* the Same'" (Blum 1985: 294). Proximity refers to the fact that one is the Other's hostage, to election by accusation, to "the *ethical* or *religious* election of the self by the Other" (305). Levinas (1976) is a more direct response to Derrida, who later (1980) continued the discussion.

78. Prefacing *Totality and Infinity*, Levinas calls Rosenzweig's *The Star of Redemption* "a book too often present in this book to be cited" (Levinas 1969: 28).

79. Typical narratives of this kind are the apocryphal story about Rosenzweig's epiphany in a Berlin synagogue during a Yom Kippur service in 1913, which changed his mind about converting to Protestantism, and Simone Weil's mystical experience of union with Christ in 1938. Similar experiences are not uncommon in the history of aesthetics. Heidegger, for example, considered the true artwork "the epiphany of the world it illuminates and protects."

80. "In his essay on Boehme in 1901 Buber writes that Boehme's dialectic of the reciprocal conditioning of things finds its completion in Ludwig Feuer-

bach's sentence: 'Man with man—the unity of I and Thou—is God'" (Friedman 1960: 51).

81. "Reading Habermas is extraordinarily like reading Luther. . . . Above all, both put their trust in 'the redeeming power of reflection' (Habermas's phrase), and hence in our ability to save ourselves through the healing properties of the Word. . . . But it is disconcerting to see how far his assumptions and vocabulary merely recast a traditional story of deliverance in secular modern dress. We are surely entitled to something more rigorous from our social philosophers than a continuation of Protestantism by other means" (Skinner 1982: 38).

82. Gadamer (1979: 321–25), in his discussion of the "hermeneutical experience,' describes the understanding of a text and the assimilation of the relevant tradition in terms of an I-Thou relation.

83. Buber defines Biblical or Hebrew Humanism, first advocated by Hamann and Herder, as follows: "By this I mean that, just as the West has for centuries drawn educative vigor from the language and the writings of antiquity, so does the pivotal place in our system of education belong to the language and the writings of classical Israel" (Buber 1968a: 211). In his paper "For a Jewish Humanism" Levinas suggests: "Monotheism is a humanism" (Levinas 1990: 275).

84. Levinas (1968a: 165) compares the Jewish and Greek notions of the foundation of justice as reflected in Tractate *Sanhedrin* and Aeschylus' *Eumenides*.

85. A commentator on the abduction of Adolf Eichmann by Israeli agents in 1960 and the subsequent trial in Jerusalem exclaims: "'Wo kein Klager, ist kein Richter'—without an accuser there is no judge, it is said in German. Now, Israel alone wants to accuse—can and must accuse. And judge also? Of course!" (Fackenheim 1973: 224)

86. Hölderlin writes in 1799: "Kant is the Moses of our nation who leads it out of the Egyptian apathy into the free, solitary desert of his speculation and who brings the rigorous law from the sacred mountain" (Hölderlin 1988: 137).

87. Derrida was to teach a course on the "Political Theology of Language" at the Ninth International Summer Institute for Semiotic and Structural Studies, held in June 1987 at the University of Toronto. In the brochure advertising the Institute, the course was described as follows: "What is a sacred language? Is a language sacred *in itself*, or through its association with sacred things or significations: What are the political dimensions of the opposition sacred/profane, sacred/secular with respect to language? The birth of a nation, its mythology, its history, its representations and fantasies constitute a privileged domain in which these questions can be tested. Through close examination of the values of alliance, promise, contract, mission, universal responsibility, messianism, eschatology, and utopia, the discourse on 'the Chosen People' in general, and primarily on the Jewish nation, will be analyzed. . . . The authors studied will include Gershom Scholem and Franz Rosenzweig, but also Walter Benjamin, Hannah Arendt, Martin Buber and Theodor Adorno."

88. Levinas's entire work since his Hebraic "turn" in the early 1950s ought to be read as a large-scale, systematic critique of Weil—political activist, anti-authoritarian philosopher, theoretician of democracy and power, theologian of suffering, and Catholic saint—and especially her denial of Jewishness. Since 1952, even before major works like her *La Source grecque* (1953) and *Oppression et liberté* (1955)

appeared, Levinas is engaged with her philosophy. "To Love the Torah more than God" (1955) proposes a "Jewish science" to counter the work of Weil "who, as everyone in Paris knows, is the last word in religious terminology" (Levinas 1979: 217). In this essay, the author exclaims: "Simone Weil, you have never understood anything of the Torah" (219).

89. Levinas's own ideas often contribute to this tyranny: "This end of philosophy is not only an event that touches a host of intellectuals and their scholarly quarrels. It is perhaps the very meaning of our age. . . . [T]he end of philosophy is the beginning of an age in which everything is philosophy, because philosophy is not revealed through philosophers" (Levinas 1990: 185).

90. "On the one hand and on the other hand. This is a pattern one finds in and among the writings of Derrida. It is a pattern one used to find in leading articles of *The Times* of London. In *The Times* the outcome was either a neutral, middle of the road compromise or a dissolution of an apparent conflict through the exposure of an equivocation in the terms in which the views of the parties to the dispute were expressed" (Llewelyn 1988: 273). The most notorious example of this strategy is Derrida 1988c. "Nonetheless, Derrida apparently wants to have it both ways: to undermine all logocentric concepts and yet to continue to use them for his own purposes. The tactic of using them 'under erasure' strikes me as less like being 'suspended over an abyss' than like trying to be on both sides of a fence" (McCarthy 1989–90: 154). In a typical gesture, when "the question of political strategy" regarding the field of women's studies is posed to him, Derrida answers: "This may not answer the question, but one way of dealing with these problems, not necessarily within women's studies, but on the whole, is to try to do both things at the same time, to occupy two places, both places. That is why deconstruction is often accused of being conservative and . . . not conservative. And both are true! We have to negotiate" (Derrida 1987: 202).

91. Compare Heidegger's linguistic aesthetics: "Mortal speech is a calling that names, a bidding which, out of the simple onefold of the difference, bids thing and world to come" (Heidegger 1971d: 208).

92. The Zionist perception of Israel defines its total independence (political, historical, geographical, cultural, ethnic) in terms of the absolute artwork. For the late romantic Cohen, who still believed in the power of civic culture, an Israeli state was unthinkable since state and culture could still support each other beneficially in Germany. For the modernist Buber, on the other hand, only an independent state—with its sovereignty modeled on the self-justifying authority of art, its right to exist, not to mean but to be—could be an absolute expression of Judaism.

93. "Where it has traded its homeland in the text for one of the Golan Heights or in Gaza—'eyeless' was the clairvoyant epithet of that great Hebraist, Milton—Judaism has become homeless to itself" (Steiner 1985: 22).

94. With its millennialist appropriation of Jewish destiny (Feldman 1990), "evangelical Protestantism has profoundly colored American civic culture. It underlies the notion of American exceptionalism: the idea that America is a redeemer nation, a people charged with a divine mission in the world. Beyond that, it has been the engine for most social-reform movements of the left and on the right, and it has sustained the idealistic, even visionary, quality in American life. Abolitionism, civil rights, women's rights, pacifism and internationalism have historically grown out of

left-wing evangelical movements with their optimistic millenarianism. Social con-servativism, nativism and jingoistic nationalism have grown out of conservative evangelical movements and pessimistic millenarianism. Both millennial traditions look forward to an end to human history, an end to politics and government" (Fitz-Gerald 1987: 38–39).

95. Compare this with the end of Barthes' book on the erethisms of the text, where he talks about the capacity of cinema "to succeed in shifting the signified a great distance and in throwing, so to speak, the anonymous body of the actor into my ear: it granulates, it crackles, it caresses, it grates, it cuts, it comes: that is bliss" (Barthes 1975: 67).

96. Contemporary messianic criticism is based on "the theology of the aesthetic critic's redemptive mission, whereby the Baptist-critic-jester, crying 'in the wilder-ness,' undertakes to 'save the text' from the Babylonian 'Fate of Reading'" (Argyros and Flieger 1987: 57) in the name of a privileged tradition.

97. "The text Hartman would save is finally part of the archive of traditional literary history and critical practice" (Rowe 1985–86: 55). "In Hartman's view, then, the aesthetic critic turns out to be a *privileged* reader, a shaman-priest-analyst-guide who navigates the dangerous eddies of theoretical currents without being pulled in. . . . The critic-cum-analyst, then, is a mediator as well, who liberates and teaches the reader whom he initiates to the textual mysteries. His function is not only analytic, or even therapeutic, but is actually messianic, even sacrificial, in character" (Argyros and Flieger 1987: 55).

98. Among the innumerable responses, the answer to the (phone)call by Ronell (1990) has been in all respects the most extravagant.

99. In the Buber-Rosenzweig translation of the Bible the name of God does not appear—God is spoken of as He. The two philosophers held quite different views about the importance of the name (Friedman 1981: 218–19).

100. For a similar effort to translate the New Testament, which assumes that the Greek text is a translation of lost Hebrew and Aramaic documents, see Schonfield (1985).

101. "One might suggest that Derrida, in proclaiming the abyss within man's personal self-identity, has merely rediscovered sin" (Young 1985: 115).

102. Bernal's *Black Athena* has been followed by Gerard Lucotte's *Introduction à l'anthropologie moléculaire: Eve était noire* (1990). They both recuperate, in very different ways, the old tradition of exploring the Jewish origin of Greek thought—for example, the Mosaic and prophetic influence on Plato: "The spirituality of the God-idea as evolved by Greek metaphysics had nothing new to offer to Israel's teachers. At a time when the Hellenic race had scarcely emerged from the savage state, the Sinaitic revelation virtually declared that no material representation could, in the remotest degree, serve as symbolical of the Supreme Being. . . . Nor had the sages of Israel much to learn from Greek ethics. All that was really sound in the teachings of the Grecian masters, which, by the way, unlike the ethics of Juda-ism, failed to influence the lives of the masses, they could find equalled, nay, sur-passed, in the inspired Word, and in native Jewish doctrines evolved from Scrip-tural principles and from the ethical concept of the God-idea taught by the Torah, the Psalmists, and the Wisdom Literature of ancient Israel" (Herzog 1974: 104).

103. Levinas is building on a common comparison which finds that faith is not

pistis but the audacity to reject absolute laws, accept nothing as impossible, and seek absolute freedom—groundlessness. This groundlessness, this absurdity, is faith—the only freedom possible. By nature, man has no freedom of choice, since he is a fallen man (Shestov 1932: 199–201). The only freedom he can choose is the freedom of "unfounded" faith which leaves him groundless—without a basis in reason. This view demands the audacity to transcend the lack of freedom by surrendering the illusion of free will. In a related discussion in *Two Types of Faith* (1950), Buber shows the similarities between Judaism and Christianity by distinguishing between a Hebraic and a Hellenic Christianity, the former based on the Jewish *emunah* and the latter on the Greek *pistis*. Hebraic faith is based on trust (in the word of God) while Hellenic on belief in the truth of propositions (concerning incarnation). Thus Hellenic Christianity is Paul's message of salvation, of Jesus as Messiah. It is the fact that Paul made the Law secondary to faith, external to action, that made *pistis* necessary. In a bold move, Buber opposes Jesus and Paul, appropriating the former for Biblical Judaism.

104. In different situations of passivity Blanchot discovers "common traits: anonymity, loss of self; loss of all sovereignty but also of all subordination; utter uprootedness, exile, the impossibility of presence, dispersion (separation)" (Blanchot 1986: 18). See also Deleuze on "passive synthesis" in *Différence et répétition* (1968).

105. At the same time, the slave of the lord turns into his independent servant: "Just as Mastery showed that its essential reality is the reverse or perversion of what it wants to be, so much the more will Slavery, in its fulfillment, probably become the opposite of what it is immediately; as repressed Consciousness it will go within itself and reverse and transform itself into true autonomy" (Kojève 1969: 20).

106. Other contemporary thinkers, like Weber, express a special interest in comparisons between East and West: "In Weber's later work the question of the evolution of modern capitalism and its distinctive morale becomes subordinate to an analysis of the enormous historical differences between the Orient and the Occident" (Fischoff 1944: 59).

107. Jakob Wassermann, in an essay of 1919, tried to account for the eminent role of Jews in literature. "The 'Jew as European, as cosmopolitan, is a man of letters; the Jew as Oriental, not in the ethnographic, but in the mythic sense, with the transforming strength for the present day which he is bound to possess, can be a creator.' Challenged by Martin Buber in the early 1920s to clarify this dichotomy, Wassermann stood by it, called the 'European' Jew sterile, formalistic, and solitary, and the 'Oriental' Jew sure of himself, of his world and his humanity. . . . 'He is free, and the others are servants. He is truthful, and the others lie.' Vague and rhetorical as these assertions are, Wassermann further reduces what little specificity they have by insisting that 'Oriental' is 'naturally' only a 'symbolic figure: I could just as soon call him the fulfilled or the legitimate heir.' To call the Jew an Oriental, which is so often intended as an insult, here becomes a source of pride and self-confidence" (Gay 1975: 50).

108. Buber's view has been criticized for confusing the reality of revelation with the relation of meeting: "God is Thou, not because Israel has met Him as Thou, not because Israel has, at a past moment of its history, addressed God with wholeness of intent, but rather because God has revealed Himself. Revelation is deeply autonomous. It is neither the labor nor the fruit of the divine-human relation. The issue

of relation comes after and without any necessary connection to the reality of revelation" (Cohen 1952: 251). Thus the two must be sharply distinguished so that God's commandment to history in regard to Israel will become apparent: "Revelation is the act of God whereby He has disclosed the way and destiny of Israel. Meeting is the act whereby that destiny, that way, and its divine source are drawn into the inner life" (253). Other commentators have suggested that the wisdom of halakhah transcends Western civilization and its secularism-religion opposition, pointing the way out of the crisis of modernity (Eidelberg 1989).

109. The aesthetic dimension of the ideal of community is highlighted by the observation that the work of art "seems to be made specifically in order to provoke communication. It is not a question of a sum of isolated pleasures to be attained but of a socially-arrived-at judgment which has no other meaning beyond itself. In art, one could almost say, communication becomes its own purpose, to use a problematic concept" (Luhmann 1985: 7). Compare Buber's community (*Gemeinschaft*) with Kant's community of aesthetic judgment, Landauer's counter-community (*Gegengemeinschaft*), Berdyaev's (Orthodox) communal society, Schmitt's (Catholic) national community, Fish's interpretive community, Derrida's community of the question, Lyotard's "community of ethical phrases" (Lyotard 1988: 125) or Eco's community as intersubjective guarantee of truth.

110. "What is proper to Judaism is to say: Well, God himself we know nothing about; there is nothing to say about it. We call that God, but ultimately we do not know what we are saying when we say God. We know nothing about it. We merely say: There is a law. And when we say 'law,' it does not mean that the law is defined and that it suffices to abide by it. There is a law, but we do not know what this law says. There is a kind of a law of laws, there is a metalaw that says: 'Be just.' That is all that matters to Judaism: 'Be just.' But we do not know what it is to be just. That is, we have to be 'just'" (Lyotard and Thébaud 1985: 9).

111. The structural study of myth applied to the story of Moses discovers a major "transformation of Land into Law, with the compensation of the vision of the promised land recorded in it" (Marshall 1980: 786). Research shows that "the myth of Moses was being transformed into a sacred text at the same time it was being reshaped to model the Israelites' problem of how, in the face of all-too-familiar evidence to the contrary, they might continue as a distinctive people without full control of an adequately sized piece of territory.... The solution offered was a double one: the identity of Land with Law, and the distinction between the individual and collectivity" (787).

112. For others, it is the fear of style and revolution canceling each other:

> The Tupamaros/An immutable truth (all right)
> I got a razor blade/An' a beautiful youth (and I like it)
> A Moto Guzzi/An' a Gaultier pants (all right)
> I got a reason girl/Was Immanuel Kant's (and I like it).
> (Scritti Politti: "Boom! There she was," from
> *Provision*, 1988, on the Jouissance label)

113. Sharing the same vague view, most critics agree: "Some indicators speak in favor of the fact that, in reaction to the mass loss of the religious certainty of salva-

tion, a new Hellenism is taking shape, that is, a regression below the level of identity reached in communication with the one God in the monotheistic high religions" (Habermas 1983: 18). Other writers worry: "I am well aware that any praise of Derrida is bound to seem folly to the Greeks. But we are almost certainly more Greek than we ought to be" (Megill 1985: 313).

114. It has been argued that there are similarities between Hasidism and postmodern society: "In Hasidic fashion, Buber adequately portrays this view of the polity when he writes that a community is 'the being no longer side by side but *with* another or a multitude of persons.' Recognizing and integrating otherness is the hallmark of the community in the postmodern world" (Murphy 1989: 141).

115. Levinas had again prepared the ground: "Oral law is eternally contemporary with the written" (Levinas 1990: 138). Compare the position of Abraham Isaac Kook (1861–1935), Chief Rabbi of Palestine, on the same relation: "The world will have its remedy to the degree that these two spiritual forces unite and mutually influence each other. The oral tradition is from heaven but is manifested on earth, and it is necessary that the land of Israel be built and the orders of priesthood, prophecy, judges, and rulers be restored; then the Oral Law will shine forth resplendent and be united to the Written Law. In the Diaspora the two had been severed and the Written Law raised to the level of holiness while the Oral Law was relegated to an inferior station. The distinction between prophecy (the Written Law) and the halakah (the Oral Law) is only a historical distinction and does not refer to their respective contents. The religious conception bridges the gap between them by placing them both on the same plane" (Rotenstreich 1968: 225).

116. "After the attack on aesthetic autonomy by structuralism, Marxism, and various political forces, deconstruction represented an effort to roll back the spread of secularization into the world of art. Hence the religious, often nearly clerical atmosphere in deconstructive seminars: the aura has returned, the master speaks, the acolytes murmur. Hence also the preference for romantic texts and metaphors of violence: now the critic is the poet-priest. The point is not comprehension but belief, *credo quia absurdum*, for the alternative would be banal logocentric rationality. Literature, beyond ratiocinative explanation (denounced as reductionist), becomes mystery, sacrament, catachresis, and studied obscurity becomes a virtue. The more religiously deconstructive critics behave, the more they effectively recover the theological origins of the thinker from whom they inherit the most: Heidegger" (Berman 1990: 9).

117. Derrida borrows the notion of grace from Levinas's 1982 discussion of Buber's ethics of the relation. Grace is an important notion in Buber's *I and Thou*: "That a meeting can never be brought about through my deed but requires a cooperation from the other side presents itself out of the inner perspective of the meeting, in such a way that when it happens, it happens 'out of will and grace in one'" (Theunissen 1984: 280). Grace is also important in Simone Weil's *La Pesanteur et la Grâce* (1950). Compare Alexander Pope's passage on originality in *An Essay on Criticism* (1711):

> Great wits sometimes may gloriously offend,
> And rise to faults true critics dare not mend;
> From vulgar bounds with brave disorder part,

And snatch a grace beyond the reach of art,
Which, without passing through the judgment, gains
The heart, and all its ends at once attains

(I, 152–57)

118. In Peter Handke's novel *Absence* (1987), three individuals are seeking an enigmatic book which promises revelation and has been left behind by an old man, the writer, who disappeared in the desert.

119. Thinking about the function of culture in the fragmented world of diverse opinions and virtues, Hölderlin wrote to his brother: "I said that poetry unites man not like the play; it unites people if it is authentic and works authentically with all the manifold suffering, fortune, striving, hoping, and fearing, with all their opinions and mistakes, all their virtues and ideas, with everything major and minor that exists among them, unites them into a living, a thousand times divided, inward whole, for precisely this shall be poetry itself; and like the cause, so the effect. Is it not true, my dear, the Germans could well use such a *panacea*, even after the politico-philosophical cure; for, regardless of everything else, the philosophico-political education already contains in itself the inconvenience that it knits together the people in the essential, inevitably necessary relations, in duty and law; yet how much is left, then, for human harmony?" (Hölderlin 1988: 139–40). The deconstructionist aesthetic is such a panacea for the inconvenience of law.

120. This kind of religious practice fits Daniel Bell's description: "*Redemptive religion*: Retreating from the (post) modernity, rooted in the intellectual and professional classes; and the growth of intellectual and professional classes; and the growth of 'mediating institutions' of care (family, church, neighbourhood, voluntary associations), opposed to the state" (paraphrased in O'Neill 1988: 497). Benjamin was the first spokesman of this position. The painter Anselm Kiefer (b. 1945) and the composer Arvo Pärt (b. 1935) are among its best-known contemporary representatives.

121. Humanist academic literalism also continues strong: "Jewish studies exemplifies the sorts of commitments that I have outlined, at a time in the history of the American university when these commitments face serious challenge. This is so, first of all, in the commitment to text as such. Textual study, whether the texts be 'classic' or modern, involves a care for the word, a demand for depth rather than breadth, a command to go slowly where others have gone before. This is a far more traditional exercise than others in the academy, suited to—and formative of—a different sort of temper. It breathes the air of bygone ages" (Eisen 1989: 29).

122. Heidegger's oracular style, parodied by Günter Grass in *Dog Years* (1963), has been compared with Derrida's Pharisaic one. In addition, the modernist populism of Heidegger's demotic use of concepts deserves comparison with Derrida's postmodern appeal to pop culture, which includes the following: the consummate "Jacques Derrida" (1982) single (later included in the album *Songs to Remember* of the same year) by Scritti Politti, in a cover that alludes to the Napoleon brandy label; deconstructed garments by French designer Jean-Paul Gaultier for various tours, from Grace Jones' "One-Man Show" (1981) to Madonna's "Blond Ambition" (1990); the Italian record label De-Construction, established in 1987, which specializes in house disco music; the work of "deconstructionist" disc jockey Christian

Marclay; the "postmodernist-deconstructionist" (Mick Jagger) stage set by British architect Mark Fisher for the Rolling Stones' "Steel Wheels" 1989 tour; and the Italian band The Difference, which emerged in 1989. In addition, Derrida's appearances on records include his reading of *"Feu la cendre"* on cassette (Antoinette Fouque, 1987) and a question-and-answer session included in the album *Minutes* (Les Temps Modernes, 1987), a compilation of archival material of voices from Jean Cocteau to rock singer Richard Jobson. Derrida has also starred in the film *Ghost Dance* (1983) by Ken McMullen.

BIBLIOGRAPHY

Aaron, Daniel. 1965. "Some Reflections on Communism and the Jewish Writer."
Salmagundi 1, 23–36.

Abel, Elizabeth, Marianne Hirsch, and Elizabeth Langland, eds. 1983. *The Voyage
In: Fictions of Female Development.* Hanover, NH: University Press of New
England.

Abrams, M. H. 1971. *Natural Supernaturalism: Tradition and Revolution in Romantic Literature.* New York: W. W. Norton and Company.

———. 1981. "Kant and the Theology of Art." *Notre Dame English Journal* 13: 3,
75–106.

———. 1989. "Art-as-Such: The Sociology of Modern Aesthetics" [1985]. In *Doing
Things with Texts: Essays in Criticism and Critical Theory.* New York: W. W.
Norton and Company.

———. 1989a. "From Addison to Kant: Modern Aesthetics and the Exemplary Art"
[1985]. In *Doing Things with Texts. See* Abrams 1989.

Adamson, Walter L. 1980. *Hegemony and Revolution: A Study of Antonio Gramsci's
Political and Cultural Theory.* Berkeley: University of California Press.

Addy, John. 1989. *Sin and Society in the 17th Century.* London: Routledge.

Adorno, Theodor W. 1941. "Veblen's Attack on Culture." *Studies in Philosophy and
Social Sciences* 9: 3, 389–413.

———. 1945. "Theses upon Art and Religion Today." *The Kenyon Review* 7: 1,
677–82.

———. 1973. *Philosophy of Modern Music* [1948]. Trans. Anne G. Mitchell and
Wesley V. Bloomster. New York: Seabury Press.

———. 1973a. *The Jargon of Authenticity* [1964]. Trans. Knut Tarnowski and
Frederic Will. Evanston, IL: Northwestern University Press.

———. 1973b. *Negative Dialectics* [1966]. Trans. E. B. Ashton. New York: Continuum.

———. 1974. *Minima Moralia: Reflections from a Damaged Life* [1951]. Trans.
E. F. N. Jephcott. London: NLB.

———. 1976. *Introduction to the Sociology of Music* [1962]. Trans. E. B. Ashton.
New York: Seabury Press.

———. 1978. "On the Fetish-Character in Music and the Regression of Listening"
[1938]. In Andrew Arato and Eike Gebhardt, eds.: *The Essential Frankfurt School
Reader.* Oxford: Basil Blackwell.

———. 1983. *Against Epistemology—A Metacritique: Studies in Husserl and the
Phenomenological Antinomies* [1956]. Trans. Willis Domingo. Cambridge, MA:
MIT Press.

———. 1984. *Aesthetic Theory* [1970]. Eds. Gretel Adorno and Rolf Tiedemann.
Trans. C. Lenhardt. London: Routledge & Kegan Paul.

Alden, Patricia. 1986. *Social Mobility in the English Bildungsroman: Gissing, Hardy,
Bennett, and Lawrence.* Ann Arbor: UMI Research Press.

Allen, J. W. 1961. A *History of Political Thought in the Sixteenth Century* [1928]. London: Methuen.

Allison, Henry E. 1966. *Lessing and the Enlightenment. His Philosophy of Religion and its Relation to Eighteenth-Century Thought.* Ann Arbor: University of Michigan Press.

Alter, Robert. 1981. *The Art of Biblical Narrative.* New York: Basic Books.

―――. 1985. *The Art of Biblical Poetry.* New York: Basic Books.

Alter, Robert, and Frank Kermode, eds. 1987. *The Literary Guide to the Bible.* Cambridge, MA: Harvard University Press.

Altizer, Thomas J. J. *et al.* 1982. *Deconstruction and Theology.* New York: Crossroad.

Altmann, Alexander. 1956. "Theology in Twentieth-Century German Jewry." *Leo Baeck Institute Year Book* 1, 193–216.

―――. 1985. "Moses Mendelssohn as the Archetypal German Jew." In Reinharz and Schatzberg 1985.

American Journal of Semiotics. 1983. "The Semiotics of Roman Jakobson" (special issue), 2:3.

Améry, Jean. 1980. "On the Necessity and Impossibility of Being a Jew" [1976]. *New German Critique* 20, 15–29.

Anderson, Perry. 1987. "The Myth of Hellenism." *Manchester Guardian Weekly,* 3 May.

Antonio, Robert J., and Ronald M. Glassman, eds. 1987. *A Weber-Marx Dialogue.* Lawrence: University Press of Kansas.

Apostolidès, Jean-Marie. 1982. "The Problem of History in Seventeenth-Century France." *Diacritics* 12: 4, 58–68.

Applegate, Celia. 1990. *A Nation of Provincials: The German Idea of Heimat.* Berkeley: University of California Press.

Arac, Jonathan, Wlad Godzich, and Wallace Martin. 1983. *The Yale Critics: Deconstruction in America.* Minneapolis: University of Minnesota Press.

Arendt, Hannah. 1968. "The Concept of History: Ancient and Modern." In *Between Past and Future: Eight Exercises in Political Thought.* New York: The Viking Press.

Arethusa. 1989. "The Challenge of *Black Athena*" (special issue).

Argyros, Alexander, and Jerry Aline Flieger. 1987. "Hartman's Contagious Orbit: Reassessing Aesthetic Criticism." *Diacritics* 17: 1, 52–69.

Armstrong, Nancy. 1987. *Desire and Domestic Fiction: A Political History of the Novel.* New York: Oxford University Press.

Aronson, A. 1946. "The Anatomy of Taste: A Note of Eighteenth-Century Periodical Literature." *Modern Language Notes* 51, 228–36.

Aston, Margaret. 1988. *England's Iconoclasts.* Vol. 1: *Laws against Images.* Oxford: Clarendon Press.

Atkins, G. Douglas. 1980. "Dehellenizing Literary Criticism." *College English* 41: 7, 769–79.

―――. 1983. "Partial Stories: Hebraic and Christian Thinking in the Wake of Deconstruction." *Notre Dame English Journal* 15: 3, 7–21.

―――. 1985. "A(fter) D(econstruction): The Relations of Literature and Religion in the Wake of Deconstruction." *Studies in the Literary Imagination* 18: 1, 89–100.

Atkins, G. Douglas, and Michael L. Johnson, eds. 1985. *Writing and Reading Differently: Deconstruction and the Teaching of Composition and Literature.* Lawrence: University Press of Kansas.

Attali, Jacques. 1990. *Lignes d'horizon*. Paris: Fayard.

Auden, W. H., ed. 1948. *The Portable Greek Reader*. New York: The Viking Press.

Auerbach, Erich. 1953. *Mimesis: The Representation of Reality in Western Literature* [1946]. Trans. Willard R. Trask. Princeton: Princeton University Press.

_____. 1953a. "Epilegomena zu Mimesis." *Romanische Forschungen* 65, 1–18.

_____. 1965. *Literary Language and its Public in Late Latin Antiquity and in the Middle Ages* [1958]. Trans. Ralph Manheim. New York: Pantheon.

_____. 1984. "Figura" [1944]. Trans. Ralph Manheim. In *Scenes from the Drama of European Literature* [1959]. Minneapolis: University of Minnesota Press.

Avineri, Shlomo. 1989. *Arlosoroff*. London: Weidenfeld & Nicolson.

Baeumer, Max L. 1976. "Nietzsche and the Tradition of the Dionysian." Trans. Timothy F. Sellner. In James O'Flaherty, Timothy F. Sellner, and Robert M. Helm, eds.: *Studies in Nietzsche and the Classical Tradition*. Chapel Hill: University of North Carolina Press.

Bahti, Timothy. 1981. "Vico, Auerbach, and Literary History." In Giorgio Tagliacozzo, ed.: *Vico: Past and Present*. Atlantic Highlands, NJ: Humanities Press.

_____. 1985. "Auerbach's *Mimesis*: Figural Structure and Historical Narrative." In Gregory S. Jay and David L. Miller, eds.: *After Strange Texts: The Role of Theory in the Study of Literature*. Tuscaloosa: University of Alabama Press.

Bailey, Peter. 1987. *Leisure and Class in Victorian England: Rational Recreation and the Contest for Control, 1830–1885*. London: Methuen.

Bainton, Roland. 1963. "The Bible in the Reformation." In S. L. Greenslade, ed.: *The Cambridge History of the Bible: The West from the Reformation to the Present Day*. Cambridge: Cambridge University Press.

Bakhtin, M. M. 1981. "Epic and Novel." In *The Dialogic Imagination: Four Essays* [1975]. Trans. Caryl Emerson and Michael Holquist. Austin: University of Texas Press.

_____. 1986. "The Bildungsroman and Its Significance in the History of Realism (Toward a Historical Typology of the Novel)." In *Speech Genres and Other Late Essays*. Eds. Michael Holquist and Caryl Emerson. Trans. Vern W. McGee. Austin: University of Texas Press.

Barnard, F. M. 1959. "The Hebrews and Herder's Political Creed." *Modern Language Review* 54, 533–46.

_____. 1965. *Herder's Social and Political Thought: From Enlightenment to Nationalism*. Oxford: Clarendon Press.

_____. 1966. "Herder and Israel." *Jewish Social Studies* 28: 25–33.

_____, ed. and trans. 1969. *J. G. Herder on Social and Political Culture*. Cambridge: Cambridge University Press.

_____. 1989. *Self-Direction and Political Legitimacy: Rousseau and Herder*. Oxford: Oxford University Press.

Barnouw, Dagmar. 1988. *Weimar Intellectuals and the Threat of Modernity*. Bloomington: Indiana University Press.

Baroway, Israel. 1933. "The Bible as Poetry in the English Renaissance: An Introduction." *Journal of English and German Philology* 32, 447–480.

Barr, James. 1966. *Old and New in Interpretation: A Study of the Two Testaments*. London: SCM Press.

_____. 1983. *Holy Scripture: Canon, Authority, Criticism*. Oxford: Oxford University Press.

Barrett, Michèle. 1987. "The Concept of Difference." *Feminist Review* 26, 29–42.

Barth, Lewis M. 1984. "Recent Studies in Aggadah." *Prooftexts* 4:2, 204–13.

Barthes, Roland. 1972. *Mythologies* [1957]. Trans. Annette Lavers. New York: Hill & Wang.

———. 1975. *The Pleasure of the Text* [1973]. Trans. Richard Miller. New York: Hill & Wang.

Bartsch, Hans Werner, ed. 1953. *Kerygma and Myth: A Theological Debate* [1948, 1952]. Trans. Reginald H. Fuller. London: SPCK.

Bataille, Georges. 1988. *Guilty* [1961]. Trans. Bruce Boone. Venice, CA: Lapis Press.

Baudrillard, Jean. 1975. *The Mirror of Production* [1973]. Trans. Mark Poster. St. Louis: Telos Press.

———. 1981. *For a Critique of the Political Economy of the Sign* [1972]. Trans. Charles Levin. St. Louis: Telos Press.

———. 1988. *America*. Trans. Chris Turner. London: Verso.

Bauman, Zygmunt. 1987. *Legislators and Interpreters: On Modernity, Post-Modernity, and Intellectuals*. Ithaca, NY: Cornell University Press.

———. 1988. "Exit Visas and Entry Tickets: Paradoxes of Jewish Assimilation." *Telos* 77, 45–77.

———. 1988a. *Freedom*. Minneapolis: University of Minnesota Press.

———. 1989. *Modernity and the Holocaust*. Oxford: Polity Press.

Beckwith, Roger T. 1985. *The Old Testament Canon of the New Testament Church and its Background in Early Judaism*. London: SPCK.

Beddow, Michael. 1982. *The Fiction of Humanity: Studies in the Bildungsroman from Wieland to Thomas Mann*. Cambridge: Cambridge University Press.

Beiser, Frederick C. 1987. *The Fate of Reason: German Philosophy from Kant to Fichte*. Cambridge, MA: Harvard University Press.

Bell, Daniel. 1946. "A Parable of Alienation." *Jewish Frontier* 13: 11, 12–19.

Bell, David. 1984. *Spinoza in Germany from 1670 to the Age of Goethe*. London: Institute of Germanic Studies (University of London).

Benjamin, Andrew, ed. 1989. *The Problems of Modernity: Adorno and Benjamin*. London: Routledge.

Benjamin, Walter. 1969. "The Task of the Translator: An Introduction to the Translation of Baudelaire's *Tableaux parisiens*" [1923]. In *Illuminations* [1955]. Trans. Harry Zohn. New York: Schocken Books.

———. 1969a. "Some Reflections on Kafka" [1938]. In *Illuminations*. See Benjamin 1969.

———. 1969b. "Franz Kafka: On the Tenth Anniversary of His Death" [1934]. In *Illuminations*. See Benjamin 1969.

———. 1977. *The Origin of German Tragic Drama* [1963]. Trans. John Osborne. London: NLB.

———. 1978. "Critique of Violence" [1920–21]. In *Reflections: Essays, Aphorisms, Autobiographical Writings*. Trans. Edmund Jephcott. New York: Harcourt Brace Jovanovich.

———. 1978a. "On Language as Such and on the Language of Man." In *Reflections*. See Benjamin 1978.

———. 1979. *One-Way Street and Other Writings*. Trans. Edmund Jephcott and Kingsley Shorter. London: NLB.

_____. 1983–84. "N [Theoretics of Knowledge; Theory of Progress]." Trans. Mark Ritter. *The Philosophical Forum* 15: 1–2, 1–40.

_____. 1983–84a. "Program of the Coming Philosophy" [1918]. Trans. Mark Ritter. *The Philosophical Forum* 15: 1–2, 41–51.

Bennett, Benjamin. 1979. "Nietzsche's Idea of Myth: The Birth of Tragedy from the Spirit of Eighteenth-Century Aesthetics." *PMLA* 94: 3, 420–33.

Bercovitch, Sacvan, ed. 1972. *Typology and Early American Literature*. Amherst: University of Massachusetts Press.

Berghahn, Klaus L. 1988. "From Classicist to Classical Literary Criticism, 1730–1806." Trans. John R. Blazek. In Hohendahl 1988.

Berlin, Isaiah. 1976. *Vico and Herder: Two Studies in the History of Ideas*. London: The Hogarth Press.

Berman, Jaye. 1989. "Exiles." *Midstream* 35: 9, 57–58.

Berman, Marshall. 1982. *All That is Solid Melts into Air: The Experience of Modernity*. New York: Simon and Schuster.

Berman, Russell A. 1990. "Troping to Pretoria: The Rise and Fall of Deconstruction." *Telos* 85, 4–16.

Bernal, Martin. 1985. "Black Athena: The African and Levantine Roots of Greece." *Journal of African Civilizations* 7: 5, 66–82.

_____. 1986. "Black Athena Denied: The Tyranny of Germany over Greece and the Rejection of the Afroasiatic Roots of Europe, 1780–1980." *Comparative Criticism* 8, 3–69.

_____. 1987. *Black Athena: The Afroasiatic Roots of Classical Civilization*. Vol. 1: *The Fabrication of Ancient Greece, 1785–1985*. London: Free Association Books.

_____. 1989. "*Black Athena* and the APA." In *Arethusa* 1989, 17–38.

Bernasconi, Robert. 1987. "Deconstruction and the Possibility of Ethics." In John Sallis, ed.: *Deconstruction and Philosophy: The Texts of Jacques Derrida*. Chicago: The University of Chicago Press.

_____. 1988. "The Trace of Levinas in Derrida." In Wood and Bernasconi 1988.

_____. 1988a. "Levinas: Philosophy and Beyond." In Silverman 1988.

_____. 1988b. "'Failure of Communication' as a Surplus: Dialogue and Lack of Dialogue between Buber and Levinas." In Bernasconi and Wood 1988.

Bernasconi, Robert, and David Wood, eds. 1988. *The Provocation of Levinas: Rethinking the Other*. London: Routledge.

Bernstein, J. M. 1984. *The Philosophy of the Novel. Lukács, Marxism, and the Dialectics of Form*. Minneapolis: University of Minnesota Press.

_____. 1987. "Unknowing." *Textual Practice* 1: 1, 98–106.

_____. 1987a. "Aesthetic Alienation: Heidegger, Adorno, and Truth at the End of Art." In John Fekete, ed.: *Life After Postmodernism: Essays on Value and Culture*. New York: St. Martin's Press.

Bersani, Leo. 1990. *The Culture of Redemption*. Cambridge, MA: Harvard University Press.

Bevan, Edwyn R., and Charles Singer, eds. 1928. *The Legacy of Israel* [1927]. Oxford: Clarendon Press.

Biale, David. 1979. *Gershom Scholem: Kabbalah and Counter-History*. Cambridge, MA: Harvard University Press.

Bialik, H. N. 1961. "Jewish Dualism" [1922]. Trans. Maurice M. Shudofsky. *Jewish Frontier* 28: 7, 19–22.

Blake, William. 1972. *Complete Writings, with Variant Readings*. Ed. Geoffrey Keynes. London: Oxford University Press.

Blanchot, Maurice. 1969."ctre Juif." In *L'Entretien infini*. Paris: Gallimard.

———. 1986. *The Writing of the Disaster* [1980]. Trans. Ann Smock. Lincoln: University of Nebraska Press.

Blenkinsopp, Joseph. 1977. *Prophecy and Canon*. Notre Dame, IN: University of Notre Dame Press.

Bloch, Ernst. 1970. *Man on his Own: Essays in the Philosophy of Religion* [1961]. Trans. E. B. Ashton. New York: Herder and Herder.

———. 1972. *Atheism in Christianity: The Religion of Exodus and the Kingdom* [1968]. Trans. J. T. Swann. New York: Herder and Herder.

Bloom, Harold. 1959. *Shelley's Mythmaking*. New Haven, CT: Yale University Press.

———. 1979. *The Flight to Lucifer: A Gnostic Fantasy*. New York: Farrar, Straus & Giroux.

———. 1982. "Free and Broken Tablets: The Cultural Prospects of American Jewry." In *Agon: Towards a Theory of Revisionism*. New York: Oxford University Press.

———. 1984. "'Before Moses was, I am': The Original and Belated Testaments." *Notebooks in Cultural Analysis* 1, 3–14.

———. 1985. "The Pragmatics of Contemporary Jewish Culture." In John Rajchman and Cornel West, eds.: *Post-Analytic Philosophy*. New York: Columbia University Press.

———. 1986. "Homer, Virgil, Tolstoy: The Epic Hero." *Raritan* 6: 1, 1–25.

———, ed. 1986a. "Introduction." In *James Joyce*. New York: Chelsea House Publishers.

———. 1987. [Interview.] In Salusinszky 1987.

———. 1988. "Literature as the Bible." *The New York Review of Books*, 31 March, 23–25.

Blum, Roland Paul. 1985. "Deconstruction and Creation." *Philosophy and Phenomenological Research* 46: 2, 293–306.

Blumenberg, Hans. 1983. *The Legitimacy of the Modern Age* [1966]. Trans. [of 2nd ed., 1976] Robert M. Wallace. Cambridge, MA: The MIT Press.

———. 1985. *Work on Myth* [1979]. Trans. Robert M. Wallace. Cambridge, MA: The MIT Press.

Boas, George, ed. 1939. *The Greek Tradition*. Baltimore: The Johns Hopkins Press.

Bocock, Robert. 1986. *Hegemony*. Sussex: Ellis Horwood; London: Tavistock.

Bodin, John [Jean]. 1945. *Method for the Easy Comprehension of History* [1566]. Trans. Beatrice Reynolds. New York: Columbia University Press.

Bolkosky, Sidney M. 1975. *The Distorted Image: German Jewish Perceptions of Germans and Germany, 1918–1935*. New York: Elsevier.

Boly, John R. 1988–89. "Deconstruction as a General System: Tropes, Disciplines, Politics." *Cultural Critique* 11, 175–201.

Boman, Thorleif. 1970. *Hebrew Thought compared with Greek* [1954, 2nd ed. 1960]. Trans. Jules L. Moreau. New York: W. W. Norton and Company.

Bordo, Susan. 1987. "The Cartesian Masculinization of Thought and the Seventeenth-Century Flight from the Feminine." In *The Flight to Objectivity: Essays on Cartesianism and Culture*. Albany: State University of New York Press.

Bossy, John. 1985. *Christianity in the West, 1400–1700.* Oxford: Oxford University Press.

Bourdieu, Pierre. 1983. "The Philosophical Institution." Trans. Kathleen McLaughlin. In Montefiore 1983.

———. 1984. *Distinction: A Social Critique of the Judgment of Taste* [1979]. Trans. Richard Nice. Cambridge, MA: Harvard University Press.

———. 1985. "The Market of Symbolic Goods" [1971]. Trans. Rupert Swyer. *Poetics* 14, 13–44.

Bourgeois, Bernard. 1970. *Hegel à Francfort, ou Judaïsme, Christianisme, Hégélianisme.* Paris: J. Vrin.

Bové, Paul. 1983. "Variations on Authority: Some Deconstructive Transformations of the New Criticism." In Arac, Godzich, and Martin 1983.

———. 1986. *Intellectuals in Power: A Genealogy of Critical Humanism.* New York: Columbia University Press.

Bowie, Andrew. 1990. *Aesthetics and Subjectivity: From Kant to Nietzsche.* Manchester: Manchester University Press.

Bowler, Maurice Gerald. 1988. *Claude Montefiore and Christianity.* Atlanta: Scholars Press.

Brand, Arie. 1987. "Weber: Man, the Prime Mover." In Diane J. Austin-Broos, ed.: *Creating Culture: Profiles in the Study of Culture.* Sydney: Allen & Unwin.

Brantlinger, Patrick. 1983. *Bread and Circuses: Theories of Mass Culture as Social Decay.* Ithaca, NY: Cornell University Press.

Breines, Paul. 1970. "Notes on Georg Lukács' 'The Old Culture and the New Culture.'" *Telos* 5, 1–20.

Breslauer, S. Daniel. 1990. *Martin Buber on Myth: An Introduction.* New York: Garland.

Brink, C. O. 1986. *English Classical Scholarship: Historical Reflections on Bentley, Porson, and Housman.* Oxford: James Clarke/Oxford University Press.

Brittan, Arthur. 1989. *Masculinity and Power.* Oxford: Basil Blackwell.

Brod, Max. 1970. *Paganism—Christianity—Judaism: A Confession of Faith* [1921]. Trans. William Wolf. Tuscaloosa: University of Alabama Press.

Bromwich, David. 1989. *A Choice of Inheritance: Self and Community from Edmund Burke to Robert Frost.* Cambridge, MA: Harvard University Press.

Brooke-Rose, Christine. 1976. *A Structural Analysis of Pound's Usura Canto: Jakobson's Method Expanded and Applied to Free Verse.* The Hague: Mouton.

Brown, Edward. 1973. *Major Soviet Writers: Essays in Criticism.* Oxford: Oxford University Press.

Brown, Frank Burch. 1990. *Religious Aesthetics: A Theological Study of Making and Meaning.* Princeton: Princeton University Press.

Brubaker, Rogers. 1989. "Traditions of Nationhood and Politics of Citizenship." *States and Social Structures Newsletter* 9, 4–8.

Bruford, W. H. 1975. *The German Tradition of Self-Cultivation: Bildung from Humboldt to Thomas Mann.* Cambridge: Cambridge University Press.

Brumm, Ursula. 1970. *American Thought and Religious Typology.* New Brunswick, NJ: Rutgers University Press.

Brunette, Peter, and David Wills. 1990. *Screen/Play: Derrida and Film Theory.* Princeton: Princeton University Press.

Bruns, Gerald L. 1987. "Midrash and Allegory." In Alter and Kermode 1987.

Brunschwig, Henri. 1974. *Enlightenment and Romanticism in Eighteenth-Century Prussia* [1947]. Trans. Frank Jellinek. Chicago: The University of Chicago Press.

Buber, Martin. 1948. "Plato and Isaiah" [1938]. In *Israel and the World: Essays in a Time of Crisis*. Trans. Olga Marx. New York: Schocken Books.

————. 1948a. "Biblical Leadeship" [1928]. Trans. G. Hort. In *Israel and the World*. See Buber 1948.

————. 1965. "Dialogue" [1929]. In *Between Man and Man* [1948]. Trans. Ronald Gregor Smith. New York: Macmillan.

————. 1967. *On Judaism*. Trans. Nahum N. Glatzer. New York: Schocken Books.

————. 1968. "Prophecy, Apocalyptic, and the Historical Hour" [1954]. In *On the Bible: Eighteen Studies*. Trans. Maurice Friedman. New York: Schocken Books.

————. 1968a. "Biblical Humanism" [1933]. In *On the Bible: Eighteen Studies*. Trans. Michael A. Meyer. New York: Schocken Books.

————. 1970. *I and Thou* [1922]. Trans. Walter Kaufmann. New York: Charles Scribner and Sons.

Buckley, Jerome Hamilton. 1974. *Season of Youth: The Bildungsroman from Dickens to Golding*. Cambridge, MA: Harvard University Press.

Buck-Morss, Susan. 1983. "Benjamin's *Passagen-Werk*: Redeeming Mass Culture for the Revolution." *New German Critique* 29, 211–40.

Budick, Sanford. 1986. "Milton and the Scene of Interpretation: From Typology toward Midrash." In Hartman and Budick 1986.

Budick, Sanford, and Wolfgang Iser, eds. 1989. *Languages of the Unsayable: The Play of Negativity in Literature and Literary Theory*. New York: Columbia University Press.

Bürger, Peter. 1984–85. "The Decline of the Modern Age" [1983]. Trans. David J. Parent. *Telos* 62, 117–30.

Burke, Joseph. 1966. "Grand Tour and the Rule of Taste." *Studies in the Eighteenth Century* 11, 231–50.

Burlingame, Anne Elizabeth. 1920. *The Battle of the Books in its Historical Setting*. New York: Huebsch.

Burns, R. M. 1981. *The Great Debate on Miracles*. Lewisburg, PA: Bucknell University Press.

Burrell, Sidney A. 1968. "Calvinism, Capitalism, and the Middle Classes: Some Afterthoughts on an Old Problem" [1960]. In S. N. Eisenstadt, ed.: *The Protestant Ethic and Modernization: A Comparative View*. New York: Basic Books.

Butler, Marilyn. 1988. *Literature as a Heritage, or Reading Other Ways*. Cambridge: Cambridge University Press.

Byrne, Peter. 1989. *Natural Religion and the Nature of Religion: The Legacy of Deism*. London: Routledge.

Cahn, Walter. 1979. *Masterpieces: Chapters on the History of an Idea*. Princeton: Princeton University Press.

Cahoone, Lawrence E. 1987. *The Dilemma of Modernity: Philosophy, Culture, and Anti-Culture*. Albany: State University of New York Press.

Cain, Maureen, ed. 1989. *Growing up Good: Policing the Behaviour of Girls in Europe*. Beverly Hills, CA: Sage.

Campbell, Colin. 1986. "The Tyranny of the Yale Critics." *New York Times Magazine*, 9 February.

―――. 1987. *The Romantic Ethic and the Spirit of Modern Consumerism*. Oxford: Basil Blackwell.

Campbell, Joan. 1989. *Joy in Work, German Work: The National Debate, 1800–1945*. Princeton: Princeton University Press.

Camus, Albert. 1955. *The Myth of Sisyphus, and Other Essays*. Trans. Justin O'Brien. New York: Vintage Books.

Cardozo Law Review. 1990. "Deconstruction and the Possibility of Justice" (special issue), 11, 919–1727.

Carroll, David. 1975. "*Mimesis* Reconsidered: Literature, History, Ideology." *Diacritics* 5: 2, 5–12.

Carroll, John. 1985. *Guilt: The Grey Eminence behind Character, History, and Culture*. London: Routledge & Kegan Paul.

Casey, Edward S. 1984. "Origin(s) in (of) Heidegger/Derrida." *The Journal of Philosophy* 81: 10, 601–10.

Casey, John. 1990. *Pagan Virtue: An Essay in Ethics*. Oxford: Clarendon Press.

Cassirer, Ernst. 1951. *The Philosophy of the Enlightenment* [1932]. Trans. Fritz C. A. Koelln and James P. Pettegrove. Princeton: Princeton University Press.

Castillo, Debra A. 1985. *The Translated World: A Postmodern Tour of Libraries in Literature*. Gainesville: University of Florida Press.

Castoriadis, Cornelius. 1989. "The End of Philosophy?" *Salmagundi* 82–83, 3–23.

―――. 1990. "Individual, Society, Rationality, History" [1988]. Trans. David Ames Curtis. *Thesis Eleven* 25, 59–90.

Caygill, Howard. 1989. *Art of Judgment*. Oxford: Basil Blackwell.

Chadwick, Henry. 1966. *Early Christian Thought and the Classical Tradition: Studies in Justin, Clement, and Origen*. New York: Oxford University Press.

Chalier, Catherine. 1982. *Figures du féminin: Lecture d'Emmanuel Lévinas*. Paris: La Nuit Surveillée.

Champagne, Roland. 1977. *Beyond the Structuralist Myth of Écriture*. The Hague: Mouton.

Charity, A. C. 1966. *Events and Their Afterlife: The Dialectics of Christian Typology in the Bible and Dante*. Cambridge: Cambridge University Press.

Charles, Michel. 1986. *L'Arbre et la source*. Paris: Seuil.

Chytry, Josef. 1989. *The Aesthetic State: A Quest in Modern German Thought*. Berkeley: University of California Press.

Clark, Robert T. Jr. 1955. *Herder: His Life and Thought*. Berkeley: University of California Press.

Clark, Stephen R. L. 1984. *From Athens to Jerusalem: The Love of Wisdom and the Love of God*. Oxford: Clarendon Press.

Clark, Timothy. 1987. "Heidegger, Derrida, and the Greek Limits of Philosophy." *Philosophy and Literature* 11: 1, 75–91.

Clifford, James, and George E. Marcus, eds. 1986. *Writing Culture: The Poetics and Politics of Ethnography*. Berkeley: University of California Press.

Coalter, Fred. 1988. *Freedom and Constraint: The Paradoxes of Leisure*. London: Routledge.

Coats, George W., and Burke O. Long, eds. 1977. *Canon and Authority: Essays in Old Testament Religion and Theology*. Philadelphia: Fortress Press.

Cocalis, Susan L. 1978. "The Transformation of *Bildung* from an Image to an Ideal." *Monatshefte* 70: 4, 399–414.

Cohen, Arthur A. 1952. "Revelation and Law: Reflections on Martin Buber's Views of Halakah." *Judaism* 1: 3, 250–56.

——, ed. 1980. *The Jew: Essays from Martin Buber's Journal Der Jude, 1916–1928.* Tuscaloosa: The University of Alabama Press.

Cohen, Arthur A., and Paul Mendes-Flohr, eds. 1987. *Contemporary Jewish Religious Thought: Original Essays on Critical Concepts, Movements, and Beliefs.* New York: Charles Scribner's Sons.

Cohen, Gerson D. 1975. "Introduction: German Jewry as Mirror of Modernity." *The Leo Baeck Institute Year Book* 20, ix-xxxi.

Cohen, Hermann. 1971. *Reason and Hope: Selections from the Jewish Writings of Hermann Cohen.* Trans. Eva Jospe. New York: W. W. Norton & Co.

Cohen, Hermann. 1972. *Religion of Reason out of the Sources of Judaism* [1919]. Trans. Simon Kaplan. New York: Frederick Ungar.

Cohen, Kitty. 1975. *The Throne and the Chariot: Studies in Milton's Hebraism.* The Hague: Mouton.

Coleridge, Henry Nelson. 1846. *Introduction to the Study of the Greek Classic Poets: Designed Principally for the Use of Young Persons at School and College* [3rd edition]. London: John Murray.

Collins, Randall. 1987. "A Micro-Macro Theory of Intellectual Creativity: The Case of German Idealist Philosophy." *Sociological Theory* 5, 47–69.

Collins, Stephen L. 1989. *From Divine Cosmos to Sovereign State: An Intellectual History of Consciousness and the Idea of Order in Renaissance England.* Oxford: Oxford University Press.

Condren, Conal. 1985. *The Status and Appraisal of Classic Texts: An Essay on Political Theory, its Inheritance, and the History of Ideas.* Princeton: Princeton University Press.

Congdon, Lee. 1983. *The Young Lukács.* Chapel Hill: University of North Carolina Press.

Connolly, William E. 1988. *Political Theory and Modernity.* Oxford: Basil Blackwell.

Conrad, Peter, and Joseph W. Schneider. 1980. *Deviance and Medicalization: From Badness to Sickness.* St. Louis: The C. V. Mosby Company.

Costa-Lima, Luiz. 1988. "Erich Auerbach: History and Metahistory." *New Literary History* 19: 3, 467–99.

Craig, Gordon A. 1982. *The Germans.* New York: Putnam.

Crane, Ronald S. 1922. "An Early Eighteenth-Century Enthusiast for Primitive Poetry: John Husbands." *Modern Language Notes* 37, 27–36.

Cranfield, C. E. B. 1964. "St. Paul and the Law." *Scottish Journal of Theology* 17, 43–68.

Critchley, Simon. 1989. "The Chiasmus: Levinas, Derrida and the Ethical Demand for Deconstruction." *Textual Practice* 3: 1, 91–106.

Cuddihy, John Murray. 1974. *The Ordeal of Civility: Freud, Marx, Lévi-Strauss, and the Jewish Struggle with Modernity.* New York: Basic Books.

Culler, Jonathan. 1975. "Jakobson's Poetic Analyses" [1971]. In *Structuralist Poetics: Structuralism, Linguistics and the Study of Literature.* London: Routledge & Kegan Paul.

——. 1984. "A Critic against the Christians." *Times Literary Supplement,* 23 November, 1327–28.

Cunningham, H. 1980. *Leisure in the Industrial Revolution, 1780–1880*. London: Croom Helm.

Curtius, Ernst Robert. 1953. *European Literature and the Latin Middle Ages* [1948]. Trans. Willard R. Trask. Princeton: Princeton University Press.

Dahlhaus, Carl. 1987. "Schoenberg's Aesthetic Theology" [1984]. In *Schoenberg and the New Music*. Trans. Derrick Puffett and Alfred Clayton. Cambridge: Cambridge University Prss.

Dallmayr, Fred. 1989. "Adorno and Heidegger." *Diacritics* 19: 3–4, 82–100.

Damrosch, Leopold Jr. 1985. *God's Plot and Man's Stories: Studies in the Fictional Imagination from Milton to Fielding*. Chicago: The University of Chicago Press.

Daniel, Stephen H. 1990. *Myth and Modern Philosophy*. Philadelphia: Temple University Press.

Danielou, Jean. 1960. *From Shadows to Reality: Studies in the Biblical Typology of the Fathers*. Trans. Wulston Hibberd. London: Burns and Oates.

D'Arby, Terence Trent. 1989. Interview by Paolo Hewitt. *New Musical Express*, 14 October.

Dasenbrock, Reed Way, ed. 1989. *Redrawing the Lines: Analytic Philosophy, Deconstruction, and Literary Theory*. Minneapolis: University of Minnesota Press.

Davie, Donald. 1975. *Pound*. London: Fontana.

Deak, Istvan. 1968. *Weimar Germany's Left-Wing Intellectuals: A Political History of the Weltbühne and its Circle*. Berkeley: University of California Press.

De Boer, Theo. 1985. "Judaism and Hellenism in the Philosophy of Levinas and Heidegger." *Archivio di Filosofia* 53, 197–215.

DeJean, Joan. 1989. *Fictions of Sappho, 1546–1937*. Chicago: The University of Chicago Press.

Deleuze, Gilles. 1956. "La conception de la différence chez Bergson." *Etudes bergsoniennes* 4, 79–112.

———. 1968. *Différence et répétition*. Paris: PUF.

Deleuze, Gilles, and Felix Guattari. 1986. *Kafka: Toward a Minor Literature* [1975]. Trans. Richard Brinkley. Minneapolis: University of Minnesota Press.

———. 1987. *A Thousand Plateaus*: Volume 2 of *Capitalism and Schizophrenia* [1980]. Trans. Brian Massumi. Minneapolis: University of Minnesota Press.

de Man, Paul. 1983. "Georg Lukács's *Theory of the Novel*" [1966]. In *Blindness and Insight: Essays in the Rhetoric of Contemporary Criticism*, [2nd ed.; 1st ed. 1971]. Minneapolis: University of Minnesota Press.

———. 1983a. "Heidegger's Exegeses of Hölderlin." Trans. Wlad Godzich. In *Blindness and Insight*. See de Man 1983.

Dembo, L. S. 1989. *Detotalized Totalities: Synthesis and Disintegration in Naturalist, Existentialist, and Socialist Fiction*. Madison: University of Wisconsin Press.

Derrida, Jacques. 1976. *Of Grammatology* [1967]. Trans. Gayatri Chakravorty Spivak. Baltimore: The Johns Hopkins University Press.

———. 1978. "Edmond Jabès and the Question of the Book" [1964]. In *Writing and Difference* [1967]. Trans. Alan Bass. Chicago: The University of Chicago Press.

———. 1978a. "Violence and Metaphysics: An Essay on the Thought of Emmanuel Levinas" [1964]. In *Writing and Difference*. See Derrida 1978.

_____. 1978b. "Structure, Sign, and Play in the Discourse of the Human Sciences" [1966]. In *Writing and Difference. See* Derrida 1978.

_____. 1978c. "Force and Signification" [1963]. In *Writing and Difference. See* Derrida 1978.

_____. 1980. "En ce moment même dans cet ouvrage me voici." In Francois Laruelle, ed.: *Textes pour Emmanuel Lévinas*. Paris: Jean-Michel Place.

_____. 1981. "Plato's Pharmacy" [1968]. In *Dissemination* [1972]. Trans. Barbara Johnson. Chicago: The University of Chicago Press.

_____. 1981a. "Economimesis" [1975]. Trans. R. Klein. *Diacritics* 11: 2, 3–25.

_____. 1982. "On an Apocalyptic Tone Recently Adopted in Philosophy." Trans. John P. Leavey, Jr. *Semeia* 23 ["Derrida and Biblical Studies" issue], 63–99.

_____. 1982a. "*Différance*" [1968]. In *Margins of Philosophy* [1972]. Trans. Alan Bass. Chicago: The University of Chicago Press.

_____. 1982b. "The Supplement of Copula: Philosophy before Linguistics" [1971]. In *Margins of Philosophy*.

_____. 1983. "The Time of a Thesis: Punctuations" [1980]. Trans. Kathleen McLaughlin. In Montefiore 1983.

_____. 1984. "Deconstruction and the Other" (interview). In Richard Kearney, ed.: *Dialogues with Contemporary Continental Thinkers*. Manchester: Manchester University Press.

_____. 1984a. "No Apocalypse, Not Now (full spead ahead, seven missiles, seven missives)." Trans. Catherine Porter and Philip Lewis. *Diacritics* 14: 2, 20–31.

_____. 1985. "Des Tours de Babel." Trans. Joseph F. Graham. In Joseph F. Graham, ed.: *Difference in Translation*. Ithaca, NY: Cornell University Press.

_____. 1985a. "Deconstruction in America" (interview). *Critical Exchange* 17, 1–32.

_____. 1986. "The Age of Hegel" [1977]. Trans. Susan Winnett. *Glyph Textual Studies* 1, 3–35.

_____. 1986a. "Shibboleth." Trans. Joshua Wilner. In Hartman and Budick 1986.

_____. 1986b. *Glas* [1974]. Trans. John P. Leavey, Jr., and Richard Rand. Lincoln: University of Nebraska Press.

_____. 1987. "Women in the Beehive: A Seminar with Jacques Derrida" [1984]. In Alice Jardine and Paul Smith, eds.: *Men in Feminism*. New York: Methuen.

_____. 1987a. [Interview.] In Salusinszky 1987.

_____. 1987b. "On Reading Heidegger: An Outline of Remarks to the Essex Colloquium." *Research in Phenomenology* 17, 171–85.

_____. 1988. "The Politics of Friendship." *Journal of Philosophy* 85: 12, 632–45.

_____. 1988a. "Letter to a Japanese Friend" [1983]. In Wood and Bernasconi 1988.

_____. 1988b. "An Interview with Derrida" [1983]. In Wood and Bernasconi 1988.

_____. 1988c. "Like the Sound of the Sea Deep within a Shell: Paul de Man's War." Trans. Peggy Kamuf. *Critical Inquiry* 14: 3, 590–652.

_____. 1989. *Of Spirit: Heidegger and the Question* [1987]. Trans. Geoffrey Bennington and Rachel Bowlby. Chicago: The University of Chicago Press.

_____. 1989a. "Biodegradables: Seven Diary Fragments." Trans. Peggy Kamuf. *Critical Inquiry* 15: 4, 812–73.

Descombes, Vincent. 1980. *Modern French Philosophy* [1979]. Trans. L. Scott-Fox and J. M. Harding. Cambridge: Cambridge University Press.

Des Pres, Terrence. 1975. "Prophecies of Grace and Doom: The Function of Criticism at the Present Time." *Partisan Review* 42: 2, 273–80.

Detienne, Marcel. 1986. *The Creation of Mythology* [1981]. Trans. Margaret Cook. Chicago: University of Chicago Press.

Dewart, Leslie. 1966. *The Future of Belief: Theism in a World Come of Age.* New York: Herder and Herder.

Dickens, A. G. 1982. *Reformation Studies.* London: The Hambledon Press.

Donougho, Martin. 1981. "The Cunning of Odysseus: A Theme in Hegel, Lukács, and Adorno." *Philosophy and Social Criticism* 8: 13–43.

Douglas, Wallace W. 1953–54. "Souls among Masterpieces: The Solemn Style of Modern Critics." *The American Scholar* 23, 43–55.

Doyle, Brian. 1989. *English and Englishness.* London: Routledge.

Dronke, Peter. 1980. "Curtius as Medievalist and Modernist." *Times Literary Supplement,* 3 October, 1103–6.

Dyck, Joachim. 1977. *Athen und Jerusalem: Die Tradition der argumentativen Verknüpfung von Bibel und Poesie im 17. und 18. Jahrhundert.* München: Verlag C. H. Beck.

Eagleton, Terry. 1986. "Frère Jacques: The Politics of Deconstruction" [1984]. In *Against the Grain: Essays 1975–1985.* London: Verso.

————. 1990. *The Ideology of the Aesthetic.* Oxford: Basil Blackwell.

Ebeling, Gerhard. 1968. *The Word of God and Tradition* [1966]. Trans. S. H. Hooke. London: Collins.

Eichrodt, Walther. 1963. "Is Typological Exegesis an Appropriate Method?" Trans. James Barr. In Claus Westermann, ed.: *Essays on Old Testament Hermeneutics* [1960]. Richmond, VA: John Knox Press.

Eidelberg, Paul. 1983. *Jerusalem vs. Athens: In Quest of a General Theory of Existence.* Lanham, MD: University Press of America.

————. 1989. *Beyond the Secular Mind: A Judaic Response to the Problems of Modernity.* Westport, CT: Greenwood.

Eisen, Arnold. 1986. *Galut: Modern Jewish Reflection on Homelessness and Homecoming.* Bloomington: Indiana University Press.

————. 1989. "Jews, Jewish Studies, and the American Humanities." *Tikkun* 4: 5, 23–29.

Eisenstadt, S. N., ed. 1987. *Patterns of Modernity* (2 vols.). London: Frances Printer.

Eisenstein, Hester, and Alice Jardin, eds. 1985. *The Future of Difference.* New Brunswick, NJ: Rutgers University Press.

Elias, Norbert. 1978. *The Civilising Process: The History of Manners* [1939]. Trans. Edmund Jephcott. Oxford: Basil Blackwell.

Eliot, T. S. 1923. "Ulysses, Order, and Myth." *The Dial* 75, 480–83.

Ellenson, David. 1989. *Tradition in Transition: Orthodoxy, Halakhah, and the Boundaries of Modern Jewish Identity.* Lanham, MD: University Press of America.

Ellis, Kate Ferguson. 1989. *The Contested Castle: Gothic Novels and the Subversion of Domestic Ideology.* Champaign: University of Illinois Press.

Ellmann, Richard. 1977. "Joyce and Homer." *Critical Inquiry* 3: 3, 567–82.

Elsky, Martin. 1990. *Authorizing Words: Speech, Writing, and Print in the English Renaissance.* Ithaca, NY: Cornell University Press.

Ettinger, S. 1961. "The Beginnings of the Change in the Attitude of European Society towards the Jews." *Scripta Hierosolymitana* 7, 193–219.

Evans, G. R. 1985. *The Language and Logic of the Bible. The Road to Reformation.* Cambridge: Cambridge University Press.

Fackenheim, Emil L. 1970. *God's Presence in History: Jewish Affirmations and Philosophical Reflections.* New York: New York University Press.

―――. 1973. *Encounters between Judaism and Modern Philosophy: A Preface to Future Jewish Thought.* New York: Basic Books.

Faderman, Lillian. 1981. *Surpassing the Love of Men: Romantic Friendship and Love between Women from the Renaissance to the Present.* New York: William Morrow.

Fanon, Frantz. 1968. *The Wretched of the Earth* [1961]. Trans. Constance Farrington. New York: Grove Press.

Feenberg, Andrew. 1973. "Aesthetics as Social Theory: Introduction to Fehér's 'Is the Novel Problematic?'" *Telos* 15, 41–46.

Fehér, Ference. 1988. *The Frozen Revolution: An Essay on Jacobinism.* Cambridge: Cambridge University Press.

―――. 1990. "The Cult of the Supreme Being and the Limits of the Secularization of the Political." In Ference Fehér, ed.: *The French Revolution and the Birth of Modernity.* Berkeley: University of California Press.

Feldman, Egal. 1990. *Dual Destinies: The Jewish Encounter with Protestant America.* Champaign: University of Illinois Press.

Femia, J. 1981. *Gramsci's Political Thought: Hegemony, Consciousness and Revolutionary Process.* Oxford: Clarendon.

Feuerbach, Ludwig. 1980. *Thoughts on Death and Immortality: From the Papers of a Thinker, along with an Appendix of Theological-Satirical Epigrams, Edited by One of His Friends* [1830]. Trans. James A. Massey. Berkeley: University of California Press.

Fiedler, Leslie, and Houston Baker, Jr., eds. 1981. *English Literature: Opening up the Canon.* Baltimore: The Johns Hopkins University Press.

Fietkau, Wolfgang. 1986. "Loss of Experience and Experience of Loss: Remarks on the Problem of the Lost Revolution in the Work of Benjamin and his Fellow Combatants" [1984]. Trans. Jonathan Monroe and Irving Wohlfarth. *New German Critique* 39, 169–78.

Finkelstein, Norman. 1989. "The Utopian Function and the Refunctioning of Marxism." *Diacritics* 19: 2, 54–65.

Fisch, Harold. 1964. *Jerusalem and Albion: The Hebraic Factor in Seventeenth-Century Literature.* New York: Schocken Books.

―――. 1977. "The Sanctification of Literature." *Commentary* 63, 63–69.

Fischer, Michael M. J. 1986. "Ethnicity and the Post-Modern Arts of Memory." In Clifford and Marcus 1986.

Fischoff, Ephraim. 1944. "The Protestant Ethic and the Spirit of Capitalism: The History of a Controversy." *Social Research* 11, 53–77.

Fish, Stanley. 1980. "Structuralist Homiletics" [1973]. In *Is there a Text in this Class? The Authority of Interpretive Communities.* Cambridge, MA: Harvard University Press.

Fishbane, Michael. 1987. "Hermeneutics." In Cohen and Mendes-Flohr 1987.

FitzGerald, Frances. 1987. "Reagan's Band of True Believers." *New York Times Magazine*, 10 May.

Foucault, Michel. 1973. *The Order of Things: An Archaeology of the Human Sciences* [1966]. New York: Vintage Books.

———. 1975. *The Birth of the Clinic: An Archaeology of Medical Perception* [1963]. Trans. A. M. Sheridan Smith. New York: Vintage Books.

———. 1977. "Language to Infinity" [1963]. In *Language, Counter-Memory, Practice: Selected Essays and Interviews*. Trans. Donald F. Bouchard and Sherry Simon. Ithaca, NY: Cornell University Press.

———. 1977a. "Revolutionary Action: 'Until Now' " [1971]. In *Language, Counter-Memory, Practice. See* Foucault 1977.

———. 1977b. "A Preface to Transgression" [1963]. In *Language, Counter-Memory, Practice. See* Foucault 1977.

———. 1978. *The History of Sexuality. Volume I: An Introduction* [1976]. Trans. Robert Hurley. New York: Random House.

———. 1979. *Discipline and Punish: The Birth of the Prison* [1975]. Trans. Alan Sheridan. New York: Vintage Books.

———. 1979a. "What is an Author?" [1969]. In Josué V. Harari, ed.: *Textual Strategies: Perspectives in Post-Structuralist Criticism*. Ithaca, NY: Cornell University Press.

———. 1979b. "Governmentality" [1978]. *Ideology and Consciousness* 6, 5–21.

———. 1979c. "My Body, This Paper, This Fire" [1972]. Trans. Geoff Bennington. *The Oxford Literary Review* 4: 1, 9–28.

———. 1984. "What is Enlightenment?" In Paul Rabinow, ed.: *The Foucault Reader*. New York: Pantheon Books.

Fowler, Alastair. 1982. "Hierarchies of Genres and Canons of Literature." In *Kinds of Literature: An Introduction to the Theory of Genres and Modes*. Cambridge, MA: Harvard University Press.

Fowler, Roger. 1975. "Language and the Reader: Shakespeare's Sonnet 73." In Roger Fowler, ed.: *Style and Structure in Literature: Essays in the New Stylistics*. Oxford: Basil Blackwell.

Fowles, Bridget. 1987. " 'The Canon' and Marxist Theories of Literature." *Cultural Studies* 1:2, 162–78.

Fox, James J. 1977. "Roman Jakobson and the Comparative Study of Parallelism." In Daniel Armstrong and C. H. van Schooneveld, eds.: *Roman Jakobson: Echoes of his Scholarship*. Lisse: Peter de Ridder.

Fraser, Nancy. 1984. "The French Derrideans: Politicizing Deconstruction or Deconstructing the Political?" *New German Critique* 33, 127–54.

———. 1989. "What's Critical about Critical Theory? The Case of Habermas and Gender" [1985]. In *Unruly Practices: Power, Discourse, and Gender in Contemporary Social Theory*. Minneapolis: University of Minnesota Press.

Frei, Hans W. 1974. *The Eclipse of Biblical Narrative: A Study in Eighteenth and Nineteenth Century Hermeneutics*. New Haven, CT: Yale University Press.

Freimarck, Vincent. 1952. "The Bible and Neo-Classical Views of Style." *Journal of English and German Philology* 51, 507–26.

Freud, Sigmund. 1964. *The Future of an Illusion*. Trans. W. D. Robson-Scott. Garden City, NY: Anchor Books.

Friedlander, Judith. 1990. *Vilna on the Seine: Jewish Intellectuals in France since 1968*. New Haven, CT: Yale Universty Press.

Friedman, George. 1981. *The Political Philosophy of the Frankfurt School*. Ithaca, NY: Cornell University Press.

Friedman, Maurice S. 1960. *Martin Buber: The Life of Dialogue* [1955]. New York: Harper and Brothers.

————. 1981. "Martin Buber and Franz Rosenzweig: The Road to *I and Thou*." *Philosophy Today* 25, 210–20.

Friedrichsmeyer, Sara. 1983. *The Androgyne in Early German Romanticism: Friedrich Schlegel, Novalis and the Metaphysics of Love*. New York: Peter Lang.

Frisby, David. 1986. *Fragments of Modernity: Theories of Modernity in the Works of Simmel, Kracauer, and Benjamin*. Cambridge, MA: The MIT Press.

Frykman, Jonas, and Orvar Lofgren. 1987. *Culture Builders: A Historical Anthropology of Middle-Class Life*. New Brunswick, NJ: Rutgers University Press.

Fussner, F. Smith. 1962. *The Historical Revolution: English Historical Writing and Thought, 1580–1740*. Westport, CT: Greenwood Press.

Gadamer, Hans-Georg. 1976. "Martin Heidegger and Marburg Theology" [1964]. In *Philosophical Hermeneutics*. Trans. David E. Linge. Berkeley: University of California Press.

————. 1979 [Rev. 2nd ed.]. *Truth and Method* [1960, 2nd ed. 1965]. Trans. William Glen-Doepel. London: Sheed and Ward.

————. 1981. "Heidegger and the History of Philosophy." Trans. Karen Campbell. *The Monist* 64, 434–44.

Gaddis, William. 1985. *The Recognitions* [1955]. New York: Penguin Books.

Galgan, Michael. 1982. *The Logic of Modernity*. New York: New York University Press.

Gans, Eric. 1985. *The End of Culture: Toward a Generative Anthropology*. Berkeley: University of California Press.

Gans, Herbert J. 1974. *Popular Culture and High Culture: An Analysis and Evaluation of Taste*. New York: Basic Books.

Gardiner, Patrick. 1979. "Freedom as an Aesthetic Idea." In Alan Ryan, ed.: *The Idea of Freedom: Essays in Honour of Isaiah Berlin*. Oxford: Oxford University Press.

Gasché, Rodolphe. 1983. "Joining the Text: From Heidegger to Derrida." In Arac, Godzich, and Martin 1983.

Gay, Peter. 1966. *The Enlightenment—An Interpretation: The Rise of Modern Paganism*. New York: Alfred A. Knopf.

————. 1975. "Encounter with Modernism: German Jews in German Culture, 1888–1914." *Midstream* 21, 23–65.

————, ed. 1968. *Deism: An Anthology*. Princeton: D. Van Nostrand.

————. 1968a. *Weimar Culture: The Outsider as Insider*. New York: Harper & Row.

Gellner, Ernest. 1988. *Plough, Sword and Book: The Structure of Human History*. London: Collins Harvill.

Gentile, Emilio. 1990. "Fascism as Political Religion." *Journal of Contemporary History* 25: 2–3, 229–51.

George, Margaret. 1988. *Women in the First Capitalist Society: Experiences in Seventeenth-Century England*. Champaign: University of Illinois Press.

Gerber, Rudolph J. 1967. "Totality and Infinity: Hebraism & Hellenism—The Experiential Ontology of Emmanuel Levinas." *Review of Existential Psychology and Psychiatry* 7: 3, 177–88.

Gerrish, B. A. 1973. "'To the Unknown God': Luther and Calvin on the Hiddenness of God." *Journal of Religion* 53: 3, 263–92.

Giddens, Anthony. 1990. *The Consequences of Modernity*. Stanford, CA: Stanford University Press.

Gilbert, Sandra M. 1985. "What do Feminist Critics Want? The Academy and the Canon." In Showalter 1985.

Gilbert, Stuart. 1963. *James Joyce's* Ulysses: A *Study* [1930]. Harmondsworth: Penguin Books.

Gilman, Sander L. 1986. *Jewish Self-Hatred: Anti-Semitism and the Hidden Language of the Jews*. Baltimore: The Johns Hopkins University Press.

Gitenstein, R. Barbara. 1983. "The Temptation of Apollo and the Loss of Yiddish in Cynthia Ozick's Fiction." *Studies in American Jewish Literature* 3, 194–201.

Gladstone, W. E. 1858. "On the Place of Homer in Classical Education and in Historical Inquiry." In *Oxford Essays, Contributed by Members of the University, 1857*. London: Parker.

Glatzer, Nahum N. 1978. "The Beginnings of Modern Jewish Studies" [1974]. In *Essays in Jewish Thought*. Tuscaloosa: The University of Alabama Press.

Gluck, Mary. 1986. *Georg Lukács and His Generation, 1900–1918*. Cambridge, MA: Harvard University Press.

Gnuse, Robert. 1989. *Heilsgeschichte as a Model for Biblical Theology: The Debate Concerning the Uniqueness and Significance of Israel's Worldview*. Lanham, MD: University Press of America.

Goldman, Ari L. 1984. "Kahane and Professor [Dershowitz] Split sharply in a Debate on Israel's Future." *New York Times*, 13 November.

Goldman, Harvey. 1988. *Max Weber and Thomas Mann: Calling and the Shaping of the Self*. Berkeley: University of California Press.

Goldstein, David I. 1981. *Dostoyevsky and the Jews*. Austin: University of Texas Press.

Goldstein, Moritz. 1957. "German Jewry's Dilemma: The Story of a Provocative Essay." *Leo Baeck Institute Year Book* 2, 236–54.

Gombrich, E. H. 1966. "The Style *all'antica*: Imitation and Assimilation" [1961]. In *Norm and Form: Studies in the Art of the Renaissance*. London: Phaidon Press.

———. 1986. *Aby Warburg: An Intellectual Biography* [1970]. Oxford: Phaidon.

Gossman, Lionel. 1986. "History as Decipherment: Romantic Historiography and the Discovery of the Other." *New Literary History* 18: 1, 23–57.

Gottcent, John H. 1979. *The Bible as Literature: A Selective Bibliography*. Boston: G. K. Hall.

Gould, Eric, ed. 1985. *The Sin of the Book: Edmond Jabès*. Lincoln: University of Nebraska Press.

Gouldner, Alvin. 1979. *The Future of Intellectuals and the Rise of the New Class*. New York: Macmillan.

Goux, Jean-Joseph. 1989. "Politics and Modern Art—Heidegger's Dilemma." Trans. Michele Sharp. *Diacritics* 19: 3–4, 10–24.

Graham, Joseph F., ed. 1985. *Difference in Translation*. Ithaca, NY: Cornell University Press.

Gramsci, Antonio. 1985. *Selections from Cultural Writings*. Trans. William Boelhower. Cambridge, MA: Harvard University Press.

Green, Geoffrey. 1982. *Literary Criticism and the Structures of History: Erich Auerbach and Leo Spitzer*. Lincoln: University of Nebraska Press.

Green, Tamara M. 1989. "*Black Athena* and Classical Historiography: Other Approaches, Other Views." In *Arethusa* 1989, 55–65.

Greenberg, Clement. 1950. "Self-Hatred and Jewish Chauvinism: Some Reflection on 'Positive Jewishness.'" *Commentary* 10, 426–33.

Greenstein, Edward L. 1983. "Theories of Modern Bible Translation." *Prooftexts* 3: 1, 9–39.

————. 1989. "Deconstruction and Biblical Narrative." *Prooftexts* 9: 1, 43–72.

Griffin, Jasper. 1989. "Who are These Coming to the Sacrifice?" *The New York Review of Books*, 15 June, 25–27.

Gross, David. 1980. "Lowenthal, Adorno, Barthes: Three Perspectives on Popular Culture." *Telos* 45, 122–40.

Grumley, John. 1989. *History and Totality: Radical Historicism from Hegel to Foucault*. London: Routledge.

Guibbory, Achsah. 1986. *The Map of Time: Seventeenth-Century English Literature and Ideas of Pattern in History*. Champaign: University of Illinois Press.

Guillen, Claudio. 1987. "On the Uses of Monistic Theories: Parallelism in Poetry." *New Literary History* 18: 3, 497–516.

Guillory, John. 1983. *Poetic Authority: Spenser, Milton, and Literary History*. New York: Columbia University Press.

Guinness, Gerald, and Andrew Hurley, eds. 1984. *Auctor Ludens: Essays on Play in Literature*. Philadelphia: John Benjamins.

Gurr, Andrew. 1981. *Writers in Exile: The Identity of Home in Modern Literature*. London: Harvester Press.

Habermas, Jurgen. 1979. "Consciousness-Raising or Redemptive Criticism—The Contemporaneity of Walter Benjamin" [1972]. Trans. Philip Brewster and Carl Howard Buchner. *New German Critique* 17, 30–59.

————. 1982. "The Entwinement of Myth and Enlightenment: Re-Reading *Dialectic of Enlightenment*." Trans. Thomas Y. Levin. *New German Critique* 26: 13–30.

————. 1983. "Does Philosophy still have a Purpose?" [1971]. In *Philosophical-Political Profiles*. Trans. Frederick G. Lawrence. Cambridge, MA: The MIT Press.

————. 1983a. "Ernst Bloch: A Marxist Schelling" [1960]. In *Philosophical-Political Profiles. See* Habermas 1983.

————. 1983b. "The German Idealism of the Jewish Philosophers" [1961]. In *Philosophical-Political Profiles. See* Habermas 1983.

————. 1989. "Work and Weltanschauung: The Heidegger Controversy from a German Perspective." Trans. John McCumber. *Critical Inquiry* 15: 2, 431–56.

————. 1989a. *The Structural Transformation of the Public Sphere: An Inquiry into a Category of Bourgeois Society* [1971]. Trans. Thomas Burger. Cambridge, MA: The MIT Press.

Hall, Basil. 1985. "*Hoc est corpus meum*: The Centrality of the Real Presence for Luther." In George Yule, ed.: *Luther: Theologian for Catholics and Protestants*. Edinburgh: T&T Clark.

Hall, Vernon, Jr. 1948. "Scaliger's Defense of Poetry." *PMLA* 63: 4, 1125–30.

Halperin, David. 1986. "One Hundred Years of Homosexuality." *Diacritics* 16: 2, 34–45.

Halpern, Ben. 1946. "Letter to an Intellectual." *Jewish Frontier* 13: 12, 13–15.

Hamann, Johann Georg. 1856. "The Merchant" [1756]. In Frederic H. Hedge, ed.: *Prose Writers of Germany* [4th ed.]. New York: C. S. Francis and Co.

Hamilton, Richard, and James D. Wright. 1986. *The State of the Masses*. Hawthorne, NY: Aldine.

Handelman, Susan A. 1982. *The Slayers of Moses: The Emergence of Rabbinic Interpretation in Modern Literary Theory*. Albany: State University of New York Press.

———. 1983. "Jacques Derrida and the Heretic Hermeneutic." In Mark Krupnick, ed.: *Displacement: Derrida and After*. Bloomington: Indiana University Press.

———. 1985. "'Torments of an Ancient Word': Jabès and the Rabbinic Tradition." In Gould 1985.

Handler, Joel F. 1990. *Law and the Search for Community*. Philadelphia: University of Pennsylvania Press.

Hans, James S. 1981. *The Play of the World*. Amherst: University of Massachussets Press.

Hansen, Frank-Peter. 1989. *"Das älteste Systemprogramm des deutschen Idealismus": Rezeptionsgeschichte und Interpretation*. Berlin: de Gruyter.

Harcourt, Hugh R. 1963. "The Hebraic Void in the University." *Theology Today* 20, 347–61.

Harpham, Geoffrey Galt. 1987. *The Ascetic Imperative in Culture and Criticism*. Chicago: The University of Chicago Press.

Harris, H. S. 1972. *Hegel's Development: Toward the Sunlight 1770–1801*. Oxford: Clarendon Press.

Hart, Kevin. 1990. *The Trespass of the Sign: Deconstruction, Theology, and Philosophy*. Cambridge: Cambridge University Press.

Hartman, Geoffrey H. 1980. *Criticism in the Wilderness: The Study of Literature Today*. New Haven, CT: Yale University Press.

———. 1981. *Saving the Text: Literature/Derrida/Philosophy*. Baltimore: The Johns Hopkins University Press.

———. 1981a. "The Poetics of Prophecy." In Lawrence Lipking, ed.: *High Romantic Argument: Essays for M. H. Abrams*. Ithaca, NY: Cornell University Press.

———. 1985. "Tea and Totality: The Demand of Theory on Critical Style" [1984]. In Gregory S. Jay and David L. Miller, eds.: *After Strange Texts: The Role of Theory in the Study of Literature*. Tuscaloosa: The University of Alabama Press.

———. 1985a. "The Advanced Study of Literature: Elementary Considerations." *ADE Bulletin* 80, 11–14.

———. 1985b. "On the Jewish Imagination." *Prooftexts* 5: 3, 201–20.

———. 1986. "The Struggle for the Text." In Hartman and Budick 1986.

———. 1987. [Interview.] In Salusinszky 1987.

Hartman, Geoffrey H., and Sanford Budick, eds. 1986. *Midrash and Literature*. New Haven, CT: Yale University Press.

———. 1989. "Criticism and Restitution." *Tikkun* 4: 1, 29–32.

Harvey, David. 1989. *The Condition of Postmodernity: An Enquiry into the Origins of Cultural Change*. Oxford: Basil Blackwell.

Harvey, Irene E. 1986. *Derrida and the Economy of* Différance. Bloomington: Indiana University Press.

Haskell, Francis, and Nicholas Penny. 1981. *Taste and the Antique: The Lure of Classical Sculpture, 1500–1900*. New Haven, CT: Yale University Press.

Hatfield, Henry Caraway. 1943. *Winckelmann and his German Critics, 1755–1781. A Prelude to the Classical Age*. New York: King's Crown.

————. 1964. *Aesthetic Paganism in German Literature. From Winckelmann to the Death of Goethe*. Cambridge, MA: Harvard University Press.

Hauge, Hans. 1989. "Paul de Man as Theologian: Deconstruction as Dialectical Theology." In Luc Herman, Kris Humbeeck, and Geert Lernout, eds.: *(Dis)continuities: Essays on Paul de Man*. Amsterdam: Rodopi.

Hawkins, Harriett. 1990. *Classics and Trash: Traditions and Taboos in High Literature and Popular Modern Genres*. New York: Harvester Wheatsheaf.

Hearn, Francis. 1976–77. "Toward a Critical Theory of Play." *Telos* 30, 145–60.

Heath, Stephen. 1978. "Difference." *Screen* 19: 3, 51–112.

Hegel, G. W. F. 1895. *Lectures on the Philosophy of Religion* (3 vols.). Trans. E. B. Speirs and J. Burdon Sanderson. London: Kegan Paul, Trench, Trübner, & Co.

————. 1900. *The Philosophy of History*. Trans. J. Sibree. New York: The Colonial Press.

————. 1955. *Hegel's Lectures on the History of Philosophy*. Vol. 1. Trans. E. S. Haldane. New York: The Humanities Press.

————. 1962. *On Tragedy*. Eds. Anne and Henry Paolucci. New York: Harper & Row.

————. 1971. *Early Theological Writings*. Trans. T. M. Knox. Philadelphia: University of Pennsylvania Press.

————. 1975. *Lectures on the Philosophy of World History: Introduction—Reason in History*. Trans. H. B. Nisbet. Cambridge: Cambridge University Press.

————. 1975a. *Aesthetics: Lectures on Fine Art*. Trans. T. M. Knox. Oxford: Clarendon Press.

————. 1984. *The Letters*. Trans. Clark Butler and Christiane Seiler. Bloomington: Indiana University Press.

Heidegger, Martin. 1959. *An Introduction to Metaphysics* [1953]. Trans. Ralph Manheim. New Haven, CT: Yale University Press.

————. 1962. *Being and Time* [1927]. Trans. John Macquarrie and Edward Robinson. New York: Harper & Row.

————. 1967. "Hegel und die Griechen." In *Wegmarken*. Frankfurt: Klosterman.

————. 1969. *Identity and Difference* [1957]. Trans. Joan Stambaugh. New York: Harper & Row.

————. 1971. "What are Poets for?" [1946]. In *Poetry, Language, Thought*. Trans. Albert Hofstadter. New York: Harper & Row.

————. 1971a. "The Origin of the Work of Art" [1935]. In *Poetry, Language, Thought. See* Heidegger 1971.

————. 1971b. " ... Poetically Man Dwells ... " [1951]. In *Poetry, Language, Thought. See* Heidegger 1971.

————. 1971c. "Building Dwelling Thinking" [1951]. In *Poetry, Language, Thought. See* Heidegger 1971.

————. 1971d. "Language" [1950]. In *Poetry, Language, Thought. See* Heidegger 1971.

————. 1972. *Of Time and Being* [1969]. Trans. Joan Stambaugh. New York: Harper & Row.

————. 1977. "The End of Philosophy and the Task of Thinking" [1969]. Trans. Joan Stambaugh. In David Farrell Krell, ed.: *Basic Writings: From Being and Time (1927) to The Task of Thinking (1964)*. New York: Harper & Row.

————. 1984. "The Anaximander Fragment" [1950]. Trans. David Farrell Krell and Frank A. Capuzzi. In *Early Greek Thinking: The Dawn of Western Philosophy*. San Francisco: Harper & Row.

————. 1985. *Schelling's Treatise on the Essence of Human Freedom* [1936, 1941–43]. Trans. Joan Stambaugh. Athens, OH: Ohio University Press.

Heilman, Samuel C. 1983. *The People of the Book: Drama, Fellowship, and Religion.* Chicago: The University of Chicago Press.

Henrichs, Albert. 1984. "Loss of Self, Suffering, Violence: The Modern View of Dionysus from Nietzsche to Girard." *Harvard Studies in Classical Philology* 88, 205–40.

Herder, J. G. 1833. *The Spirit of Hebrew Poetry* [1782]. 2 vols. Trans. James Marsh. Burlington: Smith.

Herlitz, Georg. 1964. "Three Jewish Historians: Isaak Markus Jost—Heinrich Graetz—Eugen Taeubler; A Comparative Study." *Leo Baeck Institute Year Book* 9, 69–90.

Hernadi, Paul, ed. 1978. *What is Literature?* Bloomington: Indiana University Press.

Herren, Michael W., with Shirley Ann Brown. 1988. *The Sacred Nectar of the Greeks: The Study of Greek in the West in the Early Middle Ages.* London: King's College Medieval Studies.

Herzog, Don. 1989. *Happy Slaves: A Critique of Consent Theory.* Chicago: The University of Chicago Press.

Herzog, Isaac. 1974. *Judaism—Law and Ethics: Essays by the late Chief Rabbi Dr Isaac Herzog.* Selected by Chaim Herzog. London: The Soncino Press.

Highfield, Ron. 1989. *Barth and Rahner in Dialogue: Toward an Ecumenical Understanding of Sin and Evil.* New York: Peter Lang.

Himmelfarb, Milton. 1973. "Modern, Honorable, Masculine" [1967]. In *The Jews of Modernity.* New York: Basic Books.

Hine, Edward. 1871. *Forty-Seven Identifications of the British Nation with the Lost Ten Tribes of Israel. Founded upon Five Hundred Scripture Proofs.* London: S. W. Partridge & Co.

Hobbes, Thomas. 1962. *Leviathan or the Matter, Forme and Power of a Commonwealth Ecclesiasticall and Civil* [1651]. Selected by Richard S. Peters. New York: Collier Books.

Hodgson, Geoffrey. 1983. "The Ideology of the Liberal Consensus." In William Chafe and Harvard Sitkoff, eds.: *A History of Our Time: Readings on Postwar America.* New York: Oxford University Press.

Hogan, Patrick Colm. 1985. "The Political Economy of Criticism." In Gerald Graff and Reginald Gibbons, eds.: *Criticism in the University.* Evanston, IL: Northwestern University Press.

Hohendahl, Peter Uwe, ed. 1988. *A History of German Literary Criticism, 1730–1980* [1985]. Lincoln: University of Nebraska Press.

Hölderlin, Friedrich. 1980. *Poems and Fragments.* Trans. Michael Hamburger. Cambridge: Cambridge University Press.

———. 1984. *Hyperion or The Hermit in Greece* [1797–99]. Trans. Willard R. Trask. New York: Frederick Ungar.

———. 1988. *Essays and Letters on Theory.* Trans. Thomas Pfau. Albany: State University of New York Press.

Holeczek, Heinz. 1975. *Humanistische Bibelphilologie als Reformproblem bei Erasmus von Rotterdam, Thomas More und William Tyndale.* Leiden: E. J. Brill.

Holub, Robert. 1983. "Leftist Recreation: The Politicizing of Deconstruction." *Enclitic* 7: 1, 62–65.

Holzman, Michal. 1985. *Lukács's Road to God: The Early Criticism against its Pre-Marxist Background.* Lanham, MD: University Press of America.

Hook, Sidney. 1962. *From Hegel to Marx: Studies in the Intellectual Development of Karl Marx* [1950]. Ann Arbor: The University of Michigan Press.

Horkheimer, Max. 1970. "Was wir 'Sinn' nennen, wird verschwinden: *Spiegel*-Gespräch mit dem Philosophen Max Horkheimer." *Der Spiegel* 24: 1–2, 79–84.

———. 1974. "The German Jews" [1961]. In *Critique of Instrumental Reason: Lectures and Essays since the End of World War II* [1967]. Trans. Matthew J. O'Connell et al. New York: Seabury Press.

———. 1978. *Dawn and Decline.* Trans. Michael Shaw. New York: Seabury Press.

Horkheimer, Max, and Theodor W. Adorno. 1972. *Dialectic of Enlightenment [Philosophical Fragments]* [1944]. Trans. John Cumming. New York: Seabury Press.

Horowitz, Irving Louis. 1990. "Philo-Semitism and Anti-Semitism: Jewish Conspiracies and Totalitarian Sentiments." *Midstream* 36: 4, 17–22.

Horton, Robin. 1973. "Lévy-Bruhl, Durkheim and the Scientific Revolution." In Robin Horton and Ruth Finnegan, eds.: *Modes of Thought: Essays on Thinking in Western and Non-Western Societies.* London: Faber and Faber.

Horwitz, Rivka G. 1964. "Franz Rosenzweig on Language." *Judaism* 13, 393–406.

———. 1978. *Buber's Way to* I and Thou: *An Historical Analysis and the First Publication of Martin Buber's Lectures* "Religion als Gegenwart." Heidelberg: Verlag Lambert Schneider.

Howard, Dick. 1989. *Defining the Political.* Minneapolis: University of Minnesota Press.

Hsia, R. Po-Chia. 1989. *Social Discipline in the Reformation: Central Europe, 1550–1750.* London: Routledge.

Hübner, Kurt. 1983. *Critique of Scientific Reason* [1978]. Trans. Paul R. Dixon, Jr., and Hollis M. Dixon. Chicago: University of Chicago Press.

Hudson, Anne. 1988. *The Premature Reformation: Wycliffite Texts and Lollard History.* Oxford: Oxford University Press.

Hume, Kathryn. 1985. *Fantasy and Mimesis: Responses to Reality in Western Literature.* London: Methuen.

Hutchinson, Peter. 1983. *Games Authors Play.* London: Methuen.

Hyland, Drew A. 1984. *The Question of Play.* Lanham, MD: University Press of America.

Hyma, Albert. 1937. *Christianity, Capitalism and Communism: A Historical Analysis.* Ann Arbor, MI: Published by the author.

Irigaray, Luce. 1987. "Sexual Difference" [1984]. Trans. Seán Hand. In Toril Moi, ed.: *French Feminist Thought.* Oxford: Basil Blackwell.

Jabès, Edmond. 1985. "'There is such a Thing as Jewish Writing . . . '" Trans. Rosmarie Waldrop. In Gould 1985.

———. 1986. "The Key." Trans. Rosmarie Waldrop. In Hartman and Budick 1986.

———. 1987. "My Itinerary." Trans. Rosmarie Waldrop. *Studies in 20th-Century Literature* 12: 1, 3–12.

Jakobson, Roman. 1960. "Closing Statement: Linguistics and Poetics." In Thomas Sebeok, ed.: *Style in Language*. Cambridge, MA: The MIT Press.

———. 1966. "Grammatical Parallelism and its Russian Facet." *Language* 42: 2, 399–429.

———. 1968. "Poetry of Grammar and Grammar of Poetry" [1961]. *Lingua* 21, 597–609.

———. 1980. "A Postscript to the Discussion on Grammar of Poetry." *Diacritics* 10: 1, 22–35.

Jameson, Fredric. 1971. *Marxism and Form: Twentieth-Century Dialectical Theories of Literature*. Princeton: Princeton University Press.

———. 1988. "The Vanishing Mediator; or, Max Weber as Storyteller" [1973]. In *The Ideologies of Theory: Essays 1971–1986. Volume 2: The Syntax of History*. Minneapolis: University of Minnesota Press.

Jarausch, Konrad H. 1990. *The Unfree Professions: German Lawyers, Teachers, and Engineers, 1900–1950*. Oxford: Oxford Universty Press.

Jardine, Alice A. 1985. *Gynesis: Configurations of Woman and Modernity*. Ithaca, NY: Cornell University Press.

Jay, Martin. 1973. *The Dialectical Imagination: A History of the Frankfurt School and the Institute for Social Research, 1923–1950*. Boston: Little, Brown and Company.

———. 1976. "Politics of Translation: Siegfried Kracauer and Walter Benjamin on the Buber-Rosenzweig Bible." *Leo Baeck Institute Year Book* 21, 3–24.

———. 1980. "The Jews and the Frankfurt School: Critical Theory's Analysis of Anti-Semitism." *New German Critique* 19, 137–49.

———. 1984. *Marxism and Totality: The Adventures of a Concept from Lukács to Habermas*. Berkeley: University of California Press.

Jebb, John. 1820. *Sacred Literature*. London: Cadell & Davies.

Jenkyns, Richard. 1980. *The Victorians and Ancient Greece*. Cambridge, MA: Harvard University Press.

Johnson, Barbara, ed. 1982. "The Pedagogical Imperative: Teaching as a Literary Genre." *Yale French Studies* 63.

Johnston, Otto. 1989. *The Myth of a Nation: Literature and Politics in Prussia under Napoleon*. London: Camden House.

Jusdanis, Gregory. 1991. *Belated Modernity and Aesthetic Culture: Inventing National Literature*. Minneapolis: University of Minnesota Press.

Kain, Philip J. 1982. *Schiller, Hegel, and Marx: State, Society, and the Aesthetic Ideal of Ancient Greece*. Kingston/Montreal: McGill-Queen's University Press.

Kanfer, Stefan. 1989. *A Summer World: The Attempt to Build a Jewish Eden in the Catskills, from the Days of the Ghetto to the Rise and Decline of the Borscht Belt*. New York: Farrar, Straus & Giroux.

Kasson, John F. 1990. *Rudeness & Civility: Manners in Nineteenth-Century Urban America*. New York: Hill & Wang.

Katz, Jacob. 1964. "The Term 'Jewish Emancipation': Its Origins and Historical Impact." In Alexander Altmann, ed.: *Studies in Nineteenth-Century Jewish Intellectual History*. Cambridge, MA: Harvard University Press.

———. 1985. "German Culture and the Jews." In Reinharz and Schatzberg 1985.

Kaufman, William E. 1976. *Contemporary Jewish Philosophies*. New York: Reconstructionist Press and Behrman House.

Kaufmann, Walter. 1970. "*I and Thou*: A Prologue." In Martin Buber: *I and Thou*. Trans. Walter Kaufmann. New York: Charles Scribner's Sons.

Kazin, Alfred. 1965. *On Native Grounds: An Interpretation of Modern American Prose Literature* [1942]. New York: Harcourt, Brace & World.

Kelley, Mary. 1984. *Private Woman, Public Stage: Literary Domesticity in Nineteenth-Century America*. Oxford: Oxford University Press.

Kelly, Christopher. 1987. *Rousseau's Exemplary Life: The Confessions as Political Philosophy*. Ithaca, NY: Cornell University Press.

Kermode, Frank. 1983. *The Classic: Literary Images of Permanence and Change* [1975]. Cambridge, MA: Harvard University Press.

———. 1985. *Forms of Attention*. Chicago: The University of Chicago Press.

———. 1987. "The Canon." In Alter and Kermode 1987.

Kestner, Joseph A. 1989. *Mythology and Misogyny: The Social Discourse of Nineteenth-Century British Classical-Subject Painting*. Madison: University of Wisconsin Press.

Kierkegaard, Søren. 1989. *Prefaces: Light Reading for Certain Classes as the Occasion may Require* [1844]. Trans. William McDonald. Tallahassee: The Florida State University Press.

Kilcullen, John. 1988. *Sincerity and Truth: Essays on Arnauld, Bayle, and Toleration*. Oxford: Clarendon Press.

Kilgour, Maggie. 1990. *From Communion to Cannibalism: An Anatomy of Metaphors of Incorporation*. Princeton: Princeton University Press.

Kiosse, Hara. 1987. "To 'mavrisma' tis theas." *To Vima*, 15 November, 63.

Kitaj, R. B. 1989. *First Diasporist Manifesto*. London: Thames and Hudson.

Kluback, William. 1989. *The Legacy of Hermann Cohen*. Atlanta: Scholars Press.

Kluckhohn, Clyde. 1961. *Anthropology and the Classics*. Providence: Brown University Press.

Knoll, Samson B. 1982. "Herder's Concept of *Humanität*." In Koepke 1982.

Koepke, Wulf, ed. 1982. *Johann Gottfried Herder: Innovator Through the Ages*. Bonn: Bouvier Verlag Herbert Grundmann.

———. 1982a. "Truth and Revelation: On Herder's Theological Writings." In Koepke 1982.

Koestenbaum, Wayne. 1989. *Double Talk: The Erotics of Male Literary Collaboration*. New York: Routledge.

Koester, Helmut H. 1965. "Paul and Hellenism." In J. Philip Hyatt, ed.: *The Bible in Modern Scholarship*. Nashville, TN: Abingdon Press.

Kojève, Alexandre. 1969. *Introduction to the Reading of Hegel: Lectures on the Phenomenology of the Spirit* [1947]. Trans. James H. Nichols, Jr. New York: Basic Books.

Kolb, David. 1987. *The Critique of Pure Modernity: Hegel, Heidegger, and After*. Chicago: The University of Chicago Press.

Korshin, Paul J. 1977. "The Development of Abstracted Typology in England, 1650–1820." In Miner 1977.

———. 1982. *Typologies in England, 1650–1820*. Princeton: Princeton University Press.

Kraus, Hans-Joachim. 1956. *Geschichte der historisch-kritischen Erforschung des Alten Testaments*. Neukirchen: Verlag der Buchhandlung des Erziehungsvereins.

Kristeva, Julia. 1990. *Strangers to Ourselves* [1988]. Trans. Leon Roudiez. New York: Columbia University Press.

Krüger, Gustav. 1966. "The 'Theology of Crisis.'" In Warren Wagar, ed.: *European Intellectual History since Darwin and Marx*. New York: Harper & Row.

Krupnick, Mark. 1986. *Lionel Trilling and the Fate of Cultural Criticism*. Evanston, IL: Northwestern University Press.

Kugel, James L. 1981. *The Idea of Biblical Poetry: Parallelism and its History*. New Haven, CT: Yale University Press.

Kuhn, Albert J. 1956. "English Deism and the Development of Romantic Mythological Syncretism." *PMLA* 71: 5, 1094–1116.

Labovitz, Esther K. 1987. *The Myth of the Heroine: The Female Bildungsroman in the Twentieth Century—Dorothy Richardson, Simone de Bauvoir, Doris Lessing, Christa Wolf*. New York: Peter Lang.

Laclau, Ernesto, and Chantal Mouffe. 1985. *Hegemony and Socialist Strategy: Towards a Radical Democratic Politics*. Trans. Winston Moore and Paul Cammack. London: Verso.

Lacoue-Labarthe, Philippe. 1978. "The Caesura of the Speculative." Trans. Robert Eisenhauer. *Glyph* 4, 57–84.

———. 1982. "Transcendence Ends in Politics." Trans. Peter Caws. *Social Research* 49: 2, 405–40.

———. 1989. "Hölderlin and the Greeks" [1979]. In Christopher Fynsk, ed.: *Typography: Mimesis, Philosophy, Politics*. Cambridge, MA: Harvard University Press.

———. 1990. *Heidegger, Art and Politics: The Fiction of the Political* [1987]. Trans. Chris Turner. Oxford: Basil Blackwell.

Lacoue-Labarthe, Philippe, and Jean-Luc Nancy. 1988. *The Literary Absolute: The Theory of Literature in German Romanticism* [1978]. Trans. Philip Barnard and Cheryl Lester. Albany: State University of New York Press.

———. 1990. "The Nazi Myth" [1980]. Trans. Brian Holmes. *Critical Inquiry* 16: 2, 291–312.

Lambropoulos, Vassilis. 1989. "Violence and the Liberal Imagination: The Representation of Hellenism in Matthew Arnold." In Nancy Armstrong and Leonard Tennenhouse, eds.: *The Violence of Representation: Literature and the History of Violence*. London: Routledge.

Lamm, Norman. 1990. *Torah Umadda: The Encounter of Religious Learning and Worldly Knowledge in the Jewish Tradition*. Northvale, NJ: Jason Aronson.

Lamont, Michèle. 1987. "How to Become a Dominant French Philosopher: The Case of Jacques Derrida." *American Journal of Sociology* 93: 3, 584–622.

Lampe, G. W. H., and K. J. Woolcombe, eds. 1957. *Essays in Typology*. London: SCM.

Landes, Joan B. 1988. *Women and the Public Sphere in the Age of the French Revolution*. Ithaca, NY: Cornell University Press.

Langan, Janine D. 1986. *Hegel and Mallarmé*. Lanham, MD: University Press of America.

Lauter, Paul. 1985. "Race and Gender in the Shaping of the American Literary Canon" [1983]. In Judith Newton and Deborah Rosenfelt, eds.: *Feminist Criticism and Social Change*. New York: Methuen.

Lears, T. J. Jackson. 1985. "The Concept of Cultural Hegemony: Problems and Possibilities." *American Historical Review* 90: 3, 567–93.

Leidner, Alan C. 1989. "A Titan in Extenuating Circumstances: Sturm und Drang and the *Kraftmensch*." *PMLA* 104: 2, 178–89.

Lem, Stanislaw. 1979. *A Perfect Vacuum* [1971]. Trans. Michael Kandel. London: Secker and Warburg.

———. 1984. *Imaginary Magnitude* [1981]. Trans. Marc E. Heine. San Diego: Helen and Kurt Wolff/Harcourt Brace Jovanovich.

———. 1985. *Microworlds: Writings on Science Fiction and Fantasy*. Trans. Franz Rottensteiner. San Diego: Helen and Kurt Wolff/Harcourt Brace Jovanovich.

———. 1986. *One Human Minute* [1985]. Trans. Catherine S. Leach. San Diego: Helen and Kurt Wolff/Harcourt Brace Jovanovich.

Lemon, Lee T. 1985. *Portraits of the Artist in Contemporary Fiction*. Lincoln: University of Nebraska Press.

Lentricchia, Frank. 1980. *After the New Criticism*. London: The Athlone Press.

Leventhal, Robert S. 1986. "The Emergence of Philological Discourse in the German States, 1770–1810." *Isis* 77, 243–60.

Levi, A. H. T. 1987. "The Breakdown of Scholasticism and the Significance of Evangelical Humanism." In Gerard J. Hughes, ed.: *The Philosophical Assessment of Theology*. Washington, DC: Georgetown University Press.

Levin, Gabriel. 1985. "What Different Things Link up: Hellenism in Contemporary Hebrew Poetry." *Prooftexts* 5: 3, 221–43.

Levin, Samuel R. 1962. *Linguistic Structures in Poetry*. The Hague: Mouton.

Levinas, Emmanuel. 1967. "Martin Buber and the Theory of Knowledge" [1976]. In Paul Schilpp and Maurice Friedman, eds.: *The Philosophy of Martin Buber*. La Salle, IL: Open Court.

———. 1968. "On the Trail of the Other" [1963]. Trans. Daniel J. Hoy. *Philosophy Today* 10, 34–45.

———. 1968a. *Quatre lectures talmudiques*. Paris: Minuit.

———. 1969. *Totality and Infinity: An Essay on Exteriority* [1960]. Trans. Alphonso Lingis. Pittsburgh: Duquesne University Press.

———. 1969a. "Judaism and the Feminine Element" [1960]. Trans. Edith Wyschogrod. *Judaism* 18: 2, 30–38.

———. 1976. *"Tout autrement"* [1973]. In *Noms propres*. Paris: Fata Morgana.

———. 1979. "To Love the Torah more than God" [1955]. Trans. Helen A. Stephenson and Richard I. Sugarman. *Judaism* 28: 2, 217–20.

———. 1981. *Otherwise than Being or Beyond Essence* [1974]. Trans. [of the 2nd ed., 1978] Alphonso Lingis. The Hague: Martinus Nijhoff.

———. 1982. *"Questions et réponses"* (interview) [1977]. In *De Dieu qui vient à l'idée*. Paris: Vrin.

———. 1982a. *"Le Dialogue: Conscience de soi et proximité du prochain"* [1980]. In *De Dieu qui vient à l'idée*. See Levinas 1982.

———. 1983. "Beyond Intentionality." Trans. Kathleen McLaughlin. In Montefiore 1983.

———. 1984. "Martin Buber, Gabriel Marcel and Philosophy" [1978]. Trans. Esther Kameron. In Haim Gordon and Jochanan Bloch, eds.: *Martin Buber: A Centenary Volume*. New York: Ktav Publishing House.

———. 1985. *Ethics and Infinity: Conversations with Philippe Nemo* [1982]. Trans. Richard A. Cohen. Pittsburgh: Duquesne University Press.

———. 1987. "Philosophy and the Idea of Infinity" [1957]. In *Collected Philosophical Papers*. Trans. Alphonso Lingis. Dordrecht: Martinus Nijhoff.

———. 1987a. "Meaning and Sense" [1972]. In *Collected Philosophical Papers*. See Levinas 1987.

———. 1987b. "No Identity" [1970]. In *Collected Philosophical Papers*. See Levinas 1987.

———. 1987c. "God and Philosophy" [1975]. In *Collected Philosophical Papers*. See Levinas 1987.

———. 1988. "The Paradox of Morality: An Interview with Emmanuel Levinas." Trans. Andrew Benjamin and Tamra Wright. In Bernasconi and Wood 1988.

———. 1989. "The State of Caesar and the State of David" [1971]. Trans. Roland Lack. In Seán Hand, ed.: *The Levinas Reader*. Oxford: Basil Blackwell.

———. 1989a. "Politics After!" [1979]. Trans. Ronald Lack. In *The Levinas Reader*. See Levinas 1989.

———. 1989b. "Assimilation and New Culture" [1980]. Trans. Ronald Lack. In *The Levinas Reader*. See Levinas 1989.

———. 1990. *Difficult Freedom: Essays on Judaism* [1963]. Trans. Seán Hand. Baltimore: The Johns Hopkins University Press.

Levine, Lawrence W. 1988. *Highbrow/Lowbrow: The Emergence of Cultural Hierarchy in America*. Cambridge, MA: Harvard University Press.

Levine, Molly Myerowitz. 1989. "The Challenge of *Black Athena* to Classics Today." In *Arethusa* 1989, 7–16.

Lévi-Strauss, Claude. 1963. *Structural Anthropology* [Vol. I] [1958]. Trans. Claire Jacobson and Brooke Grundfest Schoepf. New York: Basic Books.

Lewalski, Barbara Kiefer. 1979. *Protestant Poetics and the Seventeenth-Century Religious Lyric*. Princeton: Princeton University Press.

Lewisohn, Ludwig. 1932. *Expression in America*. New York: Harper and Brothers.

Libertson, Joseph. 1982. *Proximity: Levinas, Blanchot, Bataille and Communication*. The Hague: Martinus Nijhoff.

Lichtheim, George. 1968. "Socialism and the Jews." *Dissent* 15: 4, 314–42.

Liebeschütz, Hans. 1964. "Max Weber's Historical Interpretation of Judaism." *Leo Baeck Institute Year Book* 9, 41–68.

———. 1968. "Hermann Cohen and his Historical Background." *Leo Baeck Institute Year Book* 12, 3–33.

———. 1971. "Aby Warburg (1866–1929) as Interpreter of Civilisation.' *Leo Baeck Institute Yearbook* 16, 225–36.

Linder, Staffan Buvenstam. 1970. *The Harried Leisure Class*. New York: Columbia University Press.

Lindner, Burkhardt. 1986. "The *Passagen-Werk*, the *Berliner Kindheit*, and the Archaeology of the 'Recent Past.'" Trans. Carol B. Ludtke. *New German Critique* 39, 25–46.

Llewelyn, John. 1988. "Jewgreek or Greekjew." In John C. Sallis, Giuseppina Moneta, and Jacques Taminiaux, eds.: *The Collegium Phaenomenologicum: The First Ten Years*. Dordrecht: Kluwer Academic Publishers.

Lodge, David. 1977. *The Modes of Modern Writing: Metaphor, Metonymy, and the Typology of Modern Literature*. Ithaca, NY: Cornell University Press.

Loewenstein, David. 1990. *Milton and the Drama of History: Historical Vision, Iconoclasm, and the Literary Imagination*. Cambridge: Cambridge University Press.

Lord, Albert B. 1960. *The Singer of Tales*. Cambridge, MA: Harvard University Press.

Loriggio, Francesco. 1988. "The Anthropology in/of Fiction: Novels about Voyages." In Fernando Poyatos, ed.: *Literary Anthropology: A New Interdisciplinary Approach to People, Signs and Literature*. Philadelphia: John Benjamins.

Love, Nancy S. 1986. *Marx, Nietzsche, and Modernity*. New York: Columbia University Press.

Lovejoy, Athur O. 1932. "The Parallel of Deism and Classicism." *Modern Philology* 29, 281–99.

Lowenthal, Leo, and Norbert Guterman. 1949. *Prophets of Deceit: A Study of the Techniques of the American Agitator*. New York: Harper and Brothers.

Löwith, Karl. 1966. "M. Heidegger and F. Rosenzweig: A Postscript to *Being and Time*" [1942]. In Arnold Levison, ed.: *Nature, History, and Existentialism, and Other Essays in the Philosophy of History*. Evanston, IL: Northwestern University Press.

Lowth, Robert. 1816. *Lectures on the Sacred Poetry of the Hebrews* [1753]. 2 vols. Trans. G. Gregory [1787]. London: Ogles, Duncan, & Cochran.

Löwy, Michael. 1980. "Jewish Messianism and Libertarian Utopia in Central Europe (1900–1933)." Trans. Renée B. Larrier. *New German Critique* 20, 105–115.

Luft, Sandra Rudnick. 1987. "The Legitimacy of Hans Blumenberg's Conception of Originary Activity." *Annals of Scholarship* 7: 1, 3–36.

———. 1988. "'Secular Theology' in the Modern Age." *Journal of the American Academy of Religion* 54: 4, 741–50.

Luhmann, Niklas. 1982. "The Differentiation of Society" [1977]. Trans. Stephen Holmes. In *The Differentiation of Society*. Trans. Stephen Holmes and Charles Larmore. New York: Columbia University Press.

———. 1985. "The Work of Art and the Self-Reproduction of Art." Trans. David Roberts. *Thesis Eleven* 12, 4–27.

Lukács, Georg. 1970. "The Old Culture and the New Culture" [1920]. Trans. Paul Breines. *Telos* 5, 21–30.

———. 1971. *The Theory of the Novel: A Historico-Philosophical Essay on the Forms of Great Epic Literature* [1916]. Trans. Anna Bostock. Cambridge, MA: The MIT Press.

———. 1978. *Goethe and his Age* [1947]. Trans. Robert Anchor. New York: Howard Fertig.

———. 1978a. "Schiller's Theory of Modern Literature" [1935]. *See* Lukács 1978.

———. 1978b. "Hölderlin's *Hyperion*" [1934]. *See* Lukács 1978.

Luke, Carmen. 1989. *Pedagogy, Printing, and Protestantism: The Discourse on Childhood*. Albany: State University of New York Press.

Luther, Martin. 1974. "Temporal Authority: To what Extent it should be Obeyed" [1523]. Trans. J. J. Schindel; rev. Walther I. Brandt. In J. M. Porter, ed.: *Selected Political Writings.* Philadelphia: Fortress Press.

Lyotard, Jean-François. 1988. *The Differend: Phrases in Dispute* [1983]. Trans. Georges Van Den Abbeele. Minneapolis: University of Minnesota Press.

———. 1990. *Heidegger and "the jews"* [1988]. Trans. Andreas Michel and Mark Roberts. Minneapolis: University of Minnesota Press.

Lyotard, Jean-Francois, and Jean-Loup Thébaud. 1985. *Just Gaming* [1979]. Trans. Wlad Godzich. Minneapolis: University of Minnesota Press.

Macaulay, T. Babington. 1878. "Milton" [1825]. In *Essays Critical and Miscellaneous.* New York: D. Appleton and Company.

MacCabe, Colin, ed. 1986. *High Theory / Low Culture: Analysing Popular Television and Film.* New York: St. Martin's Press.

MacCannell, Dean. 1975. *The Tourist: A New Theory of the Leisure Class.* New York: Schocken Books.

Macdonald, Duncan Black. 1933. *The Hebrew Literary Genius: An Interpretation being an Introduction to the Reading of the Old Testament.* Princeton: Princeton University Press.

Macdonald, Ronald R. 1988. *The Burial-Places of Memory: Epic Underworlds in Vergil, Dante, and Milton.* Amherst: The University of Massachusetts Press.

Macfarlane, Alan. 1978. *The Origins of English Individualism: The Family, Property, and Social Transition.* Oxford: Basil Blackwell.

MacIntyre, Alasdair. 1968. *Marxism and Christianity.* New York: Schocken Books.

Macken, John. 1990. *The Autonomy Theme in the Church Dogmatics of Karl Barth and in Current Barth Criticism.* Cambridge: Cambridge University Press.

Mackey, Louis. 1983. "Slouching toward Bethlehem: Deconstructive Strategies in Theology." *The Anglican Theological Review* 65, 255–70.

Macquarrie, John. 1973. *An Existentialist Theology: A Comparison of Heidegger and Bultmann.* Harmondsworth: Penguin.

Madsen, William. 1968. *From Shadowy Types to Truth: Studies in Milton's Symbolism.* New Haven, CT: Yale University Press.

Maffesoli, Michel. 1988. *Le temps des tribus.* Paris: Méridiens Klincksieck.

Magnus, Laurie. 1928. "The Legacy [of Israel] in Modern Literature." In Bevan and Singer 1928.

Mahoney, John L. 1986. *The Whole Internal Universe: Imitation and the New Defense of Poetry in British Criticism, 1660–1830.* New York: Fordham University Press.

Mallarmé, [Stéphane]. 1977. *The Poems.* Trans. Keith Bosley. Harmondsworth: Penguin.

Mann, Thomas. 1968. *Doctor Faustus: The Life of the German Composer Adrian Leverkühn as Told by a Friend* [1947]. Trans. H. T. Lowe-Porter. Harmonsworth: Penguin.

Marcus, Judith, and Zoltán Tar. 1986. "The Judaic Element in the Teachings of the Frankfurt School." *Leo Baeck Institute Year Book* 31, 339–53.

Marcuse, Herbert. 1966. *Eros and Civilization: A Philosophical Inquiry into Freud* [1955]. Boston: Beacon Press.

———. 1969. *An Essay on Liberation.* Boston: Beacon Press.

————. 1978. "Der deutsche Künstlerroman" [1922]. In *Schriften*. Vol. 1. Frankfurt: Suhrkamp.

Marin, Louis. 1989. *Food for Thought*. Trans. Mette Hjort. Baltimore: The Johns Hopkins University Press.

Markish, Shimon. 1986. *Erasmus and the Jews* [1979]. Trans. Anthony Olcott. Chicago: The University of Chicago Press.

Márkus, György. 1983. "Life and the Soul: The Young Lukács and the Problem of Culture." Trans. Michael Clark. In Agnes Heller, ed.: *Lukács Revalued*. Oxford: Basil Blackwell.

Marshall, Donald G. 1989. "Christian Criticism: Can it/Should it Exist?" Paper presented at the MLA Convention in panel with the same title.

Marshall, Robert C. 1980. "Heroes and Hebrews: The Priest in the Promised Land." *American Ethnologist* 6: 4, 772–90.

Martin, Bernard, ed. 1970. *Great Twentieth Century Jewish Philosophers: Shestov-Rosenzweig-Buber*. London: Collier-Macmillan.

Martin, Bill, and Ivan Szelényi. 1987. "Beyond Cultural Capital: Toward a Theory of Symbolic Domination." In Ron Eyerman, Lennart G. Svensson, and Thomas Söderqvist, eds.: *Intellectuals, Universities, and the State in Western Modern Societies*. Berkeley: University of California Press.

Martin, James Alfred Jr. 1990. *Beauty and Holiness: The Dialogue between Aesthetics and Religion*. Princeton: Princeton University Press.

Martin, Wallace. 1983. "Introduction." In Arac, Godzich, and Martin 1983.

Marx, Karl. 1971. "On the Jewish Question" [1844]. In David McLellan, ed. and trans.: *Early Texts*. New York: Barnes & Noble.

Marx, Karl, and Friedrich Engels. 1956. *The Holy Family, or Critique of Critical Critique* [1845]. Trans. R. Dixon. Moscow: Foreign Languages Publishing House.

Marx-Scouras, Danielle. 1987. "The Dissident Politics of *Tel Quel*." *L'Esprit Créateur* 27: 2, 101–8.

Matejka, Ladislav, ed. 1964. *Two Essays on Poetic Language*. Ann Arbor: Michigan Slavic Materials.

Mazlish, Bruce. 1989. *A New Science: The Breakdown of Connections and the Birth of Sociology*. Oxford: Oxford University Press.

McCarthy, Thomas. 1989–80. "The Politics of the Ineffable: Derrida's Deconstructionism." *The Philosophical Forum* 21: 1–2, 146–68.

McClelland, J. S. 1989. *The Crowd and the Mob: From Plato to Canetti*. Winchester, MA: Unwin Hyman.

McCollester, Charles. 1970. "The Philosophy of Emmanuel Levinas." *Judaism* 29: 3, 344–54.

McGrath, Alister E. 1986. "Reformation to Enlightenment." In Paul Avis, ed.: *The History of Christian Theology*. Vol. 1: *The Science of Theology*. Grand Rapids, MI: Wm. B. Eerdmans.

————. 1988. *Reformation Thought: An Introduction*. Oxford: Basil Blackwell.

McGrath, William. 1974. *Dionysian Art and Populist Politics in Austria*. New Haven, CT: Yale University Press.

McHale, Brian. 1987. *Postmodernist Fiction*. New York: Methuen.

McKnight, Edgar V. 1985. *The Bible and the Reader: An Intoduction to Literary Criticism*. Philadelphia: Fortress Press.

McLaren, Peter L. 1988. "Culture or Canon? Critical Pedagogy and the Politics of Literacy." *Harvard Educational Review* 58: 2, 213–34.

Megill, Allan. 1985. *Prophets of Extremity: Nietzsche, Heidegger, Foucault, Derrida.* Berkeley: University of California Press.

Mehlman, Jeffrey. 1983. *Legacies of Anti-Semitism in France.* Minneapolis: University of Minnesota Press.

Meixner, Horst. 1971. *Romantischer Figuralismus: Kritische Studien zu Romanen von Arnim, Eichendorff und Hoffmann.* Frankfurt am Main: Athenäum Verlag.

Meltzer, Francoise. 1987. *Salomé and the Dance of Writing: Portraits of Mimesis in Literature.* Chicago: The University of Chicago Press.

Melville, Stephen W. 1986. *Philosophy beside Itself: On Deconstruction and Modernism.* Minneapolis: University of Minnesota Press.

Mendelssohn, Moses. 1983. *Jerusalem or On Religious Power and Judaism* [1783]. Trans. Allan Arkush. Hanover, NH: University Press of New England.

Mendes-Flohr, Paul R. 1982. "The Study of the Jewish Intellectual: Some Methodological Proposals." In F. Malino and P. Cohen Albert, eds.: *Essays in Modern Jewish History.* Rutherford, NJ: Fairleigh Dickinson University Press.

———. 1989. *From Mysticism to Dialogue: Martin Buber's Transformation of German Social Thought.* Detroit: Wayne State University Press.

Menhennet, Alan. 1973. *Order and Freedom: Literature and Society in Germany from 1720 to 1805.* New York: Basic Books.

Menninghaus, Winfried. 1988. "Walter Benjamin's Theory of Myth" [1983]. Trans. Gary Smith. In Gary Smith, ed.: *On Walter Benjamin: Critical Essays and Recollections.* Cambridge, MA: The MIT Press.

Merlan, Philip. 1948. "Parva Hamanniana: J. G. Hamann as a Spokesman of the Middle Class." *Journal of the History of Ideas* 9: 3, 380–84.

Merquior, J. G. 1986. *Western Marxism.* London: Paladin.

Meschonnic, Henri. 1970. "Pour une poétique de la traduction." In *Les cinq rouleaux.* Paris: Gallimard.

———. 1982. *Critique du rythme: Anthropologie historique du langage.* Lagrasse: Verdier.

———. 1988. "Interview." *Diacritics* 18: 3, 93–111.

———. 1988a. *Modernité, modernité.* Paris: Verdier.

Meschonnic, Henri, with Alex Derczansky, Olivier Mongin, and Paul Thibaud. 1988a. "Poetics and Politics: A Round Table" [1977]. Trans. Gabriella Bedetti. *New Literary History* 19: 3, 453–66.

Metzer, Bruce M. 1987. *The Canon of the New Testament: Its Origin, Development, and Significance.* Oxford: Oxford University Press.

Meyer, Michael A. 1975. "Where does the Modern Period of Jewish History Begin?" *Judaism* 24: 3, 329–38.

———. 1988. *Response to Modernity: A History of the Reform Movement in Judaism.* Oxford: Oxford University Press.

Miles, Peter, and Malcolm Smith. 1987. *Cinema, Literature and Society: Elite and Mass Culture in Interwar Britain.* London: Croom Helm.

Mileur, Jean-Pierre. 1990. *The Critical Romance: The Critic as Reader, Writer, Hero.* Madison: University of Wisconsin Press.

Miller, Ronald H. 1989. *Dialogue and Disagreement: Franz Rosenzweig's Relevance to Contemporary Jewish-Christian Understanding.* Lanham, MD: University Press of America.

Miner, Earl, ed. 1971. *Seventeenth-Century Imagery: Essays on Uses of Figurative Language from Donne to Farquhar.* Berkeley: University of California Press.

———, ed. 1977. *Literary Uses of Typology, from the Late Middle Ages to the Present.* Princeton: Princeton University Press.

Momigliano, Arnaldo. 1966. "George Grote and the Study of Greek History" [1952]. In *Studies in Historiography.* New York: Harper & Row.

———. 1975. *Alien Wisdom: The Limits of Hellenization.* Cambridge: Cambridge University Press.

———. 1977. "The Ancient City of Fustel de Coulanges" [1970]. In *Essays in Ancient and Modern Historiography.* Middletown, CT: Wesleyan University Press.

———. 1977a. "J. G. Droysen between Greeks and Jews" [1970]. In *Essays in Ancient and Modern Historiography. See* Momigliano 1977.

Monk, Samuel H. 1960. *The Sublime: A Study of Critical Theories in XVIII-Century England* [1935]. Ann Arbor: The University of Michigan Press.

Montefiore, Alan, ed. 1983. *Philosophy in France Today.* Cambridge: Cambridge University Press.

Montgomery, Marshall. 1923. *Friedrich Hölderlin and the German Neo-Hellenic Movement.* London: Oxford University Press.

Moran, William L. 1962. "A Kingdom of Priests." In John L. McKenzie, ed.: *The Bible in Current Catholic Thought.* New York: Herder and Herder.

Morawski, Stefan. 1968. "Mimesis—Lukács' Universal Principle." *Science and Society* 32: 1, 26–38.

Moretti, Franco. 1988. *The Way of the World: The Bildungsroman in European Culture.* London: Verso.

Morgan, Donn F. 1990. *Between Text and Community: The Writings in Canonical Interpretation.* Minneapolis: Fortress Press.

Morrison, Karl. 1982. *The Mimetic Tradition of Reform in the West.* Princeton: Princeton University Press.

Mort, Frank. 1987. *Dangerous Sexualities: Medico-Moral Politics in England since 1830.* London: Routledge & Kegan Paul.

Morton, Michael M. 1982. "Herder and the Possibility of Literature: Rationalism and Poetry in Eighteenth-Century Germany." In Koepke 1982.

Mosse, George L. 1970. *Germans and Jews: The Right, the Left, and the Search for a 'Third Force' in Pre-Nazi Germany.* New York: Howard Fertig.

———. 1975. *The Nationalization of the Masses: Political Symbolism and Mass Movements in Germany from the Napoleonic Wars through the Third Reich.* New York: Howard Fertig.

———. 1978. *Toward the Final Solution: A History of European Racism.* New York: Howard Fertig.

———. 1985. *German Jews beyond Judaism.* Bloomington: Indiana University Press; Cincinnati: Hebrew Union College Press.

———. 1985a. "Jewish Emancipation: Between *Bildung* and Respectability." In Reinharz and Schatzberg 1985.

Motte, Warren F. Jr. 1990. *Questioning Edmond Jabès.* Lincoln: University of Nebraska Press.

Mouw, Richard J. 1990. *The God who Commands.* Notre Dame, IN: University of Notre Dame Press.

Munich, Adrienne. 1985. "Feminist Criticism and the Literary Canon." In Gayle Greene and Coppelia Kahn, eds.: *Making a Difference: Feminist Literary Criticism*. New York: Methuen.

Murphy, John W. 1989. *Postmodern Social Analysis and Criticism*. Westport, CT: Greenwood Press.

Murray, Gilbert. 1907. *The Rise of the Greek Epic, Being a Course of Lectures Delivered at Harvard University*. Oxford: Clarendon Press.

Murray, Penelope, ed. 1989. *Genius: The History of an Idea*. Oxford: Basil Blackwell.

Murrin, Michael. 1980. *The Allegorical Epic: Essays in Its Rise and Decline*. Chicago: The University of Chicago Press.

Nadel, Ira B. 1989. *Joyce and the Jews: Culture and Texts*. Iowa City: University of Iowa Press.

Nauta, Lolle. 1985. "Historical Roots of the Concept of Autonomy in Western Philosophy." *Praxis International* 4: 4, 363–77.

Needler, Howard I. 1982. "Sacred Books and Sacral Criticism." *New Literary History* 13: 3, 393–409.

Nehamas, Alexander. 1985. *Nietzsche: Life as Literature*. Cambridge, MA: Harvard University Press.

Neher, André. 1981. *The Exile of the Word: From the Silence of the Bible to the Silence of Auschwitz* [1970]. Trans. David Maisel. Philadelphia: The Jewish Publication Society of America.

———. 1990. *They Made Their Souls Anew* [1979]. Trans. David Maisel. Albany: State University of New York Press.

Nerlich, Michael. 1987. *Ideology of Adventure: Studies in Modern Consciousness, 1100–1750* [1977]. Trans. Ruth Crowley. Minneapolis: University of Minnesota Press.

New, Elisa. 1988. "Pharaoh's Birthstool: Deconstruction and Midrash." *SubStance* 17: 3, 26–36.

The New Oxford Annotated Bible with the Apocrypha. 1977. Revised Standard Edition. New York: Oxford University Press.

Nicholls, David. 1989. *Deity and Domination*. London: Routledge.

Niebuhr, H. Richard. 1989. *Faith on Earth: An Inquiry into the Structure of Human Faith*. Richard R. Niebuhr, ed. New Haven, CT: Yale University Press.

Nietzsche, Friedrich. 1967. *The Will to Power* [1901]. Trans. Walter Kaufmann and R. J. Hollingdale. New York: Random House.

———. 1969. *On the Genealogy of Morals* [1887] and *Ecce Homo* [1908]. Trans. Walter Kaufmann. New York: Vintage Books.

———. 1983. "On the Uses and Disadvantages of History for Life" [1874]. In *Untimely Meditations*. Trans. R. J. Hollingdale. Cambridge: Cambridge University Press.

Nisbet, H. B., ed. 1985. *German Aesthetic and Literary Criticism: Winckelmann, Lessing, Hamann, Herder, Schiller, Goethe*. Cambridge: Cambridge University Press.

O'Flaherty, James C. 1950. "J. D. Michaelis: Rational Biblicist." *Journal of English and Germanic Philology* 49, 172–81.

O'Hara, Daniel. 1983. "The Genius of Irony: Nietzsche in Bloom." In Arac, Godzich, and Martin 1983.

Olender, Maurice. 1989. *Les Langues du Paradis: Aryens et Semites—Un couple providentiel*. Paris: Gallimard.

O'Neill, John. 1988. "Religion and Postmodernism: The Durkheimian Bond in Bell and Jameson." *Theory, Culture and Society* 5: 2/3, 493–508.

O'Neill, Molly. 1990. "Words to Survive Life With: None of This, None of That." *New York Times*, 27 May.

Ong, Walter J. 1982. *Orality and Literacy: The Technologizing of the Word*. London: Methuen.

The Original New Testament. 1985. Trans. Hugh J. Schonfield. London: Firethorn Press.

Osborne, John. 1961. *Luther*. London: Faber and Faber.

Ozick, Cynthia. 1970. "America: Toward Yavneh." *Judaism* 19: 3, 264–82.

––––––. 1984. "Torah as Feminism, Feminism as Torah." *Congress Monthly* 51: 4, 7–10.

Ozment, Steven. 1979. "Humanism, Scholasticism, and the Intellectual Origins of the Reformation." In F. Forrester Church and Timothy George, eds.: *Continuity and Discontinuity in Church History*. Leiden: E. J. Brill.

Paglia, Camille. 1990. *Sexual Personae: Art and Decadence from Nefertiti to Emily Dickinson*. New Haven, CT: Yale University Press.

Papadakis, Andreas, Catherine Cooke, and Andrew Benjamin, eds. 1990. *Deconstruction: Omnibus Volume*. New York: Rizzoli.

Parker, Andrew. 1985. "Response to Jacques Derrida's '*Mnemosyne*: A Lecture for Paul de Man.'" *Critical Exchange* 17, 35–44.

––––––. 1986. "Ezra Pound and the 'Economy' of Anti-Semitism." In Jonathan Arac, ed.: *Postmodernism and Politics* [1983]. Minneapolis: University of Minnesota Press.

Parker, Harold Talbot. 1937. *The Cult of Antiquity and the French Revolutionaries*. Chicago: The University of Chicago Press.

Parker, Ian, and John Shotter, eds. 1990. *Deconstructing Social Psychology*. London: Routledge.

Patrides, C. A. 1972. *The Grand Design of God: The Literary Form of the Christian View of History*. London: Routledge & Kegan Paul.

Paulson, Ronald. 1990. *Breaking and Remaking: Aesthetic Practice in England, 1700–1820*. New Brunswick, NJ: Rutgers University Press.

Payne, Harry C. 1978. "Modernizing the Ancients: The Reconstruction of Ritual Drama 1870–1920." *Proceedings of the American Philosophical Society*, 122: 3, 182–92.

Pease, Donald. 1983. "J. Hillis Miller: The Other Victorian at Yale." In Arac, Godzich, and Martin 1983.

Pelikan, Jaroslav. 1971. *The Christian Tradition: A History of the Development of Doctrine*. Vol. 1: *The Emergence of the Catholic Tradition (100–600)*. Chicago: The University of Chicago Press.

Pelli, Moshe. 1979. *The Age of Haskalah: Studies in Hebrew Literature of the Enlightenment in Germany*. Leiden: E. J. Brill.

Pellicani, Luciano. 1988. "Weber and the Myth of Calvinism." *Telos* 75, 57–85.

Pépin, Jean. 1958. *Mythe et allégorie: Les origines Grecques et les contestations Judéo-Chrétiennes*. Aubier: Éditions Montaigne.

Perl, Jeffrey M. 1984. *The Tradition of Return: The Implicit History of Modern Literature*. Princeton: Princeton University Press.

Petrosino, S., and J. Rolland. 1984. *La verité nomade: Introduction à la pensée d' E. Levinas*. Paris: La découverte.

Petschauer, Peter. 1989. *The Education of Women in Eighteenth-Century Germany: New Directions from the German Female Perspective*. Dyfed: The Edwin Mellen Press.

Pick, Daniel. 1990. *Faces of Degeneration: A European Disorder, c.1848–c.1918*. Cambridge: Cambridge University Press.

Pleck, Joseph. 1981. *The Myth of Masculinity*. Cambridge, MA: The MIT Press.

Pocock, J. G. A. 1986. *Virtue, Commerce, and History: Essays on Political Thought and History, Chiefly in the Eighteenth Century*. Cambridge: Cambridge University Press.

Poetics Today. 1980. "Roman Jakobson: Language and Literature" (special issue), 2: 1a.

Polanyi, M. 1943. "Jewish Problems." *The Political Quarterly* 14: 1, 33–45.

Poliakov, Léon. 1974. *The Aryan Myth: A History of Racist and Nationalist Ideas in Europe* [1971]. Trans. Edmund Howard. New York: Basic Books.

Poovey, Mary. 1988. "Feminism and Deconstruction." *Feminist Studies* 14: 1, 51–65.

———. 1988a. *Uneven Developments: The Ideological Work of Gender in Mid-Victorian England*. Chicago: The University of Chicago Press.

Potok, Chaim. 1972. *My Name is Asher Lev*. New York: Alfred A. Knopf.

———. 1990. *The Gift of Asher Lev*. New York: Alfred A. Knopf.

Prawer, S. S. 1976. *Karl Marx and World Literature*. Oxford: Clarendon Press.

Prendergast, Christopher. 1986. *The Order of Mimesis: Balzac, Stendhal, Nerval and Flaubert*. Cambridge: Cambridge University Press.

Preus, J. S. 1969. *From Shadow to Promise: Old Testament Interpretation from Augustine to the Young Luther*. Cambridge, MA: Harvard University Press.

Prickett, Stephen. 1986. *Words and 'The Word': Language, Poetics and Biblical Interpretation*. Cambridge: Cambridge University Press.

Rabinbach, Anson. 1985. "Between Enlightenment and Apocalypse: Benjamin, Bloch and Modern German Jewish Messianism." *New German Critique* 34, 78–124.

———. 1988. "The Jewish Question in the German Question." *New German Critique* 44, 159–92.

Ragussis, Michael. 1989. "Representation, Conversion, and Literary Form: *Harrington* and the Novel of Jewish Identity." *Critical Inquiry* 16: 1, 113–43.

Rajan, Tilottama. 1986. "The Supplement of Reading." *New Literary History* 17: 3, 573–94.

Raleigh, John Henry. 1977. "Bloom as a Modern Epic Hero." *Critical Inquiry* 3: 3, 583–98.

Rand, Nicholas. 1990. "The Political Truth of Heidegger's 'Logos': Hiding in Translation." *PMLA* 105: 3, 436–47.

Rapaport, Herman. 1986. Review of Gregory Ulmer's *Applied Grammatology*. *SubStance* 15: 2, 136–41.

Raschke, Carl. 1988. *Theological Thinking: An In-quiry*. Atlanta: Scholars Press.

Rasula, Jed. 1987. *Tabula Rasula*. New York: Station Hill.

Ratz, Norbert. 1988. *Der Identitätsroman: Ein Strukturanalyse*. Tübingen: Niemeyer.

Raulet, Gerard. 1976. "Critique of Religion and Religion as Critique: The Secularized Hope of Ernst Bloch." Trans. David J. Parent. *New German Critique* 9, 71–
85.

———. 1979–80. "What Good is Schopenhauer? Remarks on Horkheimer's Pessimism." Trans. David J. Parent. *Telos* 42, 98–106.

Reed, T. J. 1980. *The Classical Centre: Goethe and Weimar, 1775–1832*. London:
Croom Helm.

Reichmann, Eva G. 1974. "Max Horkheimer the Jew: Critical Theory and Beyond."
Leo Baeck Institute Yearbook 19, 181–95.

Reill, Peter Hanns. 1975. *The German Enlightenment and the Rise of Historicism*.
Berkeley: University of California Press.

Reilly, Patrick. 1988. *The Literature of Guilt: From* Gulliver *to* Golding. Iowa City:
University of Iowa Press.

Reimarus, [Hermann Samuel]. 1970. *Fragments*. Trans. Ralph S. Fraser. Philadelphia: Fortress Press.

Reinhart, Tanya. 1976. "Patterns, Intuitions and the Sense of Nonsense." *PTL* 1: 1,
85–103.

Reinharz, Jehuda, and Walter Schatzberg, eds. 1985. *The Jewish Response to German Culture: From the Enlightenment to the Second World War*. Hanover, NH:
University Press of New England.

Reventlow, Henning Graf. 1985. *The Authority of the Bible and the Rise of the
Modern World*. London: SCM.

Richardson, Robert D. Jr. 1978. *Myth and Literature in the American Renaissance*.
Bloomington: Indiana University Press.

Ricoeur, Paul. 1974. *The Conflict of Interpretations: Essays in Hermeneutics* [1969].
Ed. Don Ihde. Evanston, IL: Northwestern University Press.

———. 1981. "Mimesis and Representation." *Annals of Scholarship* 2: 3, 15–32.

Riddel, Joseph N. 1979. "From Heidegger to Derrida to Chance: Doubling and
(Poetic) Language." In William V. Spanos, ed.: *Martin Heidegger and the Question of Literature: Toward a Postmodern Literary Hermeneutics* [1976]. Bloomington: Indiana University Press.

Rieff, Philip. 1972. "'Fellow Teachers.'" *Salmagundi* 20, 5–85.

Riffaterre, Michael. 1966. "Describing Poetic Structures: Two Approaches to Baudelaire's 'Les Chats.'" *Yale French Studies* 36–37, 200–42.

Riley, Patrick. 1986. *The General Will before Rousseau: The Transformation of the
Divine into the Civic*. Princeton: Princeton University Press.

Ringer, Alexander L. 1990. *Arnold Schoenberg: The Composer as Jew*. Oxford: Clarendon Press.

Rizzi, Bruno. 1985–86. "The Jewish Question" [1939]. Trans. Frank Adler. *Telos* 66,
109–13.

Roback, A. A. 1929. *Jewish Influence in Modern Thought*. Cambridge, MA: SCI-Art
Publishers.

Robbins, Bruce. 1986. *The Servant's Hand: English Fiction from Below*. New York:
Columbia University Press.

Roberts, Julian. 1982. *Walter Benjamin*. London: Macmillan.

Robertson, David. 1977. *The Old Testament and the Literary Critic*. Philadelphia:
Fortress Press.

Robertson, J. G. 1924. *The Gods of Greece in German Poetry*. Oxford: Oxford University Press.

Robinson, Lillian S. 1985. "Treason our Text: Feminist Challenges to the Literary Canon." In Showalter 1985.

Rojek, Chris, ed. 1989. *Leisure for Leisure: Critical Essays*. London: Macmillan.

Ronell, Avital. 1990. *The Telephone Book: Technology, Schizophrenia, Electric Speech*. Lincoln: University of Nebraska Press.

Rorty, Richard. 1982. "Philosophy as a Kind of Writing: An Essay on Derrida" [1978]. In *Consequences of Pragmatism (Essays: 1972–1980)*. Minneapolis: University of Minnesota Press.

––––––. 1982a. "Nineteenth-Century Idealism and Twentieth-Century Textualism" [1980]. In *Consequences of Pragmatism. See* Rorty 1982.

––––––. 1983. "Against Belatedness." *London Review of Books*, 16 June, 3–5.

Rose, Gillian. 1984. *Dialectic of Nihilism*. Oxford: Basil Blackwell.

Rose, William. 1964. "Goethe and the Jews" [1931]. In *Men, Myths and Movements in German Literature*. Port Washington, NY: Kennikat Press.

Rosen, Stanley. 1989. *The Ancients and the Moderns: Rethinking Modernity*. Cambridge, MA: Harvard University Press.

Rosenfelt, Deborah S. 1982. "The Politics of Bibliography: Women's Studies and the Literary Canon." In Joan E. Hartman and Ellen Messer-Davidow, eds.: *Women in Print I: Opportunities for Women's Studies Research in Language and Literature*. New York: MLA.

Rossi, Paolo. 1984. *The Dark Abyss of Time: The History of the Earth and the History of Nations from Hooke to Vico* [1979]. Trans. Lydia G. Cochrane. Chicago: The University of Chicago Press.

Roston, Murray. 1965. *Prophet and Poet: The Bible and the Growth of Romanticism*. Evanston, IL: Northwestern University Press.

Rotenstreich, Nathan. 1959. "For and against Emancipation: The Bruno Bauer Controversy." *Leo Baeck Institute Yearbook* 4, 3–36.

––––––. 1963. *The Recurring Pattern: Studies in Anti-Judaism in Modern Thought*. London: Weidenfeld & Nicolson.

––––––. 1968. *Jewish Philosophy in Modern Times: From Mendelssohn to Rosenzweig*. New York: Holt, Rinehart and Winston.

––––––. 1989. *Alienation: The Concept and its Reception*. Leiden: E. J. Brill.

Roth, Cecil. 1964. *A History of the Jews in England* [1949]. Oxford: Clarendon Press.

Rowe, John Carlos. 1985–86. "'To Live Outside the Law, You Must Be Honest': The Authority of the Margin in Contemporary Thought." *Cultural Critique* 2, 35–68.

Rue, Loyal D. 1989. *Amythia: Crisis in the Natural History of Western Culture*. Tuscaloosa: University of Alabama Press.

Rustin, Michael. 1988. "Absolute Voluntarism: Critique of a Post-Marxist Concept of Hegemony." *New German Critique* 43, 146–73.

Ruwet, Nicolas. 1973. *Langage, musique, poésie*. Paris: Seuil.

Ryan, Michael. 1982. *Marxism and Deconstruction: A Critical Articulation*. Baltimore: The Johns Hopkins University Press.

Ryken, Leland. 1974. "Literary Criticism and the Bible: Some Fallacies." In Kenneth R. R. Gros Louis, James S. Ackerman, and Thayer S. Warshaw, eds.: *Literary Interpretations of Biblical Narratives*. Nashville, TN: Abingdon Press.

Said, Edward W. 1978. "The Problem of Textuality: Two Exemplary Positions." *Critical Inquiry* 4: 4, 673–714.

———. 1978a. *Orientalism*. New York: Pantheon.

———. 1983. *The World, the Text, and the Critic*. Cambridge, MA: Harvard University Press.

Salusinszky, Imre, ed. 1987. *Criticism in Society*. New York: Methuen.

Samuelson, Norbert M. 1989. *An Introduction to Modern Jewish Philosophy*. Albany, NY: State University of New York Press.

Santirocco, Matthew S., ed. 1987. "*Latinitas*: The Tradition and Teaching of Latin." *Helios* 14: 2 (special issue).

Sartre, Jean-Paul. 1948. *Anti-Semite and Jew* [1946]. Trans. George J. Becker. New York: Schocken Books.

Satran, David. 1987. "Hellenism." In Cohen and Mendes-Flohr 1987.

Sax, Benjamin Charles. 1987. *Images of Identity: Goethe and the Problem of Self-Conception in the Nineteenth Century*. New York: Peter Lang.

Sayre, Robert, and Michael Löwy. 1984. "Figures of Romantic Anti-Capitalism." *New German Critique* 32, 42–92.

Schacht, Richard. 1970. *Alienation*. Garden City, NY: Doubleday.

Schama, Simon. 1987. *The Embarrassment of Riches: An Interpretation of Dutch Culture in the Golden Age*. New York: Alfred A. Knopf.

Schiller, Friedrich. 1902. "The Moral Utility of Aesthetic Manners" [1796]. In *Complete Works*. Vol. 8: *Aesthetical and Philosophical Essays*. New York: P. F. Collier & Son.

———. 1902a. "The Gods of Greece." In *Poetical Works*. Nathan Haskell Dole, ed. Boston: Francis A. Niccolls.

———. 1965. *On the Aesthetic Education of Man, In a Series of Letters* [1794–94]. Trans. Reginald Snell. New York: Frederick Ungar.

———. 1985. "On Naive and Sentimental Poetry" [1795–96]. Trans. Julius A. Elias. In Nisbet 1985.

Schlegel, Friedrich. 1968. *Dialogue on Poetry and Literary Aphorisms*. Trans. Ernst Behler and Roman Struc. University Park: Pennsylvania State University Press.

———. 1971. *Lucinde and the Fragments*. Trans. Peter Firchow. Minneapolis: University of Minnesota Press.

Schlesier, Renate. 1988. "Lévi-Strauss' Mythology of the Myth" [1986]. Trans. Harold Stadler. *Telos* 77, 143–57.

Schmidt, H. D. 1956. "The Terms of Emancipation, 1781–1812: The Public Debate in Germany and its Effect on the Mentality and Ideas of German Jewry." *Leo Baeck Institute Year Book* 1, 28–47.

———. 1959. "Anti-Western and Anti-Jewish Tradition in German Historical Thought." *Leo Baeck Institute Year Book* 4, 37–60.

Schmidt, James. 1975. "Lukács' Concept of Proletarian Bildung." *Telos* 24, 2–40.

Schneidau, Herbert N. 1976. *Sacred Discontent: The Bible and Western Tradition*. Baton Rouge: Louisiana State University Press.

———. 1982. "The Word against the Word: Derrida on Textuality." *Semeia* 23, 5–28.

Scholem, Gershom. 1971. "At the Completion of Buber's Translation of the Bible"

[1963]. Trans. Michael A. Mayer. In *The Messianic Idea in Judaism, and Other Essays on Jewish Spirituality*. New York: Schocken Books.

———. 1971a. "The Science of Judaism—Then and Now" [1960]. Trans. Michael A. Mayer. In *The Messianic Idea in Judaism*. See Scholem 1971.

———. 1971b. "Toward an Understanding of the Messianic Idea in Judaism." In *The Messianic Idea in Judaism*. See Scholem 1971.

Scholes, Robert. 1988. "Deconstruction and Communication." *Critical Inquiry* 14: 2, 278–95.

Schorske, Carl E. 1980. *Fin-de-Siècle Vienna: Politics and Culture*. New York: Alfred A. Knopf.

Schulte-Sasse, Jochen. 1988. "The Concept of Literary Criticism in German Romanticism, 1795–1810." In Hohendahl 1988.

———. 1989. "The Prestige of the Artist under Conditions of Modernity." *Cultural Critique* 12, 83–100.

Schwartz, Regina M. 1988. "Joseph's Bones and the Resurrection of the Text: Remembering in the Bible." *PMLA* 103:2, 114–24.

Schweiker, William. 1990. *Mimetic Reflections: A Study in Hermeneutics, Theology, and Ethics*. New York: Fordham University Press.

Seabrook, Jeremy. 1988. *The Leisure Society*. Oxford: Basil Blackwell.

Sedgwick, Eve Kosofsky. 1985. *Between Men: English Literature and Male Homosocial Desire*. New York: Columbia University Press.

Seeskin, Kenneth. 1990. *Jewish Philosophy in a Secular Age*. Albany, NY: State University of New York Press.

Segal, Alan F. 1990. *Paul the Convert: The Apostolate and Apostasy of Saul the Pharisee*. New Haven, CT: Yale University Press.

Seznec, Jean. 1953. *The Survival of the Pagan Gods: The Mythological Tradition and its Place in Renaissance Humanism and Art* [1940]. Trans. Barbara F. Sessions. New York: Pantheon.

Shaffer, E. S. 1975. *"Kubla Khan" and The Fall of Jerusalem: The Mythological School in Biblical Criticism and Secular Literature 1770–1880*. Cambridge: Cambridge University Press.

Sharratt, Bernard. 1985. *The Literary Labyrinth: Contemporary Critical Discourses*. Brighton: Harvester.

Sheehan, Thomas. 1979. "Heidegger's 'Introduction to the Phenomenology of Religion,' 1920–21." *Personalist* 60: 3, 312–24.

Shelley, Percy Bysshe. 1898. *The Complete Poetical Works*. Vol. III. Boston: Houghton Mifflin Co.

Shestov, Lev. 1932. *In Job's Balances* [1929]. Trans. Camilla Coventry and C. A. McCartney. London: J. M. Dent & Sons.

———. 1966. *Athens and Jerusalem* [1937]. Trans. Bernard Martin. Athens, OH: Ohio University Press.

Shevelow, Kathryn. 1989. *Women and Print Culture: The Construction of Femininity in the Early Periodical*. London: Routledge.

Shklovsky, Viktor. 1973. "The Connection between Devices of *Syuzhet* Construction and General Stylistic Devices" [1919]. Trans. Jane Knox. In Stephen Bann and John E. Bowlt, eds.: *Russian Formalism: A Collection of Articles and Texts in Translation*. Edinburgh: Scottish Academic Press.

Showalter, Elaine, ed. 1985. *The New Feminist Criticism: Essays on Women, Literature, and Theory*. New York: Pantheon.

Siebert, Rudolf J. 1983–84. "Adorno's Theory of Religion." *Telos* 58, 108–14.

Silberner, Edmund. 1952–53. "Ferdinand Lassalle: From Maccabeism to Jewish Anti-Semitism." *Hebrew Union College Annual* 24, 151–86.

Silverman, Hugh J., ed. 1988. *Philosophy and Non-Philosophy since Merleau-Ponty*. New York: Routledge.

———. 1989. *Derrida and Deconstruction*. New York: Routledge.

Simonsuuri, Kirsti. 1979. *Homer's Original Genius: Eighteenth-Century Notions of the Early Greek Epic (1688–1798)*. Cambridge: Cambridge University Press.

Skinner, Quentin. 1982. "Habermas's Reformation." *The New York Review of Books*, 7 October, 35–38.

Sloterdijk, Peter. 1987. *Critique of Cynical Reason* [1983]. Trans. Michael Eldred. Minneapolis: University of Minnesota Press.

Smith, John H. 1988. *The Spirit and its Letter: Traces of Rhetoric in Hegel's Philosophy of Bildung*. Ithaca, NY: Cornell University Press.

Smith, Joseph H., and William Kerrigan, eds. 1983. *Taking Chances: Derrida, Psychoanalysis, and Literature*. Baltimore: The Johns Hopkins University Press.

Sombart, Werner. 1951. *The Jews and Modern Capitalism* [*Die Juden und das Wirtschaftsleben*, 1911]. Trans. M. Epstein. Glencoe, IL: The Free Press.

Sontag, Susan. 1966. "Notes on 'Camp.'" In *Against Interpretation, and Other Essays*. New York: Farrar, Straus & Giroux.

Sörböm, Göran. 1966. *Mimesis and Art*. Stockholm: Svenska Bokförlaget Bonniers.

Sorkin, David. 1983. "Wilhelm von Humboldt: The Theory and Practice of Self-Formation (*Bildung*), 1791–1810." *Journal of the History of Ideas* 44: 1, 55–73.

———. 1990. "Emancipation and Assimilation: Two Concepts and their Application to German-Jewish History." *Leo Baeck Institute Year Book* 35, 17–33.

Spanos, William V. 1985. "The Apollonian Investment of Modern Humanist Education: The Examples of Matthew Arnold, Irving Babbitt, and I. A. Richards." *Cultural Critique* 1, 7–72.

Spariosu, Mihai I., ed. 1984. *Mimesis in Contemporary Theory: An Interdisciplinary Approach*. Amsterdam: John Benjamins.

———. 1989. *Dionysus Reborn: Play and the Aesthetic Dimension in Modern Philosophical and Scientific Discourse*. Ithaca, NY: Cornell University Press.

Spender, Stephen. 1965. *The Struggle of the Modern* [1963]. London: Methuen.

Spiegelman, Art. 1989. "Spiegelman on Looney Tunes, Zionism, and the Jewish Question." *The Village Voice*, 6 June, 21–22.

Spinoza, Benedict de. 1951. "Theologico-Political Treatise" [1670]. In *Chief Works*. Trans. R. H. M. Elwes. New York: Dover.

Sprinker, Michael. 1983. "Aesthetic Criticism: Geoffrey Hartman." In Arac, Godzich, and Martin 1983.

Stanford, W. B. 1976. *The Ulysses Theme: A Study in the Adaptability of a Traditional Hero* [1st ed. 1963]. Ann Arbor: University of Michigan Press.

Stanley, A. P. 1907. *Lectures on the History of the Eastern Church*. London: J. M. Dent & Sons.

Starobinski, Jean. 1989. *Le Remède dans le mal: Critique et légitimation de l'artifice à l'age des Lumières*. Paris: Gallimard.

Steadman, John M. 1984. *Milton's Biblical and Classical Imagery*. Pittsburgh: Duquesne University Press.

Steele, H. Meili. 1988. *Realism and the Drama of Reference: Strategies of Representation in Balzac, Flaubert, and James*. University Park: Pennsylvania State University Press.

Steinberg, Milton J. 1937. "Judaism and Hellenism." In Emily Solis-Cohen, Jr., ed.: *Hanukkah: The Feast of Lights*. Philadelphia: The Jewish Publication Society of America.

Steiner, George. 1964. "One Definition of a Jew." *Cambridge Opinion* 39, 16–22.

———. 1967. "An Aesthetic Manifesto" [1964]. In *Language and Silence: Essays on Language, Literature, and the Inhuman*. New York: Atheneum.

———. 1975. *After Babel: Aspects of Language and Translation*. London: Oxford University Press.

———. 1976. "Some 'Meta-Rabbis.'" In Douglas Villiers, ed.: *Next Year in Jerusalem: Jews in the Twentieth Century*. London: Harrap.

———. 1978. *Heidegger*. London: Fontana.

———. 1981. *The Portage to San Cristóbal of A. H.* New York: Simon and Schuster.

———. 1984. *Antigones*. Oxford: Clarendon Press.

———. 1985. "Our Homeland, the Text." *Salmagundi* 66, 4–25.

———. 1985a. "Viewpoint: A New Meaning of Meaning." *Times Literary Supplement*, 8 November, 1262, 1275–76.

———. 1989. *Real Presences: Is there Anything in what We Say?* London: Faber.

Stendahl, Krister. 1983. "The Apostle Paul and the Introspective Conscience of the West" [1963]. In *Paul among Jews and Gentiles, and Other Essays*. Philadelphia: Fortress Press.

Stern, David. 1987. "Aggadah." In Arthur A. Cohen and Paul Mendes-Flohr 1987.

Stock, R. D. 1989. *The Flutes of Dionysus: Daemonic Enthrallment in Literature*. Lincoln: University of Nebraska Press.

Stoeffler, F. Ernest. 1973. *German Pietism during the Eighteenth Century*. Leiden: E. J. Brill.

Stolnitz, Jerome. 1961. "On the Significance of Lord Shaftesbury in Modern Aesthetic Theory." *The Philosophical Quarterly* 11: 43, 97–113.

———. 1961–62. "On the Origins of 'Aesthetic Disinterestedness.'" *Journal of Aesthetics and Art Criticism* 20, 131–43.

Strauss, Leo. 1952. "How to Study Spinoza's *Theologico-Political Treatise*." In *Persecution and the Art of Writing*. Glencoe, IL: The Free Press.

———. 1983. "Jerusalem and Athens: Some Preliminary Reflections" [1967]. In *Studies in Platonic Political Philosophy*. Chicago: The University of Chicago Press.

———. 1983a. "Introductory Essay for Hermann Cohen, *Religion of Reason out of the Sources of Judaism*" [1972]. In *Studies in Platonic Political Philosophy*. See Strauss 1983.

Struever, Nancy. 1970. *The Language of History in the Renaissance: Rhetoric and Consciousness in Florentine Humanism*. Princeton: Princeton University Press.

SubStance. 1980. "A Polylogue on Play" (special issue), 25.

Suganami, Hidemi. 1989. *The Domestic Analogy and World Order Proposals*. Cambridge: Cambridge University Press.

Sullivan, Robert R. 1989. *Political Hermeneutics: The Early Thinking of Hans-Georg Gadamer*. University Park: Pennsylvania State University Press.

—————. 1990. *Political Hermeneutics: The Early Thinking of Hans-Georg Gadamer*. University Park: Pennsylvania State University Press.

Swales, Martin. 1978. *The German Bildungsroman from Wieland to Hesse*. Princeton: Princeton University Press.

Swenson, Chester A. 1990. *Selling to a Segmented Market: The Lifestyle Approach*. New York: Quorum Books.

Szondi, Peter. 1983. "Hölderlin's Overcoming of Classicism." Trans. Timothy Bahti. *Comparative Literature* 5, 251–270.

Talbert, Charles H. 1970. "Introduction." In Reimarus 1970.

Tambiah, Stanley Jeyaraja. 1990. *Magic, Science, Religion, and the Scope of Rationality*. Cambridge: Cambridge University Press.

Taminiaux, Jacques. 1985. *Dialectic and Difference: Finitude in Modern Thought*. Trans. Robert Crease and James Decker. Atlantic Highlands, NJ: Humanities Press.

Taubes, Jacob. 1954. "From Cult to Culture." *Partisan Review* 21, 387–400.

Taylor, David. 1988. "American Dreaming." *American Book Review* 10: 5, 9.

Taylor, Isaac. 1861. *The Spirit of the Hebrew Poetry*. London: Bell & Daldy.

Taylor, Mark C. 1982. *Deconstructing Theology*. Atlanta: Scholars Press.

—————. 1985. *Erring: A Postmodern A/Theology*. Chicago: The University of Chicago Press.

Theunissen, Michael. 1984. *The Other: Studies in the Social Ontology of Husserl, Heidegger, Sartre, and Buber* [2nd ed. 1977]. Trans. Christopher Macann. Cambridge, MA: The MIT Press.

Theweleit, Klaus. 1987. *Male Fantasies. Volume I: Women, Floods, Bodies, History* [1977]. Trans. Stephen Conway. Minneapolis: University of Minnesota Press.

—————. 1988. *Male Fantasies. Volume II: Male Bodies: Psychoanalyzing the White Terror* [1978]. Trans. Erica Carter, Chris Turner, and Stephen Conway. Minneapolis: University of Minnesota Press.

Tiedemann, Rolf. 1983–84. "Historical Materialism or Political Messianism? An Interpretation of the Theses 'On the Concept of History.'" Trans. Barton Byg. *The Philosophical Forum* 15: 1–2, 71–104.

Tillich, Paul. 1959. "An Evaluation of Martin Buber: Protestant and Jewish Thought" [1948]. In *Theology of Culture*. New York: Oxford University Press.

Todd, Janet. 1980. *Women's Friendship in Literature*. New York: Columbia University Press.

Tresmontant, Claude. 1989. *The Hebrew Christ: Language in the Age of the Gospels* [1983]. Trans. Kenneth D. Whitehead. Chicago: Franciscan Herald.

Trevelyan, Humphrey. 1941. *Goethe and the Greeks*. Cambridge: Cambridge University Press.

Tucker, Robert C., ed. 1978. *The Marx-Engels Reader* [2nd ed.]. New York: W. W. Norton & Company.

Tuleja, Tad. 1989. *The Catalog of Lost Books: An Annotated and Seriously Addled Collection of Great Books that Should Have Been Written but Never Were*. New York: Fawcett Columbine.

Turetsky, Arnold S. 1990. "Light of Hope in the Face of Decadence." *New York Times*, 22 December.

Turner, Frank M. 1981. *The Greek Heritage in Victorian Britain*. New Haven: Yale University Press.

———. 1989. "Martin Bernal's *Black Athena*: A Dissent." In *Arethusa* 1989, 97–109.

Tyler, Stephen A. 1986. "Post-Modern Ethnography: From Document of the Occult to Occult Document." In Clifford and Marcus 1986.

Ulmer, Gregory L. 1984. *Applied Grammatology: Post(e)-Pedagogy from Jacques Derrida to Joseph Beuys*. Baltimore: The Johns Hopkins University Press.

van den Haag, Ernest. 1969. *The Jewish Mystique*. New York: Stein and Day.

van Reijen, Willem. 1988. "The *Dialectic of Enlightenment* Read as Allegory." Trans. Josef Bleicher, Georg Stauth, and Bryan S. Turner. *Theory, Culture & Society* 5: 2–3, 409–29.

Vattimo, Gianni. 1980. *Le avventure della differenza*. Milan: Garzanti.

———. 1988. "Bottles, Nets, Revolution, and the Tasks of Philosophy" [1981]. Trans. Iain Chambers. *Cultural Studies* 2: 2, 143–51.

———. 1989. *The End of Modernity: Nihilism and Hermeneutics in Postmodern Culture* [1985]. Trans. Jon R. Snyder. Baltimore: The Johns Hopkins University Press.

Veblen, Thorstein. 1899. *The Theory of the Leisure Class*. London: Macmillan.

———. 1964. "The Intellectual Pre-Eminence of Jews in Modern Europe" [1919]. In *Essays in our Changing Order*. Ed. Leon Ardzrooni. New York: Augustus M. Kelley.

Vergote, Antoine. 1988. *Guilt and Desire: Religious Attitudes and their Pathological Derivatives* [1978]. Trans. M. H. Wood. New Haven, CT: Yale University Press.

Vernant, Jean-Pierre, and Marcel Detienne. 1978. *Cunning Intelligence in Greek Culture and Society* [1974]. Trans. Janet Lloyd. Atlantic Highlands, NJ: Humanities Press.

Veyne, Paul. 1988. *Did the Greeks Believe in their Myths? An Essay on the Constitutive Imagination* [1983]. Trans. Paula Wissing. Chicago: The University of Chicago Press.

Vidal-Naquet, Pierre. 1980. "Interpreting Revolutionary Change: Political Divisions and Ideological Diversity in the Jewish World of the First Century A.D." Trans. Maria Jolas. *Yale French Studies* 59, 86–105.

Virilio, Paul, and Sylvere Lotringer. 1983. *Pure War*. Trans. Mark Polizotti. New York: Semiotext(e).

Vogt, Adolf Max. 1986. "The Influence of Paestum in the German and Scandinavian Speaking Countries." In Joselita Raspi Serra, ed.: *Paestum and the Doric Revival, 1750–1830: Essential Outlines of an Approach*. Florence: Centro Di.

von Campenhausen, Hans. 1972. *The Formation of the Christian Bible*. Trans. J. A. Baker. Philadelphia: Fortress Press.

von Hallberg, Robert, ed. 1984. *Canons*. Chicago: The University of Chicago Press.

———. 1985. *American Poetry and Culture, 1945–1980*. Cambridge, MA: Harvard University Press.

von Rad, G. 1963. "Typological Interpretation of the Old Testament." In C. Westermann, ed.: *Essays in Old Testament Hermeneutics*. Richmond, VA: John Knox Press.

Wagner, Richard. 1973. "Judaism in Music" [1850]. In *Stories and Essays*. Ed. Charles Osborne. New York: Library Press.

Walcott, Derek. 1990. *Omeros*. New York: Farrar, Straus & Giroux.

Warminski, Andrej. 1985. "Deconstruction in America/Heidegger Reading Hölderlin." *Criticial Exchange* 17, 45–59.

Watson, George. 1962. *The Literary Critics: A Study of English Descriptive Criticism*. Harmondsworth: Penguin Books.

Watt, Ian. 1957. *The Rise of the Novel: Studies in Defoe, Richardson and Fielding*. Berkeley: University of California Press.

Weber, Max. 1958. *Essays in Sociology* [1946]. Trans. H. H. Gerth and C. Wright Mills. New York: Oxford University Press.

―――. 1958a. "Science as a Vocation" [1919]. In *Essays in Sociology*. *See* Weber 1958.

―――. 1958b. "Religious Rejections of the World and their Directions" [1915]. In *Essays in Sociology*. *See* Weber 1958.

―――. 1963. *The Sociology of Religion* [1922]. Trans. Ephraim Eischoff [of 4th ed., 1956]. Boston: Beacon Press.

―――. 1976. *The Protestant Ethic and the Spirit of Capitalism* [1904–5]. Trans. Talcott Parsons. London: Allen & Unwin.

Weeks, Jeffrey. 1981. *Sex, Politics and Society: The Regulation of Sexuality since 1800*. London: Longman.

Weigel, Sigrid. 1990. "Body and Image Space: Problems and Representability of a Female Dialectic of Enlightenment." *Australian Feminist Studies* 11, 1–15.

Weimann, Robert. 1986. "History and the Issue of Authority in Representation: The Elizabethan Theater and the Reformation." *New Literary History* 17: 3, 449–76.

Weinberg, Henry H. 1987. *The Myth of the Jew in France, 1967–1982*. Oakville, Ont.: Mosaic.

Weindling, Paul. 1989. *Health, Race and German Politics between National Unification and Nazism, 1870–1945*. Cambridge: Cambridge University Press.

Weingartner, Rudolph H. 1960. *Experience and Culture: The Philosophy of Georg Simmel*. Middletown, CT: Wesleyan University Press.

Weinsheimer, Joel. 1985. *Imitation*. London: Routledge & Kegan Paul.

Weir, D. A. 1990. *The Origins of the Federal Theology in Sixteenth-Century Reformation Thought*. Oxford: Oxford University Press.

Wells, Susan. 1986. *The Dialectics of Representation*. Baltimore: Johns Hopkins University Press.

Weltin, E. G. 1987. *Athens and Jerusalem: An Interpretative Essay on Christianity and Classical Culture*. Atlanta: Scholars Press.

Werblowsky, R. J. Zwi. 1952. *Lucifer and Prometheus: A Study of Milton's Satan*. London: Routledge & Kegan Paul.

Werth, Paul. 1976. "Roman Jakobson's Verbal Analysis of Poetry." *Journal of Linguistics* 12: 1, 21–73.

West, Cornel. 1987. "Minority Discourse and the Pitfalls of Canon Formation." *Yale Journal of Criticism* 1: 1, 193–201.

Whallon, William. 1966. "Old Testament Poetry and Homeric Epic." *Comparative Literature* 18, 113–31.

Whimster, Sam. 1987. "The Secular Ethic and the Culture of Modernism." In Scott Lash and Sam Whimster, eds.: *Max Weber, Rationality and Modernity*. London: Allen & Unwin.

White, John J. 1971. *Mythology in the Modern Novel: A Study of Prefigurative Techniques*. Princeton: Princeton University Press.

Whitman, James Q. 1990. *The Legacy of Roman Law in the German Romantic Era. Historical Vision and Legal Change*. Princeton: Princeton University Press.

Wiener, Max. 1952. "Abraham Geiger and the Science of Judaism." *Judaism* 2, 41–48.

Wiesel, Elie. 1989. "Art and the Holocaust: Trivializing Memory." Trans. Iver Peterson. *New York Times*, 11 June.

Wilder, Amos N. 1958. *Theology and Modern Literature*. Cambridge, MA: Harvard University Press.

———. 1969. *The New Voice: Religion, Literature, Hermeneutics*. New York: Herder and Herder.

Wiley, Norbert, ed. 1987. *The Marx-Weber Debate*. Beverly Hills, CA: Sage.

Wimsatt, W. K. Jr. 1954. "Poetry and Christian Thinking" [1948, 1951]. In *The Verbal Icon: Studies in the Meaning of Poetry*. Lexington: University of Kentucky Press.

Winckelmann, J. J. 1985. "Thoughts on the Imitation of the Painting and Sculpture of the Greeks" [1755]. In Nisbet 1985.

Winkle, Sally A. 1989. *Woman as Bourgeois Ideal: A Study of Sophie von La Roche's* Geschichte des Frauleins von Sternheim *and Goethe's* Werther. New York: Peter Lang.

Winnifrith, Tom, and Cyril Barrett, eds. 1989. *The Philosophy of Leisure*. London: Macmillan.

Wistrich, Robert S. 1989. *The Jews of Vienna in the Age of Franz Joseph*. Oxford: Oxford University Press.

Witemeyer, Hugh. 1969. *The Poetry of Ezra Pound: Forms and Renewal, 1908–1920*. Berkeley: University of California Press.

Witte, Bernd. 1986. "Paris-Berlin-Paris: Personal, Literary, and Social Experience in Walter Benjamin's Late Works." *New German Critique* 39, 49–60.

Wittgenstein, Ludwig. 1963. *Tractatus Logico-Philosophicus* [1921]. Trans. D. F. Pears and B. F. McGuinness. London: Routledge & Kegan Paul.

———. 1980. *Culture and Value* [1977]. Trans. Peter Winch. Chicago: The University of Chicago Press.

Wolf, F. A. 1985. *Prolegomena to Homer* [1795]. Trans. Anthony Grafton, Glenn W. Most, and James E. G. Zetzel. Princeton: Princeton University Press.

Wolf, Immanuel. 1957. "On the Concept of a Science of Judaism" [1822]. Trans. Lionel E. Kochan. *Leo Baeck Institute Yearbook* 2, 194–204.

Wolin, Richard. 1982. *Walter Benjamin: An Aesthetic of Redemption*. New York: Columbia University Press.

———. 1990. "Utopia, Mimesis, and Reconciliation: A Redemptive Critique of Adorno's *Aesthetic Theory*." *Representations* 32, 33–49.

———. 1990a. *The Politics of Being: The Political Thought of Martin Heidegger*. New York: Columbia University Press.

Wolosky, Shira. 1982. "Derrida, Jabès, Levinas: Sign-Theory as Ethical Discourse." *Prooftexts* 2: 3, 283–302.

Wood, David. 1985. "An Introduction to Derrida." In Roy Edgley and Richard Osborne, eds.: *Radical Philosophy Reader*. London: Verso.

———. 1987. "Heidegger after Derrida." *Research in Phenomenology* 17, 103–16.

————. 1988. "*Différance* and the Problem of Strategy." In Wood and Bernasconi 1988.

Wood, David, and Robert Bernasconi, eds. 1988. *Derrida and Différance* [1985]. Evanston, IL: Northwestern University Press.

Woodmansee, Martha. 1984. "The Interests of Disinterestedness: Karl Philipp Moritz and the Emergence of the Theory of Aesthetic Autonomy in Eighteenth-Century Germany." *Modern Language Quarterly* 45, 22–47.

Worden, Blair. 1989. "Uncommon Rights of Man." *Times Literary Supplement*, 2 June, 610, 621.

Wyschogrod, Edith. 1974. *Emmanuel Levinas: The Problem of Ethical Metaphysics.* The Hague: Martinus Nijhoff.

————. 1989. "Derrida, Levinas and Violence." In Silverman 1989.

Xenos, Nicholas. 1989. *Scarcity and Modernity.* London: Routledge.

Yavetz, Zvi. 1976. "Why Rome? Zeitgeist and Ancient Historians in Early 19th Century Germany." *American Journal of Philology* 97: 3, 276–96.

Young, R. V. 1985. "Derrida or Deity? Deconstruction in the Presence of the Word." In Paul Williams, ed.: *Issues in the Wake of Vatican II. Proceedings of the Eighth Convention of the Fellowship of Catholic Scholars.* Scranton, PA: Northeast Books.

Yovel, Yirmiyahu. 1990. *Spinoza and Other Heretics.* Vol. 2: *The Marrano of Reason.* Princeton: Princeton University Press.

————. 1990a. "Spinoza, the First Secular Jew?" *Tikkun* 5: 1, 40–42, 94–96.

Zarader, Marlène. 1990. *La dette impensée: Heidegger et l'héritage hébraïque.* Paris: Seuil.

Zelechow, Bernard. 1990. "Yovel's Spinoza: The Discovery of Secularism and Beginning of Modernity." *Midstream* 36: 4, 31–35.

Zimmerman, Michael E. 1981. *Eclipse of the Self: The Development of Heidegger's Concept of Authenticity.* Athens, OH: Ohio University Press.

————. 1988. "*L' affaire* Heidegger." *Times Literary Supplement*, 7 October, 1115–17.

Zwerdling, Alex. 1964. "The Mythographers and the Romantic Revival of Greek Myth." *PMLA* 79: 4, 447–56.

Zwicker, Steven N. 1988. "England, Israel and the Triumph of Roman Virtue." In Richard H. Popkin, ed.: *Millenarianism and Messianism in English Literature and Thought, 1650–1800: Clark Library Lectures, 1981–1982.* Leiden: E. J. Brill.

INDEX

NOTE: The following words (in alphabetical order) appear too frequently in the book to require indexing: antiquity, Bible/Scripture (including Old and New Testament), Christianity, ethics/morality, faith, God, Hebraism and Hellenism (or Jews and Greeks, Israel and Greece, and the like), middle class/bourgeoisie, modernity/modernization, philosophy, politics, Protestantism, Reformation, religion, state, and theology.